CRITICAL COMPANION TO

Maya Angelou

CRITICAL COMPANION TO

Maya Angelou

A Literary Reference to Her Life and Work

JACQUELINE S. THURSBY

Critical Companion to Maya Angelou:
A Literary Reference to Her Life and Work

Facts On File, Inc.
An imprint of Infobase Learning
132 West 31st Street
New York NY 10001

Library of Congress Cataloging-in-Publication Data
Thursby, Jacqueline S., 1940
Critical companion to Maya Angelou : a literary reference to her life and work / Jacqueline S. Thursby.
p. cm.
Includes bibliographical references and index.
ISBN 978-0-8160-8093-9 (hc : alk. paper) 1. Angelou, Maya—Handbooks, manuals, etc. 2. African Americans in literature—Handbooks, manuals, etc.
I. Title.
PS3551.N464Z95 2011
818'.5409—dc22 2010032716

Facts On File books are available at special discounts when purchased in bulk quantities for businesses, associations, institutions, or sales promotions. Please call our Special Sales Department in New York at (212) 967-8800 or (800) 322-8755.

You can find Facts On File on the World Wide Web at http://www.infobaselearning.com

Text design by Erika K. Arroyo
Composition by Hermitage Publishing Services
Cover printed by Yurchak Printing, Inc., Landisville, Pa.
Book printed and bound by Yurchak Printing, Inc., Landisville, Pa.
Date printed: June 2011

Printed in the United States of America

10 9 8 7 6 5 4 3 2 1

This book is printed on acid-free paper.

Contents

ACKNOWLEDGMENTS

First, I would like to express both gratitude and indebtedness to Dr. Maya Angelou, whose life and work have been an inspiration to millions of people. It has been a privilege and honor to write this review of her life and critical commentary on many of her works. I hope it will serve to uplift and enlighten several generations of readers. My sincere thanks are extended to the Department of English at Brigham Young University and to the College of Humanities for providing me with an able research assistant, Christina Roach. I am also indebted to the Harold B. Lee Library for prompt and consistent accommodation of my various requests. Thank you to Professor Gloria Cronin, a BYU colleague, who generously shared materials, insight, and feedback about Angelou, and Janis Hansen, a design professional, who located illustrations for the book. I would be unmindful if I did not acknowledge the erudite counsel of the Facts On File editor Jeff Soloway, who responded promptly and made wise suggestions, advised, and helped to shape the work. Most important, I gratefully acknowledge my husband, who has consistently and gently helped me find a balance between scholarship and life (including golf). I acknowledge the understanding of our four beloved children, their spouses, and our grandchildren, who approve of my work and have benefited greatly from a non-hovering mother, mother-in-law, and grandmother. Oh yes, lest I forget, my appreciation also extends to our American domestic tabbies, Molly and Max, who have restored my calm many late nights with their affection and soothing purrs.

INTRODUCTION

Maya Angelou represents the talents and accomplishments of a multitude wrapped up into one person. Her wisdom, warmth, sincerity, and arresting presence have made her a worldwide sister/mother figure. Angelou became a luminary in the literary world with her first autobiography, *I Know Why the Caged Bird Sings* (1969), and her Pulitzer Prize nomination in 1972 for a collection of poems titled *Just Give Me a Cool Drink of Water 'fore I Diiie*. Her broader national and international public fame came in 1993 when President BILL CLINTON chose her as only the second poet in U.S. history to have the honor of writing and reciting an original work at a presidential inauguration. With both dignity and humility, Angelou delivered her dedicatory poem, "On the Pulse of Morning," to Americans and to the world, and those who heard her recognized that she spoke for the sake of hope and peace for all humankind.

Angelou's history and stories are told in her six autobiographies and through her poetry, where the reader learns, through candid and often penetrating words, that her life has been full and varied. Much of her poetry reflects the black experience and speaks through the vernacular of her heritage. Her works tell the story of African Americans in the United States. She has learned, and teaches constantly, that thriving positively rather than simply enduring and surviving life's unpredictable difficulties yields confidence and joy. She has danced, sung, written, and published prolifically. She has created and directed plays and films, edited, traveled, lectured, mastered at least six languages (French, Italian, Spanish, Serbo-Croatian, Arabic, and Fanti, a Ghanaian dialect, in addition to English), written for newspapers and magazines, been strongly involved in the American CIVIL RIGHTS MOVEMENT, lived and worked in Africa, and won many honors and awards—but perhaps her most satisfying accomplishment in life has been that of a devoted mother, grandmother, and friend of many.

About This Book

This text is primarily intended for high school students, undergraduates, and general readers. It is meant to be a clear and accessible discussion of critical interpretations and meanings. It is not a literary handbook of prose and poetry patterns and styles. The author and publisher hope that this book will attract more readers to the great literary contributions and wisdom of Maya Angelou. There are references throughout the text for further reading on Maya Angelou's life and works. Part I of this book provides a biography. Part II offers detailed entries on many of Angelou's works, focusing on her autobiographical novels and poetry. Also included are entries that discuss in less depth her other written works, such as television and screenplay writing, children's books, and important essays and speeches. Entries on the autobiographies include synopses of the works and critical commentary sections, as well as subentries on the individual characters in the works (listed according to significance). Part III contains entries on people, places, terms, and topics related to Angelou and her work. Part IV contains the appendixes, including a chronology of Angelou's life, chronologies of the events in each of her autobiographies, a bibliography of her corpus of work, and a bibliography of secondary sources.

A reference to a person, a term, or a topic that is the subject of its own entry in Part III is given in SMALL CAPITAL LETTERS the first time it appears in a particular entry.

PART I

Biography

Maya Angelou (Marquerite Ann Johnson)

(1928–)

Maya Angelou (mah' yuh an'jeh loh) is an African-American poet, author, playwright, film and television producer, director, and stage and screen performer. In her youth, she was a nightclub singer and dancer. Because of her many talents and skills, she has often been labeled a Renaissance woman. Though she was a thin, lanky, and insecure child, she grew into a tall, graceful woman with a quick smile and a warm, friendly manner. The scholar Joanne M. Braxton has called her "America's most visible female autobiographer" (4).

Angelou created what many consider a new genre, the serial autobiography. She wrote six sequential autobiographies of her life, the most famous of which is *I Know Why the Caged Bird Sings*. She wrote candidly of her adventures, providing unprecedented insight into her interiority and identity formation as an African-American woman. Gloria Cronin, a scholar of African-American culture and literature at Brigham Young University, writes that Angelou's "sympathies range across history, class, color lines, communities, and whole continents" (14). A remarkably gifted, generous, and prolific woman, Maya Angelou emerged from a difficult childhood and unstable youth, and yet her artistic contributions have positively impacted millions of lives. Her voice has been influential in turning literary attention to black women's voices. She conscientiously and constantly works to bring people and traditions together in authentic dialogue and understanding.

The importance of music, particularly the BLUES and the soulful hymns and SPIRITUALS of her African-American Christian religion, should not be underestimated when considering the life, accomplishments, and contributions Angelou has made. In 2005, Cherron Barnwell wrote a well-informed article called "Singin' de Blues, Writing Black Female Survival in *I Know Why the Caged Bird Sings*," which illuminates the deep meaning music, particularly the blues, has for Angelou. Barnwell wrote:

> Of the African American cultural elements present in the text, the blues is most influential in *Caged Bird*. The blues shapes its form and content, and in using the blues aesthetic, Angelou meets the challenge of writing autobiography in literature. Descending from the Negro spiritual, the blues is a music native to America, having its genesis in the African American culture, it is expressive of blackness encountering that which is commonly called American. (134–135)

Maya was raised in the COLORED METHODIST EPISCOPAL CHURCH, where spirituals and hymns strongly undergirded the pastor's message. Movement, rhythms, and words were expressions of spirituality, and the sounds and feelings were carried in the mind long after the church doors were closed. The blues, anchored in these familiar rhythms and melodies, were comforting and transformative for Angelou. "While the motif of movement is influenced by the slave narrative, the blues form treats movement as transforming" (Barnwell 2009, 138). In *Singin' and Swingin' and Gettin' Merry Like Christmas,* Angelou wrote: "Music was my refuge. I could crawl into the spaces between the notes and curl my back to loneliness" (391).

She has always expressed her culture through words. She drew from countless influential experiences gained through reading, listening, and living as she expressed different parts of her childhood and adult life through the medium of her serial autobiographies, poetry, and other writing. Angelou has shared her experiences in the world with her readers, as well as her wit, wisdom, and determined survival. From her humble beginnings, she met the world head-on, and she has given her readership and listeners easily understood keys to survival and self-respect, again and again. Angelou has lived a rich life, and her literary works blend her individual experiences with the cultural and social history of African Americans.

Maya Angelou was born Marguerite Ann (or Annie) Johnson on April 4, 1928, in St. Louis, Missouri. Her parents were BAILEY JOHNSON, SR., a carefree and breezy navy dietitian, and VIVIAN BAXTER, a beautiful woman and professional nurse

Maya Angelou, a woman of many gifts and talents: dancer, singer, actor, civil rights activist, journalist, poet, screenwriter, director, professor, producer, and friend to millions *(Courtesy Angelou-Johnson Family Archives)*

who preferred to earn her living by gambling. The first half of Angelou's professional name was given by her older brother, BAILEY JOHNSON, JR., who as a toddler called her My for "my sister." He eventually transformed that into "Maya" after reading a book about the Maya. She retained the Angelou surname after divorcing her first husband, ENISTASIOUS "TOSH" ANGELOS, (sometimes spelled Anastasios Angelopulos), a Greek-American sailor, and she put the two names together for her stage name.

After her parents' divorce, Maya (three) and Bailey (four) were labeled with notes saying "To Whom It May Concern" and put aboard a train to travel alone from Long Beach, California, to their paternal grandmother, Annie Henderson, who owned a general store in a southern backwash town named Stamps in Arkansas (*See* STAMPS, ARKANSAS.) The imprint of ten years of living in Stamps with her grandmother and her uncle WILLIE JOHNSON formed the basis for Angelou's first and best known autobiography, *I Know Why the Caged Bird Sings,* which chronicles her first 16 years. It also established an understanding of African Americans that resonated in her mind many years later when she lived in Africa. Stamps was a small, segregated, and racist place made up of whites and blacks with a long history of distrust for one another. Most of the African-American community lived in poverty, sustaining themselves by picking cotton, but they were close-knit and supportive of each member of their black community. The many APHORISMs and MAXIMs that particularly find expression in Angelou's earliest works were learned in Stamps, as was her old-fashioned courtesy. Her humorous recollections of Momma (as she called her grandmother) and Momma's training of Bailey and Maya included memories of being taught how to wash. In *I Know Why the Caged Bird Sings,* for instance, "She [Momma] used to add, with a smirk that unprofane people can't control when venturing into profanity, 'and wash as far as possible, and then wash possible'" (25).

Angelou learned life-affirming values and resiliency from her grandmother's constant strength, hard work, and positive outlook in spite of adversity, and from observing the attitudes of other members of the African-American community living in Stamps. Her first autobiography is a historical document of the vernacular of the people as well as the personal narrative of a black girl living in the segregated South. Maya Angelou not only learned life values, she learned Southern black speech; colloquial aphorisms; and the lore that has enriched and colored her prose, her poetry, and her almost countless lectures and presentations. Her writings are laced with the rhythms and black traditions of the South, though she never preferred to speak in the deep southern accents of her heritage. Because of her keen intelligence, careful ear, and voracious reading, she formed herself into a refined, powerful woman with a devoted and sustained international following.

Maya's grandmother and her semiparalyzed uncle, Willie Johnson, owned and ran the William Johnson General Merchandise Store (always capitalized as "Store" in Angelou's writing). Uncle Willie was paralyzed on his right side; though he used a cane, he walked with difficulty. The store was an informal community center as well as a source of supplies for the people. Maya and her brother watched as people came to the Store in the morning, each one hopeful that the day would be productive, and that they would earn enough to pay their bills. They worked in the cotton fields, and whole families might work together; babies and little children were sometimes taken along. The cotton plants with their sharp COTTON BOLLS tore their hands and arms, but it was the only work available. When these same people returned in the evening, dirty, weary, aching, and discouraged, Grandmother Henderson sold them SLOAN'S LINIMENT to ease their pain. But they knew that their best work was still not enough to earn the money they needed. Bailey and Maya watched and learned about African Americans' grave oppression.

Maya and her brother, Bailey, were close friends, and he was her favorite adviser. When they were children, she called him her "kingdom come" because she trusted him. *(Courtesy Angelou-Johnson Family Archives)*

Maya and Bailey experienced the black community spirit as well as strict discipline, no-nonsense religion, and moral training from their grandmother. They learned to wait on customers, and the brother and sister even became competitive in their goals of measuring flour and sugar accurately by eye. They were both bright and read the classics voraciously. Maya escaped from day-to-day life through her imagination by reading classic authors such as WILLIAM SHAKESPEARE, RUDYARD KIPLING, EDGAR ALLAN POE, WILLIAM MAKEPEACE THACKERAY, RALPH WALDO EMERSON, HORATIO ALGER, WILLIAM ERNEST HENLEY, ROBERT SERVICE, and SAMUEL BUTLER. She also read important black authors, including PAUL DUNBAR, LANGSTON HUGHES, W. E. B. DUBOIS, and JAMES WELDON JOHNSON.

Their uncle Willie watched over their education, and Angelou later wrote that there was little room for them to make errors in their educational process. Uncle Willie was strict and careful about their accuracy and accountability. There was a potbellied stove in the store, and Uncle Willie made lots of threats about throwing the children on it when it was red-hot if they failed to do their math sums correctly. He was a taskmaster, but he loved the children and never hurt them in any way. Maya did her homework efficiently and learned her numbers quickly.

The children also had chores to perform in the evening. They threw grain to the chickens and mixed ground meal with leftover food and dishwater for the pigs. Angelou fondly remembered waiting around until the pigs grunted with contentment, and then the two children playfully imitated the grunting. She never complained about those chores but, rather, made the best of the situation time after time, and she often tried to find humor in the work. She and Bailey were close friends throughout their childhood and adult years, and she remarked in her books that to her, he was one of the best and most handsome people in the world. She called him her "kingdom come" (23). Throughout their adult years, Bailey maintained his early protective loyalty and frequently acted as a sounding board, friend, confidant, and careful adviser to his sister. They had no father figure except Uncle Willie, and for Maya, Bailey was always a deeply trusted friend.

In 1935, their father took Maya and Bailey to St. Louis for a stay with their mother. The new, somewhat sophisticated environment was quite a change from rural Arkansas, but the children soon adapted and enjoyed the sights and sounds of the city, which "had many paved streets and large brick buildings, and coal dust filled the air. Buses, cars and trucks constantly moved back and forth" (Kite 1999, 25). They had plenty of good food and clothing bought in a store, each of them had a radio, and they also were given enough money to buy paperback books. It was an entirely different way of life in contrast to Stamps, and they both enjoyed it.

Their mother was often away from home working, and tragically, Maya, at eight years old, was seduced and later brutally raped by her mother's boyfriend. She revealed her assailant reluctantly, afraid to tell anyone because she had been told that if she confessed who had hurt her, her brother would be killed. The rapist's trial and subsequent death by a brutal beating (perhaps by her uncles) was perceived by Maya to be her fault. In her young mind, she felt that her words had the power to kill; consequently, she silenced her voice for about five years and spoke only infrequently with Bailey.

After her tragic experience, Maya and Bailey were returned to her grandmother, Momma, and the safe, nurturing community of Stamps. Bailey was unhappy about being returned, but he remained supportive and helpful to Maya. Many of the black people in Stamps thought Maya was retarded because of her silence, but MRS. BERTHA FLOWERS, a refined and educated black woman in Stamps and friend of her grandmother's, took a personal interest in Maya. She and Maya spent many afternoons reading, and Mrs. Flowers encouraged oral recitation of prose and poetry. At last, Maya began to speak again.

She remained in Stamps until she graduated, with honors, from the eighth grade at Lafayette County Training School in 1940. Shortly after that, Momma took her to her mother in LOS ANGELES, CALIFORNIA, and Bailey followed about a month later. Vivian Baxter (maiden name), Maya, and Bailey lived first in Los Angeles; then OAKLAND, CALIFORNIA; and then, finally, in SAN FRANCISCO, CALIFORNIA, after their mother married "Daddy" CLIDELL JACKSON. Their large home was on Post Street in the FILLMORE DISTRICT of San Francisco.

Maya attended the George Washington High School by day, and in the evening, from 1941 to 1945, she studied dance and performance at the California Labor School. She spent a few days at her father's trailer in southern California, hoping to become better acquainted with him, but she was poorly treated by Dolores, his live-in girlfriend. In *I Know Why the Caged Bird Sings,* Angelou describes a trip to ENSENADA, MEXICO, that she made with her father. The girlfriend did not want to go, and Maya's father, too drunk to drive after partying in Ensenada, passed out in the backseat of the car. Maya, who had never before driven a car, drove the harrowing roads to the border, where she had a minor accident. When that was sorted out, she and her father returned to San Diego, but it was brutally clear that the girlfriend was jealous and Maya was not welcome there.

After a quarrel, Dolores stabbed Maya. Her father took her for care and then left her at a friend's trailer for the night. The next morning, Maya found the trailer empty, made herself some sandwiches, and left for 30 days, falling in with a group of teenagers who were mostly homeless but kind and loyal to one another. When she reflected on this experience later, she realized that she first learned interracial democracy from those youngsters. They were loyal to one another, they had established a system, and they were at peace.

Bedraggled and hungry, Maya finally contacted her mother in San Francisco and returned home. She hoped to find a job, and her mother was supportive of whatever she chose to do. She saw an ad for a streetcar conductor and determinedly decided that was the job she would have. She pestered the San Francisco city offices and their resistant secretary until they finally tested her and then hired her as the first black streetcar conductor in the city. Angelou's persistence and success with that job was a foreshadowing of the drive and determination that manifested itself throughout her life. She

Maya and her only child, Guy, both gifted writers, enjoy each other's company about 1980. *(Courtesy Angelou-Johnson Family Archives)*

finished her required course of study at Mission High School and graduated in the summer. Just a few weeks after graduation, the birth of her son, her only child, began a new dimension of her life.

Maya had had doubts about her sexual inclinations and plunged into a quick affair with a handsome white neighborhood boy to determine if she was or was not a lesbian. She offered her body to him one day, and he took her to a room where they had a quick and unsatisfactory sexual encounter. She realized about three weeks later that she had conceived, but she told no one until it was almost time for the baby to be born. Her mother gracefully accepted the information, and CLYDE BAILEY JOHNSON was born shortly after her high school graduation in 1944 when she was 16 years old.

Themes throughout her other five autobiographies emphasize the bonds between Angelou and her son. The texts reveal the nature of her devoted motherhood and also her relationships with her mother, grandmother, and both familial and African-American culture. Parts of her story are familiar to many young women who bear a child without a husband. The new mother's cultural or biological heritage does not matter; it is a difficult and challenging situation. Angelou became a mother as a young teen with no marketable skills and an infant whom she wanted to support independently. She floated from one short-term job to another in California to try to support her child and herself.

Her mother's financial safety net was always available, but Angelou wanted to provide appropriate support and care for her infant son and herself without outside dependency or strings. One of her first jobs was as a cook in a café that specialized in Creole COOKING. Though she was not familiar with the flavors of Creole food, someone told her just to add peppers, onions, and tomatoes, and it would be Creole. Typical of Angelou, she learned as she cooked, and her creations were well-received. Her skill and interest in cooking led to developing self-taught gourmet skills in the culinary arts, and she has used these skills on a daily basis. Her first cookbook, *Hallelujah! The Welcome Table: A Lifetime of Memories with Recipes* (2004), reflects her tribute to many great friends and cooks she has admired, eaten with, and listened to.

Angelou worked as a dancer in nightclubs; as a body shop employee, removing paint from cars with her hands; and, for a short time, as a madam of her own prostitution business. Afraid of being arrested because of her illegal brothel, she returned to Stamps, but she was no longer comfortable with

An accomplished cook, Angelou continues to enjoy preparing gourmet meals for guests to her home. *(Courtesy Angelou-Johnson Family Archives)*

the intensely racist conditions there and returned to California. There, she tried to enlist in the army; however, her application was turned down because she had studied at the California Labor School, and that school was suspected of having communist links.

For a while, Angelou was part of a dance team called "Poole and Rita." When she auditioned in her home for Mr. Poole, she performed various positions, including an ARABESQUE, but she accidentally became fixed between a gas jet and a table leg when she did the splits. He forgave her for that, and with his guidance she mastered the dancing routine and particularly enjoyed performing in the spotlight. When Poole's former dance partner returned, Angelou's professional life as a costumed club performer came temporarily to a halt. There were other jobs, including a short episode of prostitution, and in this early and frustrating period of her life, she acquired the habit of using marijuana for escape.

When her brother Bailey's young wife died of tuberculosis and complications from pneumonia, Maya turned her attention to him in his grief. Bailey, sensing that the lifestyle Maya was living was dead-end, spoke firmly to her and persuaded her to find a more legitimate job. Before long, Maya had an opportunity to become financially independent by selling clothes for a male junkie. Though it was still not a legitimate career, the junkie's concern for Maya, in spite of his own dependency on drugs, led him to take her to a filthy gathering place of junkies and dope users. He administered heroin to himself in front of her, and she watched him lose consciousness. That was enough of a lesson, and she never used drugs again.

Angelou worked two legitimate jobs in order to afford a dependable babysitter, pay her rent, and cover expenses for herself and baby Clyde (later called "Guy" by his request). When the boy was around five, Maya began working full-time at the Melrose Record Shop in San Francisco's Fillmore District. During the 1940s and 1950s, the well-known district was also called the "Harlem of the West." It was a black music haven, and Tosh Angelos, a regular customer at the record store, became romantically interested in Maya. He was a white, Greek-American sailor who had finished his service in the U.S. Navy and had a steady civilian job in an appliance store. Tosh began to court both Maya and Guy, and before long, much to her mother's disapproval, Maya accepted his marriage proposal. Thereafter, she became a full-time homemaker styled after images in the pages of *Good Housekeeping* of that time (1949). She took pride in her cooking and squeaky clean home and dedicated herself almost completely to her husband's and son's needs. For a while, that seemed to work, but Tosh's atheism clashed with Maya's fundamental Christian faith. Soon undeniable racial issues began to emerge, and after three years of both racial and religious tension, the marriage ended in divorce in 1952.

Guy was heartbroken by the separation from Tosh, who was the only father he had known, loved, and trusted. As a consequence, he blamed and distrusted his mother. It took a concentrated effort of time and patience to reestablish Guy's confidence in her. By spending as much time as possible with him, preparing his favorite foods often and generously, and letting him choose board games to play with her in the evening, Angelou was able to mend their relationship. There were many moments during Guy's growing-up years when she reached out to him to accommodate hurts for which she felt responsible. They moved often, but in spite of that, she tried to provide a consistently safe home for him.

Angelou resorted to exotic dancing in nightclubs for a period of time to provide enough income for she and Guy to live comfortably. She worked as a dancer, not a stripper, and as a "B-girl" at the Garden of Allah nightclub in 1955. She then had an opportunity to work as a calypso dancer and singer at the famous Purple Onion club. The Purple Onion, located in the North Beach neighborhood of San Francisco, was well known as a showcase for rising performers. PHYLLIS DILLER was another entertainer and eventual star who got her start there (Gillespie, Butler, and Long 2008, 43). At that time, Maya changed her name from Marguerite Johnson Angelos to Maya Angelou. In order to enhance her exotic calypso act, she also assumed a fictional Cuban/African/Spanish identity.

At 25, Angelou had officially stepped back into the spotlight and established herself as an up-and-coming professional dancer and singer. She became a popular performer, and soon other offers for professional performances came her way. She was invited to audition as a replacement for EARTHA KITT in the revue *New Faces for 1953* and was offered the spot, but because she was under contract to the Purple Onion, there was no legal way to accept it. She honored her contract and, a short time later, accepted an opportunity to tour Europe and Africa with the Department of State production of *PORGY AND BESS*. Her mother was happy to take care of Guy, so Angelou toured with the musical company from 1954 to 1955. While on that tour, she met JAMES BALDWIN in Paris, and they established a lasting friendship.

Another telling aspect of Angelou's quest for learning is the way she handled her time on the European tour of *Porgy and Bess*. In *Maya Angelou: Journey of the Heart* (1996), Jayne Pettit wrote:

> While other members of the cast relaxed at a sidewalk café, Maya strolled through the narrow streets, past rows of old stone houses and balconies crammed with pots of bright red geraniums. Could she really be in Italy? As lines from *Romeo and Juliet* raced through her head, she thought of the times that she and Bailey had read the play to each other back in Stamps.
>
> In Venice, Maya spent her free hours exploring the wonders of the great medieval city: the churches and palaces, the marketplaces, and the canals where gondolas moved gracefully through mirrored waters. Eager to learn a new language, she bought a small pocket Italian dictionary and taught herself simple phrases. (33)

Angelou recognized that she was giving her son much of the same kind of childhood she had experienced herself. He was being left with babysitters, friends, and her mother as the need arose, but he was her first priority. She determined that when she got home, any performances she undertook after *Porgy and Bess* would be arranged so that he could travel with her, or she would not accept the opportunity. She returned to San Francisco before the tour ended because her mother let her know that Guy needed her. It was 1955, and Guy was 10. His name from birth had been Clyde, but shortly after they were reunited, he requested that he be called Guy. Maya had changed her own name, so she accepted his announcement without an argument (Gillespie, Butler, and Long 2008, 47)

Angelou began writing short sketches and song lyrics after returning from the European tour, and she was able to record six of them for Liberty Records on an album called *Miss Calypso*. She met JOHN KILLENS, a writer temporarily in Hollywood working on a screenplay of his novel *Youngblood*, and he suggested that she move to New York in order to be a member of the HARLEM WRITERS GUILD. He explained that she would receive helpful critiques from that group, which would improve her writing skill. Angelou decided to take his advice, and she and Guy—with assistance from Killen's family, who lived in Brooklyn—relocated to New York City. Guy, interested in public welfare like his mother, became active in the NATIONAL COMMITTEE FOR SANE NUCLEAR POLICY (SANE).

It was 1959, and the members of the Harlem Writers Guild were not only serious about writing, they were also informed about contemporary issues and discussed them frequently. Both African independence and African-American civil rights in the United States were in the forefront of the news at that time, and Angelou, 31, was being guided in her writing as well as becoming informed politically. Her first reading to the group was received with sharp criticism, but she began to understand that good writing meant hard work. She began to write in earnest and also became politically active in the CIVIL RIGHTS MOVEMENT. The unrest was a demand for social reform to address and change the issues of American institutionalized RACISM and create a more just society.

After attending a consciousness-raising rally in a Harlem church where MARTIN LUTHER KING, JR., RALPH ABERNATHY, and others challenged the audience to support the southern movement to end SEGREGATION, she and comedian/actor GODFREY CAMBRIDGE organized a fund-raiser ("Cabaret for Freedom") for Martin Luther King's SOUTHERN CHRISTIAN LEADERSHIP CONFERENCE (SCLC). It ran for five successful weeks at the Village Gate in

New York City. Shortly after the benefit cabaret finished its run, she was invited to become the northeastern regional coordinator of the SCLC in the New York office. Angelou was an avid supporter of Martin Luther King, Jr., who visited her office one morning, unannounced, and affirmed his support of her work. She found him comfortable to talk to, and he asked her questions about her family. She served in that administrative position for about a year until her life took a surprising and interesting turn.

In 1961, John Killens invited her to meet a South African freedom fighter, VUSUMZI MAKE, who, with OLIVER TAMBO, another African activist, was in New York to speak in behalf of his people at the United Nations. He and Angelou were immediately attracted to one another, and within a few short weeks, he proposed to her. She was engaged to a man named Thomas Allen at the time and had visions of settling down as a quiet homemaker, but she accepted Make's proposal. Soon she, Guy, and Vusumzi were sharing a luxurious apartment in New York City.

Recognized as an accomplished stage performer after the European tour, Angelou was offered the role of the White Queen in JEAN GENET's *The BLACKS*, an Off-Broadway production about the corruption of power regardless of race. Both Make and Angelou were resistant to the offer at first, but after reading the play, Make changed his mind and encouraged her to take the part if it was still available. The play was received well in New York and was eventually performed in Europe.

At this time, Angelou began to receive threatening phone calls from agents of South Africa's apartheid regime. She began to take this cruel intrusion personally, and she was determined to make the relationship with Make work, though there were warning signals in the relationship. She loved him, but their bills were not being paid, and he also had strong ideas about the place of women. After Angelou left the cast of *The Blacks,* Make moved her and Guy to Cairo, Egypt. It was exotic and fascinating to both Guy and his mother, and they competed while learning Arabic to see who could learn the words the fastest and with the least accent. Over time, Angelou learned to speak Arabic fluently as well as West African Fanti, French, Spanish, Serbo-Croatian, and Italian.

Guy completed high school in Egypt, and because of Make's lack of responsible financial management, Angelou worked as an associate editor of the *Arab Observer* from 1961 to 1962. She had learned from her housekeeper that their luxurious apartment, chosen and furnished by Vusumzi, was not being paid for; further, there were tuition and clothing expenses for Guy. Make had felt that Maya would not be able to get a job in Cairo, and also that it was not appropriate for a wife to work. Angelou had convinced him that if she were employed, he would be able to use all of his money for the South African United Front. He accepted that, and she went to work.

The relationship with Make continued to deteriorate, and in addition to the financial instability, he was not true to his relationship with Maya. (Though they had never formally married, they lived as man and wife.) Meanwhile, Guy had finished school and was ready for university studies. In 1963, Angelou traveled to Accra, Ghana, with Guy to enroll him in the University of Ghana. They liked the country from the moment they arrived in the Ghanian Airport. It was a black world, and the people were well-dressed and impressive. Maya had expected only being there long enough to enroll Guy because she had been promised a job in Liberia by dignitaries in Cairo. Those plans were changed just a few days later because of a serious automobile accident that left Guy in a body cast for months. Consequently, Angelou unexpectedly settled in Accra.

Guy mended completely, and after some wrangling about rules and regulations on Angelou's part, he was able to take his entrance exams and be admitted to the University of Ghana. Friends assisted Angelou, and soon she was hired as the assistant administrator of the School of Music and Drama at the University of Ghana. She also worked for the Ghanian Broadcast Corporation and wrote for the *Ghanian Times* newspaper. During this time, she was introduced to several important African women who valued her friendship, and there was time for her to enjoy the beauty of Accra and establish many warm friendships. Angelou recognized commonalities in the behaviors of African people and her own heritage in Stamps, Arkansas. There were factors that "influenced sensibilities and behavior, the grave formality of elders in Ghana so like her Grandmother Henderson's demeanor. It was alive in the spoken and body language of Black America, in the music and the kitchen" (Gillespie, Butler, and Long 2008, 69). The children played similar games to those she had played in her childhood, and the older people shared some of the same folktales.

During the time she worked in Ghana, she also met the wife and adopted son of W. E. B. DuBois and MALCOLM X, all luminaries in the fight for African-American civil rights. She was well known and organized a Ghanian demonstration in support of Martin Luther King, Jr.'s March on Washington in 1963. In 1964, she arranged Malcolm X's Ghanian itinerary. Meanwhile, Guy was growing up and had met a woman in Africa with whom he wanted to live. Declaring himself a man, he informed his mother that she was finished with raising him, which Angelou accepted graciously. She had been offered a position as coordinator of Malcolm X's Organization of Afro-American Unity (OAAU) in New York and felt it was time to let Guy be on his own. A little later, in 1965, she returned to the United States alone. She wrote:

> There was much to cry for, much to mourn, but in my heart I felt exalted knowing there was much to celebrate. Although separated from our languages, our families and customs, we had dared to continue to live. We had crossed the unknowable oceans in chains and had written its mystery into "Deep River, my home is over Jordan." Through the centuries of despair and dislocation, we had been creative, because we faced down death by daring to hope. (1986, 1,050–1,051)

Angelou was looking forward to working in Malcolm X's organization, and so upon her arrival in New York, among other calls, she contacted him. He invited her to spend a few days at his home with his family, but she declined because she was exhausted and anxious to return to San Francisco. She regretted that decision because Malcolm X was assassinated just a few days later (on February 21, 1965), and the tragedy left her unsure of her future once more. She was at a close friend's home when she heard the shocking news. She fell into an emotional tailspin there, and soon Bailey came after her. They both stayed at their mother's place for a short time, and then Bailey suggested that she move to Hawaii, where he was working as a chef, and resume her performing career there. Following his advice, she stayed in Hawaii about six months, but she realized that her heart was really in writing. She had no desire to move back to New York, so she decided to try Los Angeles. She had friends and connections there and was soon settled in an apartment. She decided to work just enough to support herself so she could write. She found a job as a part-time market researcher interviewing homemakers about the products they used. Her assignment was in WATTS, which, because of unemployment, poor schools, price gouging, and family disintegration, literally exploded into riots on August 11, 1965. Angelou saw it, and she understood it.

Soon after the horror of Watts, Angelou's friend ROSA GUY visited Los Angeles to promote her new book, *Bird at My Window.* Rosa persuaded Maya to make a change, and Angelou decided to return to New York and begin serious writing again when the news came that Guy had returned from Africa and had been in another serious accident. He had finished school in Ghana and had only been in the United States a few days when he was hit by a truck in San Francisco. Maya went to him there; his neck was broken again, but his prognosis was good. When his recovery was assured, she returned to Los Angeles, saved as much money as she could, and then moved to New York, where she resumed her friendship with James Baldwin, who introduced her to his family. His mother immediately added her to her large brood of children, and Angelou was once again surrounded by friends and chosen family. Baldwin and Angelou ran into some tension in their friendship when he decided to relocate to California from New York to lend a hand to ELDRIDGE CLEAVER and the BLACK PANTHER PARTY. Angelou passionately believed in Martin Luther King, Jr.'s passive resistance style, and the potential violence of Cleaver's organization unsettled her. However, time moved on, issues changed, and Baldwin and Angelou's close, supportive friendship resumed and continued.

Three years later, just after a memorial tribute for W. E. B. DuBois, Martin Luther King, Jr., asked Angelou to help in an effort to raise funds for another march on Washington. He hoped she would appeal to black ministers across the country and persuade them to donate one Sunday's church collection a year. She was pleased to be asked, but on April 4, 1968, her birthday, she received a phone call from a close friend who then went to her home to inform her that King had been assassinated. Devastated, she turned to Baldwin, who helped her work through her deep grief and disappointment. Baldwin set her path, at last, toward serious writing. He took her to the home of JULES AND JUDY FEIFFER, where their funny stories and Angelou's tales from her childhood in segregated Stamps lifted all of their spirits at this sad time. Soon after that dinner, Angelou began working on a 10-part African-American culture series for television called *Black, Blues, Black.* It was broadcast on San Francisco's National Education Television affiliate, KQED. She was both the writer and the program's host, and the essence of the series was, as Angelou stated: "We were blacks in Africa before we were brought to America as slaves, where we created the blues, and now we were painfully and proudly returning to being upstanding free blacks again" (2002, 1,163).

The Feiffers had contacted an editor at Random House named ROBERT LOOMIS and told him about Angelou's stories. He contacted Angelou and invited her to write an autobiography for their company, she responded that she sincerely doubted her ability to write such a book. Nevertheless, even after several refusals, Loomis continued to encourage her, and finally, following a tip about her personality he received from James Baldwin, he challenged her by saying that autobiography was nearly the hardest genre in which to write. At that, she said she would do it. The eventual result was her first book, the prize-winning *I Know Why the Caged Bird Sings* (1970), an autobiographical account of the first 16 years of her life.

The first reader of Angelou's manuscript was her good friend JESSICA MITFORD, who found the book fascinating and encouraged her to continue writing. It is both poignant and humorous, as is much of her other writing, and in *Heart of a Woman, Mind of a Writer, and Soul of a Poet* (1997), the critic Lyman B. Hagen wrote:

> To contrast the psychological and physically devastating forces encountered there [Stamps, Arkansas], she lavishly imbues her prose and poetry with humor. Her philosophy is that every chance one gets, one should laugh. It is interesting to note, however, that in spite of sister support in her writings, Angelou does not align herself with modern feminists because she thinks they do not have a sense of humor. While Angelou's comedy is often born out of pain and anger, she is, nevertheless, secure enough to laugh at herself and with her people. (27)

Loomis, who has continued to be her editor, stated: "Maya is her books" (quoted in Russell 1985, 8–9). Angelou was also quoted as saying: "I am a writer. Every writer is his or her books. Just as every singer is the song, while you're doing it. The dancer is the dance . . ." (8–9). A little later in the interview with Russell, Angelou remarked: "I use the first person singular and I'm talking about the third person plural all the time; what it's like to be a human being. So the person who reads my work and suspects that he or she knows me, hasn't gotten the half of the book, because he or she should know himself or herself better after reading my work. That's my prayer" (8–9).

I Know Why the Caged Bird Sings became the Book of the Month selection in 1970, was nominated for a National Book Award, and was later produced as a television movie. The first book was followed with five more autobiographies: *Gather Together in My Name* (1974), *Singin' and Swingin' and Gettin' Merry Like Christmas* (1976), *The Heart of a Woman* (1981), *All God's Children Need Traveling Shoes* (1986), and *A Song Flung Up to Heaven* (2002). She has also written several volumes of personal essays, poetry, dramas, two television plays, children's books, and two screenplays: *Georgia, Georgia* (1972) and *All Day Long* (1972).

In 1973, Angelou married PAUL DU FEU, a British builder and architect. They lived in Los Angeles, Sonoma County, and then in the Pacific Palisades. Du Feu was also a writer, and their relationship was promising in the beginning. He encouraged her to "tell the truth as a writer and not to let her writings be determined by what her readers would think" (Lupton 1998, 14). In her collection *Even the Stars Look Lonesome* (1997), Angelou wrote an essay called "A House Can Hurt, a Home Can Heal," the first sentence of which states: "My last marriage was made in heaven" (3). It began well, but as they moved from place to place and home to home, they found that not only did their furniture sometimes seem misplaced, but somehow their relationship began to feel misplaced as well.

The last home Angelou and Du Feu owned together, one that seemed to accommodate their possessions appropriately, ultimately proved to be the catalyst for the breaking point of their relationship. Nothing seemed to stay in place as they had planned: Professionally hung curtains fell off their rods, doors ceased to fit their frames, the bed collapsed in the middle of the night with no apparent

Maya Angelou with her son, Guy; Guy's son, Colin; and their wives and two young children at a Christmas celebration *(Courtesy Angelou-Johnson Family Archives)*

cause, and the last nerve-breaking straw was that even her cooking would not turn out correctly. Finally, Angelou moved to North Carolina, while Du Feu remained in California.

The same year as their divorce, 1981, Angelou was given a lifetime appointment as the Reynolds Professor and Chair of American Studies at Wake Forest University in Winston-Salem, North Carolina. She still has a rambling home there, which had 10 rooms when she purchased it and now has 18. She wrote, "My builder asked me if I was thinking of reaching the next street down from my house. This is no longer my house, it is my home" (1998, 9).

The same year as the divorce from Du Feu, Angelou published her fourth autobiography, *The Heart of a Woman.* The next 12 years of her life were extraordinarily productive. She taught at Wake Forest and prepared carefully for her classes there but continued to write, perform, and make public appearances. In 1982, she appeared on television as an actor on the *Richard Pryce Special.* She published *Shaker, Why Don't You Sing,* a collection of poetry, in 1983. Her fifth autobiography, *All God's Children Need Traveling Shoes,* was published in 1986, along with a collection of previously published poetry. She also served as a Fulbright Anniversary Distinguished Lecturer in Liberia that year. In 1988, she appeared on the PBS program *The Face of Evil* and directed Errol John's film *Moon on a Rainbow Shawl* in London. In 1989, she was listed in *USA Today* as one of 50 most important black role models. In 1989, she also appeared in a TV special with James Baldwin, *The Price of a Ticket.*

The year 1990 saw the publication of another important collection of Angelou's poetry, *I Shall Not Be Moved* (1990). It was dedicated to her mother, Vivian Baxter, and friend, Mildred Garris Tuttle. That same year, she lectured in Washington, D.C., appeared in the television special R.A.C.E., and also appeared in the televised 22nd Annual NAACP Image Awards. She also received the Langston Hughes Medal in 1991. In 1991 and 1992, she appeared on television as an actor in several specials (a Jacqueline Kennedy Onassis show, *Who Cares About the Kids?* and *Kindred Spirits: Contemporary African American Artists*). Perhaps the great honor of her life came in January 1993.

In preparation for his presidential inauguration, BILL CLINTON invited Angelou to write and read a poem. The dignity and sensitivity of her delivery of "On the Pulse of Morning" garnered Angelou both national and international acclaim. Angelou was the first poet to read at a presidential inaugural since Robert Frost at the inauguration of President John F. Kennedy. Knowledge of her work immediately became widespread, and Angelou's poems were featured in the film *Poetic Justice: On the Road to Redemption* in 1993; she also made a brief appearance in that film.

Angelou has maintained a rigorous lecture circuit, often appearing on college campuses throughout the United States. In the last 10 years or so, however, she has given up flying for a tour bus, explaining that she

> gave up flying, unless it was really vital . . . not because she was afraid, but because she was fed up with the hassle of celebrity. One of the last times she flew, her feet had not made it to the curbside of the airport before an excitable woman started shouting her name. (Younge 2002, 1)

Because she has written so much about her personal life in both her autobiographies and her poetry, many people treat Angelou as public property. Her style of speaking to a group is a mixture of aphorisms and parables. The journalist Gary Younge has written that when she is on stage, it "is like watching stand-up comedy, a university lecture and a poetry recital all in one. With stories, quips and poems, both her own and those of African-American poets both dead and living, she has them laughing, gasping and listening for over an hour" (4). Younge also tells us about her manner of speaking and Southern courtesies:

> Her voice is slow and rich—so deliberate she seems to be tasting words before she lets them leave her mouth. Her speech is peppered with Southern courtesies. You may introduce yourself with your first name, but she will address you with your second. Everybody, in her pres-

ence, becomes Mr, Mrs or Miss—legacy from a time when African Americans were denied those basic signifiers of civility by whites, and so demanded it within their own community.

"I insist upon that," says Angelou. "I did it and do it still. I do it still to Dr. Dorothy Hyde, who is 90. I'm still the young kid and very respectful." (4)

The year after she read "On the Pulse of Morning" at President Clinton's inauguration, Random House published *The Complete Collected Poems of Maya Angelou,* and Angelou also came out with a children's book *(My Painted House, My Friendly Chicken, and Me)* and appeared in several television specials. In 1995, she was recognized by Bantam Books as being the first African American to have the current longest-running title (two years for *Caged Bird*) on the *New York Times* paperback nonfiction best-seller list. That year, she also read her poem, "A Brave and Startling Truth" at the 50th anniversary of the founding of the United Nations in San Francisco, and she read her poem "A Black Woman Speaks to Black Manhood" (also called the "Million Man March Poem") at the Million Man March in Washington, D.C.

In 1996, she published another children's book *(Koji and His Magic)*, served as an ambassador for UNICEF (the United Nations Children's Fund), and received the Martin Luther King, Jr., Legacy Association National Award, as well as appearing on the television show *Touched By an Angel.*

She published a collection of essays, *Even the Stars Look Lonesome,* in 1997 and again appeared on television several times, including being a guest on *The Oprah Winfrey Show.* In 1998, she directed *Down in the Delta,* produced by Miramax, and in 1999, she was recognized by *Writer's Digest* as one of the 100 best writers of the 20th century. In 2000, Angelou signed a contract with Hallmark Cards to help create "The Maya Angelou Collection from Hallmark." Though some critics have decried the collection as inspirational kitsch, Angelou considered the series a strong medium for spreading her message of love and perseverance. The next year, she participated in a television special for the healing of AIDS and also played the role of a conjure woman in the television movie *Runaway.*

Angelou published the last of her autobiographies, *A Song Flung Up to Heaven,* in 2002. She also recorded it and won a Grammy Award for her performance. Over the next few years, from 2003 to 2005, Angelou continued to act on television, teach, and travel between Wake Forest and New York City; she considered both places her home. In 2005, she published *Amazing Peace: A Celebration,* which included "Amazing Peace," the poem she read at the lighting of the National Christmas Tree in Washington, D.C., on December 5, 2005. The next year, she became a radio talk show host for XM Satellite Radio on the Oprah & Friends station. She also published two more books of poetry, won additional awards for her writing, and appeared on television several times. In 2007, she narrated the film *As Seen through These Eyes* and was given the Martha Parker Legacy Award. Her book *Letter to My Daughter* was published in 2008.

In September 2008, Angelou introduced MICHELLE OBAMA at a Women for Obama event in Greensboro, North Carolina. Angelou wrote a short reflection on that experience for the *Washington Post* and said that sometime before the introduction, she had consulted OPRAH WINFREY, her close friend who knows the Obamas. Angelou wrote that "Oprah answered promptly and with conviction, 'She is the *real deal*'" (2009, B05). So, after sharing some of Michelle Obama's accomplishments with the audience, Angelou ended the introduction by saying, "Now ladies and gentlemen, please welcome the 'real deal'" (B05). In this short article, Angelou also reflected on North Carolinian history. She noted how much has changed there in the last five decades, which was reflected in the spirit of optimism she felt from the audience that day. Nearly a century and a half had passed since ABRAHAM LINCOLN had signed the Emancipation Proclamation stating that people held as slaves would be free, and African Americans were finally bidding for significant leadership.

In November 2008, Angelou was interviewed by Diane Rehm on National Public Radio regarding her latest book, *Letter to My Daughter.* In that interview, she read the letter that serves as the opening of the book. The last paragraph of the letter is:

> I gave birth to one child, a son, but I have thousands of daughters. You are Black and White, Jewish and Muslim, Asian, Spanish speaking, Native American and Aleut. You are fat and thin and pretty and plain, gay and straight, educated and unlettered, and I am speaking to you all. Here is my offering to you. (2008, xii)

On Friday, November 29, 2010, officials from the New York Public Library announced that they had acquired a great portion of Angelou's papers. They are to be housed at Harlem's Schomburg Center for Research in Black Culture. Included are letters from James Baldwin, Malcolm X, and other correspondence with well-known figures, as well as drafts of such important works as "On the Pulse of Morning." According to the *New York Times*, "Ms. Angelou, 82, said it dawned on her that 'I'd better make sure my papers and books are taken care of, they are somewhere people can see and read them.'"

Though Angelou has passed the age of 80, she is still an active member of the world political and literary communities. She is a constant advocate for the continuing civil rights movements and many other outreach groups. Her home remains in Winston-Salem, where she enjoys family (she now has two great-grandchildren) and frequent guests in her 18-room residence; she also has two town houses in Harlem, New York, renting one out and using the other for convenience in the city when she is there. Her Harlem town house is elegantly appointed with African-American art, and she often hosts dinner parties there.

At the July 7, 2009, public memorial for MICHAEL JACKSON, QUEEN LATIFAH recited a warm, affirming poem Angelou had written for the occasion entitled "We Had Him." Again, Angelou spoke to everyone in language clearly understood and from her heart. In February 2011, she received the Presidential Medal of Freedom from President Barack Obama.

For decades, Maya Angelou has been a role model for Americans of all ages. She is a living example of a woman who, through faith, determination, and perseverance, overcame what some might consider impossible obstacles. In a 1973 interview, she revealed that she was often asked, "How did you escape it all: the poverty, the rape at an early age, a broken home, growing up black in the South?" She replied: "My natural response is to say, 'How the hell do you know I did escape? You don't know what demons I wrestle with'" (quoted in Weller 1973, 14). Whether she has escaped all of her demons or not, she has refused to be defeated. She continues to teach the world with dignity and common sense through inspirational stories, wisdom, and engaging charisma.

In another of her early interviews, Angelou stated part of her philosophy of life. She told her interviewer, Claudia Tate:

> I try to live what I consider a "poetic existence." That means I take responsibility for the air I breathe and the space I take up. I try to be immediate, to be totally present for all my work. *I try*. This interview with you is a prime example of this. I am withdrawing from the grief that awaits me over the death of someone dear so that I can be present for you, for myself, for your work and for the people who read it, so I can tell you exactly how I feel and what I think and try to answer your questions cheerfully—if I feel cheerful—as I can. That to me is poetic. I try for concentrated consciousness which I miss by more than half, but I'm trying. (quoted in Tate 1983, 4)

Once upon a time, Maya Angelou was a traumatized, silent little girl mistaken by neighbors in Stamps, Arkansas, as a backward or even retarded child. But her grandmother "Momma" Henderson told her, "Sister, Momma don't care what other people say about you. Momma knows when you and the Lord are ready, you goin' to be a teacher" (quoted in Minzesheimer 2008). And she is a teacher; she is a university professor. She still does not plan to retire and "teaches one course each semester at Wake Forest. . . . I work all the time. I don't know how not to work. I'm not complaining. I play hard, too" (quoted in Minzesheimer).

Angelou has succeeded in her objectives and has set a positive example for the present generation and probably for many generations to come. She prefers to teach her readers deliberately and

Maya at the table before an elegant Christmas dinner *(Courtesy Angelou-Johnson Family Archives)*

simply lives what she teaches. In her essay on aging, she closes with lines of homey wisdom: "Mostly, what I have learned so far about aging, despite the creakiness of one's bones and the cragginess of one's once-silken skin, is this: do it. By all means, do it" (1998, 24).

FURTHER READING

Throughout this volume, page citations for all of Angelou's autobiographies are from *The Collected Autobiographies of Maya Angelou* (New York: Modern Library Edition by Random House, 2004).

Angelou, Maya. *All God's Children Need Traveling Shoes.* New York: Random House, 1986.

———. "At Long Last, Ready for the Real Deal." *Washington Post,* 18 January 2009, B05.

———. *The Collected Autobiographies of Maya Angelou.* New York: Random House, 2004.

———. *Even the Stars Look Lonesome.* New York: Bantam Books/Random House, 1998.

———. *Letter to My Daughter.* New York: Random House Publishing Group, 2008.

———. *A Song Flung Up to Heaven.* New York: Random House, 2002.

Barnwell, Cherron A. "Singin' de Blues, Writing Black Female Survival in *I Know Why the Caged Bird Sings.*" In *Maya Angelou,* Bloom's Modern Critical Views, edited by Harold Bloom, 133–155. New York: Bloom's Literary Criticism, 2009.

Braxton, Joanne M. "Symbolic Geography and Psychic Landscapes: A Conversation with Maya Angelou." In *Maya Angelou's* I Know Why the Caged Bird Sings: A Casebook, edited by Joanne M. Braxton, 3–20. New York: Oxford Press, 1999.

Cronin, Gloria. "Angelou, Maya." In *Encyclopedia of African-American Literature,* edited by Wilfred D. Samuels, 12–15. New York: Facts On File, 2007.

Gillespie, Marcia Ann, Rosa Johnson Butler, and Richard A. Long. *Maya Angelou: A Glorious Celebration.* New York: Doubleday, 2008.

Hagen, Lyman B. *Heart of a Woman, Mind of a Writer, and Soul of a Poet: A Critical Analysis of the Writings of Maya Angelou.* Lanham, Md.: University Press of America, 1997.

Kite, L. Patricia. *Maya Angelou.* Minneapolis: Lerner, 1999.

Lee, Felicia R. "Shomburg Center in Harlem Acquires Maya Angelou Archive." *New York Times,* 26 October. 2010, n.p.

Lupton, Mary Jane. *Maya Angelou: A Critical Companion.* Westport, Conn.: Greenwood Press, 1998.

Minzesheimer, Bob. "Maya Angelou Celebrates Her 80 Years of Pain and Joy." USAtoday.com, 26 March 2008. Available online. URL: http://www.usatoday.com/life/books/news/2008-03-26-maya-angelou_N.htm. Accessed March 29, 2010.

Pettit, Jayne. *Maya Angelou: Journey of the Heart.* New York: Puffin Books, 1996.

Russell, Sandi. "Maya Angelou." *Women's Review,* December 1985, 8–9.

Tate, Claudia, ed. *Black Women Writers at Work.* New York: Continuum, 1983.

Weller, Sheila. "Work in Progress: Maya Angelou." In *Conversations with Maya Angelou,* edited by Jeffrey M. Elliot, 10–17. Jackson and London: University Press of Mississippi, 1973.

Younge, Gary. "No Surrender." *Guardian,* 25 May 2000, 16.

PART II

Works

AUTOBIOGRAPHIES

In this book, page citations for all of Angelou's autobiographies are from *The Collected Autobiographies of Maya Angelou* (New York: Modern Library Edition by Random House, 2004).

I Know Why the Caged Bird Sings (1970)

I Know Why the Caged Bird Sings was Maya Angelou's first autobiography, and though she has written five other autobiographies and many essays and poems, it remains her most famous work. This highly acclaimed, groundbreaking book brought her international recognition and was nominated for a National Book Award.

Angelou was initially hesitant to write her autobiography, but many of her friends encouraged her to write and publish her personal stories. JOHN KILLENS, a friend and author, helped her to become active in the HARLEM WRITERS GUILD, where she shared her work with fellow novelists, essayists, and playwrights. By receiving professional critiques, she learned how to distill meanings, edit, and improve her own work. During the late 1960s, Angelou was working on a 10-part television documentary on African-American culture called *Black, Blues, Black,* and ROBERT LOOMIS, an editor from Random House publishers, called her. Her name had been given to him by Judy Feiffer, the wife of the well-known political cartoonist and writer Jules Feiffer (see FEIFFER, JULES AND JUDY), after she and her husband had a dinner at their home with Angelou and JAMES BALDWIN. Maya had been so entertaining that the Feiffers thought she should write her life stories for everyone to read.

Angelou had met the Feiffers through Baldwin, her close friend, shortly after the assassination of Dr. Martin Luther King, Jr. She was in deep grief and depression over King's death, and Baldwin felt laughter might help restore her usually positive outlook. At the Feiffers' dinner party, humorous stories were exchanged, and Angelou's quick wit and clear memory of racial tensions in STAMPS, ARKANSAS, where her grandmother had raised her, impressed all the guests. She was unsure of her ability, but she thought about the possible contribution it might make for both black and white readers, and after some persuasion by Loomis, she began writing her autobiographies.

The book was first published in January 1970. A quote from James Baldwin was printed on the original cover:

> This testimony from a Black sister marks the beginning of a new era in the minds and hearts and lives of all Black men and women. *I Know Why the Caged Bird Sings* liberates the reader into life simply because Maya Angelou confronts her own life with such a moving wonder, such a luminous dignity. I have no words for this achievement, but I know that not since the days of my childhood, when the people in books were more real than the people one saw every day, have I found myself so moved. . . . Her portrait is a Biblical study of life in the midst of death.

I Know Why the Caged Book Sings became an immediate best seller. In many ways, her six autobiographies echo the narrative style of such African-American memoirists as Baldwin, FREDERICK DOUGLASS, and ELDRIDGE CLEAVER. These narratives convey a personal story, but at the same time, they include the social and cultural experiences of African Americans.

In her first autobiography, Angelou describes much of her life experience from early childhood through her middle teen years, when she gave birth to her only child, a son named Clyde (later known as Guy). It is a story of courage and survival, but more than that, it reveals the indomitable spirit of a strong woman. Angelou has repeated many times that we are all role models for someone, and therefore, we must try to be cheerful and positive because someone is always watching and making mental notes of our behavior. The book is dedicated to her son, Guy Johnson, "and all the Strong Black Birds of Promise Who Defy the Odds and Gods and Sing Their Songs."

I Know Why the Caged Bird Sings is written in an adult voice using a child's perspectives and feelings as they are remembered. There are regional expressions throughout the text, some quite poetic, such as "laid a handful of attention on my face" (2004, 36). Some of Angelou's memories of her early life may have been unclear as she wrote, but she skillfully weaves her memory and adult perspectives together to create credible characters and events as she shares her stories.

Angelou's autobiographies have always sold well, but after the recitation of her poem "On the Pulse of Morning" at President BILL CLINTON's inauguration in 1993, both of her primary publishers, Random House and Bantam Books, saw phenomenal increases in the sales of her works. Bantam Books reprinted 400,000 copies of all of her autobiographies because of the demand, and Random House had a 1,200 percent increase over the year before (Brozan 1993).

The William Johnson General Merchandise Store, owned by Maya's grandmother, Annie Henderson, in Stamps, Arkansas *(Courtesy Angelou-Johnson Family Archives)*

SYNOPSIS

Angelou begins the introduction to *I Know Why the Caged Bird Sings* with a question from a childhood poem buried in her memory: "What are you looking at me for? I didn't come to stay . . ." (7). The setting is the children's section of the COLORED METHODIST EPISCOPAL CHURCH on Easter Sunday, and Maya is wearing a rustling, used, cut-down, lavender taffeta dress and feeling conspicuous and uncomfortable. She had thought she would look like a movie star when she wore the dress and often imagined that she was a blond, blue-eyed child temporarily bewitched by a wicked stepmother into a black girl with gapped teeth. She had dreamed, too, that someday everyone would realize that and forgive her for being skinny and nappy-haired. Now she felt ugly and knew that her dress was ugly too.

During the service, she realized that she needed to use the outhouse. She excused herself, but as she left, she tripped over "a foot stuck out from the children's pew" (9) and lost control of her bladder. Running all the way home with urine streaming down her legs, she cried but then began to laugh. She might be punished for leaving church, and the children might laugh at her, but the release would guarantee that at least her head would not explode with backed-up water. She was also delighted to be liberated from church for that day.

Chapter 1

Three-year-old Marguerite (later called Maya) and her brother, four-year-old Bailey Johnson, Jr., were shipped by rail from Long Beach, California, to Stamps, Arkansas, to their father's mother, Mrs. Annie Henderson. They wore tags on their wrists that said: "To Whom It May Concern." The tags identified the children by name and gave the "To" and "From" information. The porter who had been asked to look after them got off of the train in Arizona the day after they left California, and their tickets were pinned to Bailey's inside coat pocket. When they reached the segregated South, where JIM CROW laws were still in effect, black passengers looked after "the poor little motherless darlings" (10) and fed them from their own supply of food.

Grandmother Henderson and their uncle WILLIE JOHNSON, their father's only brother, lived in the back of Grandmother Henderson's general store, the William Johnson General Merchandise Store. (The word *Store* is always capitalized in Angelou's writing.) The grandmother had earned the money to have it built by creating a mobile lunch counter between eastern and western Stamps, where she sold hot meat pies and cool lemonade to workers at the eastern lumberyard and the western cotton gin.

The general store became an unofficial town center for the blacks of the community. They obtained supplies there and talked, exchanged news, and were always treated with respect by Mrs. Henderson. Maya and Bailey loved the store because it was like a fun house, with products ranging from food staples to oranges, peanut paddies, and even balloons.

As the children grew, they fell into the rhythm of life in Stamps. Grandmother, renamed "Momma" soon after their arrival, rose early each morning, said prayers of gratitude, and opened the store. When the cotton was ready to pick, the people—rested, hopeful, and jovial in the mornings—would stop by the store and pick up what they needed for the day, then went to the fields to work until late afternoon. At the end of the workday, they would be exhausted and frustrated that no matter how much they picked, it was never enough to earn the money to meet their expenses.

Chapter 2

Uncle Willie had been dropped and subsequently crippled as a child, but that did not hinder his role as tutor and taskmaster for Maya and Bailey. By the time they were five and six, they knew the times tables. She reflected later that she and Bailey "could rattle off the times tables with the speed I was later to see Chinese children [do correctly] in San Francisco" (13). The children she observed there used ABACUSES, but Maya and her brother had learned by working in their grandmother's store and being held to constant accountability by their uncle and grandmother.

Uncle Willie cared about the children, and though he had no wife and children of his own, Maya reflected that it would be all right if he wanted to pretend she was his daughter. After all, he was giving her better treatment than her own absent father. Once, upon returning home from school, Maya found Uncle Willie in the Store with black schoolteachers from Little Rock who were passing through Stamps. For a rare moment, Uncle Willie was standing up straight behind the counter and appeared to be whole. Maya thought, he must get tired of being a cripple; she understood and felt very close to him.

Maya and Bailey read widely as children, and WILLIAM SHAKESPEARE was her first white love. They read other great writers: RUDYARD KIPLING, EDGAR ALLAN POE, SAMUEL BUTLER, WILLIAM MAKEPEACE THACKERAY, HORATIO ALGER, and WILLIAM ERNEST HENLEY, as well as the black writers PAUL LAURENCE DUNBAR, LANGSTON HUGHES, JAMES WELDON JOHNSON, and W. E. B. DUBOIS.

Chapter 3

At the Store, Maya and Bailey waited on customers, and Maya was often able to guess correct measurements of dry staples before putting the products, such as flour or sugar, onto the scale. The Store was her favorite place. The sun entered softly in the early morning and, like opening a gift, slowly crept across the floor and up the shelves, illuminating the colorful cans, threads, and tobacco. By late afternoon, she sensed that the Store was tired, but like a human it still continued to welcome everyone until at last it was time for bed.

The children had chores, and one of their least favorite was feeding the pigs. The pigs got a mixture of used dishwater and leftover food, and as they rooted and grunted through their vittles, Maya and Bailey imitated them and laughed. One night, while they were feeding the pigs, they heard a horse come into their front yard. It was the former sheriff, warning the family that the KU KLUX KLAN was riding in the region because a "crazy nigger had messed with a white lady" (18). Fearing for the safety of Uncle Willie, the family hid him in the onion/potato bin. They emptied it and then covered him with onions and potatoes, "layer upon layer, like a casserole" (19). No one came that night, but poor Uncle Willie suffered and moaned throughout the long ordeal.

Chapter 4

Maya considered herself to be homely. She admired her brother Bailey's dark, neat beauty compared to her skin hue, which children said was shit color. Bailey had curly hair and velvet black skin. As Maya's trusted friend, he did what he could to protect her. Bailey seemed to be better than Maya at everything: He could read faster, get his chores done faster, play harder, and could even pray out loud in church. To Maya, a lonely child with faith in an unshakable God, Bailey was her "kingdom come" (23).

Now and then, Maya and Bailey were sent to town to get fresh meat. To them, the trip was an adventure, but going into the white part of town was like crossing into enemy territory. Whites were unknown and seemed like aliens. The African Americans lived on the black side of town, but "the strange pale creatures that lived in their alien unlife, weren't considered folks. They were whitefolks" (24).

Chapter 5

Even in the bitterest winter, Maya and Bailey had to bathe outside by the ice-cold well at night. They were to wash their faces, necks, arms, legs, and feet and, as Momma said, "wash as far as possible, then wash possible" (25). The bathing was followed by a coat of Vaseline on their legs. There were protocols of etiquette that the children were trained to observe. No adults were ever to be addressed by their first names. They were to be called "Mister, Missus, Miss, Auntie, Cousin, Unk, Uncl, Buhbah, Sister, Brother," or other appellations. The only ones Maya knew who did not follow these forms were the poor white-trash children. There were poor white-trash SHARECROPPERS living on Momma's land behind the Store. Now and then, they came to the Store, and Maya watched as they took liberties she would never dare. Maya thought they were ghosts without real bodies, and if one of the white children happened to get too close, Maya would pinch the child to see if he or she was real.

Raking and cleaning the soft dirt of the yard was a southern tradition. One morning, just after Maya had finished raking and making half-moon designs in the yard, some "powhitetrash" girls came over the hill and into the yard. Momma saw them and told Maya to go inside. The girls mocked Momma, and Maya watched as her grandmother stood quietly with her arms folded slowly and softly humming a hymn. She waited for the rude girls to finish their taunting, and then one girl did a handstand and displayed her naked self beneath the dress. Grandmother sang quietly, "Bread of Heaven, bread of Heaven, feed me till I want no more" (29). They finally left and said, "Bye, Annie" (29). Standing still, Momma said, "'Bye, Miz Helen, 'bye Miz Ruth, 'bye Miz Elouise" (29).

Maya writes: "I suppose my lifelong paranoia [fear of whites] was born in those molasses-slow minutes" (27). Afterward, Momma went inside the Store and behind the counter to work, softly humming. Maya returned to the yard and worked carefully to make a new design. It was a large heart with small hearts inside. She took Momma's hand and led her outside to see the pattern, and Momma said, "Sister, that's right pretty" (30). Still softly singing a hymn, she returned to her work.

Chapter 6

Every three months, the obese Reverend Howard Thomas, an African American from TEXARKANA, ARKANSAS, would arrive with his GLADSTONE BAG and visit Stamps to collect the offerings given since his last visit and to preach a Sunday sermon. He stayed overnight at Momma's and made no secret about enjoying her food. The children covertly mocked his looks and blustery words and regarded him as an unwelcome guest and buffoon. Momma always prepared a huge breakfast before church designed to hold the family from 9:30 A.M. to 3:00 P.M. When Reverend Thomas was there, he said such a long prayer before the meal that the food got cold. Maya observes that "The eggs had withdrawn from the edge of the platter to bunch in the center like children left out in the cold" (33).

On the Sundays of his visits, Reverend Thomas preached, and Maya and Bailey had to sit on the front row. Sister Monroe, one of the women in the congregation, lived in the country and could not make it to church every Sunday. When she was there, she would sometimes act like she had "got the spirit" (34) and shout, throw her arms around, and jerk her body. One time, she caused near pandemonium by climbing the steps to the dais, grabbing Reverend Taylor, and shouting wildly, "Preach it. I say, preach it" (34).

This particular day, with Reverend Thomas preaching, Maya, Bailey, and their grandmother were all wondering how Sister Monroe would conduct herself. After he began his sermon, the children heard "Preach it" from behind them. Sister Monroe approached the altar, and Reverend

Thomas moved away from her and continued to preach. She followed him and was so agitated that she hit him on the back of the head with her purse, and suddenly his false teeth flew out.

Maya was struggling not to laugh at Reverend Thomas with his "lips flapping loose like tired elastic" (38). He picked up his teeth with a handkerchief and said, "Naked I came into the world, and naked I shall go out" (38). The ushers took Sister Monroe out, and Maya and Bailey immediately let loose. They both rolled off the bench and onto the floor, hysterical with laughter. Uncle Willie gave them a terrible whipping afterward, and Maya said that in the weeks that followed, every time Bailey said "Preach it," she remembered that thrashing, hit him hard, and cried.

Chapter 7

Momma had been married three times. The father of her two sons, Bailey and Willie Johnson, deserted the family around 1900, and then she married Mr. Henderson. The third and last was Mr. Murphy. Maya never knew him, but one Saturday night he showed up and slept on the floor. The next day, he waited for their return from church, enjoyed Momma's delicious Sunday meal, and then left.

Once, Momma was summoned by the court because she and Willie had hidden a black man who was accused of "assaulting white womanhood" (40). The man said he had hid in Mrs. Henderson's store, and in turn, the judge subpoenaed Mrs. Henderson, assuming she was a white store owner. The title of *Mrs.* was something rarely used for a black. The judge, bailiff, and other whites laughed at the error. The blacks felt the title was appropriate use, considering the respect they had for her. Momma knew and understood the safe paths blacks were forced to take with whites, particularly in the South, and she made every effort to teach those life-protecting strategies to Maya and Bailey.

Chapter 8

To the impoverished blacks of Stamps, it seemed that the whites were wasteful of their money. Momma bought two bolts of cloth each year from Sears and Roebuck and made clothes and underwear for the children and herself. Only Uncle Willie had store-bought clothes. At first, the DEPRESSION did not seem to impact the black community, but when the price of cotton dropped, they knew that the bad economy had hit everywhere. Momma kept the store going by taking trades, and the people often swapped government-issued foods for her store goods.

Though Maya and Bailey often thought their absent parents might be dead, the children were surprised by Christmas gifts one year. They knew they had been abandoned by their parents, and the gifts confused them. They cried and then were scolded for ingratitude. The children thought maybe the gifts were a sign that their mother might be coming for them soon, but she did not. The day after Christmas, they destroyed the doll that Maya had received.

Chapter 9

When Maya was seven, her father appeared at the Store in a fancy car he had driven from California to Stamps. He was huge and handsome and stayed for three weeks. Maya did not know if she loved him or not, and she was relieved when she thought he was leaving. He had intruded into her private life, but she soon learned that she and her brother would be leaving with him.

To prepare Maya for life outside Stamps, Momma made jumpers and skirts for her out of giveaway clothing she had received in trade. She packed their clothes in cardboard boxes, and they left Stamps with Maya and the boxes in the backseat of the car along with fried chicken and sweet potato pie. Bailey and her dad talked and laughed in the front seat. He was taking them to St. Louis to live with their mother. Maya asked if she could go back to Stamps, but their father assured her that their mother, "Mother Dear," would not "eat them" (48), and it would be all right. No one had explained, and Maya felt betrayed. St. Louis was hot and seemed dirty, and Maya wondered if they were being driven into Hell. PIG LATIN was an emergency-only children's language, and Bailey did not like Maya to use it around adults, but she needed assurance from him that they were safe so she used the language to communicate with him. Bailey told her not to worry. When they finally arrived, they at last met their mother. "Mother

Dear" was a stunning beauty with a wide smile, beautiful teeth, and a clean, fresh-butter color. Bailey, Sr., left for California a few days later, and Maya felt that he was one stranger abandoning her to another.

Chapter 10

Their mother did not have a home large enough to accommodate them, so at first they stayed at their grandmother Baxter's house. Grandmother Baxter was nearly white. She was raised by a German family in Cairo, Illinois, and met Grandfather Baxter in St. Louis. She spoke with a German accent, and he spoke with the cadence of the West Indies. The black section of St. Louis where the Baxter family lived was rough and lawless. These were the Prohibition years of the 1930s. Grandmother Baxter was a local precinct captain, and after school Maya often walked into a living room full of needed "NUMBERS RUNNERS, gamblers, lottery takers, and whiskey salesmen" (51). Grandmother Baxter had influence with the police, and she traded her ability to get them leniency for various charges for votes to keep her in office.

Maya and Bailey were enrolled in Toussaint L'Ouverture Grammar School, where they attended for one full school year. They were ahead of their classmates, and though the teachers were trained and the building substantial, Maya and Bailey found the children "[s]hockingly backward" (52). Sometimes, after school, Maya and Bailey would meet their mother at Louie's, a dark tavern that was near the school. They enjoyed the time there with her, and besides "soft drinks and boiled shrimp," they both learned to dance.

Their mother, VIVIAN BAXTER, had one sister who had moved to California and four brothers: Tutti, Tom, Ira, and Billie. They all worked in the city, and they had a reputation for being mean. Tommy was Maya's favorite. He played ball with them and once said to Maya, "Ritie, don't worry 'cause you ain't pretty. Plenty pretty women I seen digging ditches or worse. You smart. I swear to God, I rather you have a good mind than a cute behind" (55). After several months, Maya and Bailey moved from the Baxter house into their mother's home. By this time, Bailey's name for Maya, "my sister," had become her name. Their mother had a boyfriend, Mr. Freeman, who was a big, slow southerner. She was light-skinned, educated, and quick, and Maya thought he was very lucky to have her.

Chapter 11

St. Louis seemed temporary to young Maya. It was noisy and bustling and very unlike Stamps. Maya would retreat into the imaginary world of "Robin Hood's forest and the caves of Alley Oop where all reality was unreal and even that changed every day" (57). After finishing their homework, the children were allowed to listen to *The SHADOW* or other shows on the radio. Their mother was a trained nurse, but she earned her money "cutting poker games in gambling parlors" (57). Mr. Freeman was a foreman in the Southern Pacific train yards. Both children were physically afflicted by their insecurities. Bailey stuttered, and Maya had horrible nightmares. Sometimes, to comfort her, Maya's mother would take her to sleep in the big bed where she and Mr. Freeman slept together. It was there, in Vivian's absence, that Freeman first touched and molested young Maya.

Both children loved to read and bought illustrated paperbacks with their spending money. Homework was first, but then came pleasure reading. They both enjoyed JACK LONDON's adventure stories and a variety of other popular classics. The children were good friends, and Maya confided in Bailey. However, Mr. Freeman warned Maya that if she ever told anyone that he had touched her in the bed, he would kill Bailey.

Maya enjoyed watching Bailey with his newfound friends playing games in the neighborhood. She spent much of her time in the library exploring the world of ideas.

Chapter 12

Alone together one Saturday morning in the late spring or early summer, Mr. Freeman brutally raped Maya. She was seven (or eight), and the violation made her ill. Freeman told her to get out of the house afterward and walk to the library. Though she was in great pain, she did as he directed. On the way home, she hurt severely, but she played a counting game using the cracks in the sidewalk to distract her mind. She painfully climbed the steps to her room, one at a time, hid her blood-stained panties under the mattress, and went to bed. When her mother found her apparently ill, she checked to see if Maya had a fever and then assumed Maya was coming down with the measles.

Freeman left the next morning after a fight with Vivian. That same day, Maya's bed linens needed to be changed, and a fearful and confused Maya needed to be bathed. As her mother held her, Bailey stripped the bed, and Maya's stained underpants fell from the linens and revealed the trauma.

Chapter 13

Maya was taken to the hospital, and there, reluctantly, she told Bailey what had happened. He passed the information to Grandmother Baxter, and Freeman was arrested. Maya received love and attention from the family while she was in the hospital and thought she might like to stay there for the rest of her life.

Sometime later, Maya had to testify in court. The weather was very hot, but Maya was allowed to wear her navy-blue winter coat with brass buttons that she seemed to hug to herself for protection. When the judge asked when was the first time Freeman had touched her, she froze in silence. The lawyer rephrased the question and asked if Freeman had touched her before the rape. Maya, reasoning as a child, said, "No," and knew she was lying because Freeman had touched her in the bed. The lie was devastating, and Maya instantly regretted it. She began to cry and felt she had been made to lie. She was thinking words that came screaming out of her mouth: "Ole mean, dirty thing, you. Dirty old thing" (68). If she had told of the molestation in the bed, Freeman would have received a heavier sentence. As it turned out, Freeman was sentenced to a year and a day, but someone got him off, and he was released that afternoon.

At home soon afterward, Maya and Bailey heard the doorbell ring unexpectedly. It was a policeman who had come to tell Mrs. Baxter that Freeman had been found dead on a lot behind the slaughterhouse, apparently kicked to death. The truth of the murder frightened the children. Bailey did not understand, and Maya, somehow thinking that her lying words had caused his death, decided to stop talking. She thought that her words had killed a man.

Soon the children were put on a train and sent back to Stamps. Bailey was brokenhearted to again be separated from their mother, but Maya, in sustained silence, stoically accepted whatever might happen to them. She cared about Bailey and did not care about their destination.

Chapter 14

Maya was glad to return to the "obscure lanes and lonely bungalows set back deep in dirt yards" (71). It felt like a safe cocoon. No one there seemed to expect much of the children except for mild curiosity about Mrs. Henderson's California grandchildren who had been on a glamorous trip to the fabulous St. Louis. They asked questions about buildings, elevators, and white folks. Bailey made up all sorts of tales to impress and regale the locals. He told them that there were buildings so high that for months in the winter, people could not see the top. He described watermelons as big as a cow's head, and he told them that if they could guess the correct number of seeds before it was cut open, they might win five zillion dollars and a new car.

Maya remained silent. Bailey seemed to understand her choice not to talk and treated her with kindness. Her mind was dull during this time, and both colors and her memory were clouded. The people seemed to accept her silence and blamed it on her pining for the big city. She was also known to be tenderhearted, and she was perceived to be a little delicate. Some folks thought she was retarded.

Chapter 15

For four and a half years, Maya did not speak, except to Bailey and Momma. Then she met MRS. BERTHA FLOWERS, a "gentlewoman" who wore printed voile dresses, flowered hats, and gloves. In retrospect, the adult writer Angelou writes: "She was one of the few gentlewomen I have ever known, and has remained throughout my life the measure of what a human being can be" (74). Mrs. Flowers was educated and lived in a little bungalow at the top of a hill. She bought things at the store, and Maya was embarrassed by her grandmother's grammar. That did not seem to bother the soft-spoken Mrs. Flowers. After choosing a few items in the Store one summer afternoon, Momma suggested that Bailey carry the sacks to her home. Mrs. Flowers thanked her but said she would prefer that Marguerite carry them. Maya's grandmother told her to change her clothes before helping Mrs. Flowers, and Maya got a dress from the CHIFFOROBE. Grandmother Henderson had made the dress with fabric from the MONTGOMERY WARD & COMPANY catalog, and she showed Mrs. Flowers the perfect FRENCH SEAMS she had made. The dress was as well-made on the inside as the outside, and that revealed Momma's standard for everything.

Mrs. Flowers began to talk to Maya as they walked. She told Maya that she had heard she was doing well in school. The path widened, and Maya was invited to walk beside Mrs. Flowers, who told Maya of the importance of words. She suggested that Maya read aloud and play with the sounds of sentences. They reached the house, and to Maya's surprise it smelled like vanilla. Mrs. Flowers had made tea cookies and lemonade expressly for her, and there were extras that she could take to Bailey. She told Maya about the concept of MOTHER WIT, or common sense.

After serving the cookies and lemonade, Mrs. Flowers brushed off the table and took a small book from her bookcase. In a beautiful voice, she began to read, "It was the best of times and the worst of times . . ." (79). Maya listened, but she did not really hear. She was deeply entranced by the musical quality of Mrs. Flower's voice and did not absorb the words. When Mrs. Flowers asked Maya if she liked what she had heard, she answered, "Yes Ma'am" (79), but that was all. When it was time to go, Mrs. Flower gave Maya a book of poems and asked her to memorize one so she could recite on her next visit. She gave her cookies for Bailey, and Maya returned home reflecting on the sweet friendship of this woman. She had singled out Maya, and it felt deeply affirming.

Chapter 16

Reflecting on a comment made by a white woman from Texas who said being raised black in a southern town by a successful shop owner was comparable to a white debutante gave Maya pause. She was being raised carefully, but the training was not the same. There was very little money, but black girls were taught certain refinements. Delicate handwork, manners, COOKING with care, washing, and ironing were all a part of their finishing school. Often the girls were trained to work as domestics, and when Maya was nearly 10, she began to work at the house of a homely white woman named Mrs. Viola Cullinan.

Miss Glory was the cook at the Cullinan house. She was a descendant of slaves who had worked for the Cullinans in Virginia. It was Miss Glory who taught Maya the difference between a salad plate, a bread plate, and a dessert plate. She was patient with Maya and explained the various pieces of silver, crystal, and china. There was vocabulary that Maya had never encountered before, such as *tureen, soup spoons, gravy boat, butter knives,* and *carving platter,* which suggested to her that Mrs. Cullinan lived in an Alice-in-Wonderland house.

One evening, Maya was asked to serve Mrs. Cullinan's lady friends on her porch. She was returning to the kitchen when one of the women said, "What's your name, girl?" (85) Mrs. Cullinan said, "Margaret." The woman said she would call her Mary because the other name was too long. Maya overheard the conversation and was so furious she became sick to her stomach. After throwing up in a flower bed, Miss Glory surmised that Maya might be coming down with something, so she excused her for the day.

At work the next day, Mrs. Cullinan called Maya "Mary." Miss Glory reminded her that the child's name was Margaret. Mrs. Cullinan said that was too long, and henceforth she should be called Mary. Maya was deeply offended. Blacks had been nicknamed many ugly names, and to be denied one's own name was an insult and horror. Miss Glory suggested that she ignore it; after all, "Hallelujah" was the name she was given at birth, but Mrs. Cullinan had renamed her "Glory," and she actually liked it better. Maya felt demeaned and knew she would have to figure out a way to quit the job. If she did not do it right, Momma would never allow it. For the following week, Maya arrived late and left early, did a sloppy job with the dishes, and did not work hard at polishing the silver. Miss

Glory did not complain to the mistress about it, so Maya asked Bailey for advice.

At work the next day, when Maya was instructed to serve the ladies on the porch, she deliberately dropped the empty serving tray. When Mrs. Cullinan screamed "Mary" at her, she picked up a fish-shaped casserole dish and two green glass cups, both favorites of Mrs. Cullinan's, and dropped them on the tile floor. Both Miss Glory and Mrs. Cullinan were aghast; it was Mrs. Cullinan's mother's Virginia china. The woman who had suggested the name Mary came into the kitchen and asked if Maya had done it. Mrs. Cullinan responded sharply that the girl's name was Margaret and threw a shard of the broken plate at Maya. It missed Maya and hit Miss Glory just over the ear. Maya had left the front door open so everyone could hear, and she reflected that Mrs. Cullinan had finally got her name right.

Chapter 17

One Saturday night, Bailey did not come home from the movies when expected. It was well after dark, and Momma's eyes reflected deep apprehension. The South was a dangerous place for black men and young black boys. Momma and Maya walked together in the darkness, and before long they met Bailey. He did not explain where he had been, but he seemed very sad. When they got home, Uncle Willie gave Bailey a beating with a leather belt for being late and worrying them.

Maya heard Bailey say his prayers that night, but he still sounded sad. When Bailey and Maya were doing their chores a few days later, Bailey said, "I saw Mother Dear" (92). He explained that he saw a white movie star in a film, KAY FRANCIS, who looked just like their mother. His lateness that night was because he was watching the film over and over. Two months later, another Kay Francis movie came to Stamps. Maya enjoyed the film, but she thought her mother was much prettier than Kay Francis.

The two children enjoyed the movies and their favorite stars included BETTE DAVIS, VERONICA LAKE, HERBERT MARSHALL, and CLAUDE RAINS, as well as the cartoon character MICKEY MOUSE. Typical of films of that time, blacks were stereotyped as an unwise maid and a chauffeur. On the way home, Bailey ran across some tracks just before a train went by and left Maya on the other side. After the train passed, Maya found Bailey, but she feared that at some point he would catch a freight train and run away. About a year later, he did just that but was stranded in Baton Rouge, Louisiana, for two weeks.

Chapter 18

The cotton pickers who came to the Store were painfully tired at the end of the day. Both the men and the women tried to make a show of bravado in the face of fatigue and frustration. No matter what they earned, it was never enough. Maya reflected that Momma still thanked God for even the smallest achievement, but it seemed to the girl that the more affluent people became, the less they seemed to turn to God. In spite of fatigue and hunger, these same people planned to go home, clean up, and attend a continuing revival meeting again that night. They would take their children too, reminding themselves that the Good Book said, "Raise a child in the way he should go and he will not depart from it" (95).

The revival was being held in a tent by the railroad tracks. It pulled black people in from all the denominations in Stamps—from the staid African Methodist Episcopals to the raucous Holy Rollers. The singing and shouting had a rhythm, and it went on until the minister said "Amen." When the program finally began, the minister introduced the bishop and invited him to say a prayer. The style was call and response, and after the opening prayer, the people sang another spirited hymn.

There were cardboard fans with funeral home advertisements on them, and the ladies waved white, lacy handkerchiefs. Then came the sermon. Angelou writes: "I had never heard a preacher jump into the muscle of his sermon so quickly" (99). The topic was charity, and the congregation responded vocally and passionately. There was another hymn, and then the call to dedicate oneself to Christ and charity by joining one of the denominations. That was followed by a collection and then one more hymn. The people felt that though life was hard and they continued to be downtrodden by whites,

Cotton pickers waiting to be taken to the fields where they will work many hours and then, exhausted, be returned, with little recompense for their labor *(Courtesy Library of Congress Prints and Photographs Division)*

their reward would be a justification and joy in the eternities, in the next life, if they could behave charitably in this one.

As they all walked home after the meeting, they passed a good-time house (sometimes called a juke joint) where honky-tonk music was blaring, and the people were having a rousing good time. Angelou reflected that the revival music and honky-tonk (or BARRELHOUSE BLUES) would sound about the same to an outsider, but the salient question regarding their lowly position was, "How long, oh God? How long?" (104).

Chapter 19

People crowded into the Store to listen to the radio broadcast of the world boxing match between the famous world heavyweight champion JOE LOUIS (the "Brown Bomber") and Primo Carnera. It was summer, June 25, 1935, and the store was packed. Uncle Willie turned the volume all the way up so the children on the porch would not miss anything. The fight was between a black and a white boxer, a powerful demonstration of the struggle the blacks of Stamps experienced every day. Maya imagined that if Louis lost, it would be like being thrown back into slavery, and all the insults blacks had suffered would be heaped on their heads once again. The blows continued, and at last the contender was down. The referee counted, and then the announcement was made: "The winnah, and still heavyweight champion of the world . . . Joe Louis" (106).*

The community in the Store celebrated with Coca-Cola and candy bars. Some of the men went behind the store and added white lightening (home-brewed alcohol) to their sodas, and some of the bigger boys followed them. After an hour or so, the people headed home, but those who lived far away stayed in town. Joe Louis had proven they were the strongest people in the world, and

*Primo Carnera lost the heavyweight championship to Max Baer in in 1934. When he fought Joe Louis on June 25, 1935, and was defeated, Louis was not officially declared world heavyweight champion. That occurred in 1937, when Louis defeated James J. Braddock.

it would not be safe for black families to be on the dark road that night.

Chapter 20

The summer fish-fry picnic was the outdoor event of the year. All of the churches, social groups and clubs, teachers, other professionals, and excited children were there. It may have been, in part, a celebration of JUNETEENTH—June 19—traditionally the day that southern black people celebrate as Emancipation Day and give special thanks for the end of slavery, though the date is not defined. Musicians played "cigar-box guitars, harmonicas, juice harps [Jew's Harps], combs wrapped in tissue paper and even bathtub basses" (108) (created from an upside-down aluminum bath or wash tub). There was the best food the ladies could prepare, and it included everything from crisp fried chicken and country ham to pickles and watermelon, delicious coconut, orange, and chocolate cakes, and more. Experienced fishermen caught bass and perch and handed them to girls who cleaned them. Then the girls passed them on to women who salted each one, rolled them in cornmeal, and then dropped them in boiling fat. It was a great system with delicious results.

Maya found a quiet place in a grove of trees and sat down between two protruding black walnut tree roots. Soon she was joined by a neighbor girl, Louise Kendricks. Louise found a root seat and settled in close to Maya. The girls pretended they were falling into the sky. They played by spinning around and around, tumbling, and laughing, and they became good friends. After being a "woman" for three years, Maya had once again become a girl.

One day at school, a boy passed a note to Maya. She was not quite sure what to make of it, so she passed it to Louise for a second opinion. It was from a boy named Tommy Valden, and Louise explained that it was a Valentine. Maya was not interested in love or in being anyone's Valentine, so she tore up the note and threw it away. Speaking of love seemed to trigger unpleasant feelings about the past in Maya's mind. Later, she received another note from the same boy, but this time it was signed T. V. It was kind, and Maya began to be friendlier to him when she saw him, but he lost interest in her soon because when Maya would see him, she would collapse in giggles.

Chapter 21

Bailey made a tent out of branches and a worn blanket behind the house and there, with Maya playing lookout in the so-called role of baby, he invited various girls to play "Momma and Papa" with him. It was not a consummated act but rather a wiggling of his hips as he lay on top of various girls. He was 11, and the game continued in the same way until he met an orphaned girl new to town named Joyce, who was four years older than him.

Joyce hung around the tent and ran errands for Momma. One day, Bailey and Joyce decided they would play house; Maya would stand guard. Over Maya's protests, Joyce invited Bailey to remove his trousers and complete the act. Maya was sent off, and later Bailey told her the details of the first encounter. Joyce soon ran off with a railroad porter, and Bailey fell into a melancholy silence, much like Maya's earlier sustained withdrawal from talking. Momma and Mrs. Goodman, Joyce's aunt, who liked her niece, commiserated about scriptural admonitions concerning "The Lord giveth and the Lord taketh away" (118). Bailey finally accepted Joyce's absence and never mentioned her name again.

Chapter 22

It was November, and a storm was working into a frenzy outside. The wind whistled under the door. The Store was closed early because people, fearful of a dangerous tornado, would stay inside. It was a good night for reading: Maya had *Jane Eyre,* Bailey had *Mark Twain,* and Uncle Willie was reading the *Almanac.* Momma was preparing corn cakes and vegetable soup for dinner when a rattle and a knock at the back door signaled a visitor. It was Mr. George Taylor.

Mr. Taylor's wife had died in the past summer, and neighbors had been feeding him. Uncle Willie told him that he could join them for supper anytime. Momma agreed and began to serve the meal. The man was melancholy, and Momma tried to speak wisdom about acceptance to him. Then his posture changed, his eyes brightened, and he said that just last night his wife had told him that she wanted children. He said it was not a dream, and he wanted to tell the story. Maya got up and walked away. She had wearied of folks telling "anti-life" stories in the Store and did not want to hear another one.

When Mrs. Taylor died, she had left Maya her favorite imitation gold brooch. The woman had become acquainted with the child in the Store and was fond of her, so Momma said Maya had to go to the funeral. She reluctantly went, of course, and the funeral was progressing normally with people dressed in dark clothes, mournful music, and a sermon that recounted and praised Mrs. Taylor's good works. The time came for the congregation to file by the casket for a last look and farewell, and Maya froze for a moment at the casket. She had never seen a dead person or understood the finality of death, but she reflected that Mrs. Taylor looked like "[a] mud baby, molded into form by creative children on a rainy day, soon to run back into the loose earth" (127).

Momma told Maya to come back to the table, and Mr. Taylor began his story. He said a laughing, blue-eyed baby angel had appeared to him while he was in bed the night before, and he also heard his wife moan. Then his wife's voice said, "I want some children" (128), and the little angel laughed and laughed. The story fascinated Bailey and frightened Maya. Mr. Taylor asked Momma what she thought it meant. Her suggestions did not seem to help. At last, bedtime came. Mr. Taylor slept on a pallet in Uncle Willie's room, and Maya slept near Momma for safety and refuge.

Chapter 23

Large classes were graduating from both the grammar and high schools in Stamps, and they shared one graduation ceremony. The black high school was a bare-bones facility with rusty basketball hoops and a simple field used for various outdoor sports. Maya and her eighth-grade classmates wore dresses made of yellow piqué for their graduation, and Momma had hand-smocked Maya's dress. She was at the top of her class and would be among the first called in the graduating ceremonies. Bailey gave her a gift of poems by Edgar Allan Poe, and Momma made a Sunday breakfast, though it was only Friday.

The ceremony began with the principal's welcome, followed by the Baptist minister's invocation. The main speaker was a white man from Texarkana named Mr. Edward Donleavy. He talked about improvements to be made at the white school and mentioned the great potential the white students had. He held up sports heroes like Joe Louis and JESSE OWENS to the black students, but gave no examples of black leaders and thinkers. The students dropped their heads because they were demeaned with the reminder that their expectations could only be in sports or servitude.

Donleavy was running for election and left before the ceremonies were over. The demoralized assembly continued with the graduation ceremony, but the atmosphere was heavy. At last, Henry Reed began to give his well-practiced valedictory address based on Shakespeare's soliloquy in Hamlet, "To Be or Not to Be," but then he stopped and began to sing/talk "Lift Every Voice and Sing," the unofficial Negro national anthem written by J. Rosamund Johnson. Soon everyone joined in. Hearts were lifted, and their pride returned. Angelou reflects that the voices of her people, "preachers, musicians, and blues singers" (143), were the very voices that sustained them again and again in the constant and ongoing struggle for equal opportunities, acceptance, and respect.

Chapter 24

Maya was in blinding pain because of two dental cavities that were rotten to the gums. Momma knew of a black doctor in Texarkana, 25 miles away, but decided to take Maya to the local white dentist in Stamps. Dr. Lincoln owed Momma a favor because she had helped him during the lean years of the depression. Maya, in excruciating pain, bathed and dressed, and they walked to the dentist's office. They climbed the back steps and knocked on the door. Annie, a white girl, answered, and Momma asked the girl to tell the dentist they were there.

When the dentist came to the door, Momma explained the situation. Dr. Lincoln courteously explained that he did not treat colored people.

That was his firm policy. Momma reminded him that when he came to her to borrow money, he did not have to beg. He reminded her that he had repaid her, then he said that he would "rather stick my hand in a dog's mouth than in a nigger's" (147). Turning his back, he went inside, and Momma sent Maya downstairs to wait for her.

Momma went into the office, and Maya imagined that her grandmother had verbally obliterated the dentist and ordered him out of Stamps. Finally, she came down the steps and took Maya to the kind black dentist in Texarkana. When they got home, Maya explained to the family what had happened. Though he had paid in full, Momma told him that he still owed $10 in interest. He argued a little, but he paid it, and Momma signed a receipt. She figured that if he was going to treat her poorly, he could pay for it (fair or not). Then, at last, Momma laughed.

Chapter 25

Momma decided that it was time for Maya and Bailey to join their parents in California. The decision may have been triggered by an experience Bailey had in Stamps. He saw a dead and decayed black man fished out of a pond, and he watched as a white man rolled the body over with his foot and then laughed. Bailey, along with other black male adults, was ordered by the white man to carry the corpse to a calaboose (a jail). Bailey did not understand, but he was beginning to realize the racial danger black males in the South had to learn to negotiate. Using money from the Store and railway pass reductions obtained in trade for groceries, Momma escorted Maya to California, and Bailey followed about a month later. Though their mother, Vivian Baxter, lived in SAN FRANCISCO, Momma thought it best to escort Maya to LOS ANGELES, where her father lived at that time.

Chapter 26

Vivian Baxter met them at the train looking slender and stylish in a head-to-toe beige suede ensemble. It was a friendly welcome, and Maya mentally compared the two adults to a chick and mother hen. Maya and Momma settled into an apartment, and Vivian returned to San Francisco to prepare a home for her two children. Bailey soon arrived, as planned, and Momma remained in Los Angeles for about six months. Daddy Bailey (Sr.) stopped by with fresh fruit occasionally. Angelou retrospectively marvels at the remarkable adjustment Momma made to urban life, going to church and making new friends in the city. She then returned to Stamps to care for Uncle Willie when Vivian was ready to take the children.

Maya and Bailey wondered what living with their real mother would be like, and it turned out to be fun. The first few months, they lived in an apartment in Oakland, small but adequate, and Grandmother Baxter lived with them, but soon they relocated to a big house. One night about 2:00 A.M., their mother quietly wakened them and said she was giving them a party. She was a delight to them, a beautiful woman who laughed, sang, and danced and was unflinchingly honest with her children. She worked at gambling and played pinochle or ran poker games for money and was able to earn enough to support her mother and children.

Maya and Bailey were introduced to new foods and cultures in San Francisco: Italian and Chinese dishes, Hungarian goulash, Irish stew, and other less exotic tastes such as bologna. Their mother had owned a restaurant and gambling casino in St. Louis, but her partner was slack about working. When she had confronted him, he became physically abusive and called her names. She warned him and then deliberately shot him twice and ended up with two black eyes and an overnight stay in jail. They had dissolved the partnership but remained mutual admirers. Soon after that, Vivian had moved to California. In time, she married a successful businessman the children called "Daddy Clidell," and they bought a big house in San Francisco. Bailey and Maya finally had a father figure, and their uncles Tommy and Billy as well as Grandmother Baxter lived together in the big OAKLAND, CALIFORNIA, home.

Chapter 27

The FILLMORE DISTRICT of San Francisco had once been the home of Japanese and Chinese immigrants and their children. The Japanese people were mostly NISEI, or Japanese Americans who were born and educated in the United States. It was the beginning of World War II, and Japanese families had been placed in internment camps because of the fear that they may have remained loyal to Japan and assist in Japan's war against the United States. As the Asians were quietly removed, local black families and new black arrivals from the South replaced them. There was work, and many blacks earned more money than ever before.

Maya felt comfortable in the eight-to-10 blocks of the Fillmore area where her mother's large home was located. She was a newcomer among many other newcomers, and the city seemed to have the right combination of formal and informal ambience for her. Both blacks and whites from the South poured into the city to work, and southern animosities rooted in prejudice and fear were just under the surface in many of the war plants. Racial tension had moved in with the new residents.

Chapter 28

Maya was advanced two semesters at her first high school in San Francisco, but she was soon transferred to George Washington High School, some 60 blocks from the black neighborhood where she lived. She was one of three black students there. The teacher who made the biggest impression on her was a Miss Kirwin, the civics and current events instructor. Miss Kirwin respected her students and treated them all the same. She recognized and said that Maya had a good mind and "should be doing something with it" (167).

Maya received an unexpected scholarship to the California Labor School, a college for adults. For two years, she took classes in drama and dance in the evening, six months of which were spent studying pantomime. Her day-to-day life was structured by her emulation of Grandmother Henderson's strong determination, Mrs. Flower's love of books, Bailey's love, her mother's gaiety, and Miss Kirwin's teaching of current events. In the evening, she studied dance and drama.

Chapter 29

The large house (14 rooms) that Vivian Baxter and Daddy Clidell owned in San Francisco accommodated many boarders. Along with Maya and Bailey, they were all housed on the second floor. Their mother taught the children proper behaviors, such as "personal hygiene, proper posture, table manners, good restaurants and tipping practices, Daddy Clidell taught me to play poker, blackjack, tonk and high, low, Jick, Jack, and the Game" (169). Clidell cared about Maya, and he contributed to her education by letting his friends, skilled con men, teach her how never to become "anybody's mark" (170). Mr. Red Leg, one of the con men, told her many stories about how clever blacks, acting stupid (as white marks expected), could outwit and con their victims out of money.

African Americans respected those in the black community who used their ingenuity for gain. Expensive cars and clothing worn by janitors or housekeepers reflected their ability to get what they wanted. Because of the constant oppression by whites, the blacks learned to straddle both worlds, and petty crime among their people was largely ignored. The blacks created their own cultural mores; their society had boundaries and was made safe and familiar in many ways. Another accepted example of black insider culture was the dual use of speech. In the white classroom or setting, a black would probably say, "That's not unusual" (173). Angelou writes that meeting the same situation in the street, black vernacular might be used, and the comment could be, "It be's like that sometimes" (173).

Chapter 30

Maya's father, Daddy Bailey, invited Maya to spend the summer with him and his sort-of fiancée in San Diego. They lived in a trailer that the woman, Dolores Stockland, carefully kept clean and tidy. From the beginning, Dolores and Maya had a strained relationship because Maya was required to keep her room clean but had never been taught how to do it. Daddy Bailey was a dietitian and cook and often brought home half-roasts, pieces of ham, and quartered chicken from his job in the kitchen of a U.S. Navy hospital. He created sophisticated gourmet dishes out of the leftovers. One evening, he announced that he was going to Mexico for some culinary supplies and invited Maya to accompany him. Dolores was not interested in going.

The next morning, father and daughter left for their destination, which was about five miles out

Maya, book in hand, during the summer of 1943, which she spent in San Diego, California, with her father *(Courtesy Angelou-Johnson Family Archives)*

of ENSENADA, MEXICO. The roads were steep and twisted, but they finally stopped outside a cantina where half-dressed children chased chickens around and around the yard. Daddy Bailey was warmly welcomed, and Maya recognized that he was well-liked and comfortable there. She danced and drank Coca-Cola until she realized that she did not know where her father was. She searched the cantina and then went outside. His car was there, but she still did not see him.

Maya got in the car and waited. She correctly figured he was with a woman. Finally, she saw him being helped back to the cantina by a man and woman. Maya persuaded him to return to the car, and he quickly passed out in the backseat. She decided that she could drive them home. It was a stick-shift car, which she did not know how to drive, but she kept it on the road. When she reached the guard box at the border, she lost control of the car and ran into the side of another automobile that held a large family. Everyone was speaking rapid Spanish, and finally they seemed to understand that this was a daughter driving home a drunken father after a fiesta of some kind. The people woke him up, and Maya told him there had been an accident. He reached into the glove compartment and got insurance papers and a half-full bottle of whisky. He put his arm around the shoulder of the other driver and walked with the guard into the guard hut; soon the three men were laughing. Daddy Bailey returned to the car, and he and Maya were on their way once again. Sober, he rolled down the windows to stay awake and gave her his jacket to keep warm.

Chapter 31

When they got home, Dolores was jealous that Maya had made the trip with her father, and that Daddy Bailey and his daughter seemed to be getting along so well. Dolores was upset and angry, and Bailey left the trailer, simply saying he was going out for a while. Maya overheard the argument from her room and went to Dolores to console her. Dolores said Maya should go back to her mother, whom she called a prostitute, and Maya slapped her. Dolores came after Maya with some sharp scissors and jabbed her in the side, a bad cut. Maya left the trailer and got into her father's car once again, rolled up the windows, and locked the doors.

Dolores was screaming at her, and Daddy Bailey and the neighbors came out and crowded around Dolores. He took Dolores back to the trailer and then went to help Maya. Getting into the car, he saw the blood and asked what had happened. Maya told him she had been cut and that Dolores had done it. Bailey took her to a woman who cleaned the cut and taped it. Afterward, he took Maya to friends at another trailer for the night. The next morning, she awakened to learn that she had been left alone. Her father arrived around noon, gave her $1.50 and a kiss, and said he would return in the evening. Maya decided to run away. She had about $3, made a few tuna-fish sandwiches, and walked out of the neighbor's trailer into the unknown of Southern California.

Chapter 32

Most of the day was spent wandering though sunlit streets, checking out arcades, and exploring. The library seemed like the best place to be, and the washroom there provided privacy and a place to change her bandage. Later, Maya discovered a junkyard and decided to spend the night in an old car. She settled in, ate her sandwiches, said her prayers, and finally fell asleep. When she awoke the next morning, it was to a "collage of Negro, Mexican, and white faces" (194) looking at her through the car's windows. The faces belonged to juveniles who also lived in the junkyard. Maya explained who she was, they accepted her, and one named Bootsie explained their rules and codes. They all worked at one thing or another, and Bootsie held the money, which was used communally. One boy lived with his mother but ran with the gang. On Friday nights, the girls went to his house for a bath and ironed their clothes after washing them at a laundromat.

Reflecting on this month of total, uncritical acceptance by her peers, Angelou writes: "The lack of criticism evidenced by our ad hoc community influenced me, and set a tone of tolerance for my life" (195). The group collected unbroken bottles and did odd jobs, and some of the girls worked weekends in cheap restaurants. After a month, Maya called her mother and asked her to send airfare for her return to San Francisco. She told the gang that she was leaving, and two of her new friends gave her small gifts.

When Maya arrived in San Francisco, her mother noticed immediately how thin she had become and welcomed her home with good food and a listening ear.

Chapter 33

Bailey and Maya were both growing up. Her attitude about life in general was becoming blasé, and he had taken up slang, sloe gin, and the ZOOT SUIT look that his streetwise friends wore. The main thing Maya and Bailey had in common was the jitterbug. They danced to the tunes of COUNT BASIE, CAB CALLOWAY, and DUKE ELLINGTON.

One night, Bailey came home at 1:00, two hours after curfew. Their mother was upset, and Bailey, who had taken up with an older white prostitute, said he was leaving. He went to his room, stuffed his belongings into a pillowcase, and told Maya that she could have his books. The front door slammed as he left.

Bailey moved into the boardinghouse where the woman, Betty, lived. She got a room for him, and Maya and "Mother Dear" made a visit. Bailey told Maya that their mother was getting him a job on the railroad. Maya left feeling sad about the changes but realized that another painful step toward growing up had occurred.

Chapter 34

Since Bailey was out in the world, Maya decided that she also needed to venture out and find a job. She had earned extra school credits, so she could afford the time off. She decided she wanted a job as a conductor on a streetcar. White women had replaced men on streetcars as conductors and motormen, so Maya, only 15, decided to try to get the job she wanted. Her mother warned her that colored people were not accepted on streetcars, but that only made Maya more determined. Her mother supported her and said, "I've told you many times, 'Can't do is like Don't Care.' Neither of them have a home" (203).

Maya went to the Market Street Railway Company and met resistance from the white receptionist. She decided to return the next day and try again. After leaving, Maya rode the streetcar home and felt the black/white tension from the female conductor, which reinforced her determination. For three weeks, she wrangled with the streetcar company and finally got the job.

Maya's mother did not ask what was going on, but each morning she made breakfast and gave Maya carfare, lunch money, and APHORISMS like "God helps those who help themselves" (206). Maya worked on the streetcars for a semester and then returned to school but felt different from the other students. They were focused on school happenings, and she had experienced much more. She skipped school several times, and her mother said she could play hooky as long as her schoolwork

A San Francisco streetcar from the 1940s, when Maya was the first black streetcar conductor in that city *(Photo by Daniel Schwen/Used under Creative Commons license)*

was done. That stopped the truancy, but Maya was learning how difficult it was to survive as an adult African-American female.

Chapter 35

After reading *The Well of Loneliness: A 1920s Classic of Lesbian Fiction* by Radclyff Hall, Maya became so sympathetic toward lesbians that she thought she might actually be one. Her body was tall, strong, and flat, like an AMAZON, and she began to have doubts about her femininity. She decided to talk to her mother about the issue, knowing that Vivian would love and respect her no matter what, as long as she told the truth. It was a difficult struggle, but Maya finally told her mother that she thought something unusual was growing inside her vagina. Her mother asked her to get a bottle of beer for her and to get the big Webster's dictionary. Maya relaxed a little knowing that these were not alarm signals.

Her mother guided her to the dictionary entry for vulva, and she helped Maya to understand that her body was simply developing normally. Maya accepted the explanation and then her mother laughed—not *at* her, but because Maya pleased her. Vivian assured Maya that she had asked God for a girl and a boy, and God does not make mistakes. So Maya was a girl, though very tall, underdeveloped, and thin, with big feet.

For the moment, Maya believed that she was not turning into a lesbian, but two weeks later, when a girlfriend of Maya's asked to spend the night at their home, Maya's doubts returned. The girl innocently changed her clothes in Maya's presence, and her well-formed breasts amazed and moved Maya. Again she wondered why, and she decided that she needed a boyfriend to find out if she was a normal female or not.

She casually asked a handsome white youth who lived near her home to sleep with her. He agreed to accommodate her and, without romance or particular tenderness, the act was performed. The experience did not seem to have much impact on Maya's feelings, but she soon found herself pregnant.

Chapter 36

Distraught about the pregnancy, Maya did not know where to turn. She wrote to Bailey, who warned her not to tell their mother. The pregnancy progressed normally, but Maya said nothing. When she was about halfway along, Bailey came home from serving with the merchant marine, and soon after that their mother went to Alaska to open a nightclub. Three weeks before her due date, Maya finally left a note on her stepfather's bed saying that she was sorry to bring disgrace on the family, but she was pregnant. Her philosophical mother returned from Alaska and helped her daughter face the reality of taking care of a baby.

Soon a beautiful boy was born, and Vivian, a pediatric nurse, was confident that Maya would learn how to take care of him. One night, she told Maya that it was safe for the baby to sleep with his mother. Maya was sure she would roll over and crush him, but she did not do so. In fact, her mother woke her in the night to show her how she had propped her arm in her sleep to make a tent for the baby. Her mother said, "See, you do not have to think about doing the right thing. If you're for the right thing, then you do it without thinking" (222).

CRITICAL COMMENTARY

James Olney, author of *Autobiography: Essays Theoretical and Critical* (1980), citing the literary critic John Blassingame, points out that "black writers entered into the house of literature through the door of autobiography" (15). Frederick Douglass, MALCOLM X, OLAUDAH EQUIANO, and other African-American autobiographers preceded Angelou, but in many ways, her candid recounting of her life experiences took black autobiography to a different level of disclosure and understanding. Well-known literary critics responded to her work immediately after it was published, and this signaled a shift in cultural and literary acceptance of this form.

Though *I Know Why the Caged Bird Sings* was an immediate success both commercially and critically, it has been banned in some schools as being too graphic for young-adult reading. It is an honest story of the first 16 years of Angelou's life. Her friend ABBEY LINCOLN suggested the title, which comes from Paul Laurence Dunbar's poem "Sympathy." When an interviewer asked why a caged bird sings, Angelou replied, "I believe that a free bird . . . floats down, eats the early worm, flies away, and mates. . . . But the bird that's in a cage stalks up and down, looking constantly out . . . and he sings about freedom" (quoted in Hagen 1997, 54). Like others, Angelou had little choice over her birth or circumstances, but like the caged bird, she chose to make positive use of her life and sing through her trials. This idea is integral to all her autobiographies.

In this book, Angelou demonstrates her ability to sympathize even with those who had abandoned and misused her. She speaks often and warmly of her mother, yet it was her mother's absence that created the opportunity for Angelou to become the victim of a brutal rape. Using FOLKLORE and humor, Angelou both indicts and vilifies whites and defends and supports blacks. She was raised in a segregated, rural black and white community and observed firsthand the oppression and negation of her own people. With down-to-earth metaphor and figurative language, the book "regularly throws out rich, dazzling images which delight and surprise with their simplicity" (Gross 1970, 90).

In 1997, Lyman B. Hagen reported:

> As of the mid 1980s, *Caged Bird* had gone through twenty hardback printings and thirty-two printings in paperback. Angelou's appearance at the 1993 Presidential Inauguration sent the book back to the top of the *New York Times* best seller lists and resulted in another round of printings. In fact, *Caged Bird* has never been out of print since first issued, nor it seems have any of her other books. That *Caged Bird* was once a selection of the Book of the Month Club, the Ebony Book Club, and also nominated for the National Book Award testifies to its appeal and broad popularity. *Caged Bird* alone would assure Angelou a place amongst America's most popular authors. (56)

What is it about this book that appeals to an international set of readers from all races? Is it that it has a universal message that, with a tweak here or there, could reflect the early experiences of many of its readers? Or is it a view into a little-known world within the United States that outsiders know nothing about? *Caged Bird* is a unique literary achievement that discloses Angelou's response to black female victimization by imposed powerlessness. She tells her story while often using the traditional vernacular of her people and maintaining blameless goodwill and humor.

Angelou was an adult nearly 40 years old when she spent two years reflecting on her life and writing *Caged Bird.* With the advantage of maturity and what appears to be a selective memory, she was able to recall important episodes in her youth and convey them in a way that genuinely reflected the insignificance she felt as a human being when she was a child. She showed the completed manuscript first to her friend JESSICA MITFORD, who found it fascinating, and after that the book moved rapidly into publication.

The time, language, and episodes of *I Know Why the Caged Bird Sings* trace the important memories of Angelou's first 16 years. She and her brother arrived in Stamps, Arkansas, as bewildered, abandoned children, and they struggled together toward early adulthood. The story is captivating and real. The time of their arrival was in the early 1930s, when the country was still suffering from what was called the Great Depression. Both jobs and food were scarce. Though much of the humor Angelou uses is forced laughter through grim circumstance, the point is that she does laugh.

The book opens with a flashback of an episode where the young Maya is trapped in a made-over purple dress that "sounded like crepe paper on the back of hearses" (7). It is Easter, she is in church, and her bladder is full. Hers is the key narrative voice in the story, and her use of language reveals that from the beginning of her serial autobiographies, she has a command of rhythm, dialect, alliteration, and imagery. In that first episode, she explains that she had imagined herself to really be a blue-eyed blond child who had been the victim of a spell cast by a cruel fairy godmother, and surely, when the spell was off, everyone would recognize and understand her. They would *know* that she was not really a tall, black girl with nappy hair, wide feet, and a gap between her front teeth.

Did she really feel this at that moment in her childhood? Did this episode really occur? Does that matter? Angelou writes that she had to get out of church quickly, that she imagined as she stumbled out of the pew that there was a green persimmon or lemon between her legs squeezing her. If she did not escape, her head would "burst like a dropped watermelon" (9). She made it out, and the urine burst out as well. First she cried, and then she laughed. The tension built up by this all-familiar pressure and release that all humans experience at one time or another sets the reader up for a delightful adventure. Angelou's imaginative mind has a gift for describing sensory impressions in a way that appeals to the collective human condition. The reader *knows* about fairy godmothers, and the reader *knows* about a full bladder, and the reader *knows* what it feels like not to look good, so it is no wonder that this book carries an appeal that has been embraced around the world.

Throughout *Caged Bird,* Angelou uses southern black vernacular in her remembered conversations and comments. The familiar "Sister" and "Brother" commonly used in southern conversation between people well-known to one another, and particularly from the same church congregation, is a good example: "Sister, I'll have two cans of sardines" (11), addressed to Mrs. Henderson at the Store, or aphorisms such as "I'm gonna work so fast today I'm gonna make you look like you standing still" (11). Angelou was constantly observing as the workers stopped at the Store early in the morning on the way to the fields and returned late in the afternoon. She listened to their words and expressions, and from her earliest years, her empathy for their never-ending plight demonstrated keen understanding of their anguish and the way they talked about it. That deep, empathetic understanding and respect continues throughout the text, as well as in her other autobiographies and her poetry, and she often uses traditional vernacular drawn from her own people.

Another thread Angelou runs through the text is that of the old SPIRITUALS sung in and out of church by her grandmother and others in the Stamps community. In the episode where poor white girls, feeling superior because of their skin, taunt and tease Momma, the narrative finishes with Momma stoically maintaining her dignity and resuming her song, "Glory, Glory, hallelujah, when I lay my burden down" (30). Angelou uses hymns and truisms throughout her prose and poetry to anchor it in the culture of her childhood.

The author's figurative language works to help her readers clearly visualize the memories she has of various scenes and experiences. Her description of the Store begins with what it looked like to her in the early morning: It reminded her of an unopened present from a stranger. Angelou writes that opening the doors "was pulling the ribbon off the unexpected gift. The light would come in softly (we faced north), easing itself over the shelves of mackerel, salmon, tobacco, thread. It fell flat on the big vat of lard. . . . Whenever I walked into the Store in the afternoon, I sensed that it was tired" (17). Describing Bailey at play, the reader again easily visualizes: "And when he was on the tail of the pop the whip, he would twirl off the end like a top, spinning, falling, laughing finally stopping just before my heart beat its last . . . still laughing" (22).

Angelou's descriptions of food preparation include traditional folkloric methods handed down from generation to generation and, for the most part, from woman to woman. She describes the preparation of pork sausage by the missionary ladies of the Colored Methodist Episcopal Church who helped her grandmother Momma. At one point, she writes, "they opened the knuckle of the hams with their deadly-looking knives, took out a certain round harmless bone ('it could make the meat go bad') and rubbed salt, coarse brown salt that looked like fine gravel" (23). Traditionally, there was a certain bone as well as a certain salt believed to be the only right and safe way to prepare the pork sausage. These represented material and belief traditions of folklore, and Angelou remembered and described them carefully.

Another food passage, rich with imagery, describes Momma's Sunday morning breakfasts that were to sustain the family for several hours: ". . . thick pink slabs of home-cured ham and . . . sliced red tomatoes. Eggs over easy, fried potatoes and onions, yellow hominy and crisp perch fried so hard we would pop them in our mouths and chew bones, fins and all . . . biscuits . . . three inches in diameter and two inches thick" (33). Angelou chooses the order, the vowels and consonants to contrast and create sensory perception of the food descriptions.

Humor, a frequent presence in Angelou's writing, is again demonstrated in the church episode where a member of the congregation, Sister Monroe, raises her voice with "Preach it" (35) repeatedly. The next week, the scene is re-created, and Angelou brings the humor to the level of hysteria. Sister Monroe is even more enthusiastic—"I say, preach it" (37)—and as the minister says, "'Great God of Mount Nebo,' Sister Monroe hit him on the back of the head with her purse. Twice. . . . [and] actually his teeth jumped, out of his mouth" (37). The children observe all of this enthusiasm before them and break out in peals of laughter. Angelou writes: "Laughter so easily turns to hysteria for imaginative children. I felt for weeks . . . [that] I stood on laughter's cliff, and any funny thing could hurl me off to my death far below" (39).

Angelou reveals, with grace and humor, the tragic gulf between the blacks and whites of Stamps. She writes: "People in Stamps used to say that the whites in our town were so prejudiced that a Negro couldn't buy vanilla ice cream. Except on July Fourth. Other days he had to be satisfied with chocolate" (41). Along with others in her community, Angelou was suspicious and hated whites. When her father came for a visit and then took the children to their mother in St. Louis, the intensity of her feelings is succinctly expressed by her childlike reflection on her father's manner of speaking: "He sounded more like a white man than a Negro. Maybe he was the only brown-skinned white man in the world. It would be just my luck that the only one would turn out to be my father" (48). These feelings mellowed later in her adult experience, but throughout *Caged Bird*, the suspicion and paranoia concerning whites are apparent.

In St. Louis, in addition to her mother, Angelou met four uncles, her mother's brothers. These were

Baxters, and there was a strong, loyal bond in the family. Again, in a few words Angelou expresses feeling, bonding, hope, and the vernacular of the family. She writes that her favorite uncle, Tommy, often told her: "Ritie, don't worry 'cause you ain't pretty. Plenty pretty women I seen digging ditches or worse. You smart. I swear to God, I rather you have a good mind than a cute behind" (55). The humor of the comment is embedded in it, and yet these few words of counsel reveal a deep well of sincere respect and feeling. Angelou's skill in conveying the humble humanity of her community and family repeatedly reveals itself.

Angelou's sensitivity and dexterity as a writer, even in this first autobiography, is evident in her ability to convey, without rancor, the deep trauma of her childhood rape. Her long silence, broken only occasionally with her brother and less often with her grandmother, takes the reader deep into the bleak and confused despair of those years. The contrast with such scenes as the one featuring Sister Monroe's call of "Preach it!" demonstrates Angelou's ability to put herself into the recalled moments and describe them clearly. Though parts of the narratives have been fictionalized out of necessity, Angelou's facility to convey the emotional climate of certain moments reveals her remarkable talent. In *The Writer's Presence: A Pool of Essays* (1997), which includes a sample of Angelou's work, the editors Donald McQuade and Robert Atwan state that each of her essays "features the distinctive intellectual signature that marks all memorable prose: the presence of a lively individual mind attempting to explore one's self, shape information into meaning, or contend with issues through conversation or debate" (v).

Angelou has a vast store of knowledge gained from broad, lifelong reading, and *Caged Bird* is full of metaphors and allusions to works of literature. Whether these connections and links were present in her child's mind or accumulated as she grew to a mature adult would be impossible to determine, but she was an early and avid reader and consumed literature of all kinds, from Shakespeare to comic books. FOLKTALES and various mythic figures enhance her writing. For instance, when she tells of Bailey returning home late from the movies one evening and describes her fear that something might have happened to him, she writes: "The Bluebeards and tigers and Rippers could eat him up before he could scream for help" (90).

Strands of religiosity also figure frequently in this text, from observations at church services to quoted stanzas of hymns and passionate descriptions of a typical southern Protestant revival. Angelou notes that after the revival meeting, repentant sinners, reborn in the surrender of religious emotion, returned home and could hear music from a roadhouse blaring honky-tonk music. She suggests that there really is not much difference between the music of the revival and that being danced to at the roadside juke joint, but all the people, whether they turned to religion or turned to the escape of a roadhouse, suffered in similar ways and asked "the same questions. How long, oh God? How long?" (104).

Angelou provides realistic vignettes of typical family life in the late 1930s. From community picnics to listening to broadcasts of Joe Louis fights, from Bailey's first love to her junior high graduation, the yearly turn of calendar events unfolded in Stamps, Arkansas, much the same as in the rest of the United States. Angelou elaborates her first encounter with a severe toothache and uses it as a vehicle to describe the bigotry, hatred, and distrust that festered between black and whites in the deep South, describing how her grandmother became angry at the refusal of a white dentist to take care of a suffering black child.

When the children reached early adolescence, their grandmother escorted Maya to California to rejoin her mother, and Bailey followed about a month later. In the description of the initial reunion, Angelou uses the figurative devises of metaphor and simile, suggesting their mother "was a blithe chick" and her grandmother more like a "large, solid dark hen" (156). "Momma's deep, slow voice lay under my mother's rapid peeps and chirps like stones under rushing water" (156). Later, Angelou attended high school in San Francisco and began serious study of dance and pantomime. She describes becoming wise in both academics and the street.

The skill in bringing this text to closure leaves the reader eager to read more about Angelou and her life's adventure. She has candidly described the journey from her early childhood to her beginning as a young, unmarried mother. Using humor, characterization, figurative language, sensory impressions, the religious and secular musical aura of her heritage, occasional dialect, and an accessible voice, she has created in *Caged Bird* a universal and international narrative that has continued to be well-received though it is now more than 40 years since its publication.

In the foreword to *Order Out of Chaos: The Autobiographical Works of Maya Angelou* (1990, 1994) by Angelou's lifelong colleague and friend, DOLLY A. MCPHERSON, Professor Eleanor W. Traylor writes: "Situating the most prodigious contemporary autobiographer at the apex of her literary traditions, Dolly McPherson has also centered the African American autobiography as the procreant voice in the national literature itself" (xiii). Traylor writes that Angelou's work meets the "configurations which have historically informed the discourse of the Self," and she elaborates on those configurations:

> We remember the *apology* wherein the Self defends itself for "a road taken"; the *confession* wherein the Self measures itself by a higher criterion and, though finding itself lacking, discovers the glory of itself's own truth; the *memoir*, an account of the Self's experience as that has been shaped by those whom the writer has known and by the world in which the writer/Self has assumed some state presence; the *travelogue*, the merging of the Self with the spirit of a place allowing a discovery resulting in a deeper revelation of both; the *diary* kept for multi-personal reasons, and the *journal*, the logging in of the data of flux. (xi–xii)

These elements—which represent "the discourse of self-portraiture," as Traylor tells the reader (xii)—are the structures that Angelou used to write each of her six autobiographies.

Applying Traylor's specific elements of autobiography to *Caged Bird*, it is clear that Angelou's does indeed use Traylor's traditional "discourse of the Self." The apology—Angelou's defense for decisions concerning which path to take through life—takes place in the scene at Mrs. Cullinan's house. Prior to that, Angelou had been a passive victim of neglect, abandonment, and even abuse by others. The teaching and care given to her by Mrs. Flowers strengthened her, but it was only when the incident at Mrs. Cullinan's occurred—where white female guests Maya was serving determined that her name was too long and that she should be called Mary rather than Margaret (or even her given name, Marguerite)—that she determined that she would be her own person. Unsure of the strategy she needed to quit the job (or get fired), she consulted her trusted brother, who advised her to break something valuable to her mistress, Mrs. Cullinan. She did so, pandemonium followed, and she left the house for good. Angelou explains that a black man has a "horror of being 'called out of his name.' It was a dangerous practice to call a Negro anything that could be loosely construed as insulting because of the centuries of their having been called niggers, jigs, dinges, blackbirds, crows, boots and Spooks" (86). That explanation is, in essence, the apology: Maya explains that she was determined not to let people insult her. This was when the young woman began to walk her own road.

In spite of the difficulties of her first 16 years, Angelou possessed the strength of character to discuss these early years honestly in *Caged Bird*. Confession—another of Traylor's terms, meaning to enjoy and even glory in a truth of self—is exemplified in the description of the time when Angelou openly shared the story of the rape and earlier molestation she fell victim to in her mother's St. Louis home. Later, when she had doubts about her sexual orientation, she again discussed the problem openly. This discussion opened an important door for black writers such as ROSA GUY and Alice Walker who previously had sidestepped such issues in literature.

As a memoir of shaped experience, Angelou's *Caged Bird* reveals "the growth of the individual from an innocence to knowledge" (McPherson 1994, 20). When Uncle Willie had to be hidden in a vegetable bin along with onions and potatoes because of Ku Klux Klan night riders, when Bailey came home one night after seeing a murdered black man dragged from the river, and when Maya witnessed the way the poor white-trash girls treated

Momma with no resistance from her beloved, demeaned grandmother, Maya learned something more of why she feared and hated whites. She could no longer imagine herself as a pretty little white girl with blue eyes and blond hair. She was black, and that reality was fraught with danger. She had lost the ideal innocence of childhood and accepted her racial identity. Gaining that knowledge, she recognized the behavior expected of her (especially in the South) and gained the wisdom needed to negotiate them.

A constancy of movement and changing locations is also threaded throughout *Caged Bird.* McPherson's *Order Out of Chaos* carries the traveling metaphor further by quoting Henry David Thoreau's concept of the interior self as being another "distant land" (8). Throughout *Caged Bird,* both literal travel and self-examination of the interior self are constants. The book begins in Stamps, but it soon describes the arduous trip Maya and Bailey made, unescorted, from California at the ages of three and four. In a few years, they were dropped off in St. Louis, Missouri, by their father to live with their mother, and not long after that, the children returned to Stamps. Then they were whisked to California to live in three different cities—Los Angeles, Oakland, and San Francisco—and Angelou even includes a brief trip to Mexico. Describing her experiences in each place, she conveys her curiosity and sense of the rhythms of these places. She carefully describes people, foods, and colors, and she conveys her genuine interest in gaining new cultural insights.

This early work sets up the trajectory of intelligent travel and exploration that Angelou follows in her later autobiographies. She explores herself and her responses within various settings in Europe and Africa and often seeks out native speakers in order to learn the correct pronunciation of basic words. As travelogue, the text provides context of time and place with clearly accessible explanations, and it is often so realistic that the reader can lose objectivity and almost experience the episode with Angelou rather than vicariously.

Angelou takes the reader along on her quests. From the graphic account of her rape to the description of her persistence in her bid for the streetcar conductor job, she explains, reveals, and expresses her emotional responses and her day-to day activities. McPherson reminds us that "the artistic tension between her recollected self and her authorial consciousness . . . mark points of transcendence" (9). Angelou is writing from an adult perspective and learning to know her own "distant self" in the very act of writing. She shares both joy and pain in the episode-filled pages of *Caged Bird,* a song of her eventful first 16 years.

SOME IMPORTANT THEMES AND SYMBOLS IN *I KNOW WHY THE CAGED BIRD SINGS*

Mother Wit

Mrs. Flowers advised the silent child Maya "to listen carefully to what country people called mother wit. That in those homely sayings was couched the collective wisdom of generations" (Angelou 2004, 79). Alan Dundes, in his work *Mother Wit from the Laughing Barrel* (1990) defined *mother wit* by stating:

> Mother wit is a popular term in black speech referring to common sense. Mother wit is the kind of good sense not necessarily learned from books or in school. Mother wit with its connotation of collective wisdom acquired by experience of living and from generations past is often expressed in folklore. (xvi)

In an article entitled "Mother Wit: Words of Wisdom from Black Women," published in *Ebony* in 1997, Joyce Bennett Kinnon writes:

> On the surface, the dictionary definition is simply "common sense," a natural intelligence. But dig deeper and there's a history. There is a wealth of living in the word mother wit. In Black history, the word usage began in the 1800s. Thus the word was born and distilled in the brutality of slavery and has survived to enter the new millennium. It was a code word then, and it's still a code word for the knowledge you must have to survive. It is, as author Tony Morrison says, "a knowing so deep" that the lesson has been instilled and distilled to its essence. Collectively these words are a gift—

> from your own mother, or anyone's mother. They are wise words for life's journey.

Maya Angelou used the humor of her community's anecdotes and sayings to color *Caged Bird* and her other five autobiographies. She was raised on the verbal lore of her mother and grandmother, and naturally adapted their ADAGEs or MAXIMs as she shaped her own character. Vivian Baxter repeated one homespun proverb after another as she was raising Maya. For instance, at the time Maya was trying so hard to get the job on the San Francisco streetcar, her mother stated:

> "That's what you want to do? Then nothing beats a trial but a failure. Give it everything you've got. I've told you many times, 'Can't do is like Don't Care.' Neither of them have a home."
>
> Translated, that meant there was nothing a person can't do, and there should be nothing a human being didn't care about. It was the most positive encouragement I could have hoped for. (205)

An example from her grandmother's repertoire was included in a later book, *All God's Children Need Traveling Shoes,* when Malcolm X had failed to get an important message across to a group of people. Angelou remembered her grandmother saying: "If you want to know how important you are to the world, stick your finger in a pond and pull it out. Will the hole remain?" (993). Lyman B. Hagen, who wrote a critical analysis of Angelou's writing, has noted that "Mother Wit, maxims, and warnings to live by . . . gave her a code of understanding and an underlying stability that enabled her to withstand injustices and to evaluate the morality of the world in which she lived" (148).

The African-American Grandmother

Maya Angelou's paternal grandmother, Annie Henderson—or "Momma," as Maya and Bailey called her—provided stability and consistency for the children when they were young, and her deep spiritual roots and day-to-day work ethic and honesty made a lifelong impression on the children, particularly Maya. The strong African-American grandmother figure has roots reaching across the ocean and far into the past. The powerful presence and stability of the black grandmother figure have a long history of holding both families and communities together.

For Maya and Bailey, Momma provided a safe haven. She was a tall, strong, no-nonsense person. The children learned how to work, study, take care of themselves, and accept what life handed them through her steadfastness. By her example, they learned compassion as she demonstrated, without words, the constant care of their Uncle Willie. Through her, they made connections with the black community and learned their position within that community. They also learned the boundaries of social SEGREGATION, though sometimes they tested those invisible markers and found that crossing the line could be very dangerous.

The scholar Mildred A. Hill-Lubin writes: "The Black grandmother in America, then, represents the most tenacious survival of the African extended family" (256). In West African society, where Angelou's ancestors are from according to DNA research, elders are held in the highest esteem. Their wisdom is sought after by following generations, and often it is the grandmother who has preserved the family and influenced the community through her wisdom and stability. Often young West African men, even those married with children, must leave their villages and find work in other parts of the country. They sometimes return but not always, and it is the grandmothers who have learned to survive grinding poverty and keep the family fed and together until circumstances improve.

In her essay, Hill-Lubin states that in African literature the grandmother functions in three important "capacities: one, as the preserver of the African extended family; second, as the repository and distributor of family history wisdom, and Black lore; and third, as the retainer and communicator of values and ideals which support and enhance her personhood, her family, and her community" (258). These same characteristics and attributes are clearly present in Annie Henderson, and as Maya Angelou matured, she internalized these same values.

Maya's Grandmother Baxter, her mother's mother, is another example of a determined, powerful black woman. Part white and raised by Germans, Grandmother Baxter was a tough precinct leader in a crime-filled neighborhood, but at the same time she was a woman who maintained her femininity and gracious manners while also dealing with criminals. Maya remembered her as a ramrod-straight woman with tiny pince-nez glasses and a presence no one would challenge. She held together a large family who always remained loyal and protective of one another.

A great-grandmother of Maya and Bailey's, KENTUCKY SHANNON, was another woman who evidenced the strength of her ancestors. "Maya's paternal great-grandmother declared her personal independence when slavery was abolished by taking the name Kentucky Shannon. There is . . . a grouping of Maya's female ancestors that hangs in constant view on the wall facing her as she sits at her favorite work table in her home North Carolina" (Gillespie, Butler, and Long 2008, 15). The links that forge family are made stronger by the knowledge of one's ancestors and their traditions. There are values that pass from mother to daughter and father to son, sometimes deliberately and sometimes unconsciously. Angelou, by honoring those who came before her, demonstrates respect. As Henry Glassie puts it, she understands "that tradition is the creation of the future out of the past" (176).

Coming of Age

The overriding theme in this first autobiography is Angelou's difficult journey from childhood to young adulthood. Her introspection, humor, intelligence, resilience, and confidence, in spite of constant obstacles, propelled her through her perilous first 16 years. Though the narrative is written from memory, Angelou expressively recalls her thinking and responses to many early situations, and she shows how the dominant characteristics of curiosity, energy, and self-preservation that have supported her through her adult years were in their formative stages even when she was a tiny child. The strong personality that emerged as she grew to maturity was present early in her development. She begins her story with an emergency: She had to relieve her bladder, and she was enclosed in a church pew on Easter Sunday. Though someone tripped her as she exited to the powerful strains of "Were you there when they crucified my Lord?" (9), Maya made it to the church porch and then ran home crying and wetting. At last gaining some perspective, she managed to laugh at the whole ludicrous situation.

Written from an adult perspective and distance, the text repeats the thoughts of the child as different situations are experienced. That is not entirely adult creativity; rather, it is the ongoing recollection of how Angelou felt when she experienced various events. In an interview with George Goodman, Jr., in 1972, after writing *I Know Why the Caged Bird Sings,* she said that she would "help clear the air in black America, because that's what needs to be done. . . . *Caged Bird* [will speak to] all those black men with their fists balled up who talk about nation-buildin' time and then go home to rape their nieces and step-daughters and all the little teen-age girls who don't know beans about life" (quoted in Goodman, 1972, 9). She knew how confused she became when it happened to her, and as an adult, she revived the feelings she had as a child to scold and warn others.

In her recollected story, Angelou began to recognize how narrow and stilted life was in Stamps and how independent she would need to learn to be. She recognized that her father was too self-centered to take care of her, she learned that she could always trust her brother, Bailey, she learned how to earn money, she discovered what her talents were, and she watched herself grow up. That consciousness of maturity is shared in the text. At the close of *Caged Bird,* she revealed her own confusion about lesbianism and tested her physical responses by having a meaningless sexual encounter with a boy. Three weeks later, she realized that she had conceived, and though she was only 16, she took responsibility for the pregnancy and then her infant son. Thrust into premature motherhood, she quickly made the transition and commitment to sacrifice for another human's welfare, and she never betrayed that commitment. Her childhood was over, and her adult responsibilities had begun.

Racism

At the time that Maya and her brother, Bailey, traveled by train from California to Stamps, Arkansas, the so-called JIM CROW laws were still in effect. That meant strict segregation. Under the first Jim Crow law passed in 1881, white and black southerners were required to ride in separate railway cars, and by the 1890s, all southern states required this type of separation in schools, streetcars, railroads, and railroad stations. In a very few years, racial segregation had spread to parks, playgrounds, and other public facilities, including drinking fountains and restrooms. In 1896, the Supreme Court added legal support to segregation and ruled that "separate but equal" facilities should be maintained.

Angelou writes that she did not remember much of that cross-country trip, "but after we reached the segregated southern part of the journey, things must have looked up. Negro passengers, who always traveled with loaded lunch boxes, felt sorry for 'the poor little motherless darlings' and plied us with cold fried chicken and potato salad" (2004, 10). The segregation that she speaks of was the continued enforcement of the laws from the late 1800s, racist laws that enforced separation of blacks and whites with the constant implication that blacks were inferior to whites. JOHN BROWN and GABRIEL PROSSER had failed in attempts to rebel against white oppression, and both became martyrs to the cause of African-American freedom.

The town of Stamps, which Angelou describes clearly, was segregated, and the Ku Klux Klan was a terrifying force that commanded obedient respect. The killing of black people by lynching was a reality. For this reason, after a supposed infraction of the law, Maya's crippled Uncle Willie was warned by a caring white sheriff to hide until the danger was past. He was stuffed into the onion and potato storage box and spent a miserable, fearful night there. Such continuous behavior of instilling fear in blacks was a legacy of the post–Civil War or Reconstruction period, and unfortunately, in some areas of the United States, corruption of power and instillation of fear still continue.

The historian Ronald Wright writes: "For the dozen years of postwar Reconstruction, the North came down hard on the South, and Douglass's dream—later Martin Luther King's and Barack Obama's—seemed almost within reach" (160). But it took much longer to achieve. Racism is a double-edged sword that can cut from either direction, and as Angelou progressed in experience and maturity in life, much of the misunderstanding and fear of her childhood observations were refocused and her own inherited racism dissolved.

Religion

Maya's Grandmother Henderson (Momma) was deeply Christian. A dignified woman, she lived by her beliefs and did her best to instill her religious values in her children and grandchildren. Every morning, the children heard Momma pray fervently in the vernacular of her people. Her routine was to thank her heavenly Father for the life of the new day. She used to say, "Thank you that you didn't allow the bed I lay on last night to be my cooling board, nor my blanket my winding sheet" (11). She often hummed or sang hymns and turned to the comfort of their words when her situation became stressful. Maya followed this pattern and internalized many of Momma's words, feelings, and behavior.

Throughout *I Know Why the Caged Bird Sings*, there are descriptions of religion and church. From the first page, when Maya is described escaping from the Easter service because her bladder is full, to the outrageously funny scenes when the minister's teeth fly out, to the angst-ridden dreams of Mr. Taylor when his deceased wife seems to appear to him in his dreams, observations of religion run through the story. The people hold a community interdenominational revival where all manner of spiritual manifestations seem to take place. Religion holds a mix of hope and fear, and those elements are the core psychology of these struggling but persistent people.

Survival

The theme of looking forward and carrying on—surviving—is strong throughout *I Know Why the Caged Bird Sings.* From the earliest descriptions of the downtrodden southern black people to Momma's predawn prayers of thanks for another day of life, the text reflects the will to overcome negative circumstances and go forward with hope of better circumstances. That is not to say that difficult experiences can always be left behind.

In a 1973 interview with Sheila Weller, Angelou explained that people assumed she escaped her past because of her apparent success in many undertakings, but she stated, "You don't know what demons I wrestle with" (quoted in Elliot 1989, 14). There are examples given in her autobiographies that describe the inescapable haunting of her mind caused by Mr. Freeman's molestation and rape of Maya when she was only eight years old. Because she was unable to completely describe what he had done to her, and because Freeman was ultimately beaten to death shortly after the court trial, Maya blamed herself for his death and fell silent for about five years. In *Caged Bird,* she states poignantly that "the guilt which lined my heart, even after all those years, was a nagging passenger in my mind" (193).

In one of the last passages in *A Song Flung Up to Heaven* (2002), Angelou recounts a joy ride in an automobile with people she had met in a bar. She did not know them well, and the teasing driver turned off the motor of his car on railroad tracks, knowing that a train was coming. The passengers in the car heard the whistle from around a curve of tracks that they could see. The driver did move the car in time, and other passengers in the back seat with her were cursing, but Maya was so hysterical that she was unable to say anything. "I had been frightened mute again, just like twenty-five years earlier, when I had been so terrorized that I had chosen to become mute" (1,106). Still, after the event, she showered, and "the terror released me" (1,108).

There is little doubt that some fears have haunted her throughout her life, as her poem "Still I Rise" declares. Mary Jane Lupton, one of Angelou's biographers, writes: "Although Maya is in some degree a negative character, she is a potential feminist because she is aware of the forces in society that are working against her" (73). As a child, Angelou was taught that she was black, female, and vulnerable, and yet her mother, Vivian Baxter, and the independent Mrs. Flowers in Stamps—the woman who rescued her from silence and turned her mind toward literature—both impressed upon her the vital components of looking forward with a belief in one's own ability to survive. Throughout Angelou's works and even in her interviews, she always expresses an indomitable spirit, and in *Caged Bird,* that spirit is present on almost every page.

Family and Community Solidarity

Long before the Civil War, there were organized groups of black abolitionists protesting the disregard of civil rights for enslaved African Americans. After the war and Reconstruction, there continued to be protests and appeals in favor of civil rights for African-American citizens in the United States. Prevented from owning property, voting, and even having consistent access to education, African Americans were denied basic rights. Against this, African-American families often bonded tightly to one another for both security and identity. There is wisdom in like-minded individuals standing together against a perceived common enemy, and that is apparent over the history of the world in many settings.

In a small, segregated community like Stamps, this solidarity was an imperative tool of survival in the 1940s and 1950s. The churches, the community picnics, the Johnson store as the unofficial black town hall, the segregated school, and the shared work all bound together to form a tight, supportive community. The Johnson and Baxter families, from the grandmothers to CLYDE BAILEY JOHNSON (Guy), the youngest child, continually worked together to care for, teach, and sustain one another.

CHARACTERS

Marguerite "Maya" Johnson Largely abandoned by her divorced parents, this tall, intelligent black girl negotiated survival with the odds clearly stacked against her. Her active imagination carried her through many difficult situations, and though she spent the majority of her childhood in the rural and deeply segregated town of Stamps, Arkansas, her voracious reading and creative mind worked to change proverbial lemons to lemonade. Her grandmother, Momma Henderson, owned a general store where she was required to work, and she viewed the store like a stimulating, unexpected gift from a stranger with its many colors, shapes, and smells. She had to feed the pigs at night, but rather than complain, she hung around, listened to them grunt after they fed, and then laughingly grunted with them in imitation. Momma Henderson was deeply religious, strict, and orderly, but at the same time, her grandmother loved her. The child grew to womanhood all too quickly, and with the birth of her son when she is just 16, she made her premature entry into adult responsibilities, at which point the book finishes. Even in that circumstance, her attitude was independent, laced with good humor, and she looked ahead into self-supporting womanhood.

Bailey Johnson, Jr. ("Ju" Johnson) Bailey was Maya's older brother. Small, dark, and well-read, he protected and comforted Maya as time went by, and Maya was equally loyal to him. There was a mutual trust between them, and though he would far rather have lived with their mother in St. Louis than in Stamps, he returned to Stamps with Maya after she was raped by their mother's boyfriend. He entertained himself and Maya with a variety of antics, including stealing pickles from the barrel in the store, playing mama and papa with various schoolgirls in a blanket tent in their backyard, escaping Stamps once on a slow train and ending up stranded in Louisiana, and a variety of other tricks. He was a firm support to Maya during her pregnancy, and their relationship continued to be strong through their adult years.

Momma Henderson (Mrs. Annie Henderson) Married at times to three different men—Mr. Johnson, Mr. Henderson, and Mr. Murphy—and the daughter of a former slave woman named Kentucky Shannon, Momma, as she is called in the text, was the only black female entrepreneur in Stamps, Arkansas. Finding herself with two boys (Bailey, Sr., and Willie) to raise with no husband to support them, she made fresh, hot lunches and sold them to black workers at two strategic locations in Stamps. When she had saved enough money, she established the William Johnson General Merchandise Store, which in a short time became the unofficial black community center. During the depression era, she took government-issued fish, powdered eggs, and powdered milk in trade for store goods and thus maintained her life and business. She even loaned money to some white people. Momma was a traditional southern Christian and deeply religious. Because of her wisdom and patience, she was held in the highest esteem by the people of Stamps, both black and white.

Daddy Bailey Johnson (Bailey Johnson, Sr.) A handsome and conceited man, Daddy Bailey was an insensitive, neglectful father. Angelou notes in the narrative that he used affected speech. His English was correct, but he often exaggerated sounds for effect. He worked as a doorman at the Breakers Hotel in Santa Monica, California, and then as a dietitian at a naval hospital in San Diego. He did little for Maya and Bailey. He did aid Maya when his lover stabbed her, but after providing initial medical care, he proved to be of little or no support. He is rarely mentioned in the autobiographies after the first one.

Vivian Baxter A beautiful, intelligent, and confident woman, Vivian Baxter was Maya and Bailey's mother. She was a nurse, but she earned her living primarily working in gambling parlors. Her nickname was "Bibbie," but her children referred to her as "Mother Dear" after they heard their father use that phrase. She was capable and tough with most adults but soft and indulgent with her children. Her aphorisms and truisms are often quoted in Angelou's texts, and in *Caged Bird,* her inability to care properly for Maya after one of her boyfriends rapes the child reveals a woman who is unable to cope with serious difficulties. After the tragedy, Vivian shipped the children back to her husband's mother. At the end of the text, she was helpful to Maya in teaching her how to care for the teenager's newborn baby. She offered to let Maya and her baby live at home with her, but a few months after the birth, Maya realized her own need and desire for independence.

Uncle Willie (Willie Johnson) Uncle Willie, the younger son of Momma Henderson, was dropped and badly injured by a babysitter when he was three years old. His left hand was withered, and injured muscles in his face pulled down the left side. His spine was misshapen, and he had to walk with a cane, but he worked hard in his mother's store, and both Bailey and Maya respected him. He helped them master their schoolwork, particularly math, and he was a constant presence during their years in Stamps. He was not an intellectual, but he was kind and respected by the community.

Grandfather Baxter The father of Vivian Baxter and her siblings, Grandfather Baxter was from the West Indies. He was devoted to his wife, Vivian's mother, and he was an invalid from the mid-1930s. One of his favorite sayings was "Bah Jesus, I live for my wife, my children and my dog" (50).

Grandmother Baxter The mother of Vivian Baxter and her four brothers and one sister, Grandmother Baxter was a quadroon or octoroon, meaning she only had a little black blood, and her skin and delicate features gave her the appearance of a refined white woman. She was raised by Germans in a town near St. Louis, and she spoke English with a guttural German accent throughout her life. Ladylike and feminine but an energetic, intelligent woman, she was a wise precinct leader in their St. Louis neighborhood. She had influence with the local police, and because of this, many con men and other crooks asked favors of her. Like her daughter, she had a cool, sharp mind, and she was able to overlook the probable murder her sons committed in vengeance for Mr. Freeman's savage rape of Maya.

Baxter uncles Tutti, Tom, Ira, and Billy were Vivian Baxter's brothers. Three were older, and Billy was younger. They liked Maya and let her know of their respect for her. Their home was in a tough black St. Louis neighborhood, and they enjoyed their reputation of being mean characters. They had jobs in the city, which was unusual for black men of this period. They, like their father, were intensely loyal to the family. Their father knew they were wild, but he said, "Bah Jesus, if you ever get in jail for stealing or some foolishness, I'll let you rot. But if you're arrested for fighting, I'll sell the house, lock stock, and barrel, to get you out!" (54). Because they were encouraged never to avoid a fight and also had outrageous tempers, their reputation was not surprising.

Daddy Clidell Jackson Soon after World War II began, Vivian Baxter married this conservative businessman. He was originally from Slaten, Texas, and was the first stable father figure in Maya and Bailey's lives. A successful property owner, he was genuinely interested in Maya's well-being. However, he was undereducated, and his perception of a complete education included poker, blackjack, tonk and high, and other gambling games, which he taught to Maya. He and Vivian Baxter divorced when Maya and Bailey were young adults.

Reverend Howard Thomas Reverend Thomas was the minister who presided as church elder over the district in which Stamps was located. Maya and Bailey hated him because whenever he paid visits to Stamps, he freeloaded on their grandmother. The children saw him as conceited, ugly, fat, and rude. He said such long prayers before a meal that the food became cold, flattened, and nearly ruined. The children became nearly hysterical with laughter when his false teeth fell out once during a preaching exchange with an enthusiastic and evangelistic member of their congregation.

Sister Monroe An overly enthusiastic member of Maya's church congregation, Sister Monroe hit Reverend Thomas's back with her purse and demanded loudly that he "Preach it," over and over again, until his teeth flew out of his mouth. He made a joke of the incident, and she was removed from the church by ushers.

Miz Ruth, Mis Helen, Miz Eloise White daughters of sharecroppers who taunted Momma Henderson by making fun and imitating her posture. To add further insult, one of the girls did a handstand in the dust, revealing nakedness beneath her dress. Momma Henderson stood still, said nothing, and hummed a hymn during the disrespectful display.

Mrs. Bertha Flowers A genteel, well-read Stamps matron who helped Maya regain her voice after the rape, Mrs. Flowers recognized Maya's intelligence in spite of the child's escape into silence. She wore beautiful lightweight dresses, flowered hats, and white gloves and was very different from the other women in Stamps. She made tea cookies and lemonade for Maya, whom she gently taught to memorize and recite good literature. Thus, she was instrumental in aiding the child to regain her balance and emotional strength.

Viola Cullinan Maya worked as a domestic for Mrs. Viola Cullinan, who perceived herself as a Virginia-born elite. Mrs. Cullinan thought that the name Marguerite was too long (she mispronounced it as Margaret as well), and she renamed the girl Mary. Maya was deeply offended feeling that her identity and personhood was being denied, and she retaliated by arriving at work late, breaking treasured dishes, and working slowly. Mrs. Cullinan became hysterical over her mother's favorite pieces of china being broken and fired Maya, which was exactly the outcome the girl wanted.

Louise Kendricks Louise was Maya's first and only girlhood friend in Stamps. They created a secret child's language, and they enjoyed many of the same dreams. Leaving Louise was the only regret Maya had when she left Stamps.

Tommy Veldon Without realizing it, Tommy hurt Maya by triggering confusing feelings about her past trauma. He was her first male admirer and knew nothing of Maya's past.

Joyce A 14-year-old girl who seduced Bailey, who was then only 10 years old, Joyce lived in Stamps for a short time after her parents died, and she coerced Bailey into stealing food from the Store for her. Ultimately, she ran away with a railroad porter, and Bailey fell into depression for a period of time, thinking that he loved her. He never spoke of her again after he recovered from his heartbreak.

George Taylor On a windy night with the threat of tornadoes looming, George Taylor, a lonely widower, arrived at Momma Henderson's home to tell about a dream he had. He was bald, wizened, and old, and he said that his wife's ghost had come to him in a dream with a request for children. He ate well and spent the night with the family before leaving in the morning.

Mr. Edward Donleavy A white politician from Texarkana, running for office, who demeaned the students in Maya's eighth grade graduating class. He stereotyped the black students' future by suggesting that their only heroes were athletes. He also suggested that their future work would be limited to mundane roles as domestics, farmers, washwomen, and handymen. He extolled the white graduates in a neighboring school and talked about expensive equipment with which they were going to be provided as they would be professionals. He promised the parents of the black graduates that if he won the election, they would be given the "only colored paved playing field in that part of Arkansas" (140); he also promised new equipment for the home economics building and the workshop. Then he left suddenly for more important things.

Henry Reed Henry was the valedictorian of the 1940 graduating class of the Lafayette County Training School. He had prepared to speak about Hamlet's "To Be or Not to Be" soliloquy, but sensing the depressive pall that had fallen over the graduation ceremony because of Donleavy's message, he chose instead to lead the class in singing James Weldon Johnson's "Lift Ev'ry Voice and Sing," the unofficial Negro national anthem. It lifted the spirits of everyone there, and the mood changed back to one of celebration and joy.

Mr. Freeman Vivian Baxter's boyfriend, Mr. Freeman worked for the Southern Pacific Railroad and spent a lot of time hanging around her home waiting for her to return from work. He worshipped Vivian, but he noticed Maya and after first molesting her, he brutally raped her. He warned Maya that if she revealed what he had done to her, he would kill her brother. He was expelled from the house and was later beaten and kicked to death in an alley. No one was ever charged with the murder.

Miss Kirwin Kirwin was a teacher of civics and current events under whom Maya studied at the George Washington High School in San Francisco. Miss Kirwin referred to all of her students as "ladies and gentlemen," and she impressed Maya with the consistent and democratic way she treated all of them.

Red Leg Red Leg was a friend of Daddy Clidell's, along with Just Black, Stonewall Jimmy, Cool Clyde, and Tight Coat. Red Leg regaled Maya with a long story about how he conned a white man whom he called a Tulsa CRACKER.

Delores Stockland Delores was a small, fussy woman who thought Daddy Bailey Johnson, Maya's father, was going to marry her. They lived together in his trailer in San Diego, and Maya visited there for a part of a summer when she was a young teen. Delores was jealous of Maya and stabbed her in the side with a pair of sharp scissors. Daddy Bailey eventually married someone else.

Bootsie After running away from her father's trailer in San Diego, Maya lived in a junkyard car for about a month. Bootsie was the spokesman for a group of homeless teens who also lived in the San Diego car lot. He handled the group's money and distributed it equitably.

Lee Arthur Lee was a member of the junkyard commune who lived at home and let the group use his house to take baths on Friday evenings.

FURTHER READING

Angelou, Maya. *The Collected Autobiographies of Maya Angelou.* New York: Modern Library Edition by Random House, 2004.

———. *The Complete Collected Poems of Maya Angelou.* New York: Random House, 1994.

Angelou, Maya, and Carol E. Neubauer. "Interview." *Massachusetts Review* (Summer 1987): 286–292.

Brozan, Nadine. "Chronicle." *New York Times,* 30 December 1993. Available online. URL: http://www.nytimes.com/1993/12/30/style/chronicle_1522993.html. Accessed February 23, 2011.

Demetrakopoulos, Stephanie A. "Maya Angelou and the Autobiographical Statement." In *Women's Autobiography: Essays in Criticism,* edited by Estelle C. Jelinek, 180–205. Bloomington: Indiana University Press, 1980.

Douglass, Frederick. "Our Work Is Not Done." (Speech to the American Antislavery Society, Philadelphia, Pennsylvania. December 3–4, 1863.) In *Race and Reunion: The Civil War in American Memory,* by David W. Blight, 16. Cambridge, Mass.: Harvard University Press, 2001.

Dundes, Alan, ed. *Mother Wit from the Laughing Barrel: Readings in the Interpretation of Afro-American Folklore.* 1973. Reprint, Jackson and London: University Press of Mississippi, 1990.

Elliot, Jeffrey M., ed. *Conversations with Maya Angelou.* Jackson and London: University Press of Mississippi, 1989.

Gillespie, Marcia Ann, Rosa Johnson Butler, and Richard A. Long. *Maya Angelou: A Glorious Celebration.* New York: Doubleday, 2008.

Glassie, Henry. "Tradition." In *Eight Words for the Study of Expressive Culture,* edited by Burt Feintuch. Urbana and Chicago: University of Illinois Press, 2003.

Goodman, George, Jr. "Maya Angelou's Lonely, Black Outlook." *New York Times,* 24 March 1972, 28. In *Conversations with Maya Angelou,* edited by Jeffrey M. Elliot, 7–9. Jackson and London: University Press of Mississippi, 1989.

Gross, R. A. *Newsweek,* 2 March 1970, 90.

Hagen, Lyman B. *Heart of a Woman, Mind of a Writer, and Soul of a Poet.* Lanham, Md.: University Press of America, 1997.

Hill-Lubin, Mildred. "The Grandmother in African and African-American Literature." In *Ngambika: Studies of Women in African Literature,* edited by Carole Boyce Davies and Anne Adams Graves, 257–270. Trenton, N.J.: Africa World Press, 1986.

Kent, George E. "Maya Angelou's *I Know Why the Caged Bird Sings* and Black Autobiographical Tradition." *Kansas Quarterly* (Summer 1975): 72–78.

Kinnon, Joy Bennett. "Mother Wit: Words of Wisdom from Black Women. *Ebony,* March 1997.

Lupton, Mary Jane. *Maya Angelou: A Critical Companion.* Westport, Conn.: Greenwood Press, 1998.

McPherson, Dolly A. *Order Out of Chaos: The Autobiographical Works of Maya Angelou.* 1990. Reprint, London: Virago Press, 1994.

McQuade, Donald, and Robert Atwan. *The Writer's Presence: A Pool of Essays.* 2nd ed. Boston: Bedford Books, 1997.

Olney, James, ed. *Autobiography: Essays Theoretical and Critical.* Princeton, N.J.: Princeton University Press, 1980.

Thoreau, Henry David. *Walden and Civil Disobedience.* Edited by Sherman Paul. Boston: Houghton Mifflin, 1960.

Traylor, Eleanor W. Forward. In *Order Out of Chaos: The Autobiographical Works of Maya Angelou,* by Dolly A. McPherson, xi–xiii. 1990. Reprint, London: Virago Press, 1994.

Weller, Sheila. "Work in Progress: Maya Angelou." In *Conversations with Maya Angelou,* edited by Jeffrey M. Elliot, 10–17. Jackson and London: University Press of Mississippi, 1989.

Wright, Ronald. *What Is America?* Philadelphia: Da Capo Press, 2008.

Gather Together in My Name (1974)

In *Gather Together In My Name,* her second autobiography, Maya Angelou continues to share the story of her quest for survival and identity. The time frame covered in this book is about four years, and it takes the reader through Maya's life from ages 17 to 21. During this time, she took menial jobs in order to provide for herself and her son and gain independence from her extended family, and her striving for financial security took her into some of the darkest corners of urban life.

Angelou dedicates the book primarily to her "blood brother," BAILEY JOHNSON, JR., and then she lists other "real brothers who encouraged me to be bodacious enough to invent my own life daily." Many of the men listed appear in later autobiographies, and some also helped in raising Guy, her son. The ones named are: JAMES BALDWIN, Kwesi Brew, David DuBois, Samuel Floyd, JOHN KILLENS, Vagabond King, Leo Maitland, VUSUMZI MAKE, JULIAN MAYFIELD, and MAX ROACH. She also extends a special thanks to her good friend DOLLY MCPHERSON.

The narrated experiences in *Gather Together* take the reader on a journey from SAN FRANCISCO to LOS ANGELES to San Diego and then to STAMPS, ARKANSAS, followed by San Francisco again; then Stockton, California; and finally to Oakland. Recounting different life struggles in various cities over a relatively short period of time, Angelou candidly shares her tactics for survival. She seems to hide little or nothing of her questionable, perhaps even dangerous, adventures during this four-year period. Her openness about her exploits subjected her style of autobiography to critical scrutiny from both academics and her general readership. Her disregard for conventional conduct presented a very different perspective for autobiography, but it opened the way for many other writers. Mary Jane Lupton writes: "Like Ann Moody's *Coming of Age in Mississippi* (1968) and Eldridge Cleaver's *Soul on Ice* (1968), *Gather Together in My Name* is one of several contemporary black texts that reinvent the very notion of autobiographical decorum. They tell it like it is, without obeying the strictures of language and behavior found in mainstream works" (77).

In *Gather Together,* Angelou introduced characters from her life who lived on the fringes of mainstream, middle-class society. While she was working as a cook, she met and associated with con man L. D. Tolbrook, a fatherly type who ran several brothels. She became acquainted with lesbians and prostitutes Beatrice and Johnnie Mae at a bar, and rather than separate herself from them, she went to their home for a Sunday meal, and then set herself up as their madam, with the two lesbians as her working girls. She provided a place for her friend Troubadour Martin to sell his stolen clothing, and then she learned later that he was also a heavy drug user. An unfortunate episode occurred when Big Mary, a babysitter, kidnapped Angelou's child. Even so, all of these characters had redeeming qualities, not the least of which was their recognition of Angelou's naïveté and their desire not to see her harmed.

When asked why she wrote so openly of her experiences, Angelou explained to an interviewer that it was because "I saw so many adults lying to so many young people, lying in their teeth, saying 'You know, when I was young, I never would have done. . . . Why I couldn't. . . . I shouldn't. . . .' Lying. Young people know when you are lying; so I thought . . . I will tell it" (quoted in Tate 1983, 9). And tell it, she did.

SYNOPSIS

Beginning with the celebratory mood in Europe and the United States after victory in World War II (European Victory Day [VE-DAY]) was May 8, 1945), the introduction recaps the great American war effort. From children making balls of tinfoil to supply scrap metal for the war machinery, to "black Marines fresh from having buried death on a sandy South Pacific beach" (227), to women in work pants and steel helmets, America and democracy had won. Black marketeers and prostitutes, gamblers and ministers had sacrificed for victory, and Angelou suggests that the mood was "something like a festival" (228), for the war had come to an end with victory. "Hadn't we all joined together to kick the hell out of *der Gruber*, and that fat Italian, and put that little rice-eating Tojo in his place?" (228).

Sadly, economic security also changed quickly and turned from steady, well-paying wartime jobs and respect for black workers to closed plants just two months after VE-day. Black workers were displaced and plunged back into financial insecurity. African-American military heroes were soon turned into corner slouchers, and all that was left of the spiffy khaki uniforms were the shoes—the sturdy, long-lasting shoes. Maya knew she did not want to leave her son with her mother and go back to school; she wanted to get a job, a room of her own, and she hoped to raise her son herself. She could see people leaving her mother's big boardinghouse for jobs in other cities, and she knew that Daddy Clidell would only be a stepfather and grandfather as long as the marriage with her mother lasted.

Maya and the baby were welcome to stay in the big house, and she could accept her mother's and stepfather's support and go to school, but her pride and personal sense of independence drove her to find her own way. Her mother loved the baby and imagined herself reflected in him. Her mother "saw his every virtue as a mirror for her own. He had pretty hands. . . . 'Well, look at mine'" (231). Maya's youth and her own self-doubt seemed to push her away from easy security. She needed independence, and characteristically, she went after it.

Chapter 1

Maya applied for a telephone operator job and was flabbergasted when she was told that she had failed the employee examination test. She asked the white receptionist if she could take it again and was told, "No, I'm sorry" (232). The receptionist told Maya that the company spent a lot of money training operators, and that her scores were so bad that they just could not take a chance on someone with test results like that. The woman did repeat that she was sorry and suggested that Maya consider a job as a bus girl in the cafeteria. Maya tried it, mostly clearing and cleaning tables and filling salt and pepper shakers, but she only lasted a week. It was demeaning labor, and she was actually cleaning off tables for former classmates who were on the way to becoming telephone operators. She hated the meager salary, and the afternoon she quit the job, she took the money she had earned and happily spent all of it.

Chapter 2

Maya saw a sign in the window of the Creole Café that said: "COOK WANTED SEVENTY-FIVE DOLLARS A WEEK." Maya did not know what Creole COOKING was, but she knew she could learn, so she told the proprietress that she knew how to make the Creole food and got the job. It was six days a week, starting at 5:00 in the morning, and she introduced herself as Rita, which her new boss, Mrs. Dupree, shortened to "Reet." So Maya had a job. Her assignment would be cooking dinners and putting them on the steam table. She was pleased with herself, but she needed to learn to cook Creole food quickly.

She was to report to work at 5:00 A.M. on the following Monday, and she reflected about what happened in the streets at that early hour: "Those mean streets before the thugs had gone to sleep, pillowing on someone else's dreams. Before the streetcars began to rattle, their lighted insides like exclusive houses in the fog. Five!" (233).

Chapter 3

Papa Ford, a sweet, uneducated black man probably in his late 50s or early 60s, worked for Maya's mother, VIVIAN BAXTER, in the boardinghouse. He had lived in many places and experienced both menial labor (cleaning up after elephants in circuses) and living by his wits and luck by gambling in "back rooms and shanties" all over the northern states. He cooked huge meals when Vivian was too busy to prepare dinner, and he saw to other odds and ends that needed doing. He adored Vivian, and Maya trusted him. He did not think much of Maya working as a cook—after all, she was educated—but he told her that to cook Creole, all she had to do was use onions, garlic, and green pepper. He also asked her if she could cook rice. She said she was able to do this, and he replied that, "them gauchos can't live without swamp seed" (235). He felt she was too good to be a cook and thought someone like Maya should marry and cook for "nobody but your own family" (235).

Chapter 4

Maya loved her job as the cook at the Creole Café. She felt that she had finally gained authority over something, and she prepared dishes in a mist of onion, garlic, tomato, and green-pepper steam and aromas. She felt like an alchemist discovering new creations in her quick mastery of Creole kitchen mysteries. Her mother found a good woman to take care of the baby, and Maya enjoyed the many customers who ate and then lingered for conversation. From the kitchen, she could hear French patois, the common vernacular of the light-skinned Creoles from Louisiana. She described what she heard as the "soft sounds of black talk, the sharp reports of laughter, and the shuffling feet on tiled floors" (236). She was content with learning a new cooking style and also felt entertained by the customers' conversation.

Chapter 5

With a job, a kind babysitter, and a nice room in an attractive Victorian home (with cooking privileges), Maya was beginning to feel confident that she was capable of taking care of her adult responsibilities. One evening on her day off, she was taking a walk with the sleeping baby nestled in her arm when she encountered two of her ex-schoolmates, "that rare breed, black born San Franciscans" (237). They had heard that the baby was cute and wanted to see him. Trustingly, Maya lifted the light blanket, and the girls carried on about his light skin. They said he could "pass" for white, and the most hurtful comment was, "A crow gives birth to a dove. The bird kingdom must be petrified" (238). The comment cut deeply, and Maya reflects, "Motionless, I froze, as Lot's wife must have done, having caught a last glimpse of concentrated evil" (238). The girls asked the baby's name, but Maya did not answer. Instead, she covered him and left them without any more conversation. She hid her feelings but felt deeply wounded.

Their response shook her, and when she reached her apartment, she put her baby on the chenille bedspread and examined his fine features carefully. He was five months old and looked a little like a tiny Buddha with soft and curly black hair. Most significant was his hairline: It was exactly like hers, and she knew that this plump, healthy baby was "undeniably" hers, in spite of her self-perception that she lacked grace, style, and beauty.

Chapter 6

Maya reflected and wondered why people described the different skin colors of African Americans in terms of good foods. Butter, honey, lemon, chocolate, nutmeg, cinnamon, peaches-and-cream, and cream itself were common adjectives. The Creoles had skin of many different shades, and the food descriptors of skin color were curious to her. As she was thinking about that, a handsome man with glistening dark-brown skin walked into the restaurant. Maya was so taken with his appearance that she suggested it was "surely the second coming of Christ" (239). His name was Curly, but Maya felt that was a poor name for someone so attractive and elegant. He even ate slowly and carefully. He noticed Maya and called her over to him to get acquainted. Starting the conversation by asking her how long she had been cooking like that, they talked a little, and when she got off at 1:00, he went to see her baby. He said he did not think much of the baby's father for not taking care of Maya, and she agreed, temporarily forgetting that she had been the one to instigate the act that got her pregnant. She reflected on the way she had conceived and enjoyed a moment of self-pity, knowing well that she had invited the sexual encounter that led to her pregnancy. She writes: "Self-pity in its early stage is as snug as a feather mattress. Only when it hardens does it become uncomfortable" (241).

After taking Maya to visit the baby, Curly invited her to go to his hotel room. She was nervous and unsure of the whole situation, but she went and let the act unfold there as she had hoped it would. She was treated with respect and physically loved by this tender gentleman. She had first experienced violence as a young child in regard to sex, and then indifference, but this man treated her gently and with care. She was thankful for that and cried from relief afterward. The next day, she was so happy and grateful to Curly for his kindness that she went to a jewelry store and bought him an onyx ring with a diamond chip, and she charged it to her stepfather's account.

Chapter 7

The man's real name was Charles, and Curly was his nickname. He was honest enough with Maya to tell her that he had a girl who worked in the San Diego shipyard whom he was going to marry. Their plan was that when her job was finished, they would be going to New Orleans, marry, and settle there. He was 31 and seemed older because of experiencing the terror of World War II. He was honest about having a fiancée, and Maya thought she had accepted that as fact, but she was not prepared for the emotional letdown when his girl arrived in San Francisco.

Curly had admired her baby, made love to her, and then ended the relationship just as he said he would. He had taught her how to love a man, and he was kind, but his departure was deeply painful. Angelou writes: "The loss of first love is so painful that it borders on the ludicrous" (244). After he left, Maya began to lose weight and slipped into sort of a depression. She stopped taking good care of herself and looked unkempt. She writes: "By eighteen I managed to look run down if not actually run over" (245).

Maya's brother, Bailey, returned to San Francisco after many months away at sea as a merchant marine, and he saw immediately that something was seriously wrong with Maya. It seemed to anger him more than worry him, and he let her know that he wanted to talk and identify the problem. With the baby crawling and playing on the floor, Maya told her brother about the affair and also told him about the way her schoolmates had treated her when they saw the baby. He listened and suggested that it was probably time she move to another city. She resisted the idea at first, mostly because she was feeling sorry for herself. She dramatically imagined herself "as the heroine, solitary, standing under a streetlight's soft yellow glow. Waiting, Waiting. As the fog comes in, a gentle rain falls but doesn't drench her. It is just enough to make her shiver in her white raincoat (collar turned up)" (246). Bailey knew her well and said, "If you want to stay around here looking like death eating a soda cracker, that's your business" (247). Maya decided to move to Los Angeles.

Her mother approved of the idea and reminded her that whatever she did, she was to do it well. Maya's mother was a veritable walking collection of APHORISMS—saying, for example, "Be the best of anything you get into. If you want to be a prostitute, it's your life. Be a damn good one. Don't chirpy at anything. Anything worth having is worth working for" (247). Vivian Baxter was facing the probable end to her own marriage, and there would be a considerable change in her own income because of it. She was negotiating her own problems and would not stand in the way of Maya's future.

Chapter 8

The Los Angeles Union Railway Terminal was a Moorish Spanish style with a high, domed ceiling. Palm trees and long benches made it feel even more exotic, but the thing Maya noticed most when she arrived was the casual dress. Men wore flowered shirts, and the women lounged in cotton dresses. She was dressed formally and wore a black dress with a rhinestone brooch and white gloves. The baby, about a year old, had all but destroyed her appearance by climbing on her, but she straightened herself out, maintained her dignity, and promptly called her Los Angeles relatives, the Baxters. One of her aunts answered the phone and told Maya to get a taxi, which they would pay for, and come on to Federal Avenue, where they lived.

The Baxter clan gathered to meet Maya and baby Clyde, and they passed the baby around for inspection. They removed his little bootees and admired his feet. A round head was a genetic Baxter trait, and Clyde not only had the round head but looked like his grandmother Vivian. Though the Baxters were polite, there was no invitation to stay there. Maya knew that these were people who had no patience with any kind of weakness and expected people to be independent. They asked if she needed money, and they asked if they could give her a ride to the train station. There was little warmth and even less welcome.

Maya had imagined warmer hospitality from her mother's family, but she quickly realized that they were not really interested in her or the baby. They assumed she would be moving on to San Diego to stay with her father, but Maya knew that staying with her father was not a possibility. She realized that she and Clyde would have to make their own way, and though she had a plan, life itself seemed to take over and lead her the way it wanted to. She decided to go on to San Diego.

Chapter 9

Maya found a hotel in San Diego where she and Clyde stayed for the night, and the next day she went to an address given to her by a helpful maid at the hotel. It was the address of a woman, Mother Cleo, who had a reputation for taking good care of children. Because Maya had so much makeup on when she arrived, Mother Cleo's first impression was that she was a hooker. Maya assured her that she was a chef and was going to apply for a job as a waitress at the Hi Hat Club. The woman took Clyde into her arms and was immediately captivated by his beauty. She told Maya that she would charge her less than what she charged her white moms. She felt a little used as a "mammy" by those mothers, who were mostly from the South, and thought their children might someday say that they had a colored mammy in their early childhood. She seemed delighted to take care of Clyde.

Mother Cleo held Clyde, and "Her face softened and her voice blurred" (253). He began to cry loudly. Maya had a struggle getting past his cries of terror and took the baby back to comfort him. Mother Cleo told Maya that she was too soft, assuring her: "They all do that till they get used to me" (254). She gently took the baby again, and though Clyde did all that he could to let Maya know that this was not to his liking, Mother Cleo confidently promised Maya that he would be fine, and she began to sing softly. Maya paid the woman for the first week, and then she left with the sounds of her son yelling. "His screams were lightning, piercing the dark cloud of her music. I closed the door" (254).

Chapter 10

The Hi Hat Club had a purple stucco facade with glitter on the outside and a dark inside illuminated only by red bulbs overhead and a jukebox with flickering green, red, and yellow lights "like an evil robot from a Flash Gordon film" (254). The bar's population seemed to be made up of underworld characters, sailors, and women from the street. Thieves entered the bar late at night and made deals on stolen goods, and the pimps bought items from them with money their prostitutes had earned. The air felt thick with cigarette smoke, Lysol, perfume, bodies, and stale beer. Maya had the impression that the customers thought that smart women were prostitutes and dumb ones were waitresses. Her tips for serving as a waitress were good "because I was fast and had a good memory" (255).

After the first week, Mother Cleo and her husband decided to offer Maya a room in their home. The woman said, "I see you a good girl coming over here to see your baby ever [*sic*] day" (256). Maya accepted the offer from the couple, and soon her life began to have a rhythm. She was well aware of her youth, but she was able to establish a daily routine and independence. She found a dancing school "where a long-haired white woman gave classes to a motley crew of Navy wives" (256), and she balanced her life between work, dancing lessons, and playing with Clyde. She perceived the baby as her own living doll.

Chapter 11

Two black women, a little like Mutt and Jeff, were nightly regulars at the Hi Hat Club. Johnnie Mae was tall, thin, and dark-brown-skinned, and Beatrice was short, plump, and colored yellow. The two were lesbians, and they only spoke to Maya and to each other. The fact that they were lesbians did not bother Maya, who found them interesting. They invited her to Sunday dinner at their home with a promise of chicken, ham, and a watermelon. Another waitress warned her that they were "bull daggers" who loved women rather than men, but Maya told her she was not a lesbian. The two women gave her their address and told her to come to their place at 2:00. They knew from overhearing the conversation Maya had with the waitress that she was not into their game, but the invitation stood anyway.

Chapter 12

Maya had been trained to be a churchgoer from early childhood, and she went to church in San Diego, but she thought that her bed seemed to have more appeal on Sunday morning than on weekdays. The church nearest to her apartment (or room) was often crowded, and the congregation was verbally passionate in response to the minister's message. Her southern black upbringing had prepared her for these kinds of services, but the "rocking crowd of strangers" (259) left her a little uncomfortable. Still, she understood the people: "The fact of my Southern upbringing, the fact that my born blackness meant that I was for the rest of my life a member of that righteous band, and would be whether or not I ever went to church again" (260).

Maya went to the home of Johnnie Mae and Beatrice for Sunday dinner that afternoon. They seemed glad to see her, welcomed her in, and invited her to look over their house. There seemed to be no pictures or books, but they had a lot of overstuffed furniture. Their bed was round and covered with a blue satin spread. Never at a loss for words, Maya complimented them on their home and then sat nervously on the couch with a glass of wine they had given her. The meal preparation was just starting, so Maya knew she would be there for some time. The two women kissed rather passionately in front of her, but Maya was unmoved and unimpressed; she just thought they were stupid.

At some point, Maya asked them where they worked, and they openly said they were prostitutes and did tricks all night twice a week there in their home, earning about $200 between them. They told her they were going to have to move because the landlord did not like gay people. His son was gay, and that had turned him against them. They had painted the place themselves and did not really want to move. Then they asked her why she was working as a waitress since she must have a diploma. Maya explained that she could not type or take shorthand, so she just had to take the kind of work she could get. Johnnie Mae said that Beatrice was the same. The two lesbians had met when they worked for a wealthy woman as a cook and housekeeper. They fell in love there, and the two paired off and had stayed together since. They had painted the walls in the living room sort of a pea yellow, and they had also planted roses and tried to make a home to share with one another.

Chapter 13

Beatrice and Johnnie Mae offered Maya marijuana (or *grifa*). Though Maya had never used it, she decided that under the circumstances she might as well. When she tried it, it burned and choked her. They laughed at her when she smoked and taught her how to use it. Maya coughed a lot, but she smoked until it was time for dinner. They said Maya had a "buzz," and from Maya's perspective, she thought she had never tasted better food. Then they laughed, knowing they had managed to get her high, and Maya felt she might have to design a way to take revenge against them for racist comments they had made like "Now baby, you don't want no black chicken, do you?" (262) and "If that chicken gets any darker than you, I'll have to whip your rusty dusty" (262). They turned to music and asked Maya to dance for them. She did, and Beatrice got up to dance with her. She was too close, and they nearly fell, but mercifully, the music ended. Maya went to the bathroom, and during her time there, she thought of a money-making plan.

Maya excused herself to use their bathroom for the second time, and when she came out, she suggested that they put their rented place in Maya's name, and three or four nights a week, they could turn tricks. She said she could cut in white cab drivers who could furnish the customers. They could all split the money, and soon Beatrice and Johnnie Mae could buy their own house. Maya lied and told them that she had managed something like this before and was working as a waitress as a cover because the "cops" were after her—well, actually not her but after one of her "girls." They decided to go with her plan and gave her the landlord's name and address. They had a drink together to seal the deal, and Maya left with her head ringing with liquor and marijuana. She felt a need, somehow, to use and hurt them because they were what they were, and they had been teasing and rude to her. Only 18, she was now the manager of two prostitutes and a whorehouse.

Chapter 14

Maya boldly approached a cab driver about giving him $5 for each prostitute-seeking navy man he brought to her new business enterprise. The driver accepted the business opportunity, and Maya was proud of herself now that she had her own independent source of income. She felt a snobby superiority to Beatrice and Johnnie Mae; after all, she was a madam and they were just prostitutes. She also felt superior to the customers at the club, perceiving that she was brighter than common bar people. She felt free and thought she was more confident than most young women her age, married or not.

Maya enlisted Hank, a bouncer she had met at the club, for help with her enterprise. He would watch out for her and provide protection at the house if she or the lesbians needed it. He was unpredictable, but he liked Maya, and she promised to pay him one-third of her earnings. She wanted him to watch over the house, look out for police, and keep track of the money. Maya felt she had put things together pretty well, but she worried that if Mother Cleo found out, she would not only lose her room and her son's caretaker, she would also lose the Christian reputation she had established with Mother Cleo and her husband. As it turned out, the babysitter and landlady assumed that Maya had a boyfriend because she was coming home later. Maya let it go at that.

Maya's "business" lasted two and a half months and provided a dresser drawer of money for her to spend as she wished. She bought a "pale-green Chrysler, '39 vintage, convertible" (273). She told Mother Cleo that her boyfriend had bought the car for her, but the caretaker was worried that the boyfriend might be married or, even worse, white. Maya assured her that he was neither. And so the ruse continued. Maya thought of herself as a widow with invisible "widow's weeds" (274), but the reality was that she was still mourning the loss of Curly, her first real love as she viewed it, and he had returned to someone else and moved to Louisiana.

Chapter 15

Because Maya felt she was living in a dark, forbidden world, the gloomy Russian novel writers FYODOR DOSTOYEVSKY, Maksim Gorky, Anton Chekov, and Ivan Turgenev seemed to appeal to her. Dostoyevsky's novel *Crime and Punishment* held her focus because her own life seemed to be made up of opposites. Life took on an aura of Russian mists, and she seemed to live in a "murky, unjust world" (274). She copied her dance teacher's way of dressing (long gathered skirts, Mexican peasant blouses, beads, and thongs) and lived as a "waitress, dreamer, madam, and mother" (275). But life soon took another turn.

One firm rule of the prostitute house was that no "tricks" were ever to be there when Maya arrived to pick up the money. One night as she was gathering the money, a white sailor, nude from the waist down, stumbled out of the bedroom. Maya was angry. The women, jealous and defensive, let Maya know how unfairly they thought she had treated them. They accused her of thinking she was too good to turn a trick, and they did not like Hank guarding them all the time. After a hot exchange, Maya told Hank, the bouncer, that he could have the prostitute house along with the prostitutes; then she asked the cab driver to take her home.

As she left, Johnnie Mae threatened to tell the police how Maya got the money to buy the car. This scared Maya.

Maya decided to leave San Diego as quickly as possible. When she got to her room, she stuffed all of her possessions into the suitcases Bailey had given her in San Francisco and planned to run away at daybreak. Mother Cleo knocked at the door to remind Maya about using lights (electricity) in the middle of the night, and Maya told her that her mother was sick in San Francisco and that she and the baby would have to leave right away. When the hour to leave came, Mother Cleo and her husband blessed them, and Mother Cleo said, "You're just what I wanted for a daughter" (279). Maya had presented the ideal young woman image to them, but as soon as she was on her way she tore to the train station. She wiped down the steering wheel to get rid of fingerprints, just in case someone might try to trace the owner, and she left the car in a no-parking zone, then boarded a train and did not look back.

Her destination was Stamps, Arkansas, and the embrace of her beloved and trusted grandmother, Mrs. Annie Henderson.

Chapter 16

Returning to the South was no romantic illusion for Maya. It was a poor, racially divided world of prejudice and poverty-stricken blacks. The South seemed to be viewed by many Americans as a place of soft white women, impressive black magnolia trees, and considerate gentlemen set against a background of "harmonious black music" (280). For blacks, the realities were racial prejudice and bare survival. To Maya, it "was flesh-real and swollen-belly poor" (280). Maya' s grandmother understood how prejudice in the South worked, and by working hard and thinking clearly, she managed to own a country store as well as other property, and she had the respect of the community. Maya and her brother called her Momma, and she welcomed them home with familiar foods and welcoming words. Maya relaxed and wept with relief within the comfort of the familiar. She waited on people in the Store for four days and let them look her over. Maya was the Stamps girl who had gone to California and returned. No one asked why.

One night, Maya went for an evening out at the Dew Drop In café with friends who lived locally. She heard her name spoken there, and it turned out to be L. C. Smith. As she remembered from years past, he was a quiet fellow, but he asked her to dance. He had been watching Maya drink Coke and sloe gin, and knew her old "friends" were just trying to make her look foolish. She started to get up, but she "noticed that the building moved. It rippled and buckled as if a nest of snakes were mating beneath the floors" (285). He got a glass of water for the intoxicated Maya and then led her outside for fresh air. She threw up, and L. C. explained that her friends wanted to leave Stamps and were jealous of her. She had escaped then returned, and they could not understand why she had not changed more. She was still dressed like them in long, flowered skirts and simple white peasant blouses but bragging about her wonderful experiences in San Francisco.

L. C. walked her home, and at the back door of the store he gave her some breath freshener so she would not upset "Sister Henderson." On the walk home, he explained that he would probably never leave Stamps. He was devoted to his father, but his father was a drunk and would use L. C.'s salary from cotton picking before he could buy groceries for the week. He said that he was grateful to Maya's grandmother for food. She was generous about extending credit to him. He told Maya that he had thought about leaving, but he had no skills except picking cotton and hoeing potatoes. He left her there at the back door of the Store and disappeared into the darkness. About a year later, on the day of his father's funeral, Maya heard that he had committed suicide.

Chapter 17

Maya dressed herself up San Francisco–style, meaning white gloves, high heels, a girdle, and deodorant, and walked three miles to a shop in the white town. She thought she was demonstrating to all women there, black and white, that she knew how a lady should dress for shopping. She realized later that what she was really demonstrating was a haughty pride. It was midmorning, and the walk was on a gravel road. Her high heels slipped on the "small, grabbing stones" (289), but she held her head high and shoulders square and paraded to the store.

Maya asked for a specific pattern from the young white clerk who waited on her. The girl said they did not have it but could order it and have it for her in three days. Maya wrote her name for the order and then walked out of the store into the noon heat. The road was empty because it was extremely hot, and wisdom suggested that people should avoid being outdoors during the blistering afternoon. Being prideful, she would not walk home in the shade of the trees that lined the road but instead walked with the hot sun beating down on her head and shoulders. She strode along with the same demonstration of dignity and pride she had determined to exhibit earlier. By the time she reached the Store, she was exhausted and nauseous from the oppressive heat, but she hid it from Momma.

The days passed slowly, and Momma was engrossed in the charm and wonder of baby Clyde. He was just as pleased with her and followed Momma everywhere she went. Three days passed, and again, it was a very hot day, but Maya knew her pattern had arrived, so she dressed up again and walked the three miles to town. The sun was beating down relentlessly, but "arrogance and stupidity" (291) seemed to drive her, and she felt that her "thighs scudded like wet rubber" (291). When she entered the shop aisle, she discovered that a tall white saleswoman was in the same aisle headed in the opposite direction. They both moved to let the other pass, but this did not work. Finally, the saleswoman strongly suggested that Maya stand still and she would pass by. Maya said, "No," and told the woman that she would pass her. About that time, the girl who had waited on Maya previously walked into the same aisle. The tall woman asked Maya's name, and Maya said, "Miss Johnson" very firmly. Maya felt offended and sarcastically told them she would call them "Miss Idiot, Miss Stupid, [or] Miss Fool." (293). She told them where they could put their pattern and left arrogantly.

Maya felt so self-righteous that she did not even feel the heat as she walked home. She congratulated herself and felt "cool as a fountain" (293). When she was nearly to her grandmother's store, she saw Momma standing on the porch. She recognized that something was very wrong and sensed Momma's tension by the way she was standing. Momma had been telephoned, and she knew exactly what had happened at the shop. Maya began to explain that her behavior was based on "the principle of the thing" (294), when she suddenly felt Momma's hand slap her face not once but several times. Each time Maya would say it was a principle, Momma would strike her again. Maya's behavior had placed herself in grave danger in Klan-ruled Arkansas. She had invited the inevitability of being sexually violated or even worse. Her grandmother knew the potential violence of the Klan and had already packed Maya's and her son's belongings and made arrangements for someone to take them to Lewisville (spelled Louisville in the text), about five miles west of Stamps. Suddenly, they were removed from Grandmother Henderson, Uncle Willie, and Stamps.

Chapter 18

Maya soon returned to San Francisco, and while she was on the train, she wondered if there would be a warrant for her arrest there. Momma had never hit her before, and reflecting on the whole experience left her hating whites all the more. She looked meanly at every white face she encountered on the train. When she arrived, there was no warrant awaiting her, and she felt let down that her absence had not been noticed. She went to her mother's new 14-room house, and it felt like she had just returned from a vacation.

Her first job in San Francisco was as a short-order cook in a cheesy restaurant that she called "a tiny greasy spoon" (295). There was a record store across the street, and the music comforted her, so she spent a lot of time there. She used her salary to pay board at her mother's, and the rest she spent on records and books. There was a friendly white woman at the record shop who did not seem to condescend to Maya. When Maya told her the kind of music she really liked, the woman found records she knew Maya would enjoy.

Maya's mother reminded her that she should be doing more with her life. Maya was bright, and her mother was ambitious for her. Vivian reminded her about various young friends and what they were doing, and she also told Maya that she needed either job training or more education. After finding dead-end jobs in the paper, Maya suddenly decided to join the U.S. Army. Reflecting on a chauffeuring job she had held in the past where she wore a uniform and enjoyed the people she worked with, she thought that might be what she could do in the army. She took the idea to her mother, but Vivian did not think much of it. In fact, she said that being in the army would be like being in jail. Even so, she said she would support Maya if that was what she decided to do, and she reminded Maya that the decision belonged to her, and her alone. She also told Maya that whatever she decided to do, she should not "be a funky chippie. Go with class" (299).

Chapter 19

Maya went to the United States Recruitment Center in the whitewashed, prefabricated building at the foot of Market Street in San Francisco. She went through the many procedures required to join the army, lied delicately now and then, and tried hard to make a good impression because she hoped to qualify for admission to the Officer Candidate School. Her mother had told her to aim high, and that was what she was doing. She went through the rigors of testing, including a RORSCHACH TEST, and was examined from top to bottom, literally. Then she went back to her mother's house to await the results. In a few days, the phone call came, and she was told that she had passed her tests and would be included in the "March–April quota of personnel to enter Officer Candidate School" (301). She was so happy she could not speak. She was instructed to return to the recruitment center to sign a loyalty oath.

Her mother was pleased but not surprised; however, Bailey was furious. He reminded her that men were trying to get out of the army, yet she was trying to get in. Bailey worked for the Southern Pacific Railways as a waiter, and he had become hard and remote. Maya could not find explanations about what had changed him, but he was a different Bailey than she had known before.

Chapter 20

Maya's records and favorite books were to be kept at her mother's house while she was in the army, but her old clothes and other unneeded personal belongings were given to the Salvation Army. Everything seemed to be in order when she received a call to report immediately to the recruitment center because of a discrepancy in her documents. As it turned out, it was because she had attended the California Labor School when she was 14 and 15. That school was on the House Un-American Activities list and suspected of being communist. There was no discussion; she was dismissed.

Maya returned home realizing that she now had no job, her clothes were gone, and the U.S. Army had rejected her. She wanted to talk to Bailey like they used to talk, but he was not home. She went to his dark, empty room and decided to freshen it up for him, including changing his bed linens and adding some flowers to perk things up. As she pulled the sheets and pillows off the bed, a small package bounced off with them. Cigarettes, thin and brown, were in the package. Maya lit one, sat down on the bed, and laughed, reflecting on the army's stupidity for rejecting her application.

Chapter 21

Maya found a job as a swing-shift waitress in a 24-hour restaurant called the Chicken Shack. She also began smoking grass—"Mary Jane, hash, grass, gauge, weed or pot" (309)—which was easy to get. It relaxed her, and for the first time, life began to amuse her. She enjoyed walking, eating her mother's huge dinners, and playing with the baby. The grass seemed to put a positive slant on everything.

A woman at the record shop gave Maya's address to a man named R. L. Poole. He was a rhythm tap dancer from Chicago and needed a dance partner. She had been trained to dance but not in the specifics about which he was asking. He called on her at her mother's house, and Maya, wanting to show him how flexible and graceful she was, began to slide into a split to demonstrate her agility. He was amazed, but unfortunately she became stuck between the legs of her mother's heavy oak table and a gas jet. Maya tried to maintain her dignity, but she was stuck. She jerked her foot a couple of times to loosen it, and the "pipe came away from the stove, and gas hissed out steadily like ten fat men resting on a summer's day" (312). R. L. reached over and turned off the jet, and in spite of her pride, Maya rolled over on the floor and began to cry. R. L. did not laugh at her, but rather kindly told her that she had nice legs. He took her to a rehearsal hall and tap-danced like the wind was carrying him. Maya learned quickly how to be a flash partner—that is, one who "frames and highlights the principal dancer when he is tapping out complex rhythms" (313). She felt free on the dance floor, and "fell promptly in love with him" (313).

Chapter 22

Maya wanted a show-business career and practiced until her ankles ached. R. L. recognized that she was ready to perform, so Maya went to a theatrical store and put together a scanty outfit. He did not approve of it and rented a red, white, and blue costume much like a bathing suit. She added a top hat and cane, and they were ready for their debut at a small club a little south of San Francisco.

Their names were announced, and they entered the performance floor at the cue of "Poole and Rita." Poole came out dancing, but Rita came out and froze. He flashed by her a few times whispering, "Come on, Rita. Break. Break!" (316). When she finally began to dance, she completely forgot their rehearsal routine and became, as she put it, "the world's dancing fool" (316). R. L. finally put his arm around her, firmly, and they danced off the floor. The audience clapped them back, and Maya returned for another bow. She was hooked. She was happy. She was in show business.

Chapter 23

Vivian Baxter, Maya's mother, had many male friends and suitors. At the time of this chapter, her live-in was Good-Doing David, a dapper and very black man. Another friend, seaman John Thomas, called unexpectedly and said he was in town. Vivian's relationship with Thomas was like brother and sister, and so she invited him to her home and made biscuits and fried chicken to welcome him.

Maya left the house to pick up Clyde at the sitter's and was shocked to find police arresting her mother when she returned home. When Good-Doing David returned from wherever he had been, he found John Thomas in the kitchen eating. Jealous and angry, David insisted the man leave and pulled a knife to threaten him. Vivian got her pistol and slapped David across the face with it. It cut him, and he screamed, "Bibbie, you cut me!" (320). She answered, "You lucky I do not shoot you on top of it" (320). She told John Thomas to make himself scarce, and then she called the police and ambulance. Vivian explained the incident to her daughter, first telling her that many people seem to think they can take advantage of black women. Then she reminded Maya that her mother had raised her to think, "'If you have not been trained at home to their liking tell them to get to stepping.' Here a whisper of delight crawled over her face. 'Stepping. But not on you'" (320).

Bailey fell in love with an old classmate from school named Eunice. He was happy, in good humor, and Maya visited them at their apartment, where they talked, laughed, and congratulated themselves for being young and intelligent. Maya was grateful to Eunice for saving her brother. Many of his contemporaries, young black men, were caught up in drugs and crime. Eunice loved him, and he wanted to be good for her. Bailey was drawn toward a looser life, but Eunice had turned him toward a better direction.

Chapter 24

Rita and Poole were doing well and had a contract at the Champagne Supper Club. Maya quit her waitress job at the Chicken Shack and committed herself to her job in show business. Investing in Maya's career, her mother loaned her money and expected success. Vivian Baxter had achieved diplomas in various vocations and expected her children to be successful.

When Maya went to Bailey to ask for a small advance, she learned that Eunice was in the hospital. Bailey was deeply preoccupied, unkempt, and the apartment was neglected. Eunice was very sick. Her brother told her that her illness was like a bad cold. Maya sensed she was intruding and did not press the cause for her visit.

Opening night of the next gig at the Champagne Supper Club finally arrived. R. L. was handsome in his powder-blue tuxedo, and Maya was glamorous in her swimsuit costume. They had rehearsed unceasingly and performed well, but Maya felt the audience did not really appreciate them as much as she expected. There were small gigs after that, but things changed when R. L.'s former partner, Cotton Candy Adams, arrived. She was beautiful, with a cute walk and a "little girl mince" (326). R. L. turned from Maya to Cotton Candy, and Maya felt her career had ended before it had really begun. She again found herself without a job, a man to love, or a predictable future.

Her mother reminded her that during the war, when things were easy financially, she could have become idle. But rather than do so, Vivian had studied a variety of vocations, including barbering and cosmetology, shipfitting, tool-and-dye making, and even welding. She had earned several diplomas, and she had qualified herself for many different jobs should she need them. She hoped Maya would follow her example and prepare to take care of herself and her child.

Chapter 25

Maya's mother had a friend who owned a restaurant in Stockton, about 80 miles from San Francisco, and a fry cook was needed there. Southerners, Mexicans, Filipinos, and others in Stockton were looking for ways to earn money to support their families, but Maya thought she would be able to get the job. The law was not strict or particularly enforced there at that time, so gamblers and prostitutes from San Francisco inhabited Stockton as well as other kinds of criminals—including drug dealers. Drugs were easy to get there. Maya was hired and worked an afternoon shift. After work, she often hung out in a bar wearing glamorous evening clothes, observing people, and rejecting men.

A woman named Big Mary kept the baby on a weekly basis in Stockton, and Maya trusted her. She drank heavily once a month, but on those weekends, other arrangements were made for the children. She was from Oklahoma and part Native American, with distinctive high cheekbones and the dark black-brown skin of her heritage. She was good with children, and Maya felt Big Mary would take good care of her son. Because Maya had given away most of her wardrobe thinking she would be donning a uniform, she concentrated on work and earning enough money to rebuild her wardrobe.

Her future was still uncertain, and she dreamed of a husband who would provide for her, love her, and be there for her, always, as a father to her son, and perhaps to her imagined next child, a girl—the imagined child that never happened. One night, as Maya was waiting for her replacement cook at the restaurant, a group entered and wanted a midnight breakfast. She had already changed into her evening clothes, but one of the customers came to the kitchen door and asked her to stay and cook for them. He recognized that she was about to leave and gave her a $10 bill. Maya needed the money, so she took it and went back to the dressing room to change back into work clothes. His name was Louis David Tolbrook (L. D.), an older professional gambler who was dressed elegantly in the manner of an affluent gentleman.

The next night, he returned to ask Maya (then calling herself Rita) if he could spend some money on her. Maya found that interesting and went out with him after work. He said he wanted her to meet a woman named Clara in Sacramento with whom he had some business. Maya recognized the place they went to as a red-light house, but they were not there long, and it did not particularly bother her. L. D. courteously returned her to the rooming house where she was staying, and the next evening, he was waiting outside her workplace when she finished her shift. This time, they drove to Tulare, where Maya met a woman named Minnie who ran the same kind of house as Clara. Maya liked the way she was treated by L. D. He was kind, but she did not quite understand where this new friendship was headed. When he returned her to the rooming house, he pressed a crumpled $50 bill into her hand and told her that he had a big game to attend down in San Francisco and would not see her for a few days. He promised to return before long.

Chapter 26

Maya's friendship, nothing more, continued with L. D. He never did really explain his business, and she did not ask. For three weeks, she rode along California highways with him while he gave gifts to various women and said business was good. L. D. gave Maya money to buy clothes more appropriate for her age: low shoes and anklets, blouses and pretty skirts, and ribbons for her hair. When he saw her dressed in teen clothes, he called her "Bobby Sock Baby" (338). Then he took her to a room, asked her to wash, and made love to her.

Maya enjoyed being Bobby Sock Baby, and she also continued using marijuana. L. D. recognized that she was using it and told her it could destroy her nature. She promised she would quit, and he told her about his wife, who had been ruined by pot use. Maya believed him, and their relationship continued, but she did not stop smoking the marijuana. It made her giggle for about an hour, and then she would lose the hysteria and behave normally again. She dreamed of a long-term relationship with him and hoped they might even establish a family someday.

For three days, L. D. did not visit the restaurant. When he did show up, he looked ungroomed and tired. He told Maya that he had lost everything gambling, and he said that he was in debt to "the big boys" (353) for more than $2,000. Maya offered to be a prostitute for him (after L. D. manipulated her into thinking it was her idea). He said that when this time was over, he would divorce his wife and marry his Bobby Sock Baby.

Chapter 27

Maya had an interview of sorts with Clara, a madam, and Bea, one of Clara's prostitutes. She was instructed about how to turn tricks, how to keep a record of her tricks, and when she could be with her own man. The women had a good-luck ritual that Maya had never seen before, and they shared it with her. One of the women attached two long strings to tacks that were pressed into the lintel (horizontal crosspiece) of the living-room door. Then one of them took matches from her pocket and lit the ends of the strings that nearly touched the floor. She explained, "You burn string in the morning for luck, Rita. When it reaches the first knot the tricks begin to walk" (346).

Maya's first customer was an Indian-looking man who spoke Spanish and was told that Maya was a schoolgirl. They went into a room, and Maya did what was expected of her.

Clara gave Maya more tips, but Maya sensed the shame of it. There were cooks who served them dinner each day, and Maya rationalized that all of this was simply to help her man. Bea, one of the prostitutes Maya met when she first went there, told Maya that she would like her job better when her sponsor daddy (L. D.) would give her "white girl," or cocaine. Maya did not believe her because L. D. did not even approve of weed. There were other stories, other examples, but Maya felt she was different. She believed L. D. would marry her. She also realized that Bea was better at the job than she was.

Bea and Clara burned strings faithfully every morning. They explained to Maya that turning a trick was just that, a trick. She was not to pretend to really be making love with the customers. Maya thought differently, and she knew she was not a very successful prostitute. One evening, L. D. picked her up for a date, but he let her know that she was not earning enough, and that he also expected her to call him Daddy. Maya hated it, but she obeyed him. She picked up the baby, and then L. D. gave her money for a movie and said he would see her later.

Chapter 28

Maya was conscious that she was not spending much time with baby Clyde. The babysitter, Big Mary, bluntly questioned her about her work, but Maya evaded her. When she returned him to the sitter, she received news that someone in San Francisco had been trying to reach her. Maya returned the call and learned that her mother was in the hospital recovering from surgery and not doing well. She left the baby with the sitter and took a Greyhound bus to San Francisco.

Maya found her mother slowly recovering, and Bailey was in her hospital room slumped in a chair, asleep. Eunice had died unexpectedly, and it was also Bailey and Eunice's one-year anniversary. Vivian asked Maya to take care of her brother. Maya awakened him and took her brokenhearted brother to their mother's home. At the house, he cried long but ate well, and then he began to talk. Eunice had had tuberculosis and double pneumonia, and though he had not expected it, she had died that very morning. After explaining what had happened, he slept on his mother's bed curled up in a fetal position like a baby. In the morning, he showered and sang, but when he was in the kitchen, he was edgy and cooked breakfast for himself. He took another bath and later told Maya that after the funeral, scheduled the next day, he never wanted to hear Eunice's name spoken again. His smile was odd, and he wore a white tennis outfit to the funeral and talked of quitting his job.

Maya told him what she was doing in Stockton, and Bailey demanded to know who was the man "who turned you out" (361). He would not tolerate his sister working as a prostitute and gave her money for a round-trip back to San Francisco. He ordered her to get the baby and come home, so she left that afternoon for Stockton.

Chapter 29

When Maya returned to Stockton to pick up her son, Big Mary's house was boarded up and vacant. In her fear and anxiety, Maya learned from a neighbor that Big Mary had taken her son to Bakersfield. Maya turned to L. D. for help, and though it was forbidden, she went to his home. A beautiful woman, L. D.'s wife, answered the door. L. D. was angry with Maya and said, "What put it in your head to come to my house? . . . Don't you have better sense than to come to my house?" (364–365). He told her to go to her apartment and wait. Maya realized that she had been duped and that she had been stupid again. She slept at her apartment and determined to go to Bakersfield the next morning.

When Maya arrived in Bakersfield, she asked around about Big Mary Dawson and learned that Mary's brother was John Peterson. She found their home and her little boy. In the emotional moments of the child's first clinging to her, she finally realized that the child was a person with feelings and not just "a beautiful appendage of myself" (368). Big Mary wanted to keep him, but Maya promptly gathered up her child and informed Big Mary that she was taking him with her. Still young, Maya realized in those moments that Clyde was not a "cute doll"; rather, he was "an entire person" (368). He was three, and she was 19, and the child was old enough to understand. He was furious that she had left him and let her know it. They departed for San Francisco immediately.

Chapter 30

Maya and Bailey both stayed for a while at their mother's comfortable house, where music, good food, and icy drinks seemed to restore them. Bailey had grown up in many ways. He did not smile as often, and he did not tease as much as he had done before. His arrogance was gone, and there were no more comments about Maya's height. They looked for jobs, and Bailey made it clear to Maya that what she had been doing was bad in every way. Looking at her sharply, he said, "And let me tell you another thing, a prostitute is the saddest and silliest broad walking. All she hopes is to beat somebody out of something, by lying down first and getting up last" (370). Maya knew he was right. Both seemed confident that they would find their way in life successfully, and they continued to lean on each other for support with their mother's home as a safety net beneath them.

Maya found a job in OAKLAND managing a restaurant and worked for an entrepreneur named James Cain, who had amazing half-carat diamonds in his two front teeth. Cain had many business interests and wanted to upgrade his Oakland restaurant. Southern foods were the specialties, and on the menu were neck bones, short ribs, hog maws, pork chops, and red snappers. Maya upgraded the menu for him to chicken à la king, Irish stew, veal cutlets, T-bone steak, peach cobbler, sweet potato pie, ham hocks, and mustard greens. The customers were black gamblers, pimps, and sometimes prostitutes, and they enjoyed the simple foods they had known most of their lives. However, Maya realized that business was dropping off because of the new menu, so after a while they went back to the old one.

Cain decided that he could use Maya in another job, and he asked her to drive boxers out to Lake Merrit to exercise. The men would get out of the car and run, and she was to follow them in a car. So she worked as a chauffeurette. Cain outfitted her in brown suede and introduced her to the world of boxing, which she did not understand. She watched one of the men she knew getting beaten in the ring, turned to her boss, and said, "Stop them, Cain" (376). Maya carried on, and soon he told her to "Shut up" (376). She yelled several things at him finishing with, "Marquis de Sade son of a . . ." (376), and she threw her purse at Cain. She was terribly upset at the brutality of boxing and abruptly ran out of the arena, knowing she would lose her job. After she was fired, she then slid into another emotional loss of confidence in herself and her future.

Chapter 31

Troubadour Martin was a customer at Cain's restaurant, where Maya first met him. He asked if he could keep some clothes at her house for women to try on and buy, promising her a percentage of the money. She agreed, and the arrangement worked. Maya had each day with her child, and the women came to try on clothes in the evening. She hoped a serious relationship, possibly even marriage, would happen with "Troub," but he was a heavy drug user.

She let him know her feelings for him, and he responded by taking her for a ride to a building on the waterfront where she could see for herself what dead-end lives drugs can lead people to. It was a hotel. "People sat and lounged on every available place. Three bodies were draped over a bed, and men and women sat on the floor backs supported by a wall. Two women sat in one chair and all, black and white, were dozing off or waking up or fast asleep" (382). Then Troub showed her how he shot up. It was horrible. She watched, and then he made Maya promise that she would never use "shit" because, he said, "It is" (383). She made the promise. He took her home and told her to keep the clothes and sell them for money if she needed to. Maya knew she would keep the promise about never using drugs again, and she felt a return of innocence, but sadly, her future was once more uncertain.

CRITICAL COMMENTARY

Gather Together in My Name, Angelou's second autobiography, was first published in 1974. Many of the themes of this work echo her first, *I Know Why the Caged Bird Sings,* and they also foreshadow the autobiographies to follow. In this work, which covers a period of about four years in her life from age 17 to 21, she describes her life as an undereducated teenage mother, candidly shares her experiences with drugs and illegal behaviors, and gives a clear account of her bare economic survival. The literary critic Priscilla R. Ramsey writes: "Her autobiographies and poetry reveal a vital need to transform the elements of a stultifying and destructive personal, social, political and historical milieu into a sensual and physical refuge" (76).

Angelou opened a new level of truthfulness and openness for other black female writers. Cheryl A. Wall, in a short article about Maya Angelou, Toni Morrison, and Alice Walker, comments: "Relatively few autobiographies by black women had been published before Angelou wrote hers. None had delved as deeply into the writer's intimate life. In the process, the book helped break a long-standing public silence around the issue of sexual violence" (970). Wall adds that Angelou's "exploration of family violence, sexual oppression and abuse, and the corrosive effects of racism and poverty . . . ran counter to the then prevailing mood in popular black consciousness of righteous anger and triumphant struggle" (970).

Angelou first described the horror she experienced as a child in *I Know Why the Caged Bird Sings,* but in *Gather Together in My Name,* she openly shares the consequences of the abuse she had suffered by narrating the dire circumstances and unfortunate choices of an independent but desperate young mother. During this period of her life, she narrowly escaped tragedy many times. Her pluck and idealism gave her strength in spite of deep insecurities and confusion, and it was fortunate that she came out on top of the difficulties she had during this period of her life.

The book's opening is set in San Francisco and describes the celebratory mood following the end of World War II. Angelou discusses the social and cultural changes taking place at the time and sets a context for black experience and attitudes following the war. It was a bittersweet aftermath for California racial relations because the war effort had required that people learn to work together regardless of race or creed. Blacks, whites, and Jews worked shoulder-to-shoulder in factories and shipyards in order to support the military effort, and there was little time to think about racial or cultural differences. When the war ended, many black people lost the best jobs and income they had ever had because white soldiers and sailors had returned and were given the jobs the black minorities had filled while they were gone. Black workers were laid off permanently, and it was doubly hard because they had become accustomed to having enough money to provide their families with homes, food, and clothing.

This devastating and humiliating return to poverty caused confusion, fragmention, and alienation. Racial lines were again drawn among Americans, and many blacks who had relocated to cities from the rural South because of the work were thrown back into menial jobs or even total unemployment. All Americans were jubilant about winning the war, but within a few months, some blacks in San Francisco were even offered tickets back to their homes in the South. However, because of their wartime experience and service in the cities, where they were treated with dignity, earned good wages, and rode nonsegregated busses and streetcars, it was next to impossible to return to their earlier subservience and hopelessness. As Angelou writes, "more times than not [they] were called Mister/Missus at their jobs or by sales clerks" (228). There was no way they could passively return to the demeaning SEGREGATION, poverty, and fear present in their southern hometowns.

Gather Together depicts a wide variety of black people from different socioeconomic levels and in particular describes the creative and varied methods they employed to earn the money needed to survive. There are discussions of their encounters with day-to-day life, racial relations and challenges, and descriptions of life patterns and behavior in environments ranging from brothels to boxing matches. Again and again, Angelou exposes the spirit of the black people within an often hostile society and reveals her own insights through her descriptions and stories about them. She often uses folk vernacular and traditions to describe her experiences; as the literary critic Lyman B. Hagen states, "A significant linkage of these works [of hers] is the frequent embracing and reflection of the folklore of her race" (2). Angelou has an insider's perspective that exposes the realities of being black in the United States during this time period, and she also reveals clear examples of why the hegemonic white society needed to change.

Gather Together depicts Angelou's life in her late teens and early 20s. Based on her experience to this point, she had little or no reason to trust whites. She was raised in the racially segregated town of Stamps, Arkansas, and her observations of white power after the war left her with bitter hatred and reinforced suspicion of white people. She sometimes doubted if whites were human since many of her people considered them to be devils, lore that she had heard repeated many times. However, Angelou represents her personality as adaptable, and she demonstrates in her narratives that she was able to respond to hardship creatively and yet continue to play the role of her son's nurturer and protector. Her optimism reveals black hope in the American Dream. To Angelou and most of her acquaintances, including the people she worked with, it was almost unthinkable to consider that conditions would not improve at some time in the future. On the other hand, there was always a thread of uncertainty, which often led to desperate behavior, including her own, which she candidly describes in *Gather Together.*

Within a milieu of postwar change, Angelou describes her desire to be independent of her mother's support and find a way to take care of herself and her two-month-old child. She felt that neither her mother or her mother's relatives understood her: "They were not equipped to understand that an eighteen-year-old mother is also an eighteen-year-old girl" (250). At 17, the mother of an infant, and without marketable skills, she had little to offer the dominant white society in which she lived. She really had no idea what she would do with her life, but she believed that her intelligence, determination, and her belief in God would carry her forward. As Angelou reflected and wrote her narratives, she often used a three-part autobiographical style: that is, *anticipation,* meaning a projection of what might happen; *recognition*, an understanding of realities to be faced; and *fulfillment,* meaning that in spite of obstacles, she would always survive and be all right. As examples typical of this style, Angelou describes *anticipation* by being confident of finding a way to support herself and her child. She *recognized* that she would need to compromise herself to accomplish this, and in spite of obstacles and foolish mistakes, she managed to accomplish that huge task and emerge at the end of this second autobiography having *fulfilled* her first priority, the safety of her son. She recognized the many lessons she had learned in this early adult period of her life and looked forward hopefully to a successful, but unknown, future.

Angelou's search for economic and physical survival included traveling from San Francisco to Los Angeles, San Diego, and Stamps; then back to San Francisco; to Stockton and Oakland, California; and finally to her mother's home in San Francisco after realizing the danger of drugs from an explicit lesson given by a confirmed drug addict. In *Gather Together,* Angelou also sheds light on the reason for the initial move from Stamps to California, described in the last part of the first book. Her grandmother had viewed California as a land of opportunity. It was safe for black people, and she believed that Bailey and Maya might both have a realistic chance at a good life there.

The four-year period described in *Gather Together in My Name* was a fragmented and alienated time in Angelou's life, but the text reveals her attitude and unrelenting search for identity, as well as a more mature understanding of how to maintain innocence and survive life. She also candidly reveals her youthful idealism and dreamy evaluations of men. Her romanticism and emotional neediness blinded her judgement to the point that, as Priscilla Ramsey stated: "In the final analysis, each of these men exploits her because all are morally and characterologically flawed in ways her own emotional neediness causes her to miss as her fantasy life recreates their personalities" (86). In this segment of Angelou's life, one man used her while he was stationed nearby and then returned to his sweetheart. Not long after that, a pimp used her as a prostitute, feigning debt but using the money Maya provided to buy gifts for his wife. This was part of a series of humiliating mistakes in judgment that resulted in a stronger sense of depth and dignity, and Angelou did mature. Her pathetic choices, near-tragic and often bordering on the bizarre, are tied together and unfold in a readable and often amusing style.

Angelou admired her mother's beauty, light skin, and many talents but seemed unable to quite understand her real persona. Vivian Baxter's character in *Gather Together* is not fully developed. Angelou gives examples of her mother's behavior, and she relies on African-American aphorisms and folklore at times to carry her mother's characterization, but the reader is not given clear insight into Vivian's deeper personality. For instance, Angelou shares a song her mother sang that extolled marijuana:

> Dream about a reefer five foot long
> Vitamin but not too strong
> You'll be high but not for long
> If you're a viper.
>
> I'm the queen of everything
> I got to get high before I can swing
> Light some tea and let it be
> If you're a viper.
>
> Now when your throat gets dry
> you know you're high
> Everything is dandy
> You truck on down to the candy store
> And bust your conk on peppermint candy
>
> Then you know your brown body scent
> You do not give a damn if you do not pay your rent
> Light some tea and let it be
> If you're a viper. (2004, 309)

Françoise Lionnet wrote an essay about Maya Angelou's problematic sense of audience: How does she represent characters in her autobiographies in a manner that would be understood and revealing to her readers. Lionnet suggests that perhaps Angelou, experiencing an "anxiety of authorship," attempted to draw Vivian Baxter's character in the same manner of Daniel Defoe's Moll Flanders, whom he designed to be understood as an "inescapably alienating . . . individualistic heroine" (Lionnet 1999, 152). Lionnet states further:

> Vivian Baxter is such an individualist, and in *Gather Together in My Name,* the narrator does attempt to adopt her mother's lifestyle. But in sharing ideals of beauty and independence which are beyond reach, the daughter only alienates herself. (152)

Angelou ultimately embraced life very differently than her mother chose to do. Through her own experiences and self-education, she made independent and contrasting choices for herself and her son. Though they were both nurturing parents, her mother's choices were material and physical; Maya's choices were more intellectual and civically oriented.

Angelou candidly tells the story of her association with unsavory characters who make a living on the fringes of mainstream society. Though she became deeply involved with some of them, her early religious training by her Grandmother Henderson had embedded the concept of daily trials and ultimate reward. Within the context of a large and baffling society, young Maya learned to be thankful for the most meager good luck that might come her way, and she learned through the folk religion of her heritage that ultimately there would be a transcendence of worldly suffering for her people. Everyone, including Maya, would be at peace and have their dreams fulfilled. She was naive, and by reflection through writing this segment of her autobiography, she candidly reveals that naïveté but also reveals her ingenuity in surviving often devastating consequences and bad choices.

The elegant pimp L. D. Tolbrook came into Angelou's life while she was working as a short-order cook. Without recognizing what he was, she fell in love with him and fantasized that he would provide her with a home and security. Instead, he deceived her after capturing her interest by saying that he was a gambler and deeply in debt. He asked her to prostitute herself for him so that he could get out of a financial jam. In the passages describing the experiences she has in a brothel, Angelou uses personal disclosure to bring the shameful reality of that life to the reader. It is obscure information for most, but Angelou describes it with careful analogy to create a vivid, if sordid, picture in the reader's mind. "Trick time. . . . Bea came running into the room, and the sound of her footsteps was a little more audible than my heartbeat. The moment of truth had gotten stuck in my throat and saliva refused to go around it" (347). She frankly describes her participation, but she somehow maintains her own integrity in the youthful process. The experience was repugnant to Maya, and she finally climbed out of its sordid depths when her son went missing. She learned that she had again been deceived on many levels, found her son, and once again returned to the safe San Francisco home of her mother. One of the book's important messages is that individuals can emerge successfully from dark associations and experiences and establish a life on an entirely different level.

Overall, the book was received positively by literary critics, though a few expressed concern about its ethics and moral message. Others, including Selwyn R. Cudjoe, suggested that "the incidents of the book appear merely gathered together in the name of Maya Angelou" (Cudjoe 1999, 69). Angelou's jobs, from cook to dancer to a brief stint as a brothel madam to prostitute are told clearly and carefully, and some critics praised her writing skill. Lyman B. Hagen suggests that her books "abound in engrossing narratives, dramatic perspectives, and unique similes and metaphors" (1).

Hagen also suggests that by including the more unsavory elements of this period of her life, Angelou accomplished several objectives. Her family encouraged her to be honest, and her writing conveys a strong message about her ability to survive. Furthermore, Angelou wanted wide circulation of her stories and was aware that candid experiences concerning sex sell well (Hagen 1997, 77). ZORA NEALE HURSTON, the author of *Their Eyes Were Watching God,* wrote that the black "woman is de mule uh de world so fur as Ah can see" (14). Often deserted by their men and oppressed by many whites, African-American women in the United States have suffered and endured. Angelou reconstructed and told her experiences as she remembered them more openly than black autobiographical writers preceding her.

Angelou's autobiographies tell of a new, rising class of black women. Formally or self-educated, many are well-informed readers. Angelou has referred to her books as elevators out of an almost hopeless lifestyle, and she was encouraged by her editor at Random House, ROBERT LOOMIS, to tell the whole story of her experiences. Her second husband urged her to tell her real and whole experiences: "Tell it. Because if it happened to black girls it happened to black boys, happened to white girls it happened to white boys. This is true" (quoted in Lupton 1997, 77).

Angelou tells her experiences chronologically as her life progressed through different periods. The narrative style is in segments, with a beginning, middle, and conclusion to each short story, and occasionally there is a flashback, a shared memory or a glimpse into the past that contextualizes the presenting story or episode. An autobiographical narrative such as this cannot ever quite finish because as life continues, the story continues. Like life, or an unfinished work of art, it is a work in progress. James Olney has stated that the means for this style of writing is "by its very nature, the self is (like the autobiography that records and creates it) open-ended and incomplete: it is always in process or, more precisely, is itself a process" (25).

Various critics of *Gather Together* have pointed out the fragmentation of Angelou's life at this period. Reflecting Olney's "in process" writing concept, Angelou's life was in process: She was leaping from job to job and place to place as she struggled to find a source of income that would provide a consistent level of security. That quest was not met until many years later, but the process itself led Angelou on an enlightening journey. Frequent relocations also appear in *I Know Why the Caged Bird Sings,* and it was not until much later in life that Angelou was able to secure a more settled lifestyle. Her life has been lived in episodes, and therefore she writes the story of her life in episodes. There is not always a clear connection between the book's episodes, just as there is not always a clear connection between those in people's real-life experiences.

Angelou grew up with a rich assortment of aphorisms and truisms that came back to her time and again to help her mature into wisdom about her choices. The concept of training African-American children to avoid the danger of living in a white-dominated world, particularly in the South, is well represented in various interchanges in this work. The warnings, MAXIMS, and aphorisms serve a critical purpose. For instance, there is the incident in Stamps when Maya becomes antagonistic and then belligerent with two white clerks in a general store in the white part of town. Her grandmother slaps her, warns her of the danger she has put herself in, and then sends her away. Maya defends herself to her grandmother by repeating that it is the principle of the thing. Using typical language and African-American vernacular that her grandmother would have used, Angelou writes:

> "You think 'cause you've been to California these crazy people won't kill you? You think them lunatic cracker boys won't try to catch you in the road and violate you? You think because of your all-fired principle some of the men won't feel like putting their white sheets on and riding over here to stir up trouble? You do, you're wrong. Ain't nothing to protect you and us except the good Lord and some miles" (294).

The autobiography is enriched repeatedly by Vivian Baxter's maxims and aphorisms. They are meant to be counsel, and they are embedded in Angelou's memory. These are sometimes followed by aphorisms derived from her own voracious reading. When Angelou finalizes her decision to move to Los Angeles from San Francisco, her mother counsels, "Be the best of anything you get into. If you want to be a prostitute, it's your life. Be a damn good one. Don't be chippy at anything. Anything worth having is worth working for" (247). Maya's reflection on that counsel is: "It was her version of Polonius' speech to Laertes. With that wisdom in my pouch, I was to go out and buy my future" (247). In WILLIAM SHAKESPEARE's play *Hamlet,* Polonius gives Laertes advice on many matters, and like Polonius, Baxter was warning Maya to be true to herself and never settle for less than performing at her best and excelling in everything she might undertake.

On the other hand, though Vivian gives to both Maya and Bailey words of wisdom and encouragement, her lifestyle and codes of living did not offer her male child the foundation and support he needed to survive. He called her "Mother Dear" and sought bonding with her, but her erratic patterns and many male friends did not include much real time for establishing close ties with him. As shown in *I Know Why the Caged Bird Sings,* when he and Maya were young children growing up in Stamps, Bailey watched for the appearances of KAY FRANCIS in films at the local movie house because he thought Francis looked like his mother. Maya had hope for him when he met and married Eunice, but after the early death of his wife from tuberculosis and pneumonia, he seemed to sever his ties to both his mother and sister and began to sink into heavy drug use. Angelou, using multiple adjectives and figurative language, writes: "The potential sharp-tongued lawyer, keen-eyed scientist and cool-hand surgeon, changed his mind about jimmying the locks and took to narcotics so he could float through the key hole" (321).

Frequent literary devices used in *Gather Together in My Name* are simile, metaphor, compound words, and colloquialisms. The text is infused with clever plays on words, and a few examples demonstrate Angelou's versatility: "my guilt, which I carried around like a raw egg" (230); "looking like death eating a soda cracker" (246); "Self-pity in its early stage is a snug as a feather mattress" (241); "It just so happened that life took my script away and upstaged me" (251). Angelou uses compounds such as "never-could-have-happened land" (282) and "flesh-real and swollen-belly poor" (280). She also skillfully incorporates colloquial language, as when Momma scolds Maya after her behavior downtown in a general store—"you was downtown showing out" (294). In that passage, Henderson slaps Angelou repeatedly, which further juxtapositions the southern black's real terror with the concept of fair play and justice. Angelou repeats, over and over again, "It was a principle, Momma" (294), and the response was a sharp slap to the face with the comment, "Here's your principle" (294). There are few passages in the book that reveal the clash of terror and fear of punishing retribution toward the blacks as clearly as this. Angelou's use of creative language enlivens almost every page of the book, but rather than detracting from the readability, it draws the reader in and creates empathy for both the suffering and the moments of joy.

Though *Gather Together* includes extensive scatological humor (crudely referring to body functions) and profanity, Angelou deliberately uses those elements to add realism to her stories. She quotes, she invents, and she expects the reader to understand that this language fits the setting and is used appropriately. She has spent much of her time among counterculture people living on the edge, and part of their survival tactics come through the use of crude language that reflects their stress and attempts to cope with life. On the other hand, Selwyn R. Cudjoe writes that the use of language in this second autobiography is its saving grace:

> Where there were mere patches of beautiful writing in *Caged Bird,* there is a much more consistent and sustained flow of eloquent and almost honey-dipped writing. The simplicity of the speech patterns remains, yet there is a much more controlled use of language. The writing flows and shimmers with beauty; only the rigorous, coherent and meaningful organization of experience is missing. (69)

Throughout the text, Angelou demonstrates her constant sense of responsibility, even though her judgment was in error now and then. She took responsibility for herself and her son, and the echoes of both Momma's and Vivian's words remained alive in her mind. She gained experience and strength through this portion of her life, and her maturity as a woman was expressed after she was exposed to the human end product of drug use. In a sense, she felt a rebirth into a more conscious and responsible person. In the last lines of this book, she reflects: "I had no idea what I was going to make of my life, but I had given a promise and found my innocence. I swore I'd never lose it again" (384).

SOME IMPORTANT THEMES AND SYMBOLS IN *GATHER TOGETHER IN MY NAME*

Motherhood

Raising a child alone and providing support for both the child and one's self is difficult. Even if there is economic security, which in Angelou's situation there was not, the parent still has a myriad of responsibilities for the child that are difficult to meet without a partner. Throughout *Gather Together,* the theme of motherhood and child care are returned to repeatedly, though some of the situations were too complicated to be satisfactory to either Maya or her son.

In one of the most tension-filled episodes of the book, Maya has to leave Clyde with a sitter named Big Mary Dalton while she returns to San Francisco to be with her mother, who has suffered complications after a surgery. When she arrives at her mother's hospital room, she learns that Bailey's wife has died, and he is there mourning and crumpled in a chair in the corner. Maya meets her family responsibilities, but when she returns to get baby Clyde from the caretaker, she finds the sitter's house empty and boarded up. After following a few clues and encountering several difficult obstacles, Maya discovers that Big Mary had decided to relocate to Bakersfield, California, and keep Clyde. The sitter sincerely believed that she could give the boy better care than a frequently absent mother. Though there is no doubt of Maya's love and concern for her child, her necessary absences made it impossible to be the kind of full-time mother she wanted to be.

There was little that Angelou could do about the dilemma of not being with Clyde more, and the theme of trying and sometimes failing to be all she hoped to be as a parent continues through the other autobiographies. Overall, however, even under frequently difficult circumstances, the child was kept safe, and Maya was able to instill in him the standards and responsibilities of contemporary society and culture. Angelou has often acknowledged the guidance and support she has received from many friends, male and female, who helped her raise her son.

Clothing

In everyday life, appearance and manner can denote a person's age and social status, but it is also important to remember the old cliché that one cannot always judge a book by its cover. In varied economic classes around the world, clothing (self-presentation) and decorum (behavior) are often revealing clues to identity and leave inevitable impressions; however, the perceived impressions are sometimes well off the mark. Angelou's *Gather Together in My Name* includes references to clothing enough to indicate its importance to her. In this, her second autobiography, clothing is often mentioned in relation to what people do or the image they are trying to project. Of course, clothing also occasionally projects an image that is not contrived but rather a true representation of the individual's status or self-perception.

On the first page of *Gather Together,* Angelou mentions people who have come to the city from the South "who have only known maid's uniforms and mammy-made dresses" (229). These people put on work clothes to labor in the war-industry factories and shipyards. Angelou suggests that prostitutes did not even take time to remove their expensive shoes or charge as much as the shoes cost. There are other examples throughout the text, including the pimp's suggestion that Angelou dress like a teenager in order to project a certain innocence to some customers.

In this narrative, Maya is trying to find her own identity. She rids herself of her common clothes thinking that in the future, after her discharge from the army, she will dress in classic clothes of skirts, blouses, and sweaters. (Though Angelou thought she would enter officer's training in the U.S. Army, she was not allowed to enlist because a school she had attended had communist associations.) In *I Know Why the Caged Bird Sings,* the first autobiography, Vivian Baxter is described as a beautiful woman and classy dresser. When she met Maya and Momma at the train station after their trip West from Stamps, she was wearing a "light-tan suede suit, shoes to match and a mannish hat with a feather in the band . . . gloved hands . . . [and a] lipsticked mouth" (156). Baxter's husband, Daddy Clidell, is described as wearing "expensively tailored suits and a large yellow diamond stickpin. Except for jewelry, he was a conservative dresser and carried himself with the unconscious pomp of a man of secure means" (170).

Maya's choices of clothing, and her budget to meet the needs she had, posed difficulties. Bailey occasionally gave her money as she needed it, and the gambler/pimp gave her money to buy the teen look he wanted for her. The entrepreneur purchased a matched head-to-toe outfit for chauffeuring, but for the most part she bought her own wardrobe. From evening gowns to clothes for church, she did not try to project a false image. Rather, her goal seemed to be to dress appropriately for each situation. Clothing was basically important to her, but her intention was to dress in what she thought was the right way for the given occasion, and that ranged from G-strings to driving clothes. When Troubadour left the wardrobe of fine apparel for her, it was a windfall of good, classic clothing. Her effort was to dress, even as a young woman, as the woman she perceived herself to be. It was important in the determination and definition of her own interior authenticity.

Work

In the desperate effort to find enough income to remain independent and take care of her child, Angelou attempted many kinds of jobs. She never shirked the responsibility of working, but because of her youth and lack of training, it was difficult to find any one job that paid enough to cover her expenses for a babysitter, rent, food, and clothing. She describes working first as a cafeteria clean-up person, then as a cook, prostitute, waitress, restaurant manager, and short-order cook. She found a few jobs in clubs as a dancer, and those early performances, coupled with dancing lessons and consistent practice, finally opened up a successful career in dance and singing. That foundation led to the later tour with PORGY AND BESS elaborated in her third autobiography, *Singin' and Swingin' and Gettin' Merry Like Christmas.* Her short experience as a 19-year-old madam of a two-girl brothel and another experience as a prostitute herself were soundly condemned by her brother and not repeated. In *Gather Together,* Angelou represents herself as young and extraordinarily naive, but through her experiences she accumulated insight about the kind of life she knew she did not want.

CHARACTERS

Maya Angelou (Rita, Reet, Ritie) At the time of the action she describes in *Gather Together,* Angelou was in her late teens and determined to support herself and her child, independent of her extended family. She worked at various menial jobs and tried again and again to make secure arrangements for her child and take good care of herself. In this book, she reveals many attempts at employment and describes meeting many people who lived on the fringes of mainstream society. She also moved several times during this restive, unsettled time period.

L. C. Smith A friend in Stamps who at 11 could pick cotton like a grown man. When Maya took baby Clyde to visit Stamps, she was invited to join old "friends" at a café for drinks. They wanted to make a fool of her, but L. C. warned her and took her home. His life was difficult because his father was a drunk dependent on L. C. Having no hope for the future, he committed suicide on the same day as his father's funeral, about a year after Maya had been in Stamps.

Charles (Curly) A dark brown man who became acquainted with Maya as she was working in a San Francisco greasy spoon called the Creole Café. He seduced Maya, with her permission, but was honest enough to tell her that he had a girlfriend and would be moving back to New Orleans to marry when she finished her work at a San Diego shipyard.

L. D. Tolbrook Maya was working as a cook and just getting off work when L. D. Tolbrook, a handsome, dapper older gentleman, entered the restaurant with friends. He returned the next evening and slowly began to court Maya. She thought he was a successful gambler and dreamed that he was the partner she had been looking for. Tolbrook was a con man and pimp, and he manipulated Maya into working as a prostitute for him, supposedly to help him pay off gambling debts. Maya was 19 and naive, and she believed most of what he told her until she learned that he was married, and that he actually kept prostitutes under his control by supplying them with cocaine. Bailey ordered Maya to get away from him and return to San Francisco immediately, which she did.

Beatrice Maya met Beatrice, a lesbian, while working at the Hi Hat Club in Los Angeles. In a short time, Beatrice and her partner, Johnnie Mae, were working for Maya as prostitutes.

Johnnie Mae Maya met Johnnie Mae, a lesbian, while working at the Hi Hat Club in Los Angeles. In a short time, she and her partner, Beatrice, were working for Maya as prostitutes.

Troubadour Martin A tall, thin drug addict who peddled fine stolen clothing, Troubadour invited Maya to house his merchandise at her home to enable her to stay at home with her child. Troubadour realized that Maya was using marijuana, and he knew that was a dead-end habit. He took her to a hotel on the waterfront so she could see for herself what happened to people who got hooked and could not stop using drugs. Maya observed the vacant-eyed people—some awake, some asleep, all unkempt—and was saddened by their state. Then Troubadour prepared himself to shoot up heroine, and Maya nearly fainted at the sight of the process. He was a good, protective friend and made Maya promise that she would never use any illegal drugs again. She kept her promise.

Big Mary Maya left her son with Big Mary, a babysitter who would keep children for several days if necessary, while she made an emergency trip from Los Angeles to San Francisco to see her mother, who was in the hospital. When she returned to Stockton, outside of Los Angeles, to pick up Clyde, Big Mary's house was boarded up, and there was no forwarding address. A neighbor told her that Big Mary had a brother in Bakersfield, and Maya went there immediately. She learned that the last name of the family was Peterson, located the place, and recovered her son. Big Mary explained that she thought she could give the child better care than Maya. "He was the prettiest of them all," she said, "And you was always going somewhere" (369).

Clyde The name Maya gave her son was Clyde. He was a pretty, light-colored baby with fine features, and he was very dependent on his mother in spite of his many caretakers. He was three when Big Mary kidnapped him.

assorted junkies When Troubadour Martin took Maya to the wharf-side hotel, he showed her what happened to people who got hooked on drugs and lost all hope for the future. There were people there of various ages, all vacant-looking and often draped over one another with only a vague perception of their dead-end lives.

Vivian Baxter Maya's mother, Vivian lived in San Francisco and had a large, beautiful home. She rented rooms to boarders and was married to Daddy Clidell. She was a professional nurse and had many other diplomas, but she preferred to earn her living by gambling in clubs and renting rooms in her substantial homes.

Bailey Johnson At the time of this book, Bailey Johnson, Maya's beloved brother, had married Eunice, the love of his life, a girl he had known at school. She died about a year after their wedding of tuberculosis and pneumonia. He had been a merchant marine previously, but he had taken a job as a dining-car waiter on the railroad. The death was hard for him, but he did his best to cope with it and said he never wanted his late wife's name mentioned again after her funeral.

Daddy Clidell Jackson Daddy Clidell was Vivian Baxter's husband and the only stable father figure Maya was to know.

Momma (Mrs. Annie Henderson) Maya's grandmother in Stamps, Arkansas, Momma raised Maya and Bailey until they moved to California. Maya took baby Clyde and visited her grandmother during the time depicted in *Gather Together*, but the visit did not last long. Momma was wise and respected in the town, but when Maya became arrogant with white women in a general merchandise store where they worked, trouble developed.

Maya, having been treated overall as an equal in California, was very rude about what she perceived as the white women's condescension toward her. By the time she walked home from the general merchandise store in the white part of town, her grandmother had been telephoned and knew what had happened. She slapped Maya several times for behaving the way she did and told her she had already packed Maya's bags. The fear was that the Klan would punish Maya for her rudeness to the white women. If Momma did not make arrangements to get her out of town, both Maya and perhaps even Momma would suffer the consequences. Maya and her baby were immediately put in a horse-drawn wagon and driven to Lewisville, Arkansas, about five miles west of Stamps.

R. L. Poole Poole was a very fine dancer, and when his partner became hooked on drugs, he needed to find another entertainer to assist in his act. Maya was recommended to him by the owner of a record shop where Maya often listened to music and bought records. Poole hired her, trained her, and they performed together until his regular partner, Cotton Candy Adams, returned and took Maya's place.

FURTHER READING

Angelou, Maya. *The Collected Autobiographies of Maya Angelou.* New York: Modern Library Edition by Random House, 2004.

Bloom, Harold. *Maya Angelou.* New Edition. Bloom's Modern Critical Views. New York: Bloom's Literary Criticism, 2009.

Cudjoe, Selwyn R. "Maya Angelou and the Autobiographical Statement." In *Maya Angelou.* Modern Critical Views, edited by Harold Bloom, 55–74. Philadelphia: Chelsea House, 1999.

Gillespie, Marcia Ann, Rosa Johnson Butler, and Richard A. Long. *Maya Angelou: A Glorious Celebration.* New York: Doubleday/Random House, 2008.

Hagen, Lyman B. *Heart of a Woman, Mind of a Writer, and Soul of a Poet.* Lanham, Md.: University Press of America, 1997.

Hurston, Zora Neale. *Their Eyes Were Watching God.* 1939. Reprint, New York: Harper & Row, 1990.

Kanin, Ruth. *Write the Story of Your Life.* New York: Dutton, 1971.

Lionnet, Françoise. "Con Artists and Storytellers: Maya Angelou's Problematic Sense of Audience." In *Maya Angelou.* Modern Critical Views, edited by Harold Bloom, 143–172. Philadelphia: Chelsea House, 1999.

Lupton, Mary Jane. *Maya Angelou: A Critical Companion.* Westport, Conn.: Greenwood Press, 1998.

———. "Talking with an Icon: An Interview with Maya Angelou." June 16, 1997. Unpublished.

Olney, James. "Autobiography and the Cultural Moment: A Thematic, Historical, and Bibliographical Introduction." In *Autobiography: Essays Theoretical and Critical,* edited by James Olney. Princeton, N.J.: Princeton University Press, 1980.

Ramsey, Priscilla R. "Transcendence: The Poetry of Maya Angelou." In *Maya Angelou, Modern Critical Views,* edited by Harold Bloom, 75–90. Philadelphia: Chelsea House, 1999.

Tate, Claudia, ed. *Black Women Writers at Work.* 1983. Reprint, Jackson: University Press of Mississippi, 1989.

Wall, Cheryl A. "Maya Angelou, Toni Morrison, Alice Walker." In *A New Literary History of America,* edited by Greil Marcus and Werner Sollers, 968–972. Cambridge, Mass.: Belknap Press of Harvard University Press, 2009.

Singin' and Swingin' and Gettin' Merry Like Christmas (1976)

The title of Maya Angelou's third autobiography comes from what she called rent parties that took place in the decades of the 1920s and 1930s. Friends would gather on Saturday night around nine o'clock and then party until the next morning, when they would go to church. That would be followed with a Sunday meal. By Sunday evening, "everyone was encouraged to sing and swing and get merry like Christmas so one would have some fuel with which to live the rest of the week" (Tate 1983, 10). Those were economically hard times for most people in the United States, black or white, and the parties gave everyone something to look forward to each week and then something to remember.

This book is dedicated to "Martha, and Lillian, Ned and Bey, for the laughter, the love, and the music." Music is one of the central themes in this text; contemporary lyrics seemed to speak to Maya and trigger dreams of meeting the right man and living a life like those described in popular women's magazines of the time. Other important themes in this book are motherhood, the guilt of separation from her son, and race. The text covers a period of about five years, and within its narrative, Angelou meets and marries her first husband, TOSH ANGELOS. She also made a trusted friend in Ivonne Broadnax.

Angelou recounts here that she toured Europe for about a year performing in the opera *PORGY AND BESS*, but the separation from her son produced deep feelings of guilt, which she resolved upon her return. Additionally, in this segment of her serial autobiographies, there are more than 50 statements concerning black attitudes about whites. Critic Lyman B. Hagen writes: "This heavy concentration on the black perception of whites rather than the travel to exotic countries and the fun at parties is primarily what makes *Singin' and Swingin'* worthy of consideration" (92). Most of Angelou's racial attitudes emerged from her experiences growing up in a segregated southern town, but perspectives learned from her mother and grandmother also influenced her negative emotional responses to whites.

SYNOPSIS

Chapter 1

Maya loved music; it nurtured her. She spent as much time as she could listening and exploring sounds at the Melrose Music Shop on Fillmore Street in SAN FRANCISCO, CALIFORNIA, and in her own apartment: "In my rented room (cooking privileges down the hall), I would play a record, then put my arms around the shoulders of the song. As we danced, glued together, I would nuzzle into its neck, kissing the skin, and rubbing its cheek with my own" (391). Louise Cox, the Store's white co-owner, was friendly to her and, after a while, invited her to work there. Cox tried to keep a stock of every record "made by Negro artists" (396), and as a result, her store was successful. Maya could not quite understand why she was offered the job, but it meant she could quit working the two jobs she had. The best benefit of that was that she could spend more time with her child.

> Outside on the evening street, I examined the woman's intention. What did I have that she wanted? Why did she allow me to walk away with her property? She didn't know me. Even my name might have been constructed on the spot. She couldn't have been seeking friendship; after all she was white, and as far as I knew, white women were never lonely except in books. White men adored them, Black men desired them and Black women worked for them. There was no ready explanation for her gesture of trust. (393)

At this point, Maya was boarding her child out six days and five nights a week in order to work two jobs, but she had avoided the humiliation and dependency of welfare. This offer would be her first introduction to an amiable black-white relationship, and she was grateful for the offer. The higher salary increased her self-respect, and she felt she could move back to her mother's house, pay rent, and start looking for a house of her own.

One evening, while Maya and her five-year-old son were taking a walk, they encountered a street preacher. They stopped and listened for a while, and Clyde (later Guy) asked if there really was a God. Maya quickly realized that she had taught him little or nothing about God, so she began to remedy the omission that very night.

Chapter 2

Maya, along with most young women in the security-conscious 1950s, dreamed of a refuge with a husband, a white picket fence, a station wagon, and a few more children. Pondering the romantic music she heard each day in the music store, she dreamed the same dreams of both black and white girls of her age. Society's choice, it seemed, was for young women to be nurses, teachers, or homemakers.

Louise Cox and her mother were Christian Scientists, and they invited Maya to visit their church with them. The quiet austerity of the church unsettled Maya because her experiences had been in churches where "one made 'a joyful noise unto the Lord'" (404). Afterward, Louise gave her a copy of MARY BAKER EDDY's *Science and Health,* which taught that humans could and should think of themselves as spiritually prosperous, and that people were never alone. Reflecting on her years of poverty and loneliness, even in her mother's house, Maya could not affirm that for herself.

Enistasious (Greek for Thomas) "Tosh" Angelos, a handsome white sailor, frequented the music store. He was knowledgeable about black music, Maya was attracted to him, and he seemed interested in her. She was also searching for spiritual truth. Christian Science was too austere, and because the shop's other co-owner, David Rosenbaum, was Jewish, she consulted him and visited the synagogue Beth Emanu-El. She reflected on the DIASPORA and persecutions of both Jews and blacks, and she thought she might find a friendlier God there than the threatening one of her childhood. She visited with the leader at the synagogue, Rabbi Alvin I. Fine, who gave her a reading list. In response to his questions about her curiosity concerning Judaism, Maya admitted that she was afraid to die. She did not tell him that, imaginatively, she could almost smell her "flesh frying and see [her] . . . skin as crisp as pork cracklins" (410). Over the next year, she read the books, but she did not see Rabbi Fine again for two decades.

Chapter 3

Tosh Angelos was discharged from the navy, took a job in an electrical appliance shop, and moved into the black neighborhood. He continued as a frequent customer at the music store and suggested to Maya that she and Clyde go to the park with him sometime so he could teach her son a little about playing baseball.

A few days later, Maya let Clyde go out with Tosh for an afternoon. When Clyde returned, he was happy and full of stories about things they had done and things they would do soon. Maya realized that Tosh was courting her through Clyde. This triggered deep reflection within her about the ugliness of white prejudice. Not long after that, he proposed. She was so astounded that she could not answer.

Maya's mother exploded at the thought of Maya marrying a poor white man. Maya could not say yes to her mother's question about whether she loved Tosh, but she did explain that she was going to marry him because he had asked her. Her mother seemed to accept that answer. Maya invited Bailey to her mother's house for dinner and to meet Tosh. The two men discussed literature. As Bailey left, he let Maya know that he approved of Tosh, and that since Tosh had asked her and she wanted to accept, she should. He said, "Marry him, Maya. Be happy and prove them all [people with racial prejudices] fools and liars" (415).

Three days before the courthouse wedding ceremony, VIVIAN BAXTER moved her 14 rooms of furniture to LOS ANGELES. She strongly disapproved of the marriage. The newlyweds rented a large flat, and Tosh asked Maya to quit her job. She became a careful homemaker, and Tosh believed that Clyde was the most intelligent child in the world. Tosh was protective and controlling about Maya's and Clyde's friends and associates, but he was an excellent husband and provider.

After about a year, tension began to appear in their relationship because Tosh told Clyde there was no God. Maya believed differently and began to contrive strategies to get out of the flat on Sundays and attend church, alone. This filled a need she had been trained to have in her childhood; her family believed in God passionately, and their faith had become hers also. She could live in Tosh's godless world, but she found that it kept the peace in their home by simply avoiding the topic.

Chapter 4

Over time, Maya began to encounter small reminders of the racial differences between herself and Tosh. People, black and white, often looked askance at them. Clyde began to wish for what he called "good hair" like Tosh's, straight and smooth. Maya though the solution might be found in study, so she made a plan to become a historian, sociologist, and anthropologist by reading in the library.

She thought that she might be able to resolve their racial and cultural differences by learning more about differing cultures and societies. She planned to make just one more church visit, and then her self-education at the library would begin.

At that last planned visit to the Baptist church, Maya seemed to be overcome by the spirit. She was deeply touched by the sermon and surrendered herself to passionate emotion. Her pattern in visiting various churches had been to fill out a visitor's card with her maiden name. This time she filled it out with her real name and address, and Tosh found out about it because a woman from the Baptist church made a house call about a fee for a baptismal robe. Tosh questioned Maya, but Maya "made no protest, gave no confession" (423); she just stood silent.

Chapter 5

Maya began to realize that her marriage to Tosh had deteriorated to little or no affection or pleasure. The routine of everyday life was not fulfilling, and she felt that even their greetings and responses had become a "relationship of pretense" (423). One morning, he shouted about not being able to find a dry towel and then snapped at Clyde during breakfast. He told Maya the breakfast was poorly prepared. Maya confronted him about the way he was acting, and he said simply, "I think I'm just tired of being married" (425). Then he left for work.

Rather than let Tosh decide her future, Maya decided to leave him. She went to a bar, drank too much, and was put to bed (though not abused) by a decent stranger. When she awakened, she went to the home of Ivonne Broadnax, her closest friend, and slept on Ivonne's couch. She called Tosh from Ivonne's but felt nothing for him as they spoke. She did return to their home, but before long she developed appendicitis and was hospitalized longer than expected because the recovery was complicated. After spending several weeks there, she told Tosh that she really wanted to convalesce in Arkansas with her grandmother. What she did not know was that her grandmother, "Momma," had died the day after Maya's emergency surgery. That news was an unforeseen shock, and Maya grieved deeply because this loss was her first encounter with the death of a close loved one.

Chapter 6

Vivian Baxter and her friend Lottie Wells returned to San Francisco a few months before Tosh and Maya separated. They opened a soul food café, and Wells, a loving and tender person, became Maya's and Clyde's Aunt Lottie.

A year later, the marriage ended in divorce, which filled Clyde, now about eight, with heartbreak and doubt. If Maya could leave his "Dad," could it not follow, he wondered, that she might leave him? Maya worked hard to rebuild their relationship by cooking his favorite foods and spending time with him in various mother-and-son games and diversions. They were soon close again, but she realized that her small bank account was dwindling fast, and that she needed to find a job that could support the two of them.

Maya, along with five other women, auditioned for jobs as exotic dancers at a club called the Garden of Allah. Maya danced in a blue bra and G-string that would have fit in a cigarette box, and along with three of the others, she was hired. Her job was to be a B-girl, meaning she would hustle male customers to buy drinks for her, and she would get a percentage of the cost of the drink. She would dance six times a night, six nights a week for 15 minutes each performance wearing the mini-costume. She was not to strip. Her salary was $75 a week, and she would be served ginger ale or 7Up rather than liquor as she sat with customers. She was also warned never to go home with any man.

Her friend Ivonne grinned at the news of the job, and then they laughed together. Ivonne knew that Maya could take care of herself. "Ivonne was wise without glitter, while I, too often, glittered without wisdom" (441).

Chapter 7

Maya went to a costume store and bought what she needed for her three acts. She would present herself as Cleopatra (carrying a stuffed cobra); Scheherazade, with red sequins and ankle bells; and Sheba, with brown feathers and no props. One of the members of the band told her the songs they would play for her performances ("Caravan,"

"Night in Tunisia," and "Babalu"), and he said the others in the band liked her energy. She performed to a lukewarm audience, and for the first week she dressed and left quickly each night.

Jack, the drummer, reminded her that part of her job was to get men to buy drinks for her. She began to do that, and a sassy confidence grew from the experience. Some men seemed to like her dancing, but many seemed equally to enjoy her witty personality and "Quick, brittle words" (448).

Chapter 8

Maya was earning enough money at the Garden of Allah to dress her son and herself well. She and Clyde, now close to nine, enjoyed movies and ate out at nice restaurants, and she was also able to save some money toward a hoped-for vacation. Things were going well until she was given two weeks' notice at the club because the other girls were jealous of her ability to make more money from customers than they could. They made false claims against her and suggested that she made promises to sleep with the customers.

The next night, knowing that she was on two-week notice and dancing to please herself, she was aware that four well-dressed strangers in the bar were observing her closely. After dancing, she went to the dressing room and changed her clothes. When she returned to the bar, they introduced themselves to her and told her that she danced divinely. They told her that she was famous locally, and that they worked at a nearby nightclub called the Purple Onion. The strangers were Jorie, a chanteuse (ballad singer); Barry Drew, the club manager and emcee; and Don Curry and Fred Kuh, bartenders. After that, the group dropped in each evening to watch her dance and told her she was welcome at their club any time she could get away.

Chapter 9

One evening, Maya was invited to attend a wine party at Jorie's apartment. There were only two other black people there, and Maya sipped wine, observed, and listened. After most of the guests had left, Maya and her four new friends sat and talked. Jorie was leaving San Francisco for a job in New York, and Barry said that it was too bad that Maya did not sing because they would need a replacement for Jorie. Maya said she knew calypso (a style Jorie did not understand or like) and then demonstrated the music's beauty by singing "Run Joe" by Louis Jordan. As she sang, she moved with the rhythm of the song and added arm and hip motions to demonstrate its message.

Maya's small audience applauded and smiled and suggested that she audition at the Purple Onion. They started thinking about a stage identity for her, and because she spoke a little Spanish, they settled on Rita, the Cuban Bombshell. She contrived a new personal history (a Watusi chieftain for a father and a dark-eyed Spanish girl for a mother—and wealth as well), and her new friends were astounded at her quick imagination.

When sharing all of this with her friend Ivonne, the idea of Maya performing calypso at the Purple Onion in the guise of a Cuban-African performer sounded tasteless and crass. Maya performed for her to prove that she could do it, and Ivonne said, "I'll say this for you, Marguerite Johnson, you've got a lot of nerve" (464).

Chapter 10

The Purple Onion was located in the North Beach neighborhood of San Francisco. The area was a Bohemian mix of ethnic groups, beatnik poetry, gay bars, and trendy cabarets. Maya auditioned for members of the Rockwell family, who owned the Purple Onion, and signed a six-month contract with a three-month option. She met the drama coach, Lloyd Clark, and the piano player. They were experienced and intimidating, and she was certain that neither seemed impressed with her talent at first. However, after watching her perform, they were both convinced of her talent and excited about hiring her at the Purple Onion.

The next step was to find a convincing stage name. "Rita" did not seem believable, and after brainstorming, they settled on Maya Angelou. "Maya" was her brother Bailey's name for her, and "Angelou" was adapted from her married name, Angelos.

Frequent practices, stage coaching, and costume fittings followed during the next few weeks. Maya was to have a 12-song repertoire, and she needed to memorize all of the songs. She often practiced

Maya gained public recognition for her professional calypso dancing. She was trained in New York by the great Pearl Primus, a Trinidad-born anthropologist, choreographer, and dance teacher. Here she is performing in the 1950s. *(Courtesy Library of Congress Prints and Photographs Division)*

at home for Clyde, who wondered how she could remember so many words. At last she performed for an audience, and she was a hit. Maya knew that her main goal was to have a real income; she writes: "The truth was, I simply wanted an end to uncertainty" (468). While she was still working at the Purple Onion, another performer auditioned and was accepted at the club. With silly hats, boas, and sarcasm, she was also a hit. She used her real name, PHYLLIS DILLER.

Chapter 11

Young Clyde was healthy and doing well, and Maya was happily engaged with her developing career. One evening, her mother, Clyde, and several other friends and family members visited the Purple Onion to see the show. Phyllis Diller directed her comedy to Clyde and Joyce (Ivonne's daughter), and the children convulsed with laughter. Soon it was time for Maya's act. She sang, and Clyde unexpectedly sang along on the first song. Maya was embarrassed, but after taking a bow, the child remained quiet. The performance was important to Maya not only because her family was there but also because the well-known performers Paul Lynde and Alice Ghostley were in the audience. After the first show, they invited Maya for a drink and visited until it was time for her to perform again. A few nights later, they suggested she audition for *New Faces of 1953* because EARTHA KITT, the velvet kitten, had come to the end of her contract and was going to perform in a high-paying Las Vegas club. Maya auditioned and got the job, but because she was under contract at the Purple Onion, she had to let the opportunity go and fulfill her contractual obligation, much to her disappointment.

Chapter 12

One day, during the Joseph McCarthy period of blacklists, perceived communist threats to the United States, and the HOUSE COMMITTEE ON UN-AMERICAN ACTIVITIES, Clyde remarked at school that he would go to jail before expressing admiration for any branch of the military service. The day before had been Armed Forces Day, and the teacher was leading a discussion about which military branch the students admired most. The teacher called Maya for an explanation of Clyde's comments.

Maya went to the school promptly, kept a trembling Clyde at her side during the discussion, and though the teacher suggested Clyde surely did not get such ideas at home, Maya assured her that he did. Soon Clyde gained confidence and clearly explained what he had said the day before about the money-making aspects of war. The teachers were silenced. Maya excused herself and Clyde from their presence, and the two of them went "to a movie that showed ten Disney shorts" (484); it was total diversion.

Chapter 13

After her show one night, Maya met an older white gentleman who asked if he could see her home. She took him to her mother's house, and Vivian made a breakfast meal for them. The friendship between Maya and George Hitchcock, a playwright, lasted some time, but there was no romance. They both enjoyed poetry, and she often recited the poetry of WILLIAM SHAKESPEARE and PAUL LAURENCE DUNBAR to him.

Maya answered the phone one time and heard a mysterious male voice with an Eastern European accent paying compliments to her about her beauty and intelligence and inviting her to dinner on a houseboat. George drove her there and said he would pick her up at 11. Inside, Maya met Yanko Varda, a Greek painter who called her Rima. He explained that Rima was a half-bird, half-woman creature who visited the earth now and then to sing melodies and lighten human hearts. He mentioned W. H. Hudson's book *Green Mansions*, noting that the heroine was called Rima, and he also said the book's story was based on Maya's magic.

Soon after that, Maya was again a little embarrassed after her performance at the Purple Onion by the applauding and shouting of a group she did not know. Friends of Yanko's, they invited her to sit with them and then extended an enthusiastic invitation for her to join them for a party on Sunday. The party was on Yanko's houseboat, and the guests were a mix of ages and cultures. Maya was made to feel very much a part of the group, and they invited her to sail with them the following Sunday. They also invited Clyde, and Yanko remarked, "Bring him. The sea is a female. And females desire young and masculine life. Bring him and we shall pacify the mother of us all. Bring him" (2004, 495). They were a fanciful, somewhat strange new group of friends, but Maya enjoyed them and found that some of the magic of Yanko's "world stayed around her shoulders" (495).

Chapter 14

Porgy and Bess, the opera, was extraordinarily well-received in San Francisco. One evening, Maya took off work to see the production, and she found herself captivated by a talented dancer who seemed to let the music fly through her body. Maya thought the musical opera was "the greatest array of Negro talent I had ever seen" (479). One night, the great singers from the opera attended Maya's act at the Purple Onion. Afterward, they went to a restaurant together, and they said they would be at the club again the next night and would invite the dancer Elizabeth Foster, the performer Maya particularly admired, to accompany them. They followed through, and among the group was Frederick Wilkerson (Wilkie), a voice teacher who soon became Maya's trainer. The next evening, the producer of *Porgy and Bess,* Robert Breen, and his wife, Wilva, visited Maya at the Purple Onion and invited her to audition for a singing and dancing role in their opera. With them were the business manager and the company drama coach, who were enthusiastically supportive of the invitation extended to Maya.

Maya auditioned, and she was offered the job three days later. They told her they would be conducting auditions for at least two more months, but they had to find a lead dancer before they could return to Europe. She realized that accepting the opportunity would not interfere with the three months left in her Purple Onion contract, and the reality of all of it left her excited and somewhat stunned.

Chapter 15

A few days before her contract at the Purple Onion ran out, Maya was invited to audition for a part in a New York play called *House of Flowers;* if she got it, she would play opposite PEARL BAILEY. If she won the role, she would have to give up the idea of going to Europe with the *Porgy and Bess* company. Her mother, Lottie (her mother's good friend), and Wilkie (the voice coach) encouraged her to try for the part. Maya went for the audition and saw a long line of people waiting for their turn to try out. She was admitted immediately, but her song, "Love for Sale," did not go over very well as the piano and Maya were out of sync. She then offered to do a calypso number, and apparently it was impressive as a few days later, she received a note telling her she had won the role. Almost immediately, she received a call from the *Porgy and Bess* company inviting her to leave for Italy in four days to play the part of Ruby on a world tour. Maya made her decision quickly, accepting the *Porgy and Bess* role and turning down the new Broadway show. She had always wanted to see more of the world, and the opportunity had come.

Chapter 16

Leaving Clyde with her mother was hard for Maya. Memories of growing up with her grandmother in Stamps came back to her and triggered feelings of guilt. The boy was in good hands, and Maya hoped that someday she would be able to take her son to the places she would see on the tour. They would both adjust.

Maya read the Ira and GEORGE GERSHWIN version of *Porgy and Bess* and joined the troupe in Montreal. Warmly welcomed and fascinated by the professional singers, she was curious about the vocal exercises they used before a performance. It amazed her, too, that the actors could so quickly throw off the dramatic personae of their roles and instantly be themselves when they walked off the stage. When it was time for her to rehearse her own part as Ruby, the dancing came easily, but because she could not read music, singing correctly became a challenge. She was willing and able to practice, and she knew that she would be ready to open with them for her first performance in Venice, Italy.

Chapter 17

Maya enjoyed being in Montreal. It was an international city with the sounds of many languages. There were all kinds of people there, and even the whites were less intimidating. After all, Canada had been the final destination of the UNDERGROUND RAILROAD and represented black freedom. Most of the cast members dressed expensively, but there were some who were more modestly attired and always seemed to keep themselves a little apart from the more flamboyant members of the group. Maya preferred their company because they were friendlier and not so showy about their stardom.

Once they finally got through customs and boarded the plane, several arrogant cast members began making rude demands of the flight attendants. The stewardesses handled the situation by serving the meals when it was time and then disappearing into the front of the plane, wisely not catering to their rude passengers. The group finally arrived in Milan, where they were transported to Venice by bus. They stopped in Verona for a meal, and in her imagination Maya could hear lines from *ROMEO AND JULIET*. She saw balconies on the charming houses there, and it triggered reflections of Shakespeare's great romantic tragedy.

When she shared some of her feelings of awe about where they were with other cast members, they seemed to find her naive. At that point, Maya decided to keep her enthusiasm to herself. She wanted to learn what she could of languages and culture, and she carefully observed many of the details of new scenes around her. Soon a crowd of Italians surrounded the cast in a warm welcome, and the cast seemed to enjoy the attention. There was a little confusion among the Italians about who would be playing Porgy, but Rose Tobias, the public relations person for the cast, straightened it out, and the encounter was another slice of European culture for Maya.

Chapter 18

After Maya registered at the hotel, she went out to see Venice on her own, finding the canals and then the city square called the Piazza San Marco. At a small table facing the square, she ordered a cup of coffee and soon found that she was the object of stares. Strangers invited her to join them at their table. Maya did not hesitate to join the friendly group and later learned the Europeans, like American southerners, differentiated between whites and blacks, but that often "Blacks were liked whereas white Americans were not" (529).

Chapter 19

The Teatro la Fenice (named for the Phoenix), the opera house in Venice, was ROCOCO style, with rich red fabrics, gold mosaics, and white marble decor. Maya performed superbly, and she reflected that for as long as she was a part of the cast, the deep pathos of the story and the impressive role-playing of the actors never grew stale. Their opening night in Venice was a hit, and they performed there to a sold-out house for a week.

The next city was Paris. People in Venice had treated them like royalty with dinners and gifts, and to Maya Venice seemed like an object of art itself. On the Blue Train to Paris, she and friends from the cast—Lillian, Martha, and Barbara Ann—began to sing. Maya thought that the smoothness of Martha's voice sounded "like hot silver being poured from a high place" (533). When they arrived at the Gare de Nord train station in Paris, the cast was greeted by Maya's friends from San Francisco with baskets of fruit, cheese, wine, and loaves of bread in her honor. The five friends, including Yanko, took her to a sidewalk café and explained they were all in Europe for different reasons and had learned that Maya would be performing there. They promised each other that they would meet and attend the Paris opening night of *Porgy and Bess.*

Chapter 20

Unexpectedly, *Porgy and Bess* was held over in Paris for several months. One evening, a group of black American entertainers who lived and worked in Paris came backstage and invited Maya to go with them to see the city's nightlife. They took her several places, including the Rose Rouge on the Left Bank, where the owner said that he wanted her to perform in his club. If that was agreeable to her, he said he would arrange it.

Later that same night (or morning), Maya was taken to the Mars Club. The owner was named Ben, an American from New York who featured black entertainment at the club. He invited her to give him a song, and he enjoyed it. After dancing and singing some calypso songs for Ben, Maya was invited to perform there nightly, after the opera performance. Because she was sending part of her salary to San Francisco for Clyde's care, she was glad to find a source for extra money. Friends from the cast dropped in to see her perform, and one evening Martha, the singer who sang Bess in the opera, also performed for the cast and others at the club. One by one, the others performed as well, to the great enjoyment of the owner, the bartenders, and the patrons. Maya knew her talent was good

When the European tour of *Porgy and Bess* came to Venice for a few days in 1954, Maya went to the Piazza San Marco and ordered coffee at an outside café. She soon found herself surrounded by friendly, curious Italians. *(Courtesy Library of Congress Prints and Photographs Division)*

enough to entertain them, but she also realized that her presence had drawn the stars from *Porgy and Bess.* That was very good for Ben's business.

Chapter 21

Maya continued to work very hard in Paris. She performed nightly in *Porgy and Bess* and did shows afterward at the Mars Club and then the Rose Rouge. She was so well-received in Paris that she considered sending for Clyde and making it their home until she experienced another kind of cultural experience. One night after the Rose Rouge show, a tiny woman sitting at a table with friends asked Maya to join them. The woman asked Maya to sing at a reception in honor of PIERRE MENDÈS-FRANCE, a French socialist statesman and premier of France from 1954 to 1955. Maya said she would, and when the night arrived, two gentlemen friends from Senegal escorted her. When they arrived at the reception, the woman's chill of intolerance against the men from Africa was obvious. Maya performed and was paid, but she ultimately decided that Paris and its prejudices were not for her.

The next destination for the tour was Yugoslavia, so Maya bought a language dictionary and found someone to tutor her in Serbo-Croatian.

Chapter 22

Yugoslavia was behind the Iron Curtain, and Maya's troupe was the first group of American singers ever invited to perform there. There were many restrictions about fraternization with the country's people, and Maya also learned that being a black in Yugoslavia brought a lot of unwanted stares and attention. Strangers reached out to touch her, and one evening when she was taking a walk, she marched right through the crowd that had gathered around her. She made her way into a music store to look for a mandolin, and as she examined and strummed it, the man's children and heavy wife tumbled into the shop from a back room to get a look at this tall black American. After Maya's repeated greeting to the wife, the woman said, "PAUL ROBESON," and she began singing "Deep River." The children and husband joined in with her singing. Maya was deeply touched but did not have the words to express her feelings. They all shared a dismal past history and hope for a better future. She paid the shopkeeper for the instrument, and both he and his wife embraced her. Then Maya took her beautiful mandolin and returned to the hotel.

From Serbo-Croatia, in Yugoslavia, they went to Belgrade and the Moskva hotel, where Maya, Martha, and Ethel were required to sleep in one lumpy bed. They were awakened early in the morning by a call from someone called Mr. Julian, who wanted to speak with Maya. He told her that he had seen her dance, and that he was in love with her. He suggested, dramatically, that because of this love, he could throw himself into the Danube and die for such a passion. He would have his heart sent to her. Maya was mostly amused, and after continuing for a while, the voice said, "Good-bye, lovely legs leaping" (554).

Maya worried all day that he really would somehow have his blood-dripping heart sent, and when she got to her dressing room, she was told that a small package had been delivered for her. She opened it, and inside was an inedible cake made of dough and water and decorated with bits of glass, paper doilies, tatters of lace, dead leaves, and dried flowers. Glued to the surface were also grains of rice, barley, and wheat.

Mr. Julian continued to make 8 A.M. calls, and Maya's rudeness on the phone did not deter him. One time, another Slavic man entered their room, fell on the floor, and pledged himself to Ethel. She and Maya dragged him out into the hall.

A young couple named Dovic, a photographer and a dancer, visited Maya's dressing room after a performance one night and invited her to their home for a pre-Christmas party. It was against government rules, but Maya accepted. Another young singer, Helen Ferguson, was invited and also accepted. A crowded truck came to pick them up and take them deep into the countryside to a house party of artists. There were Yugoslavian writers, musicians, photographers, and others drinking and talking. There was also an elderly couple, the grandparents of the house, who found their black guests very interesting.

After the party, Maya and Helen were returned to the hotel, where the desk clerk opened the door for them and knew exactly where they had been. The next morning, a strange white American lectured Maya about the transgression, but she felt he was being discourteous and closed the conversation. Nothing further was ever said about the evening with the Dovics.

The evening before they left Yugoslavia, Maya finally consented to meet Mr. Julian. He told her that he was an Olympic swimming champion, and that intrigued her. She met him after the show, and he was a tiny old man. He bought her coffee, wished her well, and then Maya returned, alone, to her friends.

Chapter 23

The company was glad to leave the oppressive atmosphere of Yugoslavia. They boarded the train to go, and Mr. Julian showed up to say good-bye to Maya. He threw a package in her lap and leaped off the train. The train was the fabled ORIENT EXPRESS, which took them to Greece. They caught a glimpse of Athens, but they boarded buses quickly and were taken to the port city of Piraeus, where they were invited to a champagne party on a ship. The party was hosted by Lee Gershwin, the wife of the song lyricist Ira Gershwin.

The ship was headed for Alexandria, Africa, and Maya had changed into evening clothes to join the party. A ship's purser stopped her on the way to her table and let her know the trip would be rough. He advised her to drink no liquor and eat very little. He warned only her, perhaps, she thought, because she had been married to a Greek. Maya told the others, but they ignored her, saying they never got seasick; however, the roiling sea soon proved them wrong. Their company and another group on board, an English movie company with a French star, BRIGITTE BARDOT, were also very sick. Maya ate little except for some cold chicken and bread and did not become ill, but she was frightened by the choppy sea and the rocking ship. She did not like not being in control of her surroundings.

In the morning, the ship docked safely in beautiful, sparkling Alexandria. Tall white buildings stood out, and Maya remarked that "the sun shines on Africa" (579). The handsome ship's doctor invited her to dinner at her hotel, and she accepted. Maya was with the cast of performers for the evening until the doctor arrived with his cousin and an in-law. After dinner, Maya spent the night with him and then learned that he was really interested in using her as a passport to the United States. She returned to her hotel alone, but on the way she was almost attacked by a filthy, aggressive beggar family. She made it back to the hotel safely after learning the realities of disease and poverty in Africa, her ancient homeland.

Chapter 24

The cast traveled from Alexandria to Cairo. There were beggars hounding their footsteps there too, but the opera was accepted well, and it was a good experience for Maya. The company toured the city together, and then Maya returned to the pyramids and reflected about the history of the region and the slaves who had built the tombs and even died there. Going to a party one evening, she and her companions had to step through deep mud on what was basically a walkway. They were offered house blacks to clean their feet, but they did not feel right about accepting that assistance; they felt too close to slavery themselves to be comfortable with such service. When they left, wooden planks had been placed over the muddy walkway.

The next experience was at a beauty parlor. Several of Maya's friends decided to have their hair straightened. Maya could not tolerate the burning green foam the beauticians used on them and washed it out of her hair immediately. Her friends went through with it, but the following week, their hair started falling out, and they had to get wigs to wear until it grew back in. Maya's mother, who had read about the incident in a San Francisco paper, thought that maybe Maya's hair had fallen out too, but Maya had no aftereffects of the treatment.

The Greek ship returned the company to Alexandria. The doctor, with his idea of a romance with Maya and then using her as his ticket to the United States, clearly explained his hopes and expectations. Maya coolly advised him to stay with his wife and told him to go away. She said, "I'm not marrying anyone. And surely it would not be another Greek" (591). The cruise was easy, with no storms or complications, and though Maya received a little appropriate teasing from cast members about the doctor, the trip was easy and uneventful.

Chapter 25

"The opera was well-received in Athens" (592), and the group proceeded from there to Tel Aviv. The streets in Israel were clean, and there were no beggars. American JAZZ musicians were performing in the city, and everyone got along well, though opera performers and jazz musicians usually do not associate much. Next was Morocco and then Barcelona. The whole group was getting tired, but that did not interfere with their flawless performances. They went on to perform in Switzerland, Marseilles, and Turin.

A birthday party held in Turin ended up in social chaos. The troupe was tired, and the liquor led to many mistakes. A classical soprano and the associate conductor accidentally collided on the dance floor, and things went downhill from there. Friendships were broken, and Maya felt ready to resign and go home to Clyde. As it turned out, good humor returned to the cast, and the ridiculous and confused events of the party evening slipped into the past. Friendships were restored.

Chapter 26

A premiere performance of the troupe was scheduled for La Scala, the famous opera house in Milan, Italy. *Porgy and Bess* was the first American opera to be performed there. They knew that the audience at La Scala would boo a poor performance, not unlike the Apollo Theater in HARLEM, so they worked extra hard to polish every movement and song. It turned out to be the best performance they had ever given. It was a performance of love, and the cast was happy with it. Afterward, they were full of compliments for each other.

The next assignment was Rome, and it was important to Maya to visit the Bricktop Bar there because her friend Bernard Hassel had recommended it. Maya went, identified herself as part of the *Porgy and Bess* cast, and was generously welcomed by Bricktop, the bar owner herself. Bricktop enjoyed the reputation of a living legend. In the 1930s, she, Josephine Baker, and Mabel Mercer had been the toasts of Europe (2004, 602). Bricktop's club was still Rome's most fashionable. After a visit, Brickie gave Maya what would come to be important information. She said, "Fact is, I know where to find anything and everyone in Rome" (609).

Chapter 27

Maya soon received news that the arrangement at home in San Francisco was changing. Among other things, Wilkie, the voice coach who had been boarding at her mother's large home, had moved into his own studio. Her mother was moving to Las Vegas to become a dealer in a Negro casino there. Clyde had developed a rash that was resistant to treatment, and Maya knew she needed to go home. She wrote that she would be home in a month.

She gave one month's notice to the company, but was told that she would have to pay her own airfare home as well as pay for a first-class ticket for her replacement from wherever she could be found. When she realized she needed over a thousand dollars for fares alone, Maya cried. She went to Brickie to ask for guidance on how to earn money in Rome, and again, Brickie was generous. For the next two months, Maya sang at Bricktop's after the opera, and she also taught African dance movements, by request, to the dancers at the Rome Opera house.

When Maya had earned the money she needed, her friends gave her a lavish farewell party, and at last she headed home. She did not sleep well on the voyage because of guilt about taking so long to return home, but she arrived safely in San Francisco and was happy.

Chapter 28

Maya was welcomed home warmly. Clyde sat on her lap with his arms wound tightly around her neck, and her mother said if they lived on a farm, she would have killed the fatted calf because her prodigal daughter had returned. During the early hours of the next morning, Clyde came to her room. He had been crying and simply asked when she would be going away again. Maya held him, and they cried together. She promised that if she ever had to go away again, she would take him with her or she would not go. He fell asleep in her arms, and she gently returned him to his own bed.

Chapter 29

Maya was home with Clyde, but she was not feeling comfortable with her life. Clyde's severe skin disorder and her guilt for leaving him put her into a serious state of melancholy. One morning, she decided that she needed to find some sort of professional help. She managed to get an appointment with a psychiatrist, but when she actually faced him, a well-dressed white man, she felt there was no use in trying to explain her life and problems to him. She left and went to see Wilkie. She babbled, and he ordered her to sit down and write out the things she felt thankful for. Her list included positive things: "I can hear. I can speak. I have a son. I have a mother. I have a brother. I can dance. I can sing. I can cook. I can read. I can write" (612). She followed his directions and it helped, but she said she felt silly by the time she got to the end of the page.

Reflecting on what she had just remembered about herself, Maya had an epiphany and a turnabout in her feelings. Wilkie had also reminded her that she was a good mother and that she should forgive herself. He advised her to stop by a theatrical agency on the way home and sign up for work. She did as he suggested, and at the agency she specified that any contract she might receive had to provide transportation and accommodation for her son as well as for her. She returned home with a lighter heart; she had made some good choices for her future, and she had kept her word to her son.

Maya told stories to Clyde and her mother about the fun experiences she had had on the tour, and her appetite perked up. Clyde, who was nine years old, was allowed to skip school for a week, and he and Maya spent the time riding bikes and having picnics. After trying out several names, Clyde settled on being called Guy, and he kept the name permanently. It took about a month, but finally everyone in his family circle was trained, and no one ever called him Clyde again.

Chapter 30

Maya was invited to sing and dance in a Hawaiian hotel owned by women. Provisions were made for Guy, and the women welcomed him with leis and smiles. They were provided with adjoining rooms, but when Maya awakened in the morning, Guy was not in his room. All of his clothes were there, and after searching every place she thought he might be, Maya called the police to help her find her son. Very soon, the police found a sand-covered Guy wearing only swimming trunks.

Guy seemed amazed that his mother was worried. His grandmother had given him the swimming trunks, and he had charged his breakfast by telling the waiter that his mother was the great singer whose name was on the big sign outside. He had been swimming alone. Guy was a strong-spirited, intelligent, and precocious child. Maya relaxed and reflected that this was her "wonderful, dependently independent son" (617).

CRITICAL COMMENTARY

Maya Angelou's serial autobiographies broke new ground in many ways. Writing individual but chronological segments in serial book form was a new way of approaching the genre. Further, though there were elements of repetition in the books to provide context and continuity, the books were not redundant. In *Maya Angelou: A Critical Companion* (1998), Mary Jane Lupton discusses Angelou's method in a brief section entitled "Narrative Point of View":

> *Singin' and Swingin' and Gettin' Merry Like Christmas* marks an historical moment in the history of African American autobiography. At this time [1976], no other well-known black female autobiographer had taken her story into a third volume. Maya Angelou's decision to keep going affects point of view, for there is now a narrator who is telling her life story in three distinct but connected segments, each linked to the other by the changing central character and by the first-person point of view. In extending her story into a third frame, Angelou deviates from the more contained autobiographical pattern, which tends to begin in a moment of revelation and to end at some decisive moment in the autobiographer's life. (98)

The autobiographical plot patterns of anticipation, recognition, and fulfillment mentioned in the discussion of *Gather Together in My Name* are slowly developed over Angelou's autobiographies, and though this third in the series of six does not yet reach fulfillment, the narrative reveals Angelou's maturing recognition of her own talents and serious responsibilities toward her son. In her earlier years as a young mother and teenager without skills, she had dreamed of some kind of miraculous rescue. That protection appeared most often in the form of an attentive husband for her and father for her son. As she matured—and that maturity process is clearly evident in *Singin' and Swingin'*—she realized that as a strong individual, she was able to make life work for both her son and herself without a man to support them.

Angelou also began to recognize that through focused practice, work, and performance, she had developed a much sought-after and marketable talent. She could dance, and she could sing. These talents did not fulfill all of her dreams, but they provided a reliable and adequate income. In this period of life, she experienced a sort of metamorphosis, both externally and internally. Outwardly, she transformed from the ugly duckling she had always felt herself to be to a graceful swan. Her beauty and talent were recognized and sought after. In turn, her confidence and belief in herself and her ability to handle both her son's and her own future were affirmed. This is not to say that there were no challenges ahead, but the difference was that she had begun to recognize her strengths, and she had also begun to realize that she would have a successful future.

This autobiography begins with Angelou's reflection on her love of music. Her relationship with music and its use runs through this entire narrative. She writes: "Music was my refuge. I could crawl into spaces between the notes and curl back to loneliness" (392). Working two jobs (in a dress shop and a small real estate office) in San Francisco to support herself and to pay for a babysitter, she was still young, and music was a dependable companion. Her distrust of whites was still strong, but the white female owner of a record shop she frequented offered her a job there. Angelou did not trust the woman because she was white but recognized that she could earn enough there to quit both of her other jobs and still come out ahead financially. She was suspicious of the woman's motives, but she accepted the job offer and learned that her distrust was unfounded.

The shop's other co-owner was white, male, and Jewish, and he, too, helped Angelou to learn that she could trust them. The co-owners responded to Maya's expressed need for religious focus and offered her glimpses into their own belief systems. The woman was a Christian Scientist, and the man was a Jew. Maya was deeply rooted in her Grandmother Henderson's COLORED METHODIST EPISCOPAL CHURCH traditions, but she wanted to find a belief system that did not depend so heavily on guilt and a sustained fear of a threatening God. She visited both churches and found connections between the Jewish musical tradition and her own black heritage, but she soon realized that she was more comfortable with the style of prayer and the music she had learned in her childhood. She attended black services and felt more at peace there.

In time, she met Tosh Angelos, a young white man and regular customer at the record shop, who shared her fascination with black music. He courted both her and her son. In spite of her reservations about whites, she found they had much in common, and she accepted his proposal of marriage. Her youthful fantasies included scenes from American movies that often concluded with happily-ever-after endings, and she thought she could find total happiness through marriage and family. Tosh was a Greek American, and she entered into the marriage thinking he would fulfill her dreams; however, the only "forever" element of the union turned out to be her later adaptation of his surname for her stage name.

Carol E. Neubauer writes that "Angelou had accounted for her illusory belief that she had finally met the man of her dreams who would give her everything she had always lacked—love, domestic tranquility, security, children, and a house in the suburbs modeled after *Better Homes and Gardens*" (34). The marriage lasted about three years, and a disappointed Angelou found her next job as a scantily dressed dancer at a local bar.

Over a relatively short time, her talent, audacious and entertaining personality, and audience appeal were discovered, and she began to perform at a well-known San Francisco nightclub called the Purple Onion. Many show business luminaries performed there, including Phyllis Diller (who made her stand-up debut at the club), Woody Allen, the Kingston Trio, the Smothers Brothers, and Richard Pryor. Performing at the Purple Onion led to public fame and many opportunities, and it was at this point that Angelou realized that she was a legitimate and marketable commodity. There were interviews and photographs, and she was even invited to audition for a Broadway production of TRUMAN CAPOTE's *House of Flowers,* in which she would have shared star billing with Pearl Bailey. She was selected for the part after her audition, but she turned it down. There were other performing opportunities, which included a world tour, and travel was one of the dreams Angelou had hoped to fulfill.

Eleanor W. Traylor writes that motion has been a dominant motif in Angelou's life and is present even in the titles of some of her autobiographies. Referring to Angelou's works, Traylor stated that "*motion,* by its recurrence, impresses itself upon a reader with remarkable force. I suggest that rhythmic motion dominates the whole symphony heard in these narratives of being" (98). Angelou's decision to join the cast of *Porgy and Bess* and go on a European tour in 1954 affirms Traylor's view. Despite her dedication to Clyde (later Guy), still a young boy in elementary school, she made the decision to leave him with her mother and take the opportunity to travel.

It was a hard parting, and Angelou was beset with guilt and memories of her own displacement as a child. Schools were being integrated throughout the nation because of the successful court case of *BROWN V. BOARD OF EDUCATION OF TOPEKA, KANSAS* in 1954, a significant step in the CIVIL RIGHTS MOVEMENT. Maya knew that Clyde would be fine and ultimately concluded that they would both adjust positively. Someday she would be able to take him to these faraway places she would see with the tour company.

The four-year European tour of *Porgy and Bess* in the mid-1950s was scheduled to perform in Italy, France, Germany, Yugoslavia, Greece, Israel, Egypt, and Russia (which at that time was locked behind the Iron Curtain). Maya accepted their offer to join them as a lead dancer, assured herself that her son would have excellent care, and she wrote that she "enjoyed every minute of it except when she thought about him" (606).

The entourage included "fifty-eight actors, seven backstage personnel, two conductors, assorted wives and office workers, six children and their schoolteacher, three journalists, two dogs, and one psychiatrist," according to Truman Capote in his book *The Muses Are Heard* (3), and through these experiences Angelou was exposed "to a progression of intelligent, keen, vital people, [which] increases her self-esteem and sophistication" (Hagen 1997, 91). She made the best she could of this opportunity to travel in Europe, and she worked to learn the language of each country where the opera was performed. Using dictionaries and native speakers, she gained proficiency in many languages, and this was a practice she continued throughout her future travels as a point of pride. Lyman B. Hagen points out: "Language facility seems to hold a special meaning to Angelou and is often mentioned . . ." (92).

In sharing some of the unexpected, humorous, and sometime poignant experiences she had while in Europe, Angelou reveals her own empathy for the suffering and hopes of people whose lives hold little promise of change and improvement. In Belgrade, she and two other female performers shared the same room, and indeed even the same large, lumpy bed. An admirer, Mr. Julian said that if she would not see him, he would send her his heart. Her friends loved the humor in the situation with Mr. Julian and teased Angelou without mercy. Angelou handled Julian's declarations of love calmly, and soon she received a package from him. She wondered if he had cut out his heart, as he had said he would do, but it turned out to be an inedible cake. She continued to put him off, courteously, until finally agreeing to meet him on the troupe's last evening in Belgrade.

Angelou and her friends had been told that some Yugoslavian men were aggressive, and that they hoped to be rescued by Americans and taken to the United States. Mr. Julian had been particularly persistent, but Maya agreed to meet him after the final performance, alone. As it turned out, he was a fragile-looking old man with polished metal teeth and wearing a bright green suit. Maya let him buy her coffee at a café but was firm about his not escorting her back to her hotel. Early the next morning, he came to her on the train and, with tears on his face, tossed a package into her lap, then left. Her friends still teased her and continued to make negative remarks, but Maya cried. "He persevered. And he was nice, I mean, he never failed to call and he had to get up very early to be at the station before we left. I admire that in anyone" (569). Angelou's careful telling of the memory, including her own sympathetic reflections on Mr. Julian's perhaps feigned devotion, revealed her deep caring and nurturing sensibilities for those less fortunate than her and the colleagues in her world.

Another incident, telling again of the deep understanding and feeling Angelou had for others, occurred when she left her Yugoslavian hotel and went out to do a little shopping. She was tall and black, and her very presence attracted a crowd of followers as she walked down the street. She wanted to buy a mandolin and entered a small music store where instruments were for sale. The shop owner helped her, and soon a beautiful mandolin, inlaid with mother-of-pearl, was in her hands. She strummed it, and almost immediately the owner's wife and several children came from a back room into the shop. Angelou said, "Good morning, Madam." The woman said "Paul Robeson," and then she began to sing (550). Her husband and children joined the woman with the poignant words of "Deep River." They knew it well, and Angelou reflected tearfully on the meaning of the words both to her and to them. The lyrics of the song made promises of something better, and though the Serbo-Croatian language Angelou had learned so far was inadequate to express her love of them and an understanding for their pain, they all hugged and understood their shared anguish. Through the song, they shared the unsure future of their people, past and present.

The extended *Porgy and Bess* tour has a central place in this third autobiography. As Angelou traveled, she was also sensitive to attitudes and behaviors of blacks and whites. She describes an experience at a party in the Yugoslavian countryside where an old woman, probably the grandmother of the house, wandered from her room into the party. Startled at seeing a black woman, and frightened, she quickly turned and headed back to her room. The party hostess gently retrieved the grandmother, and Angelou said "Good Evening, Madam" in Serbo-Croatian. The woman returned the greeting. Curious, the elderly woman touched Maya's cheek and hair, and then ordered that food be brought for this guest. Then she began to talk. It was too fast for Maya to understand, but the old lady again touched Maya's face and knee and then, laboriously, returned to her room. This, again, reveals Angelou's great sensitivity and empathy. She patiently let the old woman touch her and accept her, and her description of the woman and her response is drawn vividly.

Thoughtful reflections she had when she entered Africa for the first time reveal Angelou's curiosity, sensitivity, pride, and then pity and fear. She first saw men in long robes and tiny skullcaps and noted that they did not look much different from men in her own family. She noted also that the beautiful tall buildings, gleaming in the bright sunlight, were designed by people who shared her own ancestry. And yet it was not long before Angelou saw the squalor of poverty and need, as yet ignored by their new, independent government. She went out alone for a walk one morning and was soon surrounded by people with their arms and hands outstretched and begging. They were dirty and hungry, and one mother showed her two of her children: One was blind with a thick white substance seeping from his eyes, and the other had only a stump left of his arm. Maya gave them what money she had and turned back toward her hotel, but they followed her. As she walked, more and more destitute people followed her with "supplications, loud and cacophonous" (584). When the doorman of the hotel saw what was happening, he rushed to escort her to safety. Again, her sense of responsibility, along with guilt for being American and prosperous by contrast, left her frustrated. Inwardly, it was another experience along the journey to maturity and understanding of the world's peoples.

Repeatedly, Angelou cites incidents either observed or experienced on the tour. Though she had overcome much of her inherited prejudices against whites because of their generous treatment of her and support for her professional advancement, she realized that black Americans were more accepted in Europe than in the United States, particularly in France and Italy. These descriptions of foreign cultures, unfamiliar to many untraveled American readers of her works, have contributed to the books' popularity. Angelou opened her own experiences to her readership, knowing well that many were never able to move or travel beyond their own variants of STAMPS, ARKANSAS.

Angelou returned home before the performance in Russia. While the cast was performing in Rome, she received a letter from her mother saying that circumstances were changing, and that Clyde had a severe rash that was not responding to treatment. Vivian was moving to Las Vegas to take a job in a club as a dealer, and Angelou's son needed his mother. Because Maya had to pay transportation costs for her replacement dancer as well as her own travel expenses, she continued to perform in the opera, danced and sang at a nightclub, and was invited to conduct classes in African movement to dancers at the Rome Opera House. About two months after receiving the letter from her mother, she was on a boat headed for California. Fearful of flying, crashing, and leaving her son motherless, a guilt-wracked Angelou sensed that returning across the ocean in a ship would be the safest way to make the journey. Friends counseled her otherwise, but wisely true to her own instincts, she went home the way she had planned. This reflection, and the determinedness it represents, again suggests the movement toward maturity that Angelou was experiencing. There are many kinds of motion in this third autobiography, and one of the most important was her inward journey to maturity.

In "Reconstruction of the Composite Self," critic Sondra O'Neale discusses a passage from Angelou's *I Know Why the Caged Bird Sings* concerning ethics and black society. In that book, Angelou writes: "The needs of a society determine its ethics, and in the Black American ghettos the hero is that man who is offered only the crumbs from his country's table but by ingenuity and courage is able to take for himself a Lucullan Feast" (173). O'Neale explains the very things that Angelou realized as she lived through the period represented in *Singin' and Swingin'*:

> Whether from vivid recollection of fond fellowships in rural schools contrasted with the better remembrance of a segregated system designed to animalize Black students that one finds in *Caged Bird,* or from the startling reminiscences of Black entertainers who managed to evade Hitlerism and form enclaves of Black performers in Europe during the war years (e.g., Josephine Baker, Bernard Hassel, Mabel Mercer, "Brickie" Bricktop, Nancy Holloway, and Cordon Heath) that one finds in *Singin' and Swingin' and Gettin' Merry Like Christmas* . . . Angelou's message is one blending chorus: Black people and Black women do not just endure, they triumph with a will of collective consciousness that Western experience cannot extinguish. (44)

After returning from Europe, Maya found herself wanting in many ways. She whipped herself mentally for going on the tour and leaving her child, and soon she slipped into depression. Early in the book, she states: "Indeed no men at all seemed attracted to me. . . . No, husbands were rarer than common garden variety unicorns" (400). Her friend Ivonne had married, and though Maya was no longer pining for a husband, it was difficult to see her friend settled and happy with her man. Maya felt she had failed at both marriage and mothering, and at this point she was not sure of her direction or mental stability. Trying to come to grips with her emotions and lack of self-esteem, she again demonstrated her inner strength and resourcefulness.

In retrospect, Angelou expresses her own understanding and strength by being able to present the narrative of this difficult time in realistic detail. In the course of her internal anguish, she recognized her mistakes and learned from them. In *Maya Angelou: A Critical Companion,* Mary Jane Lupton writes: "Maya's personality is often ambiguous: uncertain, indefinite, and unsettled. And yet, it is because of these negative characteristics that Angelou engages readers in the awesome reality of her personality" (102).

Maya thought she might need a psychiatrist. The one available to her was white, and though by this time she had overcome many of the negative attitudes she had harbored toward white people, Maya rejected the possibility of a white psychiatrist really being able to understand her. She made and kept an appointment, but given her confused and multilayered feelings, in part related to her race, she did not feel that he could be of any help. Instead, she turned to her pragmatic friend and former voice coach, Frederick "Wilkie" Wilkerson. He told her to write down what she was thankful for, and as she wrote the long list, the realization of multiple positives in her life awakened her from her lethargy. She recognized that she was the only one inflicting guilt upon herself and was finally able to let it go. This was an epiphany for Angelou. It was a realization of her real worth and responsibilities, and she finally gained a clear understanding that she had not deliberately neglected or harmed her son.

Wilkie advised Maya to find work right away, so she stopped at a theatrical agency on the way home from his studio, and soon she had accepted a contract in Hawaii. By the end of this third autobiography, she and her son—now calling himself Guy—had traveled there, and Maya was beginning to realize many truths about herself. After hearing DELLA REESE sing so well one evening, she realized that singing was not her own best talent. She also knew herself well enough to know that she did not have the interest or drive to improve her singing much either. She also knew that though she was a well-trained and talented dancer, her career would not last forever. She really wanted to write. Grateful that her son had emerged as a healthy, clever boy, Maya decided that it might be time to turn toward a serious career.

Overall, *Singin' and Swingin' and Gettin' Merry Like Christmas* was accepted well by critics. Kathryn Robinson writes: "This latest segment in Angelou's autobiography will be received with the same enthusiasm as earlier books. . . . Angelou continually succeeds in sharing her vitality, and *Singin' and Swingin'* should find a wide audience" (144). Another critic, R. E. Almeida, writes:

> Most Angelou-philes will find [*Singin' and Swingin'*] a pleasant sequel. . . . It is her perceptions of herself as a black, a woman, and a mother as well as her impressions of those she meets which distinguish this account. Her religious strength, personal courage, and her talent prevail. (1,763)

DOLLY MCPHERSON, one of Maya Angelou's closest friends and her biographer, includes an intriguing chapter about *Singin' and Swingin'* called "The Adult Self in Bloom" in her book *Order Out of Chaos: The Autobiographical Works of Maya Angelou* (1990). Written from the perspective of a friend and professional colleague at Wake Forest College where the two worked together for many years, McPherson sheds personal insight on Angelou's growth during this particular time of her life. To McPherson, this third autobiography is "a graphic portrait of the adult self in bloom. . . . The third volume marks years of joy in Angelou's life" (80).

Though the narrative takes place at a time in Angelou's experience when poverty is ever-present and failure is a very real possibility, McPherson points out that "like the cunning heroine in a picaresque novel, this self conceived picaresque heroine has learned to live by her wits, to survive, and at times to prosper" (81). Sensitively, she points out the tension and conflict that Angelou experienced as she began to realize that not all white people were dishonest or bad. Angelou almost bathed in self-righteousness and self-indulgence because of injuries she had felt from whites in the past, and she had courage enough to admit this to herself and her audience:

> Oh, the holiness of always being the injured party. The historically oppressed can find not only sanctity but safety in the state of victimization. When access to a better life has been denied often enough, and successfully enough, one can use the rejection as an excuse to cease all efforts. (2004, 461)

Here, Angelou seems to drop her stereotyped perceptions of whites and realize that her self-pity had been immature and limited. McPherson describes Angelou's attitudes as she married and then outgrew her idealistic fantasies of the safe white-picket-fence haven that she dreamed wedded bliss would be.

Angelou's story reflects a growing understanding of the myriad complexities of race relations. As she discovered a wider world through her experiences with the cast of *Porgy and Bess,* and through her own personal experiences in the streets, hotels, shops, restaurants, and bars of places that ranged from Venice to Paris to Belgrade, her understanding of people grew. She began to recognize that there were varied responses among people toward African Americans, and she also realized that her own peace of mind about these issues must come from deep within herself. Mary Jane Lupton writes that "the rich ambivalence of *Singin' and Swingin'* could only have been achieved by a writer who had abandoned 'ignorance' for a conscious self-exploration" (186).

McPherson concludes her discussion of *Singin' Swingin'* by stating:

> When one meets Maya Angelou in her story, one encounters the humor, the pain, the exuberance, the honesty, and the determination of a human being who has experienced life fully and retained her strong sense of self. Both the writing and the story fulfill the promise of the title. Angelou has a remarkable ability to recreate scenes from her life. In narrating retrospective accounts of incidents and dialogue, there is necessarily some contrivance,

but there is always the ring of authenticity in the telling. (90)

SOME IMPORTANT THEMES AND SYMBOLS IN *SINGIN' AND SWINGIN' AND GETTIN' MERRY LIKE CHRISTMAS*

Music

This text begins: "Music was my refuge" (392). Maya worked at the Melrose Music Shop on Fillmore Street in San Francisco. As she listened to music with lyrics like "You'd be so nice to come home to," she often dreamed of finding the ideal husband, having two more children, and living in a nice house with a well-tended garden. But the reality was that she had to work hard to meet her expenses because she was determined not to turn to the welfare system. The music comforted her, and it was at the music store that she met Tosh Angelos, a Greek American interested in black music. They courted, and soon she accepted his proposal of marriage. Though she had not overcome her prejudice against whites at that time, she rationalized that he was not really a white man because he was of Greek descent. She thought that fact exempted him from the RACISM of white people.

The marriage lasted about three years, and after it ended, Angelou turned to dance and performance to earn a living. She had extensive dance training as she was growing up, and it was time to put her love of music and dance together and see if she could earn a living with her talent and skills.

The music of black Americans—including folk songs; religious, dance, and vocal creations; instrumental pieces; and, since the late 1800s, ragtime, blues, and jazz—is anchored in West Africa, "the place of origin for the ancestors of most black Americans" (Southern 1971, xv). The rich voices and sense of rhythm seemingly innate in many African Americans have attracted listeners for centuries. One early American black writer, Martin Delaney, wrote in *Blake: or The Huts of America* (1859):

> In the distance, on the levee and in the harbor among the steamers, the songs of the boatmen were incessant. Every few hours landing, loading and unloading, the glee of these men of sorrow was touchingly appropriate and impressive. . . . If there is any class of men anywhere to be found whose sentiments of song and words of lament are made to reach the sympathies of others, the black slave-boatmen are that class. . . . They are seemingly contented by soothing their sorrows with songs apparently cheerful, but in reality, wailing lamentations. (quoted in Southern 1971, 147)

Angelou grew up with the sounds of music in the background. In Stamps, Momma hummed and sang SPIRITUALS, the church was a place for everyone to sing the hymns, and annual picnics included homemade instruments and Jew's harps. Maya's mother, Vivian Baxter, played music in her home constantly. According to Maya, "The spirituals and gospel songs were sweeter than sugar" (quoted in Lupton 1999, 179). Her talent and dance training in high school led her to naturally turn toward dance performance as a profession, and at each bar where she entertained, she was surrounded by the popular sounds of the music she craved.

Later, after many trials and disappointments, Maya was hired as a singer, dancer, performer at the Purple Onion, a well-known nightclub in San Francisco. She was soon recognized as a rising star, and her growing popularity as an entertainer opened the door to performance in the opera *Porgy and Bess.* She was once again wrapped in a community of music. Being in that opera gave her association with some of the most talented black singers, dancers, and instrumentalists on stage at the time. The sounds of music ring behind the words of this text, and the allusions range from blues to calypso to children's songs to opera.

See also BLUES, THE.

Travel

This text moves from one inward and outward journey to another. In the beginning, Maya was working in San Francisco at the Melrose Record Shop. In time, she moved from there to Montreal and then on to the tour of Europe and Egypt playing a lead dance role with the star-studded cast of *Porgy and Bess.* The European tour is described in *Singin' and Swingin'* with a series of sights and experiences in the varied places where they performed, as well as descriptions of the train, bus, and ship journeys in between. Angelou discusses some of the foods and beverages she encountered on tour and the insights and comments of Europeans as they observed black Americans. She mentions more than once the preference of Europeans for black Americans more than white. While on tour, she apparently did not hesitate to express her own views as well.

For nearly a year during the European tour, Angelou picked up foreign language dictionaries and studied them as she moved from place to place. She often found native speakers to tutor her, and by doing that consistently, she learned native pronunciations and mastered many languages conversationally. Because of her friendliness and genuine interest in people, she had opportunities to interact with many who opened even more knowledge to her. Her keen perception of human nature and her own kind disposition continued to draw strangers to her. She met many men during these travels, and many would have been happy to make her their own, but that was not to be.

More than one-third of *Singin' and Swingin'* is devoted to Angelou's depiction of the *Porgy and Bess* tour, but because she shares not only descriptive information but her own and others' reactions to where they were, it is much more than a travel account. At the end of the experiences described in the book, she returned to San Francisco and her son and nursed herself back to emotional health after a near-tragic brush with guilt-caused depression. She determined then that any traveling she did in the future would include her son.

Separation

Clyde was eight years old when his mother left to go tour in Europe and Egypt, and he stayed with Vivian Baxter at her large home in San Francisco. He was well cared for but developed a serious skin disorder in Maya's absence. Angelou repeatedly expresses her feelings of guilt about leaving him with her mother during this time, reflecting on the abandonment she felt as a child, when she and her brother had been sent to Arkansas to live with their grandmother because their parents were too unsettled to raise them. The European tour made a difficult separation for both mother and son, and when Maya returned to San Francisco, she specifically promised to take Clyde with her if she were ever again to take a job in a distant city.

Realizing that Clyde's skin condition was probably caused by their separation, Maya accused herself of neglect. After her return, her son would panic and run into her room to assure himself that she was there. She became obsessive and wanted to touch him, hold him, and even carry him all the time, but she resisted those impulses.

It was her friend Wilkie who suggested that she stop by a theatrical agency on the way home from an unsuccessful session with a psychiatrist and that she also try to forgive herself. He said, "Don't ask God to forgive you, for that's already done. . . . So forgive yourself" (612).

Maya went to an agency and signed contracts stipulating that if they found work for her, transportation and accommodations would also be provided for her son. She went home feeling reborn and laughing. She began to share stories about the European tour that were funny rather than just dwelling on how miserable she had been without Clyde, and soon her son began to heal. Before long, his sense of security returned, and he announced that he was to be called Guy instead of Clyde. His mother had changed her name for show business, and he felt he could do the same, so the name became permanent. The next job she accepted was in Hawaii, and Guy went with her. The separations were over.

Race

Maya's perception of Tosh Angelos as a Greek rather than a white man frustrated her mother and was not anchored in the reality of Angelos's whiteness. He had Greek heritage, but he was a white man. Issues began to rise in the relationship that caused tension, including Clyde's desire to have "good hair" like Tosh. Maya's mother anticipated problems in the marriage, which dissolved after about three years. There were other reasons, not the least of which was differing opinions on religion, but race was part of the divisive tension.

Angelou interpreted the preference of many Europeans for black rather than white Americans as an affirmation and recognition of the humility and guilelessness of her race. When the cast of *Porgy and*

Bess encountered Lionel Hampton's band in Israel, she noted how delighted the African Americans were to connect with other African Americans. Performing and interacting constantly with white audiences and associates in Europe was not always comfortable; a deep-seated distrust of white people was often evident. Even though those they associated with in Europe were not white Americans, the discomfort was still present simply because of stereotypical constructions attached to skin color and maintained by prejudice.

CHARACTERS

Maya Angelou During the period of this text, Maya was in her 20s, and she met and married her first husband, Tosh Angelos. After three years together, they divorced, and she sought jobs performing in nightclubs. After stints at a few lesser-known clubs, she began performing at the Purple Onion. Her talent gained recognition, and she was offered a position as a dancer with the tour company of Gershwin's *Porgy and Bess*. The opera was scheduled for a one-year tour in Europe, leaving from Montreal. This period of her life was one of maturing and self-discovery. Though she made choices that she regretted later (primarily that of leaving her son), her resiliency and determination were constantly represented. Inward and outward movement, changes, and realizations were apparent as she moved away from dependency on her mother and brother and became her own person.

Louise Cox Louise Cox was a white woman and co-owner of the Melrose Record Shop on Fillmore Street in San Francisco. She and her daughter were practicing Christian Scientists and invited Maya to visit their church service. Louise offered Maya a job after noting her interest in and knowledge of black music. Maya was distrustful of the woman's motivation but recognized the offer as a good opportunity and took it. In a short while, she realized that Louise was sincere, and it was the beginning of her shedding the lifelong prejudices she had held, almost religiously, against white people.

David Rosenbaum A white man, a Jew, and co-owner of the Melrose Record Shop on Fillmore Street in San Francisco. Maya was curious about his religion, and he recommended that she speak with Rabbi Fine at Beth Emanu-El Synagogue. Rosenbaum's kindnesses, like Louise Cox's, formed another important stepping-stone for overcoming the prejudice Angelou maintained regarding white people because of her childhood training and experiences.

Clyde (Guy) Age nine at the end of this autobiography, Maya's son was a bright, independent, and precocious child, and he held her heart in his hands. After Maya returned from Europe, the boy renamed himself Guy; the changed name may have been influenced by his mother's change from Marguerite Johnson to Maya Angelou, her adopted stage name. His choice was promptly accepted by Angelou and the rest of the family.

Enistasious "Tosh" Angelos Tosh Angelos was Maya Angelou's first husband. He was a Greek-American sailor who has just been released from the navy after World War II, and he particularly liked black music. He and Maya met at the Melrose Record Shop, and he began to court her in a roundabout way by taking Clyde for various outings. Clyde liked him very much, and Tosh said he thought that Clyde was the smartest little boy in the world. The three of them often went to see old movies, and Tosh particularly enjoyed Mae West's DIAMOND LIL. He had an interest in literature and had studied it at Reed College in Oregon, which also helped ingratiate him to both Maya and her brother Bailey. He proposed, and Maya accepted. Their marriage lasted about three years.

Vivian Baxter At this time, Maya's mother was still living in San Francisco, but when she realized that Maya was going to marry a white man in a courthouse ceremony, she moved her entire 14 rooms of furniture to Los Angeles three days before the ceremony. In this period of of time, Maya began to recognize significant differences between herself and her mother. Though they were close, Maya wanted a different kind of life for her son and herself. Vivian was educated and had diplomas from several vocational programs, but Maya desired a more intellectual life. There was peace between them, and Vivian's APHORISMs and advice, laced with wit, wisdom, and FOLKLORE, had a deep influence on Maya.

Momma (Mrs. Annie Henderson) About a year before the divorce from Tosh, Maya became ill and was hospitalized with appendicitis. She developed complications and was in the hospital several weeks. Her plan was to go to Stamps to recover, both physically and mentally, but she learned that her grandmother had died the day after her appendectomy. The last time Maya had been to Stamps, Momma had slapped Maya several times because Maya had been disrespectful to two white women at a general store in the white part of town, then sent her and Clyde away. Maya loved and respected her grandmother, and she internalized the strong spiritual training she had been given. Again, Momma's Christian grounding is a theme that runs through all six of Angelou's autobiographies.

Mr. Julian When Angelou was on tour in Europe with the cast of *Porgy and Bess,* Mr. Julian was one of many males who would feign undying love for a cast member. The reality was that these local visitors hoped someone in the cast would return the affection and take them to the United States. In Belgrade, the capital of Yugoslavia, Maya was sharing a room with two other women (Ethel Ayler and Martha Flowers). One morning, the phone rang for Maya, and the caller introduced himself as Mr. Julian, a new fan who had seen her perform. He professed love for her, saying things like: "It's that I'm loving you . . . and your lovely legs jumping" (553). He told her he would send her his heart and that he was a swimming champion. He sent a heart he had made. It was an attempt at an artistic creation made of flour and water with various baubles of lace, paper doilies, dried flowers, leaves, and it had assorted grains stuck to it. She finally agreed to meet him, and he turned out to be a "small, very wiry old man" (567). They had coffee and visited pleasantly, and then she promptly returned to her friends.

Ivonne Broadnax Ivonne Broadnax was one of Maya's closest friends during this period of time in San Francisco. Ivonne lived on Ellis Street and was 25 but already raising an eight-year-old daughter and a 15-year-old sister. Angelou writes that Ivonne was levelheaded and "had the clear, clean eyes of a born survivor" (396). Ivonne eventually settled into a happy marriage at a time when Maya's life felt confusing. She introduced Maya to her new husband just after Angelou had returned from the European tour of *Porgy and Bess* to an ailing Clyde (soon to be called Guy) and to her own misgivings about her separation from Clyde, no husband, and their future. It was difficult for Maya to see Ivonne's joy when she was so low.

Frederick "Wilkie" Wilkerson Maya's voice coach and friend of her mother's, Wilkie was a trusted friend. When Maya returned from Europe, she was plagued with guilt and depression for having been away from her son for so long. Wilkie gave her very wise, fatherly counsel, and he helped her get started once more in a positive direction.

FURTHER READING

Almeida, R. E. "Singin' and Swingin' and Gettin' Merry Like Christmas." *Library Journal* 101 (1976): 1,763.

Angelou, Maya. *The Collected Autobiographies of Maya Angelou.* New York: Modern Library Edition by Random House, 2004.

Barnwell, Cherron A. "Singin' de Blues, Writing Black Female Survival in *I Know Why the Caged Bird Sings.*" In *Maya Angelou.* Bloom's Modern Critical Views, edited by Harold Bloom, 133–146. New York: Bloom's Literary Criticism, 2009.

Capote, Truman. *The Muses Are Heard.* New York: Random House, 1956.

Gillespie, Marcia Ann, Rosa Johnson Butler, and Richard A. Long. *Maya Angelou: A Glorious Celebration.* New York: Doubleday/Random House, 2008.

Hagen, Lyman B. *Heart of a Woman, Mind of a Writer, and Soul of a Poet: A Critical Analysis of the Writings of Maya Angelou.* Lanham, Md.: University Press of America, 1997.

Lupton, Mary Jane. *Maya Angelou: A Critical Companion.* Westport, Conn.: Greenwood Press, 1998.

———. "Singing the Black Mother: Maya Angelou and Autobiographical Continuity." In *Maya*

Angelou. Modern Critical Views, edited by Harold Bloom, 173–199. Philadelphia: Chelsea House, 1999.

McPherson, Dolly A. *Order Out of Chaos: The Autobiographical Works of Maya Angelou.* New York: Peter Lang, 1990.

Neubauer, Carol E. "Displacement and Autobiographical Style in Maya Angelou's *Heart of a Woman.*" In *Maya Angelou.* Modern Critical Views, edited by Harold Bloom, 25–40. Philadelphia: Chelsea House, 1999.

O'Neale, Sondra. "Reconstruction of the Composite Self: New Images of Black Women in Maya Angelou's Continuing Autobiography." In *Maya Angelou.* Modern Critical Views, edited by Harold Bloom, 41–53. Philadelphia: Chelsea House, 1999.

Robinson, Kathryn. "Singin' and Swingin' and Gettin' Merry Like Christmas." *School Library Journal* 23 (September 1976): 144.

Southern, Eileen. *The Music of Black Americans: A History.* New York: W. W. Norton, 1971.

Tate, Claudia, ed. *Black Women Writers at Work.* New York: Continuum, 1983.

Traylor, Eleanor W. "Maya Angelou: Writing Life, Inventing Literary Genre." In *Maya Angelou.* Bloom's Modern Critical Views, edited by Harold Bloom, 91–105. New York: Bloom's Literary Criticism, 2009.

The Heart of a Woman (1981)

The Heart of a Woman, Maya Angelou's fourth autobiography, is a complex narrative of the changing relationship between Angelou and her only child, Guy (born CLYDE BAILEY JOHNSON). It also describes her interactions with male luminaries and consorts. By this point in her life, Angelou had recognized that her talent was authentic and important. Her devotion to the successful rearing of her son in a world still largely unsafe for black men threads through the story, and her growing maturity led her to turn toward serious racial issues. Though she was not an overt militant, her voice and actions made a difference during the CIVIL RIGHTS MOVEMENT.

The text covers a period of about five years, and Angelou's fine literary style, laced through with metaphors and even fantasy, carries her story from California to New York and then to Africa. Though there is a sense of fatalism in the narrative, Angelou's personal strength convinces the reader that she will survive and triumph over whatever challenges present themselves. From the vitriolic comments of BILLIE HOLIDAY to the exotic and persuasive charm of her African consort, freedom fighter VUSUMZI MAKE, Angelou handled many tough situations with grace and dignity.

In an interview with Judith Paterson in 1982, Angelou stated: "Surviving is important, but thriving is *elegant*" (quoted in Paterson 1989, 118). Though she fictionalizes most of the dialogue in *The Heart of a Woman,* she does it in a credible and captivating style, and she thrives elegantly. Her anecdotes are rich and unaffected, and she tells the stories as she remembers them. Her skill at creating visual context takes the reader almost literally into the United Nations building, a ballroom, a race around the lobby of the Waldorf Astoria, and a crude hospital setting in Ghana. Jokes, poems, and occasional candid personal revelations demonstrate her growing command of her talent and her compelling drive to share it.

SYNOPSIS

The Heart of a Woman is dedicated to Angelou's grandson, Colin Ashani Murphy-Johnson, Guy's son, and a list of 14 sister/friends. This autobiography has a short introduction and 20 chapters.

An epigraph at the beginning of the first page is taken from a traditional African American spiritual: *"The ole ark's a-moverin', a-moverin', a moverin', the ole ark's a -moverin' along"* (Cain 1938). The lyrics are apt because Angelou and Guy traveled and moved many times during the period represented in this book (1957–62). The epigraph also refers to the racial unrest in the United States. The introductory lines mention the tennis player ALTHEA GIBSON, the politician STROM THURMOND, the boxer Sugar Ray Robinson, and the writer JACK KEROUAC, all luminaries in the significant cultural changes of the time.

Angelou also mentions that she and Guy lived on a houseboat with culturally sophisticated whites, and that was followed by a rented home in an upscale Los Angeles white neighborhood, Laurel Canyon. Not long after Maya and her son moved there, Frederick "Wilkie" Wilkerson, her voice coach, asked if she would like to meet the famous JAZZ vocalist Billie Holiday. Holiday had a reputation for using heavy drugs and having a vulgar mouth. When Wilkerson arrived with "Lady Day" (so nicknamed by saxophonist LESTER YOUNG), Maya realized that the rumors were true.

Holiday liked Guy, finding him bright and well-informed. At the end of this first evening, she sang a good-night song for Guy, and then Maya returned Lady Day to her hotel. The visit lasted four days, with Holiday staying from morning until evening and ending each visit with a bedtime song for Guy. The last night, she sang her signature song,"Strange Fruit," a protest song describing the tragedy of black lynchings in the South. Guy interrupted to ask some questions about the metaphors in the song, and Holiday spat out an offensive response that hurt Guy and stunned his mother.

Holiday attended Angelou's vocal act at the nightclub that evening, and again used her "waterfront" mouth. She was ill, and a few months later, she died in a New York hospital. Guy felt his mother should have protected him from Holiday's crudeness, and tensions between them escalated further when he soon got into trouble at school. He had explained the facts of life to two white girls who were discussing the topic and was soon given a letter stating that he was to be transferred to another school at the end of the term. Angelou immediately found a home in the integrated Westlake district, where their tensions eased and both of them felt more comfortable.

Chapter 1

Guy did well in the Westlake school, and Angelou began to write song lyrics for Liberty Records; she also wrote a few unpublished short stories. JOHN KILLENS, a black writer from New York, had come to Hollywood to write a screenplay for his novel *Youngblood.* He read some of Angelou's work and felt that she had writing talent, so he suggested that she move to New York and become active in the HARLEM WRITERS GUILD, where her work could be read and critiqued. He knew that associating with the professional writers there would help strengthen her developing talent.

Angelou wanted to relocate, but she knew she would have to explain her choice to her son and to her mother, VIVIAN BAXTER. Vivian wanted to get together with Maya at the newly integrated Desert Hotel in Fresno, California, located halfway between LOS ANGELES and Vivian's home in SAN FRANCISCO. When Angelou got home from Fresno, her next task was to inform Guy that they were moving again. Because of her work, they had moved 11 times in his nine years of schooling, so Guy had been repeatedly uprooted from schools and friends. She told him that John and Grace Killens were looking for an apartment in New York for them, and that Ray, her boyfriend, would stay with Guy while she was away. Guy was cool to her, but he quietly accepted the news. Angelou and Ray parted on friendly terms, and he consented to stay in the house and send Guy to her in two weeks.

Chapter 2

The Killens family welcomed Angelou to their brownstone home in Brooklyn, New York. Over the next several days, she got to know the general personalities of each Killens family member. They were warm and friendly with her, but it seemed that every time a familiar black person's name was mentioned (for instance, the civil rights leader MARTIN LUTHER KING, JR., the murdered EMMETT TILL, the singers and entertainers HARRY BELAFONTE and MIRIAM MAKEBA, and others), the story included negative elements of racial oppression, delayed racial progress, and future possibilities of racial INTEGRATION. Maya was not comfortable with these discussions.

Maya found an apartment not far from the Killens's and promptly painted and furnished it with like-new furnishings. Guy was condescending when she picked him up at the airport because he had been left in California with a disinterested caretaker who deserted Guy and left him on his own after she was gone a week. She took him to the apartment, and while Guy was arranging his room, Angelou reflected on the challenges of being a single, black mother. Outside of their own home, authority was in the hands of whites who simply did not look, think, or act like blacks, nor did they understood African Americans. After dinner that first night, however, Guy challenged her to a game of Scrabble and asked nonconfrontational questions about the dictionary and New York television. Things seemed to be back to normal between them.

Angelou's first encounter with the Harlem Writers Guild held at John Killens's home created intense anxiety within her. She read from her new play, *One Love, One Life,* and found that she could not correctly gauge the speed of her tempo. In describing these moments later, she writes: "Time wrapped itself around every word, slowing me" (656). When she finally finished reading, no one said anything for quite a while. Finally, the criticism began. One fellow remarked, "*One Life, One Love?* I found no life and very little love in the play from the opening of the act to its unfortunate end" (657). Internally, Angelou was seething. She was trying to leave when she heard, "Maya, you've got a story to tell" (658). It was John Henrik Clarke, who had criticized her so harshly. He told her that they were glad to have her there, and that an important part of talent was the willingness to work very hard.

John Killens drove her home, and they talked about writing. Though he told her that short stories were the most difficult to produce, Angelou, nearly always up for a challenge, said that she would have a short story ready to read to the group in about two months. She reflects: "Trying to overcome was black people's honorable tradition" (661).

Chapter 3

Maya needed money and managed to find a job in a club on the Lower East Side. Several people she admired were doing important work: ABBEY LINCOLN and MAX ROACH (who married in 1962) were performing in jazz concerts focused on liberation; LORRAINE HANSBERRY had a play on Broadway about black American families; JAMES BALDWIN had published *The Fire Next Time;* and John Killens had published *And Then We Heard the Thunder,* about black soldiers in an army of whites. Harry Belafonte had added a South African singer to his concert. Though Angelou wanted to quit show business, she was soon invited to appear at the Apollo, a theater in HARLEM. PEARL BAILEY, DIZZY GILLESPIE, COUNT BASIE, DUKE ELLINGTON, and other famous black entertainers had performed there; its prestige for African-American performers was on the same level as the Met or La Scala for white singers.

On the last day of Maya's performances at the Apollo, the Killenses, their children, and Guy attended the show. When she got to "Uhuru," an African song she had introduced there that invited audience participation, the Killens family and Guy joined in enthusiastically. After they left, there was one more show, at which hecklers quickly grew strident and vocal about not wanting to sing with her. Rude words were called out, and Maya was afraid there would be a fight, but a woman began to sing "Freedom, freedom, freedom" (669), and though the tune was not quite right, others in the audience began to join in and things returned to normal. After the show, Angelou and her manager were both smiling. He paid her, and Maya remembered her mother's advice: "Since you're black, you have to hope for the best. Be prepared for the worst and always know that anything can happen" (670).

Chapter 4

The actor GODFREY CAMBRIDGE was introduced to Angelou at a Greenwich Village party. She invited him to dinner, and Guy and Godfrey immediately bonded. At the end of the evening, he gave Maya what she called a brother's kiss, and that established the grounds for their friendship. Soon after, Godfrey and Angelou attended a fund-raiser for the SOUTHERN CHRISTIAN LEADERSHIP CONFERENCE (SCLC). The speakers were all ministers: Wyatt Walker, Fred Shuttlesworth, RALPH ABERNATHY, and Martin Luther King, Jr. King had just been released from jail, and part of the purpose for the meeting was to inform northerners of the fight for equal rights taking place in the South. When it was his turn to speak, King went to the podium and told of the changes and violence in their southern homeland. He reminded his audience that it was time to "take fear and by love, change it into hope" (674).

Afterward, Godfrey and Angelou walked from Harlem to the Hudson River and began to make a plan for a fund-raising show with actors, singers, and dancers to benefit the SCLC. Angelou knew many unemployed singers from the production of PORGY AND BESS with which she had toured Europe, and she agreed to talk to them. They had to get permission to use the SCLC's name for their fund-raiser, and Godfrey knew an actor named Hugh Herd who had contacts and excellent organizational skills. He and Maya had a tentative plan for a benefit show within an hour.

Maya immediately made an appointment at the SCLC office. The director, BAYARD RUSTIN, had been called away, but Maya met with Stanley Levison, who called in Jack Murray, a writer in the next office, and explained her proposal. Murray mentioned the possibility of using the Village Gate for the benefit. It was a popular Greenwich Village nightclub, and having the fund-raiser there might draw a good crowd. He knew the owner, Art D'Lugoff, and said that he would talk to him.

Bayard Rustin arrived, welcomed her, and began to ask questions. Angelou explained again, and Rustin said that he would like to see a script. If it was approved, they would loan the theater group their SCLC mailing list. Soon they had made arrangements with actors, singers, and dancers, and they had permission to use the theater on Sunday, Monday, and Tuesday nights. Though the plans were coming together, Angelou was struggling to get a script written. Nothing exciting seemed to be coming to her, and she was producing one boring plot after another.

Godfrey had been driving his taxi (his part-time job), dropped off a fare near Angelou's apartment, and stopped for a visit. She told him how she was struggling, and he suggested that they do a "cabaret kind of thing" (682). The performers could do songs, dances, and skits that were particularly black in style. Before Godfrey left to pick up his next fare, Maya came up with a title: *Cabaret for Freedom.* Soon rehearsals began, and the cabaret began to come together.

Chapter 5

Every seat was filled at the Village Gate on opening night of *Cabaret for Freedom.* Well-known stars, including SIDNEY POITIER, were there as well as newspaper reporters and editors, a lawyer, and a few politicians from Harlem. There were comedians who made the audience laugh, singers who performed familiar romantic songs, and skits including LANGSTON HUGHES's "The Emperor of Haiti." The somber reminder from that presentation was that "as black people we had a dignity and a love of life, those qualities had to be defended constantly" (684). Orson Bean was the only white actor in the cast, and his rambling remembrance also brought laughter. "Lift Every Voice and Sing" was sung by the cast as a finale, and Godfrey hugged Angelou and whispered, "We've got a hit. A hit, damn, a hit" (685).

While Maya worked in New York, Guy explored the city and enjoyed school. He became good friends with Chuck Killens, a son of the writer John Killens, a champion of Maya's work. *(Courtesy Angelou-Johnson Family Archives)*

D'Lugoff told them afterward that they could use his nightclub without charge for five weeks, and he would let them use his mailing list to advertise. But the fine summer of 1960 finally came to a close, and so did *Cabaret for Freedom.* Angelou was out of work, and "Rent was due again" (688). But the Village Gate had filled to capacity with people who had paid to see the review, and they were able to raise a significant sum of money.

Maya was offered a two-week job in Chicago singing at a new club called the Gate of Horn, but the question that opportunity presented was how to take care of Guy. She found a part-time housekeeper and cook. Guy was not happy with the idea until his mother suggested that there may be crime in the neighborhood. He found this interesting and accepted the arrangement.

Angelou enjoyed the Irish flavor of the Chicago club and learned that the oppression of the Irish was not much different than the oppression of blacks. As she was paying her hotel bill at the end of the engagement, a uniformed black man approached and told her that she had a phone call from New York. It was John Killens about a problem concerning Guy, but he would not tell her any details. He said that Guy was all right and was staying at their home.

Maya flew home immediately and learned that the story was about some wild boys who had threatened Guy. The Killenses explained that it was a gang called the Savages, who were threatening Guy that they were going to beat him severely. The gang was so violent they even terrorized the police. Guy told her that he did not want to move away from their current home no matter what happened. He was trying very hard to assert himself as an adult, and his mother recognized that this was a time to allow him his dignity. When they arrived home, Guy made a pot of coffee for her, and he told her what had happened.

Mrs. Tolman, the temporary housekeeper, had a 15-year-old granddaughter, Susie, whom she had brought along to the house one day. Susie developed a crush on Guy, but he already had a steady girlfriend and turned her away. Later that day, the doorbell rang, and Jerry, Susie's boyfriend, was standing there. He had heard that Guy had hit Susie and said he would be back later with his gang. The morning after hearing the story from Guy, Maya called a musician friend in Manhattan and asked for a favor—the loan of a small gun. She then called Mrs. Tolman and told her she would like to come over to her home and pay her for her services.

Upon her arrival at the Tolman home, Maya paid the housekeeper and then asked to see Susie. The girl was just waking up, and Jerry was there as well. Mrs. Tolman introduced Maya to Susie's mother, who was nursing a baby. Susie came out of the bedroom, and Maya said she would like to see Jerry also. Susie got him, and after Maya introduced herself, she told Jerry that she knew he was the head of the Savages, that even the police were afraid of him, and that he had threatened her son. She informed him that if Guy came home damaged in the slightest way, she would not call the police. Her hand moved to her purse as she said she would shoot Susie's grandmother, mother, and even the baby if anything happened, and then she would find Jerry's house and "kill everything that moves, including the rats and cockroaches" (700). At that point, she showed the borrowed pistol to the family, put it back in the purse, and left. Later, Guy told her that he had told the Savages an invented story about his gang in California always fighting to the death. Guy said he told them that he would meet Jerry and one other guy somewhere and fight it out. Then he asked what was for dinner. Maya mused about whether or not either of them was bluffing and found she could not answer the question.

Angelou's first published short story was accepted by *Revolución* in Cuba, and she knew that because of the publication, she had become an in-member of the elite Harlem Writers Guild. ROSA GUY, born in Trinidad but raised in New York, was a founding member of the guild and opened her home for the next reading, to be combined with a party in Angelou's honor.

Chapter 6

Maya was called for an appointment with Bayard Rustin at the headquarters of the Southern Christian Leadership Conference. Rustin told her that the SCLC was looking for someone to take his place there as coordinator, and he had suggested her. She was offered the position with the SCLC, which would mean a living wage, a secretary, and many responsibilities. Shocked, she courteously thanked Rustin, saying she needed to think about it and would call the office the next day. Though she was worried about her skills, she accepted the offer and took charge of the SCLC office as civil unrest was increasing in the South.

From white Long Island high school volunteers to steady black volunteers from Harlem neighborhoods (black), Maya organized and instructed people how to help. She organized volunteer captains, and she assigned tasks that ranged from envelope stuffing to sweeping to scrubbing the steps leading to the office. Maya and the black staff did not miss the irony of white students doing the work blacks had done for them for centuries. In the meanwhile, Martin Luther King, Jr., was in jail, North Carolina black students were dragged out by a white diner where they had tried to be served, and North Carolina's black community was angry but still peaceful. MALCOLM X continued to be seen challenging white television reporters, and in Harlem, MARCUS GARVEY's UNIVERSAL NEGRO IMPROVEMENT ASSOCIATION and the Ethiopian Association were being revived.

One day, Maya walked into her office, and sitting at her desk with his back to her was Martin Luther King, Jr. He turned and stood up, greeted her warmly, and stayed a while to visit with her. He thanked her for her support and asked about herself and her family. She told him about Stamps and her brother, BAILEY JOHNSON, JR., who was in Sing Sing for selling stolen goods. With understanding, King said, "That's why we must fight and win. We must save the Baileys of the world. . . . Never give up on him. Never deny him. And remember, he is freer than those who hold him behind bars" (709). As King left, he reminded her that "for every fair-minded white American, there is a Bull Connor [an ardent segregationist] waiting with his shotgun and attack dogs" (709).

Maya's work at the headquarters continued as street-corner speakers called for reform; groups of blacks and whites and visiting African diplomats partied together; and the Harlem community was kept informed about who was doing what, including successes and failures, by G. Norwood's social and political columns in the local *Amsterdam News*.

Abbey Lincoln, Rosa Guy, and Maya decided to organize a group of talented black women to perform in various ways to raise money for organizations working in the Civil Rights movement. They could read poetry, sing, write, give fashion shows, and take other creative actions in order to raise funds.

Chapter 7

Maya continued as coordinator of the SCLC for about six months and mastered the tasks she needed to know. It was always busy, and she enjoyed the work, but when she returned home to life as a single mother with a 15-year-old son, rent to pay, and loneliness, she no longer felt like a successful young executive. She frequented a safe bar in the neighborhood, made friends with the bartender (for just-in-case protection, as her mother had advised her), and over time enjoyed a joking relationship with him. After some time, a man named Thomas Allen introduced himself to her. He was a bail bondsman and divorced, and he clearly wanted to know Maya better.

Angelou's friends in the Writers Guild were not impressed with the news that Allen was a bail bondsman, but Maya announced that she was going to marry him (he had not yet proposed). She felt ready for a significant life change and was again entertaining thoughts of a quiet, secure life as a homemaker. Later, she told Allen that she wanted to marry, and he agreed. Guy had no special regard for Allen, but he accepted the news "gravely" (717), commenting that he guessed they would have to move again. Allen gave Angelou an engagement ring and told her that in three months they would marry in Virginia, where his parents had been wed. Then they would drive to Florida, where he could fish in the Gulf of Mexico, and Guy would stay with his family. Maya ignored the authoritarian warning signals.

Chapter 8

Because of her work, Maya missed a lecture that Vusumzi Make presented in Harlem. The South African freedom fighter had come to the United

States to petition the United Nations against his country's racial policies. Maya asked her friend Hazel, one of the workers at the SCLC office, to take notes to share with her on Monday. Hazel then reported that Make's speech was even more eloquent than his previous presentation, which she had heard. He talked about both the black American struggle and South African colonialism. He knew the history of both well and stated that he "had found the oppressor to be a formidable but opposable foe" (721).

On Thursday morning, John Killens phoned and invited Maya to meet Make and his traveling companion, OLIVER TAMBO, at their home on Friday night. He told her that Make was the representative of the Pan-African Congress and Tambo was the head of the African National Congress. Though the two were different politically, they were compatible. Maya said she would try to be there, and the next morning she told Guy that he should go to the Killenses for dinner and she would meet him there later. When Angelou arrived at the Killens' home, Guy was in the kitchen. He had already met the guests and expressed excitement about Make's brilliance. John Killens introduced her to Tambo and then to Make, calling them South African warriors.

When Make spoke to the group, it was with passion about the influence of Martin Luther King, Jr., and the SCLC, saying they had been encouraged by Malcolm X and the Muslims to "set themselves apart from their oppressors" (721). Maya asked if the problems of South Africa could be solved with nonviolence, and he suggested that what worked in the United States could not have the same success in Africa. After his talk, Make offered to walk Guy and his mother home, but Guy courteously answered that he was seeing his mother home, and they left. Guy told his mother that obviously Mr. Make did not know she was engaged.

The next morning, the author PAULE MARSHALL called and invited Angelou to a party that night, explaining that Tambo and Make would be there. Maya decided against it and went home after work, but she soon began to think about the party; within 30 minutes, she was there. Make made no further moves toward her, and after listening to the two men speak again, Maya called a cab and went home.

The American Society for African Culture had its annual formal ball on a Saturday night in midtown New York. Thomas Allen was working, so Maya met Rosa Guy and her escort in Manhattan, and they attended together. A table was reserved for the SCLC, and Make made his way to where she was seated and asked her to dance. With overt admiration, he announced that he was going to take her to Africa. She told Make that she was engaged and went home early to call her fiancé. He was tired but planned to take her to the movies the next night, and on that date, Maya realized sadly that Thomas had little interest in the very issues that were most important to her.

Maya returned to work on Monday and through the following days received bouquets of mixed flowers and vases of red roses, all accompanied by notes from Vusumzi Make. The same week, Thomas sent more wedding gifts. Vusumzi kept asking her to lunch, and Thomas kept asking her to visit his apartment; she refused both. She was stressed and not sure of her direction.

Chapter 9

On Thursday, Maya agreed to have lunch with Vusumzi, and they met at Wells Restaurant, one of the finest dining places in Harlem. He had told Paule Marshall by telephone that his plan was to marry Maya and take her to Africa. At the restaurant, after sharing some of his history and personal experiences, he proposed to Maya, who excused herself to go to the restroom and began to cry. She rolled the elements of her situation over in her mind and impulsively decided to accept Vusumzi's offer, then called Abbey Lincoln on the phone and asked her to stand by. When she returned to the table, she accepted the proposal. Vusumzi claimed an engagement kiss, and Maya calmly went back to work for the rest of the day.

That evening, they had dinner at Max Roach and Abbey Lincoln's home, and afterward Maya told Vusumzi that she would break off with Thomas Allen immediately. When she was ready to leave, he put her in a taxi for Brooklyn. When she got home, she had to face Guy's anger because he did not know where she had been and neither did any of her friends. She knew that was unfair to Guy when she expected always to know where he was, and again, she was frustrated by inadvertently hurting him again.

Maya broke off with Thomas the next day, and though he took the news calmly, she was sure he would never want to see her again. She let the men at the SCLC and John Killens know of her decision. She still needed to inform Guy, but Vusumzi—called Vus for short—had said he wanted to be the one to tell him. That evening, Abbey and Max had a performance, so Vus prepared dinner for Maya at their apartment. He told her about the "lights and shadows" of Africa, led her into the guest bedroom, and gave her a gift of beautiful amber beads. Maya accepted him and wearing the beads was "made beautiful for her chief" (742). The next evening, Vus came to their home for dinner, and shortly after the meal, he asked Guy if he could speak to him in his room. Maya cleaned up the kitchen while they talked, and at last, the two of them emerged, smiling. Guy congratulated his mother, and they spent the remainder of the evening making happy plans. After Vus left, Guy told his mother that Thomas really did not love her, but that Vus respected her, "and maybe for an African, that's better than love" (746).

Friends arranged parties and dinners for the two of them, Guy took up lodgings at a friend's home in Brooklyn, and Maya and Vus left for England. On the plane, he suggested that they be married in Oxford, but Maya said that she wanted to wait until her mother and son could be present at the wedding. He agreed and said that in England they would say they were married in America, and in America, they would say they were married in England. Marriage was never mentioned again.

Chapter 10

Vus and Maya stayed in an apartment near Finsbury Park in London while he attended the conference. The conference was to last two weeks with the purpose of creating a charter for a strong, peace-making south and southwest African organization for freedom fighters. Soon, Oliver Tambo's wife invited Maya and several other guests to the house in Maida Vale where the Tambos were staying. The African women invited to the party were beautiful, interesting, and intelligent. One of the women said that she found it quite stupid to be holding a conference about colonialism's foot on Africa's neck in London, the heart of colonialism. She quoted an African saying, "Only a fool asks a leopard to look after a lamb" (748). Other women spoke with purpose and shared some of their stories as fighters in their homeland. Tales were told of African women from every level of society who had outwitted the British, French, or BOERS, and Angelou told the story of HARRIET TUBMAN, a small, black woman nicknamed "Moses" who led many slaves out of the South to freedom in the North. She also told the story of SOJOURNER TRUTH, who spoke powerfully to an equal rights meeting in 1851. Truth was accused of being a man by one of the white men in the hall, and after soundly speaking history and truth to the audience, she bared her huge bosom and said, "And ain't I a woman?" After the story, the African women stood up crying, stamping their feet, and applauding this sister from an earlier century. They agreed to carry the stories back to their native lands.

After the London conference, Vus had to go to Cairo, and he gave Maya money to find an apartment in New York City with instructions to furnish it well. When she returned, both Guy and the Harlem Writers were fascinated by the tales she shared about London and the African women. She prepared the apartment for Vus's return, and she helped Guy adjust to his new school. Vus came home after about a month and told Guy and his mother that they would soon be living in Cairo.

Vus was unhappy with Maya's furniture choices. He had extravagant tastes and also let Maya know that her role as his "wife" was to be a gourmet cook and an absolutely perfect housekeeper. Angelou was disappointed and uncomfortable with the arrangement, but her friend Abbey offered little sympathy and even said, "A man's supposed to be in charge. That's the order of nature" (755). Before long, Vus left for a conference in India.

Chapter 11

The CULTURAL ASSOCIATION FOR WOMEN OF AFRICAN HERITAGE (CAWAH), an organization Maya had helped create, drew up a charter with the purpose of raising money for any gathering or group genuinely engaged in developing a just society. Arrangements were being made for a huge African-themed fashion show when Rosa Guy told Maya that Patrice Lumumba, a radical African leader the American blacks supported, had just been assassinated. An announcement of the tragedy was to be made public in a few days by Adlai Stevenson, the U.S. delegate at the United Nations. The two women were in Harlem, and they were soon drawn to a corner where the Nation of Islam was having a mass meeting. Malcolm X stood by a microphone and clearly expressed his "love and understanding of black folks and his loathing of whites and their cruelty" (758).

For Rosa and Maya, the talk contained the truths they believed, and they felt they had to do something. They called the members of CAWAH together to brainstorm and decided to attend the general session of the United Nations where Stevenson was to make the announcement about Lumumba's death. Their idea was that when Stevenson began to speak, they would stand with their faces covered with black mourning veils. They informed the Harlem community of their plan.

A huge crowd from Harlem showed up for the announcement, and though it was quiet for a moment, the observers interrupted Stevenson's first word. There was a sudden scream, which was followed by shouts of "Murderers," "Lumumba, Lumumba," "Killers," and more. The houselights came on, and security guards rushed in at the upper and lower levels. Blacks and whites were exchanging insults, and there was a near riot. Mounted police outside the building rode through the crowd to restore some sort of order. Finally, the crowds dispersed and people went home. Rosa and Maya had dinner together that night. Afterward, they watched the demonstration on television and learned that the unrest in Harlem was now public knowledge. Rosa and Maya decided that the next step was to contact the Black Muslims.

The appointment with Malcolm X was easy to make, but his words were not what they expected. He was not supportive. He told them that Muslims do not demonstrate and warned that, like Peter in the Christian Bible, black leaders would deny their work that very evening. As it turned out, he was right. That evening, on radio, television, and in the newspapers, conservative black leaders stated: "That ugly demonstration was carried out by an irresponsible element and does not reflect the mood of the larger black community" (781).

Chapter 12

Vus returned from the conference in India. Angelou writes that at this time, Guy was connected primarily to the refrigerator and the telephone. She realized that she had not engaged in real conversation with anyone for some time. Max Roach invited her over to read a script with Abbey, and when she arrived, she heard musicians tuning up beside their piano. The script was for JEAN GENET's play *The BLACKS*, an Off-Broadway production. Abbey and Maya read the unfamiliar play with the producer, Sidney Bernstein, listening. Maya did not understand the script's theme and message, which was that no matter who was in power, black or white, the dominant group would be oppressive, arrogant, and greedy. She strongly disagreed with that theory, and Max became impatient with her.

A few days later, Maya was called and invited to be in the play, but she declined. Abbey had accepted the invitation to be in it, and she thought Max should talk to Vus about Maya's refusal. Vus agreed to read it, and after examining the script, he felt that she should be a part of it because of its important message. Maya agreed to read for the director and was cast in the role of the White Queen. There were many well-known black actors and actresses in the cast, including Godfrey Cambridge, JAMES EARL JONES, and CICELY TYSON. Rehearsals began, and the "white" roles were played by actors wearing exaggerated masks and performing from a high platform above the stage. On the morning of opening night, Gene Frankel, the director, informed the cast that Max Roach and Abbey Lincoln had dropped out; consequently, there was no music for the play. There was an understudy for Abbey's part, but there was no music. Quickly, Maya went outside to a telephone and called Max for permission to write the needed tunes. Max did not care and assured her that there would be no hard feelings, so Maya and Ethel Ayler, an understudy who had musical training and had been in *Porgy and Bess* with her, put together the two songs within an hour. The play was a success for both black and white audiences, but Maya questioned why people enjoyed it. The message was clear, and still they came.

Chapter 13

Vus was carelessly leaving telltale evidence of his infidelity where Maya could not avoid finding it. Women's makeup was often on his clothes, so she confronted him. He denied doing anything wrong by saying that she was his wife and that was all she needed to know. Guy and Vus had built a good rapport, and though Maya was hurt and frustrated, she washed away the makeup stains and tried to accept the situation.

The play continued, and Maya began to go to the theater early and return home with reluctance. One evening, she received a peculiar phone call from a man who said that Vusumzi would never return home again. That was all that was said. She told Vus about the call, and he responded coldly that their phone number would have to be changed. He then said that he was surprised it had taken so long for the call to come. It happened a second time a few weeks later, and Vus explained that people representing the South African police often called wives of freedom fighters and told them frightening lies about their husbands or children.

Ethel Ayler accepted a role in a new Broadway play and planned to leave *The Blacks,* but she and Maya had never been compensated for the songs they had written. They approached Sidney Bernstein and asked to be paid for their compositions, but he said that they really had not composed anything. At that point, both women were furious. Ethel left, and Maya met Vus and James Baldwin, who were waiting for her. She told them what had happened, and Vus said that she would never return to that theater. Angelou explained that as a member of the theatrical union, she could not just quit, but Baldwin told her that Vus understood the episode exactly. Vus went to the nearest Western Union office and sent a message that said: "Mrs. Maya Angelou Make will not be returning to *The Blacks* or the St. Mark's Playhouse. She resists the exploitation of herself and her people. She has closed. Signed, Vusumzi Linda Make, Pan African Congress, Johannesburg, South Africa. Currently Petitioner at United Nations" (807). He then said that would be the last of that unless Bernstein wanted an international incident.

Chapter 14

Black and white activism was increasing in the United States. Among others, RALPH BUNCHE, the U.S. ambassador to the United Nations and Nobel Prize winner for his work as a mediator and negotiator for the Palestine conflict, spoke out when his son was denied membership in an all-white tennis club. Bunche said, "I know now that until the lowliest Negro sharecropper in the South is free, I am not free" (809). Guy was busy with school, Vus was traveling in Africa, and Maya was left at home, isolated. She even withdrew from the Harlem Writers Guild.

After Vus returned from Africa, he and Maya attended a dinner dance at the Waldorf Astoria Hotel. He did not stay with her, and no one else made her feel welcome either, so she drank alone and too much as she watched Vus flirt with other women. Realizing that she needed to eat, she went to the kitchen. Rather than food, a woman there produced a bottle of gin from her purse and Angelou drank more. Vus burst through the door, and the steam in the room clouding around him reminded Angelou of "Aladdin's Djinn, only bigger" (812). She began to laugh, reflecting that the cook's gin bottle was the lamp she had been rubbing. Vus was angry and left abruptly.

Maya finally left the kitchen and headed to the elevator, where Vus gave her a scolding, but she just kept laughing. They entered the elevator together, and when they reached the main floor, Vus tried to restrain her, but she dodged him and ran around the plush Waldorf Astoria lobby, sidestepping several people. He was yelling, and she was running. Finally, she dove into the revolving door, then heard a thud: Vus, the clerk, and a policeman had hit the door at the same time and tumbled into a heap. Maya grabbed a cab and went to Rosa Guy's home, where they laughed together. The next morning, Vus came to Rosa's with perfume for Maya and flowers for Rosa. They never again mentioned his flirtation that night or her display in the lobby.

Vus had not been paying the rent for their apartment, and they were evicted. He found a dingy furnished apartment, and the three of them moved into it immediately. Maya and Guy lived there for about three weeks, and during that time Vus went to Egypt to prepare a place for them there. Before leaving for Cairo, Maya and Guy went to San Francisco to see her mother. Vivian met them when they arrived, but she was not the source of strength Maya had hoped she would be. Her new husband was a heavy drinker, and she needed comforting herself. It was disconcerting for Guy to see the two women's roles reversed. A short time later, Vus called to tell them their tickets were waiting for them at a nearby travel agency. At last, Angelou and Guy were heading to Egypt.

Chapter 15

Mother and son arrived in Cairo on a beautiful and clear afternoon, but Vus was not at the airport to meet them. They did not have his address and felt understandably frustrated. Finally, two black men in Western suits approached them, introduced themselves, and explained that they were to pick them up and take them to Vus's office. They made their way through crowded streets of shiny European cars; large cows with horns; wild taxies; and dense throngs of pedestrians, goats, mules, camels, and children. They finally reached a whitewashed office building, and the men left promptly after unloading their luggage in the library. After a while, Vus came through the open doors, shouted, and hugged them both. He told them that their apartment was across the street, and their luggage would be brought to them.

At the end of a corridor in the opposite building, Vus unlocked a large carved door and led them into a luxurious apartment furnished with the very best of everything, including tapestries, antique Oriental carpets, and antique French furniture. Unfortunately, the kitchen was almost nothing. There was a lamplike Sterno stove but little else. Maya was uncomfortable with all of it and let her feelings be known, but soon she joined Vus and Guy on the balcony (overlooking their private garden) and said, "This is the most gorgeous house I've ever seen" (825). The moment had passed, and things were all right again.

Angelou hired a cook-housekeeper who knew how to manage COOKING with the little Sterno lamp. Guy went to the American College at Mahdi, 15 miles out of Cairo by bus, where he did well in his high school studies. He was learning and happy, and the two of them engaged in a contest to see who could learn the most Arabic words with the least accent. Vus soon introduced her to the American David DuBois, who was the adopted son of W. E. B. DUBOIS and a journalist in Cairo. It was refreshing for both DuBois and Angelou to hear the other's American cadence. There were many cocktail parties at the Make home, and DuBois attended occasionally. He and Maya would sometimes find a quiet space where they could talk about the folks back home. Sometimes they sang black American SPIRITUALS for the guests, and David always started with his favorite, "Glory, Glory, Hallelujah, When I Lay My Burden Down" (829).

Chapter 16

One summer afternoon, Omanadia, the housemaid, spoke to Maya about the household finances and told her that payments on the house furnishings had not been made for two months. She pressed the woman for more information and learned that the rent was also two months in arrears. Maya realized that she needed to find a job, immediately. She called David DuBois and told him that she had an emergency. He met her at a downtown tearoom, and she reluctantly told him the story. Two days later, he took her to Dr. Zen Nagati, the founder of a magazine called the *Arab Observer*. David told Dr. Nagati that Maya was an American journalist married to a freedom fighter, and that she was also an experienced administrator. Dr. Nagati offered her a position as an associate editor, reached for her hand, and told her that she could begin on the following Monday.

David then showed Maya where his office was located on another floor in the same building. She knew Vus would be against her working, but they needed the money. Guy came home and gave her another notice for school fees. Vus returned a few days later, and Angelou told him of her intention to work. He talked about the slim chances of her working in Egypt, and she countered with the truth about the overdue bills. He repeated that she could never find a job in Cairo, and when she told him she already had one, the expression on his face turned to rage. As he vilified her verbally in every way he could, Maya realized that she no longer loved him. After a while, he told her she would have to refuse the job, and she explained that she had already given her word. Later that same afternoon, David arrived and assured Vus that Angelou had taken the job to relieve some of Vus's burdens, and that her job also demonstrated Vus's revolutionary attitudes by allowing his wife to work. David's persuasiveness was successful, and the African mellowed.

There were cultural protocols to be honored. Vus accompanied Maya to the office the next day, and David met them. He greeted Vus first and then introduced him to the men in the office before introducing Maya. This was the correct form. Vus and David left, and Maya waited at her desk. After a while, Dr. Nagati arrived and explained the responsibilities of each of the men in the office. Then he took her to the lower floor of the building where the paper was printed and introduced her to the typesetters. He reminded her that all of the men were capable but had never worked with women before except, perhaps, secretaries. He assured her that she would do well, and then he left.

Maya returned to her desk and pondered the reality that she did not know enough. Then two of the reporters came to her and suggested that her desk be placed in the library, where there were hundreds of books in English. Maya was relieved and delighted. She remembered the old story of JOEL CHANDLER HARRIS's BRER RABBIT and the TAR BABY, reissued in JAMES MASON BREWER'S collection called *American Negro Folklore* (1968). Brer Rabbit told his captor that the worst thing that could be done to him, even worse than boiling and skinning and eating him, would be to throw him into the briar patch. He protested and pretended that the briar patch would be a terrible fate for him, and because of all that protest, that is just what the captor did. Brer Rabbit was tossed into the briar patch, and the twist was that the briar patch was where he was born. It was home.

From earliest childhood, books had been Maya's companions, and she had raised Guy the same way. After her desk had been pushed and shoved into the library, she looked over the crowded bookshelves with their unfamiliar titles and authors and reflected happily that she still felt "just like Brer Rabbit in the briar patch" (842).

Chapter 17

Maya spent the first two weeks of her job studying in the library using every free moment to learn about journalism, writing about Africa, printing, publishing, and editing. Her work was accepted, and she was at the *Arab Observer* for over a year. Vus was still indulging in other romantic interests, and his work in helping South African escapees was escalating. Maya had cultivated the friendship of two African women, A. B. (Banti) Williamson and Kebidetch Erdatchew Mesfin; they were both wives of diplomats. Banti was the wife of Joe Williamson, the Liberian chargé d'affaires, and Kebidetch was the wife of Jarra Mesfin, the Ethiopian Embassy's First Secretary and also a son of the royal Selassie House.

It was hard to make friends among the Egyptian women because Maya's background was so different, but even so she was able to enjoy many warm acquaintances and a few confidants. Hanifa Fathy, a poet and the wife of a judge, admired Maya's work and invited her to meet some female Egyptian writers, scholars, and teachers. Hanifa was fun and clever, and they often spent afternoons together sitting outside on the Cairo country club veranda. Life was good for a while, but there was never enough money.

Banti Williamson gave a women-only birthday party in honor of a well-known female Liberian doctor. It was a beautiful event, and as the party progressed, individual women from different parts of Africa danced native dances. Maya performed the twist and the swim and received laughter and approving applause. The party was nearly over when a beautiful young woman in West African national dress took the floor and began to dance. Her name was Mendinah, and she was from northern Nigeria. Her body was beautiful, and her dance was a sly, sexy style, complete with flutters and vibrations. The women enjoyed her performance, and afterward she explained that she was an unmarried girl with a good dowry and had come to Cairo to study Arabic.

Chapter 18

David DuBois found that Maya could write commentary for Radio Egypt for four pounds a review, and she could earn an extra amount for each broadcast she narrated herself. Guy was getting acceptable grades, and Vus was still traveling. Maya finally had some friends, and the latest gossip among the African diplomatic corps was that Mendinah, the dancer, was morally loose. She had propositioned several ambassadors, and they had reported to their wives. Of course, Vus was not immune to her charms.

One evening, an Egyptian woman acquaintance of Maya's African friends gave a party. Banti, Kebi, and seven other ladies were already there; Maya and Vus joined them. They were talking when Mendinah interrupted and said that Mr. Make had been trying to reach Maya all day, adding that he was looking for someone to help her at the office. Maya was incensed but, strengthened by the presence of her friends, told Mendinah that the job had been filled. Furthermore, she said (among other stronger words), "you would never do" (852). She was shaken afterward, but the women told her that she had handled it well. They were warm and consoling, and her friend Banti leaned forward and said in her charming Liberian country accent, "Old man say, 'If you mess with Jesus Christ, god will make you shit'" (852). Maya smiled and nodded and then walked toward Vus. She casually asked if he knew the girl playing records. He looked at Mendinah and said that he did not know her. She knew that was a lie and walked away from him. After they arrived at home, Vus asked her to join him in the living room for a talk. Maya finally had the courage to tell him that she no longer loved him, and he said he felt the same way but that he knew they had admiration and mutual respect for each other. She then asked him about Mendinah, and he said "Women like that are only good for one, almost two experiences" (2004, 851). At that, Maya finally told him that she was going to leave him.

The next day, she received an unexpected call from Banti, who invited Maya to join her and her husband around nine o'clock after dinner that night. When Maya stepped into Banti's living room, she saw about 20 people sitting in a half-circle of chairs. Kebi, Jarra, and Banti were together, and no one smiled. She was shown to a seat beside Vus. Joe Williamson explained that a palaver [a conference or a discussion] had been called. One side of the room was to argue for "our sister, Maya, and this side for our brother, Vus" (858). Both Vus and Angelou were asked many questions. It was decided that she was in the right, but at the close of the meeting, she was asked if she would give the relationship another six-month trial. She agreed to that, and then Joe Williamson announced that it was time to celebrate their reunion.

Chapter 19

There was tension in Maya's office because of the conflict between President John F. Kennedy and the Soviet premier Nikita Khrushchev over the independence of Cuba. She was an American, she smoked, she was not a Muslim, and the office staff somehow made her feel responsible for the tense political situation. By this time, Guy had graduated from high school and was on a trek in the Sahara with Egyptian friends. Vus and Maya were trying to make it through the trial period, but the stress had caused him to gain weight and her to lose weight. Banti and Kebi were constant friends and would often send crates of liquor and food to her apartment with notes saying they had over-ordered. At last, Angelou went to Joe Williamson and said that she was ready to leave. She wanted Guy to go to the University of Ghana, and she needed a job. It had been five months, but there was no sense in pushing the failed trial any further. Williamson told her that there was a job for her in the Liberian Department of Information, and that she would be an asset to Liberia. Vus did not resist the decision and said he would get tickets for Guy and Maya on United Arab Airlines. He also knew people in Ghana where she could stay for a few days.

Once good-byes were over and Guy and his mother were finally on the plane, Maya became reflective and emotional. Crossing over the vast Sahara, she looked down from the plane window and watched the changing land. Her reflections led her to think about the suffering of the many people who lived there both presently and in the distant past. She thought about the victims of slavery long ago, and then images of black lynchings in the southern United States began to run through her imagination. Guy quietly took care of her while she wept. She could not talk or explain it, but the warm tears of sorrow lasted a long time as she mourned for her ancestors.

The airport at Accra was amazing to both of them because everyone was black and for the most part very well-dressed. Maya thought her TOBY, (the southern black word for a lucky talisman) had led her right (865). A taxi took them to the home of Vus's acquaintance Walter Nthia, and he told them that he was divorced and lived alone, and they could stay as long as they liked. He had invited five guests to meet them: Richard, a tall thin Yoruba man and his Canadian wife, Ellen; a South African man with an unpronounceable name; and three black Americans named Frank, Vickie Garvey, and Alice Windom. They discussed Egypt and politics, and spoke of KWAME NKRUMAH, the president of Ghana, and said that he was a "man pass man. Iron cut iron" (867). Guy spoke up and said, "He is a man who surpasses other men. An iron so strong that it cuts iron" (867). Richard and Ellen invited both of them to a picnic in two days. Maya declined, but Guy expressed his wish to go.

The next day, Maya visited the Mayfields, people she had known in New York. JULIAN MAYFIELD was handsome, and his wife, Anna Livia Cordero Mayfield, was a petite and opinionated Puerto Rican physician. Julian assured her that he would keep an eye on Guy while she was in Liberia. Her new American acquaintance, Frank, returned her to Walter's home, and she and Guy said good night.

The next day, Guy was badly injured in a car accident on the way home from the picnic. Richard had become drunk at the picnic, and Guy was driving back for him. The car stalled, and when he got out of the car, he was hit by a truck. At home, Maya was beginning to worry because they had not returned and it was getting late. She finally heard a car on the driveway, and a bloody Ellen explained that Guy was alive but injured and in Korle Bu Hospital. She found Guy caked with blood and unconscious. X-rays were taken to determine if any bones were broken, and he also seemed to be in a coma. When Maya returned the next day, Guy was awake and recognized her. He had been pulled from the wreckage and was left by the side of the road when an old couple happened by, found him, and drove him to the hospital. His diagnosis was a broken arm, broken leg, and possible internal injuries.

After spending the day in Guy's hospital room, Maya went to the Mayfields' house. When Anna Livia opened the door, Maya collapsed into her arms in hysterics. The tiny doctor said she would make a visit to Guy that evening. Soon Anna Livia called Maya and told her that Guy's neck was broken in three places. He was to be put in a body, arm, and leg cast and to be moved to the military hospital as soon as the cast had hardened. He would receive the best care there, and Anna Livia would be able keep an eye on him. Maya went to the hospital and reflected that her beloved son looked like a "pale-yellow angel in a long white gown" (874).

Chapter 20

During the time Guy was healing, Julian Mayfield introduced Maya to Efuah Sutherland, a poet, playwright, and head of Ghana's theater. He knew Efuah had many connections and could help Maya find work. After talking to Maya, Efuah arranged for a meeting with Professor J. H. Nketia, an ethnomusicologist and head of the Institute of African Studies. The process moved quickly, and soon Maya had a job at the University of Ghana as an administrative assistant in the music and drama department. She was delighted with the position, its connection to the arts, and the talented people she knew she would meet. It placed her on the university campus, and she was able to gain both an academic and insider's view of professional attitudes and perspectives there. This was the school where her son would receive his university education, and though the job she was given did not pay very well, it met her needs. Arrangements had been made for her to stay in the home of an instructor who was on a six-month leave, so she had a kitchen to use. Guy was released from the hospital, and they celebrated his homecoming with roast chicken and dressing, their favorite foods.

Circumventing red tape and the British university admissions system, Guy applied to the University of Ghana. Dr. O'Brien, vice chancellor of the university, assured Maya that he had read Guy's admission exam and said that it was excellent. Guy had been reading O'Brien's book *To Katanga and Back* (1962) and was well prepared for the questions. His registration papers were approved, and permission to enter the university was granted. O'Brien even said, "We want minds like that in the university" (878). Soon Guy was well and ready to move into one of the campus dorms with his friends. He assured his mother that he was prepared and ready to make the changes, and after wrapping his arms around her, he said, "I love you, Mom. Maybe now you'll have a chance to grow up" (878). After he left, Maya closed the door thinking that great waves of emotion would hit her. They did not. Rather, she thought, "At last, I'll be able to eat the whole breast of a roast chicken by myself" (878).

CRITICAL COMMENTARY

The effort to find an appropriate language in which to tell the story of one's life has always been a concern in the black autobiographical tradition. Many writers have switched between a standard "white" voice and a voice more specific to the African-American community. Maya Angelou carefully and intelligently shares the voice of her people in *The Heart of a Woman,* her fourth autobiography, in a language all readers can understand. She mainly uses standard prose, and yet African-American vernacular is apparent throughout. To both devoted Angelou readers and newcomers to her work, her autobiographical serials have exposed and explained many elements of black tradition. Angelou has shared her experiences with family solidarity, community optimism and humor, continuity of purpose, and triumph over suffering. In doing so, she has provided her readership a window that reveals an enduring culture.

Angelou has command of the language and of herself in this text, and by this time her writing demonstrates a powerful maturity. She is telling her story, but she is also telling the story of her people, their community, their hopes, and their disappointments from an insider's point of view. This autobiography is set during the years of 1957–62, when political upheaval in the United States over discrimination against African Americans was at a peak. Contrived boundaries that held black Americans back from full participation in education and other areas had begun to crumble. The integration of Schools in Little Rock, Arkansas, after the Supreme Court decision in *Brown v. Board of Education of Topeka, Kansas,* the entry of blacks into professional sports, voting rights for all citizens, open restaurants, and other advances were finally occurring, and people committed to eliminating the restrictions of JIM CROW laws were dying in the cause of freedom, not only for black Americans but for all people in the United States. It was also a time of upheaval against colonialism in Africa, and Angelou was often in the midst of civil rights activities in New York, Egypt, and Ghana.

Angelou's prose moves quickly, taking the reader into the heart of her experiences, and at times she leaves the reader wanting more when the story comes to a close. Her characters and the narratives are realistic and engaging. She has had to adapt to difficult situations creatively, and she conveys this to her readers. Mary Ann Lupton has written the following about Angelou's work: "Like an unfinished painting, the autobiographical series is an ongoing creation, in a form that rejects the finality of a restricting frame. Its continuity is achieved through characters who enter the picture, leave, and reappear, and through certain interlaced themes—self-acceptance, race, men, work, separation, sexuality, motherhood" (172). Of *The Heart of a Woman,* the critic Eleanor Traylor writes: "This book is alive. It breathes as it pilots, pivots, taxies, and flies the lucky reader though a journey from San Francisco through New York to Egypt, landing in Accra in Ghana, West Africa" (91).

In 1965, Angelou left San Francisco to try her hand at writing. The Harlem Writers Guild listened to her early works, and though she initially resisted their critiques, she ultimately accepted them and let the professionals teach her. She was friends with other writers, including Lorraine Hansberry, James Baldwin, John Killens, and Paule Marshall, and she could see that they were making serious contributions in the movement toward reaching equality for African Americans.

For some time in New York, Angelou earned her living as a performer and entertainer, but then she turned away from that to participate in the Civil Rights movement. Caring for Guy, looking for a companion, writing and studying, and becoming more and more active in the work of equal rights, she assisted with putting on a benefit show for the Southern Christian Leadership Conference (SCLC), and as a consequence of that success, she became the organization's New York office coordinator. She found a man, a bondsman, and he was the person she dreamed would give her the quiet life and stability she thought she wanted for Guy and herself. But she soon met someone else. Though engaged to Thomas Allen and having accepted many gifts from him (though she suspected they were stolen), she then broke the engagement and compulsively accepted a romantic proposal of marriage from a dark African stranger. The book moves quickly as Angelou leaves the familiar United States behind, packs up her son and herself, and embarks on new life in Cairo, Egypt.

It was a culture she did not know because of the generations removed, but like many African Americans, she hoped to find a sense of home there. She also dreamed of having a glimpse of long-buried roots. In spite of what she did not know, she moved forward and never floundered. In this fascinating and fast-moving narrative, Angelou shares her experiences, her heartbreak, her successes, and her failures, and with clarity she draws her readers into what is for many an unfamiliar world. She describes the leaders she met, their homes, their conversations, and their dreams in straightforward prose, providing insight into values and cultural mores little known in the United States.

The Heart of a Woman moves quickly across a variety of events. Angelou was consistently engaged with issues concerning civil rights. Her quasi-marriage with an African freedom fighter, Vusumzi Make (Vus), was in part because she supported what he was trying to do for the people of South Africa. When Congo's leader Patrice Lumumba was assassinated, she became personally involved in an angry response with others at the United Nations, hoping to demonstrate African-American awareness of the significance of that tragedy. Her understanding and commitment to the American Civil Rights movement remained steady and focused even while she was in Africa. (She continued her interest and support when she returned to the United States four years later.)

Angelou recognized that she wanted to make a more valuable and lasting contribution than entertainment; as Sondra O'Neale writes: "Her own experiential development as traced thus far in the latest work, *The Heart of a Woman,* teaches that no option—marriage, entertainment, any dependent existence—is as much a lasting or consummate reservoir" (48). Of her new direction, Angelou writes: "I made the decision to quit show business. Give up the skin-tight dresses and manufactured smiles. The false concern over sentimental lyrics. I would never again work to make people smile inanely and would take on the responsibility of making them think" (662–663).

When she and her son flew from the United States to Cairo, Egypt, Angelou found echoes of her heritage but also soon discovered that her "marriage" to Vus was in many ways a repeat of her earlier marriage with ENISTASIOUS "TOSH" ANGELOS. Though the current relationship was not legally binding, she tried her best to make it work, but soon she realized, even before leaving the United States, that Vus Make was not a faithful partner. She felt deceived, oppressed, and somewhat trapped but hoped things would be better in Africa. The distrust and betrayals did not stop, and his expectations of her as a wife, cook, and hostess were high and demanding. He was behind on their rent and various other payments both in New York and Cairo, and he did not bother to tell her. Angelou found work through a friend and became a writer for the *Arab Observer* in Cairo in order to keep Guy in school and pay their debts. The liaison with Vus eventually ended, but not without a community palaver (conference). All of these experiences are recreated skillfully and realistically in the narrative.

Angelou's ability to survive negative experiences without losing confidence or hope in the future comes through with particular power in this volume. Her friend and biographer DOLLY MCPHERSON's discussion of this element of Angelou's personality includes a psychological explanation for Maya's ability to leave the past behind and maintain hope for the future: "When an individual can live with his or her past without being bogged down by it, the individual remains adaptable, but more importantly, capable of continued growth" (80). As Angelou relates her experiences, evidence of her survival of devastating pain and disappointment resonates. Though these kinds of experiences may have defeated a lesser personality, they did not defeat her, and that is an analogy for the survival of the spirit of black Americans. Part of her purpose in publishing her story was to help others know that they also can survive such trauma. As she matured over the various periods described in this and the previous autobiographies, the reader observes the emergence of a confident and talented but still humble and teachable woman.

When Angelou published *The Heart of a Woman* in 1981, the United States was still reverberating with the power, passion, and consequences of the Civil Rights movement. In the book, she describes the change that seemed to be everywhere in the 1960s:

> One hundred and twenty-fifth street was to Harlem what the Mississippi was to the South, a long traveling river always going somewhere, carrying something. A furniture store offering sofas and fake leopard-skin chairs shouldered Mr. Micheaux's book shop, which prided itself on having or being able to get a copy of any book written by a black person since 1900. . . . Black men and women had begun to wear multicolored African prints. They moved through Harlem like bright sails on a dark sea. (664)

In another strong passage representing the dynamic spirit of the time, Angelou writes:

> The spirit in Harlem was new and old and dynamic. Black children and white children thronged the streets, en route to protest marches or to liberation offices, where they did small but important chores. Black Nationalists spoke on street corners, demanding freedom now. Black Muslims charged the white community with genocide and insisted on immediate and total segregation from the murdering blue-eyed devils. . . . The *Amsterdam News* was vigilant in its weekly attack against the "forces of evil," and G. Norwood, one of its social and political columnists, kept the community informed on who was doing what, to whom and with how much success. (710)

Coupled with those many protests were societal changes evolving through the rise of feminist voices. Raised public consciousness among all classes in the United States finally triggered the beginning of long-awaited change and redress for African Americans, for other minorities, and for women. Sondra O'Neale reminds readers that both men and women led the drive to equality: "Black progress has been attained in this country not only because of the leadership of Black men but also because of the unsung spirit of noncompliant Black women. This is the revelation she [Angelou] intends the careful portrayals of major women in her life to celebrate" (1999, 47). Angelou painted character portraits of her mother and grandmother throughout all of her serial autobiographies, and their voices echoed in her mind over and over again, teaching, reminding, and warning. In maintaining their presence throughout the works, she represents herself and black women in general as strong, adaptable, and enduring.

As a single black mother, Angelou's issues and challenges were embedded in both the African-American and feminist movements, and in *The Heart of a Woman,* she demonstrates her grace under fire. The book reveals her developing skill as an autobiographical writer who has learned to skillfully use narrative description and allusion. She frequently uses the voice of black oral tradition in her prose, and her narrative is laced with folkloric references and subtle connotations as well as a variety of literary devices. She again draws from the metaphor of a caged bird for the title of this fourth autobiography because in the relationship she had with Make, she found herself trapped and blocked from the freedom she had known before meeting him. Georgia Douglas Johnson's poem "The Heart of a Woman" contains the same metaphocial imagery as PAUL LAURENCE DUNBAR's "Sympathy," as in her second stanza: "The heart of a woman goes forth with the dawn / . . . The heart of a woman falls back with the night, / And enters some alien cage in its plight" (Johnson 1996, 971). The woman in the poem tries to forget past dreams.

Though Angelou was no longer planning to pursue a theatrical career, she was invited to perform in Jean Genet's play *The Blacks* at St. Mark's Theater off Broadway. She did not like the play at first because it represented blacks as displaying the same lust for power and control as whites if they were given the opportunity. However, Vus, with whom she and Guy were living, read the play and encouraged her to take part in it. It was a statement about human foible, and Angelou used her role as the White Queen to jeer and make fun of the whites who she felt had been unfair to her over time. She assumed a haughty attitude and thoroughly enjoyed the role. The play was a success, and Angelou had an opportunity to work with some of the leading black actors and actresses in the United States. She left the cast over a disagreement with the producer concerning payment for music she and another actress, Ethel Ayler, had written for the play. She was wary of breaking her contract, but Vus supported her, and there were no negative consequences.

Angelou's ability to dramatize her narratives with metaphors and allusions enhances her autobiographies, and her ability to describe characters and events economically but accurately demonstrates her polished writing skills. After she had moved to Cairo and taken the job as a journalist for the *Arab Observer,* she learned that she could not be comfortable sharing the same space with the patriarchal male journalists. She was offered an opportunity to work in the library, an area separated from the men by glass, and this delighted her. Not wanting to appear too anxious, she was circumspect in her response the offer, but in telling the story in retrospect, she remembers and relates the feeling she had at the time by recounting the folkloric Brer Rabbit's sly escape from danger. Like Brer Rabbit, who protested that the worst thing that could ever happen to him was to be thrown into the briar patch when that was where he really wanted to be, she had been moved into ideal surroundings for her hungry and scholarly mind: a book-lined library filled with texts in her own language. In using this analogy, Angelou shows her ability to build a story with both tension and humor.

The Heart of a Woman tells the story of one difficulty after another. The insecurity of unpaid bills while living in what appeared to be New York luxury, Angelou's continued difficulties with her own self-definition, and her sensitivity to her son growing into a sometimes rebellious and independent young man were frustrating experiences. In 1992, Angelou had an interview with Judith Paterson, a writer for *Vogue* magazine, in which she talked about the concept of *thriving* as opposed to *enduring:* "But the human being is not at his or her best when he or she simply endures. Still, it is important, at a stage, to endure so you can overcome. Surviving is important, but thriving is elegant" (quoted in Paterson 1989, 118). *The Heart of a Woman* tells the story of Angelou's ability to thrive, elegantly and, as she put it, "with gusto." Her forthright honesty and wit are again unfolded in this book, along with her self-reliance and resilience.

Angelou's focus at the time related in the book was always Guy. She wanted to help him through the unsettled adolescent years and into early adulthood. In order for her to thrive, she needed to provide the framework in which *he* could thrive. Her thoughtful and reflective parenting is echoed in her ability to express the logic of her deliberations and decisions concerning Guy.

Angelou also reveals the depth of African-American culture to readers by skillful descriptive glimpses into their everyday lives. The traditional elements are not isolated or foregrounded; rather, they are embedded in the story's natural progression. In the book's first pages, she candidly discusses her hair as a "wide, unstraightened hedge" (624). In those few descriptive words, the challenge of caring for African-American hair is made clear. An example from chapter 7 relates another code of behavior between most southern blacks "which," she wrote, "is as severe and distinct as a seventeenth century minuet or an African initiation ritual" (714). The explanation is given in the midst of another vignette, and it is almost like an aside to the reader. She met Thomas Allen, her fiancé before meeting Vusumzi Make, in a public tavern and observed the code for women in a bar:

> There is a moment to speak, a tone of voice to be used, words to be carefully chosen, a time to drop one's eyes, and a split second when a stranger can be touched on the shoulder or arm or even knee without conveying anything more than respectful friendliness. A lone woman in a new situation knows it is correct to smile slightly at the other women, never grin (a grin is proper only between friends or people making friendship), and nod to unknown men. This behavior tells the company that the new woman is ready to be friendly but is not thirsting after another woman's mate. (714)

There are examples like this throughout the text, the final example of which is related in chapter 19. In the narrative, it is just moments before Angelou learns of the serious automobile accident that almost took Guy's life. She has a premonition and reflects, "The old Arkansas toby, unimpressed by spanned oceans, quivered under her skin" (869). The toby is a good-luck charm that is kept out of sight. This descriptive omen re-creates the fearful tension of the moment, the distance from home, and the soon-to-be-learned reality that her beloved son's body has been broken in many places.

APHORISMS, proverbs, and other types of wise, homey sayings are also used throughout the narrative, often presented as originating with Angelou's mother or grandmother, though other characters in the story shared them as well. John Killens, the writer, is quoted as saying, "Old folks say, Every shuteye ain't sleep and every goodbye ain't gone. You fail, you get up and try again" (704). Angelou learned many more in Africa used effectively for compliments, resolutions of tense situations, and to pass wisdom along. After a female African lawyer from Sierra Leone described injuries and showed scars she had sustained in prison because of fighting against imperialism, other African women surrounded her and repeated, "A true daughter of a true mother" (749).

The descriptions of several important luminaries in Angelou's experience are brief and economical but capture the essence of each person. Billie Holiday, dissipated, crude, and failing, spent several days in Angelou's home but left a trail of harshness and bad memories. Using Guy's discomfort from being a victim of Holiday's vulgarity, Angelou paints her character succinctly and accurately. The same sparse but effective descriptions are created for Martin Luther King, Jr., "an easy friendliness, which was unsettling" (708), and Malcolm X, whose "voice was black baritone and musical. . . . Up close he was a great red arch through which one could pass to eternity" (779). Throughout the text, seemingly simple descriptions of individuals, created with very few well-chosen words, give them dimension and presence.

The transitions that Angelou uses to interject occasional memories related to situations in the narrative are smooth and carefully contrived. At the point in chapter 14 when Guy learns that Vus has not paid the rent on their New York apartment and they are about to be evicted, Maya's son silently seems to question her ability to take care of him. Angelou's thoughts retrieve a memory of a serious automobile accident years before in which she had lost consciousness. When she came to, Guy had become violent instead of relieved and began striking out at her, screaming, and backing away. He had trusted her, and in his child's mind she had let him down by getting hurt. His look eight years later seems to hold the same disappointment and accusation. The anxiety passes, but the descriptive prose creates a seamless presence between this time and the similar emotions of the past. Angelou was devoted to her son, but the reality was that she had to leave him many times for the sake of her career and their financial survival.

Throughout *The Heart of a Woman,* there is a constant, almost tangible, juxtaposition of tension in the present and abstract hope for the future. Her understanding of life and her place in it is clearer to her, but Angelou continues to yearn for a companion for herself and a father figure for Guy. Though that did occur temporarily—that is, for a while she thought she had found it in Make—it dissipated because he was not true to himself or to her. In spite of her doubts, however, over time she was able to provide the stability that her son needed.

The epigraph and opening lines of the introductory chapter are clearly journey metaphors and allusions, and the narrative takes us on a colorful and interesting journey through Angelou's continued soul-searching and travel that takes place across time and space. By the close of this part of her life, her son had reached maturity and left for his university studies, and she was headed positively into an unknown but promising future. Angelou's fourth autobiography ends at a point where she has accepted herself and trusts her ability to take care of herself. It is positive, and she is strong.

SOME IMPORTANT THEMES AND SYMBOLS IN *THE HEART OF A WOMAN*

Civil Rights

In *The Heart of a Woman,* the vital concept of civil rights is an ever-present theme. The narrative setting is in a time of great unrest in the United States and parts of Africa because of continued oppression and prejudice against blacks by dominant white society. Angelou was deeply aware of the issues and worked in both the United States and Africa to try to further movements toward equality for all people. From serving as an executive administrator in Martin Luther King, Jr.'s Southern Christian Leadership Conference to leading a protest group to the United Nations, to living in Egypt and writing, to supporting Martin Luther King, Jr.'s March on Washington with a counterpart demonstration in Ghana, Angelou used what influence she had in the attempt to right many wrongs.

Family

The figures of Angelou's grandmother, mother, brother, son, and other important but earlier life figures are present in *The Heart of a Woman,* and she also reveals the particulars of her quasi-marriage to Vusumzi Make, a well-known leader in the struggle for South African freedom. Other primary themes in the text are personal family relationships, particularly the changing nature of the mother/son attachment between Angelou and Guy over time in the midst of change and crisis. During the years they lived in Africa, they came to welcome and appreciate the ties they had to their ancient cultural heritage, an appreciation that is discussed with sensitivity.

The importance of Guy's education is another theme that runs through this segment of Angelou's autobiographical series. Though their journeys in the United States and in Africa caused him to change schools often, his mother's example and strong, unwavering guidance kept him focused both on broad, varied reading and a consciousness of his responsibilities in social reform. The story informs the reader that, like his mother, Guy involved himself intelligently in the social issues of the day. *The Heart of a Woman* closes with his outstanding performance on his entrance exams at the University of Ghana, and then leaving Maya to find his own independence within an African university experience.

Self-Discovery

The Heart of a Woman, like her preceding three autobiographies, continues Maya Angelou's life narrative and describes her challenges and difficulties as a single mother and a multitalented African American. Many themes run through this narrative, and Angelou candidly weaves the personal and the public sides of her life and her own tumultuous misjudgments, disappointments, and survival within the tumultuous public events of the late 1950s and early 1960s.

The Heart of a Woman represents Angelou's character as it metamorphoses from a young and unsure black woman to a confident and accomplished African-American adult. Her concerns about racist America are observed and discussed with openness, and her participation in the Civil Rights movement and interaction with important social reformers demonstrate her personal growth.

Heritage
Angelou deeply respected the people of Africa. Her admiration for them was based on her own understanding of the African-American experience in the United States and her own African heritage. In Africa, she was among the majority race, and she was proud of their accomplishments—their fighting for independence, education, and survival, but in time she realized that she was of another world, and she belonged, realistically, to another culture.

Freedom
The title of this work is tied to Angelou's past autobiographies, particularly *I Know Why the Caged Bird Sings*. It was borrowed from a poem of the same title by HARLEM RENAISSANCE writer Georgia Douglas Johnson. Johnson's eight-line poem "The Heart of a Woman" is a succinct comparison between the heart of a woman yearning for freedom and the figure of a bird beating itself against cage bars, seeking escape from an unhappy environment. This lyric poem suggests there is freedom for both the woman and the bird some of the time, but that return is inevitable and that brings entrapment, powerless, and futility, a theme Angelou struggled against but seemed to conquer particularly during the time depicted this autobiography.

CHARACTERS

Abbey Lincoln A jazz vocalist, songwriter, and actress, Abbey Lincoln met Maya in Los Angeles through black music performance circles, and they worked together in New York in Jean Genet's Off-Broadway play *The Blacks*. Abbey Lincoln and her companion, musician Max Roach, were friends of Maya during the time she and Vusumzi Make were courting.

Art D'Lugoff Art D'Lugoff owned the well-known Village Gate nightclub. He allowed Cambridge and Angelou to use the club for the "Cabaret for Freedom" fund-raiser for five weeks without charge, and the show was a hit.

Banti Williamson A. B. Williamson, called Banti, was the wife of Joseph Williamson, the chargé d'affaires of Liberia in Cairo, Egypt. Banti was one of the first women Maya met when she moved to Cairo. Banti introduced her to other women in Cairo, wives of various diplomats, and they eventually became good friends. After an encounter at a party with a young woman, Mendinah, who had her eyes on Vusumzi Make, Maya told the girl off. Banti took Maya's hand to calm her and said, "Old Man say, 'If you mess with Jesus Christ, God will make you shit'" (2004, 852). Banti and Maya remained close friends during Maya's time in Cairo.

Billie Holiday When Maya and Guy lived in Laurel Canyon, Wilkie Wilkerson, her friend and voice coach, made arrangements for Billie Holiday to spend a few days at Maya's home. Maya found the well-known singer to be abrasive and crude. Before Guy went to sleep at night, and before Maya returned Holiday to her hotel at night, Holiday would sing to Guy. On the last visit, Holiday sang him her signature song, "Strange Fruit," a protest song about Southern lynching. There was much in it that Guy did not understand, so he interrupted her. Holiday was furious and scornful toward Guy. Her crude remarks deeply offended Guy, and he blamed his mother for exposing him to such an ill-behaved person. Holiday died a few months after her visits with Maya and Guy.

David DuBois The adopted son of W. E. B. DuBois, David befriended Maya in Cairo and helped her find work as a journalist at the *Arab Observer* when Vusumzi Make (Vus) failed to provide financially for Maya and Guy. He also found radio news spots for her to do. He was a kind, supportive friend throughout Maya's two-year stay in Cairo.

Godfrey Cambridge Maya met Cambridge, an unemployed actor, at a Greenwich Village party. The two became friends (not romantic) and soon attended a consciousness-raising meeting sponsored by the Southern Christian Leadership Conference. Afterward, they decided to raise money for the organization by putting together a show called "Cabaret for Freedom."

Guy Johnson At the time Maya and Guy moved from New York to Cairo, Guy was still in high school. Maya enrolled him in a private school in Cairo, and he completed his secondary education there. Maya and Guy later moved to Accra, Ghana, where Guy entered the University of Ghana and completed his university degree. Guy grew from a youth to a man during this time, and though there were the usual tensions between mother and son, they maintained their good relationship.

John Henrik Clarke A southerner, writer, historian, and professor, and a member of the Harlem Writers Guild, Clarke was the first to level real criticism at Angelou during her first reading at the Harlem Writers Guild. He taught her, that night, that writing is work. She understood and returned to receive the help she recognized she needed.

John Killens Maya met John Killens in 1961 when he had traveled to Hollywood to write the screenplay for his novel *Youngblood.* He read some of Maya's work, liked it, and was instrumental in encouraging her to move to New York City so that she could be part of the Harlem Writers Guild. The Killens and Maya and Guy remained close friends thereafter.

Malcolm X Maya became involved in a quasi-protest at the United Nations in New York City after Patricia Lumumba was assassinated in Africa. The reaction in the media was harsh after the near riot, so Maya and her friend Rosa Guy solicited Malcolm X for advice. He was not supportive and warned them that some Negro leaders, "like Peter in your Christian Bible" (2004, 780) will deny you. And they did. Some leaders said that the demonstration was "undignified and unnecessary" (2004, 781).

Martin Luther King, Jr. When Maya was coordinator of the New York office of the Southern Christian Leadership Conference, Martin Luther King, Jr., visited her at work one day. He was courteous and complimentary, and the two had a chat about Maya's family. King reminded her that many people, black and white, were working for the common good.

Max Roach Max Roach, an American jazz drummer and composer, and companion (later husband) of Abbey Lincoln, was a friend of Maya's. He and Abbey and Maya worked together on the Off-Broadway play *The Blacks,* by Jean Genet, until he and Abbey withdrew from participation. Abbey, Max, and Maya remained close friends.

Maya Angelou At the beginning of *The Heart of a Woman,* Maya had just returned to San Francisco from a yearlong tour in Europe of *Porgy and Bess.* During this period of her life, she and her son, Guy, moved to New York, then Egypt, then Accra, Ghana, where Maya worked and Guy began studies at the University of Ghana.

The Mayfields Author and journalist Julian Mayfield and his wife, Anna (Ana in *All God's Children Need Traveling Shoes*) Livia Cordero Mayfield, a medical doctor, renewed their friendship with Maya soon after she and Guy arrived in Accra, Ghana. The Mayfields gave Maya information about the university, where Guy planned to enroll, and then when Guy was severely injured in a car accident, Anna Livia took responsibility for his care. The Mayfields, Maya, and Guy remained very close friends throughout Maya's stay in Accra.

Oliver Tambo A South African leader of the African National Congress, Tambo met Angelou at John Killens's home in New York in 1960. Tambo had come to the United States to gain support from the United Nations and the people of the United States against apartheid in South Africa. He was at the Killens' home with Vusumzi Make.

Richard and Ellen Richard, a Yoruba man, and Ellen, his Canadian wife, were among the first people Maya and Guy met in Accra, Ghana. They were all at a house party at Walter Nthia's home, and they invited Maya and Guy to a picnic the next day. Maya declined, but Guy went. Richard became drunk at the picnic and asked Guy to drive them back. There was an accident on the return home, and Guy was nearly killed. Maya had a struggle to forgive Richard and Ellen for their carelessness with her only son.

Rosa Guy Rosa Guy was a founding member of the Harlem Writer's Guild. Born in Trinidad but raised in Harlem, she and Maya became lifelong friends. She gave a party in honor of Maya's first published article.

Susie and Jerry Susie and Jerry were sleeping together in her grandmother's (Mrs. Tolman's) apartment. When Maya heard the story of how Jerry threatened Guy, she went to the apartment, paid Mrs. Tolman, and then threatened to kill the whole family (including Susie's mother and baby) if Jerry even dared to touch Guy.

Thomas Allen Maya met Thomas Allen in New York. They courted and became engaged. He was a bail bondsman and a dependable person, but Angelou broke off the engagement when she was swept off her feet by Vusumzi Make, the South African freedom fighter.

Mrs. Tolman Mrs. Tolman was hired to take care of Maya's apartment and keep an eye on Guy, who was 15, while Maya took a nightclub job in Chicago for two weeks. She let her teenage granddaughter Susie accompany her, and though nothing happened between Susie and Guy, Susie's boyfriend, a gang leader, became jealous and threatened Guy.

Vivian Baxter Maya's mother, Vivan Baxter, was going through a difficult period during the time described in this book. She had divorced and remarried, and her new husband drank too much. A strong woman, well able to take care of herself, she was emotionally needy, and their roles as mother and daughter seemed to be reversing.

Vusumzi Make (Vus) Make, a South African freedom fighter, was in the United States to petition the United Nations to redress South Africa's discriminatory racial policies. Maya and he met at a party at the Killens' home. Make and Maya both recognized an attraction between them, and soon Maya accepted Make's proposal of marriage, broke off with Thomas, and within a short time joined him, with Guy, in Cairo. Make proved to be an undependable provider and a womanizer. When Guy finished high school in Cairo, he and Maya went to Accra, Ghana. Guy enrolled at the University of Ghana. Make faded into the background. Maya and Make never married.

FURTHER READING

Angelou, Maya. *The Collected Autobiographies of Maya Angelou.* New York: Modern Library Edition by Random House, 2004.

Brewer, J. Mason. *American Negro Folklore.* New York: New York Times Book Company, 1968.

Cain, Noble. "Ole Ark's a-Moverin'." Traditional Negro Spiritual (Concert Version). New York: Harold Flammer, 1938.

Hagen, Lyman B. *Heart of a Woman, Mind of a Writer, and Soul of a Poet: A Critical Analysis of the Writings of Maya Angelou.* Lanham, Md.: University Press of America, 1997.

Johnson, Georgia Douglas. "The Heart of a Woman." In *The Norton Anthology of African American Literature,* edited by Henry Louis Gates, Jr., and Nellie Y. McKay, 971. New York: W. W. Norton, 1996.

Johnson, Guy. *Echoes of a Distant Summer.* New York: One World/Ballantine Books, 2002.

———. *Standing at the Scratch Line.* New York: Stivers Row/Villard/Random House, 1998.

Lupton, Mary Ann. "Singing the Black Mother: Maya Angelou and Autobiographical Continuity." In *Maya Angelou.* Modern Critical Views, edited by Harold Bloom, 173–189. Philadelphia: Chelsea House, 1999.

McFeely, William S. *Frederick Douglass.* New York: W. W. Norton, 1991.

McPherson, Dolly. *Order Out of Chaos: The Autobiographical Works of Maya Angelou.* New York: Peter Lang, 1990.

Neubauer, Carol E. "Displacement and Autobiographical Style in Maya Angelou's *The Heart of a Woman.*" In *Maya Angelou.* Modern Critical Views, edited by Harold Bloom, 25–40. Philadelphia: Chelsea House, 2009.

O'Neale, Sondra. "Reconstruction of the Composite Self: New Images of Black Women in Maya Angelou's Continuing Autobiography." In *Maya Angelou.* Modern Critical Views, edited by Harold Bloom, 41–53. Philadelphia: Chelsea House, 1999.

Paterson, Judith. "Interview: Maya Angelou." In *Conversations with Maya Angelou,* edited by Jeffrey M. Elliot, 115–124. Jackson and London: University Press of Mississippi, 1989.

Traylor, Eleanor W. "Maya Angelou: Writing Life, Inventing Literary Genre." In *Maya Angelou.* Bloom's Modern Critical Views, edited by Harold Bloom, 91–105. New York: Bloom's Literary Criticism, 2009.

All God's Children Need Traveling Shoes (1986)

The title for Maya Angelou's fifth autobiography is derived from a well-known spiritual called "All God's Chillun Got Wings"; most of the story takes place in Ghana, Africa. One of the book's important themes is Angelou's personal search for place as she describes becoming friends with a number of black American expatriates living in Ghana as well as several well-educated Africans. She also describes being taken to observe various ritual ceremonies to help her understand some of the ancient tribal traditions. There are clever stories, short poems, and jokes in this work, as well as scriptures and APHORISMs learned early in her life from her mother and grandmother. Angelou's candid autobiographical style is once again captivating, and it appeals to a wide interracial audience because it is both informative and entertaining.

All God's Children Need Traveling Shoes is not organized into chapters; instead, there are spaces between the sections. Written and published in 1986, the prose is sophisticated and reflects Angelou's confidence in her talent and skill as a writer. The book is dedicated to JULIAN MAYFIELD, MALCOLM X, "and all the fallen ones who were passionately and earnestly looking for a home," and the characters in the book are mostly friends rather than family members. In these pages, Angelou has become an independent woman who feels a deep, family-like kinship with the African people.

At the beginning of *All God's Children,* Maya and Guy are in Africa with plans for his university education and her future career in public service. Their plans are unpredictably disrupted by a serious automobile accident in which Guy is severely injured. By the end of this book, Maya is returning to the United States, alone, having gained invaluable experience in life and in writing. She had been able to enjoy a glimpse of her own roots and the history of her ancestors, and realizes that she has left Africa by choice, not by force, as generations centuries ago were made to do. She has learned and understood the legacy of hope her ancestors had bequeathed to her.

SYNOPSIS

After living two years in Cairo, Maya and Guy traveled to Accra to enroll him in the University of Ghana. Maya was planning to get him settled and then go to Liberia for a job with the country's Department of Information. For two days, they happily explored the streets of Accra, and then their world was turned upside down. While on a pleasure outing with new friends, Guy was seriously injured in a collision. He had pulled over to look at a map, the car stalled, and a truck hit the car he was using. His neck, one leg, and one arm were broken. Encased in plaster, Guy was stoic, but Maya was terrified that he would not pull through. She was worried and lonely and felt like "a blinded bull in a metal stall" (890).

The accident was the result of the host driver becoming drunk at a picnic. Maya had been invited to go to the picnic as well, but she had declined. Guy's host had passed out in the backseat of the car, and though Guy knew how to drive, the car had stalled. Tragically, while trying to get it started, it was hit by a truck. He was thrown from the car and knocked unconscious. He was found beside the road, taken to a local hospital, and given immediate but incomplete treatment.

Guy's host visited the hospital, drunk again (or still), and apologized for the accident he felt he had caused. Guy was light and cordial with him, but Maya was so upset that she found it difficult to be civil; she was cool but courteous. Maya and Guy had been invited to stay with a friend of friends, émigrés, and had just barely become acquainted with them when the accident occurred. The people were kind and helpful under the circumstances, but

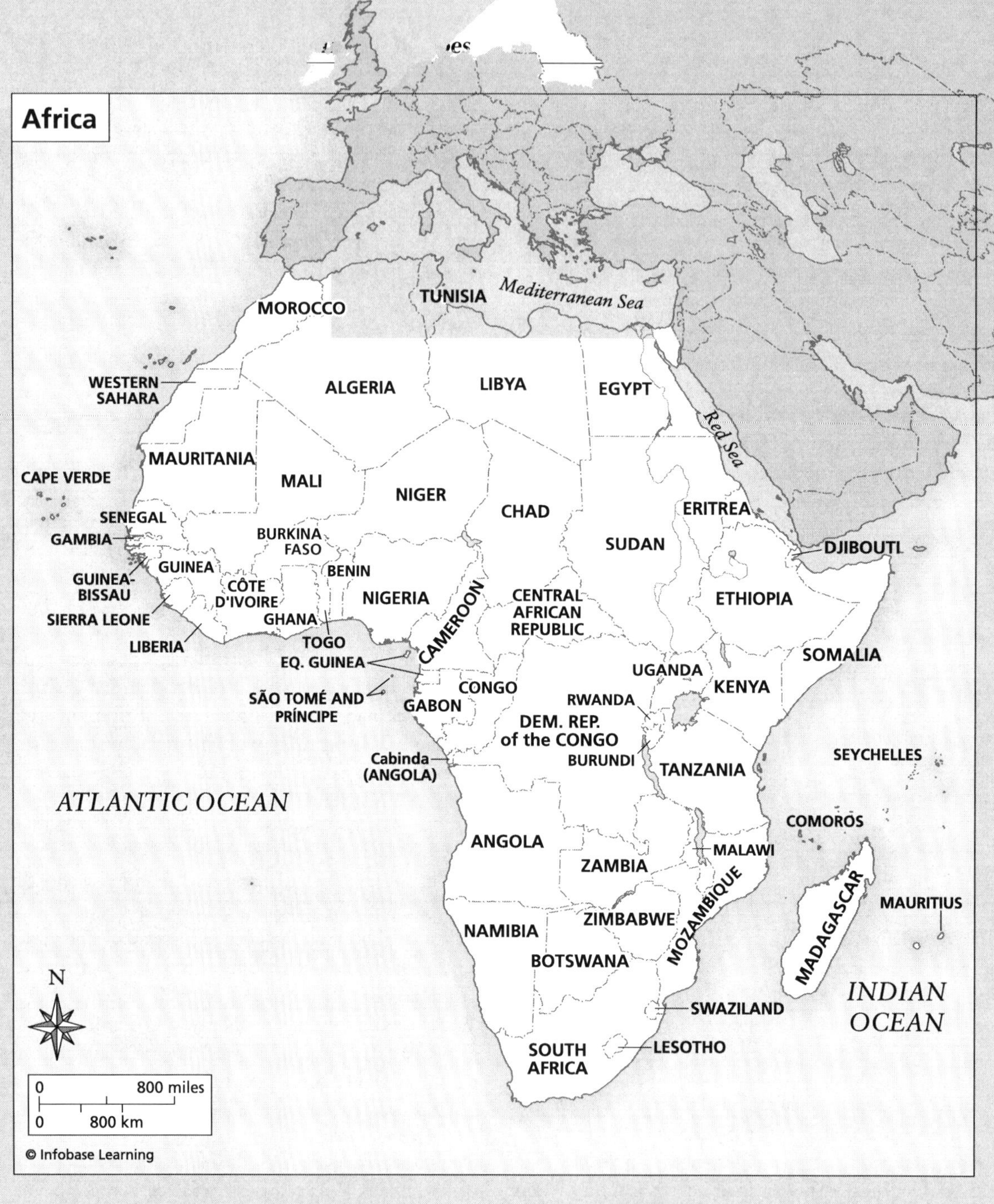

Africa
Mediterranean Sea
MOROCCO
TUNISIA
WESTERN SAHARA
ALGERIA
LIBYA
EGYPT
Red Sea
MAURITANIA
CAPE VERDE
MALI
NIGER
CHAD
ERITREA
SENEGAL
GAMBIA
BURKINA FASO
SUDAN
DJIBOUTI
GUINEA
GUINEA-BISSAU
CÔTE D'IVOIRE
BENIN
NIGERIA
CENTRAL AFRICAN REPUBLIC
ETHIOPIA
SIERRA LEONE
GHANA
LIBERIA
TOGO
CAMEROON
EQ. GUINEA
SOMALIA
UGANDA
SÃO TOMÉ AND PRÍNCIPE
CONGO
KENYA
GABON
RWANDA
DEM. REP. of the CONGO
BURUNDI
Cabinda (ANGOLA)
SEYCHELLES
TANZANIA
ATLANTIC OCEAN
COMOROS
ANGOLA
MALAWI
ZAMBIA
MOZAMBIQUE
MAURITIUS
MADAGASCAR
ZIMBABWE
NAMIBIA
BOTSWANA
INDIAN OCEAN
N
SWAZILAND
LESOTHO
SOUTH AFRICA
0
800 miles
0
800 km
© Infobase Learning

because of her grief and fear. One sunny morning, Julian Mayfield showed up in the YWCA lobby. He was firm with her and said she needed a woman to talk to. Then he drove her to meet Efua (Efuah in *The Heart of a Woman*) Sutherland, a poet, playwright, teacher, and head of Ghana's National Theater. This elegant woman was also a mother, and she reached out to Maya as a sister and friend, letting her cry, and inviting her into Efua's home as an "aunt" to her children. She made certain that Maya was well fed and then said, "Your son is now my son. He has two mothers in this place" (896).

Maya emerged from her depression and promptly took herself in hand. She cleaned her room, washed her clothes, and began to dress well again. Alice Windom and Vicki Garvin, friends from the YWCA, took her to see Accra and the sights, and Efua Sutherland took her to the chairman of the Institute of African Studies at the University of Ghana. After talking to her, Professor J. H. Nketia gave her a job at the school. Meanwhile, Ana Livia Mayfield, a physician, had taken over Guy's care and discovered that his neck was broken, a diagnosis missed earlier. Under her care, Guy was improving, and Maya, surrounded by new friends and able to relax somewhat about her son's survival, had begun studying the local language, Fanti. Life was looking more positive.

When Guy was released from the hospital, he and Maya moved into the furnished home of an on-leave professor for three months. The black American immigrants in Ghana continued to welcome them into their eclectic community of movers and shakers. Soon after arriving in Ghana, Ana Livia Mayfield had set up a women's clinic. Julian, her husband, was a journalist. Among others in the group were well-educated sociologists, a painter, electricians, grade-schoolteachers, a plumber, and a union organizer. These were African Americans who felt that relocating to Africa was like going home, and they were all eager to contribute to Ghana's culture and society.

The president of Ghana, KWAME NKRUMAH, welcomed black Americans to Ghana, and he

During the first few days that Maya and Guy were in Accra, Ghana, they enjoyed exploring the marketplace together. The colorful sights and melodious sounds of the language entertained both of them. *(Photo by Hiyori13/Used under Creative Commons license)*

also supported southern and East African revolutionaries who were working to end regional colonialism in their countries. There were nearly 20 black Americans living in Ghana during the time Maya and Guy were there. Ghana had become a democracy in 1957, and since that time many African-American professionals, medical and academic, including the great American black activist W. E. B. DuBois and his wife, Shirley Graham, "had been personally invited to spend the rest of their lives in Ghana" (904).

Guy moved to the dormitory at the university, and Maya was able to live two more weeks in the absent professor's home before moving back to the YWCA. She took her evening meal at the Y's cafeteria, where one evening a woman from Sierra Leone began complaining long and loudly about the absence of rice. It sounded like a serious complaint, so Maya went to the cook and told him of the woman's plea. When the cook learned that the woman was from Sierre Leone, he said, "They die for rice. I will bring her some" (907). And with that, he wordlessly served a large platter of rice. When he was almost back to the kitchen, "the room exploded in applause" (907). There were regulations about the food, but the cook had decided that the traditions of the people were more important, and it was Angelou who helped them remember that.

Maya enjoyed working at the university. In her position as administrative assistant, her responsibilities ranged from tracking student development to typing a professor's book manuscript to performing in the lead role of a play, *Mother Courage,* by Bertolt Brecht. She was surrounded by beautiful Moroccan architecture, fascinating markets and sellers, native costumes made of beautiful fabrics, and the fragrance of flowers. Guy was well and independent, and she felt that her life was "getting itself in joint" (909).

Maya and her friends, Vicki and Alice from the YWCA, found a pretty white bungalow to share with three bedrooms and a large living and dining room. Both of Maya's housemates had bachelor's and master's degrees; one was a union organizer and the other a sociologist. The women shared expenses, but Maya's 75 pounds on the first of each month (about $200 in the United States) was budgeted entirely for living expenses and tuition for Guy. That amount left her nothing to save, and she knew she needed to find extra work.

Maya applied to the editor of the *Ghanaian Times,* T. D. Kwesi Bafoo, first, but quickly learned that writing for them would earn her very little. However, he did ask for a 300-word article on America, capitalism, and racial prejudice to be completed by the following Friday. Next she tried the Ghana Broadcasting office but encountered a brick wall in the form of a condescending receptionist, so she turned and left. She reflected on why so many Ghanaians treated American blacks with such disdain. Not able to answer that quandary, she resolved to be positive about Ghana and try again another day.

Maya decided that she would try to have her hair done in Ghanaian fashion. The beautician who styled it, Comfort Adday, was full of chatter and worked roughly with the hair, stretching and pulling and tying it with black thread. At last it was neatly styled like any other Ghanaian woman, coiled into neat patches "exact as the design in tweed cloth" (916). Maya paid her, and the woman said she liked to laugh with Maya and would be back in two weeks. Maya reflected that she had not laughed during the procedure even once.

The living room at Alice, Vicki, and Maya's home became a gathering center for black American immigrants. Many came from the United States expecting almost a maternal welcome home to the continent, but those who had been there longer knew better. Africa had lost so much to colonization, and even the land had been neglected. The newcomers needed to give something to Africa as well as embrace their ancient roots. Because Maya and her housemates were forthright about dispelling the myth of Mother Africa, some newcomers were put off by them. Language was often a barrier, but on the other hand, many did seem to find a form of welcome there.

Maya received an unexpected telephone call telling her that she was wanted at the *Ghanaian Times.* Unsure of the reason, she went immediately. She had written the article on U.S. capitalism and racial prejudice, and T. D. Bafoo, the editor, liked it. He told Maya that he and his wife would soon have a new baby; consequently, he invited her and the whole crowd to an "outdooring" in the country after the birth. Beginning at dawn, an outdooring gives family and friends an opportunity to welcome the new soul. As Bafoo hurried away (he was always rushing), he gave her the address and insisted that she come to his house that very afternoon for a visit.

Bafoo's home was a modest bungalow, pretty but not showy, and his wife was certainly well along in her pregnancy. Beer and pleasant conversation followed Maya's arrival, and when she left after nightfall, she had been given directions to his country place. She hoped she might get a glimpse of the elusive tribal soul of Africa through this couple. She knew that there were slave traders among Africans in ancient times, and she could only wonder what her own family history might really have been. The Bafoos were from two different tribes, Fanti and Ewe, and they used stereotypical characteristics to tease each other. Their teasing offered some insight into the lighthearted play a mixed marriage might have, but Maya wanted to learn so much more.

Professors, lecturers, and some administrators gathered for conversation in the Senior Common Room at the Institute of African Studies of Legon University. One day, Maya entered unobtrusively and heard them discussing black Americans. There had been a rift in HARLEM that was front-page news in Ghana, and the conversation centered on the bestiality of black American behavior. When the conversation turned to democracy, a British man spoke up and said, "Democracy was never created for the lower classes. Everyone knows that. Just like at Ghana" (926). Maya felt they had insulted her people as well as the country of Ghana, so she spoke up. She did not think first, however, and she blubbered out insults and swearwords to these people, who she felt were being so careless with their own words.

As she left, the room steward stopped her and softly suggested that the insulting words of those people were nothing and did not matter: "They are like ice on an elephant's back. They will pass" (928). Maya knew that the steward was wise, but she also knew that he had never experienced the insults of blacks in America; he was at home and confident.

In a very formal way, the steward asked Maya if she would speak to a good boy from his village named Kojo. She said she would, and the boy offered himself to her as a house worker; he wanted only tips and not a salary. The boy, who was about 14, reminded her of her brother Bailey's appearance because he had dark brown skin, small hands, and a well-shaped, round head. He provided good service, and after some weeks, it was time for him to return to school. He was staying in Accra, and he asked if he could continue to be Maya's "small boy" (932). As it turned out, Kojo needed tutoring, and Alice, Vicki, and Maya all helped him. It was a little like déjá vu because Maya had been through all of this with Guy. The boy was so like Bailey that Maya was a little enchanted.

Efua invited Maya to a durbar, a thanksgiving harvest feast to be held about 30 miles away in Aburi. A mixed socioeconomic celebration, everyone was welcome to give thanks. There was rhythmic drumming, and people were happily swaying to the music until suddenly everything was silent. In the distance, it sounded like hundreds of giant cicadas were making a rasping sound by rubbing their legs together. Then, also in the distance, royal drums began to beat out their rhythm. The sound grew closer, and men began to emerge from the dust. They were supporting palanquins (a covered litter), each carrying an elaborately bedecked chief. Efua had given Maya a handkerchief to wave, and along with thousands of others she chanted *na-na, na-na, na-na* as the chief and their *kras*—young boys believed to carry the implanted soul of the chief for his protection and safety—passed by.

At the dance later, Maya saw a huge man dressed in a white-lace African costume. A small man who was with the other one approached Maya and told her that Sheikhali, the tall one from Mali, wanted to invite her for dinner. She accepted, perhaps too quickly, and went to her home to change into something elegant. Soon he arrived, but Maya wanted to wait for her friends Alice and Vicki to return before they went out. She left them a note, and he took her to the restaurant in a silver

1963 Coupe de Ville Cadillac. After dinner, he announced that they would go to the Continental Hotel. He did not explain, and Maya was a little shocked. She was relieved when she learned that they would dance and enjoy a long evening together. After dancing, he asked if she would like to return to her home or go to his apartment in the hotel. Maya considered the pleasant evening they had just had, and she chose to go to his room to "rest for a time" (941).

Three days after Maya met Mr. Sheikhali, he sent her a large new refrigerator for her home. Maya returned it and also refused his offer to pay her rent and give her money for her car. He wanted to marry her, take her to Mali, and have her educate his other wife and his eight children. He had made an elaborate plan, but it was a business-like proposition rather than a romantic one, and she found it easy to refuse. Kojo was sad because he felt she was hurting the Mali man by refusing his kindnesses.

After Kojo had been with her about two months, he came to her and said there were people in the backyard. She looked out and saw a large group of people dressed in rich cloth and gold. She told Kojo to take them around to the front door, and she would welcome them in. They told her that they were Kojo's family from Akwapim, and that they had traveled by truck to thank her. The oldest man of the family signaled to younger members to "Bring the thanks" (945), and they retrieved crates of fruits, vegetables, and other foods (including snails the size of kittens). The old one told her that the family owned many farms, and each month according to the season, their household would be supplied with food.

Kojo offered to get Maya some tea. She accepted and retired to her room with the hot tea and some gin. She reflected on the deep roots of the African people and thought that in spite of political bondage and exploitation, "they had retained an ineradicable innocence" (947). Maya could perceive the difference between American and African blacks. The American blacks wore "the badge of a barbarous history" (947) and had lost their innocence. She drank the gin and set aside the tea.

Because of President Nkrumah, the people of Ghana were taking pride in their heritage; he called it "The African Personality" (947) and included Americans and West Indians in his affirmation of the value of all black people. Then, though three previous attempts had failed, the president was almost killed in an assassination plan. The national mood became stricken, and joy was muted at all levels from people on the street to professors. Suddenly, there was much distrust and a search for spies. The finger of suspicion was pointed at one group after another, and finally black Americans were accused of this atrocity. A few were deported, all were watched, and in time things returned to normal, but the black Americans were less sure of themselves than they had been before.

For two weeks, Maya assisted Efua in putting together a Chinese play. When she returned to her office, she learned that Grace, Ghana's chief traditional dancer, had lost her whole pay packet. Maya was working though a stack of backed-up work in her office when she discovered Grace's pay packet in the pile. She took it to her immediately, and Grace was overjoyed. She told Maya that she would be thanked, and Maya was thanked, amazingly, over and over again by many people.

Maya went to a different eating hall a few weeks later and heard a story about the protection and hospitality village tribal members had given a white couple who had traveled about 50 miles into the bush. The whites telling the story were condescending as they unfolded their narrative about the graciousness an old African chief had extended to them. They had planned to sleep in their car, but the chief had felt the white couple were human beings and decided to help them by providing a place to sleep. He believed strongly that humans should sleep indoors. The tellers were not respectful about the experience, noting that the old man had refused any payment, saying, "We did not make you human. God did that. You are traveling in a strange land. What less could we do?" (955). A comment was made by another person listening to their story, who said, "Can't you just imagine the old codger caught in a revolving door in New York expecting somebody to help him because God made him?" (956). An English woman in the group stood and said she was embarrassed by the behavior of the storytellers. She said, "You and your husband sound like ungrateful clods, and the African has the grace of Saint Augustine" (956). Maya was thankful for the English woman's words and was sorry that she would not have an opportunity to know her better.

Early one morning, Grace Nuamah, the woman whose check Maya had found, came to Maya at her university office and said she wanted to take her to lunch. She was still thanking her for finding the money. Maya drove according to Grace's directions, and they arrived at a luxurious home, but Grace would not reveal who lived there. The two women were escorted to the opulent living room by a servant, and then Abatanu, the host, appeared. He was a handsome, sophisticated man, but Maya took an instant dislike to him; she was suspicious of his polished suaveness and seeming conceit. Grace had hoped that Abatanu and Maya would like each other and that something might develop between them. Their meeting would have been her gift to Maya. It did not work, and the afternoon visit fell into silence. Grace was disappointed in the outcome and said that she knew that American blacks were very different, but she finished her sentence there without explaining further. She could not understand Maya's instant feeling of alienation from Abatanu.

Maya was still seeing Sheikhali, but this night he was two hours late for their date. Maya drove to the Star Hotel, ordered from the menu, and ate dinner. Sheikhali finally showed up with Mamali, his aide and interpreter. For the last time, he told Maya that she would be his educated wife, and he would take her to Mali. Maya again thanked him for the proposal, but she declined. Sheikhali told her that this was her last chance. She again declined, and he said condescendingly that she was only a "functionaire" (962), a civil servant. She did not think that sounded too bad in French, and it was quite all right with her that their relationship was finished.

Ghana was a bustling country of 7½ million people, and it seemed to Maya that each day most of the people were crowded into Accra. It was a moving, noisy place, and Maya decided to escape by driving to the country for a day in the bush. She bought some simple food and drove past both the Cape Coast Castle and the nearby Elmina Castle, where captured slaves had been held prisoner centuries ago. It was said that the cries of the prisoners still echoed in the thick stones walls, and the whole concept of her own ancestors being among those suffering brought her to tears.

She drove to her destination, Dunkwa, the birthplace of one of her students, and she found it to be typical of African villages with vendors, girls and boys, and "market women, huge and impervious" (964). Maya approached one of the women because there was no hotel, and the woman, in turn, took her to Kobina Artey, "the old man," who was a member of the village counsel. The old man tried to guess her African tribal origin and decided she was a Bambara from Liberia. He had worked so hard at determining her origin that Maya decided not to reveal that she was an American. It felt good to her to be given, even briefly, an African identity. Arrangements for her lodging were made with a kind newlywed couple. Not unlike customs in the U.S. black community, people soon dropped by quietly with food for the couple and guest. When time came for the meal, the table was spread with wonderful things to eat. The next morning, Maya bathed, ate, and took leave knowing that sometimes, in spite of history, American blacks' roots were still identifiable.

Maya was summoned to see Nana, as the first African vice chancellor of the University of Ghana was called. He had been replaced by Conor Cruise O'Brien, an Irishman, who was to serve as the new head of the University of Ghana. Maya had met Nana Nketsia, an important political figure and member of royalty, when she enrolled Guy in the University. Maya was escorted to a beautiful living room that had a tree growing up through the ceiling. There were African mats on tile floors, beautiful sofas, and burl tables. She called it a woodland fantasy.

At last she met Nana, but she was instructed not to speak directly to him but rather through Kwesi Brew, his minister of protocol. They had a few drinks, and Nana talked about the pride of being black. He then revealed that he knew Maya's exact circumstances and offered her a job in Kaneshie with a new car and bungalow. It was the center of the diamond industry, and her work would be much like she was doing at the university—a girl Friday. Maya accepted the offer. Before she left, Nana wanted her to meet some of his children, whom she enjoyed, and she asked permission to see them again. Nana said an appointment would be made, and Maya was taken home. Upon reflection, however, she knew she was not qualified for the job that had been offered. They assumed that she had degrees, and she knew she had not. She decided to recommend Alice or Vicki when Nana telephoned.

Julian Mayfield received a package from Washington, D.C., which contained pork sausages and up-to-date American newspapers. His home had become a frequent meeting place for many of the black Americans in Ghana, and they were soon there and shared the sausage and discussed what they in Africa could do to support MARTIN LUTHER KING, JR.'S March on Washington. Plans for a rally were made, and the university students were also informed and invited to participate. Maya and her friends decided to write a stinging protest declaration and present it to the U.S. ambassador to Ghana at the American Embassy.

The Washington march and the Ghanian march were scheduled to begin at the same time on August 27: 7 A.M. in Washington and 2 P.M. in Ghana. There was a seven-hour difference in the time zones. A large crowd gathered in Accra across from the American Embassy, and it included Guy, Alice, friends, and many others. When Julian arrived, he told them quietly that Dr. DuBois, 96, had just died. Because he was a great and wise black leader, they decided to inform the assembly. As the word spread, the crowed became hushed. They marched, and a hard rain began. One of the African marchers explained: "It is the way spirits welcome a great soul to the land of the dead. They wash it first" (986).

At dawn, the crowd assembled in front of the American Embassy, many of them protesting against the oppression of minorities in the United States. There were armed marines on the rooftop, and voices from the crowd shouted rude comments. This was ironic because soldiers and others at the embassy were not enemies. In the early afternoon, Julian, Maya, and others presented their statement to the first secretary who was standing in for the absent ambassador. His secretary told them that his own wife was marching in Washington with Reverend King. The march was over, and they all went home to rest.

Malcolm X had been to Mecca to make the required Muslim pilgrimage, and he stopped in Accra on his way back to the United States. His behavior was light and calm, very different from the bombastic man Maya had met two years earlier. He told them that America's racist prohibitions for blacks had not changed, but his visit to Mecca had changed his mind about white people. He had been with many good ones at Mecca and learned that they were not all devils. On his way to Accra, he had met government officials in Cairo to enlist their support for his presentation on behalf of African Americans to the General Assembly of

Malcolm X visited Accra in 1964 and met with Ghanaian dignitaries in an effort to gain their support. Maya Angelou was one of his unofficial aides and guides while he was in Ghana. *(Courtesy Library of Congress Prints and Photographs Division)*

the United Nations. The Accra group pooled their thoughts to determine what leaders in Ghana there would be of most use to him.

The group was able to introduce Malcolm to many important Ghanaian leaders, as well as the Cuban and Chinese ambassadors. Before he left Ghana, the Ghana Press Club gave a party in his honor. People danced merrily, and Malcolm rose to give an invited speech. He said he could not dance because of thoughts of suffering in the United States, the Congo, and in South Africa. People were momentarily sobered, but then the happy dancing continued. Maya reflected on one of her grandmother's ADAGEs: "If you want to know how important you are to the world, stick your finger in a pond and pull it out. Will the hole remain?" (993).

Malcolm X spoke at Legon University and was well received. His many experiences had given him a charismatic aura, and when he finished, the audience rose to its feet in a standing ovation. He quieted them and asked for questions, which he answered clearly. One student said that he did not understand why Malcolm called himself a black. He suggested that Malcolm looked more white than black. Malcolm laughed and said he had been waiting for that question to come to him in Africa. He said that he defined himself as "a Black Muslim man with African heritage" (995). Some blacks have light skin. He briefly explained the slave master's genetic influence on the black culture through rape of female slaves, but rather than pursue that line of thought, he asked for the next question.

Though the African Americans in Accra were able to get audiences for Malcolm X with Nana Nketsia and other influential leaders, they were unable to arrange an audience with President Kwame Nkrumah. That was a disappointment because Nkrumah was known for his wisdom, and to have his advice would have been invaluable. When he was alone with Maya and her friends, Malcolm advised them to return home to the United States because they were needed there. The movement in America would be strengthened by their voices, and there were many ways he knew they could help. Turning from such a serious topic, he happily shared pictures of Betty, his beloved wife, and photographs of his daughters. When he was with larger groups of black American expatriates, he told humorous stories about his family and laughed easily. But onstage, he had a different demeanor altogether, and his words spoke fiercely in favor of revolution.

The last night Malcolm X was in Ghana, a party was held at the Chinese Embassy. When Shirley DuBois arrived, she whisked him away for about an hour. Afterward, she announced that he needed to meet Kwame Nkrumah, and an appointment was set up for 9:00 the next morning. Maya was furious that Shirley DuBois had waited until the last hour to make this arrangement. After the morning meeting, the Chinese, Guinean, Yugoslav, Malian, Cuban, Algerian, and Egyptian ambassadors arrived in their luxury cars to follow him to the airport. Malcolm and his friends were getting ready to enter their cars, and the boxer Muhammad Ali came out of the hotel. Still a member of the Nation of Islam, with which Malcolm had severed ties, Ali turned his back on him. Malcolm called after the man and said he still loved him, but Ali and his group turned and walked away.

Malcolm said he wanted to ride in the car with Maya and Julian. On the way, he asked Maya what she thought of Shirley DuBois. Maya let loose with her anger. Malcolm then spoke harshly to her and said she was dangerously immature. He said that she needed to broaden her mind and understand that she must not condemn others for not thinking as she thought or thinking as fast as she thought. Maya understood and told him that she would think about what he advised. After he left, there was little to say. The African Americans in Accra were once again a little group of black adults looking for a sense of home.

Maya began to feel a sense of discomfort in Ghana. She was treated well and had many friends and a good life, but she felt too self-conscious. Guy had also created discomfort. One night, a Ghanaian friend brought a bottle of gin and some deeply disturbing gossip. He opened the bottle, poured some on the ground for the spirits, and then told her about Guy's 36-year-old girl friend who was an American and worked for the American Embassy. There was gossip, and Maya said she would see to her son. When she spoke with Guy, he verbally rejected her and walked away. Maya realized that she could do little about the affair he was having, and she also understood that he had clearly declared his independence from her. She was ready to move away from the whole scene, and she contemplated going to Asia or Europe. At that time, the thought of going back to the United States did not enter her mind.

Maya received an invitation to perform in *The* BLACKS in Berlin for four days and then follow that with a run in Venice for three additional days. The timing was good, and her expenses would be paid. She could visit old friends in Cairo after the play, and she could also attend a conference of non-aligned countries meeting there. She soon learned that the Mayfields were planning to attend the Cairo conference, and that finalized her decision to go. She informed Guy, who at first seemed slightly concerned but then, almost too quickly, wished her a wonderful time.

Maya knew she needed to prepare herself to rejoin the dramatic group with whom she had once worked. They were true professionals and had been working at their craft all the time she had been in Africa. She read and reviewed the play while she was on the flight from Africa to Frankfurt, and then memorized it there before going on to Berlin. Finally, in Berlin, she bathed and then dressed in a beautiful lavender silk "Grand Bou Bou" (African costume) and renewed her friendships with the cast. CECILY TYSON, JAMES EARL JONES, and others greeted her. It did not take long for Maya to realize she was glad to be among black Americans. They were frank and volatile, much more so than Africans, who seemed to build their society on protocol and contrived courtesies.

On the afternoon before the first performance of *The Blacks* in Berlin, Flash Riley, one of the actors in the company, visited each dressing room and reminded them to remember the African-American athlete JESSE OWENS. Hitler would not award Owens his four gold medals at the 1936 Olympics in Berlin because he was not an Aryan.* Though no one in the company talked further about that long-ago insult, it strengthened their resolve to be strong and do their best.

After the successful performance, a German couple approached Maya and invited her to accompany them to a nightclub. Maya replied that she was tired but had never been in a German home, and she asked if she could visit their home the next day. They agreed, and they said they would pick her up at 10:00 the following morning. They also invited her to bring a friend. Later that evening, she met a Jewish actor who was on tour, and she invited him to accompany her. As it turned out, the German family welcomed both of them and served an elegant and rich morning meal.

After the meal, Maya found the small talk boring and suggested they share jokes or stories they knew. She told them that if you know "what a person eats, how and if he prays, how he loves and what makes him laugh, you can claim to understand him; at least a little" (1,017). Maya told them the story of BRER RABBIT and how, like blacks, he used his wit to survive. Torvash, the Jewish actor, reluctantly told the next narrative. He told of a Jewish man during World War II in Germany whose life depended on discerning which of his captors' two eyes was false. The victim replied, "I know, sir, I know. I know because the false one looks so human" (1,018). When Herr Dieter courteously rose to help his wife clear the table, neighbors who were also guests revealed that Herr Deiter had one false eye, though they knew Torvash did not know that.

The Dieters cheerfully returned from the kitchen with rich desserts and fruit, and after everyone was served and coffee poured, Dieter told a German folktale about a German worker who, on his way to work one cold winter morning, found a small, thoroughly chilled bird. He warmed it, but had to rush to his job at the factory and could not keep the bird with him. He noticed a warm cow pat on the ground and pushed the little bird into the dung so it would survive. The bird was revived and began to peep. A hungry wolf heard the peep and ate the bird.

Dieter continued and said there were three morals to the story: One was that someone who places

*Hitler was present only on the first day of the Olympics. He snubbed all non-Aryans and shook hands only with German victors.

you in a dangerous situation is not necessarily an enemy; someone who rescues you is not necessarily a friend; and if you find yourself in dung, you should keep your mouth shut. The emotion of the moment, the rich food, and perhaps the poor sleep she had the night before made Maya realize that she was going to vomit, so she rushed for the door to the garden. Dieter had insulted both of them with this oppressive story.

When she returned from the garden, Maya asked to be returned to her hotel. Dieter collected African art and asked if she would like to enter into trade with him when she returned to Ghana. Maya declined the invitation. When they were finally back at the hotel, Torvash suggested that she needed to be very careful. Roscoe, her friend in the cast, also reminded her that perhaps she had become "dangerously young" in Africa.

The remainder of *The Blacks* tour went well, and the black cast particularly enjoyed making fun of the whites in the audience. Afterward, Maya reflected that she was not really who she seemed to be on the outside. She felt that over time in Africa, she had become creolized (a person of mixed descent), and she was not comfortable with that.

The performances in Berlin came to a close, and the company moved on to Venice without regret. Maya had performed in Venice before with the PORGY AND BESS cast, and they all felt welcome there. This time, however, there were religious protests against the play they were presenting. It was not a dangerous protest, but it was disturbing. Roscoe bid her good-bye as she left Venice for Cairo. He reminded her, "If it don't fit, don't force it" (1,026). They laughed, and she left.

Maya was welcomed in Cairo by the Williamson children and their driver. Banti their pregnant mother, and Joe, their very busy father (the Liberian ambassador), were preparing to entertain the Liberian president, William V. S. Tubman, who would be in Cairo for the conference. Maya was welcomed to their home. Soon, after their meal, Banti told Maya that she and Joe would like her to sing for the president. Maya asked what she should sing, and Banti said he had learned "Swing Low, Sweet Chariot" in the American South and wanted to sing that with Maya Angelou.

After a formal dinner, the large group of guests went into the decorated parlor, and Maya was asked to sing. She began with a traditional blues song, and then the president requested "Swing Low, Sweet Chariot." Soon he joined her in singing, and the others sang too. Maya reflected that these Liberian Africans, many of whom were descendants of freed African-American slaves who had settled in Liberia about four generations earlier, could not really understand the anguish that had produced the song.

When Maya returned to Accra, Guy met her at the airport with fine chocolates and a piece of beautiful African cloth he had chosen himself. He drove her home, and she was welcomed with the aroma of fried chicken he had prepared because he knew she hated airplane food. He had something to say to her, and told her that her mothering of him was deeply appreciated, but he was now a man and their relationship as it had been was now over. Then he hugged her, thanked her again, said he had other plans for dinner, and left.

Efua, Maya's good friend, appeared at her door one day looking devastated. She told Maya that the body of an Ashanti man had been found and had lain unclaimed in the morgue for two days. This had never happened before. He had a name, a place, but no one had claimed him. Fearful of angry African gods, Efua mourned, "Oh, My Africa" (1,034). After she left, Maya reflected on the contrast of value placed on black lives in Africa and black lives in the United States. It was so different. As it turned out, the family came from the north to collect the body, and Maya was relieved.

Maya's hairdresser, Comfort, was losing weight rapidly and was very weak. Comfort explained that a woman, whose husband had fallen in love with her, had "power medicine" (1,037) and was determined to destroy Comfort. Maya asked her to tell more because she had often seen classified advertisements in U.S. newspapers for HIGH JOHN THE CONQUEROR roots, but she knew little about magic or magic practitioners. Comfort explained that the man's wife had come to her house to ask her questions, and Comfort had been unusually rude to her. Consequently, the woman told her that she would lose everything. Comfort told Maya that she knew someone in Sierra Leone who could help her and said she would return in two months. Two weeks later, however, a friend of Comfort's informed Maya that she had died after a week in Sierra Leone. There was no more explanation, except the friend told Maya that Comfort loved to laugh with her when she did Maya's hair.

Malcolm X was a dedicated correspondent, and he kept the group informed. Sometimes he gave clear directives, and he always included important news. He and MEDGAR EVERS had both received death threats, and Malcolm had great hopes that the Organization of Afro-American Unity (OAAU) would help eliminate some of the tension between groups involved in the CIVIL RIGHTS MOVEMENT. Maya knew she was a good organizer and wanted to help Malcolm with the OAAU. She decided it was time to go home and help her people there. She told Guy, and he agreed. She had learned so much and made many genuine friends in Africa, and she particularly loved the children, but it was time to return to the United States.

Nana Nketsia invited Maya to accompany him and his two daughters by car to the Togo border, where he would then leave them. Maya had not seen Eastern Ghana, so she accepted the invitation. They drove for about three hours and then stopped to spend the night at Aflao. The customs officer there was Mr. Adadevo, and his daughter Frieda took care of Nana's daughters and Maya. Maya retired early, right after dinner, and she awakened early and got up to wish Nana and his driver well on the rest of their journey. She then went to the kitchen to have some coffee.

Mr. Adadevo entered the kitchen to eat some oranges and asked why Maya was only now visiting East Ghana. She replied courteously, and then he asked if she would like to see the nearby village of Keta. It was only 30 miles away, so Maya said yes, thinking she would be able to leave with the girls for Accra in the early afternoon. They went in Mr. Adadevo's large car; the girls rode in the back seat, and the driver, Mr. Adadevo, and Maya rode in the front. The scenery was good but not particularly unusual or unexpected. When they approached a bridge, Maya panicked for some unknown reason. She commanded that the driver stop, so she and the girls could walk across. She said they could meet on the other side.

After the girls were safely back in the car, Mr. Adadevo asked Maya what had frightened her so much. He asked if she had heard stories about the old bridge and explained that bridges before had been poorly built, and many people had insisted on walking across. Maya knew nothing of that. He also explained that the town of Keta would someday disappear because of the ocean and rising waters of a lagoon behind the town; Keta was caught between them.

They entered the marketplace where Mr. Adadevo's sister had a stall. When Maya met her, they laughed at their inability to communicate either in English or French. Soon Maya left them in order to climb up some narrow steps into another part of the market. A large woman was on the stairs, and she began to yell at Maya, mistaking her for someone else. When Mr. Adadevo showed the woman Maya's driver's license, the mood changed and the woman became kind. To Maya, the woman looked a little like her grandmother.

The woman asked them to follow her, and she took them to another stand. She lifted her arms, clasped her hands and placed them on her head, moaned, and rocked a little from side to side in a peculiar way. Mr. Adadevo explained that was a mourning behavior, and Maya remembered her grandmother telling Maya and her brother, Bailey, not to do that because it was bad luck. When they got to the stand, the women there also made that gesture, and Maya was both confused and curious.

Mr. Adadevo tried to explain that Keta was a place where, in the past, nearly everyone was either killed or enslaved. Parents killed children to prevent them from being taken as slaves. The only survivors were children who hid in the bush and watched. Those very children rebuilt the village, and the story was repeated again and again among the people. The children were raised by people in nearby villages, and when they grew up, they rebuilt Keta. These women were grieving because Maya looked like them and even sounded like them. They thought she was a descendent of those who were taken, and they were mourning for those lost ones. Maya was taken from stall to stall, and each time the women would seem to mourn, and then they would give Maya goods. For Maya, it was both sad and happy, because she knew that no matter what they had all suffered, their community had survived.

When Maya left Ghana, she was not sad. Her many friends and Guy were there at the airport to see her off, and she knew that her people had never really completely left Africa. The music, rhythms, singing, and dancing had carried over, and even the proud physical characteristics continued. She left the African continent feeling that somehow her own ancestors were laughing.

CRITICAL COMMENTARY

The title of this autobiography comes from a spiritual about walking to heaven. Sung in many black and white Christian congregations in the United States, it begins with "I've got shoes, you've got shoes, all God's children got shoes." Shoes here symbolize the capability to improve, to move on. It is a capability with which most people are endowed, but too often it is a capability buried by despair. Sadly, improvement is not always possible, but betterment can come with a change of attitude, and that kind of change is the essence of *All God's Children Need Traveling Shoes.* In this brief autobiography, covering the two years that Angelou lived in Ghana, she moves forward with continuing insight and maturity. She has emerged from a broken "marriage" determined to keep her dignity and privacy. In the process, she lets go of some of her own racial prejudices and recognizes that the guilt of prejudice is not limited to whites.

Though Africa is regarded as a homeland among many African Americans as strongly as Israel is the homeland for scattered Jews, Angelou came to the realization at the end of this narrative that to contribute to the cause of eliminating RACISM, she needed to return to the United States. "As in her four previous autobiographies, she explores the theme of displacement and the difficulties involved in creating a home for oneself, one's family, and one's people" (Neubauer, 205). She loved her son deeply, and though there had been marked tensions and separations over the years, he was growing up into a strong, intelligent adult. He had become a man, and she was wisely planning to let him find himself and his place. It was time to enroll him at the University of Ghana and allow him to become independent and make his own journey of self-discovery.

This book begins with a recap of Guy's automobile accident and recovery shortly after their arrival in Accra. Before the tragedy, they had enjoyed a few days of exploring the city's marketplace and streets and had listened to the musical lilt of the many languages. For those hours, they laughed, discovered the city, and enjoyed each others' presence. Then, on the third day after their arrival, Guy was almost mortally injured in an automobile accident that fractured a leg and an arm and left him with a broken neck.

Black American expatriates living in Accra came to their rescue. Guy received excellent medical care from Julian Mayfield's wife, Ana Livia Mayfield, a doctor, and Julian watched over all of them like an older brother. Angelou had known of them in New York because he was a recognized and published writer, and they were among many American expatriates living in Accra. Later, she recorded their histories and stories, and DOLLY MCPHERSON compared her work to that of earlier great American writers such as Henry James and Ernest Hemingway, who also recorded the history of American expatriates abroad (McPherson, 104). After the accident, Maya nearly fell apart with worry for fear that Guy would not survive. She was not taking care of herself, and Julian felt that she needed a female friend to help pull herself out of the deep fear and depression she was suffering. He introduced her to the poet and playwright Efua Sutherland, and the two found much in common in their reading, work, and devotion to family, and as Guy healed, Efua introduced Maya to her culture and colleagues, and in time helped her find a job at the University of Ghana.

All God's Children takes place in Ghana in the early part of the politically restive 1960s. Because of the unrest in the United States, many of the Americans Maya met in Accra had gone there to escape the tensions of their homeland and live more comfortably as the majority race. When she told her new friends Alice Windom and Vicki

Garvin that she was just staying in Ghana long enough to get Guy well and settled in school, and that her plan was to move on to Liberia, one said, "Well, when you leave Ghana, going to Liberia, you ain't going to Africa, in fact you ain't going nowhere" (1986, 893). Alice said, "Honey, you better stay here and get a job and settle down. It can't get better than Ghana, and it could be a lot worse" (2004, 893–894).

Ghana, according to Angelou, was progressive, with a dynamic and intelligent president named Kwame Nkrumah, who offered a safe haven for American Negroes and African revolutionaries working to end colonialism in southern Africa. Liberia, on the other hand, had an unsettled history. It had been founded as an independent republic in 1847 by groups of freed slaves, freeborn blacks, and mulattoes from the United States. Over time, political and economic unrest, tribal tensions, and inconsistent policies had led to near totalitarianism. Angelou's new friends discouraged her from going there.

There are many kinds of oppression, and Angelou encountered another when she was invited to perform in the revival of *The Blacks* by JEAN GENET. She traveled to Berlin to take part in the play, and there she encountered the intense prejudice and twisted humor of an intelligent German male. A German couple had approached her after a performance and asked her to have a drink or meal with them. The next morning, she went to their home for a meal with a new Jewish acquaintance, and soon they both experienced such subtle but penetrating oppression that Angelou became ill and had to go out into the garden to throw up. As it turned out, the German man wanted to use Angelou to buy art pieces from Africa at a cheap price and then he would resell them expensively in Germany. This racist experience both frightened and educated her. Of this interesting episode in Angelou's narrative, Mary Ann Lupton writes: "The Berlin setting offers Angelou an unusual perspective. She is remote enough from Africa to gain new insights into the behavior of black Americans and the nature of white racism, both reflected against the German terrain. . . . African Americans [to her] seem more spirited than the Africans she has encountered in Ghana" (142).

Throughout this autobiography, there is an unfulfilled search for a sense of self and a deep, real sense of yearning for a homeland. The African-American immigrants in Accra had traveled from various parts of the United States to Africa with a hope of finding a sense of belonging because the continent was their ancestral land. For most, their quests ended in disappointment. As people of any race or creed usually learn in time, change is inevitable, and the concept of nurturing and peace that "home" is perceived to represent is really something wise humans learn to carry within themselves. As shown in the text, African Americans experiencing Africa were often surprised to find that they were not as universally welcomed as they had expected. The quest, however, was justified in the minds of those searching, and often an awareness and sense of self was discovered along with an understanding of personal place in the scheme of history.

As in *The Heart of a Woman*, in this book Angelou is still on a quest to not only know her ancestral homeland but also to know herself. The search for the authentic self was a part of what Angelou needed to find. In a 1974 interview with Stephanie Caruana, she said:

> Until I was thirteen, when I left Arkansas, I was known as Mrs. Henderson's California granddaughter. When I went back to California, I was called the Southern girl. And when I went to New York to study dance, I was the tall girl from California. Wherever I went, I belonged somewhere else. But in Ghana, I was called the child who has returned home. I wore African clothes, and I learned to speak a few African languages, including Fanti. Because of my accent, people thought I was from the Gambia. When I said I was American, they would say, "No, no tell the truth. What are you, where are you from? You must be Bambara." Then when I proved I was an American, they said, "Aah, a child who has returned home." (quoted in Caruna, 33)

Dolly McPherson has studied the concept of personal interiority in Angelou's serial autobiographies. Reflecting on McPherson's insights, Eleanor Traylor writes that McPherson

> reads the narratives following *Caged Bird* as preceding readings principally had not. This study [McPherson's] . . . characterizes the growth of the young narrator in *Caged Bird* as the epiphanic discovery of two worlds; the world of externality constructed as reality and the world of "St. Elsewhere"—the imagination—in which any thoughtful, much more, extraordinary consciousness must reside to find states of nurture. (99)

As Angelou relates the stories of Ghana to the reader, she reveals this inner and outer consciousness in the following passage:

> Each person had brought to Africa varying talents, energies, vigor, youth and terrible yearnings to be accepted. On Julian's side porch during warm black nights, our voices were raised in attempts to best each other in lambasting America and extolling Africa.
>
> We drank gin and ginger ale when we could afford it, and Club beer when our money was short. We did not discuss the open gutters along the streets of Accra, the shacks of corrugated iron in certain neighborhoods, dirty beaches and voracious mosquitoes. And under no circumstances did we mention our disillusionment at being overlooked by Ghanaians.
>
> We had come home, and if home was not what we had expected, never mind, our need for belonging allowed us to ignore the obvious and to create real places or even illusory places, befitting our imagination. (901)

From the earliest days of slavery, songs and stories created a sense of longing for a time and place before the slave times. Songs about going home are still sung, and that concept refers both to Africa and to the hope for a better life in the hereafter. Angelou writes: "For centuries we had sung about a place not built with hands, where the streets were paved with gold, and were washed with honey and milk . . . no one would wage war against us again" (902). Many African Americans hoped to feel at least a little of that safety and comfort in Africa. At the same time, Angelou sensed that there was a strength in African Americans that she did not find in the people of Ghana. In this segment, she again provided the reader with her perspectives of the people and the culture. Not unlike her earlier travels in Europe with the cast of *Porgy and Bess,* she explored and described her experiences. She welcomed various invitations to village ceremonies and celebrations, savored them, and shared them with her readers. Her work is both entertaining and educational because she has traveled and explored regions that much of her readership will never visit or see.

Coupled with this deep quest for understanding of other cultures and their meanings is Angelou's own deep sense of respect for all people. She practiced courtesy consistently, even if she was treated poorly. There are multiple examples of her southern manners and consideration for others' feelings throughout this work, and they reveal a black middle-class woman who has become a mature, caring individual with the primary objectives of working hard, being kind, learning, and serving others.

The text is skillfully enriched again with figurative language and beliefs. There are metaphors, exaggerations, and even FOLKLORE and superstition. When describing some of the difficult experiences of African Americans in the United States, she uses descriptive phrasings: "There we had to learn to live on the head of burnt matches, and sleep in holes in the ground" (987). When she was seeking an interview at a newspaper office and was treated condescendingly by the receptionist, she reflected metaphorically, "She knew herself to be a cat, and I was a wounded bird" (912). Angelou also shared some of the folk beliefs of the Ghanaian people expressed after the death of the great civil rights leader W. E. B. DuBois. In August 1963, there was a heavy rainstorm with wind and noise that drenched participants in a march held concurrently with Martin Luther King, Jr.'s March on Washington. "The African marchers said they could have forewarned us. They knew that a driving rain always followed the death of a great soul." Maya asked if God was weeping, and they said, "Of course not. It is the way the spirits welcome a great soul to the land of the dead. They wash it first" (986).

Maya was hired as journalist for the *Ghanaian Times*, and the editor, T. D. Kwesi Bafoo, invited her to an "outdooring," an African rite of passage for a new child. His wife was expecting a baby, and eight days after a child's birth, there was a celebration to give friends and family a first glimpse of the child and an opportunity to welcome "the newest soul" (920). Maya accepted the invitation eagerly. She again shared with her readers that she wanted very much to "get a glimpse of Africa's ancient tribal soul" (923).

Another occasion was a thanksgiving feast in Aburi that Maya was invited to attend. Thousands of people had gathered, and they were all gaily dressed and happily singing and dancing. Suddenly, the drums stopped, and out of distant clouds of dust came a procession of men carrying different kinds of drums. Then, in succession one after another, palanquins carrying richly robed chiefs with a "Kra" at their side passed by the crowd. She explained that the "Kra," a young boy, carried the implanted soul of the chief for its protection should anything happen to the chief. The people waved thousands of white handkerchiefs in respect for the royalty. Angelou describes these joyful traditional events in some detail, using adjectives that pull the reader into the scenes.

On the other hand, she is candid about her feelings concerning the slave trade, which had been practiced for centuries throughout Europe and Asia. She realized that slavery did not just concern the Africans taken to America, but also those who remained. As she looked at the happy, energetic and bustling Accra marketplace, she wondered how one African could sell another. She reflected, "Suppose my great-grandfather was enslaved in that colorful town by his brother. Imagine my great-grandmother traded by her sister in that marketplace" (924).

Because of the quiet, reflective tone of this book, and because of the revealing discussion of African culture and heritage, it can stand apart from Angelou's other autobiographical works. It is both historical and insightful, and Angelou dwells on racism time and time again from various perspectives. She shares her understanding of the changes in Malcolm X after his pilgrimage to Mecca. In that experience, he met people of all races and learned that not all white people are devils, a concept he had taught passionately for years before that trip of homage to his God and his Islamic belief. One of the most poignant moments for Malcolm was when he met the great and humble Ghanaian statesman and leader Nana Nketsia. When Angelou returned Malcolm to his hotel, he told her, "'Now I have met African royalty. A chief. True, true. He knows his people and he loves them, and they love him.' Malcolm's face wore a mask of wistfulness so telling I had to look away" (993).

Just before the conclusion of this book, Angelou reflects about having searched but recognized that she had not found the roots she had sought:

> If the heart of Africa still remained allusive, my search for it had brought me closer to understanding myself and other human beings. The ache for home lives in all of us, the safe place where we can go as we are and not be questioned. It impels mighty ambitions and dangerous capers. We amass great fortunes at the cost of our souls, or risk our lives in drug dens from London's Soho to San Francisco's Haight-Ashbury. We shout in Baptist churches, wear yarmulkes and wigs and argue even the tiniest points in the Torah, or worship the sun and refuse to kill cows for the starving. . . . My mind was made up. I would go back to the United States as soon as possible. (1,041–1,042)

At the conclusion of this book, Angelou describes being at the airport with her son and a large gathering of friends she had met in Ghana. The group included academics, performers, expatriates, children, and others. John Gruesser, Deborah E. McDowell, and other literary critics have suggested that the narrative ends on a "stereotyped and unauthentic note" (McDowell 1986, 17). Gruesser suggests that the ending is "too easily manufactured at the last minute to resolve the problem [searching for home] of the book" (18). It is true that Angelou is once again leaving her son and going her own way, but the passage quoted above gives evidence that she had brought her experiences to closure. She had sought a certain illusive center as she explored the parts of Africa that opened themselves to her, but what she found was a new and deeper understanding of herself and other human beings. She had met and accepted human beings very different from her or anyone she had known. She had observed dignity and squalor, tradition and indifference, racism and democracy, and she realized that her responsibility as a writer and spokesperson for her people was genuine. She knew that it was time to return to the United States and use her voice for change.

SOME IMPORTANT THEMES AND SYMBOLS IN *ALL GOD'S CHILDREN NEED TRAVELING SHOES*

Defining "Home"

Many of the individuals Angelou associated with in Ghana were black Americans who had relocated to Africa because of the United States's painful racial history. Some expected to be welcomed as warmly as returning children and found it difficult to understand the African people's frequent indifference to them. There were about 40 families in Accra as well as American government employees. One African-American couple, newly arrived in Ghana, visited Maya and her roommates at their rented home, where visitors often came to talk. They tried to explain their purpose in relocating to Africa by saying, "We have come to Africa to suckle from her breasts" (917). The women tried to explain why that metaphor did not really work, and finally one of the women said, "They didn't want to know that they had not come home, but had left one familiar place of painful memory for another strange place with none" (919).

Maya arrived in Ghana with Guy to register him for his university studies. His unfortunate automobile accident kept her there, and she, too, thought at first that she had come home. While there, she visited villages and associated with many Africans of varied social, economic, and political interests. But by the end of her sojourn there, she realized that though her family history stretched far back into Western Africa, her home was in the United States. She also recognized her responsibility to inform her own people of their rich heritage and their rights.

Motherhood

Though Maya was busy with her own responsibilities in Ghana, and Guy was living in the dorms and attending classes, her caring about Guy did not diminish. Having established himself as a young adult, he told her that her years of mothering him had come to an end. In a later interview, Guy stated that Maya was a wonderful, giving, supportive mother. She was a very strong person, and he knew he had to get out from under her power, but regardless, she was a magnificently successful mother for him. In Ghana, when she tried to counsel him about a 36-year-old girlfriend, he was sarcastic with her. She warned him that she, Maya, would "knock him down," and he responded by patting her head and saying, "Yes' little mother. I'm sure you will" (1,005). She accepted that, but it was very difficult for her. Even so, she realized that she had to let him find his own way.

Shortly after that exchange with Guy, Maya was invited to perform in Berlin in the play *The Blacks*. When she returned to Accra after the performances, Guy met her at the airport and drove her to her house. He had prepared one of her favorite dinners, and after a little talk, he told her that their relationship had changed, "Your life is your own, and mine belongs to me" (1,033). He did not stay for dinner, but thanked her for being a good mother and left. Painfully, she accepted his declaration of independence, but her sense of motherhood and caring for him did not diminish. Not long after, she returned to the United States and left Guy to complete his university studies in Ghana.

Signifying

SIGNIFYING means saying one thing and meaning another. Henry Louis Gates, Jr., has written about the relationships between African and African-American vernacular traditions and literature by explaining an unusual system of interpretation and speaking traditions that were carried to the New World by black slaves. Angelou uses these traditions by allowing black characters in her autobiographies and her poetry to speak for themselves in their own way. The use of motifs, figures of speech, and punning in her work reflects the practice of signifying. It is an understood meaning expressed in reverse.

In *I Know Why the Caged Bird Sings,* there is an excellent example of signifying. In Chapter 25, Angelou writes about not really knowing her grandmother: "Her African bush secretiveness and suspiciousness had been compounded by slavery and confirmed by centuries of promises made and promises broken" (150). She follows by writing: "We have a saying among Black Americans which describes Momma's caution. 'If you ask a Negro where he's been, he'll tell you where he's going'" (150). The private nature of communication between those who are insiders with understanding has been a pattern in both African and African-American communities.

In *All God's Children Need Traveling Shoes,* Angelou is in Africa searching for the essence of her motherland. In one episode, when she is exploring the bush (the countryside) and stopping in a village where there is no hotel, she is welcomed, and neighbors carry abundant foods to her lodging. She remarks that this is a version of a similar practice she had observed in STAMPS, ARKANSAS, where she had grown up. Practicing the same courtesy as would be observed in Stamps, the guest does not acknowledge that the host or hostess has not prepared all of the food. In this instance, Maya said, "Oh, Sister, you went to such trouble," and the response was, "It is nothing, Sister" (968). The references to the quest for freedom, the journey itself, and the similarities in behavior she sees echo the customs and voices of both her ancient and recent ancestors.

One of Maya's important reflections on black Americans in Africa is the following: "We carried the badge of a barbarous history sewn to our dark skins. It had often been said that Black people were childish. . . . Those actions which appeared to be childish most often were exhibitions of bravado, not unlike humming a jazz tune while walking into a gathering of the Ku Klux Klan" (947). Signifying is used with understanding; what one sees or hears may not be the meaning but rather a metaphorical pointed finger at a meaning.

In the last few pages of *All God's Children,* Angelou describes a visit she was invited to make to Keta, in Eastern Ghana. Keta was a remote place in the bush, an area where slaves were once captured. While there, she was recognized as a relative or descendant of the local people by her voice and appearance. The women wept and mourned for their lost ancestors when they saw her, and they showed her off one to another. Maya quietly accepted the experience with a "curious joy" (1,050) because she realized that no matter what cruelties they had endured, they had survived. The legacy of it all was an enduring hope for a better future. Angelou was eager to tell the stories to people in the United States because she knew and saw that these Africans have "faced down death by daring to hope" (1,051).

CHARACTERS

Maya Angelou Angelou was in her 50s when she wrote her fifth autobiography, the story of her sojourn in Accra, Ghana. Her plan had been to work in public service in Liberia, but Guy was in a serious accident so she stayed in Accra and worked as an associate administrator at the University of Ghana and also as a journalist. Initially she stayed at the YWCA, but in time Angelou and new African-American friends she met in Ghana, Alice Windom and Vicki Garvin, rented a bungalow together. Their home became a gathering place for many African-American immigrants and other visitors to Ghana, including the American civil rights leader Malcolm X.

Guy Johnson Maya's only son, Guy had graduated from high school in Cairo, Egypt, and then traveled with his mother to Accra to be enrolled in the University of Ghana. On their third day in Ghana, he was seriously injured in an automobile accident and placed in a body cast. He recovered fully from his injuries and entered his university studies. As his mother wrote, "He had grown from a precocious adolescent into an adept young man" (893). In time, he forced the separation from his mother by a declaration of his independence and manhood. However, his mother continued to pay for his education and living expenses until he later returned to the United States.

Julian Mayfield Maya had known of Julian Mayfield's journalistic work in New York. His wife, Ana (Anna in *The Heart of a Woman*) Livia, was a medical doctor who discovered that Guy's injuries from the automobile accident were more serious than the diagnosis at first suggested, and she oversaw his recovery. Julian was a progressive journalist and wrote articles for American and African journals, as well as for the *Ghana Evening News*. In time, he and Maya became close friends, and he introduced her to many people while she was in Ghana. He helped her find work and also served as a guide for her. The Mayfields also let Maya store her books and clothes at their house while she stayed at the Accra YWCA waiting for her son to recover. Having a room to herself allowed her the privacy to mourn his serious physical condition. It was Julian who recognized when it was time for Maya to gain a better perspective on the situation, and he introduced her to a woman, Efua Sutherland, who helped her to overcome much of the anxiety she was suffering.

Alice Windom An African American and witty friend from St. Louis, Missouri, Alice was one of the first black Americans Maya and Guy met in Accra. She was a social worker with a master's degree from the University of Chicago. She had been raised in a family of university professors, and her powers of verbal expression and argument were powerful. Alice had hoped to associate with African social workers, but somehow that did not occur, and she became a secretary in one of the foreign embassies.

Vicki Garvin An African-American woman from New York City, Vicki was one of the first black Americans Maya and Guy met in Accra. She had been a union organizer in the United States and was respected internationally. Vicki was well-educated with both bachelor's and master's degrees, but the only job she could find in Ghana was as a typist in one of the foreign embassies.

Efua Sutherland (Efuah Sutherland) A beautiful woman as well as a poet, playwright, and head of Ghana's National Theatre, Efua had three children and introduced Maya to them as their Auntie Maya. Befriending Maya during the worrisome early period of Guy's convalescence from the automobile accident, Efua said, "Sister, you are not alone. I, myself, will be at the hospital tomorrow. Your son is now my son. He has two mothers in this place" (2004).

Comfort Adday A stenographer and hairdresser, Comfort became Maya's regular hairdresser. She was witty with commonsense, and she said that she enjoyed laughing with Maya, for whom she created a Ghanaian hairstyle. She told Maya that she, Comfort, was very ill because a jealous wife had cast a spell on her, and perhaps the woman poisoned her. Comfort sought help from spell practitioners in Larteh, Ghana, and then went to Sierra Leone for more treatment, but unfortunately no one could cure her, and she died.

Kojo Kojo was a village boy who asked to work for Maya. He did housework for her, and Maya, Alice, and Vicki tutored him on his schoolwork three evenings a week. One evening, several of his relatives arrived from their village with a variety of foods for Maya and her friends. They thanked them for helping Kojo and told the three women that they would supply food for their household as it came into season.

Sheikhali A wealthy businessman from Mali, Sheikhali imported thoroughbred horses and beef to Ghana. He wanted to marry Maya and take her back to his other wife in Mali to have Maya educate that wife and his children.

Nana Nketsia An African leader and the first African vice chancellor at the University of Ghana, Nana welcomed Maya into his family circle.

Malcolm X Malcolm was an American civil rights leader whose Ghanaian itinerary was arranged by Maya Angelou and other black American expatriates.

FURTHER READING

Angelou, Maya. *The Collected Autobiographies of Maya Angelou*. New York: Modern Library Edition by Random House, 2004.

Bloom, Lynn Z., and Ning Yu. "American Autobiography: The Changing Critical Canon." *a/b: Autobiographical Studies* 9, no. 2 (Fall 1994): 167–180.

Caruana, Stephanie. "Maya Angelou: An Interview." 1974. In *Conversations with Maya Angelou*, edited by Jeffrey M. Elliot, 29–37. Jackson and London: University Press of Mississippi, 1989.

Cudjoe, Selwyn. "Maya Angelou and the Autobiographical Statement." In *Black Women Writers*, edited by Mari Evans, 6–24. New York: Anchor Books/Doubleday, 1984.

Dundes, Alan, ed. *Mother Wit from the Laughing Barrel: Readings in the Interpretation of African American Folklore*. Englewood Cliffs, N.J.: Prentice-Hall, 1973.

Elliot, Jeffrey M., ed. *Conversations with Maya Angelou*. Jackson and London: University Press of Mississippi, 1989.

Gruesser, John C. "Afro-American Travel Literature and Africanist Discourse." *Black American Literature Forum* 24 (1990): 5–20.

Hagen, Lyman B. *Heart of a Woman, Mind of a Writer, and Soul of a Poet: A Critical Analysis of the Writings of Maya Angelou*. Lanham, Md.: University Press of America, 1997.

Lupton, Mary Jane. *Maya Angelou: A Critical Companion*. Westport, Conn.: Greenwood Press, 1998.

McDowell, Deborah E. "Traveling Hopefully." *Women's Review of Books* 4 (October 1986): 17.

McPherson, Dolly. *The Autobiographical Works of Maya Angelou*. New York: Peter Lang, 1990.

Neubauer, Carol E. "Maya Angelou: Self and a Song of Freedom in the Southern Tradition." In *Maya Angelou*. Modern Critical Views, edited by Harold Bloom, 191–218. Philadelphia: Chelsea House, 1999.

Traylor, Eleanor W. "Maya Angelou: Writing Life, Inventing Literary Genre." In *Maya Angelou*. Bloom's Modern Critical Views, edited by Harold Bloom, 91–105. New York: Bloom's Literary Criticism, 2009.

A Song Flung Up to Heaven (2002)

A Song Flung Up to Heaven is the sixth and last of Maya Angelou's serial autobiographies. It begins with Angelou's return alone from Africa to the United States and recounts her experiences during the turbulent years of 1965–68. In the short period covered in this book, MALCOLM X and MARTIN LUTHER KING, JR., were both assassinated, and the entire country was caught up in the often violent struggles of the CIVIL RIGHTS MOVEMENT. History was in the making, and Angelou contributed to many of the significant changes in American society that grew out of that turmoil. It was difficult to be separated from Guy once again, but he had become an adult and was finishing his university education in Ghana. He was ready to be independent, and she understood and respected his need.

The book ranges from deep sorrow and fear for the future to high comedy, particularly when Angelou and her newly found African-American friend, DOLLY MCPHERSON, discover they have both been used and lied to with exactly the same lines by the same handsome, Oxford-educated, and charming African man, Angelou in California and McPherson in New York. Over time, McPherson and Angelou became lifelong friends, and eventually both became professors at Wake Forest University.

In this work, Angelou reveals how she enjoyed her developing artistic talent and received both recognition for her past writing and invitations to write more. Another important theme in the book is her perseverance, in which she was aided by the support of many good friends. Her religious background is also evident throughout the text. She acknowledges and give her thanks to seven of her teachers: the Reverends Frederick Buechner; Eric Butterworth; Serenus T. Churn, Sr.; H. Beecher Hicks; Barbara King; Cecil Williams; and Andrew Young. This is an important acknowledgment because it reveals, once again, that she has sought and listened to many important religious orators, a practice that is constantly reflected in her writing.

In this book, Angelou discusses the realities of life in the United States during the mid-1960s. When Malcolm X was shot to death, she was in California, and the indifference to his death that she observed among people there was shocking and produced deep anger within her. It was difficult for her to accept that her own people did not seem to care. It seemed to her that the people in the region where her mother lived just considered Malcolm X to be some sort of noisy radical.

When Martin Luther King, Jr., was assassinated, Angelou was living in New York. It happened the day of her 40th birthday, and she received the news in the midst of preparing for a birthday celebration. It was JAMES BALDWIN ("Jimmy"), a black writer and close friend, who pulled her out of her depression and set the wheels in motion for her to begin writing her first autobiography. This sixth autobiography thus closes the series that began with *I Know Why the Caged Bird Sings,* a series that takes Angelou's life from 1931 to 1968.

SYNOPSIS

Chapter 1

Maya seated herself on a Pan Am jet headed to the United States and realized immediately that she was among more white people than she had seen in the four years she had lived in Africa. She was wearing African dress and felt out of place because she was accustomed to being among her own race dressed much the way she was. Soon her thoughts turned to the political unrest and fear that were acutely present in both Africa and America. Maya's hope was that she could be an effective worker in Malcolm X's new Organization for African American Unity (OAAU). She had written to him to inquire if she could help, and in response she had received a letter from him promising to give his support to her participation in the current campaign. Her 19-year-old son, Guy, remained in Ghana at the university, and adult Ghanaian friends would be there for him if he needed them.

In South Africa, NELSON MANDELA and Robert Sobukwe, leader of the Pan-African Congress, had been in prison for years. Maya's former partner, VUSUMZI MAKE, and other leaders in South Africa believed that they could rid their country of apartheid and change the hearts of the authoritarian BOERS. Maya believed that Malcolm's new organization would lift all people to rid themselves of RACISM, once and for all, and at last—as Martin Luther King, Jr., taught—freedom would ring. There would be freedom for blacks in Africa and in the United States.

Maya worried about leaving Guy, but she also knew he could take care of himself in his transition to adulthood. She thought about the control her quasi-husband, Vus, had had over her, and she knew she would never miss that. When she disembarked from the plane in the United States, she immediately responded to the noise, which she called the cacophony of New York's Idlewild Airport. It was disturbing and nearly overwhelming to her because Africa's noise had seemed so much less aggressive.

She called Malcolm X, and he told her that he would leave home immediately to pick her up, but Maya felt she could not jump right into the urban clamor of New York City. She told Malcolm she was going to SAN FRANCISCO for a month to be with her mother and brother. She also had others to call: MAX ROACH and ABBEY LINCOLN; ROSA GUY, with whom she could have stayed; and James Baldwin, whom she had met in Paris in the 1960s when she toured with *PORGY AND BESS.* She and Baldwin had become close friends in New York City through their association in the HARLEM WRITERS GUILD and because he tutored her for her role as the White Queen in JEAN GENET's *The BLACKS.* However, Maya thought it would be best not to call him because he would persuade her to stay; she could never resist him.

Chapter 2

Maya met her beautiful mother—VIVIAN BAXTER—and beloved brother—BAILEY JOHNSON, JR.—in San Francisco. Bailey had flown in from Hawaii, where he was a professional hotel chef, and welcomed her back to the United States. Vivian said she had read in the papers that Maya was going to work with Malcolm X in his organization. She disapproved, and Maya began to defend her decision, but Bailey cautioned her not to try. Since they had been young children growing up together in STAMPS, ARKANSAS, with their grandmother and uncle, Bailey, less than two years older than Maya, had always been her mentor and protector. They had lived with their mother in St. Louis for a while when Maya was seven and eight, and it was exotic and interesting until Maya was brutally raped by her mother's boyfriend.

The man was killed shortly after a court trial, and Maya blamed her own voice for his death. She had been mute by choice for several years.

The children were returned to Arkansas, and Bailey was the only one Maya talked to for years. She loved him and believed that because of that love, her voice would not hurt him. When they reached their teens, Bailey and Maya joined their mother in California.

After Maya's return from Africa, the first weekend at her mother's Fulton Street home was filled with delicious food, great conversation, and friends dropping by. Maya had deep feelings of guilt about Guy remaining in Africa, and in spite of her mother's warm welcome home, her son was in her thoughts almost constantly. He wanted to stay in Africa as an independent male, and he resisted any efforts Maya made to talk to him about his future.

Chapter 3

On Sunday morning, Maya visited Aunt Lottie Wells, who had once been in business with her mother and had helped her raise Guy. While she was there, her good friend Ivonne called. It was good to hear her voice, but Ivonne wondered why Maya had returned to the United States. She reminded Maya that blacks were doing crazy things in the States, in fact; she said, "they have just killed that man in New York" (1,071). Maya knew immediately that "that man" was Malcolm X.

Chapter 4

Maya was sleeping at Lottie Wells's home when Bailey's anxious voice awakened her. She was devastated by the news of Malcolm X's assassination. Lottie knew Maya needed to rest after the long trip from Africa, and she had encouraged her to sleep. Bailey quietly took her out for the walk home, and Maya was surprised that black people were not rioting because of what had happened to Malcolm X. Bailey told her that they knew but did not care. To prove his point, he took her into a random lounge (Havana Bar) and ordered drinks. He then asked the bartender if he had heard what had happened to Malcolm X. The bartender simply said, "Well hell, man. They shot him. You know they say, you live by the sword, you die by the sword" (1,073). Maya was furious, but Bailey stopped her, and they moved on to Jack's Tavern, their mother's hangout. Bailey warned her to keep her opinions and reactions under control. Their mother's friends greeted them warmly, and to avoid another possible run-in with a bartender (an old friend of Maya's named Trumpet), Bailey escorted her to a table. He told her that she should not go back to New York and invited her to go to Honolulu with him. When they returned home, her mother expressed her sympathy. In spite of her criticism of Maya's choice to work for Malcolm, Vivian Baxter respected the fact that he and Maya had been good friends and was sorry for her daughter's loss.

Chapter 5

Maya remained in San Francisco when Bailey left, but she continued to despair about people's indifference to Malcolm's death. Bailey found a nightclub job for her in Hawaii and said she could stay with their mother's sister, evangelist Aunt Lea, until she could find a place of her own. She took him up on the offer. Her supportive and good-humored mother made tasty meals for her until she was on her way, and she also bought Maya an expensive new wardrobe. Maya realized that she was "ready to search for a path back into life" (1,078).

Chapter 6

Maya stayed a while with her Aunt Lea and her husband, Al. Maya addressed him as Uncle Brother, and the two of them got along very well. Lea lived for and spoke often of her religion; Al was a down-to-earth general contractor from the Arkansas Ozarks and had the "strength of John Henry" (1,079). His good humor helped Maya survive the constant talk of religion.

Chapter 7

Maya's return to singing in a nightclub was easy. She held the crowd's attention and entertained them with calypso folk songs and GEORGE GERSHWIN and DUKE ELLINGTON love songs. She usually included one African song in each set, and the audience seemed to enjoy it. She found a furnished flat that gave her the solitude she needed to reflect. Guilt about Guy haunted her, but she tried to be philosophical. Bailey assured her that Guy would become a man of principle.

DELLA REESE, a very talented singer, was performing at the Aloha Club nearby, and Maya recognized Reese's dedication to the art of singing, which contrasted with her own lack of commitment to it. Singing would not be a career for her, and she decided to go back to the mainland and find a job she really liked. Uncle Brother gave her keys to a car he had left in LOS ANGELES. Life was moving along for her, and she learned that BETTY SHABAZZ, Malcolm's widow, had given birth to healthy twin boys and friends OSSIE DAVIS, RUBY DEE, the attorney Percy Sutton, and the biographer ALEX HALEY were taking care of her. Friends from Africa also reported that Guy was doing better. Maya's mood was lighter, so on her last performance in Hawaii, she danced rather than sang. It was good entertainment and earned a tremendous ovation from the audience. Bailey gave her a wad of money and promised her that she would go far. Maya headed for Los Angeles, her Uncle Brother's car, and an unknown but confident future.

Chapter 8

When Maya reached Los Angeles, she quickly sought out Frances Williams, a member of Actors' Equity and a friend of Maya's for over 10 years. Williams and her brother owned a large house with apartments, and Maya soon rented one from her. Maya painted and carefully furnished her new home and then began to look for a job. Frances found her first job, which was in "Random Research" (1,087). Maya was assigned to the WATTS neighborhood of Los Angeles, and her job was to knock on every fourth house and ask questions that were listed on a form. Watts was safe, but not as carefully tended has it had been at one time.

Maya had specific prewritten lines she was supposed to use for openers, but she knew wary black women well enough to know they would not open any doors. She remembered a good story Martin Luther King, Jr., had once told about a tactful black woman who knew how to answer questions without offending. When asked why she did not speak more directly, she answered: "Honey, when you have your head in a lion's mouth, you don't snatch it out. You reach up and tickle him behind his ears and you draw your head out gradually. Every black woman in this country has had her head in a lion's mouth" (1,089). So Maya simply said to the women in Watts, "Good morning. I have a job asking questions" (1,089).

Chapter 9

The riots in Watts (1965) began with street fights and escalated into fire and destruction. Cars were overturned, and rocks, stones, and cans of beer and soda were thrown at police. Screaming sirens turned Watts into a nightmare as men and women carried or pushed their household appliances to safety and gangs of young men blocked fire trucks from entering the area. Looting was rampant, and at last the National Guard was called in to get the area under control. In a few days, jails began to fill, and there were rumors that the police were arresting anyone even "suspected of being black" (1,094).

Maya, out of curiosity, went to the site of the riots twice. The first time, she was nearly attacked, and the second time, parked only a block from the conflagration, she heard hecklers hurling insults aimed at both the soldiers and each other. In front of a pawnshop, she heard someone say to a National Guardsman; "Hey, man, don't you feel stupid keeping people from stealing something that was already stole in the first place?" (1,095). The soldiers stood fast. Maya felt invisible in the black community of Watts; she watched with comprehension as the five-day riot burned itself out.

The consequences of the riots and the burning forced people who could help to get involved with rehabilitating the neighborhood. Better jobs, a medical clinic, affordable grocery stories and markets were basic provisions desperately needed by the people, and BUDD SCHULBERG, an award-winning writer, was among many who went to Watts and helped as they could. Schulberg founded the Watts Writers Workshop, while wives of film moguls formed a group called Neighbors of Watts and learned how they could help. One of the greatest needs was safe child care so that women could go to work with peace of mind about their children.

James Baldwin gave Maya's name to a French journalist who visited her for an interview. She knew the man could not really understand the rage manifest behind the Watts riots, but she told him "some of what he wanted to hear and some of what she wanted to say" (1,101).

Chapter 10

Beah Richards, Maya's next-door neighbor at the apartment house, was a black actress second only to the great Ruby Dee. Frank Silvera, owner of a theater company called "The Theatre of Being," had hired Beah to play the lead role in Medea. Maya was cast in the role of a nurse and was also Beah's driver. The nurse was important, and Maya studied to master the character, but she felt undervalued. A week before the opening, she made up like an old woman and joined the cast for final rehearsals. Reviews of the play were mixed. Beah Richards was lauded, and now and then a review mentioned the elderly actress who played the nurse so well.

Chapter 11

Maya made new friends and felt welcome at nearby Sid's Café and Bar, where Louisiana-type food was served. A new group of friends there welcomed her and introduced themselves. One fellow she met, Phil, said he was a liar and could be ornery. Maya said that she might sit someplace else, but Phil and his friends asked her to stay. They wanted to hear about Africa and Hawaii. She told them about her life in those places, and one morning they came to her home, shared some wine, and invited her to go on a ride with them. She did, but Phil played a mean trick on the group by parking on some train tracks when a train could be heard coming around a bend not far away. He turned off the motor. Everyone in the car (except for one asleep) began to scream at him, and he slid the car off the tracks seconds before the train sped by. Maya, frightened, became mute. Phil asked if she wanted to go home, and, unable to talk, she nodded. The terror made her recollect some of the horror of her childhood rape, and that fear did not leave her until she had showered. Phil was a cruel tease, and Maya avoided him after that incident.

Chapter 12

Maya received an unexpected phone call from someone who identified himself as her husband. They were not married; she thought he had been her greatest love, but it did not work because he had expected her to worship him. He said he was in New York and headed for Los Angeles to retrieve her and take her back to Africa. One factor against returning to Africa was that she also knew Guy was nearly finished with school and would probably be returning to the United States. She called her mother for advice, and her mother assured her that Los Angeles was big enough for the ex and Maya.

He arrived at her apartment and filled her heart and soul for a few days. He said that "the American Negro represents the best the African can hope for" (1,109). Maya's longtime friend Nichelle Nichols invited the two to dinner with the intent of helping Maya, but she, too, was spellbound by him and thought Maya was very lucky to be courted by such a powerful man.

Chapter 13

The relationship between Maya and her lover from Africa did not go well as he was consistently condescending. They had never been married with a license, but there had been a private ceremony in Africa with friends. His intent was to take Maya, his "wife," back to Africa. After a Doris Day and Rock Hudson movie, he remarked that he wondered "why can't we be to each other the way they are?" (1,111). Maya did not respond positively, and he wondered if American Negros were "just stupid or merely pretending" (1,112). Maya was furious. She had already prepared dinner and set the table with her best tablecloth and china. The food was on the table, but she picked up the tablecloth by the four corners—including food, plates, glasses, and silverware—dragged it to the living room, and left it in front of him, saying, "Here's dinner if you want it. I'm leaving" (1,112).

Maya went to her friend Nichelle's home and called her mother. Bailey was at her mother's home, and both Bailey and her mother arrived at Nichelle's home in Los Angeles the next morning. By afternoon, the African was on a flight to Mexico to visit Kwesi Brew, Ghana's ambassador to Mexico, and his wife, Molly. Before Bailey and Vivian left they gave Maya a good scolding for putting herself into such a predicament. Maya did not like their reprimands, but she was glad they had rescued her.

Chapter 14

Maya wrote a play entitled *All Day Long.* It was about a 13-year-old poor southern black boy who discovers what living in the North is like. Not unlike Bailey and Maya, the boy is amazed at the gadgets in the city. Unfortunately, Maya was unable to find anyone to produce her play. At this same time, President Kwame Nkrumah of Ghana was deposed, Malcolm X had been gone for two years, and Watts was still a sad place with hundreds of homeless and injured.

Chapter 15

Maya felt that the time had come for a change in location and decided to return to New York. She had been offered two places to stay: with Dolly McPherson, who Maya understood to be an elderly friend of her African male lover, and with Abbey Lincoln and Max Roach, longtime friends. Bailey and her mother both supported her decision to move back to the East, but the plan was changed when Guy, who had returned to California from Africa, was in another serious automobile collision. His neck was broken again when a truck hit his parked car. Guy recovered and stayed at his grandmother's in San Francisco to gain strength and find a job.

Chapter 16

Because of many friendships and gratitude to those who had helped her, leaving Los Angeles for New York was harder than Maya had expected. Even so, one of her mother's truisms came into her thoughts: "Take as much time as you need to make up your mind, but once it is made up, step out on your decision like it's something you want" (1,122). Guy was fine, and Maya had enough money to travel to New York and maintain herself for at least two months. She optimistically figured that she would have a job by that time.

Maya was getting ready to return to New York from California when Guy was in another automobile accident. After he was released from the hospital and recovering well, he stayed in California with his maternal grandmother, Vivian Baxter, pictured here with Guy. *(Courtesy Angelou-Johnson Family Archives)*

Chapter 17

Maya had not been in New York long when Rosa Guy decided to have a party. Maya asked if she could invite Dolly McPherson since she, too, had offered Maya a place to stay in New York. When Dolly arrived, both she and Maya collapsed in laughter. The African, as Angelou refers to him in his book, had tricked both of them by saying that the other one was old; in fact, he had referred to both of them as "the old goat" (1,124). As it turned out, both were amazed to find the other beautiful, youthful, and intelligent. Clearly the African had fooled both of them.

Chapter 18

One of the things Maya felt she had to do when she returned to New York was to visit the Audubon Ballroom, where Malcolm X was shot on February 21, 1965. She looked through the dusty windows and pondered how different things might have been for her if she had stayed in New York when she arrived back in the United States from Ghana.

Chapter 19

Maya found a patron and genuine friend in the New Yorker Jerry Purcell, who owned a swank supper club. She had sung there once and contacted him for advice about work. He was kind and generous to her, with no strings attached, and for two years he treated her as a valued employee. Her job was to bring people to the restaurant, take the bill, add her tip, and sign it. She helped his business, and he graciously helped her by taking care of her living expenses, which allowed her to focus on her writing.

Chapter 20

Maya found an apartment in a new building on Central Park West. It was empty, and as New York friends heard about it, they began giving her gifts of fine furnishings. Sam Floyd, who was a close friend of James Baldwin's, introduced himself to her, and they also became close friends. Sam gave her a small rug and said, "People think New Yorkers are cold, but that is only when they are prevented from helping people who really don't need help" (1,128).

Chapter 21

Dolly McPherson and Maya became good friends. She had a brother who reminded Maya of Bailey so much that she wanted her mother to meet him. She and Dolly also became friends with Bea Grimes, a black woman who owned an antique shop. She taught Maya about antiques, and she helped Maya finish furnishing her new apartment. With that accomplished, Maya had a party and invited old friends from the Harlem Writers Guild, including James (Jimmy) Baldwin, PAULE MARSHALL, and JOHN KILLENS. It was a houseful, and Maya was happy to see her many friends (more than 50 guests) having a "New York good time" (1,130).

Chapter 22

James Baldwin, who came from a family of nine children, took Maya home to meet his mother. She was soft-spoken and friendly, and she liked Maya so much, she asked Maya to call her "Mother Baldwin" (1,132).

Chapter 23

Maya interviewed with Norman Cousins for a job with the *Saturday Review*. He asked her to write five précis of articles in five international journals by Monday. She felt it might be a way to eliminate her chance of getting the job there, but with the help of Dolly and Dolly's secretary, she accomplished the task. When she returned to see Cousins on Monday afternoon, a secretary told her that both Cousins and his secretary were out. Maya laid her work on the desk of the unfriendly secretary and left quickly.

Chapter 24

James Baldwin and Maya were friends, but they had a disagreement about the BLACK PANTHER PARTY and, specifically, ELDRIDGE CLEAVER. Maya liked the Black Panther organization but felt Cleaver was "an opportunist and a batterer" (1,134). Jimmy Baldwin was heading to California to help Cleaver with his organization. He respected Cleaver as a thinker and felt strongly that going to help was the right thing for him to do, despite Maya's reservations. There was a tension caused by their differing points of view, but for Jimmy, it was a matter of conscience to become more involved.

Chapter 25

Maya was invited to a dinner at Jerry Purcell's elegant apartment on the East Side of New York, where she was asked to read her poetry. Afterwards, Purcell told her that he wanted to give her a monthly allowance to enable her to work on her play and continue writing poetry. She was flabbergasted. He also warned her about any drug use, and she assured him that she had learned that "painful lesson" (1,139) from her brother. Purcell wanted Rosa to stay at the apartment with him after Maya left, but she declined, though she was attracted to him.

Chapter 26

One day, the phone rang and it was the African from Ghana, telling Maya that he would be in the United States to speak at a university. He asked if Maya would like a car, and then he asked if she would hostess a party for him for 12 guests at her apartment. He wanted to invite some people he had not seen since his last trip. Maya said she would, and then she called Dolly for a good laugh and a little planning for some discreet revenge.

When he arrived at her apartment the evening of the party, Maya was prepared with the accustomed welcoming drink, schnapps, and was put off when he ceremoniously dropped a few drops of libation to the gods on her Karastan rug. Soon other guests arrived dressed in the beautiful robes of Africa. At a point in the party, Maya asked him if he thought African or European men were more faithful to their women. He was answering when Dolly McPherson walked in, put her hand on his shoulder, and said, "Hello there" (1,143).

The African was momentarily stunned, but he regained his composure, and for about five minutes he was able to handle his realization that the two American women he had used knew one another. Then Maya and Dolly excused themselves and went to the kitchen to enjoy a good laugh. Soon he was ready to leave but not without a few words to Maya that revealed his embarrassment and hurt. He told Maya, privately, "You have tried to belittle me. That is beneath the Maya I know and still love" (1,145). Both Dolly and Maya realized they would never see him again, and he left after twisting the situation so they felt ashamed of themselves.

Chapter 27

The 100th anniversary celebration of the birth of W. E. B. DuBois was held at Carnegie Hall, and many luminaries made presentations and provided entertainment including, Ossie Davis, Pete Seeger, James Baldwin, and Martin Luther King, Jr. Maya sat in a box provided for the family and friends of James Baldwin. Toward the end of King's moving speech that night, the audience, one by one, began to stand and then responded with resounding applause.

King was impressed with Maya's energy and charismatic charm. He was grateful to her for the work she had done previously for the Southern Christian Leadership Conference, and he knew that the work she had planned with Malcolm X had vanished with his death. After King's speech and the other ceremonies, he approached Maya and asked if she would work for him for a while. He asked for a month of her time to help build support for the poor people's march to be held in Washington, D.C. King wanted her to travel the country and persuade black congregations to donate one week's collection to the effort. Believing that the march would help the people, Maya consented to help.

Chapter 28

Maya had been helped by many male friends who had advised her in Guy's upbringing, and her son had turned out to be a very nice young man. He was strong, independent, and had his own perspectives on matters that did not always agree with his mother's views. He was to be in New York for one day, and Maya planned a party in his honor. Most of the guests would be the very men who had helped advise her as she raised him. As she was leaving the supermarket, Maya happened to encounter a young man named Hercules who had been a freedom fighter in Rhodesia; she and Guy had met him in Cairo. She spontaneously invited him to the party for Guy, completely forgetting some of the less savory parts of Hercules' character.

The guests arrived and things were going well until Hercules introduced his girlfriend to Maya. The young white woman was outspoken and rude, and Maya ultimately asked them to leave. It was poorly handled, but Maya thought it necessary to excuse them. Guy spoke to her afterward about it and threatened to sever their relationship if she ever spoke like that to a woman he brought home. Maya told him that he was right to a point, but if he ever brought home someone that stupid and rude, his next job would be to sever their mother/son relationship. Guy thought her response was excellent.

Chapter 29

Maya was preparing an excellent meal for the celebration of her 40th birthday on April 4, 1968. She had just finished cleaning, polishing, and COOKING when the phone rang. It was Dolly who asked if Maya had been listening to the radio or television. She had not been, and Dolly made her promise not to turn them on, saying that she would be over immediately. Martin Luther King, Jr., had been shot in Tennessee and was dead. Maya seemed to black out, temporarily, and then went to HARLEM with John Patterson, her neighbor. The outpouring of grief there was for both King and Malcolm X, and it was an extremely sad time.

Maya had worked in New York with Martin Luther King, Jr., in the 1960s Civil Rights movement as northern coordinator in the New York City office of the Southern Christian Leadership Conference. King had invited her to work for him again when, on her 40th birthday, April 4, 1968, he was assassinated in Memphis, Tennessee. *(Courtesy Library of Congress Prints and Photographs Division)*

Chapter 30

Maya became a hermit for a few weeks. Dolly stayed in daily contact, and Jerry Purcell sent dinner over every other day. Soon James Baldwin insisted on taking her out to laugh, and he took her to dinner at JULES AND JUDY FEIFFER's apartment. There was little serious conversation, and everyone thought of funny stories to tell. It helped Maya and pulled her out of the grief-induced depression she was suffering.

Chapter 31

Maya was approached by some northern California producers and asked to put together 10 one-hour programs on African-American culture for NET (now PBS) and their San Francisco affiliate station, KQED. Jerry Purcell became her manager, and she got a contract for a series called *Black, Blues, Black.* It would reflect literature, music, and art and point to the similarities and influence of African heritage on African-American arts. It would also compare the African and African-American arts to that of influential European music styles.

Chapter 32

Before Maya left for San Francisco, she received a phone call from ROBERT LOOMIS, an editor at Random House Publishing Company. He said that Judy Feiffer had spoken to him and said that Maya told fascinating stories. He then invited her to write an autobiography. She told him she was not old enough and explained her series project. He asked for a California phone number and called her again there. Again, she refused. Loomis called again after the *Black, Blues, Black.* series was finished, and Maya agreed to try to write an autobiography. She told him she would begin the next day.

Chapter 33

Rosa Guy, Dolly, and Maya spent the last weekend in California with Vivian Baxter. Vivian was proud of these three young women and said so many times. Maya reflected on the low status of black women and how they had learned to rise in spite of adversity, and then she began to write. She began with, "What are you looking at me for. I didn't come to stay" (1,167). It was the first line of *I Know Why the Caged Bird Sings.*

CRITICAL COMMENTARY

In her sixth and last autobiography, Angelou's narrative ends on a note that turns it back to the beginning lines of *I Know Why the Caged Bird Sings. A Song Flung Up to Heaven* deals with the turbulent 1964–68 period in the United States. In the opening pages, Angelou describes her boarding of the Pan American jet that will take her across the ocean to the United States. She was dressed in traditional African clothing, and she realized immediately that she was surrounded by a sea of white faces. Angelou had decided to return from Ghana to participate in the Organization of African-American Unity with Malcolm X. He had written to her to invite her to become involved, and he even wrote: "You can communicate because you have plenty of (soul) and you always keep your feet firmly rooted on the ground" (1,061). She felt uncomfortable leaving Guy at the university in Accra, but she had a purpose in returning to the United States.

As the plane crossed the ocean, Angelou reflected on the tension, violence, and political upheaval raging in South Africa and in the United States, but she felt that it was time to do what she could to make change happen. When she arrived in New York City, she decided to go on to San Francisco to see her mother. She called Malcolm X to tell him of her plan, and then she called her friends Abbey Lincoln and Rosa Guy. Angelou thought she would be back fairly soon, "when I get my bearings" (1,064). Home was good, but before she had been in San Francisco two full days, she received a call from her old friend Yvonne, who told her about a black man in New York who had been killed. That man was Malcolm X, and it was 1965. Just three short years later, her good friend Martin Luther King, Jr., one of the great leaders of the Civil Rights movement, was also assassinated. That was in 1968. Martin had offered her work in fund-raising for him, and now he, too, was gone.

She received support from family and a close network of friends during these times of crisis, and she emerged in the end matured and ready to write her personal narrative. The message in part of this last autobiography is the example of how she survived the crisis of seeing both of these great leaders killed, her job offers from both of them lost, and still moved on to a remarkable and award-winning career as a writer. This segment of her life reveals her personal self-fulfillment. It is as though she was in a refiner's fire, faced the hardest and most difficult of all challenges, and yet her strong interior power carried her forward to her most creative works.

Not all critics responded favorably to this last segment of Angelou's narratives. A poet named Wanda Coleman wrote a book review in the *Los Angeles Times,* published on April 14, 2002, that suggested Maya had used "dead metaphors," "empty phrases," "sweeping generalities," and "clumsy similes" (quoted in Lupton 2009, 87). Debate ensued between critics who agreed with Coleman's assessment and those who strongly supported Angelou's work.

Focusing on other issues with the book, the critic John McWhorter was particularly critical of what he perceived to be a smug voice in this work, which he dubbed an "Odetta tone" in his review, entitled "Saint Maya." He described a performance by the black folksinger Odetta at his college in the early 1980s. She had worn "African garb" and "weaved together inspirational songs and savory anecdotes garnished with ancient wisdom" (1). He initially enjoyed the experience, but his roommate dismissed the woman as someone whose "obvious expectation [was that] her audience bow to her moral superiority without question" (1). McWhorter surmised that his friend would have the same opinion of Angelou's serial autobiographies based on what he perceived to be her implicit dare to the reader "to question her private line to God and Truth" (1).

On the other hand, many critics lauded the work. The critic Harold Bloom, in his anthology of criticism of Angelou's work, described the many literary critics who "are generous in their insistence on human rights, and justly proud of Maya Angelou as an exemplary autobiographer of the social struggle" (vii).

As in her earlier works, Angelou tells her stories as she remembers them, openly and candidly. Though she does not claim to be deeply religious, she carries the code of her Christian upbringing, and she also carries with her the voices of strong black and white people who have recognized her talent and who have helped her along her way. Rather than smug, her work is honest and sometimes even embarrassing. It is a series of stories too bizarre to be untrue. No matter what their color or culture, humans learn over time that truth is often stranger than fiction, and Angelou's narratives reveal that simple truth. She was often in the right place at the right time. Doors opened a crack, and she pushed them back all the way and walked through to whatever was waiting on the other side.

While visiting with Lottie Wells, a friend of the family, Maya received a phone call from her friend Yvonne. Yvonne asked, "Maya, girl, why did you come home? Why did you come back to this crazy place?" (1,071). During the course of the conversation, Yvonne revealed that a black man had been shot to death in New York, and Maya realized it was Malcolm X. She felt ripped apart. People in her family's San Francisco circle did not seem to understand or even care about the significance of what had happened. Even her mother was resistant to the idea of anyone telling her how liberation or freedom could be found and maintained. Vivian Baxter felt that she determined her own freedom, and though somewhat sympathetic toward Maya because of her loss of a friend, Vivian could not quite understand Maya's anguish.

Maya did not have a job, so her brother coaxed her into joining him in Hawaii, where he was working as a chef. She went there and worked at a hotel as a singer and entertainer, but her heart was not in it. After observing Della Reese in a nearby club and admiring her incredible talent, Maya realized that she had neither the talent nor the commitment for a lifetime of show business singing. She recalled her grandmother's words: "Sister, change everything you don't like about your life. But when you come to a thing you can't change, change the way you think about it. You'll see it new, and maybe a new way to change it" (1,081). Angelou reflected deeply about her future in the privacy of her small apartment in Hawaii, and she knew she was now on another corridor of doors. The last night she performed at the club, she danced rather than sang, and then she returned to the mainland to find another job.

In describing the realities of her life, Angelou conveys the wider challenges of African-American life with metaphors that touch the readers' minds. She cared deeply about Guy, and she reflects, "Leaving Guy in Africa had become a hair shirt that I could not dislodge" (1,083–1,084). Her role as a mother was always important to her, but her son had become a man and had to find his way. By the time this book was published (2002), life had changed appreciably for most African Americans. But at the time it depicts, the future was uncertain. According to Angelou:

> The African-American leaves the womb with the burden of her color and a race memory chockablock with horrific folk tales. Frequently there are songs, toe-tapping, finger-popping, hand-slapping, dancing songs that say, in effect, "I'm laughing to keep from crying." Gospel, blues, and love songs often suggest that birthing is hard, dying is difficult, and there isn't much ease in between. (1,081)

Friends in Los Angeles found Maya work as a researcher. Her job was to go from house to house asking housewives about the homemaking products they used. She was assigned to the pre-riot Watts neighborhood. The area was depressed, and she knew that the women were wise to outsiders. She wrote, "Behind the women's eyes, however, there is a wisdom that does not pretend to be unaware; nor does it permit gullibility" (1,088). She shares with her readers the real reasons for the depressed state of the people in Watts that she learned from these women: Many, if not most, of the men were unemployed; the women often worked as domestics outside of the area and did not have dependable sitters for their children; the price of groceries and other goods was inflated in Watts, so they shopped elsewhere; and, most dangerous of all, teenagers had formed into roving and hostile gangs. Maya creates anticipation for the reader, and then, as she develops the tension of the story, she describes how Watts exploded and burned.

There were riots and numerous arrests, and the region was burned to ashes. It was a prelude to other riots in cities throughout the country. In the text, Angelou shares comments she overheard youngsters say to National Guardsmen stationed outside of shops to prevent looting. In front of a pawnshop, one cried out, "Hey, man, don't you feel stupid keeping people from stealing something that was already stole in the first place?" (1,095). Such questions reflect the cynical mind-set of Watts at the time.

This short book is written in brief episodes and in a conversational style. Though it only covers a small segment of Angelou's life, it circles back over past events and experiences so the reader gains context and understanding of the themes and movement of her experiences. There is a sense of maturity and confidence in this text in spite of the sorrow of losing two good friends and leaders and in spite of the continued civil unrest in the United States. The reader can sense Angelou's confidence and recognize that her prose is as much about perseverance as it is about the life she has lived during this period. She has become the strong, confident artist that she was destined to be.

Maya's brother and mother were funny and generous to her when she arrived from Ghana, but behind that fun was "the specter of my distant son [who] cast the only shadow" (1,068). Bailey and Vivian helped her put that unease to rest by assuring her that it was his age and maleness that created the arrogance he was practicing. Her passages about the angst she felt in leaving him behind are described well and colored by her metaphors. Her mother said, "Don't worry about him. You have raised him with love. The fruit won't fall too far from the tree" (1,069). Upon reflection, Maya thought, "what if the fruit fell and was picked up by a hungry bird?" (1,069). She also thought, "I, who had been his shade since he was born, was leaving him under the broiling African sun" (1,069). These and other metaphors carry the narrative episodes and allow the reader to view Maya as a concerned mother a half-world away from her only son.

Angelou became involved with African-American theater artists in Los Angeles. Though she had no major stage roles, she did play the part of a nurse in the Euripides' version of *Medea.* The lead character, Medea, was played by the black actress Beah Richards. Though Maya's role was small, she did her best to put forth a convincing performance and memorable appearance. "I bought some stage gray hair and ghoulish makeup. . . . I brought the gray-haired, limping, singing nurse onto the stage" (1,103). In reflecting on the reviews, she writes: "All lauded Beah Richards, and a few had kind words for the elderly actress whom no one knew but who played the nurse so well" (1,104).

After a few more memorable experiences, including the episode that describes a courting African male shared with Dolly McPherson (an educated black woman who became a lifelong friend, confidant, colleague, and Angelou biographer), Maya returned to New York. As she reflected on the might-have-beens and perhaps the should-have-beens, she realized that she was where she wanted to be, and she would turn to her writing. She found work with restaurant owner Jerry Purcell, who, recognizing her writing talent, agreed to support her if she would never use drugs. She wrote, "His patronage was a gift as welcome as found money bearing no type of identification" (1,127).

After returning to New York, Maya felt compelled to visit the Audubon Ballroom where Malcolm X had been shot. Many stars had entertained there in the past, including the writers LANGSTON HUGHES, ZORA NEALE HURSTON, and Arna Bontemps. Famous big bands had performed there, but now it was a vast emptiness. "I approached the building slowly. The windows were dusty and the doors barred. . . . I could see no shadow inside; no chimera arose and danced. I walked away" (1,125). Seeing the place raised unanswerable questions in her mind, but she had now seen it, and it helped bring closure to the loss of her good friend Malcolm X.

At a concert celebration held at Carnegie Hall to honor the 100th anniversary of the birth of W. E. B. DuBois, Martin Luther King, Jr., approached Angelou and asked if she would help raise funds for his upcoming poor people's march. He wanted her to travel throughout the country and collect funds from black churches. King felt that she could persuade black ministers to donate congregational collections made for just one week of each month. Angelou said she was working on a play, but she would do the fund-raising after her birthday on April 4, which was coming up in about a month. Things seemed to be going pretty well. Guy had a job working for Western Airlines as their first black junior executive, and he was planning to return to Africa fairly soon to create a photographic safari service.

As it turned out, Martin Luther King, Jr., was assassinated on April 4, 1968, Angelou's 40th birthday. She had invited friends over and was just completing preparations for her birthday party when the phone rang. It was Dolly, who told Maya not to turn the radio on, and that she would be right over. When the devastating news reached Maya, she closed herself off from the world. Concerned friends, including Dolly McPherson and James Baldwin, stayed in close contact with her during this time, and Jerry Purcell made sure food was delivered daily.

Finally, Baldwin decided it was time to pull her out of her mourning. He took her to a small dinner party at Jules and Judy Feiffer's home, and soon Angelou was regaling them with stories from her past, including stories about SEGREGATION in Stamps, Arkansas. She told them, "The white folks are so prejudiced in my town, a colored person is not allowed to eat vanilla ice cream" (1,160). Angelou includes a quote from James Baldwin in this text:

> We put surviving into our poems and into our songs. We put it into our folk tales. We danced surviving in Congo Square in New Orleans and put it in our pans when we cooked pinto beans. We wore surviving on our backs when we clothed ourselves in the colors of the rainbow. We were pulled down so low we could hardly lift our eyes, so we knew, if we wanted to survive, we had better lift our own spirits. So we laughed whenever we got the chance. (Baldwin, quoted in Angelou 2004, 1,160)

The Feiffers enjoyed her stories very much and thought she should write them down. Not long after that, she was contacted by National Education Television (now Public Broadcasting System) representatives from San Francisco, and they asked if she would write a 10-part PBS series on black culture, history, and African influence on American blacks. Maya "designed a series called *Black, Blues, Black.* We were blacks in Africa before we were brought to America as slaves, where we created the blues, and now we were painfully and proudly returning to being upstanding free blacks again" (1,163). It was produced for San Francisco's affiliate PBS station in San Francisco. In the meanwhile, Jules Feiffer had spoken to Robert Loomis, an editor for Random House, and Loomis challenged her to write her autobiography. She was resistant at first, but decided to do it. Once again, life circled around, and after completion of the PBS series, she began to write the first of her well-known serial autobiographies.

The first line of *I Know Why the Caged Bird Sings* is: "What are you looking at me for? I didn't come to stay . . ." (7). In this book, Angelou's great gifts of autobiography and poetry, primarily to express the joys and sufferings of her people, are immediately evident. A form of autobiography called AUTOETHNOGRAPHY is a style of writing that has gained increased attention from scholars, authors, and literary critics in the last 20 years or so. By situating her life stories within a cultural and historical context, Angelou has constructed narratives and poetry that reflect not only her life but also the historical and cultural context of her experiences. This informs the reader of a larger historical and social setting as well as her relationship and function within it, a style that can be defined as autoethnography. Ethnography gathers information by collecting data from fieldwork, analyzing it carefully, and writing the data in an understandable manner. Autoethnography is more than objectively gathering, analyzing, and reporting. It is a subjective autobiography that situates itself in culture. Angelou has created a representation of herself and contextualized her work within African-American culture. She has told the story of black people's struggles and triumphs in the United States and Africa over her lifetime, as well as her own personal struggles and triumphs.

Angelou's first autobiography begins with finding herself uncomfortable in her grandmother's church on Easter Sunday because she needed to relieve her bladder. She speaks from the perspective of a child, and yet she gives a clear account of where she is, how she feels about it, and her escape. These conversational narratives, recognizable and familiar to many of her readers, are the key of her appeal to millions. Her life has never been one of ease, but she has warmly invited people into her world and told many of her stories in an autoethnographic style. She not only broke ground with her first autobiography and her frank discussion of abuse, but she was also a pioneer in the methodology of autoethnography.

Before returning to New York, Maya, Rosa Guy, and Dolly McPherson visited Maya's mother in Stockton, and her mother expressed her pride in this trio of intellectual young women. She said, "Black women are so special. Few men of any color and even fewer white women can deal with how fabulous we are. Girls, I'm proud of you" (1,166). In a follow-up to her mother's comment, Angelou replayed the scene of supporting three young women later, at another time and place. In an interview with Claudia Tate, she shared the story:

> Once I left church, and as I walked down the street, three young black women stopped me and asked if I would have a glass of wine with them I said, "Yes." One is a painter; one is an actress, and one a singer. We talked, and when I started to leave, I tried to tell them what it means to me to see young black women. I tried to tell them, but I could hardly explain it. My eyes filled with tears. In one way, it means all the work, all the loneliness and discipline my work exacts, is not in vain. It also means, in a more atavistic, absolutely internal way, that I can never die. (quoted in Tate 1983, 2)

IMPORTANT THEMES AND SYMBOLS IN *A SONG FLUNG UP TO HEAVEN*

Artistic Development as a Writer

The literary critic Harold Bloom, in his introduction to an edition of critical reviews and discussions of Angelou's work, describes her poetry as "popular poetry." He also states that Angelou's sense of self is a part of an African-American paradigm of what he calls "the little me within the big me" (1).

In the African-American tradition, "little man, big man" FOLKTALES are metaphorical in many ways. Often the little man is smart and wily while the big man is represented as slow-witted and foolish. These tales often suggest that blacks outwit whites repeatedly and for different purposes. The church sermons in many African-American churches, including the COLORED METHODIST EPISCOPAL CHURCH congregation where Angelou grew up, were exhortations of great passion with a constant goal of building faith and self-empowerment among the listeners. The oratory of highly skilled black pastors is legendary, with Martin Luther King, Jr., as a profound example. Passionate, sincere, and motivating, Angelou developed her own legendary charisma in part from listening and learning from the black PREACHERS' sermons.

Angelou learned to express her own experiences and at the same time depicted the real lives of African Americans in the United States. Bloom writes: "I think that this is part of the secret of Angelou's enormous appeal to American readers, whether black or white, because her remarkable literary voice speaks to something in the universal American 'little me within the big me' . . . Angelou achieves a unique tone blending intimacy and detachment" (1–2).

When Angelou wrote her autobiographies, essays, and poetry, she drew from many sources. She combined her own experience and heritage with the folk sayings and APHORISMs from her mother and grandmother. She used her extensive knowledge of SLAVE NARRATIVES and blended all of those resources with fiery church sermons and her sense of the BLUES aesthetic. Taking parts of her past experience, both from childhood and through several decades of her adult life, her writing blended, as one critic wrote, "the strategies of beauty from . . . ancestral forebears: the tortured, yet life-enduring holler from the field, the life-enhancing cadence of the spirituals, the shout of affirmation of the gospels, the dance of life cadence of the blues, the comprehensive vocabulary, the improvisational genius, the cool confidence of the jazz mode" (Traylor 2009, 103). The results were the serial autobiographies, laced with a rich knowledge of her people and herself. Angelou has said, "The spirituals and gospel songs were sweeter than sugar. I wanted to keep a mouthful of them and the sounds of my people singing fell like sweet oil in my ears" (2004, 417). The autobiographies reflect her love of her own heritage and her growing artistic development.

It is important to remember that though Angelou published her first autobiography in 1970 and the last one in 2002, and that her serial autobiography style launched a new genre, African-American women had been writing and publishing since the 1700s. Angelou had read many black women writers' work, and they shaped her voice along with her own experiences. Like many of her black female forbearers (Georgia Douglas Johnson, Frances Harper, Anne Spencer, and Jessie Fauset, among others), she wrote not only to celebrate victories but to "acknowledge defeat, not for the purposes of reinforcing a sense of defeat or victimization but to insure that we all learn to recognize what constitutes vulnerability in order to avoid its consequences in the future" (Tate, xxiv)

Black Experience in the United States

As the narrative in *A Song Flung Up to Heaven* unfolds, Angelou gives example after example of how the black community in the United States reached out across family boundaries and extended helping hands to one another over and over again. When she returned to Los Angeles from Hawaii, Frances Williams of Actors' Equity provided a place for her to live and to work. When she moved to New York, Jerry Purcell immediately gave her an opportunity to contribute to his business, and he provided financial backing to allow her to write. When she found an apartment, friends gave her elegant pieces of furniture to help her make a home of it. She was introduced to Bea Grimes, who had the only black-owned secondhand furniture store on Broadway, and Grimes sold her fine pieces of furniture for very little money. When Martin Luther King, Jr., was assassinated, Dolly McPherson, James Baldwin, and, indirectly, Jerry Purcell looked after her through her mourning withdrawal. Throughout *A Song Flung Up to Heaven,* the reader learns not only of Maya's experiences and responses to challenges and successes but also the responses of the black community to one another when there is a need.

Continuity

The drive to find herself and her place as a contributing adult to a larger world than her family or even her theatrical profession gives evidence of Angelou's psychological continuity. She had been told many times and many ways as she grew up, and in her adult years, that whatever she was to undertake, she was to do the job well. Her perseverance and resistance to defeat is constant.

Motherhood

Throughout all six of Angelou's autobiographies, there is a constant theme of devoted motherhood. Angelou was dependable and loyal to her son, and she never failed to provide for him in protective and sensible ways. Even in his early adult years, she expressed her love and provided financial support and generosity. She represents herself as a fair and tolerant parent throughout the autobiographies, surrounding her son with the best male role models she could find. Though there was no steady father figure in Guy's life, Maya choose carefully among people who cared about her and him, and she saw that he associated with the types of men she wanted him to emulate both in Africa and in the United States.

CHARACTERS

Maya Angelou *A Song Flung Up to Heaven* begins in 1965, when Maya left Africa and returned to the United States. In the more than three following years, she was devastated twice by the assassinations of men she deeply admired and supported, Malcolm X and then Martin Luther King, Jr. She was also in Los Angeles at the time of the Watts riots and witnessed firsthand the poverty, overcrowding, high unemployment, drug use, and crime in the shabby district of Watts not far from the Los Angeles International Airport. She had done some canvassing in Watts, and she was on hand to see the mob mentality in the summer heat of 1965.

Angelou was active in the theater in Los Angeles, and after she relocated to New York, she was invited to put together a 10-part series for PBS in San Francisco called *Black, Blues, Black.* It demonstrated how African and African-American music, art, and other aspects of black culture influenced one another. One of her good friends, James Baldwin, introduced her to the cartoonist Jules Feiffer and his wife, Judy, and they in turn spoke to an editor, Robert Loomis at Random House, on her behalf. Convinced that she should write an autobiography, Loomis kept calling until she finally agreed, and *A Song Flung Up to Heaven* ends with the beginning lines of *I Know Why the Caged Bird Sings.*

Guy Johnson Guy remained in Africa to continue his studies at the University of Ghana when his mother returned to the United States in 1965. He was 21 and had clearly declared himself an adult and an independent man before she left. Even so, his mother was still covering his expenses. When he returned to the United States, he was in another serious automobile accident and reinjured his neck. He convalesced at his grandmother Vivian Baxter's home San Francisco when his mother returned to New York.

Malcolm X As discussed early in the narrative of *A Song Flung Up to Heaven,* Malcolm X was shot and killed at Manhattan's Audubon Ballroom. It was February 21, 1965, and he was speaking to a meeting of the Organization of Afro-American Unity (OAAU) when three men shot him to death in front of friends and family. The men were apprehended and sentenced to life in prison, but it was never made clear exactly who was behind the assassination. Angelou had only recently arrived in California when the assassination occurred, and she was devastated by the news. She was going to work for the OAAU and had received a letter from Malcolm X just before she left Africa promising his support for her participation. In *A Song Flung Up to Heaven,* she expresses her disappointment at the indifference of the black people in San Francisco to the assassination. They seemed to feel removed from the civil rights action in the East, and Angelou began to realize the remarkable difficulty serious black leaders were facing.

Martin Luther King, Jr. On April 4, 1968, Martin Luther King, Jr., was assassinated in Memphis, Tennessee, by JAMES EARL RAY, who was imprisoned and then died in 1998. Though a wider conspiracy was suspected, it was never proven. The day of the assassination was Maya Angelou's birthday. She was not able to accept the tragic loss for some time, and she became despondent and fell into a period of serious depression. It was largely through the support of James Baldwin and other friends that she healed emotionally and was able to move on with her life. African Americans throughout the country mourned both King and Malcolm X, and that grief triggered destructive riots in American cities much like the Watts riots that took place in Los Angeles in 1965.

Abbey Lincoln A jazz vocalist, songwriter, and actress, Abbey Lincoln met Angelou in New York City. She was married to musician and jazz drummer Max Roach from 1962 to 1970, and her voice can be heard on many of his album recordings. Their music was popular in the United States and Africa. When Maya decided to relocate from California to New York, Abbey and Max invited her to stay with them until she got settled.

Max Roach The drummer Max Roach was one of the experimental founders of modern JAZZ. Roach and his wife, Abbey Lincoln, invited Angelou to stay with them when she returned to New York from Ghana, and he also encouraged her to perform in the play *The Blacks.*

Bailey Johnson When Maya returned to San Francisco from Ghana, her brother, Bailey, was there to greet her, and they resumed their supportive sibling relationship. Malcolm X was assassinated shortly after Maya arrived home, and Bailey helped her cope with that crisis. Later, when Guy was in another serious automobile accident in San Francisco, Bailey was again there to help Guy and the family through that ordeal. He was always available to her as a friend and wise adviser.

Vivian Baxter Maya's mother was living in San Francisco when Maya returned from Ghana, and Vivian was a constant friend and adviser. She took care of Guy during his convalescence so that Maya could relocate to New York and resume her writing.

Ivonne Broadnax Ivonne was a good friend of Maya's in Los Angeles. Ivonne called Maya in San Francisco shortly after Maya's return and wondered why she had decided to leave Africa. She said, "These Negros are crazy here. . . . otherwise, why would they have just killed that man in New York?" (1,071). Maya know that man was Malcolm X.

James Baldwin A prominent writer and civil rights activist, James Baldwin met Angelou in Paris many years before when she was in the cast of *Porgy and Bess.* He was a constant and supportive friend, as well as a member of the Harlem Writers Guild. After the assassination of Martin Luther King, Jr., it was Baldwin who took the responsibility of pulling Maya back from a deep depression, insisting that she go out to a party with him at the home of Jules and Judy Feiffer. Maya told engaging stories from her childhood and other experiences, and through the Feiffers' literary connections with Robert Loomis of Random House, she was persuaded to write the first of her groundbreaking serial autobiographies.

Mother Baldwin James Baldwin's mother warmly welcomed and semi-adopted Maya into their large family circle in New York.

Uncle Brother After Maya returned from Ghana, Bailey persuaded her to work in Hawaii, where he was employed as a professional chef. For a while, until she could find her own apartment, Maya stayed with her Aunt Lea and Uncle Brother. He was a general contractor from the Ozark region in Arkansas. His sense of humor helped Maya endure her aunt's constant talk of religion.

Aunt Lea Vivian Baxter's sister and an ardent evangelist, Aunt Lea and her husband, Uncle Brother, took Maya into their home until she found a furnished flat of her own.

Della Reese A singer, actress, and ordained minister, Della Reese sang rhythm and blues, gospel, pop, jazz, and traditional songs. When Maya was employed as a performer in Hawaii, she visited the Aloha Club and heard Reese sing. She recognized Reese's incredible dedication and talent and realized that her own commitment was not as strong as it needed to be for a career as a singer; her talent was in dancing. She decided to return to the mainland and find a different job.

Beah Richards An African-American actress, Beah Richards lived in an apartment next door to Maya's in Los Angeles. While there, Richards played the lead role in *Medea,* a play presented at the Theatre of Being. Maya was cast in the same play in a supporting role as the nurse, which she played well.

Dolly McPherson An emeriti professor of English, Dolly McPherson was one of the first African-American tenure-track professors at Wake Forest University. She and Maya met through a mutual African suitor who had lied about each of them to the other. It was a laughing matter, and afterward the two became lifelong friends and colleagues.

FURTHER READING

Angelou, Maya. *The Collected Autobiographies of Maya Angelou.* New York: Modern Library Edition by Random House, 2004.

Bloom, Harold. Editor's Note and Introduction. In *Maya Angelou.* Bloom's Modern Critical Views, edited by Harold Bloom, vii, 1–2. New York: Bloom's Literary Criticism, 2009.

Lupton, Mary Jane. "'Spinning in a Whirlwind': Sexuality in Maya Angelou's Sixth Autobiography." In *Maya Angelou.* Bloom's Modern Critical

Views, edited by Harold Bloom, 85–90. New York: Bloom's Literary Criticism, 2009.

McWhorter, John. "Saint Maya." *New Republic,* 20 May 2002. Available online. URL: www.tnr.com/article/saint-maya. Accessed February 9, 2010.

Schramm, Katharina. "Imagined Pasts–Present Confrontations: Literary, and Ethnographic Explorations into Pan-African Identity Politics." In *Africa, Europe, and (Post) Colonialism: Racism, Migration and Diaspora in African Literature,* edited by Susan Arndt and Marek Spitzok von Brisinski, 243–256. Bayreuth, Germany: Bayreuth University, 2006.

Tate, Claudia, ed. *Black Woman Writers at Work.* New York: Continuum, 1983.

Tinnie, Wallis. "Maya Angelou." In *The History of Southern Women's Literature,* edited by Carolyn Perry, Mary Louise Weaks, and Doris Betts, 517–524. Baton Rouge: Louisiana State University Press, 2002.

Traylor, Eleanor W. "Maya Angelou: Writing Life, Inventing Literary Genre." In *Maya Angelou.* Bloom's Modern Critical Views, edited by Harold Bloom, 91–105. New York: Bloom's Literary Criticism, 2009.

Essay Collections

Wouldn't Take Nothing for My Journey Now (1993)

This set of essays is dedicated to OPRAH WINFREY, and some of the work was published in the December 1992 issue of *Essence* magazine. It is a collection of short lessons in living, which Angelou states she "had learned over many years" (Angelou 1993, Acknowledgments). As in her autobiographies, family members and friends are mentioned now and then, and their presence contextualizes and adds wisdom to many of the pieces. In the first few pages of the book, Angelou includes a quote that she identifies as being from the Book of Acts in the New Testament: "Wisdom was created before all things, and prudent understanding from Eternity." This is the crux of Angelou's messages—that is, in enduring, one learns "prudent understanding."

SYNOPSIS

In 24 short essays, Angelou takes the reader on a life journey with her. Many important topics discussed in the work including being a woman, faith, charity, respect, and RACISM. In each of these, Angelou offers counsel to help shape positive attitudes and understanding of common human obstacles and encounters. The first short essay is called "In All Ways a Woman," and it begins by reminding the reader that phrases like "A woman always has the right to change her mind" are essentially negative. A woman needs a strong sense of self, and Angelou writes: "It is imperative that a woman keep her sense of humor intact and at the ready" (7). She closes the essay with: "The struggle for equality continues unabated, and the woman warrior who is armed with wit and courage will be among the first to celebrate victory" (7).

"The Sweetness of Charity," the third essay, instructs that "giving liberates the soul of the giver" (15). The giver is enriched, Angelou writes: "When we cast our bread upon the waters, we can presume that someone downstream whose face we will never know will benefit from our action, as we who are downstream from another will profit from that grantor's gift" (16).

In "Power of the Word," Angelou recalls her grandmother Annie Henderson's faith. She relates that her own imagination would soar "each time Momma drew herself up to her full six feet, clasped her hands behind her back, looked up into the distant sky, and said, 'I will step out on the word of God'" (74). Angelou learned this for herself from a voice coach. He had her read from a book called *Lessons in Truth*, published by the Unity School of Christianity. The line was "God loves me," and the coach had Angelou repeat it again and again. Around the seventh time, she began to believe it, and she writes: "That knowledge humbles me. . . . And it also liberates me. I am a big bird winging over high mountains, down into serene valleys. I am ripples of waves on silver seas. I'm a spring leaf trembling in anticipation" (75–76).

"Voices of Respect" reminds the reader that much courteous behavior has been lost "when too many children run mad in the land" (10), and Angelou calls for a return to self-respect. In the slave society, when owners generally treated the people harshly and with little respect, there were courtesies practiced among African Americans that provided dignity. A man might be addressed not as Joe but, rather, as Uncle Joe. A woman was not Mariah but Aunt Mariah.

In "Our Boys," Angelou tells us: "Our young must be taught that racial peculiarities do exist, but that beneath the skin, beyond the differing features and into the true heart of being, fundamentally, we are more alike, my friend, than we are unalike" (124).

CRITICAL COMMENTARY

Wisdom is sometimes hard to acquire and even more difficult to remember when it is most needed. Positive tips for improved human interrelations often fall into the self-help category, but these essays are written with Angelou's talent of mixing classical information, such as the Scriptures, with black oral tradition. Her universal concerns reach the ordinary reader. When she writes, "Many people utter insults or disparaging remarks without thinking, but a wise or stylish person takes the time to consider the positive as well as negative possibilities in each situation," the message is clear.

She explains that nicknames from slave times for young girls and boys, such as "Sister, Sis, or Tutta" and "brother, Bubba, and Bro and Buddy" (102), were tender and affectionate and are still used within her cultural setting. However, with a lack of respect, those same names can be misused by misunderstanding or imitative outsiders. Angelou's wisdom has been gained slowly over her lifetime, and the short essays in this book are both entertaining and authentic in teaching many points of social behavior.

FURTHER READING

Angelou, Maya. *Wouldn't Take Nothing for My Journey Now.* New York: Random House, 1993.

Even the Stars Look Lonesome (1997)

Even the Stars Look Lonesome is a continuation of Angelou's 1993 collection *Wouldn't Take Nothing for My Journey Now.* Her clear voice transcends commonality in the way the words are used, and the reader is captivated by both the rhythm and the wisdom of her prose. Angelou again shares some of what she has learned from a life of overcoming adversity, but somehow she seems to present her reflections in a manner that make adversities seem to be more like blessings.

SYNOPSIS

"A House Can Hurt, a Home Can Heal," the first essay in this collection, is a narrative about an ending and a beginning. From 1973 to 1981, Angelou was married to Paul Du Feu, a builder from London, and twice they moved into California homes that she describes as "bad houses." Something was always going wrong, and perhaps that was symptomatic of the marriage too. The beginning of the end came when she made the decision to move to North Carolina. She bought a huge house, added more rooms, and made it her home. Both laughter and forgiveness come easily to her now, and she knows that she is home.

"Poetic Passage" is an essay about Oprah Winfrey, and it is a short profile of the woman of whom one loyal fan said, "We can thank Oprah for some of the sanity in our country. She is America's most accessible and honest psychiatrist" (quoted in Angelou 1997, 61). Angelou paints Winfrey as a person with "a determination to leave wherever she is and her only certain destination is somewhere other than where she has been" (61). Warm and sensitive, intelligent and curious, Oprah brought herself up from poverty, worked hard, kept her integrity, and has helped countless people. At the end of her tribute to Winfrey's success, Angelou writes: "Oprah is making her journey at what might seem to be a dizzying pace, but it is her pace and she alone has set her tempo" (62).

The last essay, "Even the Stars Look Lonesome Sometimes," recounts the story of an acquaintance of Angelou's who left her small hometown for the "high life in the big city" (143). She did not find a good life but instead sank deep into an unfulfilled and wasted life. Those choices and the consequences reminded Angelou of the biblical story of the prodigal son. It was pretty much the same story, and the son ended up alone until he reached out to his family for forgiveness and aid. The point of the essay is that humans do not always need to be in a crowd. Solitude is good, and our children would benefit if we could teach them that being alone can be good, "and in the quietude," Angelou writes, "we may even hear the voice of God" (145).

CRITICAL COMMENTARY

Maya Angelou has said that she has written the black American experience, and she has. Many of her books, essays, and poems describe the oppression, disenfranchisement, and displacement of her people, but only rarely do readers get a glimpse inside this wise and gentle writer. This series of essays, and the ones before and after, reveal the heart of Angelou's philosophy and strength. She relies on her God, her heritage, and her inner strength to do what she is inspired to do, and that is to share her own methods of self-empowerment with her people.

When asked how she felt about her past works, Angelou replied, "Generally I forget them. I'm totally free of them. They have their own life. . . . The work, once completed, does not need me. The work I'm working on needs my total concentration. The one that's finished doesn't belong to me anymore. It belongs to itself" (quoted in Tate 1983, 9). And it belongs to the millions of readers who wait for and learn from her work, her wit, and her wisdom.

FURTHER READING

Angelou, Maya. *Even the Stars Look Lonesome.* New York: Random House, 1997.

Tate, Claudia, ed. *Black Women Writers at Work.* New York: Continuum, 1983, 1–11.

Letter to My Daughter (2008)

On the back-cover jacket of *Letter to My Daughter,* there is a quote from Maya Angelou's preface to this book, clearly stating whom she is addressing: "I gave birth to one child, a son, but I have thousands of daughters. You are black and white, Jewish and Muslim, Asian, Spanish-speaking, Native American and Aleut. You are fat and thin and pretty and plain, gay and straight, educated and unlettered, and I am speaking to all of you. Here is my offering to you" (xii). This is a book of inspirational wisdom, but it also sings. With a mixture of poetry and prose, it guides, shares memories both good and not so good, and entertains. In her frank disclosures and openness, Angelou again teaches from her experience and both mesmerizes and entertains the reader.

SYNOPSIS

In 28 sections, Angelou takes the reader on a ride through her extraordinary life. Each entry is short, just a few pages, and yet each one carries a message gleaned from her commonsense experience. In "Home," the first essay, she reflects on Thomas Wolfe's warning that "you can't go home again," with which she disagrees. She feels that we carry home with us "the shadows, the dreams, the fears, and dragons of home under one's skin" (6). She continues a little later: "I am convinced that most people do not grow up" (8). We look like we are grown up, with all the accoutrements of what we think are adult (credit cards, marriage, children), but she suggests that "I think what we do is mostly grow old" (7), and within we carry the once-upon-a-time innocent child we were. The message of "Home" is that home is inside us. We must learn to be comfortable with our own memories and experiences, and then we can be at home.

In another essay, "To Tell the Truth," Angelou suggests that we speak truth to one another. To teenagers, one might say, "That ragged hairstyle may be trendy, but is also unattractive" (38), or a reminder that a hanging-out shirt does not look stylish or cool; rather, it looks "unkempt and uncared for" (38). Angelou reminds us that we are often asked the question, "How are you?" We seldom answer, but she suggests we do. If the person does not ask next time around, so be it. That will simply result in your having more time to take care of yourself.

The essays discuss people Angelou has known and learned from and cultural transgressions stemming from social blunders of her own. In "Senegal," she shares an embarrassing learning moment. She once walked on an exquisite oriental rug in the home of a Senegal woman who was living in Paris. Angelou arrived for a dinner party and noticed that the guests were all standing around, conversing and admiring the rug. She assumed that the hostess had instructed her guests not to walk on the rug, and because she did not approve of such instructions, she walked across it several times while admiring the art hung on the walls. Soon servants entered the room, rolled up the rug and replaced it with one of equal beauty along with glasses, silverware, napkins, and food. The guests sank to the floor, and it turned out that the beautiful rugs were tablecloths for the dinner. She learned that "In an unfamiliar culture, it is wise to offer no innovations, no suggestions, or lessons" (91).

In a beautiful essay entitled "Poetry," Angelou pays tribute to African and African-American poets she has admired and asks, "How can exaltation be wrenched from degradation? (154). She quotes poetry from LANGSTON HUGHES, Aimé Césaire, Mari Evans, and Sterling A. Brown, and she talks of the difficulty of writing in colonial language the "poetry that opposed colonialism" (156). The chapter closes with Langston Hughes's "I, Too, Sing America." It is a nod to Walt Whitman and the promise that America belongs to everyone.

CRITICAL COMMENTARY

Elements of compassion, modesty, and humor glow in these essays. They are lessons Angelou has learned through experience, and in her radiant and charismatic voice, she both tells and teaches the reader what she has gleaned, saying that she is giving it away so others need not experience the same difficulties. Her openness has been discussed many times, and it has been labeled by less friendly critics as common and not helpful. However, it is Angelou's very openness that teaches without being didactic. Readers know that self-presentation is important, but when they are reminded, as they are in this book that multiple holes in lips, noses, ears, and elsewhere on the body are more defacing than attractive, and that someday those very same holes carrying adornments now will be wished away if possible, maybe they will listen.

Angelou has traveled and experienced many cultures in different ways. She has admitted to making a number of cultural faux pas. She has taken up with bad men and survived. She is a mature narrator with a personal tone that expresses many basic truths that others probably have not yet learned. The humble teachings of her grandmother, the commonsense APHORISMs of her mother, and the passionate words of pastors and the tender black SPIRITUALS have shaped her spirit, and she has risen to be who she is. She is "home" to millions, and she has earned that honor. It is to be hoped that her "daughters" will read, think, and learn that hard work, being nice, and loving are the keys to self-respect and peace.

FURTHER READING

Angelou, Maya. *Letter to My Daughter.* New York: Random House, 2008.

POETRY

INTRODUCTION TO MAYA ANGELOU'S POETRY

The poetry of Maya Angelou speaks clearly to her African-American community. She knows the content of her culture's experience, and she knows her audience. She uses feeling and attitude, often reflective of centuries of displacement, along with humor and occasional caprice and whimsy. Though many literary critics and academic poets have written negative reviews about her works, both when they were published and in retrospect, it must be understood that her poetry was not written for them. It was written with imagination, emotion, and significant meaning for her worldwide community. She has chosen to use familiar and accessible words so that her work will ring in the ears of people of all races, educated or not, to lift them toward higher self-respect. Her poetry serves as an expression of their angst and their victories. Angelou uses words with care, employing both standard American English and black vernacular tradition. Her perspective seems to be the same as COUNTEE CULLEN's: ". . . do write, create what we will, our only concern being that we do it well and with all the power within us" (Cullen 1969, vi).

Though there are elements of Angelou's vernacular that may not be understood by all readers, the poetry speaks in an accessible language and contributes to building a community of understanding and meaning without being preachy or didactic. Her poetry, unlike any other emerging from the black community until her time, reveals many kinds of liberation. She candidly expresses how she feels about a myriad of topics from sexual experience to paying the rent, to civil rights abuses, to growing old. She uses poetic devices that span language from the beautiful and sublime to the vulgar and even scatological, because that is how real life is. Her phrasings range from tailored language to street talk, and she creates musical sounds of celebration using a BLUES aesthetic, yet she imbues the sounds with gospel emotion.

Most of Angelou's poetry is created using short lyrics and animated rhythms. Her poems are particularly popular among young people because they have a recognizable beat and the messages are often clear and uplifting. She uses alliteration, short lines, and familiar vocabulary. Though some critics have suggested that her work is ordinary and lightweight, others praise her for her courage to boldly address entrenched sociocultural practices that have denied opportunities for many citizens for centuries in the United States.

Angelou's poetry includes bold examples of oppression, endurance, and victory. She speaks to those who will hear using what Northrop Frye calls a *demotic style*—a "style shaped by the diction, rhythms, syntax, and associations of ordinary speech" (Harmon and Holman 1996, 145). Making use of the black folk language of her culture, she speaks in imagery and allusion that is meant to be understood on many levels. Lyman B. Hagen writes: "Most lines of her three-stanza poems are trimeter; others, particularly those in the unstructured poems, are from two to four syllables long" (119). Creating accessible poetry has not been a quick process for Angelou, and she has said many times that she works from many words and reduces them to a few choice selections to express her meaning. According to Hagen, Langston Hughes believed that poems should be short (119), and she has followed his pattern.

Angelou was an early reader, and as she matured, she continued to read and listen to people's words, stories, expressed feelings, slang, and dialects. She has said in many interviews that she does not like slang and rarely uses it in her own speech, yet she does use it occasionally in her poetry to reflect the language of her people. Her Protestant, mostly Baptist, leanings resulted in familiarity with the King James translation of the Bible, and words and phrases from the Scriptures often appear in her poetry. In "Black Ode," for instance, she uses John 5:8 from the New Testament: "Take [or pick] up your bed and walk" (Angelou 1994, 41). Her decades of reading of both black and white writers has yielded a sense of poetic rhythm, and the call and response of the COLORED METHODIST EPISCOPAL CHURCH, not unlike the call-and-response exchange between leaders and their people in Africa, influenced her work as well. Hagen notes that another "shaping force derived from childhood chants, songs, and rhyme games long familiar in folklore" (120) influenced her, and these are still heard on playgrounds today.

Angelou's poetic voice also uses an expressive vernacular tradition of African-American people called SIGNIFYING. Beyond her informed understanding of poetic technique and rhetorical structure, Angelou uses the linguistic sign language of her people. "The ideal 'linguistic sign,' according to Saussure [a noted linguist], is made up of two elements, a signifier (such as a sound-image) and a signified (such as a mental concept), and the relation between the two is arbitrary, conventional, and 'unmotivated'" (Harmon and Holman 1996, 482). Without explaining or using too many words, Angelou often uses concrete or very plain words (signifiers) that are loaded with layered meanings to those who really know the culture. For instance, if she uses the words like *thirteen, noosed, cane straps,* or even *dichty* (snooty or high hat), the people of her cultural community know what the words represent. They understand within the abstract memories of their minds, in their own family histories, and from their own personal experiences.

Signifying is an implicit rhetorical strategy in the black literary tradition, and it covers a broad understanding of experience and spectrums of meaning not included in Standard American English. Geneva Smitherman, a linguist, writes that "Signifyin(g)" is a way of black speaking "that is a synonym" (121) for many other implied meanings. Henry Louis Gates, Jr., writes:

> For her [Smitherman], Signification has the following eight characteristics:
>
> 1. indirection, circumlocution
> 2. metaphysical-imagistic (but images rooted in the everyday, real world)
> 3. humorous, ironic
> 4. rhythmic fluency and sound
> 5. teachy but not preachy
> 6. directed at person or persons usually present in the situational context
> 7. punning, play on words
> 8. introduction of the semantically or logically unexpected. (Gates 1988, 94)

Angelou uses similes, metaphors, humor, and sometimes bizarre, pathetic, and tragic words and phrases that reflect the experiences and vernacular expressions (folklore) of her people. She even plays with the concepts of white supremacy in ways that expose it for what it is, but at the same time, her wry wit is expressed with grace and humor, as in her poem "On Working White Liberals." The last two lines are: "So, I'll believe in Liberals' aid for us / when I see a white man load a Black man's gun" (Angelou 1994, 47). Priscilla R. Ramsey notes of Angelou: "Her autobiographies and poetry reveal a vital need to transform the elements of a stultifying and destructive personal, social, political and historical milieu into a sensual and physical refuge" (76). Hagen, author of *Heart of a Woman, Mind of a Writer, and Soul of a Poet,* includes a quote from Langston Hughes that expresses the aim of Hughes's works: "To explain and illuminate the Negro condition in America" (Hughes, quoted in Hagen 1996, 4).

Though there have been many harsh critics of Angelou's poetry, Harold Bloom writes: "Of Angelou's sincerity, good-will towards all, and personal vitality, there can be no doubt. She is professedly an inspirational writer, of the self-help variety, which perhaps places her beyond criticism" (9). Bloom calls Angelou's poems "popular poetry," and there is no doubt that it is popular poetry for millions. But even so, numbered among those millions are more than a few literary academics who admire the rational sensibilities of her poetry.

ROBERT LOOMIS, Angelou's Random House editor, stated:

> I've always believed that those who have reservations about Angelou's poetry simply don't understand what she is doing. She is very strongly in a certain tradition of Black American poetry, and when I hear her read or declaim the works of other Black American poets, I can see very clearly what her heritage is and what her inspiration is. Furthermore, Maya is not

writing the sort of poetry that most of us grew up in school admiring. What she is writing is poetry that is very definitely in the oral tradition. That is, what she writes can be read aloud and even acted. When her words are spoken, they are extremely effective and moving. They always sound just right. (quoted in Hagen, 123)

FURTHER READING

Angelou, Maya. *The Complete Collected Poems of Maya Angelou.* New York: Random House, 1994.

Bloom, Harold, ed. *Maya Angelou.* Bloom's Major Poets. Broomall, Pa.: Chelsea House, 2001.

Cullen, Countee. *Color.* New York: Arno Press, 1969.

Emanuel, James A. *Langston Hughes.* New York: Twayne, 1967.

Gates, Henry Louis, Jr. *The Signifying Monkey: A Theory of African-American Literary Criticism.* New York: Oxford University Press, 1988.

Hagen, Lyman E. *Heart of a Woman, Mind of a Writer, and Soul of a Poet: A Critical Analysis of the Writings of Maya Angelou.* Lanham, Md.: University Press of America, 1997.

Harmon, William, and C. Hugh Holman. *A Handbook to Literature.* 7th ed. Upper Saddle River, N.J.: Prentice Hall, 1996.

Ramsey, Priscilla R. "Transcendence: The Poetry of Maya Angelou." In *Maya Angelou,* Modern Critical Views, edited by Harold Bloom, 75–90. Philadelphia: Chelsea House, 1999.

Smitherman, Geneva. *Talkin and Testifying: The Language of Black Americans.* Boston: Houghton Mifflin, 1977, 118–134.

POETRY COLLECTIONS

Just Give Me a Cool Drink of Water 'fore I Diiie (1971)

Just Give Me a Cool Drink of Water 'fore I Diiie was Angelou's first published collection of poems, and it was nominated for a Pulitzer Prize. According to Lyman B. Hagen, some of these poems "were originally published as songs. The volume includes many of the lyrics from her 1969 recording of 'The Poetry of Maya Angelou' for GWF Records" (122). Many of the poems are personal and self-searching in a quest for self-definition. Hagen also suggests that most of these stir "emotional responses. Much of it is meant to show fun with the familiar" (122). As for the title, in a 1983 interview with Claudia Tate, Angelou said that it "refers to my belief that we as individuals in a species are still so innocent that we think we could ask our murderer just before he puts the final wrench upon the throat, 'Would you please give me a cool drink of water?' and he would do so. That's innocence. It's lovely" (quoted in Tate 1989, 155).

Personal and introspective, Angelou is exploring what Yasmin Y. DeGout has called "liberation ideology" (125). Issues of gender and economic stratification as social or cultural designations are raised here, and common class-based assessments of men and women are challenged. Angelou represents the self and personal experience, and she offers a healing balm, couched in accessible language, to evoke racial self-respect and pride.

This collection contains the following poems:

Part One: Where Love Is a Scream of Anguish

"They Went Home"
"The Gamut"
"A Zorro Man"
"To a Man"
"Late October"
"No Loser, No Weeper"
"When You Come to Me"
"Remembering"
"In a Time"
"Tears"
"The Detached"
"To a Husband"
"Accident"
"Let's Majeste"
"After"
"The Mothering Blackness"
"On Diverse Deviations"
"Mourning Grace"

"How I Can Lie to You"
"Sounds Like Pearls"

Part Two: Just Before the World Ends

"When I Think About Myself"
"On a Bright Day, Next Week"
"Letter to an Aspiring Junkie"
"Miss Scarlett, Mr. Rhett and Other Latter-Day Saints"
"Times-Square-Shoeshine-Composition"
"Faces"
"To a Freedom Fighter"
"Riot: 60's"
"We Saw Beyond Our Seeming"
"Black Ode"
"No No No No"
"My Guilt"
"The Calling of Names"
"On Working White Liberals"
"Sepia Fashion Show"
"The Thirteens (Black)"
"The Thirteens (White)"
"Harlem Hopscotch"

Oh Pray My Wings Are Gonna Fit Me Well (1975)

The poems in this collection attempt to reach Angelou's readers with sparse but meaningful words, rhythmic expression, and significant meaning. Carol E. Neubauer suggests that Angelou "has developed a rapport with her audiences who await each new work as a continuation of an ongoing dialogue with the author" (194). There is power in this collection. Eleanor Traylor writes that Angelou's poems contain six predominant matters, each important, and each, until Angelou wrote them in a voice that could be understood, unnamed. These six matters are "the matter of Africa; the matter of mid-passage; the matter of slavery; the matter of America; the matter of 'we folk' (home place, home speech, home agency, home critique, and home invention); and the matter of self-definition" (97). The poems in this collection, and in Angelou's other poetry, address these matters and subsume them under principles of continuity and unity.

This collection contains the following poems:

Part One:

"Pickin Em Up and Layin Em Down"
"Here's to Adhering"
"On Reaching Forty"
"The Telephone"

Part Two:

"Passing Time"
"Now Long Ago"
"Greyday"
"Poor Girl"
"Come, And Be My Baby"
"Senses of Insecurity"
"Alone"
"Communication I"
"Communication II"
"Wonder"
"A Conceit"

Part Three:

"Request"
"Africa"
"America"
"For Us, Who Dare Not Dare"
"Lord, In My Heart"
"Artful Pose"

Part Four:

"The Couple"
"The Pusher"
"Chicken-Licken"

Part Five:

"I Almost Remember"
"Prisoner"
"Woman Me"
"John J."
"Southeast Arkanasia"
"Song for the Old Ones"
"Child Dead in Old Seas"
"Take Time Out"
"Elegy"
"Reverses"

"Little Girl Speakings"
"This Winter Day"

And Still I Rise (1978)

This is a collection of poems meant to empower the reader. Its themes include love and the pain of loneliness, the difficulties for African Americans living in the South, the importance of family, and the nature of women. By this point in her career, Angelou was speaking to a dedicated audience.

This collection contains the following poems:

Part One: Touch Me, Life, Not Softly
"A Kind of Love, Some Say"
"Country Lover"
"Remembrance"
"Where We Belong, A Duet"
"Phenomenal Woman"
"Men"
"Refusal"
"Just for a Time"

Part Two: Traveling
"Junkie Monkey Reel"
"The Lesson"
"California Prodigal"
"My Arkansas"
"Through the Inner City to the Suburbs"
"Lady Luncheon Club"
"Momma Welfare Roll"
"The Singer Will Not Sing"
"Willie"
"To Beat the Child Was Bad Enough"
"Woman Work"
"One More Round"
"The Traveler"
"Kin"
"The Memory"

Part Three: And Still I Rise
"Still I Rise"
"Ain't That Bad?"
"Life Doesn't Frighten Me"
"Bump d'Bump"
"On Aging"
"In Retrospect"
"Just Like Job"
"Call Letters: Mrs. V.B."
"Thank You, Lord"

Shaker, Why Don't You Sing? (1983)

Angelou's fourth volume of poetry was published two years after her autobiography *The Heart of a Woman.* Both books are focused on the will to survive after failure and loss of security in an important relationship, broken dreams of a predictable and secure future, and even a sense of being cornered by circumstances. In the collection, Angelou expresses her determination to go forward in spite of these threatening difficulties, and her poems ring with a soaring spirit that refuses to be defeated. Never surrendering to hopelessness, she expresses her loneliness and the betrayal she has experienced. She has lost her love, and she, the "Shaker," can no longer sing. Besides poems that mourn the loss of love, this collection also has many that are about black oppression. They describe the anguish and frustration, but they also convey the strength of hope and looking toward a different and better future.

This collection contains the following poems:

"Awaking in New York"
"A Good Woman Feeling Bad"
"The Health-Food Diner"
"A Georgia Song"
"Unmeasured Tempo"
"Amoebaean for Daddy"
"Recovery"
"Impeccable Conception"
"Caged Birds"
"Avec Merci, Mother"
"Arrival"
"A Plagued Journey"
"Starvation"
"Contemporary Announcement"
"Prelude to a Parting"

"Martial Choreograph"
"To a Suitor"
"Insomniac"
"Weekend Glory"
"The Lie"
"Prescience"
"Family Affairs"
"Changes"
"Brief Innocence"
"The Last Decision"
"Slave Coffle"
"Shaker, Why Don't You Sing?"
"My Life Has Turned to Blue"

I Shall Not Be Moved (1990)

Throughout this volume of poetry, the overriding message is from the second poem "Human Family." Toward the end of the poem, Angelou writes: "We are more alike, my friends, than we are unalike." This is a MAXIM that has been quoted many times because Angelou has said it often in interviews and talks. The collection is about empowerment. It discusses the matter of self-definition and the power of personal strength. There are praise poems and love poems, poems of oppression; there is confusion and hints of the Gospel; and in all of them runs a thread of resistance, of self-empowered will, and of the immovability of conviction.

This collection contains the following poems:

"Worker's Song"
"Human Family"
"Man Bigot"
"Old Folks Laugh"
"Is Love"
"Forgive"
"Insignificant"
"Love Letter"
"Equality"
"Coleridge Jackson"
"Why Are They Happy People?"
"Son to Mother"
"Known to Eve and Me"
"These Yet to Be United States"
"Me and My Work"
"Changing"
"Born That Way"
"Televised"
"Nothing Much"
"Glory Falls"
"London"
"Savior"
"Many and More"
"The New House"
"Our Grandmothers"
"Preacher, Don't Send Me"
"Fightin' Was Natural"
"Loss of Love"
"Seven Women's Blessed Assurance"
"In My Missouri"
"They Ask Why"
"Ailey, Baldwin, Floyd, Killens, and Mayfield" (also titled "When Great Trees Fall")

Celebrations: Rituals of Peace and Prayer (2006)

Celebrations is a collection of some of Angelou's most iconic poems. Written for both public readings and private occasions, the poems reveal Angelou to be a constant advocate for peace, a careful historian, and both mentor and friend to many. The collection includes a number of public poems, most notably "On the Pulse of Morning" (written for and read at Bill Clinton's 1995 inauguration), "Amazing Peace" (presented at the 2005 National Christmas Tree lighting), and "A Brave and Startling Truth," read at the celebration of the 50th anniversary of the United Nations. More personal poems in the collection include "Mother: A Cradle to Hold Me," "Ben Lear's Bar Mitzvah" (Lear is her nephew), and a birthday poem written for Oprah Winfrey.

The collection contains the following poems:

"On the Pulse of Morning"
"A Brave and Startling Truth"
"Continue"
"Sons and Daughters"
"When Great Trees Fall"

"A Black Woman Speaks to Black Manhood"
"Amazing Peace"
"Mother: A Cradle to Hold Me"
"In and Out of Time"
"Ben Lear's Bar Mitzvah"
"Vigil"
"Prayer"

FURTHER READING

Angelou, Maya. *Now Sheba Sings the Song.* Illustrated by Tom Feelings. New York: Plume/Penguin Group, 1987.

DeGout, Yasmin Y. "The Poetry of Maya Angelou: Liberation Ideology and Technique." In *Maya Angelou.* Bloom's Modern Critical Views, edited by Harold Bloom, 121–132. New York: Bloom's Literary Criticism, 2009.

Hagen, Lyman B. *Heart of a Woman, Mind of a Writer, and Soul of a Poet: A Critical Analysis of the Writings of Maya Angelou.* Lanham, Md.: University Press of America, 1996.

Loomis, Robert. "Letter to L. B. Hagen" (June 3, 1998). In *Heart of a Woman, Mind of a Writer, and Soul of a Poet,* by Lyman B. Hagen, 123. Lanham, Md.: University Press of America, 1996.

Neubauer, Carol E. "Maya Angelou: Self and a Song of Freedom in the Southern Tradition." In *Maya Angelou.* Modern Critical Views, edited by Harold Bloom, 191–218. Philadelphia: Chelsea House, 1999.

Tate, Claudia. "Maya Angelou." In *Conversations with Maya Angelou,* edited by Jeffrey M. Elliot, 146–156. Jackson: University Press of Mississippi, 1989.

Traylor, Eleanor W. "Maya Angelou: Writing Life, Inventing Literary Genre." In *Maya Angelou.* Bloom's Modern Critical Views, edited by Harold Bloom, 91–105. New York: Bloom's Literary Criticism, 2009.

SELECTED POEMS A TO Z

"Accident"

This poem was published in Angelou's first poetry collection, *Just Give Me a Cool Drink of Water 'fore I Diiie* (1971); it was included in Part One: Where Love Is a Scream of Anguish. "Accident" was published not long after Angelou's first autobiography, *I Know Why the Caged Bird Sings,* was received with popular acclaim. Her poetry was not received with the same praise; critical reviews written by professionals, often poets, were mostly negative. However, Lyman B. Hagen reminds us that her "poems are written for people not other poets" (121). In a 1983 interview with Claudia Tate, Angelou addressed the title of this collection by explaining that: ". . . we as individuals . . . are still so innocent that we think if we asked our murderer just before he puts the final wrench upon the throat, 'Would you please give me a cool drink of water?' and he would do so. That's innocence. It's lovely" (quoted in Tate 1983, 155). Some of the poems in this first published collection were first recorded as song lyrics in her 1969 recording of "The Poetry of Maya Angelou" for GWP records. The first half of this collection, where "Accident" appears, contains various reflections on love.

SYNOPSIS

A short poem of 21 lines arranged in two stanzas, this unrhymed work uses imagery that projects an emotional flatness. In "Accident," the magic of love or infatuation is over, and she no longer feels emotion. His "brain-dust of rainbows" has fallen on indifferent eyes. The color of emotion has faded, and all that is left is "the naked Black-White truth."

CRITICAL COMMENTARY

This terse work is a poem of recognition and truth. In it, Angelou is awakening to the negative aspects of her lover. "Your vulgarness not of living; your demands not from need." It is a closure of affection; it is an exposure of the shallow understanding of one who has used another.

FURTHER READING

Angelou, Maya. *The Complete Collected Poems of Maya Angelou.* New York: Random House, 1994.

Hagen, Lyman B. *Heart of a Woman, Mind of a Writer, and Soul of a Poet: Critical Analysis of the Writings of Maya Angelou.* Lanham, Md.: University Press of America, 1996.

Tate, Claudia, ed. *Black Women Writers at Work.* New York: Continuum, 1983.

"Africa"

"Africa" and "America" are contrasting paired poems. Both are in Part Three of the collection *O Pray My Wings Are Gonna Fit Me Well* (1975). They are about the nationhood of the two countries, and both poems contemplate the acts and consequences of captive slavery. Angelou included other contrasting poetic pairs in this collection: "Communication I" and "Communication II," and also two contrasting pairs in other collections: "Phenomenal Woman" and "Men" and "The Thirteens (Black)" and "The Thirteens (White)."

SYNOPSIS

The first stanza of "Africa" begins with an idyllic metaphor of Africa as a woman "sugarcane sweet, deserts her hair golden her feet, two Niles her tears." The second stanza contrasts sharply with the first and brings brutality: "white brigands ungentled icicle bold." The third stanza closes with "her history slain now she is striding although she had lain" (84). The line "thus she had lain" is repeated three times, twice in the first stanza and once in the second. In the third, which begins "Now she is rising," the reader is reminded that Africa is not defeated. The poem is a metaphor for colonialism and white supremacy, but it is also a warning to colonists and others that the continent's power is rising.

CRITICAL COMMENTARY

An unsigned review in *Booklist* commented that the contrasting poems "Africa" and "America" elevate nationhood to a "higher yet deeper plane" (279). At the time Angelou published this collection (1975), deep and permanent changes were occurring in South Africa. New countries were being formed (Mozambique and the People's Republic of Angola), and there were government announcements that all black children in both countries would be provided with a free education. But at the same time, there were uprisings and violence. South Africans were stirring more and more strongly against apartheid, which had been in place officially since 1948, though the practice was much older than that. Angelou's response in "Africa" to the indignities perpetrated against the people in South Africa at first indicates a passive acceptance—"thus she had lain"—but the power comes in the line "Now she is rising." The words almost hiss when read aloud, and the "deeper plane," the anonymous *Booklist* reviewer suggests, is a rumbling of righteous and potentially violent anger.

FURTHER READING

Angelou, Maya. *The Complete Collected Poems of Maya Angelou*. New York: Random House, 1994.

Unsigned review. *Booklist* 72, no. 4 (October 1975): 279.

"America"

The poem "America" appears in Part Three of Angelou's collection *Oh Pray My Wings Are Gonna Fit Me Well* (1975); it was paired with the contrasting poem, "Africa." The collection was published a year after the autobiography *Gather Together in My Name* (1974) and is a clear denunciation and bitter criticism of the America that African Americans were forced to accept from the time of slavery.

SYNOPSIS

The poem begins with the line "The gold of her promise has never been mined." After the Civil War, African Americans were made many promises, but they were not fulfilled. To the contrary, with JIM CROW laws and other government restrictions (for example, blacks could not vote), America's "proud declaration are leaves on the wind." Angelou's use of metaphor and rhythm in this poem strike the reader with hard truth, and she clearly conveys the justified anguish and disappointment of the black people.

CRITICAL COMMENTARY

Maya Angelou's poetry is clearly influenced by the church hymns and responsive readings she heard in the COLORED METHODIST EPISCOPAL CHURCH of her childhood. Her poetry sings with cadences from her past. Eleanor W. Traylor writes that the many volumes of Angelou's work and the independent poems she wrote for various occasions "continue the six predominant matters of African poetry with their subsequent emphases, until now unnamed: the matter of Africa; the matter of mid-passage; the matter of slavery; the matter of America; the matter of 'we folk' (home place, home speech, home agency, home critique, and home invention); and the matter of self-definition" (97). For centuries, America used and abused the blacks and many immigrant groups. Angelou speaks to that travesty of democracy and closes this poem by pleading, "I beg you, discover this country" (86).

FURTHER READING

Angelou, Maya. *The Complete Collected Poems of Maya Angelou.* New York: Random House, 1994.

Traylor, Eleanor W. "Maya Angelou: Writing Life, Inventing Literary Genre." In *Maya Angelou.* Bloom's Modern Critical Views, edited by Harold Bloom, 91–105. New York: Bloom's Literary Criticism, 2009.

"After"

"After" appears in Angelou's first published collections of poems, *Just Give Me a Cold Drink of Water 'fore I Diiie* (1971).

SYNOPSIS

The short stanzas evoke an empty place with silence, empty shelves, and few cars in the street. It is late (or early), and the stars seem to throw a stony, cold brilliance. We wonder, "After" what? The last stanza sighs, "The bed yawns beneath the weight of our absent selves." It is over, and it is after.

CRITICAL COMMENTARY

Lyman B. Hagen writes: "Some of the poems in her first volume, *Just Give Me a Cool Drink of Water 'fore I Diiie* were originally published as songs. . . . [This poem] is purposely lyrical. It is designed to elicit stirring emotional responses. Much of it is meant to show fun with the familiar" (122). "After" has a lyric quality, but it projects a tired emptiness. Words such as *moaning, scowl, scanty,* and *weight* all have a negative connotation. Is this about a failed liaison? It is a flat conclusion to something that perhaps should not have happened.

FURTHER READING

Angelou, Maya. *The Complete Collected Poems of Maya Angelou.* New York: Random House, 1994.

Hagen, Lyman B. *Heart of a Woman, Mind of a Writer, and Soul of a Poet: A Critical Analysis of the Writings of Maya Angelou.* Lanham, Md.: University Press of America, 1996.

"Ain't That Bad?"

"Ain't That Bad?" is in Maya Angelou's collection *And Still I Rise* (1975).

SYNOPSIS

"Ain't That Bad?" is written in the black oral tradition and is a message of black pride. It stereotypes black behavior—"Dancin' the funky chicken / Eatin' ribs and tips . . . Puttin' down that do-rag / Tightenin' up my 'fro"—in a friendly, affirming way. Light and fun, the poem mentions well-known American blacks (Stevie Wonder, Leontyne Price, Jesse Jackson, Alvin Ailey, Barbara Jordan, PEARL BAILEY, Arthur Ashe, Muhammad Ali, André Watts, and Andrew Young), and it reminds the reader that these well-known figures represent them as a people.

The last stanza repeats "An' ain't they Black? An' ain't they bad?" To recognize and affirm the culture, mores, customs, and leaders in African-American life, the narrator repetitiously chants the familiar cultural markers. The poem is written in short lines with positive connotations throughout.

CRITICAL COMMENTARY

Lyman B. Hagen explains the meaning of "Ain't That bad?":

> In black West African English (Sierra Leone) *I gud baad* means "it's very good." Thus "bad" as used extensively in this poem carries a favorable

> connotation, meaning to be "very good, extremely good." This meaning has been incorporated into everyday black vernacular and therefore is commonly understood. The last word in the last line of the poem sustains the positive connotations and provides a closure. (127) [The last line is: "An' ain't we fine?"]

Another way to consider this poem is as a shouting poem (that is, calling out truth). Though shout poetry traces back to earlier periods in black history, and in fact to Africa, the urgency of this style came through in the BLACK AESTHETIC MOVEMENT of the mid-to-late 20th century. Some of Angelou's poetry reflects that passion, and its loudness screams for attention to the injustice African Americans have endured for too long.

FURTHER READING

Angelou, Maya. *The Complete Collected Poems of Maya Angelou.* New York: Random House, 1994.

Hagen, Lyman B. *Heart of a Woman, Mind of a Writer, and Soul of a Poet: A Critical Analysis of the Writings of Maya Angelou.* Lanham, Md.: University Press of America, 1996.

"Amazing Peace"

Though Maya Angelou prefers that poetry be enjoyed privately, she is always willing to contribute her talent to important celebrations and occasions. This poem was read by the poet at the lighting of the National Christmas Tree in Washington, D.C., on December 1, 2005.

SYNOPSIS

The beginning lines of the poem refer to the rumbling of nature and perhaps negative human influence upon it. We wonder, she suggests, if we have affronted nature and possibly even God. Addressing God, she asks, "Does the covenant you made with us still hold?" We worry, but "Christmas enters," and the world sings "carols of forgiveness." The poet calls it "the Glad Season," and reflects that at this time of the year, "we make our way to higher ground." She speaks of hope, joy, and peace in their different forms, and then she suggests a "comfort of courtesies" and "security" for "our beloveds and their beloveds."

This is a poem of peace and promise. Recognizing that Christmas has become an internationally inclusive celebration, Angelou's deeply moving poem embraces everyone. Beckoning all people of the world to come to understanding and peaceful relations with one another, she invites "Baptist and Buddhist, Methodist and Muslim . . . Jew and the Jainist, the Catholic and the Confucian . . . to look beyond complexion and see community." She offers Jesus Christ and his birth as being given to all of "the great religions of the world." The last stanza of the poem is again all-inclusive: "We, Angels and Mortals, Believers and Nonbelievers . . . speak the word aloud. Peace. . . . Peace, My Brother. Peace, My Sister. Peace, My Soul."

CRITICAL COMMENTARY

Angelou's deep, personal understanding of the teachings of Christ and his ethics are evident throughout this poem. Along with prophets and teachers of other belief systems, Christ taught love and consideration—essentially, the Golden Rule. Though it may be worded a little differently from philosophy to philosophy, the concept of treating others as one would be treated oneself has been taught for centuries throughout the world. At an historically sensitive time of conflict between varied cultures, and considering threats to the planet's very survival, Angelou wrote and read a poem that was designed not to offend. The repeated words of invitation, perhaps reflecting her long experience in the call-and-response tradition of the African-American people, are comforting, welcoming, and true.

FURTHER READING

Angelou, Maya. *Amazing Peace: A Celebration.* New York: Random House, 2005.

"Amoebaean for Daddy"

"Amoebaean for Daddy" is in Angelou's 1983 volume of poems, *Shaker, Why Don't You Sing?* It is a sad narrative of a wife and daughter who did not understand and a husband/father who only wanted to be understood.

SYNOPSIS

This poem begins with the narrator's explanation of how pretty she was as a baby. The line "All black babies Are Cute" suggests the stereotypical response many whites have toward babies of other races. The stanza continues with the mother's nickname for the child, "Bootsie," and then she starts to say the father's nickname for her, but the stanza ends instead with "(Nobody listened to him)."

The second stanza reveals that the father is a bowing, scraping Union Pacific dining-car waiter, a job that her mother scorns by telling him to stand up straight. However, his tips have provided a big house for her, though she never seems to acknowledge that.

The father is silent at their dinner table; the china and silver spoons have been stolen from the railroad. In the last stanza, the man finds his child happily playing outside in the night and seems to want to say something to her, but all he is able to say is: "All I ever asked, all I ever asked . . ."

The narrator's father apparently dies soon after that last failed encounter, and the poem is an overdue plea, in a way, for forgiveness.

CRITICAL COMMENTARY

The word in the title of the poem, *amoebaean,* is an adjective that means answering or responding to each other, somewhat like the responsive reading in a church. In this four-stanza poem, the story is told of a man who provided generously for his family by compromising his integrity. Neither the mother nor the child understood what he had sacrificed to give them until it was too late. The title word suggests that the exchange that might have been was offered, but it came too late.

"Arrival"

This short poem is included in the collection *Shaker, Why Don't You Sing,* published in 1983, not long after Angelou's fourth autobiography, *The Heart of a Woman* (1982). Its 18 lines express a compulsive exuberance at the appearance of someone beloved.

SYNOPSIS

The first line of "Arrival" comprises two words: "Angels gather." Celestial imagery follows with a "rush of mad air" and "wing tips' brushing across "black anemones." Hosannahs and harps sound, and "Hallelujah! Hallelujah!" is shouted in greeting.

CRITICAL COMMENTARY

The excitement projected in this poem is not unlike the spiritual enthusiasm in a southern Christian church on Easter Sunday, but for whom is this celestial excitement directed? Is it Christ? Is it a family member being welcomed home after a long absence? Or is it a lover, a sweetheart who triggers undulating and sensuous meanings from the sounds of a harp? The short, terse lines, rich with metaphor and symbols of celestial joy, leave the reader wondering at the ambiguity.

FURTHER READING

Angelou, Maya. *The Complete Collected Poems of Maya Angelou.* New York: Random House, 1994.

"Artful Pose"

Angelou's collection *Oh Pray My Wings Are Gonna Fit Me Well* (1975) includes "Artful Pose" in Part Three. This collection was published a year after the autobiography *Gather Together in My Name.*

SYNOPSIS

The 15 lines of "Artful Pose" begin with tender poetic thoughts such as "falling leaves and melting snows" and "melodies tendering my nights sweetly" but turn quickly to "hate and hateful wrath" in describing feelings about a false lover. The soft vowels in the first seven lines turn into harsh consonants and sharp words as the speaker feels her anger rise. She cannot continue posing as an artful writer with such outrage clouding her muse.

CRITICAL COMMENTARY

Angelou's poetry and autobiographies have a confessional quality and have often carried an additional political message addressed to the black dilemma, particularly the challenges that face black American women. Though the context of this poem is unknown, the assertive power of righteous anger speaks to the black collective. The scholar Ruthe Sheffey wrote:

> Genuine rhetoric, indeed all verbal art, coexists with reason, truth, and justice. All of the traditions of rational and moral speech are allied to the primitive idea of goodness, to the force of utterance. Because the past is functional in our lives when we neither forget it nor try to return to it, the new Black voices must reach the masses in increasingly communal ways, must penetrate those hidden crevices of our beings only recognizable and reachable by poetry. (8)

Some critics discussing this new collection suggested that Angelou was suffering from too much fame too quickly. James Finn Cotter writes, "Too much fame too soon has been the ruin of many poets" (103–104), but other reviewers have been more generous. "Angelou's new volume is slim, with good heritage ballads and excellent lyrics such as 'Child Dead in Old Seas,' and the colorful, pleasant 'This Winter Day,' which reminds one of genre painting. The poems work best read aloud" (Harris 1975, 1,829).

FURTHER READING

Angelou, Maya. *The Complete Collected Poems of Maya Angelou.* New York: Random House, 1994.

Cotter, James Finn. Review of *Oh Pray My Wings Are Gonna Fit Me Well* by Maya Angelou, *The Women and The Men* by Nikki Giovanni and *The Peacock Poems* by Shirley Williams. *America* 134, no. 5 (February 1976): 103–104.

Harris, Katherine Giggs. Review of *Oh Pray My Wings Are Gonna Fit Me Well* by Maya Angelou. *Library Journal* 100, no. 17 (1975): 1,829.

Sheffey, Ruthe. "Black Poetry." In *A Current Bibliography on African Affairs,* edited by Roger W. Moeller, 8:107. Amityville, N.Y.: Baywood, 1985.

"Awaking in New York"

"Awaking in New York" is the first poem in Angelou's fourth collection of poetry, *Shaker, Why Don't You Sing?* (1983), published two years after her fourth autobiography, *The Heart of a Woman.*

SYNOPSIS

This simple 11-line poem depicts Angelou's early morning waking experience, when "the city drags itself awake on subway straps." She awakens "as a rumor of war, . . . stretching into dawn, unasked and unheeded." The poem evokes a sympathy for loneliness and a clouded future.

CRITICAL COMMENTARY

When *Shaker, Why Don't You Sing* was published, one critic wrote: "She evokes the unsung notes from her own experience. 'Awaking in New York' . . . reaches an 'Unmeasured Tempo' [the fifth poem in this collection] for everybody with her wide, deep range of sympathies" (Sylvester 1985, 19–20). In "Awaking in New York," Angelou is conveying the loneliness of the unknown. The phrase *rumor of war* gives a sense of anxiety and of a lack of control over one's own destiny. Many of Angelou's poems convey this concern.

FURTHER READING

Angelou, Maya. *The Complete Collected Poems of Maya Angelou.* New York: Random House, 1994.

Sylvester, William. "Maya Angelou." In *Contemporary Poets,* 4th ed., edited by James Vinson and D. L. Kirkpatrick, 19–20. Chicago: St. James Press, 1985.

"Black Family Pledge, A"

Maya Angelou wrote this poem to be recited at the seven-day African-American celebration of Kwanzaa, an observance held between Christmas and New Year's Eve. "The name Kwanzaa derives from the Swahili phrase *matunda ya kwanza,* meaning the first fruits of the harvest" (Scott 2009, np). The celebration honors family, community, and culture, and honors universal African heritage and its cultural legacy. The homes celebrating Kwanzaa are decorated with *kente* (a colorful African cloth), there are fresh fruits, and women often wear African kaftans. Children are included in the celebration. Kwanzaa is also marked by participants lighting a kinara (candleholder). This African-American observance was begun in 1966 by Dr. Maulana Karenga, professor and chairman of black studies at California State University, and it is the first official African-American holiday. Some non-African Americans celebrate the holiday as well.

SYNOPSIS

Each of the seven days of Kwanzaa is dedicated to one of the principles of Kwanzaa, or Nguzo Saba (the seven principles of blackness). The principals are: Unity, Self-Determination, Collective Work and Responsibility, Cooperative Economics, Purpose, Creativity, and Faith. "A Black Family Pledge" is meant to be recited on New Year's Eve, and each stanza is read by a different family member, with the pledge at the end recited in unison. It begins as follows:

> BECAUSE we have forgotten our ancestors,
> our children no longer give us honor.
> BECAUSE we have lost the path our ancestors
> cleared
> kneeling in perilous undergrowth,
> our children cannot find their way . . .

CRITICAL COMMENTARY

The words of the pledge serve as consciousness-raising reminders of responsibilities people have one to another. As the stanzas and then the pledge are read by those present and participating in the New Year's Eve ceremony, each person who hears the words is made aware of the many elements that make up a successful society. These words are also reminders of common failures.

FURTHER READING

Kwanzaa. "The Founder's Welcome." Available online. URL: http://www.officialkwanzaawebsite.org/index.shtml. Accessed November 16, 2010.

Mayes, Keith. *Kwanzaa: Black Power and the Making of the African American Holiday Tradition.* New York: Routledge, 2009.

Scott, Megan K. "Kwanza Celebrations Continue, but Boom Is Over." *Buffalo News,* 17 December 2009.

"Black Ode"

"Black Ode" is included in Angelou's first published collection of poems, *Just Give Me a Cool Drink of Water 'fore I Diiie* (1971). Angelou wrote openly and candidly about her intimate relations with lovers, and she also wrote many mournful poems about the pain of losing them. This topic had been skirted previously by black writers, both male and female, but she opened the door to expressions of intimacy, and she left it open for others.

SYNOPSIS

The lines express awareness, passion, and completion. They also imply that there is no sin in this enjoyment—"a being / Rounded / Up Baptist aisles, / so moaning / And moist sounds / Bless her heart. Take your bed and walk." In the King James Version of the Bible, Christ is quoted as saying, "Take up thy bed and walk" (John 5:8). The context is Christ's forgiving and healing of a crippled man. In this poem, the narrator is also forgiven for being human.

CRITICAL COMMENTARY

Yasmin Y. DeGout suggests that in this poem and others like it, "Rather than the female body through the male gaze or even the male body through the female gaze, what is eroticized is sexual intimacy itself" (125).

FURTHER READING

Angelou, Maya. *The Complete Collected Poems of Maya Angelou.* New York: Random House, 1994.

DeGout, Yasmin Y. "The Poetry of Maya Angelou: Liberation Ideology and Technique." In *Maya Angelou.* Bloom's Modern Critical Views, edited by Harold Bloom, 121–132. New York: Bloom's Literary Criticism, 2009.

Holy Bible: King James Version. Salt Lake City, Utah: Church of Jesus Christ of Latter-day Saints, 2004.

"Brave and Startling Truth, A"

Maya Angelou read her poem "A Brave and Startling Truth" at the 50th anniversary of the United Nations in SAN FRANCISCO on June 26, 1995. Lyman B. Hagen has quoted Angelou as stating that "'public' and 'poem' go together like buttermilk and champagne. . . . She prefers her poetry to be a private experience, but answers when called upon if the cause is noble" (135).

SYNOPSIS

In the dedication of the small book containing this powerful poem, Angelou has written, "This book is dedicated to the hope for peace, which lies, sometimes hidden, in every heart." The phrase *When we come to it* begins almost every stanza of the 11 that comprise the poem. It suggests that as we travel though our life experience on earth, we may someday come together. The poem reminds readers that we wait for a curtain to fall on violence—"let the rifles fall from our shoulders." Stanza follows stanza with powerful sensory language—for instance, "the incense of burning flesh"—and the poem builds, reminding us that to enjoy both nature and human-made monuments is not enough. We must come to a unified peace, a "climate" where people "Can live freely without sanctimonious piety" or "crippling fear" (9).

This is a poem of celebration honoring the people of the earth, but it comes with a warning that we have not yet come to world peace. Yet, she intones, "When we come to it," we can. "We the people on this small and drifting planet" must learn an imperative, "a brave and startling truth" (8). "When we come to it," she continues, hate, battlefields, and "identical plots in foreign soil" will end, and there will be a lasting time when children can "dress their dolls in flags of truce" (2, 4). There will be a time "When the curtain falls on the minstrel show of hate / And faces sooted with scorn" (an allusion to BLACKFACE) will be scrubbed clean (2).

In delivering the message of this poem, Angelou makes numerous historical geographical allusion from the Pyramids and across the Gardens of Babylon to the Grand Canyon, the Danube, Mount Fuji, the Amazon, and the Mississippi, encompassing many of the natural wonders of the world. But the message is that the people are the real wonders of this world we share. "We, this people . . . Have the power to fashion this earth . . . Without crippling fear." That can only happen, she warns, when people realize that "We are the miraculous, the true wonder of this world . . . That is when . . . we come to it" (5, 6).

CRITICAL COMMENTARY

"A Brave and Startling Truth" has orchestral power as it expresses the hope of genuine peace on earth. It begins softly and quietly, pianissimo, with gentle phrases such as *casual space, aloof stars,* and *indifferent suns* and then builds in anticipation, stanza following stanza, "when we come to it." The tension builds, like a slow crescendo, and adds the clashing dissonance of "the minstrel show of hate" and "screaming racket" (2, 3). The poem peaks at the horror of "nightmares of abuse." At last, the decrescendo occurs, and then "Come songs of such exquisite sweetness" that in "awe" people can create. At last, on this planet, "on this wayward, floating body" a lasting peace can begin (7, 9).

When Angelou reads her poetry aloud to an audience, there is an eloquence embedded with power that few other speakers can match. She reads with passion and drama, but more than that, she reads with deep conviction that her message will move her listeners to understanding and perhaps even action. That passion engages the listeners, and her message is understood. In this lyrical, repetitive poem, the point is driven home that though the world is a beautiful place made of wonders, both natural and human-made, it is and has always been a place of war, rape, destruction, and fear. The primary wonder of it is the miracle of human beings. What happens on this earth is up to the people who inhabit it.

In her autobiographies, essays, poems, plays, and other works, Angelou's constant message is that no matter what harsh experiences any people might encounter, there is always a way to work it through and move on. She teaches dignity, pride, and self-respect, and the message of this poem, written in celebration of the United Nations' golden anniversary, is that she asks for the world to release its "fists of hostility and allow the pure air to cool our palms." Angelou did not always feel this way about all of the people of the world, particularly whites, but over time and through experience, she learned that all people are more alike than different, and she has said that many times.

After a 1987 interview with Angelou, Valerie Webster reported:

> Tolerance is a strong element in her character and one in which she has schooled herself over the years. In her progress from childhood in the segregated South to international literary fame and a professorship at a 95-per-cent White North Carolina private university her attitude to Whites has inevitably changed. "When I was a child I didn't think they were human. No members of the human race could behave as they did. Now I share the view of Terence, the Roman playwright who was himself a freed African slave, and who wrote 'I am a human being therefore nothing human can be foreign to me.'" (182)

For accuracy, Webster added, "Actually Terence said 'I am a man' but Maya Angelou would forgive him that, on the grounds of cultural difference" (182).

Angelou's constant plea is that in spite of every imaginable kind of oppression, the human spirit must not be hardened. It must endure and learn that its responses to whatever happens are its responsibility. People own their reactions to experiences, good or bad, and when the human family of this world really learns that simple truth, it will be the time "When we come to it."

FURTHER READING

Angelou, Maya. *A Brave and Startling Truth.* New York: Random House, 1995.

Hagen, Lyman B. *Heart of a Woman, Mind of a Writer, and Soul of a Poet: A Critical Analysis of the Writings of Maya Angelou.* Lanham, Md.: University Press of America, 1996.

Webster, Valerie. "A Journey through Life." In *Conversations with Maya Angelou,* edited by Jeffrey M. Elliot, 179–182. Jackson and London: University Press of Mississippi, 1989.

"Brief Innocence"

"Brief Innocence" is included in Angelou's collection *Shaker, Why Don't You Sing?* (1983).

SYNOPSIS

Ten lines describe the peace and innocence of early morning. The first line states: "Dawn offers innocence to a half-mad city." The narrator considers letting go of the day's intentions for a moment of "soft nuzzling," being "sleep-besotted," and simply sleeping with angels a little longer in the dawn.

CRITICAL COMMENTARY

Maya Angelou often uses her own experiences to develop her poetry, knowing that others share much of the same life experience. She and her readers have all experienced warm, quiet mornings like this one where there is quiet peace cocooned in tranquil comfort. How welcome mornings like this are, and how rare they are for many individuals.

FURTHER READING

Angelou, Maya. *The Complete Collected Poems of Maya Angelou.* New York: Random House, 1994.

"Bump d'Bump"

"Bump d'Bump" is in Part Three of the collection *And Still I Rise.* It is a poem on the topic of achieving self-empowerment by being alert but inconspicuous. The narrator has fine-tuned her survival with seeming indifference.

SYNOPSIS

The narrator, a little like BRER RABBIT, taunts, "Play me a game like Blind Man's dance / And bind my eyes with ignorance" and still I will just bump along. Name calling will not assert superiority, either, because one can play possum or shut the ears against insult. Dreams of rising up in life are steady, but in the meanwhile, the welfare line is there (though the narrator may be last in line). The black voice clearly declares that it will not be defeated, no matter what the racists may perpetrate against it.

CRITICAL COMMENTARY

Houston A. Baker, Jr., suggests that black writing uses "readily discernible Afro-American expressive cultural referents" (89). Angelou uses signifiers in her work that carry meaning beyond what is on the page, and in this poem, the repetitive "Bump d'bump bump d'bump" suggests a dance that invites both the BLUES aesthetic and resistance to defeat. Stereotypical insults to blacks are named (liquor signs, junkie reel, liver lips, satchel mouth), and though they are acknowledged, they are ignored. This again affirms the innate pride and indifference of the victimized.

FURTHER READING

Angelou, Maya. *The Complete Collected Poems of Maya Angelou.* New York: Random House, 1994.

Baker, Houston A., Jr. *Blues, Ideology, and African American Literature: A Vernacular Theory.* Chicago: University of Chicago Press, 1987.

"Caged Bird"

"Caged Bird" is included in Maya Angelou's volume of poems entitled *Shaker, Why Don't You Sing?* (1983). The title of her first autobiography, *I Know Why the Caged Bird Sings* (1970), was taken from a line in PAUL LAURENCE DUNBAR's poem "Sympathy." The song of the caged bird is a prayer for freedom—a plea. This poem tells the story of a free bird and a caged bird.

SYNOPSIS

In five stanzas, the narrator expresses both freedom and a lament for it in alternating verses. There are two about the free bird and three about the caged bird, and the emphasis on the trapped one is a metaphor for the entrapment her people suffered for many centuries. Perhaps as a nod of gratitude to Paul Dunbar for the line Angelou borrowed for the title of her first book, this poem expresses sorrow and hope for renewal and freedom. Her musical lyrics in the stanzas about the free bird create a feeling of openness and autonomy: "A free bird leaps on the back of the wind and floats downstream." The next stanza contrasts the meaning by stating that a caged bird "can seldom see though the bars of rage." The words *Stalks, cage,* and *rage* have hard sounds, and they reflect the frustration of the caged bird whose "wings are clipped" and "feet are tied." And yet, full of hope, he "opens his throat to sing."

The caged bird is fearful of the unknown, but he still hopes for liberation. The free bird has enough to eat, and he has a sense of ownership—"he names the sky his own." The trapped bird "stands on a grave of dreams." He can hope, but he cannot escape until someone allows him to. Thus, his song is a prayer for freedom.

CRITICAL COMMENTARY

With rhythm and enchanting imagery, Angelou contrasts the beauty of freedom and the tragedy of confinement in this poem. It is a metaphor for enslavement, and it testifies to the faith and prayer for continued hope that many people use to sustain themselves through very uncomfortable lives. The caged bird in the narration will never know freedom, and perhaps it senses that, but its spirit is still unbroken. Perhaps the free bird hears the suffering one from "the distant hill" and either feels helpless or indifferent to its plight.

FURTHER READING

Angelou, Maya. *The Complete Collected Poems of Maya Angelou.* New York: Random House, 1994.

Gates, Henry Louis, Jr., and Nellie Y. McKay, eds. *The Norton Anthology of African American Literature.* New York: W. W. Norton, 1997.

"Calling of Names, The"

"The Calling of Names" is included in *Just Give Me a Cool Drink of Water 'fore I Diiie*. Democratic and political changes in the United States have resulted in ever-changing designations for minority groups. There are many variants and styles of names for most groups, and current questions are whether to hyphenate or not, or capitalize or not. Should it be African American, African-American, Afro-American, blacks or Blacks? As W. E. B. DuBois and other great black leaders have said, the most important issue is that individuals and groups be treated equitably and with respect.

SYNOPSIS

One of the many frustrations for African Americans has been society's constant indecision about name designation. Angelou expresses it in this poem, which begins by saying, "He went to being called a colored man after answering to 'hey, nigger.'" Then, she writes, the designation was changed to "Negro, With the N in caps." And "Now you'll get hurt if you don't call him 'Black.'"

Angelou has tried to build pride among African Americans through her writing, and this poem expresses an ongoing dialogue, with the pronoun *I* operating as a synecdoche for the group, a conceit she often employs in her other poems. Most important, however, is that the message be delivered firmly that African Americans must be treated with the same respect and dignity as any other group of people. There was a time when black children of slaves were taken from their families and placed in the big house as a companions and PLAY PRETTIES for the children of the house. They were called by many names, and the spoken dialects of the black children and white children influenced one another.

CRITICAL COMMENTARY

Alan Dundes's edited collection *Mother Wit from the Laughing Barrel: Readings in the Interpretation of Afro-American Folklore* (1990) includes a 1944 article entitled "Designations for Colored Folk," written by H. L. Mencken, a respected journalist of the time. The issue Mencken was discussing was a decision made by the *New York Times* in 1930 announcing "that it would capitalize the word *Negro* thereafter" (quoted in Dundes 1990, 144). In his introduction to Mencken's article, Dundes commented:

> The issue is far from dead as both Negroes and whites continue to wrestle with it. Some of the lexical choices are partly determined by age. For example, many members of the older generation of both Negroes and whites are comfortable with the term "colored." Middle-aged people tend generally to use "Negro" while the younger generation is leaning strongly toward "black." Not only is there an age factor, but there is the more crucial matter of geographical area and particular social situation. The term used depends upon who is speaking to whom in the presence of what third parties. It is probably safe to assume that no one term is likely to please everyone. (143)

The confusion about an African-American designator is an old one. In 1937, Dr. Kelly Miller suggested that "the slaves were simply called *blacks*" (quoted in Dundes 1990, 145). Dundes also wrote that a query about what term to use as a descriptor for African Americans was directed to Booker T. Washington by a member of the U.S. House of Representatives. Booker's "reply indicated a personal preference for Afro-American, which would have the advantage of being political rather than racial. Nevertheless, Booker T. Washington reluctantly suggested that the term Negro be employed" (Dundes 1990, 142–143). W. E. B. DuBois, when asked, "claimed that the name wasn't what was important but having pride in one's race was" (143). Angelou seemed to conclude that blacks would no longer take part in this naming game.

FURTHER READING

Angelou, Maya. *The Complete Collected Poems of Maya Angelou*. New York: Random House, 1994.

Dundes, Alan. *Mother Wit from the Laughing Barrel: Readings in the Interpretation of Afro-American Folklore*. Jackson and London: University Press of Mississippi, 1990.

"Changes"

"Changes" was published in *Shaker, Why Don't You Sing?* (1983). It is a short narration about a love betrayal, but the survivor will not lose in the end.

SYNOPSIS

This three-stanza poem, with some rhyming, reveals the narrator's hurt in love, but it also reveals that comfort and confidence will return. "Fickle comfort steals away," it begins, and the ambiguity of fickle behavior it describes is treated lightly. It reveals the pain of love, but there is a light attitude that is almost a warning. The second stanza suggests that "The severed nerves, The jagged mind, [and] The shattered dream" are realities, frolic, are only temporary. In the third stanza, the narrator lets the reader know that though confidence has been lost from the experience, "Tomorrow it returns to me."

CRITICAL COMMENTARY

This poem is written with harsh consonants and many two-syllable words, which suggests the jarring of sensibilities through change and ambiguity. Maya Angelou wrote many poems about lost love and loneliness. This one is a little different and more confident. Though it was not published until 1983, it may reflect an earlier time when Angelou learned that her male companion in Cairo was not only untrue to her but had also failed to pay his debts. She reveals pain in this short poem, but she also reveals that her self-esteem will return, and that she will be fine.

FURTHER READING

Angelou, Maya. *The Complete Collected Poems of Maya Angelou.* New York: Random House, 1994.

"Changing"

"Changing" is included in Maya Angelou's collection *I Shall Not Be Moved,* published in 1990. This poem observes changing behavior in someone who was close but seems to be drifting away.

SYNOPSIS

The narrator notes that her friend (or lover) enjoys others, but he never smiles around her. The "wit is honed to killing sharpness," but there are no smiles for the narrator. The friend is sending dismissive signals, and the narrator understands that and seems to accept it, but it is uncomfortable.

CRITICAL COMMENTARY

Maya Angelou often wrote poetry about disappointing love relationships and loneliness. In "Changing," she is expressing a foreshadowing of lost interest. The relationship has not quite ended, but the unmistakable signs of dismissal are there. The narrator's friend no longer enjoys her company.

FURTHER READING

Angelou, Maya. *The Complete Collected Poems of Maya Angelou.* New York: Random House, 1994.

"Chicken-Licken"

"Chicken-Licken" is included in the collection *Oh Pray My Wings Are Gonna Fit Me Well* (1975). The last line, "Autopsy read: dead of acute peoplelessness," causes the reader to pause, reflect, and perhaps read the poem again. Some critics have suggested that this poem may have been about a lesbian Angelou knew or heard about, or at least it may be about a woman who greatly feared men.

SYNOPSIS

The poem, with an outside narrator, begins with "She was afraid of men." She locked her door and "Put a chain across / her door and closed / her mind." She died there, and "Her bones were found / round thirty years later." She died, the "Autopsy read: / of acute peoplelessness."

CRITICAL COMMENTARY

Angelou is open-minded and curious about different kinds of people and life choices. Rethinking gender roles is the issue in this poem. The woman feared and hated men, but perhaps she knew she would not be accepted by the world as an lesbian (if that is what she discovered she was), so she locked herself away from everyone.

FURTHER READING

Angelou, Maya. *The Complete Collected Poems of Maya Angelou.* New York: Random House, 1994.

"Child Dead in Old Seas"

"Child Dead in Old Seas" is included in Part Five of Angelou's collection *Oh Pray My Wings Are Gonna Fit Me Well,* published in 1975.

SYNOPSIS

In three stanzas, the morbid tragedy of a lost child, probably one who lost his or her life aboard a slave ship during the Middle Passage, is told from his watery grave at the bottom of the ocean. In the slaves' stowage, which was only three feet high, there was no light or fresh air, and no sanitary provisions. The reek and heat of this space was indescribable. There was little water, and the captives were manacled. Many died and were thrown overboard. The slave spirits beneath the water wait, "Waves undulating / corn rows around my / black feet." There they wait and dream "of lost savannahs / green and / drums." They wait for release of their spirits from the sea.

CRITICAL COMMENTARY

Angelou was deeply moved and disturbed as she flew from Egypt to Ghana and watched the land below from the airplane window. She looked down on deserts and forests knowing that these were the lands where her ancestors had been chased, captured, and shipped, in dreadful conditions, into slavery. The lyrics of this tragic ballad narrative create a chilling sensory response: It is cold, it is wet, and it is dark. It is the lost grave of a child.

The Atlantic slave trade lasted for over three centuries, and people were captured in many parts of Africa, not just the West Coast as is sometimes believed. The logs of slave ships mention various points of embarkation but rarely list the origin of their human cargo. As colonial demands for slave labor grow, the slave trade grew and flourished. That it was a travesty to human beings is beyond questioning. Death was common. Captured slaves were marched in long lines and forced to wear iron collars linked together by chains. The slaves were packed between the decks of the ships, two by two, and then they were taken across the ocean in what was called the Middle Passage. It took several weeks, and many died because of spoiled food, disease, jumping overboard, or choking themselves with their chains. Dead bodies were thrown overboard, and sharks trailed the ships. Because of the deplorable conditions maintained in the passage from Africa to the West Indies, and because of the severe training or breaking the slaves underwent in the islands before being sold in America, it is known that large percentages of these kidnapped people died before ever reaching the States.

Angelou grieved for her ancestors and the ancestors of her people. Her son comforted her, as best he could, on that long trip from Cairo to Accra, but to no avail. In time, she wrote this poem, grieving for those who were needlessly lost. There were many religious beliefs about the soul in Africa. One is that the spirit of an individual, his *akra,* "which is given at birth, may venture out of the body while a person sleeps, and it departs at death" (Raboteau 32). In this poem, it is implied that the spirit waits under the sea for its redemption.

FURTHER READING

Angelou, Maya. *The Complete Collected Poems of Maya Angelou.* New York: Random House, 1994.

Raboteau, Albert J. *Slave Religion: The "Invisible Institution" in the Antebellum South.* New York: Oxford University Press, 1980.

"Coleridge Jackson"

"Coleridge Jackson" is included in Angelou's 1990 collection *I Shall Not Be Moved.* This important poem narrates how a strong black man can be reduced to becoming a bully and abuser in response to continually demeaning words by a cruel white employer.

SYNOPSIS

The poem begins, "He weighed sixty pounds / more than his sons and one / hundred pounds more than his wife." A large, strong man, even his friends respected his presence. And yet, "his puny boss, a little / white bag of bones" could reduce him to nothing with name-calling and demands.

When Coleridge went home, he beat his family. The boss heard about the battered family and "that scrawny man / grinned." For a while, he was fair to Coleridge, and then he was cruel once again. After having been called names, Coleridge just kept "sliding / away, lurking at something else."

CRITICAL COMMENTARY

"Coleridge Jackson" provides insight into the degrading mistreatment dealt to some black men who labor for their living, and yet these victims are unable to quit because they must earn a livelihood for themselves and their children.

Michelle Howe writes: "Speaking about the impact of that particular poem, Angelou said, 'I read that poem in public. And a young black man came up to me and thanked me. He said: "Now I understand my father." We hugged each other and cried'" (C4).

FURTHER READING

Angelou, Maya. *The Complete Collected Poems of Maya Angelou.* New York: Random House, 1994.

Howe, Michele. "Angelou's Poetry Builds Bridges Between Peoples." *Star-Ledger* (Newark, New Jersey), 3 June 1990, C4.

"Communication I"

"Communication I" is included in *Oh Pray My Wings Are Gonna Fit Me Well,* published in 1975. This poem is a companion poem to "Communication II."

SYNOPSIS

In "Communication I," we read how a literate, passionate lover bestows upon his partner physical warmth and tenderness, all the while speaking and reminding her of faraway places and romantic literary allusions. He named Greece, the birthplace of democracy; the Parthenon, a fifth-century Doric temple built on the Acropolis in Athens; and Cleopatra's barge, a sumptuous riverboat with purple sails and oars of silver that is described in one of WILLIAM SHAKESPEARE's famous speeches in act 2, scene 2 of *Antony and Cleopatra.* As the lovers approach the water's edge, the narrator quotes "Pope and Bernard Shaw" / and "*Catcher in the Rye,*" but becomes detached from the girl, who has lost her sandal in the ocean. Why?

In the last stanza, the girl tells her mother that "Of all he said, I understood / he said he loved another." He communicated many things from his accumulated knowledge, but he lost her in the plethora of too many allusions.

CRITICAL COMMENTARY

Maya Angelou sometimes uses movement in her poems as metaphors for tender acts of love. Here she has drawn a sensual poem wherein both partners are wrapped in their pleasure of one another and their own interests. The man quotes literary allusions; she savors the feel of the water. Their communication is lost, and she loses interest in him. The intimate experiences each enjoyed did not involve the other, and their communication was futile.

FURTHER READING

Angelou, Maya. *The Complete Collected Poems of Maya Angelou.* New York: Random House, 1994.

"Communication II"

"Communication II" is included in Part Two of *Oh Pray My Wings Are Gonna Fit Me Well,* published in 1975. It is a companion poem to "Communication I."

SYNOPSIS

This short poem is written in two parts, "The Student" and "The Teacher." It is dedicated to a woman named Adele. The first poem suggests that the young student does not understand "the dust of ancient pages" he has been given because of his "young un-knowing." "The Teacher" shares the past, or tries to, of "etched Pharonic walls" (Africa) and "Reconstruction's anguish" (post–Civil War America), but she fails to communicate the meaning of the words and the suffering they represent so the student can understand. Both "Reconstruction's anguish" and her own "resounded down the halls."

CRITICAL COMMENTARY

Communication from one generation to another is almost always difficult until each learns to connect and understand the other's perspectives. "Young-unknowing" children grow up and eventually learn the truth of the world and its ways. In this poem, the gap of understanding creates tension and a frustrated mourning in the teacher. The child seems oblivious, but perhaps the stories are heard and internally recorded after all, to be replayed, redefined, and maybe understood at a later time.

FURTHER READING

Angelou, Maya. *The Complete Collected Poems of Maya Angelou.* New York: Random House, 1994.

"Conceit, A"

"A Conceit" was published in Angelou's second book of poetry, *Oh Pray My Wings Are Gonna Fit Me Well* (1975). In a literary sense, the word *conceit* can mean many things. It can be a fanciful expression, witty and clever, or it can be a metaphor, simple or elaborate.

SYNOPSIS

In this brief poem, Angelou is suggesting that, for her, physical touching works better than words. It is a short, simple expression of love, and the first and last lines say simply, "Give me your hand." It represents a balanced relationship, "to lead and follow," and it suggests that other pairs of people might share words of love and losses in the past, but this pair would rather enjoy the security of touching in the present moment.

CRITICAL COMMENTARY

Some reviewers disliked this collection, but perhaps they missed the point of it. Angelou writes with a sparse style rather than in soaring, pretentious verse. She writes for ordinary readers, not other poets, and the message in this poem is of choice. It is a poetic metaphor, and in this poem of love, the comparison is between enjoying the moment in a touch or reflecting on a regretful past recalled in poetic words. How much more desirable is hand-to-hand touching in the present rather than evoking the losses of the past. The analogy is that a comfortable, safe present is preferable to a sad reverie of the past.

FURTHER READING

Angelou, Maya. *The Complete Collected Poems of Maya Angelou.* New York: Random House, 1994.

"Contemporary Announcement"

"Contemporary Announcement" is included in *Shaker, Why Don't You Sing,* published in 1983. It is a poem about survival in spite of an unknown future.

SYNOPSIS

Calling for a celebration, "Ring the big bells, / cook the cow," the poem begins on what seems like a high note. In the second stanza, there is caution and a change in tone. Here the poem reveals its underlying irony: The narrator has money to pay the rent, but her job was lost two weeks ago.

CRITICAL COMMENTARY

Angelou wrote many of her poems to raise the spirits of people when they were facing hard times. Larry Neal, a critic and spokesperson for the black community, writes: "The Black artist takes this [the work] to mean that his primary duty is to speak to the spiritual and cultural needs of Black people" (1,960). Losing a job is a serious situation for most people, and it is even more threatening when one earns so little that sustaining life is a marginal bet from week to week. In this poem, Angelou uses irony to represent the devastation and even possible starvation that may come as a result of losing one's source of income. The narrator is trying to be light and cheerful in tone, but her words belie that attitude.

FURTHER READING

Angelou, Maya. *The Complete Collected Poems of Maya Angelou.* New York: Random House, 1994.

Neal, Larry. "The Black Arts Movement." In *The Norton Anthology of African American Literature,* edited by Henry Louis Gates, Jr., and Nelly Y. McKay, 1960–1972. New York: W. W. Norton, 1997.

"Elegy"

Angelou includes "Elegy" in Part Five of *Oh Pray My Wings Are Gonna Fit Me Well,* published in 1975. The poem is dedicated to HARRIET TUBMAN and FREDERICK DOUGLASS, great warriors for freedom in the 19th century.

SYNOPSIS

The first stanza catches the reader unaware because it is a message from the dead to the living. They watch with pride, Tubman and Douglass, "Proud blooms / above the weeds of death." In the next stanza, they wonder if they are remembered, but that is not the focus of the poem. Rather, it is that they are what they are, and that they still care about the "roots of my / children born." They know that their work was for the future.

They know, too, that the children will join them at some time, but the responsibility was "only need to / fertilize their birth." They worked to make a richer life for their children (meaning future generation). The final stanza conveys acceptance and peace: "I lie down in my grave / and watch my children grow."

CRITICAL COMMENTARY

Angelou often pays homage to her cultural heroes in her poetry. Some individuals she alludes to are widely known, but some are drawn more privately from her wide circle of family and friends. In this poem of four stanzas, she pays respectful tribute to Harriet Tubman and Frederick Douglass and leaves the reader with a sense of historical memory. These are the ancestors of today's blacks. These are they who gave their lives and energies so that life could be free and full of equal opportunity, unlike how it was in their time. Lyman B. Hagen writes: "In 'Elegy,' the speakers are early black activists, Harriet Tubman and Frederick Douglass, who proudly observe successors to their cause, 'the torch bearers they spawned'" (129).

FURTHER READING

Angelou, Maya. *The Complete Collected Poems of Maya Angelou.* New York: Random House, 1994.

Hagen B. Lyman. *Heart of a Woman, Mind of a Writer, and Soul of a Poet: A Critical Analysis of the Writings of Maya Angelou.* Lanham, Md.: University Press of America, 1997.

"Equality"

This poem is included in the collection *I Shall Not Be Moved,* published in 1990. Angelou has a talent for combining personal experience and political discourse, and in this rhythmic poem, she has combined her personal anguish with a plea for sexual equality.

SYNOPSIS

With six rhyming stanzas separated by three couplets, this poem beats out a rhythm like the sound of a drum. It begins with an accusatory tone, saying that although the narrator stands before the opposition boldly, her body is only seen dimly, nor is she heard. The drums continue, and "the rhythms never change." The two-line couplet repeats three times, "Equality, and I will be free. Equality, and I will be free." Then, more subjectively, the narrator says, "You announce my ways are wanton, / that I fly from man to man," and the next, "We have lived a painful history, / we know the shameful past, . . ." The political discourse here is the inequality of woman. The personal is the pain that she expresses because of being made to feel so inconsequential and only a shadow. The narrator pleads that this oppressor "Take the blinders from your vision, / take the padding from your ears," and she waits. The tempo and rhythm of the poem continue, "and the rhythms never change," but not until equality comes will she be free.

CRITICAL COMMENTARY

Here, Angelou speaks for many with an almost childish hysteria, quietly, persistently begging to be recognized, validated, listened to. Her internal idealism never wavers, and she recognizes the vital need to be identified. There is no reconciliation here, no more than in the continuing global struggle for equality, but she continues, "my drums are beating nightly, and the rhythms never change." They do not change because they are moral. And they will not change until others listen.

FURTHER READING

Angelou, Maya. *The Complete Collected Poems of Maya Angelou.* New York: Random House, 1994.

"Family Affairs"

"Family Affairs" was published in the collection *Shaker, Why Don't You Sing?* in 1983.

SYNOPSIS

"Rapunzel" is an old fairy tale about a beautiful young girl trapped in a tower by a witch because of a transgression the girl's parents made before she was born. The father had taken rampion, a leafy vegetable like lettuce, from the garden of the witch while the mother was pregnant with their child. It was their only child, and the witch took the baby as restitution for the theft when it was born. The girl's name is derived from the name of the plant. The witch has the girl let down her hair and uses it as a ladder when she wants to be with her. A prince overhears the witch call to the girl, imitates the call, joins the girl, and after a variety of complications, the prince and the girl live happily ever after.

Real life often does not work this way, and that is the message of the poem. Those who are destined to live in ivory towers can seldom understand the deep pain and suffering of many who have either directly or indirectly been victimized by the tower dwellers' insensitivity.

In this poem, the narrator contrasts the opulence of the girl's circumstances and the "seas of golden hair" with the African girls' "dusty braids." "Princes and commoners / climb over waves to reach / your vaulted boudoirs," and, as the poem continues, the woman in the tower "Lay, birthing masters for / My sons, and for my / Daughters." Finally, the female in the tower wakens, somewhat, and wants to take the hand of the slave, "Smiling, call me / Sister." But no, that cannot be, not yet. "Allow an age / Of dust to fill / Ruts left on my / Beach in Africa."

CRITICAL COMMENTARY

This poem, with its images of the centuries-old fairy tale "Rapunzel," "shrewdly encloses centuries of black history in a verse-play" (Cosgrave 1983, 336). The contrast between "seas of golden hair" and "pulled by dusty braids" reflects the oblivious position of the princess in the tower, benefited by the labor of the enslaved. There are overtures made constantly between some blacks and some whites in today's world that still cannot bridge ancient wounds. There is often little trust, and Angelou speaks to that and asks that understanding and patience are needed before all of these bonds between differing cultures can be established.

If a person outside of a culture knows little of the other's real history and values, and simply hopes to magically wave those differences away with a handshake or invitation to lunch, it cannot be successful. There has been too much abuse. Angelou tries to raise the self-respect and pride of her people, and she requests in this poem that people be patient. It is about empathy, a plea for others who have benefited from the suffering of the blacks to wake up to the reality, try to understand the pain, and share the responsibility. Like the collective "I" in much of African-American poetry, the inclination is to blame a collective "you." When those generalities are understood, then respectful relationships will be a possibility. We must know, understand, and forgive one another's histories. Time has passed since this collection was published in 1983, and some healing has taken place between the races, but that is not to say that it is complete.

FURTHER READING

Angelou, Maya. *The Complete Collected Poems of Maya Angelou.* New York: Random House, 1994.

Cosgrave, Mary Silva. Review of *Shaker, Why Don't You Sing?* by Maya Angelou. *Horn Book Magazine* 59, no. 3 (June 1983): 336.

"Fightin' Was Natural"

"Fightin' Was Natural" is included in the 1990 collection *I Shall Not Be Moved.* Nearly every character in Angelou's autobiographies, poetry, and essays works hard, and the boxer in this poem is no exception.

SYNOPSIS

In three stanzas, Angelou describes the literal pain associated with boxing. In the first, the narrator says that "hurtin' was real" and the glove was heavy, but it was a way "to the top of the hill." There is money, recognition, security, and yet, "Fightin' was real." The second stanza begins: "The sting of the ointment"—a price to pay for cuts, but it is okay. The crowd is screaming, and "Boxin' was real." Finally, the fight turns to "four hammers, / new bones in my jaw," and the pain increases. "Fightin' was livin'." "Livin was . . . hell."

CRITICAL COMMENTARY

In *I Know Why the Caged Bird Sings* (1970), Angelou describes a fight being broadcast on the radio. JOE LOUIS was fighting for a world title, and the people from her community were packed into Grandmother Henderson's store to hear. Everyone was there, and it was an exciting event. When Angelou was older and living in California, she took a job managing a restaurant kitchen whose owner was an entrepreneur with an investment in boxing. It became part of Angelou's responsibility to take boxers out to a wilderness area where they could run and work out. She knew how hard these men had to work to be competitive.

This poem can be read literally, as the pain of the boxer during his training and in the ring, or it can be read as a metaphor for another reality that was the struggle for freedom, including the right to vote. "Fightin' Was Natural" in many different ways. There were no easy tickets in Angelou's world; neither are there many free rides in anyone's experience. The "ride to the top of the hill" requires hard work, constant focus, and often painful moments before the dream is realized.

FURTHER READING

Angelou, Maya. *The Complete Collected Poems of Maya Angelou.* New York: Random House, 1994.

"Forgive"

"Forgive" is included in the 1990 collection *I Shall Not Be Moved.* That collection contains poems that express the strength and determination of African-American people to maintain their dignity and their hope for a better future.

SYNOPSIS

The first stanza reflects the hard life that blacks in Virginia experienced before the Civil War. This little poem seems to beg them for forgiveness without acknowledging the sorrow and indignities the blacks had been trapped in for centuries. The poem mentions "CAMPTOWN RACES," a song written by Stephen Foster in 1850. The original title was "Gwine to Run All Night" and was sung in a stereotypical African-American dialect. The song, about a group of transients in a camp town who bet on horse races to make money, is considered racist because it was written and performed in the minstrel tradition with black, painted-on faces to mock African Americans. "Camptown Races" still appears in American elementary and secondary school handbooks.

Another line in Angelou's poem talks of "ships pregnant / with certain cargo." There is no doubt that line refers to the black slaves chained in the holds of ships, without adequate air, food, or water, during the Middle Passage from Africa to the United States. Slave owners benefited for over two centuries from the hard, oppressive labor of blacks, and those centuries left an unforgettable mark on their victims.

The second stanza paints a picture of peach petals and dogwood blooms falling tenderly on the blacks, begging forgiveness, but it is laced with a harshness as "sad as summer / parasols in a hurricane." The essence of the poem is that the past cannot be brushed away lightly. To forgive means to give up all resentment, and though that is ideal, it often does not come easily. The white community cannot expect instant forgiveness for all the abuse and suffering many of them heaped upon blacks. Forgiveness is sometimes a long process.

CRITICAL COMMENTARY

Maya Angelou has held conflicting feelings throughout her life in regard to whites. As a child, she did not even think whites were human. She believed that the blacks she knew were people, but she was not altogether sure what the whites were. She saw SEGREGATION and fear firsthand, and distrust for whites was deeply embedded within her. As time went by, she was occasionally treated well by whites, and as she became a successful public performer, such goodwill increased. However, she has always been more comfortable with her own people than with others, a common preference for most humans.

Angelou's own great-grandmother had been a slave, born in 1850, the daughter of Washington Wofford. Angelou's grandmother had such a disdain for the institution of slavery that she renamed herself KENTUCKY SHANNON. Angelou's dignity and pride, developed through her own refusal to let life defeat her, rings through this poem. She can forgive, but it takes time.

FURTHER READING

Angelou, Maya. *The Complete Collected Poems of Maya Angelou.* New York: Random House, 1994.

"For Us, Who Dare Not Dare"

"For Us, Who Dare Not Dare" is included in Part Three of the collection *Oh Pray My Wings Are Gonna Fit Me Well* (1975).

SYNOPSIS

In the first line of this poem, the narrator seems to take on the persona of a pharaoh who can command that pyramids be built. The pharoah had that power, and there were many slaves. The narrator continues and commands that the reader see the Nile, and then later, that the reader swim in the Congo, swing on vines, sing like the birds, and taste the fruit. The narrator wants the reader to "Know me / Africa." In using "me" rather than "my," and in "Swim me Congo" and "Taste me fruit," the narrator provides the poem with a sense of African English. The poem is lyrical with a steady rhythm, and one wonders if that could be the faraway beat of a drum giving the reader a figurative sensory experience of hearing. This poem is beautiful when read aloud.

CRITICAL COMMENTARY

There is a thread of ambiguity in this poem. Who is the narrator? Is it the people, collectively, or is it Africa speaking? Is it the pharaoh mentioned in the first line, or is it the chief who appears in the third stanza? Is it a priest or scribe, who once penned hieroglyphics on the walls of palaces and tombs? Or is it the wind of Africa? This is a sensory poem with images of grand pyramids, brightly colored birds quickly passing through bright leaves, the cool waters of the Congo, and the taste of fruit.

In this poem, the voices of Africa call to the reader to come and see it, swim it, taste it, and feel it. Many African Americans did not identify with the vast continent of their ancestors until black artists of the 20th century brought their heritage and pride to life. Angelou's voice, and others, have changed the world, and claiming lineage from Africa is now as proud and mentioned as much as lineage from any other place in the world.

FURTHER READING

Angelou, Maya. *The Complete Collected Poems of Maya Angelou.* New York: Random House, 1994.

"Gamut, The"

"The Gamut" is the second poem in Angelou's first published collection, *Just Give Me a Cool Drink of Water 'fore I Diiie* (1971).

SYNOPSIS

The words in this poem first create a hopeful atmosphere of gentle light and sound by using words such as *dusty sun, golden,* and *silver throats* (of birds). The first stanza indicates an arrival. The second reflects the eagerness of conversation, the attentiveness of caring what the lover has to say. But the third and closing stanzas turn to death. Here, there is mourning because separation from love feels like death to the narrator, because her "true love is leaving." The imagery in this short, three-stanza poem changes quickly from light to dark—from anticipation to disappointment.

CRITICAL COMMENTARY

The parting or separation of lovers for any reason is an emotionally painful experience. Using connotative language, the stanzas in this poem lead to a "deathly quiet" and separation. "My shroud of black be weaving" is perhaps an allusion to Penelope, who, during the absence of her husband, Odysseus, in the *Odyssey,* wove a death shroud in the daytime and unraveled it at night after promising the suitors that she would choose one of them when the shroud was finished.

FURTHER READING

Angelou, Maya. *The Complete Collected Poems of Maya Angelou.* New York: Random House, 1994.

"Georgia Song, A"

"A Georgia Song" was one of the poems written for Angelou's fourth collection, *Shaker, Why Don't You Sing?* (1983). It is set after the violence of the fight for civil rights in the 20th century, but it echoes with the legacy of 19th-century African Americans. The poem is both a celebration and a lament for true southern peace in which American blacks can trust and feel safe.

SYNOPSIS

The first line of this poem is "We swallow the odors of Southern cities," and the implication is that their joy and sorrow remain in memories of what was once a slave state. This poem cries the BLUES: "Remember our days, Susannah"; "Cry for our souls, Augusta." The image held in the collective memory of American blacks through years of trial and remembered history is the hope that at some point a song will be sung, "A song / Of Southern peace." Many African Americans in the South still do not fully enjoy promised freedoms. Threats and hidden boundaries remain too often, and their sorrow is lifted by the wailing and comforting sounds of the blues.

CRITICAL COMMENTARY

As in her autobiographies, Angelou expresses a wide range of understanding learned from her own experiences and self-reflection. She has listened to her people, and she has sung of both their sorrow and their rage in her poetry. This poem is written against a backdrop of black rhythm with a counterpoint of personal conviction. Her expressions in this poem are drawn from mature reflection of memories of the power white southern Georgia once held over an enslaved people who had stoically learned to live with what little they had. Her childhood in STAMPS, ARKANSAS, held much of the same frustration and threat as in Georgia. Times have changed, and protective laws have been put in place, but the sorrow continues, and the hope is that wholesome and genuine democracy will prevail.

FURTHER READING

Angelou, Maya. *The Complete Collected Poems of Maya Angelou.* New York: Random House, 1994.

"Glory Falls"

"Glory Falls" is a poem about the importance of enduring great pain by staying together and helping each other grow. It was published in 1990 in *I Shall Not Be Moved.*

SYNOPSIS

The poem begins with a blast of power in the first few lines, "Glory falls around us / as we sob / a dirge of / desolation on the Cross." The setting may be a church or a religious meeting where people have gathered to strengthen one another, or it could be a home. The cross represents Christ and his atoning sacrifice, but at the same time, it can also represent the terror of the KU KLUX KLAN, the scourge of the South. The hard words continue: "hatred is the ballast of / the rock." But rather than let it take away their hope, the people have woven silken tapestries, clothed themselves in beauty, and learned to soar in spite of "hate / and blind despair." They grow, they mature, and they endure, "despite the / horror." They outlast the evil, because they are determined to "bring honor / to our brothers, / and to our sisters cheer."

CRITICAL COMMENTARY

Angelou has explained that when she uses "I" or "we" in many of her poems, she is speaking of the collective whole of her people. There are poems when her inner self merges so completely with the concepts she is writing about that the reader can feel both her spirit and the spirit of her people. This is a strong poem, though it has not been reprinted or discussed in many critical reviews or anthologies. *Glory* itself is a strong word in most religious traditions. A noun, it means, basically, adoration or praise for doing something exceptionally well, not only for oneself, but also for others. A person is given glory sometimes for doing something valuable for society or even for an individual, and the words *gloria in excelsis deo* mean "glory to God on high." Another related combination of words is *gloria patri,* which mean "glory be to the father." In this poem, the glory belongs to the people. They have chosen to survive, and they have chosen to help one another.

A Christian lament, the depth of suffering, is described in terms of both the worship of Christ and the soaring spirituality and inspiration that can occur in a religious service. There is a collective purpose here, and the rhythms and the exchanges move faith to action. That action is dignified respect and compassion for one another's suffering. Angelou was raised in the southern evangelical tradition. The church was and is where the minister exhorts his people to repent, passionately. It is where the choir sings with deep feeling, harmonies, and rhythms to bring tangible vibration to the service with an objective of helping people feel the spirit of the message on many levels. In these services, call and response are traditional. This is not simply a staid scriptural exchange between a reader and the congregation; rather, it is sometimes a spontaneous calling-out, a praise song to God. The rhythm and sounds of the words in these stanzas evoke the deep, quaking sounds of the organ and the treble of the sopranos. There is depth under the words, and there is soaring life and glory falling upon a long-abused people.

FURTHER READING

Angelou, Maya. *The Complete Collected Poems of Maya Angelou.* New York: Random House, 1994.

"Good Woman Feeling Bad, A"

"A Good Woman Feeling Bad" is included in *Shaker, Why Don't You Sing?,* published in 1983.

SYNOPSIS

The first stanza contrasts different kinds of BLUES. There are deep feelings of sadness and blues that come from loneliness, but as described in the first stanza, "persecuting / Blues I've known / Could stalk / Like tigers, break like bone," this is a description of the deep pain of unwarranted oppression and victimization. The second stanza begins with the word *Pend,* which means to await a decision or punishment. In this instance, the narrator implies that many American blacks have lived under the threat of lynching throughout their lives, and it has pulled down their spirits. When "a gallows tree" is mentioned in the second stanza, it "Make me curse / My pedigree"—an unnecessary and sad commentary based on skin color. Black people have been subject to abuse in the United States for centuries, and rather than well-deserved pride, the pedigree of African blood almost guarantees harassment.

The third stanza expresses bitterness and "A psalm to love that's left unsung," because of despair. The fourth stanza expresses lost hope and death. Slaves in the South tried to escape, over and over again, but they were often caught and put to death: "Funeral music / In a going-home mouth." They would have been beaten and lynched if caught, or they might be sold to new owners and sent to places far from their families.

The final stanza suggests that blues are used in many riddles, all sad, but those mentioned in the poem are only a part of what the narrator has experienced in life so far.

CRITICAL COMMENTARY

Some of Maya Angelou's poetry seems to swing with the blues, and "A Good Woman Feeling Bad" is one of them. The narrative is about the tragedy of lynching, a black mark in American history and a fearful practice by mobs who ruled the South for centuries. *Shaker, Why Don't You Sing?* is a collection of short narrative poems that delve deeply into the pain of African-American people. Sometimes they narrate a love lament, sometimes a story of bad luck, but the deepest of all is fear, and in this poem the fear is focused on lynching. Between the years of 1882 and 1968, there were thousands of lynchings, and nearly twice as many blacks as whites were put to death in this heinous way.

This poem, about the grief of a good woman, speaks for many black mothers, grandmothers, aunts, and sisters who have lost loved ones to slavery or lynching. It is about mob violence used to exercise control over vulnerable people. After the Civil War, freed black men were given the right to vote, and the dominant culture felt threatened by the political power that vote could wield. There were communities that participated in the rampant violence in the South during the late 19th century, and there were communities that did not. Sherrilyn A. Ifill, a professor at the University of Maryland School of Law, investigated white participation in lynchings in the South and revealed that nearly 5,000 African Americans were put to death in this manner in the United States between 1860 and 1890.

When BILLIE HOLIDAY spent several days in Angelou's LOS ANGELES home as a guest, Angelou's son, Guy, was a young boy, and each night, before Holiday returned to her hotel room, she sang a bedtime song to Guy. One night, she sang "Strange Fruit," her signature song. Guy did not understand the lyrics and asked about it. The words were written by Abel Meeropol about the lynching of two men, and later he also claimed to have written the music to accompany the lyrics. There has been some dispute about who composed the music, but the song became a popular protest against violence in and around New York City. Ultimately, Holiday performed the song, and it was so well received that it became a regular part of her performance repertoire.

Strange Fruit

Southern trees bear strange fruit,
Blood on the leaves and blood at the root,
Black body swinging in the Southern breeze,
Strange fruit hanging from the poplar trees.

Pastoral scene of the gallant South,
The bulging eyes and the twisted mouth,
Scent of magnolia sweet and fresh,
Then the sudden smell of burning flesh!

Here is fruit for the crows to pluck,
For the rain to gather, for the wind to suck,
For the sun to rot, for the trees to drop,
Here is a strange and bitter crop.

Because of the song's profound message and popularity, Holiday sang it with much emotion. Many African-American people knew the song, and "A Good Woman Feeling Bad," written by Angelou for the African-American people as a reflection of the sorrow they suffered, does more than represent their voice; she *is* their voice. Angelou is much like a GRIOT, a West African poet, praise singer, or musician who, by hereditary right, tells the stories of his or her people. Angelou's poems are rich with the social and political past and present of her people; she speaks for them and to them.

FURTHER READING

Angelou, Maya. *The Complete Collected Poems of Maya Angelou.* New York: Random House, 1994.

Ifill, Sherrilyn A. *On the Courthouse Lawn: Confronting the Legacy of Lynching in the Twenty-First Century.* Biddeford, Maine: Beacon Press, 2007.

"Lynching Statistics by Year." Statistics provided by the Archives at Tuskegee Institute. Available online. URL: http://www.law.umkc.edu/faculty/projects/ftrials/shipp/lynchingyear.html. Accessed March 10, 2010.

"Strange Fruit." *Wikipedia.* Available online. URL: http://en.wikipedia.org/wiki/Strange_Fruit. Accessed March 10, 2010.

"Greyday"

"Greyday" is included in the collection *Oh Pray My Wings Are Gonna Fit Me Well* (1975). It is a sad poem, personally introspective, and one anonymous review suggested that the last stanza, "No one knows / my lonely heart / when we're apart" is "banal" (Anonymous, 1,439).

SYNOPSIS

In three stanzas of three lines each, the narrator conveys a sense of loneliness. Words such as *heavy, loose,* and *grey* in the first stanza evoke an oppressed feeling. The second stanza begins with "A crown of thorns," an allusion to the crown of sharp briars placed on the head of Jesus Christ during the time he was being scourged and beaten prior to his crucifixion. He had claimed to be the Messiah, the son of God and savior of the world, but there were many who did not believe him. Perceived to be blasphemous, he was physically abused and subjected to mockery and derision. The false crown scornfully marked him as the king of the Jews.

The "shirt of hair" referred to in the next stanza is an allusion to rough vestments worn next to the skin by Christians during a time of penitence or as a reminder of piety. Made of burlap or coarse animal hair like that of a goat, the practice of wearing one (or a sash around loins made of a similar material) was meant to promote humility and repentance from worldly pleasure.

In this short poem, the narrator feels such pain from her loneliness that she perceives it as punishment akin to Christ's crown of thorns and the wearing of a hair shirt. In the last stanza, the narrator simply states that no one can understand this level of loneliness.

CRITICAL COMMENTARY

In regard to this poem, Lyman B. Hagen writes:

> The sound should echo the sense, as Alexander Pope suggested, and Angelou does achieve a correspondence of sound and sense in many of her poems. The monotonous rhythms and diction of her poem "Greyday" seem to echo the feeling of loss and emptiness without the presence of a loved one. The lines clearly depict the perception of a time of loneliness. (133)

"Greyday" is a personal, introspective poem as are many in this collection. It represents a vision of the human condition and interior self that all people experience at one time or another. When read aloud, it has a flat sound that successfully represents genuine loneliness.

FURTHER READING

Angelou, Maya. *The Complete Collected Poems of Maya Angelou.* New York: Random House, 1994.

Anonymous Review. *Choice* 12, no. 11 (January 1976): 1,439.

Hagen, Lyman B. *Heart of a Woman, Mind of a Writer, and Soul of a Poet: A Critical Analysis of the Writings of Maya Angelou.* Lanham, Md.: University Press of America, 1997.

"Harlem Hopscotch"

"Harlem Hopscotch" was first published in the 1971 collection *Just Give Me a Cool Drink of Water 'fore I Diiie.* It is one of Angelou's best-known poems.

SYNOPSIS

In "Harlem Hopscotch," the narrator defines the life of a typical African American in HARLEM, metaphorically describing a tenuous struggle for survival. With rhythm that echoes the game of hopscotch and the sound of the feet, the first stanza begins with hopping. The game is "hot," and it is moving along. In the next stanza, things are up in the air, the food is gone, the rent is due, and life moves on less predictably. In the third stanza, another metaphor for insecure economic conditions appears: "All the people out of work," they try to continue, and then "they count you out." The last stanza reveals the people's dignity and stamina: "They think I lost. I think I won." The last line reveals the inner knowledge and perspective that guarantees survival. It is an attitude.

CRITICAL COMMENTARY

Angelou used this poem to make a point in a 1973 interview with Bill Moyers. In response to a question he asked concerning whether white critics had or did not have the right to judge the artistic work of blacks, she replied that she thought it was all right as long as they understood the work they discussed. She reminded Moyers and her listeners that there are layers to black arts, and that makes a difference in what people hear. Whites may hear the rhythm and understand the social implications of the work but may not hear its hidden cultural implications of a poem as a listener in Harlem would. She said that in ordinary hopscotch, the rhythm is "Da-da-da, da-da-da, da-da-da. But in Harlem, there's—that's basic. But there are other counter-rhythms that are going on, so that the kids stamp, 'Dadadatadatadatam,'" (quoted in Elliot 1989, 27). She concluded the interview by quoting the last line in the poem a little differently than it was printed in the published collection. She said, "The game is down. They think you lost and I think you've won," and in the published poem the words are, "The game is done. They think I lost. I think I won." There is contrast in those meanings, but the essence is that by a self-determined identity that has defined who they are from within their own culture, blacks have won the freedom and dignity they sought, but the reality is that most blacks were never really without it.

Of this poem, Carol E. Neubauer writes: "Life itself has become a brutal game of hopscotch, a series of desperate yet hopeful leaps, landing but never pausing long. . . . Yet in the final analysis, the words that bring the poem and the complete collection to close triumphantly announce the poet's victory. . . . 'I think I won'" (210).

FURTHER READING

Angelou, Maya. *The Complete Collected Poems of Maya Angelou.* New York: Random House, 1994.

Elliot, Jeffrey M., ed. *Conversations with Maya Angelou.* Jackson and London: University of Mississippi Press, 1989.

Neubauer, Carol E. "Maya Angelou: Self and a Song of Freedom in the Southern Tradition." In *Maya Angelou.* Modern Critical Views, edited by Harold Bloom, 191–218. Philadelphia: Chelsea House, 1999.

"Health-Food Diner, The"

"The Health-Food Diner" is included in *Shaker, Why Don't You Sing?* (1983). Food fads come and go, and medical studies about which foods are best for our bodies also seem to come and go. This is Angelou's response to the national obsession with health food, and though this was published in 1983, the debate continues.

SYNOPSIS

This poem begins, "No sprouted wheat and soya shoots / and brussels in a cake," and the first stanza ends with "(Today I need a steak)." "No smoking signs" are noted, and Angelou ends the poem with a few words that again clearly state her perspective. She will be happy to visit "any place that saves a space / For smoking carnivores."

CRITICAL COMMENTARY

This is a clever six-stanza poem that is both amusing and realistic for readers who are not vegetarians. The sensory elements of this work are strong, and there are almost photogenic word paintings. Further, who cannot conjure up the fragrance of a Sunday roast after the line "(I'm dreaming of a Roast)"? In an article about ZORA NEALE HURSTON's and Angelou's visual imagery, Marion M. Tangum and Marjorie Smelstor write: "Authors, subjects, and readers are enmeshed in a web of intersubjectivity and then torn apart. But the aesthetic vision of the artists abruptly unravels that web, riveting our attention on the artistic object that has been created. The result, according to [Margaret] Olin, is a text that 'repeatedly protests, down to its last sentence, that it is only about to begin'" (50).

As the different vegetables and meats the poet uses for examples are mentioned, they build and lead to the poem's denouement. Angelou enjoys COOKING and has developed her culinary skills to a gourmet level. The narrator in this poem rejects faddish vegetables and clearly reveals a preference for good red meat. The poem's message is that life must be guided by solid reason rather than fads of the times.

FURTHER READING

Angelou, Maya. *The Complete Collected Poems of Maya Angelou.* New York: Random House, 1994.

Olin, Margaret. "'It Is Not Going to Be Easy to Look into Their Eyes': Privilege of Perception in *Let Us Now Praise Famous Men.*" *Art History* 14, no. 1 (March 1991): 92–115.

Tangum, Marion M., and Marjorie Smelstor. *Hurston's and Angelou's Visual Art: The Distancing Vision and the Beckoning Gaze.* In *Maya Angelou.* Bloom's Modern Critical Views, edited by Harold Bloom, 49–65. New York: Bloom's Literary Criticism, 2009.

"Here's to Adhering"

"Here's to Adhering" is found in Part One of the Collection *Oh Pray My Wings Are Gonna Fit Me Well* (1971).

SYNOPSIS

This is a narrative about the imaginary aspects of a nonexistent lover. To *adhere,* an intransitive verb, means to stick to something—that is, to remain steadfast and firm. In this story, it means to remain loyal to an apparently imagined lover who only appears in parts. The narrator cannot find the lover all pulled together. She recognizes pieces of this laughing person—the hands, chest, and face—in different places, but he never appears all together as a reality. She is unsettled and lonely, but she has friends. As she travels to different places, from Hollywood to the Congo, she thinks she has found him—"I heard you laugh," "I found your hands," "I found your chest," "I saw your face"—but he is still incomplete. He will not appear, even though she adheres to his image.

CRITICAL COMMENTARY

This poem is more abstract than many of Angelou's works, but it is worth pondering. Angelou has been unable to achieve permanent male companionship through most of her lifetime. Idealistic and needing a man, she often became involved physically, emotionally, and romantically before really knowing those with whom she became infatuated. There may or may not have been a psychological problem stemming from her tragic childhood assault. In a paper read at the African American Literature and Culture Society conference in Salt Lake City in October 2000, Suzanne Lundquist, English professor at Brigham Young University, combined related psychological and social theory in explaining Angelou's failed relationships with men as happening because she "chooses men who re-create her childhood abandonment and abuse issues—who perpetuate her victimage. Until such women become fully conscious of what needs to be healed in themselves, they will continue to move through failed intimacy relationships. . . . Female victims of rape and incest often trust easily, don't know how to create good boundaries, and tend to buy into the glamorous stories proffered by predatory males" (7–8).

In "Here's to Adhering," the narrator is creating a physically ideal male who will meet her needs. She sees him everywhere, or at least parts of him, but she is unable, even once, to make him whole. This parallels Angelou's personal experience, yet she survived it well and turned to her work for fulfillment. She knew and used the rhythm of JAZZ and the BLUES in much of her work, and this poem has a consistent rhythm. It is particularly pleasant to hear read aloud. Eleanor Traylor writes: "It is the *do-op*, the swing, the beat, not exact but close enough to hear the play and bring the smile" (97). Angelou's multiple talents and interests have played a great part in her survival, and using her gifts to foster strength and dignity in her people has empowered her, independent of any sustained male relationship.

FURTHER READING

Angelou, Maya. *The Complete Collected Poems of Maya Angelou*. New York: Random House, 1994.

Lundquist, Suzanne Evertsen. "Maya Angelou's *The Heart of a Woman* as Auto-ethnography." Unpublished paper presented at the African American Literature and Culture Society Conference, Salt Lake City, Utah, October 25–29, 2000.

Traylor, Eleanor. "Maya Angelou: Writing Life, Inventing Literary Genre." In *Maya Angelou*. Bloom's Modern Critical Views, edited by Harold Bloom, 91–105. New York: Bloom's Literary Criticism, 2009.

"How Can I Lie to You"

"How Can I Lie to You" is included in Part One of Angelou's collection *Just Give Me a Cool Drink of Water 'fore I Diiie* (1971), which was nominated for a Pulitzer Prize.

SYNOPSIS

There is no question mark at the end of the poem's title. This might be interpreted as indicating that a decision has already been made to tell a lie, though it was not made without much thought. In this very brief poem, perhaps written after the style of LANGSTON HUGHES's poems, the narrator is struggling with telling what she believes is a necessary lie based on a "sad and wise" decision. With careful reflection, this narrator speaks lightly, disguising deep feelings. The poem is shorter than most of Angelou's works, but the rhythm and rhyme *(eyes, disguise, wise)* conveys through the sounds of the language she has chosen a cool, sad finish to a valued relationship.

CRITICAL COMMENTARY

Many of Angelou's poems include a refusal of the human spirit to be subjugated. In this cryptic verse, the narrator reveals a firmness and willingness to do what is best. Somehow there has been a betrayal, and perhaps some fear, but the decision has been made to lie in order to carry through the intention of ending the relationship.

FURTHER READING

Angelou, Maya. *The Complete Collected Poems of Maya Angelou*. New York: Random House, 1994.

"Human Family"

"Human Family" is the second poem included in Maya Angelou's 1990 collection, *I Shall Not Be Moved*.

SYNOPSIS

In nine stanzas and a few more lines at the end, this poem describes the people of the world the narrator has observed. In the first two stanzas, the differences in life approaches are noted: "Some of us are serious, / some thrive on comedy," some are profound, and others simply claim that they live reality. The third and fourth verses reveal that the narrator has traveled widely, "sailed upon the seven seas," and has yet to see "one common man." In so many ways, no people are exactly alike. She has known women, twins, and lovers, and they all differ in one way or another. In the seventh and eighth stanzas, different places and different human responses to life are noted, and yet, says the poem, "In minor ways we differ, / in major we're the same." She has noted differences in race and gender and responses to the human condition around the world, and then summarizes her observations by wisely stating: "We are more alike, / my friends, / than we are unalike."

CRITICAL COMMENTARY

In many interviews, Maya Angelou has stated, "We are more alike, my friends, than we are unlike." That line is repeated three times at the conclusion of this poem, and the statement is the summative message of most of her work. She has taught that her autobiographies, essays, plays, and poems are meant for all people regardless of race, creed, or gender. She speaks with wisdom to everyone. We are a part of one human family, we share one fragile planet, and we are only alive for a short while. Her message is to lift ourselves and each other to make a better life for everyone.

FURTHER READING

Angelou, Maya. *The Complete Collected Poems of Maya Angelou.* New York: Random House, 1994.

"I Almost Remember"

"I Almost Remember" is in Part Five of *Oh Pray My Wings Are Gonna Fit Me Well* (1975). It is a nostalgic poem for a time, perhaps, that never was.

SYNOPSIS

In this four-part poem, the narrator reflects on a past time, perhaps a time when smiling was uninformed and innocent. But as time moved forward, and an awareness of real conditions in the world became known, "News-eyed I watch / channels of hunger," knowing that the unjust tragedies of the world temper the innocent smile. Children with malnutrition and "bursting bellies" and "black / brown hands and / white thin yellowed fingers" speak of starvation and suffering forgotten and disdained, perhaps, by those who could rescue others from suffering. The narrator concludes with a time of reverie in her own garden. It is quiet, late in the evening; the grass sleeps and the streets are empty except for mist, and the long-ago memories of innocence, a time of unknowing smiling, return.

CRITICAL COMMENTARY

In this poem, the narrator speaks of a long-ago time of not knowing. The message is that there is no innocence in not learning where one's cultural and social responsibilities are, and then becoming personally active in improving the lives of others. Angelou has reached the hearts of her readers, black, white, and brown, through her common language spoken to everyone. Her message is that the responsibility for suffering belongs to all of us, and we can assist others when we understand that we are, collectively, a worldwide village of people. As she has repeated, we are more alike than not alike.

FURTHER READING

Angelou, Maya. *The Complete Collected Poems of Maya Angelou.* New York: Random House, 1994.

"In a Time"

"In a Time" was included in Part One of *Just Give Me a Cool Drink of Water 'fore I Diiie* (1971), which was nominated for the Pulitzer Prize.

SYNOPSIS

The poems in the collection *Just Give Me a Cool Drink of Water 'fore I Diiie* are a mixed selection of narratives about lost love and the anguish that comes from romantic disappointment. In addition, they represent black life and oppression and include descriptions of different lifestyles with warnings away from dead-end choices. "In a Time" is a three-stanza poem with a rhyming pattern, and it reveals a betrayed heart. The first stanza describes the first passion of a secret love, "Left knows not what right is doing," and it reveals all the passion and confusion that comes with early infatuation.

The second stanza reveals a time of "Sweet hellos and sad goodbyes," but it is also foreboding in its mention of "Half-truths told and entire lies." In the third stanza, the romance is over. Joy and happiness turn into pain. Perhaps one was ready to end the relationship, and the other was not.

CRITICAL COMMENTARY

Maya Angelou knows well the pain of broken relationships, and she also knows how often that occurs. Her poems in this collection are sometimes very tender, and her voice is so real that the depth of pain is clearly communicated. She has had two legal marriages, and it appears there were two unofficial unions. Ceremonies took place, commitments were made, and still the relationships failed. Always trying to pass on knowledge to her readers without being didactic, Angelou speaks from her own experience. Each reader will have their own memories and experiences of close relationships, but Angelou's insights and openness about her life and struggles are enlightening and help the reader gain wisdom about their own interiority.

FURTHER READING

Angelou, Maya. *The Complete Collected Poems of Maya Angelou.* New York: Random House, 1994.

"John J."

"John J." was included in Part Five of the collection *Oh Pray My Wings Are Gonna Fit Me Well* (1975). It is a narrative about the plight of abandoned black children.

SYNOPSIS

This poem begins with the concept of curdled milk as a metaphor for a childhood gone wrong. It mentions "childhood's right"—that is, the right to protection, nurturing, medical care, food, a care's presence (always), education, and joy. This is a poetic narrative about the consequences of neglect when these "rights" are not met. The poem repeats, several times, that "his momma didn't want him." In the second stanza, the reader learns that John J. was a beautiful child with "turn-around, fall-down curls." But, in spite of his beauty and intelligence, he was not wanted. The third stanza reveals his bright grin and energy. He respected his teacher, and he played conjure man to coax lightning from a summer sky. High-spirited and happy, he played and grew to be a man. The last stanza tells the consequence of his being neglected. Unhappy, he found a woman, "a flinging singing lady," for comfort, but she did not want him either. His life was not really guided by anything but his instincts, and the poem sounds a warning to those who do not care properly for children.

CRITICAL COMMENTARY

Though most responsible adults realize the importance of a balanced childhood in producing healthy adults, childhood is never quite perfect. Angelou had a mixture of experiences in her own childhood and teens; as a child, she was brutally assaulted sexually, and she moved repeatedly over her formative years. At the same time, she received several years of loving stability under the hand of her strong grandmother, Annie Henderson, in STAMPS, ARKANSAS. Her mother did love her, and she was returned to VIVIAN BAXTER for her teen years.

Writers, sociologists, psychologists, and parents have studied concepts of how to make healthy, contributing adults out of children. Some of the first focused studies were in the first part of the 20th century. In 1905, W. Leslie Mackenzie, a sociologist, told the Royal Society of Edinburgh that the most important thing he and his colleagues had learned from the studies they had conducted was that "if we would fit the man [or woman] for his [her] environment, we must begin with the child. 'The child is the father [mother] of the man [woman]'" (50). Studies over centuries winding back to biblical times have repeatedly verified that truth, and a myriad of books, courses, and lectures have continued through the 20th century and on into the 21st century to help adults realize the positive consequences of providing a nurturing environment for children and teenagers. Parenting is one of the most serious of responsibilities and one of the least understood by people of all socioeconomic levels and races. It is relatively easy to produce a child biologically, but it is an altogether different matter to raise a child and provide his or her "childhood rights." Maya Angelou was a working mother, but her priority all along was her son. In writing a poem on this topic, she was again educating her readership.

FURTHER READING

Angelou, Maya. *The Complete Collected Poems of Maya Angelou.* New York: Random House, 1994.

Mackenzie, W. Leslie. *The Health of the School Child.* London: Methuen, 1906.

"Junkie Monkey Reel"

The "Junkie Monkey Reel" was published in Part Two of Angelou's collection *And Still I Rise* (1975). It is a somber, repellent poem that graphically illustrates the binding force of drug dependency.

SYNOPSIS

Like an organ grinder's monkey tethered to a street vender's leash, a drug user is tied to the quasi-comforting effects of drugs. The narrator uses this analogy to create a grim vision of what can happen when a user turns to drugs instead of food to nourish the body: "Shoulders sag"; "knees thaw"; teeth, loosened from the gums by crack or weed, "rock in fetid gums"; and "Brains reel." The narrator asks, "How long will / the monkey dance?" For some there is escape, but for many the journey back to a better life, is lost: "The / routes are gone beneath the tracks."

CRITICAL COMMENTARY

Not only can a monkey be tethered to an organ grinder's leash, or a junkie to his or her habit, innocent young people can be drawn into dead-end lives out of unwholesome neediness and loneliness. In her second autobiography, *Gather Together in My Name,* Angelou describes how pimps, for instance, look for lonely but unfocused young people; befriend them with their time and gifts, including drugs; and capture them through their dependency and innocence, like a spider catching a fly. That dependency is used as a trap for the captured ones to serve as prostitutes. They turn their tricks, and they are given drugs and a little money, but the money is not enough to support their habit or their living expenses. It is too little, too late in this tragic system, and it is a lucrative industry throughout the world. In this poem, using strongly descriptive words and phrases, Angelou gives a warning. There is no folk language here; she simply employs graphic and disturbing images that realistically describe the peril and waste of illegal drug use.

FURTHER READING

Angelou, Maya. *The Complete Collected Poems of Maya Angelou.* New York: Random House, 1994.

"Just for a Time"

"Just for a Time" is a poem included in Angelou's collection *And Still I Rise* (1975). Most of the poems in this collection express self-assurance and a strong belief in the power of the self to overcome any oppression.

SYNOPSIS

In this poem, the narrator is a male. It begins with the memory of how the loved one walked and talked and her "insouciant" (nonchalant) smile. She was an early love, but perhaps not the first. She caused him to sing. The narrator says that he does not like to look back, but he treasures the memory of his relationship with the girl, which was "Just for a time."

CRITICAL COMMENTARY

The collection *And Still I Rise* includes poems on the themes of love and the pain of loneliness, poems about the difficulties for African Americans living in the South, and also poems about the importance of family and of the nature of women. This poem, "Just for a Time," is a reverie.

Early romances often leave lifetime memories. This rhythmic poem sounds like a love song, and it could easily be set to music as a ballad. Angelou had many relationships with men over time, and it may be that some remember her with this warmth and honesty. On the other hand, this narrative of reverie could be a commentary on how men walk away from women. A common pattern (and it can go either way) is that a young woman or young man gives themselves to another thinking that this is to be a forever relationship, only to find that the partner does not have the same feelings. Knowing how often this happens is part of the reason Angelou wrote so many poems about love and loneliness. She experienced it, and she knows that others have had the same experience. There is comfort in knowing that one is not alone in loneliness and rejection.

FURTHER READING

Angelou, Maya. *The Complete Collected Poems of Maya Angelou.* New York: Random House, 1994.

"Just Like Job"

"Just Like Job" appears in the collection *And Still I Rise* (1975). This collection includes poems about love and loss, the black struggle in the South, and the vital importance of endurance to all people.

SYNOPSIS

This is a poem urging trust in God's perfect will in spite of losing everything, as Job did in the Bible. It paraphrases many Scriptures beginning with "My Lord, my Lord, / Long have I cried out to Thee." This is a plea seen in different forms in the Old and New Testament. From human nothingness, "When my blanket was nothing but dew, . . . I chanted Your name, / Just like Job."

The second stanza promises total commitment to the Father in Heaven: "My life give I gladly to Thee," no matter the future, no matter the fears, "O Lord, forget me not." Obedient, I (the narrator) am leaning on your arm, trusting your love, calling on your name, and the key phrase to the poem comes at the end of the third stanza: "I am stepping out on Your word." That means giving the Lord total trust. *Stepping out* means going on or going out someplace with joy. It also means that though the narrator may not understand, the Lord will always give what is best for that individual's well-being eternally. It may be confusing in the moment, but in the long run, total faith in the Lord means trusting him to be true to you, so it is totally wise for the narrator to be "stepping out on Your word."

The "word" means the Son of God, and a line in the fourth stanza, "My beautiful Rose of Sharon," is thought by many to refer symbolically to Christ. Though Christ is never referred to specifically as the rose of Sharon in the New Testament, there is a reference in the Old Testament, saying, "I am the rose of Sharon, and the lily of the valleys" (Solomon 2:1). Further, there is a plain in Palestine, the birthplace of Christ, called Sharon.

In the fifth stanza, the narrator reminds the Lord of his promises: "You said that You would take me to glory . . . and I'm stepping out on Your word." And in the last stanza, any place I may go—alleys, byways, streets, passing liars, night rovers, and others—I will trust you and your teaching (and implied, I will live them to the best of my ability), since "I'm stepping out on Your word."

CRITICAL COMMENTARY

Angelou obviously based this spiritual poem on the trials of Job, and she uses his faith-filled example to carry her narrator through the story. Job never denied or blamed God no matter how much he lost (including family, friends, livelihood, home, and his health). No matter what happens, this narrator (Angelou) will keep faith in the Lord. Having been raised in the strong religious grounding of her Grandmother Henderson, Angelou held onto the tenets of belief in an almighty God. Her grandmother used the phrase, "I will step out on the word of God" (1993, 74), and Angelou embraced it. In her serial autobiographies, she has shared her many prayers for her family, friends, and herself and her dependence on the beneficial will of God. She has lived what she has shared, and she has reminded her readers of the deep power within each individual that can be tapped and used constantly in life.

FURTHER READING

Angelou, Maya. *The Complete Collected Poems of Maya Angelou.* New York: Random House, 1994.

———. *Wouldn't Take Nothing for My Journey Now.* Toronto: Random House of Canada Limited, 1993.

"Kin"

"Kin" is included in Part Two of Angelou's 1975 volume of poetry *And Still I Rise.* It is dedicated to her only brother, BAILEY JOHNSON, JR., who was one year older than she. In *I Know Why the Caged Bird Sings,* Angelou writes that her brother was her hero. She had thought of him as her "Kingdom Come," because he was always there for her, and he always gave her wise counsel. Like Maya, he was a voracious reader and exceptionally intelligent.

SYNOPSIS

Bailey and Maya grew up together in an atmosphere of brutal inhumanity in the South. The poem begins with "We were entwined in red rings / Of blood and loneliness," which alludes to the context of fear and abandonment they felt living in a segregated backwater, after having being left in the care of their paternal grandmother following their parents' divorce. "Before," the narrator writes in an idealistic voice, there was the freedom of another time and place (Africa), but wherever, "I was your sister."

The next stanza speaks of her brother's going away and her search for him in other men. That was a wish never fulfilled, and her brother felt that their very birth may have been the seed of their destruction or failure. She agrees, momentarily, but her attitude is more positive. He turned to drugs, and she mourned for the "Regions of terror" from which he did return, but not without great suffering. In the reverie of the closing stanza, the narrator returns to happy memories of their childhood in Arkansas, "the laughter of children," fireflies bursting, and the "Arkansas twilight."

CRITICAL COMMENTARY

Bailey, Maya's brother, confidant, and friend, was bright, wise, and full of common sense. For several years after her childhood rape, Bailey was the only one she trusted enough to talk to and communicate her feelings. Many of the poems in this collection, *And Still I Rise,* speak either of love or of racial bigotry in the South. "Kin" reveals another aspect, and for some readers there may be a message. This tribute to her brother reveals the depth of pain she felt when he fell into the trap of drug addiction. He was married for a time, and his beloved wife and companion died, a year after their wedding, of tuberculosis complicated by pneumonia. His world was shattered, and though he continued to be a friend and adviser to Maya, they were separated by many miles. Maya lived in New York and then Africa; Bailey lived and worked in California and Hawaii. Maya understood his sorrow and discomfort, and she understood the difficulties under which black males lived in the United States. Some critics have suggested that her friendship with the writer JAMES BALDWIN may have been an unconscious search for the close relationship she had with Bailey for so many years. Baldwin was dark and physically small, as was Bailey. Both men were genuinely interested in her well-being.

FURTHER READING

Angelou, Maya. *The Complete Collected Poems of Maya Angelou.* New York: Random House, 1994.

"Kind of Love, Some Say, A"

"A Kind of Love, Some Say," is found in Part One of the collection *And Still I Rise.* It is a furious poetic narrative of domestic abuse.

SYNOPSIS

The poem begins with a question that asks for truth. Can "the ribs . . . tell / The kick of a beast from a / Lover's fist?" The narrator expresses brutally inflicted pain: "swollen lids," "sorry eyes," "spoke not / of lost romance, but hurt." The second stanza states that hate can be confused and that "Love, by nature, exacts a pain"—a pain so devastating that it is worse than a rack.

CRITICAL COMMENTARY

In 2000, the American Bar Association's Commission on Domestic Violence reported: "Approximately 1.3 million women and 835,000 men are physically assaulted by an intimate partner annually in the United States. . . . Women are more likely to be victims of sexual violence than men" (Tjaden and Thoennes 2000, iv, v). Domestic violence has many forms, including physical aggression, intimidation, and even financial deprivation. Though the abuse is not limited to female victimization, nor entirely to male/female relationships, it is a serious crime and too often leads to purposeful or accidental death. Victims, often in helpless situations economically, frequently blame themselves and return again and again to the perpetrator.

In *Letter to My Daughter* (2008), Maya Angelou describes her own brush with death at the hands of a dangerous boyfriend named Mark, who had cajoled her into thinking he was an ideal suitor. When he suspected her of seeing someone else, he beat her nearly to death with his fists and a wooden slat. He hid her in his rented room, but her mother, VIVIAN BAXTER, was informed by friends what had happened and who had done it. "No one knew where he lived or worked or even his last name" (Angelou 2008, 31). Through the grapevine and fortunate coincidence, Angelou's mother learned where her daughter was, recruited three willing men from the pool hall she owned, took them to the rooming house where Mark was living, broke down the door, and saved Maya's life.

Angelou attributes her rescue to answered prayer, but all too often, the prayers of beaten women seem unheeded. This is a tragic, unnecessary violence, centuries old, that is a grave crime. Perpetrators of this violence must be reported and dealt with by the law. The problem is that it is seldom even reported.

FURTHER READING

Angelou, Maya. "Accident, Coincident, or Answered Prayer." In *Letter to My Daughter.* New York: Random House, 2008, 29–34.

———. *The Complete Collected Poems of Maya Angelou.* New York: Random House, 1994.

Patricia, Tjaden, and Nancy Thoennes. U.S. Department of Justice, NCJ 183781, *Full Report of the Prevalence, Incidence, and Consequences of Violence Against Women.* Washington, D.C.: U.S. Department of Justice Office of Justice Programs, 2000. Available online. URL: http://www.ojp.usdoj.gov/nij/pubs/pdf/ipv01.pdf. Accessed March 24, 2010.

"Known to Eve and Me"

"Known to Eve and Me" is included in Angelou's 1990 collection, *I Shall Not Be Moved.*

SYNOPSIS

Using the metaphor of a beautiful, sinuous, but dangerous snake, this is a poem about the anguish parents sometimes feel when their beloved children grow up and leave home. The title, "Known to Eve and Me," implies that mothers understand the mixed sorrow that has to be negotiated and accepted when children mature into young adults and go their own way. The narrator uses allusions and figurative language to describe the close supportive relationship between the child and herself. The mother lifted him into the sunlight, and "He was guileless and slid into my embrace." They shared pleasant meals, and they basked in "Love's warmth and Aton's sun / disc." His skin was as "sugared ginger" [golden], and "amber / drops of beryl [a hard mineral] on the tongue."

In the second stanza, the rhythmic imagery of a slithering snake seems to hold the narrator fast "in taut security." And then, suddenly, "he left me; And nothing / remains." Now there are two puncture marks at the site of her heart and only the sound of her own snake body "moving in the dark."

CRITICAL COMMENTARY

Using harsh sounds of alliteration, like the hissing of a snake, along with the soft vowels of mother love, Angelou has created an undulating feeling to this poem. The son "slid into my embrace," but then there is contrast in the mother's reflection, "Love's warmth and Aton's sun" (Aton was a deity in ancient Egyptian mythology), as the son and mother have divergent hopes. In the second stanza, the reader meets the foreboding: "His lidless eye slid sideways," and his betrayal, as the mother views it, is set. He deceives her with what she thinks is love by winding his presence around her heart, and then, suddenly, he is gone, and she is left with two puncture wounds over her heart.

This is a remarkably dramatic expression of a child leaving home, demonstrating how Angelou herself, with a poet's heart, was anguished when her only son and companion departed from her. Her autobiographies indicate that she knew it was time for him to grow up, and that was simply the reality. From all accounts, they continue to have a very warm familial relationship and deep, mutual respect.

FURTHER READING

Angelou, Maya. *The Complete Collected Poems of Maya Angelou.* New York: Random House, 1994.

"Lady Luncheon Club"

"Lady Luncheon Club" is included in Part Two of the collection *And Still I Rise.* Many of the poems in this volume are written in a language very close to everyday speech. Angelou's poems are often like narratives, though some might also be successfully set to music.

SYNOPSIS

This nine-stanza narrative poem tells the story of a lady's club luncheon with a serious speaker who fails in his talk, though the ladies do not pay much attention—including the one in charge of inviting the speaker. The club could be made up of the idle rich from any racial group, but the speaker's hostess has decided that the women need to think more deeply about the issues of the day and perhaps even be motivated to action. An informed speaker has been invited, a man "who would make them think." The narrator's selection of a male speaker in the poem is subtly telling. Are men the only ones who can awaken people (particularly women) to thinking? "Our woman checked her golden watch," remembering the speaker is on a plane schedule (a frequent speaker?), and she is relieved that dessert is served promptly. The reader wonders if she even paid attention and asked herself what the speaker said. The speaker leans forward, probably realizing the women were not attentive, and he feigns sincerity. He talks about "female rage," Eve's lust (for knowledge), and "Delilah's / Grim deceit." Our woman in the audience, we observe, "thinks." That was the point of having the speaker, but she is thinking that her "cake is much too sweet."

The speaker continues, discussing the tragedies of life, and "Our woman notes: / (This coffee's much too strong)." She joins in the applause but notes in her pad that "(Next time the / Speaker must be brief)."

CRITICAL COMMENTARY

It is not clear whether the poem's ladies' club is black, white, or mixed, but Angelou's description of it is more common than many members of some women's clubs would be quick to admit. Ellen Lippmann, in a review of *And Still I Rise,* has suggested that this poem "is a tongue-in-cheek description of an overly intellectual speaker at a women's club" (108). Robert B. Stepto, a literary critic, suggests that it "bear[s] strong resemblances to several poems of [Gwendolyn] Brooks' pre-Black Aesthetic period in *Annie Allen* and *The Bean-Eaters*" (313–315). These reviews are accurate. It is a tongue-in-cheek description, and there is a similarity to Brooks's lines in *Annie Allen* that are meant to move a reader from self-centeredness to taking part in a broader community, but there is a further message that Angelou is urging in this poem.

In various interviews and presentations over her lifetime, Angelou has mentioned that one of the differences between black and white women is in how the males of their respective races treat them. She teaches that the black women have never had an alternative to going to work, in part because even after slavery, the males had difficulty making enough money to support a family. White women, on the other hand, were cloistered in their homes for decades while the men served in the public sphere and supported the family. For Native American, Asian, and Hispanic women, the situation was primarily the same as that of black women, who had to work in addition to tending to the families.

Angelou identifies herself with the WOMANIST movement, which is linked to the perspective of African-American women rather than the largely white (and often academically driven) feminist movement, though she has respect for the works and fruit of both. Historically, African-American women were not struggling to be liberated from the confines of home. Rather, they were struggling for education and equal rights for black men and women so they could have a choice.

"Lady Luncheon Club" is about idle women. Many women's groups were formed in the 19th and 20th centuries to work actively for suffrage, temperance, and other rights that should have been equal between men and women of all colors and social standing. These groups continue today, of course, but there are many groups or clubs that are strictly social, with only a nod to good works, and that is the focus of this poem. The speaker is engaged to awaken the women's consciences because of bad times, to help them think about what they could contribute to improve the common good, but they are not paying attention. Perhaps his message is not sincere and the women sense that, but there is much to do to make the world a better place, and Angelou is making that point within the poem's narrative.

FURTHER READING

Angelou, Maya. *The Complete Collected Poems of Maya Angelou.* New York: Random House, 1994.

Lippmann, Ellen. Review of *And Still I Rise* by Maya Angelou. *School Library Journal* 25 (November 1978): 108.

Stepto, Robert B. "The Phenomenal Woman and the Severed Daughter (Maya Angelou, Audre Lourde)." *Parnassus: Poetry in Review* 8, no. 1 (Fall–Winter 1979): 313–315.

"Late October"

"Late October" is one of the poems in Angelou's first published collection, *Just Give Me a Cool Drink of Water 'fore I Diiie* (1971).

SYNOPSIS

The first stanza of two in this short poem describes the waning of the leaves of autumn, "the tinny / sound of little dyings," and it evokes images of "ruddy sunsets" and "roseate dawns." The stanza continues and "roils ceaselessly," metamorphosing into "cobweb greys and turn / to black," as the grim winter approaches.

The second stanza turns to a lament of ending love. It suggests that "Only lovers / see the fall as a signal end to endings." Another love will begin at another time, the poem says, the lovers "stop / in order simply / to begin / again."

CRITICAL COMMENTARY

The poems in *Just Give Me a Cool Drink of Water 'fore I Diiie* address romantic failures and various facets of racial issues in the United States. When love is working, the poems seem to soar with joy and hope, but when it is over, Angelou speaks to the loneliness and pain that the broken relationship brings. This poem uses a metaphor of the autumn season, the time when much of nature shuts down to go into hibernation, to express the dying of a romance. And yet there is the hope that another will begin. Angelou's own romantic relationships have never been sustained permanently, and her personal quest to find her perfect companion has never been fulfilled. Her understanding of this heartache leads to knowing that many others suffer in the same way, and she has tried many times to put this meaning into her poems to comfort both herself and others.

FURTHER READING

Angelou, Maya. *The Complete Collected Poems of Maya Angelou.* New York: Random House, 1994.

"Lesson, The"

"The Lesson" is included in Part Two of the collection *And Still I Rise* (1975).

SYNOPSIS

This little poem is made up of 13 lines. That may or may not have been deliberate, but the essence of the poem is that no matter what, the narrator resists dying. It begins with the idea that because of collapsing veins, the narrator has almost died again and again. The thought of old tombs and the decay of the body are haunting, but still, the teller is not ready to give up the challenge of living. "The years / And cold defeat live deep in / Lines along my face." And yet, serious illnesses continue to come, and the person keeps on (almost) dying, "Because I love to live."

CRITICAL COMMENTARY

This is a poem about not dying. Human beings are genetically wired to cling to life no matter how awry things may go. There are exceptions, of course, but death is final, and no human really knows exactly what is going to happen when we draw our last breath and our heart ceases to beat. Angelou knows that, and she also know that there are illnesses and injuries that may be interpreted as worse than death.

In 2000, Angelou wrote the foreword to a book compiled from a traveling photographic exhibition about growing older. *Elder Grace: The Nobility of Aging* was written by Chester Higgins, Jr., a staff photographer for the *New York Times* since 1975, and Betsy Kissam, a freelance writer living in New York. It includes photographs of African-American elders and their reflections about growing older. Most of Angelou's foreword is written in the form of a poem, and the book contains stunning and dignified personal portraits of aging African Americans. A note on the back cover, borrowed from Angelou's foreword, states: "Those Elders of Grace show that poverty need not grind the spirit into dust, nor should prosperity separate the fortunate from the needy." One of the stanzas in the foreword states: "The somberness of their eyes is evidence of the demons they have faced down and the despair they have overcome." As we live, we learn, and the short poem "The Lesson" gives us an important message to remember about living and learning.

FURTHER READING

Angelou, Maya. *The Complete Collected Poems of Maya Angelou.* New York: Random House, 1994.

Higgins, Chester, Jr., and Betsy Kissam. *Elder Grace: The Nobility of Aging.* New York: Bullfinch Press/ AOL Time Warner Book Group, 2000.

"Let's Majeste"

"Let's Majeste" was published in Angelou's first collection of poems, *Just Give Me a Cool Drink of Water 'fore I Diiie* (1971).

SYNOPSIS

Using a "Sleeping Beauty" fairy-tale framework for this poetic story, the narrator has taken on the role of a queen rather than a princess. She begins by suggesting that her story is set in a time when "Kings are rare" and scullery maids are little valued. In other words, there are no worthwhile men around, and further, they used the girls at hand for sexual gratification instead of making serious commitments.

In the second stanza, the narrator refers to deluding the "commoners who genuflect and cross their fingers." They live in hope, like any oppressed people, that the hierarchy will be kind and fair. But, as history shows, power usually corrupts, and the people know that. The third stanza shows the queen on her bed, sleeping as the years go by. In the final stanza, she asks: "Why must it always be a fairy, and / only just a Prince?" She wants a king; she wants a companion of assured wealth and power who is committed to her, rather than a prince with only a tentatively promised empire.

CRITICAL COMMENTARY

There are no easy answers to the question Angelou poses in the last stanza of this poem, but part of finding a king is about being cautious with both imagination and reality. Humans dream, and growing up or maturing is about separating the dreams of imagination from the reality of day-to-day commitment and living. Kings and queens do not fall out of the sky (neither do fairies), and it sometimes takes a lifetime of learning to distinguish infatuation and lust from genuine love and caring. Respect is what lasting relationships require, and that concept is a hard one for many people to understand.

FURTHER READING

Angelou, Maya. *The Complete Collected Poems of Maya Angelou.* New York: Random House, 1994.

"Letter to an Aspiring Junkie"

"Letter to an Aspiring Junkie" is included in Angelou's first volume of poetry, *Just Give Me a Cool Drink of Water 'fore I Diiie* (1971). In this poem, and in a similar one, "Junkie Monkey Reel," she uses powerful imagery to expose the grim consequences of drug use.

SYNOPSIS

Using linguistics, regionalisms, and language from the black oral tradition, the narrator dances, like a grim reaper, with a tap, tap rhythm through this poem of warning. It begins, "Let me hip you to the streets, / Jim, / Ain't nothing happening." Pointing out losers who have chosen a life of gambling or peddling cocaine or other drugs so people can ride "that / cold, white horse," the poet paints a dark picture of the consequences of life in the streets. From "A worn-out pimp" to "African dreams on a buck-and-a-wing and a prayer," her words are chosen with care. "A grey old monkey on their back" and "some fool" jar the reader's sensibility with the reality of street choices. "Nothin happening"—no, nothing good is happening out there.

CRITICAL COMMENTARY

When Angelou was a young, single mother trying to determine how to support her son and herself independent of her family, she learned that marijuana provided a comfortable escape from her anxieties. One of her friends, a man who cared about her enough to teach her, took her to a place where people hooked on drugs hung out together. The place was a dump, and the man shot drugs into his vein in front of her so she could see how devastating and destructive the long-term use of mind-altering drugs could really be. The people she saw lived on the stuff and, consequently, had no other life or future. Angelou never used marijuana again.

With rhythm and black slang ("bug-a-loo and a shing-a-ling"), Angelou warns the reader clearly about what can happen to people who make these choices. It is a dangerous place and a dead-end life.

FURTHER READING

Angelou, Maya. *The Complete Collected Poems of Maya Angelou.* New York: Random House, 1994.

"Life Doesn't Frighten Me"

"Life Doesn't Frighten Me" is included in the collection *And Still I Rise* (1975). This poem was also in 1993 published as a children's book, illustrated by Jean-Michel Basquiat. The book won the *Publishers Weekly* "Best Book of 1993" award. Jean-Michel Basquiat, a promising young artist, died in 1988 at the age of 27.

SYNOPSIS

Shadows, noises, bad dogs, and big ghosts do not frighten this narrator. Nor does "Mean old Mother Goose" or "Lions on the Loose"—no, "Life doesn't frighten me at all." The narrator boos the enemy, makes fun of them, does not cry, and "They go wild." "I've got a magic charm" in my sleeve, and I can do anything, it says, even "walk the ocean floor / And never have to breathe." No, life does not frighten this narrator.

CRITICAL COMMENTARY

This brave, defiant poem reminds every reader of the courage to be found within. The cover of *Life Doesn't Frighten Me* states: "From the scary thought of panthers in the park to the unsettling scene of a new classroom, fearsome images are summoned and dispelled by the power of faith in ourselves." In the children's book version of this poem, only a few words have been edited out (for example, "Tough Guys in a fight" has become "Tough guys fight") and Jean-Michel Basquiat's illustrations are stunning, powerful, and daring, with brilliant colors, sharp edges, and imaginary shapes that evoke an emotional response. Deep black and bright white create startling contrasts, and the use of red as a highlight for emphasis is strong. Both the poem and illustrations are manifestations of liberation ideology, a major theme in Angelou's work.

FURTHER READING

Angelou, Maya. *Life Doesn't Frighten Me.* Illustrated by Jean-Michel Basquiat. New York: Stewart, Tabori & Chang, 1993.

"Little Girl Speakings"

"Little Girl Speakings" was published in Angelou's collection *Oh Pray My Wings Are Going to Fit Me Well* (1975).

SYNOPSIS

In this poem of three stanzas, the narrator is a little girl. When challenged about her world, she asserts that there "Ain't nobody better'n my Daddy," "my dollie," or "my Mommy." The child is strong, self-assured, and safe. A reader might wonder why she is being questioned. In the first stanza, she is offered a quarter and tells the one who extends it to her, "You keep yo' quarter." Another appears to pat the head of her doll, and she says, "Don't pat her head." At last, "No lady cookinger than my Mommy." Perhaps an adult is teasing and asking for her affection, or perhaps another little girl is coveting her doll and wants to own it. The poem can be understood at a literal level, but there may be other layers of meaning less clear.

CRITICAL COMMENTARY

In order to help others cope with the brutality of childhood abuse, Angelou has been open about being the victim of a brutal rape when she was seven or eight years old. This poem may be a reflection of being coaxed unsafely into what might seem like trust but is actually danger. Children are usually loyal to their parents, even if the parents have been abusive, and children are usually possessive about their toys and other possessions. Angelou has always had a strong personality. She is a survivor, and in this little poem, she may be suggesting that it takes determination and resistance to survive the inevitable dangers that girls and women of all races encounter.

FURTHER READING

Angelou, Maya. *The Complete Collected Poems of Maya Angelou.* New York: Random House, 1994.

"Lord, in My Heart"

"Lord, in My Heart" was published in the 1975 collection *Oh Pray My Wings Are Gonna Fit Me Well* and was dedicated to one of her literary heroes, COUNTEE CULLEN.

SYNOPSIS

This poem is an honest confession of feelings. The narrator expresses distress in this poem because her experiences have made her doubt her ability to maintain her early Christian teachings. She remembers "Meshack and / Abednego," characters in the Old Testament who, through righteousness and obedience to principles taught to them, avoided burning to death in a fiery furnace. She recalls the "Golden chariot / swinging low" and feels she can recite those old stories in her sleep. But, she wonders about the "Golden Rule" and asks, "Could I turn my / cheek aside" when hurt or offended? Though taught to forgive by her early teachers, she finally says, "Here then is my / Christian lack: If I'm struck then / I'll strike back."

CRITICAL COMMENTARY

Angelou has admired the work of Countee Cullen because of his use of high European poetic forms to express his feelings and perceptions. One of the ways African-American authors she read in her youth proved their intellectual abilities was to use classical styles of writing. This is noted in a discussion of Cullen's work in *The Norton Anthology of African American Literature* (1997):

> In their adherence to a traditional poetic format, on the one hand, and their troubled perception of the issue of race, on the other, the lines "Yet do I marvel at this curious thing: / To make a poet black, and bid him sing!" may rightly serve as the signature couplet for the brilliant poet Countee Cullen, who produced some of the most haunting lyrics of the Harlem Renaissance. (Gates and McKay 1997, 1,303)

Cullen's poem "Heritage" poses some of the same questions and misgivings as "Lord, in My Heart." He writes: "Jesus of the twice-turned cheek. . . . Quick and hot to anger rise / To smitten cheek and weary eyes. / Lord, forgive me if my need / sometimes shapes a human creed" (in Gates and McKay 1997, 1,313). It is difficult to forgive and turn away when oppression and insult are constantly being heaped upon a person. In "Lord, in My Heart," a poem of simple, rhyming couplets,

Angelou is expressing honest human anger and response to insult, and yet is she is struggling with her own Christian creed of turning the other cheek and walking away from offense.

FURTHER READING

Angelou, Maya. *The Complete Collected Poems of Maya Angelou.* New York: Random House, 1994.

Gates, Henry Louis, Jr., and Nellie Y. McKay, eds. *The Norton Anthology of African American Literature.* New York: W. W. Norton, 1997.

"Love Letter"

"Love Letter" is included in the collection *I Shall Not Be Moved,* published in 1990.

SYNOPSIS

The poem begins with the narrator alone and speaking aloud the private words she plans to write. In the next stanza, she imagines her handsome lover sitting beside a shoji (a translucent sliding panel or screen often used in Japanese homes as a room divider or door). She imagines his "light lips and hungry / hands writing Tai Chi urgencies / into my body." The poem ends on a note of power she feels when they seem to "match grace." It is a tender, sensuous poem of passion.

CRITICAL COMMENTARY

Michelle Howe, a literary critic and reviewer, writes that this poem is about the equal power of a woman, and quotes Angelou as saying: "Power is a metaphor for strength but not the kind that gives you power over another human being. It addresses the strength to be yourself in a relationship and to be an equal in a love affair" (quoted in Howe 1990, 20).

FURTHER READING

Angelou, Maya. *The Complete Collected Poems of Maya Angelou.* New York: Random House, 1994.

Howe, Michele. "Angelou's Poetry Builds Bridges between Peoples." *Star-Ledger* (Newark, N.J.), 3 June 1990, 20.

"Me and My Work"

"Me and My Work," which appears in *I Shall Not Be Moved* (1990), expresses the pride and dignity of a responsible black family man.

SYNOPSIS

"I got a piece of a job on the waterfront," the hardworking black male narrator states, and "the wife works too." He and his wife have "three big children to keep in school," feed, and dress, and they provide them with a few extras of things they desire to "keep them out of the street." They are good children, and he is not complaining. In the conclusion of the poem, the narrator makes clear that what he really does not need is sympathy from strangers. Sympathy is not the same as caring.

CRITICAL COMMENTARY

There are several issues addressed in this poem that call for commentary. Though the man only works three days a week, his job pays well enough to cover the rent and food. It does not provide luxuries, but with his wife working, there is enough money to reasonably give the children things they want so they do not turn to the streets (drugs or worse). They are good children, he says, and they are cared for. He mentions that there are others worse off than him and his family, and he mentions the difference between "strangers' sympathy" and "caring." Sympathy can easily slip into a condescending pity. It can be a slippery concept, and this dignified man wants or needs no part of that. "Caring"—that is, empathy and understanding—is welcome. He has humility as well as hard-earned pride, and he deserves genuine respect.

The man represented in the poem has purpose. He has a family, a place to live, and the strength and good health to carry him along. His children have "always been good," which means he is probably investing time and interest in them. Different people have different talents, and to be able to support and love a family, and give a positive example, demands a form of creativity. For many, to bring home a dependable paycheck and be there to respond to the needs of the family is their talent, the gift of creativity they have been given.

In an interview with Mary Ardito about creativity, Maya Angelou stated:

> You can't use up creativity. The more you use, the more you have. Sadly, too often creativity is smothered rather than nurtured. There has to be a climate in which new ways of thinking, perceiving, questioning are encouraged. People also have to feel needed. Frequently we just offer a job and "perks." We don't always offer people a purpose, a need for being there to use their skills and creativity. When people feel there is a purpose and that they're needed, there's not much else to do except let them do the work. (quoted in Ardito 1982, 32)

Creativity, like love, varies. It may sometimes be more creative to dry the dishes than to write a poem or paint a picture. All humans have gifts to develop, and when Angelou writes poems for her people and shares her wisdom, just about everyone who stops to think about the message can improve their own contributions and creativity.

FURTHER READING

Angelou, Maya. *The Complete Collected Poems of Maya Angelou.* New York: Random House, 1994.

Ardito, Mary. "It's the Thought that Counts." *Bell Telephone Magazine* 1 (1982): 33.

"Memory, The"

"The Memory" is included in the collection *And Still I Rise* (1975).

SYNOPSIS

The setting for this poem is the cotton fields. "Cotton rows crisscross the world," and the workers are left dead-tired at night. Babies cry, and the workers continue to work because there is no other alternative. Their days are dying, and so are they.

CRITICAL COMMENTARY

Maya Angelou spent most of her childhood in STAMPS, ARKANSAS, which is cotton-growing country. The fields stretched far and wide across from her Grandmother Henderson's general store, and the cotton pickers, who were black, usually stopped at the store in the morning on the way to the fields to pick up a sweet or other snack to sustain them during the day. They also stopped by on the way home, weary, aching, and hungry. Angelou observed them and listened to their tales, and she saw the difference between the energy and hope of the morning told by their bodies and the defeat and hopelessness they seemed to feel in the evening. Many of her poems speak to the empowerment and liberation her people needed, and she has continued throughout her life to speak not only for her people but for all who suffer.

FURTHER READING

Angelou, Maya. *The Complete Collected Poems of Maya Angelou.* New York: Random House, 1994.

"Men"

This poem is found in Angelou's collection *And Still I Rise* (1975). "Men" was written as a contrasting poem to Angelou's well-known "Phenomenal Woman."

SYNOPSIS

Peeking from behind curtains, the narrator watches men as they pass "up and down / The street." She is curious, and she thinks they know she is watching. When she reaches a point of readiness for more than watching, she learns that caution is wiser than curiosity. A metaphor of a raw egg midway in the poem contrasts fragile female femininity with strong, male dominance. After being raped, she knows her body has been changed forever, and maybe now she will be wiser and maybe more cautious.

CRITICAL COMMENTARY

Some men use women only for their own gratification, and some do not. Angelou, a tall and imposing woman with a strong, gifted personality, had many kinds of relationships with men, from her brother, whom she admired and adored, to her

Uncle Willie, whom she both respected and felt sorrow for; to her father, who was a benign and down-at-the-heels playboy; to the horrid boyfriend of her mother's who secretly and brutally raped her when she was a young child. As she grew up, there were other serious relationships with men and a few marriages, but these relationships, which seemed to begin with so much promise, never lasted. Her lovers and husbands were bossy, deceitful, unfaithful, or incompatible in one way or another.

The narrator in this poem changes from wanting to know what men are like physically ("Jacket tails slapping over / Those behinds") to caution about learning any more. When she physically experiences a man, who rapes her, she realizes that learning has changed not only her body but her thinking. She becomes cautious, though not cautious enough to lose—really lose—her curiosity.

FURTHER READING

Angelou, Maya. *The Complete Collected Poems of Maya Angelou.* New York: Random House, 1994.

"Million Man March Poem"
("A Black Woman Speaks to Black Manhood")

On October 16, 1995, a mass gathering was held in Washington, D.C., under the leadership of Louis Farrakhan. Farrakhan was the head of the Nation of Islam, and black men from throughout the United States were eager to take part in the event in order to demonstrate to the world a positive image of African-American males. Unfortunately, controversy plagued the demonstration, largely because of Louis Farrakhan's disagreeable comments about race relations in the United States. During the program, which included many notable speakers, Maya Angelou read a poem she had written for the occasion.

SYNOPSIS

"Million Man March Poem" begins with the recognition that African-American people have suffered for centuries: "The night has been long / . . . The pit has been dark." The poem jarringly references the kidnapping of Africans while others, standing by and seeing their loved ones captured, looked on helplessly. Then the first stanza is repeated. It moves on through history, and those assembled for the march are reminded that today "Across the years, across the centuries / Across the oceans / . . . slavery's chains / Have paid for our freedom." The first stanza repeats again, and then the promise of change is made, and "I say, clap hands and let's come together in this meeting ground." Angelou calls for courtesy, gentleness, and care, and the last line echoes other poems she has written with a statement of victory: "And still we rise."

CRITICAL COMMENTARY

Angelou's poem is an appeal to her black brothers. It uses powerful imagery to evoke history and encourage courtesy and pride. The poem has a strong cadence, and in 1995, when Angelou read it to the crowd—estimated at about 800,000 people, though the exact number is unknown—the massive gathering was quiet and listened to her respectfully.

FURTHER READING

Angelou, Maya. "Million Man March Poem." Available online. URL: www.poemhunter.com/poem/million-man-march-poem/. Accessed July 10, 2010.

Nelson, William E., Jr. "Black Church Politics and the Million Man March." In *Black Religious Leadership from the Slave Community to the Million Man March: Flames of Fire,* edited by Felton D. Best, 243–249. Lewiston, N.Y.: Edwin Mellen Press, 1989.

"Miss Scarlett, Mr. Rhett, and Other Latter Day-Saints"

"Miss Scarlett, Mr. Rhett and Other Latter-Day Saints" is included in Angelou's collection of poetry, *Just Give Me a Cool Drink 'fore I Diiie* (1971), which was nominated for a Pulitzer Prize.

This is a well-known poem that brutally describes the actions of Southern blacks' enemies.

SYNOPSIS

Nine stanzas tell the grisly narratives of whippings, the KU KLUX KLAN, torture, burning, and death. To a background of righteous chanting by Klan novitiates (innocents who have little understanding), blacks are bound to whipping posts and beaten. The narrative continues, describing a scene where "Priests glow purely white" against the background of a plantation. The Klan rides, and with hidden identity, it frightens and tortures. Then, in three lines set to a song, "Scarlett" and the oppression she perpetrated on blacks are gone. "Requiescat in pace" (rest in peace).

But the narrative's tragedy continues as blood is splashed on tombs furnished with bodies drained of life from work in the cotton fields: "Hosanna, King Kotton," it says. This is followed by a prayer to the "Maternoster," Latin for "our mother," and a nod to "Hallowed Little Eva," the white child in Harriet Beecher Stowe's *Uncle Tom's Cabin.* Then comes another tragedy, the reminder of the "charred bones of four . . . very young children." The minister makes a novena, a special nine-day prayer for favors, and in the meanwhile, black men die. The last stanza praises Scarlett (she is gone) and blesses "Rhett, the Martyr," which is ironic.

CRITICAL COMMENTARY

This is a powerful diatribe against the travesties of racial oppressors. Angelou was familiar with the Ku Klux Klan's night riders. Her own uncle, a man with a crippled body, was hidden away in a cold and damp vegetable storage box to protect him from the wrath and violence of these anonymous criminals. In a lyrical style, Angelou narrates the horrors of deliberately inflicted suffering, culminating in the most heinous of all, the bombing murder of four innocent little girls at a Baptist church in the South. The shame of that lives on as reflected in last stanza, "(Oh Sing) / Hallelujah, pure Scarlett, / Blessed Rhett, the Martyr." To Angelou, Scarlett represent white greed and ambition; Rhett represents indifference.

The main characters in the book *Gone with the Wind* (1936), by Margaret Mitchell, are Scarlett O'Hara and Rhett Butler. A Civil War story of tragedy told from the Confederate perspective, it is a romantic epic of frustrated love and of ultimately building a new life thanks to a lumber business that is successful during the South's Reconstruction. The movie version won many awards and is still very much a part of American culture. Scarlett, the protagonist, never did quite learn what the war was really about, and Rhett, her great love (after all others), ultimately walked away from it all.

FURTHER READING

Angelou, Maya. *The Complete Collected Poems of Maya Angelou.* New York: Random House, 1994.

Mitchell, Margaret. *Gone with the Wind.* New York: MacMillan, 1936.

"Momma Welfare Roll"

"Momma Welfare Roll" is found in Part Two of Angelou's collection *And Still I Rise* (1975). It may have been written in honor of MALCOLM X's mother, who, according to Malcolm, had died because of red tape and the ineptitude of social workers poorly administering welfare accounts. In the poem, Angelou describes how an aging black mother feels demeaned when asking for and accepting much-needed financial help from the government.

SYNOPSIS

The mother in this poem has grown older and heavy. Grown and gone, her children are possibly involved in street crime. She is alone and reduced to government support because no one is left to provide for her. To keep her self-respect, she says to herself, "They don't give me welfare. / I take it."

CRITICAL COMMENTARY

The literary critic Robert B. Stepto, suggests that some of the poems in this collection, including "Momma Welfare Roll," "bear strong resemblance to several poems in [Gwendolyn Brooks's] *Annie*

Allen [1950] and *The Bean Eaters* [1960]" (53). He also writes that "those comparisons help us define Angelou's particular presence and success in contemporary letters . . . and publishing" (53).

In today's world, after the 2005 tragedy of Hurricane Katrina, which devastated New Orleans, the news media pointed out the large number of southern Louisiana residents, black and white, who were on government welfare rolls. As demeaning as that was and is, it was suggested that generations of some families had survived using federal assistance almost as a lifestyle. As Angelou's poem suggests, there may be no alternative for many who have no marketable skills because no one has cared enough to help them become educated and self-sufficient.

FURTHER READING

Angelou, Maya. *The Complete Collected Poems of Maya Angelou.* New York: Random House, 1994.

Stepto, Robert B. "Critical Views on 'Still I Rise.'" In *Maya Angelou.* Bloom's Major Poets, edited by Harold Bloom, 52–54. Broomall, Pa.: Chelsea House, 2001.

———. "The Phenomenal Woman and the Severed Daughter" (Maya Angelou, Audre Lourde). *Parnassus: Poetry in Review* 8, no. 1 (Fall–Winter 1979): 313–315.

Mother: A Cradle to Hold Me

Published in 2006 by Random House, the press Angelou has used most, *Mother: A Cradle to Hold Me* is a tribute to mothers throughout the world. It was designed for Mother's Day, a day set aside to honor mothers in the United States, but it is a tribute to mothers everywhere.

SYNOPSIS

This long poem is chronologically progressive, beginning with the time the mother's "arms were molded / Into a cradle to hold me, to rock me." The narrative, insightful and tender, reveals deep understanding of both the mother's and the child's role in the relationship. The second stanza states that in those early days, "I did not dream that you had a larger life which included me," for to a very young child, all of life is wrapped up in the care and tenderness of her or his mother. Though there have been painful separations now and then, the mother calms the child and tells her that she cannot "stay in your lap forever." Leaving and returning each time, the child gains confidence and observes the mother's smiles, frowns, and "The way you had of singing" even when sad. The poem continues: "You were always / The heart of happiness to me." Reflecting on the condescending attitude of teenage, Angelou remarks that when she was older, she "Was stunned to find how much knowledge you had gleaned, and so quickly." The poem ends on a note of love, thanking the mother for always finding something in the child "to cherish, to admire, and to love."

CRITICAL COMMENTARY

In many ways, Angelou had several mothers during her formative years. VIVIAN BAXTER, her birth mother, was unable to care for Maya and her brother after her divorce from BAILEY JOHNSON, SR., Maya's father. Sent to STAMPS, ARKANSAS, to live with her paternal grandmother, Annie Henderson, Maya was cared for and loved, though strictly within the boundaries of fundamental Christianity and a segregated community. She was returned to her mother for a brief period of time and horribly assaulted by Vivian's live-in boyfriend. Shocked and made mute, she was then returned to Grandmother Henderson. Soon, Mrs. BERTHA FLOWERS came into her life and, with poetry and classical reading, coaxed the child into talking once again. In time, Maya joined her mother in California, and they maintained an amiable relationship until Vivian passed away many years later.

Maya Angelou loved her mother, grandmother, and Mrs. Flowers deeply. She was conscious of what each of them had given her, and though her mother did leave and return throughout Angelou's life, there was trust and understanding. CLYDE BAILEY JOHNSON, Maya's only son, known as Guy, respects and loves Angelou as well. He has been quoted expressing his deep love for her and also the knowledge that she was a very devoted mother.

FURTHER READING

Angelou, Maya. *Mother: A Cradle to Hold Me.* New York: Random House, 2006.

"Mothering Blackness, The"

"The Mothering Blackness" was published in Part One of Angelou's first volume of poetry, *Just Give Me a Cool Drink of Water 'fore I Diiie* (1971).

SYNOPSIS

This poem speaks of the deep anguish the narrator feels after experiencing Africa as a visiting daughter. "She came home running / back to the mothering . . . smothering blackness" of her homeland. She returns to the United States, her homeland, back to "black arms waiting . . . creeping." Her heart has missed America, but she had seen much in Africa, so much that "white tears icicle gold plains of her face." She knows the suffering of her people there and at home, and she knows that she is genetically African, "black yet as Hagar's daughter / tall as was Sheba's daughter." Hagar was the handmaiden of Sarah and Abraham, whose story is told in the Old Testament. Sarah seemed barren, so Hagar was given to Abraham and bore the child Ishmael. Sheba, whose story is also told in the Old Testament, was a queen who made a famous visit to King Solomon, the son of King David. Angelou had great respect for these ancient people, and she also knew that the grim circumstances for blacks were not of her doing. She returned to the United States blameless, but she felt a responsibility to use her voice and lift her people as best as she was able.

CRITICAL COMMENTARY

When Maya and her only son, Guy, flew over the desert on their plane trip from Cairo, Egypt, to Accra, Ghana, about two years before she returned to the United States, she looked down at the vast Sahara desert from the airplane window. She began to weep, and she continued weeping for most of the flight as she reflected on the hundreds of thousands of her people, among them her own ancestors, who had been kidnapped and taken from their homeland. She knew of the consequences of that forced DIASPORA, and it burdened her heart. She looked down on the desert—"threats of northern winds die on the desert's face"(22)—and wondered how horrible that time must have been. When she returned home later having gained a surer sense of her own identity, she knew that she could write and contribute to uplifting the pride and dignity of her own people.

FURTHER READING

Angelou, Maya. *The Complete Collected Poems of Maya Angelou.* New York: Random House, 1994.

"Mourning Grace"

"Mourning Grace" is included in the collection *Just Give Me a Cool Drink of Water 'fore I Diiie* (1971). The poems in this collection address either failed love relationships and the consequent pain that one suffers afterward or various issues concerning liberation ideology.

SYNOPSIS

In 14 very short lines, "Mourning Grace" asks a question—essentially, if I die, "Will you / have / the / grace / to mourn for / me?" In this poem, the narrator is having doubts about a romantic relationship, and she is wondering if the partner would even care should death come. It begins, "If today I follow death, / go down its trackless wastes," which is a dismal consideration, but insecurity in the relationship drives the question.

CRITICAL COMMENTARY

Maya Angelou had one failed love relationship after another. She searched for male companionship and lived with the hope that she would find, at some point, a father figure for her son and a companion for herself. Lyman B. Hagen, a literary critic and proponent of Angelou's writing, states:

> This search allows the introduction of a variety of male characters [into her various autobiographies] and allows Angelou to express normal sexual interests. This is an accepted topic of the

> culture of the time. Angelou reports on a series of lovers associated with her search for a suitable husband and father. Most fall short of her requirements. Angelou does try throughout the book to balance an honest appreciation of ordinary sexual adventures with the wholesome and desirable goal of stability. This is another message of hope for those young women disturbed by their sexuality and unable to come to terms with desires and expectations. (101)

Though Angelou did not find a lifelong male companion, she has maintained enduring friendships with many men, and she has contributed generously to the dignity and well-being of her people, male and female.

FURTHER READING

Angelou, Maya. *The Complete Collected Poems of Maya Angelou.* New York: Random House, 1994.

Hagen, Lyman B. *Heart of a Woman, Mind of a Writer, and Soul of a Poet.* Lanham, Md.: University Press of America, 1997.

"My Arkansas"

"My Arkansas" appears in Angelou's 1975 volume of poetry, *And Still I Rise.* Angelou and her brother, BAILEY JOHNSON, JR., spent their formative childhood years in deeply segregated STAMPS, ARKANSAS, living in the back of general store owned by their paternal grandmother, Annie Henderson. The only other adult in their grandmother's home was their uncle WILLIE JOHNSON, who was severely crippled from an early childhood injury. The family clearly experienced the divisions between blacks and whites. Wise and knowledgeable black adults taught their children both the dangers of racial SEGREGATION and the requisite skills needed to survive it.

SYNOPSIS

The words chosen for this poem project an undercurrent of brooding and unresolved foreboding. The line "Old crimes like moss pend [wait] / from poplar trees" suggests lynchings, and the earth, being "too / red for comfort," evokes images of spilled blood. The second stanza begins with "Sunrise seems to hesitate." Is it afraid? In the third and last stanza, "Old hates and ante-bellum lace are rent / but not discarded." Freedom has not yet come to Arkansas, the poet suggests: "It writhes / in awful waves of brooding."

CRITICAL COMMENTARY

Maya Angelou grew up in frightening circumstances on many levels. In the segregated South, where blacks were perceived to have little value, young girls lived in danger of rape, while boys lived in danger of abuse and murder. Her crippled Uncle Willie, in fact, was hidden overnight in a vegetable bin to protect him from marauding KU KLUX KLAN night riders; Maya and her brother helped temporarily bury him there with cold, damp vegetables. At this writing (2010), Arkansas is fully integrated and no longer as dangerous for blacks as it was, but Angelou writes with the voice of her time to the oppressed black people of the South.

This poem, unfortunately, describes pockets of the United States where hate groups continue to thrive, choosing their enemies based on culture, religion, gender issues, and skin color. Prejudice and bigotry have still not been entirely eliminated in the United States.

FURTHER READING

Angelou, Maya. *The Complete Collected Poems of Maya Angelou.* New York: Random House, 1994.

"My Guilt"

"My Guilt" is in Part Two of *Just Give Me a Cool Drink 'fore I Diiie* (1971). The poems in this collection reflect the sadness of love relationships that end too soon or the oppression African Americans have felt in the United States over different periods of time since the blacks were first brought to the northeastern shore of North America in 1619.

SYNOPSIS

The poem is written in three stanzas and contains a powerful message of oppression, guilt, crime, and sin. The narrator confesses to not working harder to overcome the subjugation and tyranny of racial hatred that whites feel toward the blacks. The first stanza recalls "slavery's chains" and the cruel sales of slaves that separated family members forever. The narrator's tears are for the "clang of iron" that was heard over and over again. The second stanza laments the loss of many heroes who gave their lives to change the attitudes of whites and alleviate the unjust oppression of blacks. Included in the lament are Denmark Versey, NAT TURNER, and GABRIEL PROSSER, who were leaders of insurrections against whites in the early 1800s; and MALCOLM X, MARCUS GARVEY, and MARTIN LUTHER KING, JR., leaders of African Americans in the 20th century. "They fought too hard, they loved too well," the narrator says, and the crime felt by Angelou, the poem's composer, is that "I'm alive to tell." The third and last stanza includes the tragic "hanging from a tree," or lyching, the ultimate public humiliation of over 5,000 (or possibly more) blacks in the South. The narrator says, "My sin lies in not screaming loud."

CRITICAL COMMENTARY

There have been many skilled African-American speakers and writers who have tried to enlighten people about the oppression of the blacks and old racist behavior that was particularly virulent in the United States. In this regard, Remus Bejan writes:

> The system of racial stratification characteristic of the American society has deep roots in 18th century European classification schemes, in the eugenics movement and the racialized history of imperialism. Slavery exaggerated existing ideas of racial difference and the inferiority of colored people, serving as a rationalization of the exploitation of Africans in America. That same racist ideology continued, in metamorphosed form, after the emancipation of the slaves, guaranteeing their subordinate status for generations. This particular experience has produced in time a number of competing representations of the Nigrescence. (148)

Over time, black writers have tried to tell the public—that is, anyone who would read—the whole story of what has been done to them. Pierre A. Walker writes: "Since emancipation, African-American authors have used the same strategy to fight the belief in racial hierarchies that relegated them to second-class citizen status. One way to do this was to produce 'high art,' which was supposed to be one of the achievements of the highest orders of human civilization" (18).

In his book *Malcolm X Speaks,* Malcolm X explains the loss of dignity and pride of simply being black because white imperialists had declared that white was superior, in every way, to black. Consequently, black people used the white measure of beauty and became convinced that they were inferior simply because they were not the same. Malcolm states:

> [White people] very skillfully make you and me hate our African identity, our African characteristics. You know yourself that we have been a people who hated our African characteristics. We hated our heads, we hated the shape of our nose, we wanted one of those long dog-like noses, you know; we hated the color of our skin, hated the blood of African that was in our veins. And in hating our features and our skin and our blood, why, we ended up hating ourselves. And we hated ourselves. (169)

Understanding these strategies to push black self-respect down into self-hatred reveals why blacks have fought so hard to gain the rights that belonged to them all along. Angelou's contribution to the gaining of pride among African Americans cannot be overemphasized. She has written her poetry in a way that any reader can understand. The messages are strong and clear, and her voice, raised with so many others, has changed the attitudes of many people in the United States and the world.

FURTHER READING

Angelou, Maya. *The Complete Collected Poems of Maya Angelou.* New York: Random House, 1994.

Bejan, Remus. "*Nigrescence: Mapping the Journey in Maya Angelou's* I Know Why the Caged Bird Sings." In *Maya Angelou.* Bloom's Modern Critical Views, edited by Harold Bloom, 147–155. New York: Bloom's Literary Criticism, 2009.

Malcolm X. *Malcolm X Speaks.* New York: Grove Press, 1966.

Walker, Pierre A. "Breaking Out of the Cage: The Autobiographical Writings of Maya Angelou." In *Maya Angelou.* Bloom's Modern Critical Views, edited by Harold Bloom, 17–35. New York: Bloom's Literary Criticism, 2009.

"New House, The"

"The New House" is included in the collection *I Shall Not Be Moved* (1990).

SYNOPSIS

When a used home becomes a buyer's new home, there are usually questions about the people who lived in the house previously. In this narrative poem, questions are asked about words and feelings that may have been spoken or experienced there. "What words / have smashed against / these walls. . . ?" "What feelings, long since / dead, / streamed vague yearnings / below this ceiling / light?" We can only wonder. In the final stanza, the narrator wonders "what among / these shades will be / left of me."

Some homes have a welcoming atmosphere; some do not. There are now popular horror films that feature homes with hidden, mysterious, and often dangerous secrets that can stir up quite a suspenseful plot. Supposed ghosts, poltergeists, vapors, and sounds can create a terrifying sense of evil; this is fiction, but it is engaging, harmless entertainment. Angelou uses the word *shades* in the last line of this poem, and that word can evoke the image of a phantom or specter. Maybe some houses are left with wandering spirits, good or bad, that influence the atmosphere of the place. No one knows the answer for certain.

CRITICAL COMMENTARY

In Angelou's book of essays *Even the Stars Look Lonesome* (1998), there is a piece entitled "A House Can Hurt, a Home Can Heal," in which she discusses her marriage (1973–81) with a British builder, PAUL DU FEU. He had not known American blacks before meeting Maya at a literary party in London, but he was proud of her, and they shared many homes in California. At one point, he led guests "to a small study where the walls [were] hung with his wife's honorary doctoral degrees from Smith College, Mills College, and Lawrence University; a certificate proclaiming her a Chubb Fellow at Yale; framed parchments announcing her appointment by President Ford to the Bicentennial Council, by President Carter to the International Women's Year Commission; and her Tony Award nomination for best supporting actress for *Look Away* in 1972" (Inge 1999, 99). It was a good marriage, but the beginning of the end apparently occurred when Angelou and Du Feu moved into an abstraction of a futuristic house in California that jutted out over a canyon.

As indicated by its title, Angelou developed the essay with the thesis that a house must be made into a home. Du Feu felt that their new house was pretentious, and they both felt that, with all its modern conveniences, it was somehow separating them, so they moved into a home that was more suitable for their furniture and treasures. However, that house did not work, either. In fact, Angelou writes, "Within a month I realized the house hated me" (1998, 6). She is an excellent cook, but her recipes would not turn out properly, the bed fell apart in the middle of the night, drapes fell off the runners, doors did not fit their frames, and the piano would not hold a tuning. Within a year, Maya and Paul decided to divorce.

Their parting was amicable, and Angelou decided to leave California altogether and move to Winston-Salem, North Carolina, where she has taught for many years at Wake-Forest University. She found a big house there, had it remodeled, and added to it so it would be exactly as she wanted it. In this way, she found herself truly at home.

The elements of her poem "The New Home" echo the uncomfortable atmosphere of both homes described in Angelou's essay. A house, apartment, or trailer needs to be made into a home. By Angelou's criteria, it is a place that is clean and, though lived-in, fairly neat, as pretty and comfortable as it can be made, welcoming, and with aromas of delicious food. Certainly her home in Winston-Salem holds that welcome for her, her family, and her friends.

FURTHER READING

Angelou, Maya. *The Complete Collected Poems of Maya Angelou.* New York: Random House, 1994.

———. "A House Can Hurt, a Home Can Heal." In *Even the Stars Look Lonesome.* New York: Bantam Books, 1998, 3–10.

Inge, Arline. "Maya Angelou" (1978 interview). In *Conversations with Maya Angelou,* edited by Jeffrey M. Elliot, 97–101. Jackson and London: University Press of Mississippi, 1999.

"No Loser, No Weeper"

"No Loser, No Weeper," a poem about personal loss, was published in Maya Angelou's first volume of poetry, *Just Give Me a Cool Drink of Water 'fore I Diiie* (1971).

SYNOPSIS

In four stanzas, the narrator describes the loss of something valuable, but as the poem progresses, the thing of value becomes something of more worth. It begins with the loss of a dime, then a doll, then a watch, and finally—the message of the poem—the loss of a valued boyfriend. Angelou uses some common vernacular in the poem—"Cept" instead of "except," "bout" instead of "about"—but it is not really black folk-speak, it is more common language for a person speaking English in a relaxed mode. Possessiveness is the key element in this poem: The narrator expresses her hate of losing things, and it implies that someone has taken her "lover-boy" away. No threat is made, but it is a clear expression of an emotional reaction.

CRITICAL COMMENTARY

Angelou, like her literary forebears, Mark Twain and ZORA NEALE HURSTON, has a keen ear for dialogue and dialect, a talent she developed by listening carefully and mentally registering the sounds of language. This is, in part, why she was able to learn so many languages other than English (Fanti, Croatian, Spanish, French, and others). In this poem, a girl's passionate and romantic possessiveness about losing her boyfriend is expressed with an underlying tension of real anger. Angelou's skill at layered meaning has been well noted. Using very little dialect, the age of the narrator is revealed, and the complaint and possible danger clearly registers with the reader.

FURTHER READING

Angelou, Maya. *The Complete Collected Poems of Maya Angelou.* New York: Random House, 1994.

"No No No No"

This poem was published in Angelou's first volume of poetry, *Just Give Me a Cool Drink of Water 'fore I Diiie* (1971), which was nominated for the Pulitzer Prize. This poem, published while the Vietnam War was still raging, is urgent and accusative, reflecting the passion and despair of broken dreams. In it, Angelou sent a message to the world, and especially to blacks, as she protests the morality of the United State's involvement in Vietnam.

SYNOPSIS

The first stanza presents victims, described as "babies / in napalm coats"—a tragic metaphor for the realities of war. The last line, "JUST GIVE ME A COOL DRINK OF WATER 'FORE I DIIIE," links past to present; Angelou once explained that this line was a plea from blacks before being put to death by racists in the South. In this poem, the victims of war beg for life.

The second stanza metaphorically refers to the Statue of Liberty, which, in the name of the United States, has invited Europeans to come to her shores. But the lines do not employ Angelou's usual jolting rhythm and passion. Harshly naming those guilty of ignoring the plight of blacks and the immorality of war, she points out whites having cocktail afternoons in a "white, layered pink world" and, in another stanza, "red-shoed priests riding

/ palanquined" as mothers sort through feces for "undigested beans" to help their children survive.

The blacks wait "On the back porches / of forever," she writes, against continued rejection from the "cold marble steps" of the White House. Hopes and dreams are broken, and she comments, "What a pity / that pity has folded in upon itself." The last line resolves the loss of hope: "I have no pity."

CRITICAL COMMENTARY

Eleven stanzas express the angst of war with disturbing imagery, poignant metaphor, repetition, and parody. The title, "No No No No," repeats throughout the poem in rejection of the travesties both of war and of RACISM. Though crude imagery sets the tone of the message, it pierces the reality of apathy and indifference also reflected in this work.

The poem jars the reader with its jolting rhythm and passion. The literary critic Carol E. Neubauer writes that this poem "is about the rejection of American myths that promise justice for all but only guarantees freedom for a few" (208). Observing what the U.S. government was doing in Vietnam, and knowing the long history of minorities being denied equal rights in the United States, Angelou has slashed the concept of hope. She knows that an extraordinary number of her black brothers will not survive the conflagration in Vietnam, and she wonders if anyone cares.

FURTHER READING

Angelou, Maya. *The Complete Collected Poems of Maya Angelou.* New York: Random House, 1994.

Neubauer, Carol E. "Maya Angelou: Self and a Song of Freedom in the Southern Tradition." In *Maya Angelou.* Modern Critical Views, edited by Harold Bloom, 191–218. Philadelphia, Chelsea House Publishers, 1999.

Now Sheba Sings the Song

Now Sheba Sings the Song was written and published in 1987 and illustrated by the artist TOM FEELINGS. MALCOLM X introduced Angelou to Feelings in Ghana in the early 1960s.

SYNOPSIS

This sensitive work is made up of a combination of arts, both poetic and illustrative. There are 82 drawings of beautiful black women used to illustrate the poem, and as the pages are turned, and the poem continues line-upon-line in tandem with the pictures, the reader feels the women's dignity and beauty. The drawings are created in sepia tones; Feelings had sketched them over a 25-year period in different settings throughout the world.

Next to a head-and-shoulders portrait of a beautiful young black woman, the poem begins: "Mother told her secrets to me / When I rode / Low in the Pocket / Between her hips." Illustrations of black women fill the pages with their mesmerizing beauty, and Feelings has also included a few sketches of children. Glorifying the beauty of African hair, one stanza states: "My hair, a hive of honey bees / is a queenly glory / Crackles like castanets / Hums like marimbas." That stanza is followed by many views of hairstyles, including cornrows and various braids. The poem ends on an empowering note with "I am mate to Kilimanjaro . . . He who is daring and brave will know what to do." The poem and many of the drawings are sensuous, expressing the beauty and power of black women.

CRITICAL COMMENTARY

Maya Angelou's voice is one of the most original and creative of the 20th century. Her personal quest for survival and security, and the grave difficulties she has encountered in that quest, have developed both her spirit and intellectual capacity to the part where she has become a spokesperson for many of the women (and men) of the world. In this poem, illustrated with sensitive sketches of black females from many countries, she has embraced all women. Her words laud identity and power and black women's absolute refusal to be misunderstood or subdued. The portraits emphasize the individuality and validity of each woman's experience. The faces radiate with pride and confidence.

FURTHER READING

Angelou, Maya. *Now Sheba Sings the Song.* Illustrated by Tom Feelings. New York: Plume/Penguin Group, 1987.

"Old Folks Laugh"

"Old Folks Laugh" is included in Angelou's 1990 collection *I Shall Not Be Moved.* This is a light, delightful, and honest poem, expressing the joy "Old Folks" can still find in living.

SYNOPSIS

This poem is 25 lines long, and it is a charming picture of the wisdom of the elderly. The narrator begins by observing: "They have spent their / content of simpering, / holding their lips this / and what way, winding / the lines between / their brows." By *content,* it is suggested that they had just so much of posing to do, and they are through with it. They have spent the last of their "content," and now, "The hollers [laughter] / rise up and spill / over any way they want." They are free from society's perceived constraints, and finally, they can relax and just let themselves be themselves. The narrator describes saliva glistening at the corners of their mouths and heads held unsteadily on brittle necks, but "their laps / are filled with memories." Old folks, the poem says, "forgive life for happening / to them."

CRITICAL COMMENTARY

Maya Angelou is someone who respects all people, including the elderly. As is evident in this poem, she observes and she understands that individuals reach a time in life when pretense and catering to appearances are put aside, and life can be lived freely and comfortably by just being oneself. Individuals fortunate enough to live long lives carry with them the experiences of decades and memories of how things were. When they laugh and "allow their bellies to jiggle like slow / tambourines," as the poem says, it is a joy to observe.

When Angelou was in Africa and visited a village in the wilderness of Ghana, she saw the elders of the village. These were aged folks, wise in the ways of their people and generous to a stranger if they felt a certain trust. There is an ability learned over time that seems to allow older people to judge accurately whether people should be trusted or not trusted. The village elders were right in trusting Angelou. The innocence of youth includes vulnerability and often gullibility; old age suggests that people have made many right choices in order to live as long as they have. They have learned caution and how to make decisions carefully. They have learned to trust their instincts. Wisdom comes with experience and age, and when old folks laugh, they mean it.

FURTHER READING

Angelou, Maya. *The Complete Collected Poems of Maya Angelou.* New York: Random House, 1994.

"On a Bright Day, Next Week"

"On a Bright Day, Next Week" was published in Angelou's first volume of poetry, *Just Give Me a Cool Drink of Water 'fore I Diiie* (1971), which was nominated for a Pulitzer Prize.

SYNOPSIS

Just Give Me was published while the United States was engaged in a seemingly futile and endless war in Vietnam. The world's collective memory of the atomic holocaust had not faded, and with each succeeding decade, more and more powerful weapons were invented. The fear of human annihilation was, and is, a reality. In this terse poem, the narrator ponders what will happen, "Just before I die." She wonders if her tears will turn to black powder, "black and hot and dry." And, most important, she wonders if mercy to her people will tumble from the sky at last.

CRITICAL COMMENTARY

In three short, four-line stanzas, Angelou takes the reader from "a bright day" to an apocalyptic doom. Still, she weaves in a modicum of hope and wonders, "Then will mercy tumble . . . on the children . . . falling from the sky." Her poetry of liberation is often ambiguous, but it carries significant meanings, promises, and ever-present hope.

FURTHER READING

Angelou, Maya. *The Complete Collected Poems of Maya Angelou.* New York: Random House, 1994.

"On Aging"

"On Aging" is included in Part Three of *And Still I Rise,* published in 1975. It is a poem of strength and wisdom.

SYNOPSIS

In the first two lines of this three-stanza poem, the narrator is sitting quietly but warns her readers that chattering is not needed because "I'm listening to myself." No pity or sympathy is wanted or needed; "Understanding if you got it / Otherwise I'll do without it!" In the second stanza, the narrator sassily suggests that no rocking chair is needed. In the third stanza, the plucky personality of the elderly narrator is clear, and there is a warning to read the situation correctly: "'Cause tired don't mean lazy." A few lines later, the narrator remarks that she is the same as she was long ago, just "A little less hair," chin, lungs, and wind, "But ain't I lucky I can still breathe in."

CRITICAL COMMENTARY

For most people, the privilege of living to be old is just that, a privilege, but often younger people do not view it that way. For them, *old* means used up, not okay, to be pitied. After all, the old ones are just going to die. Angelou knows the wisdom that comes from age, and this little poem reflects her knowledge and understanding.

In 2000, Chester Higgins, Jr., published a photographic essay entitled *Elder Grace: The Nobility of Aging,* for which Angelou wrote the foreword. That book has been mentioned in this text because it, too, is a reflection on the grace and dignity of age. A few of the QUOTATIONS in the book are well worth pondering along with the poem discussed here.

In *Elder Grace,* Stephanie Burns, a beautiful woman wearing long white braids in her portrait, says, "When I was younger, I trusted everybody. When I grew older, I learned everyone is not alike. Now, I know more about people, and I'm more careful" (30). Another graceful-looking woman, Marie Brooks, says, "Your values change as you walk your journey. I have found that the things I value today have made me happier. I can bounce off bad things and keep on going. I have resilience" (14). A lovely old woman, standing straight and tall in a feminine, soft-looking dress, says, "I sit on my steps and I see everybody. I'm the same person I've always been" (14). The great actor OSSIE DAVIS advises: "Live and live fully. There is always an unanswered question, and if you live long enough, the secret might well be revealed. I think truth is worth waiting for, and age is an access to truth" (67).

It is always wise to listen to people who have been through life and accumulated years of experience. Life itself teaches, and there is little understanding among many of how much these older members of our culture can teach, if people would only listen.

FURTHER READING

Angelou, Maya. *The Complete Collected Poems of Maya Angelou.* New York: Random House, 1994.

Higgins, Chester, Jr. *Elder Grace: The Nobility of Aging.* New York: Bullfinch Press/AOL Time Warner Book Group, 2000.

"On Diverse Deviations"

The themes of the poems in Angelou's first published collection, *Just Give Me a Cool Drink of Water 'fore I Diiie* (1971), focus either on the pain of love thwarted or on varied approaches to liberation ideology. In Part One of the collection, "Where Love Is a Scream of Anguish," this poem is a scream of frustrated hope. *Just Give Me* was nominated for a Pulitzer Prize.

SYNOPSIS

"On Diverse Deviations" is a short narrative speaking of love as "a shimmering curtain / Before a door of chance." The narrator is repeatedly frustrated in romantic relationships and feels that the world of love is a "world in question." It speaks of amorous relationships as a "macabrous dance," being "Of blinded eyes," and a place where life is stale and weary. The poem is only 14 lines long, and it is a long sigh of frustration. In the last stanza, the third line is the title of Part One of the volume, though it is slightly changed: "Where love is the scream of anguish." The narrator dreams of a better, less painful relationship in love, but love relationships are described as elusive and unpredictable, and because of the hope and emotions they raise and then squelch, they are frightening.

CRITICAL COMMENTARY

Maya Angelou repeatedly entered romantic relationships, and unfortunately they failed each time. She maintained many friendships and professional associations with men and women, but to her deep disappointment, she was unable to find a male life companion. Some scholars have suggested that her childhood assault and rape was to blame for her inability to establish an enduring relationship with a male companion, and that may be so. On the other hand, she is multitalented and very dedicated to sharing her intellectual gifts with others. Along with many others, she has tried (and succeeded) in helping to build a sense of self-respect within African-American people. It may be that she simply did not have the time to build and sustain a male/female companionship, and the men she chose were perhaps neither generous nor secure enough to willingly support her outreach activities, which have been stimulated by her own intelligence, drive, experience, and sincerity. This poem is both a lament and warning about romantic liaisons, and it reflects a guardedness that Angelou developed over time because of the frequent emotional disappointments from which she had to heal.

FURTHER READING

Angelou, Maya. *The Complete Collected Poems of Maya Angelou.* New York: Random House, 1994.

"One More Round"

"One More Round" is in Part Two of Angelou's collection *And Still I Rise* (1975).

SYNOPSIS

This poem has eight stanzas and the rhythm of a work song. The even-number stanzas have a repetitive refrain: "One more round / And let's heave it down, / One more round / And let's heave it down." The other stanzas repeat that "I"—a collective pronoun in this usage—"was not born / to be a slave." The narration describes that the work was hard, but there was no complaint. The protest was not about the work itself—"I was born to work up to my grave"—but, rather, about being forced into slavery. Acceptance of hard work is all right, "but I ain't no mule." This poem has a strong rhythm and is best when read aloud.

CRITICAL COMMENTARY

In a review of *And Still I Rise,* Robert B. Stepto writes: "The idea of somehow binding 'work' and 'protest' forms to create new art is absolutely first rate, but the mere alternation of 'work' and 'protest' stanzas does not, in this instance, carry the idea very far" (53). Angelou's work is directed at her readers, who are primarily African Americans. Though many blacks are highly educated professionals, like President Barack Obama and his wife, Michelle, who are graduates of prestigious universities and successful lawyers, the great majority of African Americans have not had the same opportunities. The most educationally limited are those born before the middle of the 20th century. Angelou, who never attended college as a student and yet has been awarded multiple honorary doctoral degrees and a full professorship at Wake Forest University, struggled to write her poems, and she worked through them word by word. She has mentioned in several interviews that she rents a quiet room and works daily by writing many pages of ideas and words on a yellow pad before distilling them into a narrative poem that carries her message. Like many others in *And Still I Rise,* this poem protests the oppression of slavery, but it also projects the constancy of accepting the wait and working hard until times improve or until death.

FURTHER READING

Angelou, Maya. *The Complete Collected Poems of Maya Angelou.* New York: Random House, 1994.

Stepto, Robert B. "Critical Views on 'Still I Rise.'" In *Maya Angelou.* Bloom's Major Poets, edited by Harold Bloom, 52–54. Broomall, Pa.: Chelsea House, 2001.

"On Reaching Forty"

Oh Pray My Wings Are Going to Fit Me Well (1975) has poems that are about both everyday considerations and racial issues. "On Reaching Forty" is in Part One of the collection and has an unforeseen twist at the end.

SYNOPSIS

The narrator in this poem is not very happy about reaching 40. It is as though other birthdays slid by almost unnoticed—"Other acquainted years / sidle / with modest / decorum"—but this one "stomps / no-knocking / into the script / bumps a funky grind . . . and delays the action." The poem has two stanzas; one has 17 lines, and the other has six. The ending is startling and unexpected because it suggests that it might be better simply to die at 39.

CRITICAL COMMENTARY

The 40th birthday is often a shock because people usually feel very young at 40, and yet it literally means four decades of life, which is perhaps a midway mark. The old ADAGE "Life begins at 40," derived from the ancient Greek tradition that their vestal virgins served in the temple until 40 and were then released from the duty, seldom seems a happy truth to those whose 40th birthday has arrived. The narrator's attitude seems to be one of defeat, with dread of the years to come.

Angelou's own experience with her 40th birthday was a tragic and difficult one. As she was preparing for a celebration with good friends and associates, the telephone rang. It was her close friend DOLLY MCPHERSON, who said she would be right over and that Maya must promise not to turn on the television or radio. When McPherson arrived, she told Maya that MARTIN LUTHER KING, JR., had been assassinated in Memphis, Tennessee. Maya was deeply shocked and broken by that news. The birthday was forgotten, and it seemed in many ways that the hope for change she had dreamed of, as did King, might be gone forever.

FURTHER READING

Angelou, Maya. *The Complete Collected Poems of Maya Angelou.* New York: Random House, 1994.

"On the Pulse of Morning"

President BILL CLINTON invited Maya Angelou to write and deliver a poem at his presidential inauguration in January 1993. Both of them had grown up in Arkansas, and both had experienced the struggles of poverty as children. They also shared the belief that in the United States, anyone with determination and a willingness to work hard could succeed. Though Angelou was already well-known as an actress and writer in the United States, her eloquent poem, dignified delivery, and universal message catapulted her to enduring international fame. Angelou stood on the steps of the Capitol that cold January morning, wrapped in a warm coat, and greeted the collective nation and world with a message of peace, justice, harmony, and a meaningful "Good Morning."

SYNOPSIS

"On the Pulse of Morning" invites the audience, "clad in peace," to come to a river that "sang and sings on" with a message of diversity and equality. She reaches far back in time to begin her message, mentioning the ancient mastodon and dinosaur "who left dried tokens of their sojourn here." But the poem moves on quickly to a message to people of today, and the river beckons for people to "Come, rest by my side." In a later stanza, she incorporates words from a well-known spiritual song written by John W. Works: "Yet today I call you to my riverside, / If you will study war no more." There is a subtle hint of sacred and secular mythologies in the poem, as well as old African-American SPIRITUALS. References to the image of a tree, well known in myth and belief systems around the world; the rock, for eons known as a symbol of stability; and the river itself as a metaphor for life, draw from familiar motifs to create a natural unity. She names many groups that have come to America—the Asian, the Hispanic, the Jew, the African—and those who have always been here—the Native American—as well as others of all creeds and ages, suggesting that they hear the call for peace and the dream of freedom.

The poem calls for the people to use their own hands and shape freedom into their private and public needs. Near the end of the work, the mood shifts toward future horizons for everyone. "Angels," "Midas" (a mythological Greek king whose touch turned things to gold), and to "study war no more" reflect Angelou's broad cultural and literary knowledge. These references enrich the poem and make it even more inclusive. In the last stanza, she invites all people to look into one another's eyes and say simply, "Good Morning."

CRITICAL COMMENTARY

Angelou's metaphorical message carries with it an invitation for all people to come together with regard for one another and the land. Though she has never claimed to use the language and rhythms of academic poetry or the technical tools of metric composition, her poems reflect a studied precision aimed at didactic messages advocating harmony, human rights, and self-respect. Her work is penetrating, and it triggers both attention and reflection in the audience.

In "On the Pulse of Morning," the words succeed in creating the essence of the river by the use of assonance, a rhythm and pattern of vowel sounds that subsume the harsher sounds of consonants. The first stanza begins with an earlier time, and the strong vowel sounds seem to carry the poem with words like *rock, river, tree, hosts, long, marked, dried, tokens,* and *sojourn.* The frequency of the vowel sounds throughout the poem is soft and like the gentle flowing of the river. Angelou wants to convey the message that things change—slowly, gently, sometimes for good, and sometimes not.

Using the metaphor of a river to represent the changing demographics in the United States over time, the poem lists various groups of citizens and then invites all of them to "Come to me, / Here beside the River. / Plant yourself beside the River." By enumerating the diverse groups in the country, and repeating the line "I, the Rock, I, the River, I, the Tree," the message is reinforced that everyone belongs, and we are a community.

MARTIN LUTHER KING, JR., delivered a great speech that still rings in the hearts of many Americans. Called "I Have a Dream," it analogously echoes the enduring words on the Statue of Liberty, "Give me your tired, your poor." In "On the Pulse of Morning," Angelou invites all people to have hope, and it also invites us to honor each other and the precious land we share.

FURTHER READING

Angelou, Maya. *The Complete Collected Poems of Maya Angelou.* New York: Random House, 1994

Works, John W. "Study War No More." In *American Negro Songs.* 1949. Reprint, New York: Dover, 1998.

"Our Grandmothers"

Maya Angelou and her brother, Bailey, were shipped into the care of their grandmother Mrs. Annie Henderson in STAMPS, ARKANSAS, when they were young children. They were with her for several years and witnessed their grandmother begin each day before sunrise with a prayer and then open her general store to serve both goods and wisdom to the black people of her community.

In the poem "Our Grandmothers," Angelou begins by discussing the strength and determination of other African-American women who lived long before her time. As history stumbles forward and reveals the past, we know that African Americans suffered every indignity imaginable during the time of slavery in the United States. Angelou wants us to understand that her people were strong even under that oppression, and like her own grandmother, they maintained within themselves a deep and fixed dignity.

SYNOPSIS

"Our Grandmothers" reflects the terror and fear that black women in the South felt for over two centuries. By paying close attention to the words of the poem, we can feel the terror of those times, and for many, the challenges continue today. "She lay, skin down, in the moist dirt. . . . The ransack of hungers crackling the near branches." The woman gathers her young, and they wonder if the "Master going to sell you / from us tomorrow?" Slavery meant that families were often separated and valuable human beings were sold, like animals, to the highest bidders. But for the sake of her posterity, the mother chants in answer to every threat, "I shall not be moved."

Angelou names many of the powerful women who left a legacy of dignity and strength to posterity: Sheba and SOJOURNER TRUTH, HARRIET TUBMAN and ZORA NEALE HURSTON, Mary Bethune and Angela Davis, Annie Mae Perry and Zenobia. Here, Angelou draws from her own experience and generalizes the name *Momma.* The grimacing, suffering faces pictured here are rescued by a carefully chanted litany of names representing the strong, black, immovable women in history. To this day, some people claim royal linage from the queen of Sheba and Solomon; Sheba is first mentioned in 1 Kings 10. Sojourner Truth, a 19th-century preacher and abolitionist, fought for women's rights. Harriet Tubman ran an UNDERGROUND RAILROAD from the slave culture of the South to freedom in the North. Zora Neale Hurston was a folklorist and writer who rose to prominence in the HARLEM RENAISSANCE. Mary Bethune was a great educator and civil rights leader. Angela Davis is a political activist and university professor who was both controversial and prominent during the CIVIL RIGHTS MOVEMENT. Annie Mae Perry, who died in 2000, was a beloved and legendary civil rights figure. Zenobia was a third-century queen who may have been a descendant of the Egyptian queen Cleopatra. Called a "warrior queen," she led her people in a fight against the atrocities of ancient Rome. This record of indomitable black women, and the repetition of the phrase "for I shall not be moved," reinforces through rhythm and language Angelou's message of endurance and resistance to defeat.

CRITICAL COMMENTARY

As a writer, Angelou has often commented about improving black women's self-esteem. In an interview published in *Black Women Writers at Work* (1983), Angelou states: "Image making is very important for every human being. It is especially important for black American women in that we are, by being black, a minority in the United States, and by being female, the less powerful of the genders. . . . If we look out of our eyes at the immediate world around us, we see whites and males in dominant roles. We need to see our mothers, aunts, our sisters, and grandmothers" (quoted in Tate 1983, 1). By holding up these strong women to her readers, Angelou is saying that all black women can stand fast with dignity and make a good life for themselves and their descendants.

Angelou's poems are largely autobiographical, and both her prose and poetry are enriched with figurative language, imagery, repetition, and often subtle irony. Her intention is to be a catalyst for deep understanding of the pain her people have endured, particularly women. Angelou's poetry has been criticized by academics for its didactic and supposedly shrill, strident tone. Angelou's response to this sort of literary criticism has been to simply continue writing. She is viewed as a "grassroots" poet rather than a scholarly or "ivory tower" poet, but her voice, through both prose and poetry, has awakened countless readers to a more sensitive consciousness of history's realities.

Her poems often have a depth that can be explored by peeling back the stanzas, like the layers of time. This exposes not only multiple decades of struggle but also demonstrates that by steady resistance and a knowledge that one's choices are right, hardships can be borne with dignity.

Angelou's personal experiences and strength are reflected in the rich power of her words. In "Our Grandmothers," she takes us on a sensory journey into the reality of the struggle during slave times where, through imagery and repetition, we feel, taste, smell, hear, and see fear and oppression met firmly by grit and tenacity. Angelou has stated: "All my work is meant to say, 'you may encounter many defeats, but you must not be defeated'" (quoted in Kirkpatrick 2004, 44).

FURTHER READING

Angelou, Maya. *The Complete Collected Poems of Maya Angelou.* New York: Random House, 1994.

Kirkpatrick, Patricia. *Maya Angelou.* Mankato, Minn.: Creative Education/The Creative Company, 2004.

Tate, Claudia, ed. *Black Women Writers at Work.* New York: Continuum International, 1983.

"Passing Time"

The poem "Passing Time" is included in Part Two of Angelou's collection *Oh Pray My Wings Are Gonna Fit Me Well* (1975). It is a poetic commentary on the possibility of beginnings and endings.

SYNOPSIS

In this free-verse poem of just six lines, the narrator is considering changes that can take place over time. The title is revealing. "Passing" in the African-American culture suggests passing for a white person rather than an African American if one has skin color and features that appear to be Caucasian. Addressing skin and its hue, the first lines mention "like dawn" and "like dusk." "One," the narrator says, indicates the beginning of the end. The other, or "dusk," points to the opposite, the end of a beginning.

CRITICAL COMMENTARY

This poem is somewhat like an ambiguous, unresolved riddle. "Dawn" represents a beginning, or a source of something. The Greek goddess of the dawn and sunrise is Eos; in Roman mythology, she is named Aurora. She rises from the eastern horizon, seemingly from the ocean, and brings morning light. It usually refers to the beginning of a new day, and in the epic *The Odyssey*, thought to have been written by the blind bard Homer, translations from the Greek text often use the metaphor of rosy fingers to describe the soft pink light of early morning: "Now when the Dawn showed again with her rosy fingers," (Homer 1967, 39). In *A Journey through Greek Mythology* (2008), Monica Cyrino notes: "In Greek mythology, Eos is a very promiscuous and erotic goddess, and there are many tales of how she seduces her lovers first thing in the morning" (82–83).

"Dusk," on the other hand, is most commonly used in reference to the end of a day. It is the overture to nightfall and sometimes gloomy and foreboding.

In this poem, the light of dawn is used metaphorically as the beginning of something that will certainly end, contrasting with dusk as the end of the beginning. This imagery could be a metaphor for many things. It could be a literal representation of a typical day, and yet poetry often holds different meanings for different readers. Is it an affair? In this little poem, the title is "Passing Time." Does that mean time for "passing," or simply that time goes by? The topics in the first line are light, dark, and skin. It may be about feelings, or again, it may be that the narrator is suggesting that light skin will become darker, and that dark skin will become lighter in humans over time by combining the genetics of different racial groups. Is the poem pointing to a future when lighter skin will overwhelm the darker? If so, will a culture be lost when skin markers are eliminated and light-skinned people perhaps deny their own African heritage and choose to pass as whites? Will there be a day when all skin colors and shades will be blended together? We can only wonder about the genetic direction of the human family. These are serious cultural considerations to be examined as the African-American people of the United States heal from centuries of abuse. The responsibility is to emerge as fully respected participants in American democracy, but the ancient and authentic cultures of Africa must also be preserved.

Angelou has done all she can to try to lift her people and help them, individually, feel more pride in being who they are. Jeffrey M. Elliot, the editor of *Conversations with Maya Angelou* (1989), writes: "In the long tradition of her ancestors, she has spent a lifetime fighting against defeat and denigration, against the dying of the light that is life itself" (ix).

FURTHER READING

Angelou, Maya. *The Complete Collected Poems of Maya Angelou.* New York: Random House, 1994.

Cyrino, Monica. *A Journey through Greek Mythology.* Dubuque, Iowa: Kendall Hunt, 2008.

Elliot, Jeffrey M., ed. *Conversations with Maya Angelou.* Jackson and London: University Press of Mississippi, 1989.

Homer. *The Odyssey of Homer.* Translated by Richard Lattimore. New York: Harper & Row, 1967.

"Phenomenal Woman"

This hymnlike poem honors women's beauty and expresses the dynamic force of a woman strong with inner pride, individuality, and personal glory. The poem first appeared in *Cosmopolitan* in 1978, by which time Angelou had become a recognized writer and performer. It is considered one of the finest poems in her 1978 collection *And Still I Rise,* and it was also featured in the film *Poetic Justice* (1993), produced by John Singleton. When Angelou presents "Phenomenal Woman" to an audience, she presents it with vigor and passion, and the poem's powerful imagery seems to reflect the poet herself. Her dramatic passion and unwavering, coaxing voice has regularly made this poem a peak moment, one of the most memorable, in her deeply moving public performances.

SYNOPSIS

The poem begins with an intriguing and inviting line: "Pretty women wonder where my secret lies." It follows with descriptions of the elusive endowments that create this particular phenomenal woman. Is it in her striking physical presence—more than "a fashion model's size?" Is it the "inner mystery" that seems to draw men's admiration? Is it the proud way she carries herself? Is attractiveness found in her subdued ways such as the grace of her style, a quiet voice, a confident posture, and the "not bowed" way she holds her head?

Descriptions of these powerful attributes are portrayed in the poem's four stanzas, but as it repeats at the end of each refrain, the secret lies in the simple fact that she is a woman, a "Phenomenal Woman." The poem's streetwise hip language ("fire in my eyes," "flash of my teeth," "swing in my waist," and "joy in my feet") provides a free and easy rhythm to the lyrics, and the poem triumphantly celebrates the black woman's physical beauty and power.

CRITICAL COMMENTARY

The descriptive title of this poem suggests synonyms like *extraordinary, unique, remarkable,* and *amazing,* and at the time it was written, the contributions Angelou had made to American society and culture were widely recognized. Whether the poem was meant to describe her sagacious personality and imposing height of more than six feet is not determined in the work, but the powerful rhythms and repetitions present qualities that invite attention to the both the inner and outer beauty of African-American women and, interpreted more broadly, of all confident women.

The poem implies dignity, but at the same time, it has a confronting tone. The last stanza includes the sentence: "When you see me passing, / It ought to make you proud." The message of the poem reflects the pride that black women have earned—that is, the understanding that self-empowerment has been attained by believing in one's own worth. After centuries of oppression and abuse, today's black women may openly celebrate their worth and nobility of manner. In simple, easy-to-understand words, irregular rhymes, and short, terse lines, Angelou has asserted black female pride. She writes in the black oral tradition, frequently gaining power in her poetry through the economy of sharp, monosyllabic words such as *span, curl, flash,* and *bow,* and these simple words drive home the intensity of the phenomenal woman that Angelou, a WOMANIST, has become.

FURTHER READING

Angelou, Maya. *The Complete Collected Poems of Maya Angelou.* New York: Random House, 1994.

"Poor Girl"

This poem was published in the collection *Oh Pray My Wings Are Gonna Fit Me Well* (1975). It is the fourth poem in Part Two, and the subject matter is the loss of a boyfriend to another girl.

SYNOPSIS

The title, "Poor Girl," does not refer to the narrator but, rather, to the girl who has captured the affection of the narrator's boyfriend. The narrator would like to warn this second girl, but "If I try to tell her / what I know / She'll misunderstand / and make me go." The repeated "Poor Girl just like me" at the end of each stanza reflects the empathy the first girlfriend has for the second, and it reflects that the narrator understands the boyfriend's fickle ways: "You're going to leave her too / and I know it." The narrator, was abandoned for the second girlfriend, but the second will be abandoned for another, and "Then she'll begin / to sing this song."

CRITICAL COMMENTARY

"Poor Girl" is in the same style as many of Angelou's lost-love poems. Emotional, heavy with sorrow and loss, these poems carefully reflect a wide range of feelings concerning male/female relationships that did not work out, the fate of many young people during the adolescent process. Feelings are sensitive, and hormones are strong—a frustrating combination—and there is often a repetition of deep hurt during those years. In ROMEO AND JULIET, in act 2, scene 2, lines 33–36, Juliet speaks of the feud between their families, but she expresses her sworn love and the deep hope for his love in return with these famous lines:

> Oh Romeo, Romeo! Wherefore art thou Romeo?
> Deny thy father and refuse thy name;
> Or if thou wilt not, be but sworn my love,
> And I'll no longer be a Capulet.
>
> (in Asimov, 487)

Angelou was a devoted reader of the plays and sonnets of WILLIAM SHAKESPEARE, and she has said that the great English bard was her first love. Shakespeare's well-known play *Romeo and Juliet* expresses some of the deep yearning and love that can envelop an adolescent heart. Angelou understands that passion and has kept her own idealistic and romantic notions of love throughout her life. Because of this, she is able to express the themes of deep passion and thwarted love, which dominate so much of her life and poetry. All too often, the "Poor Girl just like me" was Angelou herself.

FURTHER READING

Angelou, Maya. *The Complete Collected Poems of Maya Angelou.* New York: Random House, 1994.

Asimov, Isaac. *Asimov's Guide to Shakespeare.* New York: Avenel Books, 1978.

"Preacher, Don't Send Me"

"Preacher, Don't Send Me" was published in *I Shall Not Be Moved* (1990).

SYNOPSIS

In this poem, the narrator is pleading with a man of God not to send her to a heaven where life would be the same misery as on earth. She describes rats large enough to eat leopard-sized cats, and Sunday brunches of grits (usually coarsely ground cornmeal served as a porridge) and tripe (part of the stomach of a cud-chewing animal), and she begs that heaven will not be full of those things. She has seen huge rats and eaten mountains of grits, and she begs for "a different creed"—something better, something fine. "Streets of gold / and milk for free" do not interest her either. There is no need for gold in paradise, and she has not drunk milk since she was a little girl. What she needs and pleads for is a place where families are true to one another, and even strangers are pleasant. There would be JAZZ music, and it would be beautiful, like autumn, all the time. If it cannot be that way, she says, "Promise me that / or nothing at all."

CRITICAL COMMENTARY

This poem is written from the viewpoint of someone who is determined to have something better than life as it is known to too many who suffer genuine poverty. Human beings need hope to survive, and for many, the only hope they seem to have is the promise of a better afterlife. The Bible contains promises of streets paved with gold and flowing milk and honey, but that is not what this narrator wants or needs. How long, the narrator wonders, can I live with filth, rats, subsistence food, and suffering? There are still ghettos throughout the world, including the United States, where people live even more poorly than described in this short poem, where babies die and parents stand by helplessly and watch. Angelou hopes for a better future for her people, not just in the afterlife, but now. By warning the preacher that heaven must be better than this life, she asserts that this life can be improved as well.

FURTHER READING

Angelou, Maya. *The Complete Collected Poems of Maya Angelou.* New York: Random House, 1994.

"Prescience"

"Prescience" is included in Angelou's collection *Shaker, Why Don't You Sing?* (1983).

SYNOPSIS

Prescience means to know something beforehand, and in this poem of lost love, the narrator expresses her discoveries of how lonely heartbreak can be when a relationship, however promising, does not work out successfully. It begins with her saying she did not know that the heart breaks slowly, that it slowly dissolves. She did not know that her broken heart would be so visible to "dressed-up / dining rooms of strangers." Nor did she know that solitude would "stifle the breath, loosen the joint," and leave one physically uncomfortable. She has been wound around with "cicatrix," a scar, but no matter how her grief unfolds, she will still love him from a distance. Had she known the grief she would feel, she would have left him for the "delectation" (enjoyment) of those "who / wanted more and cared less."

CRITICAL COMMENTARY

Mary Silva Cosgrave, in a review of the collection in which "Prescience" appears, suggests that this poem "brings to mind Robert Burns's 18th-century love song of parting" (18). She is referring to one of Burns's most famous poems, "Ae Fond Kiss, And Then We Sever," which suggests that "Had we never met—or never parted, / We had ne'er been broken-hearted." His "love song of parting" was written in honor of the Edinburgh actress Agnes (Nancy) McLehose, with whom he had a close, platonic relationship. They were both married, but they corresponded under the names of Sylvander and Clarinda; the letters are known as the Clarinda Letters. Their marriages survived the friendship, but their parting was painful and emotional. "Deep in heart-wrung tears I'll pledge thee" (Burns, 175), the poem declares toward the end, and their correspondence ceased.

As Cosgrave suggests, Angelou's poem does present the same sort of anguish. She states that had she known the relationship would end in such heartbreak, she would only have loved him from a distance. Perhaps he was married and kept that from her. She would have left him to the others who "wanted more and cared less," which seems to express the essence of the parting. Experience cannot be forgotten or wished away, and though in retrospect Angelou would like to be able to erase many of her life experiences, her memories serve to keep mistakes and regrets as well as triumphs and victories alive as well-learned lessons. That is how humans learn and progress toward wisdom.

FURTHER READING

Angelou, Maya. *The Complete Collected Poems of Maya Angelou.* New York: Random House, 1994.

———. *Wouldn't Take Nothing for My Journey Now.* New York: Random House, 1993.

Burns, Robert. *Burns: Poems.* Everyman's Library Pocket Poets, edited by Gerard Carruthers. New York: Borzoi/Alfred A. Knopf, 2007.

Cosgrave, Mary Silva. Review of *Shaker, Why Don't You Sing?* by Maya Angelou. *Horn Book Magazine* 59, no. 3 (June 1983): 336.

"Prisoner"

The poem "Prisoner" is found in Part Five of Angelou's collection *Oh Pray My Wings Are Gonna Fit Me Well* (1975).

SYNOPSIS

This poem has six stanzas and a predictable rhythm; it is almost musical, and when read aloud, it has the sound of a work song. The use of consonance and sibilance ("sunlight dares") create a hard sound that supports the rhythm and message. Words like *bars, keys,* and *blood-dried guns* evoke images of violence and death. The word *clang* is used onomatopoeically, sounding hard and psychologically penetrating. The repetitive stanza "It's jail

/ and bail / then rails to run" makes the rhythm work. The narrator seeks release and hopes that if someone will post bail, they will be able to escape on the railroad to a freer place. The first line speaks of sunlight that "dares / and trembles through / my bars," and the reader is reminded that the sun warms everyone as it can, no matter where they are. Even the strict guards are privy to the pale sun, which "stumbles / through the poles of / iron" and falls upon them in their work along the prison's inner hallways.

CRITICAL COMMENTARY

Angelou's sparse style does not please every literary critic. Lyman B. Hagen writes: "These negative reviewers have failed to look beyond the apparent simplistic lines to discover the power of the message. Angelou tries to reach readers not attuned to soaring poetics but comfortable with sparse exchanges" (122). Prison life is sparse by design. It is a harsh place with few privileges that has been designed for people who disregard social boundaries. Now and then, someone is placed behind bars in error, but in the scheme of things, that does not happen very often. The people in prison have their freedom revoked for a period of time, or for a lifetime, because they refused to live by the laws and mores of society. They are a menace both to themselves and others.

The literary critic Lynn Z. Bloom states that Angelou's "superficial look at 'Prisoners' show them predictably experiencing 'the horror / of gray guard men'"—"its jail / and bail / then rails to run'" (21, 22). Angelou understands the harshness and isolation prisoners feel. She knew many individuals who had served time more for misunderstandings than for committing a crime (MALCOLM X, MARTIN LUTHER KING, JR., and other civil rights leaders). The prisoners she is presenting in the poem are less likely to be leaders than they are to be lawbreakers. They want freedom, they want someone to post bail, and they will run as far away as they can as quickly as they can by hopping trains. There are many metaphors that can be discerned in this poem concerning being caged in any circumstance. One also wonders about the guards, who, in a sense, are also incarcerated for much of their lives.

FURTHER READING

Angelou, Maya. *The Complete Collected Poems of Maya Angelou.* New York: Random House, 1994.

Bloom, Lynn Z. "Maya Angelou." In *Dictionary of Literary Biography,* vol. 38. Detroit: Gale, 1985, 10–11.

Hagen, Lyman B. *Heart of a Woman, Mind of a Writer, and Soul of a Poet: A Critical Analysis of the Writings of Maya Angelou.* Lanham, Md.: University Press of America, 1997.

"Pusher, The"

"The Pusher" is included in Part Four of Angelou's collection *Oh Pray My Wings Are Gonna Fit Me Well* (1975).

SYNOPSIS

This poem has seven stanzas and 60 lines. Using a style of street talk and black folk vernacular, this rhythmic poem is a play on black pride. It begins, "He bad," and as "bad" is used in black vernacular, that means he is good—very good. *Honky,* a slang word for white, and "honkey/poot," added to that means that the "bad" black frightens the white. The second stanza mentions that "His Afro crown raises / eyes." He is envied, and he takes care of his natural hairstyle when he is on the street. The third stanza tells us that he is wearing a dashiki, an African-style pattern. It may be a batik ("Wax-printed on his skin"), or it may be a tattoo, but again, it is worn to demonstrate pride in his African roots.

The reader is told that he has bought a paper of MALCOLM X's, probably Malcolm's biography, and then continues to explain that he has looked at the photographs, read a little of it, and is proud that he is himself. The last lines of the fifth stanza reveal proudly that he has a "fro" (Afro), is displaying the dashiki, and has the Malcolm X book. Next, he is standing near the Martin Luther King library, well-supplied with drugs ("stashed") and declaring that it is black nation time. In his hand, he has coke (cocaine), "A kill of horse," drugs that will a take a user into an "eternal night's barbiturates" nightmare. He also has "Speed" to sell. There is a mention of "Breathing / slaughter on the Malcolm X / Institute," and that may mean that he is selling a lot to blacks, particularly black youths. In the end, he peddles a deathlike existence, the poem says, without the release of death.

CRITICAL COMMENTARY

"The pusher is a typical Angelou acceleration" (Anonymous 1975, 279). Though similar to some of her other poems in using repetition, metaphor, and a rhythmic beat, this free-verse poem carries a message of tragic proportion. This is a narrative about a pusher, a character who has made himself attractive to those young African Americans and whites he wants to entice with drugs. The reality is that he peddles a dead-end, deathlike future. Angelou has again written a warning. It is engaging and, in a way, entertaining because of its irony. That "He bad" means "he good" in African-American street talk is understood, but the literal truth is that he is smart enough to be genuinely evil. He is really bad and filled with rage.

When Maya Angelou was a young mother, she used marijuana for her nerves now and then. A man who cared about her took her to a dirty, run-down building inhabited by several unkempt, down-on-their-heels drug users. He then shot heroin into his own arm in front of her to help her understand the consequences of illegal drug addiction. His method of teaching, though shocking, convinced her never to use mind-altering drugs again.

FURTHER READING

Angelou, Maya. *The Complete Collected Poems of Maya Angelou.* New York: Random House, 1994.

Anonymous Review. *Booklist* 72, no. 4 (October 1975): 279.

"Recovery"

"Recovery" is a short poem in the collection *Shaker, Why Don't You Sing?* (1983). Beneath the title, it says "For Dugald." It is a poem about recovery after the loss of someone loved.

SYNOPSIS

This poem has two stanzas, but they do not all rhyme. The last words of each stanza—*flight* and *light,* two words that represent the recovery process the narrator describes—are telling in that they comprise the poem's salient points. "A lost love," the narrator says in the first stanza, forbids "further flight." But recovery has come, and the narrator will speed "toward the light."

CRITICAL COMMENTARY

Angelou takes her poetry from personal experience, hers and others. Here, in eight short lines, she expresses that even after losing a love, or loved one, it is natural to think that the finality of it cannot be accepted or overcome. However, recovery does come, and life moves forward. Though there is no note or explanation of the dedication "For Dugald," it can be assumed that it was someone whom Angelou regarded with affection.

FURTHER READING

Angelou, Maya. *The Complete Collected Poems of Maya Angelou.* New York: Random House, 1994.

"Remembering"

"Remembering" was published in Part One of Angelou's first volume of poetry, *Just Give Me a Cool Drink of Water 'fore I Diiie* (1971).

SYNOPSIS

In just two stanzas, using metaphor and imagery, the narrator conveys her denial of hints that came earlier, whispering that her romance was hopeless. "Soft grey ghosts crawl up my sleeve," she writes, and she lies to herself about what they mean. The second stanza acknowledges that what was is now just a "ritual on my lips," and her soul is wrapped in hopelessness.

CRITICAL COMMENTARY

There are 38 poems in *Just Give Me a Cool Drink of Water 'fore I Diiie,* and many of them are brief narratives about the joy and sorrow of love. Many of the poems in this volume were also published as songs by the Hirt Music Company. Selecting her words and rhythm with care, Angelou speaks gracefully of even the most heartbreaking memories.

FURTHER READING

Angelou, Maya. *The Complete Collected Poems of Maya Angelou.* New York: Random House, 1994.

"Riot: 60's"

"Riot: 60's" was published in Maya Angelou's first published collection, *Just Give Me a Cool Drink of Water 'fore I Diiie* (1971). The poem, which appears on Part Two, is an examination of the violent African-American rage during the 1965 WATTS riots in south-central LOS ANGELES.

SYNOPSIS

During the infamous riots in Watts, 34 people were killed, more than 1,000 were injured, and nearly 4,000 were arrested. It began with the routine arrest of a suspected intoxicated driver and ended after nearly a week of furious violence and destruction. Each of the six stanzas of this free-verse poem describes a different aspect of the violence; each may also represent the six days of the conflagration.

As "Riot: 60's" opens, flames are destroying a pawnshop and eating trays of zircon rings. The next stanza takes the reader into the community homes, where "Easter clothes and stolen furs / burned in the attic," and radios and televisions were crackling with static from "racial outlets." When a "leopard-print sofa with gold legs" burst into flames at the "Friendly Finance Furniture Co.," as described in the third stanza, the mass of people outside watching the fire seemed to admire the flames and felt it was appropriate that the absentee landlord had lost his shop. The fourth stanza hints that Watts lit the way for other city riots to follow—"Detroit, Newark and New York"—and all were places where people felt their lives were controlled by policemen and welfare workers. Watts swarmed with police cars, reporters, and photographers taking pictures for the world to see. The atmosphere was violent and crude, and there were National Guardsmen trying, but largely failing, to protect businesses and homes from looting. The youth of Watts resented the presence of shiny new police cars and overturned and burned as many as they could. As noted above, many arrests were made, but in retrospect to many observers—including Angelou, who entered the area twice to observe the violence—the whole scene had a surreal atmosphere to it. A supermarket burned, and confused people ran every which way.

CRITICAL COMMENTARY

Maya Angelou had been working in the Watts neighborhood as a door-to-door survey taker just prior to the riots. She had noted that the whole area was less well-kept than she had known it to be in earlier years, and she had also noted men lounging about, apparently unemployed, and the presence of youths wandering around unsupervised. She learned that many women worked outside the Watts neighborhood as domestics, and they often bought their groceries near their places of employment because they were less expensive than in the neighborhood. It was obviously a seriously depressed area—nearly hopeless. So when a combination of events came together and the fights began between the police and street kids, anger poured forth, and it developed into a battle zone.

In 1964, Congress passed the Civil Rights Act, and it seemed that the efforts for improved race relations had been successful. However, California attempted to circumvent the new law by passing Proposition 14, which blocked parts of the act, particularly the fair housing stipulations. African Americans felt trapped in the ghettos, where many had been forced to live because of unemployment. During the riots, when the black comedian Dick Gregory tried to calm the crowds, he was shot in the leg. Community leaders from the Hollywood industry and general community of Los Angeles tried to help after the riots were over. Some improvements were made by outsiders who cared about the welfare of the people in Watts, but it was really too little, too late. Good nursery schools were established to enable the women to leave their young children in safe care, food markets with fairer prices were established, and many businesses reopened, but the area has continued to be economically depressed.

FURTHER READING

Angelou, Maya. *The Complete Collected Poems of Maya Angelou.* New York: Random House, 1994.

"Sepia Fashion Show"

"Sepia Fashion Show" was published in Part Two of Angelou's first volume of poems, *Just Give Me a Cool Drink of Water 'fore I Diiie* (1971), which was nominated for the Pulitzer Prize.

SYNOPSIS

This poem begins with an image of bone-thin, vain runway models strutting, "backed and butted." They work for the fashion industry and display clothes to entice buyers. In doing this work, the models themselves become shallow and affected. The female narrator assures herself and her readers that she cannot be sold a thing they are parading: "I'd see 'em in hell, before they's sell / me one thing they're wearing, clothes-wise."

In the third stanza, the speaker calls the models "The Black Bourgeois." The noun *bourgeois* means middle class, and it usually implies a smug or unoriginality attitude, perhaps even putting on a false front of material prosperity that is not genuine. The models are affected or pretending to be something they really are not. The narrator mentions that they say "yah" when they really mean "yeah," and their "preening" is also mentioned.

The fourth stanza drives home the point Angelou is trying to make in this poem: For all their strutting and posing, the reality is that the models earn their real living scrubbing "at Miss Ann's."

CRITICAL COMMENTARY

This poem is written in a female voice that negates what it is ironically praising. The first two lines—"Their hair, pomaded, faces jaded / bones protruding"—give the image of glamorous models, when in truth, the narrator is not complimentary. The word some critics had used to describe this concept is *litotes,* which means that a thing is praised by stating the negative of its opposite. So, where the narrator says, "They'd nasty manners, held like banners," she is saying one thing and meaning another, a form of irony. The speaker is expressing her views on the models who parade clothing on their bony figures, but she perceives them to be vain, mechanical creatures who are hypocritical about their origins. SIDDITY is a word sometimes used in African-American vernacular to describe someone putting on airs. In this poem, the narrator reminds them of their occupations and social status when she states: "Look at those knees, / you got at Miss Ann's scrubbing."

This poetic narrative suggests a false sense of place and social status sometimes dictated by society to denote who is who. In the early part of the 19th century, when the Industrial Revolution was beginning, there were many mills in Lowell, Massachusetts, where wool and cotton were spun into thread and then made into fabrics. Young, white rural women worked long hours in the mills and began to earn enough money to dress nicely, buy watches and jewelry, take classes, and give themselves advantages they did not have in their isolated country villages. In fact, many earned enough money to take care of themselves, and most sent money home to their families.

Mrs. Sarah Hale, a writer and editor in the early 19th century, wrote an article that was published in *Godey's Lady's Book* that stated (in part), "The time was when the *lady* could be distinguished from the *no-lady* by her dress, as far as the eye could reach; but now you might stand in the same room, and judging by their outward appearance, you could not tell which was which" (quoted in Eisler 1977, 184). Even gold watches are now no *sure* indication—for they have been worn by the lowest, even by "many of the factory girls" (184).

Angelou's poem castigates the girls who model and enjoy the materialistic world they find themselves in because, as she wisely views life, there are issues far more important. There is no justification in self-delusion, and that is a fault that she seems to have avoided; that is, she has always tried to dress herself well, but she has also tried to present herself honestly. Many people do not seem to practice modesty in self-presentation. In a sense, the young women in both of these cultures are playing; but for their own sake, Angelou recognizes that the models must take care not to interpret the attention, praise, and money they receive for their beauty as reason to perceive themselves as superior to other folks.

FURTHER READING

Angelou, Maya. *The Complete Collected Poems of Maya Angelou.* New York: Random House, 1994.

Eisler, Benita, ed. *The Lowell Offering: Writings by New England Mill Women (1840–1845).* New York: Harper Torchbooks/Harper & Row, 1977.

"Shaker, Why Don't You Sing?"

This poem, of the same name as the 1983 volume in which it was published, is a love lament.

SYNOPSIS

Two stanzas make use of beautiful music and worship-related words. The narrator cannot sing because of melancholy, yet she seems to frame her sadness in memories of deep, holy sounds. She is alone, and she can only reflect on the beauty of a relationship that is over. She speaks of rhythm, and "your breath moaning / a canticle [hymn, song, or chant] in my hair." She speaks also of an "unaccompanied procession" where "chanteys [a rhythmic work song sung by seamen] hummed my life alive." She is unhappy and asks, "Shaker, why don't you sing?"

The sounds outside her room—"street cries / and the triumph / of amorous insects"—remove her inward focus briefly, but she cannot be distracted. She speaks of "the anthem of your hands," "perfect harmonies which are your lips," and a "syncopated promise," but her reveries still leave her alone, and the last line repeats, "Shaker, why don't you sing?"

CRITICAL COMMENTARY

In this poem, Angelou expresses permission for women to express their perspective of sensual enjoyment. The literary critic Yasmin Y. DeGout states that in this poem, Angelou

> liberates women from gendered constraints by centering upon women's sexual aegis in the depiction of women's desire, in the use of the women's bodies (and sexuality) as the "lens" through which to view sensual and erotic experience, in the depiction of the persona's imaginative (re)creation of sexual intimacy, and in the rendering of women's erotic pleasure. (124)

FURTHER READING

Angelou, Maya. *The Complete Collected Poems of Maya Angelou.* New York: Random House, 1994.

DeGout, Yasmin Y. "The Poetry of Maya Angelou: Liberation Ideology and Technique." In *Maya Angelou.* Bloom's Modern Critical Views, edited by Harold Bloom, 121–132. New York: Bloom's Literary Criticism, 2009.

"Song for the Old Ones"

"Song for the Old Ones" is found in Part Five of Angelou's collection *Oh Pray My Wings Are Gonna Fit Me Well* (1975). When asked in a 1975 interview by Walter Blum which was her favorite of all her poems, Angelou said that this was the one:

> It is so important. Because again we're back to the revolutionaries and love. A number of young blacks decided that Uncle Toms are to be laughed at and ridiculed, and I feel just the opposite. We often don't realize how those people who were scratching when they didn't itch, laughing when they weren't tickled, and saying, "Yassah, you sho' is right, I sho' is stupid," we don't know how many times their throats closed on them in pain. They did that so they could make a little money, so they could pay for somebody to go to school, to get some shoes. So that poem is for them. A lot of my work is for them, because I know they were successful, because if they hadn't been successful I wouldn't be here to talk about it. (quoted in Blum 1975, 45)

SYNOPSIS

This poem has seven stanzas, and in it, the narrator recounts many of her people's oppressive experiences. She addresses it to "My fathers," and in each stanza, she elaborates their suffering and their endurance. "My fathers," she wrote, "sit on benches," and their bodies are marked by the slats as they sit. In the second stanza, she suggests that they are "like broken candles / all waxed and burnt profound." They had endured, and they have learned to understand many things. Memories of their past flood her mind as she looks at them, and in reverie she sees material artifacts that were used to abuse them: the chains and slavery's coffles, "the whip and lash and stock." In the fourth stanza, she speaks of their survival by submission, and in the fifth, she alludes to "the lowly Uncle Tomming / and Aunt Jemima's smiles." In the sixth stanza, phrases like *shuffled, stepp'ed 'n' fetched,* and *blues with screams,* express their acquiescence to humiliation. To survive, they submitted. In the last stanza, she says they lived on the "edge of death" and "kept my race alive."

CRITICAL COMMENTARY

Angelou has profound respect and understanding for those who have suffered, and she knows that the oppression of the African Americans is only a part of the suffering of humankind. In this poem, recounting the travesties committed against them, she places concrete evidence of the weapons of torture in front of the reader. She is teaching, but she does so subtly in order to convey the means used to subdue and oppress her people. Still, in spite of tragic injuries to their bodies and insults to their spirits, African Americans survived with grace and faith. Their purpose, as Angelou writes, was to keep their race alive.

This is a rhythmic poem, and it has a rhyme scheme that creates a tempo as the poem is read aloud. Angelou's understanding of her ancestors' history is a theme in much of her poetry; it has been called liberation ideology by several critics. She never apologizes for her perspective because she writes powerfully, in a way that makes her truth evident. Much of the criticism levied at her work has been based in the perspective of academic literary critics. Her mostly free-verse style does not follow classical poetic parameters, but Angelou was not (and is not) writing her poetry for them. Rather, she is working hard to remove the blight many of her people have felt, in spite of the CIVIL RIGHTS MOVEMENT, and help them gain pride and self-respect in the choices their forerunners had made. She wants her people to measure their success in terms of legacies bequeathed to them, and in terms of what they can do with those legacies to create better lives for themselves. Her work is greatly respected by millions of readers, and many wait anxiously to read everything she creates: poems, essays, commentary, and other contributions.

FURTHER READING

Angelou, Maya. *The Complete Collected Poems of Maya Angelou.* New York: Random House, 1994.

Blum, Walter. "Listening to Maya Angelou." In *Conversations with Maya Angelou,* edited by Jeffrey M. Elliot, 38–46. Jackson and London: University Press of Mississippi, 1989.

"Son to Mother"

"Son to Mother" is included in Angelou's collection *I Shall Not Be Moved* (1990). It is a powerful expression of confidence and the willingness to defend oneself and one's mother against misjudgment, using not violence but only carefully chosen words.

SYNOPSIS

The poem begins with a clear declaration of the narrator's abhorrence concerning the mistreatment of Jews. He will have no part of it, no "melting Stars of David" for any reason. Neither will he send missionaries to lands beyond his "borders, / to plunder secrets / and barter souls." The third of these three stanzas states, "They / say you took my manhood, / Momma," but he knows she did not, and he will defend both himself and his mother against such an accusation, but he will do it with words. He asks his mother what she would like him to say, "before I annihilate / their ignorance."

CRITICAL COMMENTARY

Maya Angelou wrote this poem, not her son, and so it is unclear if this is a message from Guy to his mother; however, the message is clear. For some reason, the narrator's mother was accused of taking his manhood away. The word *manhood,* can be defined many ways from a variety of perspectives. It may have been an accusation in reference to an excellent education that set the son apart from less-educated neighborhood friends. It may give reference to dressing in a more sophisticated way than one's peers. It may be that the son is a poet rather than an athlete. Or it may mean that the son is religious and involved in a religion or charitable works. The son's action is the same in any case. He is benign and respectful of others' heritage and creeds. He understands that people have choice, and he also understands that he and his mother have that right as well. He has no plan to hurt anyone physically in his obvious passion about being misunderstood; rather, he plans to "annihilate their ignorance." He will explain, and he will teach the accusers what he feels they should know of his mother and him and of tolerance. He could make the choice to ignore them and let them keep their misinterpretations, but he chooses to clarify and, once and for all, get rid of their distorted understanding and perhaps hurtful accusations.

Angelou raised her only child, Guy (CLYDE BAILEY JOHNSON), alone. Though she was married twice during the years he was growing up, he did not have a sustained, fatherly role model. Angelou had many reliable male friends, most of whom were professionals, and they were there for her to consult with and to guide Guy as they could. Even without the supportive presence of a long-term role model for Guy, Angelou's devotion to his well-being is known through her autobiographies. She was a serious parent, and she tried to be there for him as he grew up. She saw to his educational needs and provided secure homes all along the way. He has said in interviews that she was an "awesome" parent. She was strong, and that was what he needed, but the time came when he had to leave her and be his own man, and she recognized and allowed that. They remain very close.

FURTHER READING

Angelou, Maya. *The Complete Collected Poems of Maya Angelou.* New York: Random House, 1994.

"Sounds Like Pearls"

"Sounds Like Pearls" is in Part One of Angelou's first published collection, *Just Give Me a Cool Drink of Water 'fore I Diiie* (1971).

SYNOPSIS

In this eight-line free-verse poem, the message is embedded in a simile. "Sounds / Like pearls" are words, smooth and unvarying, like carefully chosen and finely matched pearls. Gentle sounds whisper away "Doubt and fear," perhaps causing a blush as trust is secured.

CRITICAL COMMENTARY

This sensuous poem reveals an intimate moment between two lovers. He whispers smooth words of love, and she relaxes, trusts, and responds without fear.

FURTHER READING

Angelou, Maya. *The Complete Collected Poems of Maya Angelou.* New York: Random House, 1994.

"Starvation"

"Starvation" is included in Angelou's collection *Shaker, Why Don't You Sing* (1983). It is an ironic narrative, told in the voice of a starving mother.

SYNOPSIS

Taking on the persona and disguise of an eager bride, the narrator has invited starvation or death into her home. "Come through the keyhole," she suggests, as she is too weak to open the door. Never mind the rotting sashes at the windows, just come in. Her voice is inviting—inviting death to "Hurry! Hurry!" In the second stanza, she mentions the largest pot, which is shiny because it is not used anymore. Her purse is empty, as is both the bread bin and the cold oven. "Hurry up! Hurry down!" she coaxes again. In the final stanza, she reveals the "sour beast which / fills the bellies of my children," and says that she has received multiple eviction notices. "Come!" she begs. Death by starvation would relieve the misery she and her children are enduring.

CRITICAL COMMENTARY

In this great land called the United States, there are pockets of depressed communities where families starve. Unemployment, abandonment, lack of education, mental incapacity, and other life circumstances cause people to lose hope, withdraw into themselves, and starve. Those realities, compounded with the oppression that skin color can invite in too many situations, can leave mothers and children completely at the mercy of fate. Starvation happens, though it is a consequence rather than choice.

Angelou did survey work in the WATTS neighborhood of Los Angeles before she moved to New York City to write. She saw the depressed, neglected black neighborhoods prior to the devastating riots that took place there in 1965, and it is probable that scenarios like the one described in this poem were taking place in the very neighborhoods where she was doing her work. She also saw hardship in Africa when she lived there and was well aware that death by starvation was a reality. She seems sensitive to every kind of suffering that occurs in life, and in this poem she is conveying to her readers that there are people who face this kind of death. Reaching out, paying attention, helping, and serving others is what she hopes everyone will awaken to and do. Everyone has responsibilities to help others as they can.

FURTHER READING

Angelou, Maya. *The Complete Collected Poems of Maya Angelou.* New York: Random House, 1994.

"Still I Rise"

The collection entitled *And Still I Rise* was published in 1975, the same year as *Oh Pray My Wings are Gonna Fit Me Well.* "Still I Rise" is the title poem and first one in Part Three, also called "And Still I Rise." It is a poem about strength and self-empowerment, a defiant statement on behalf of African Americans.

SYNOPSIS

The poem begins with a challenge and continues throughout with powerful energy: "You may write me down in history / With your bitter, twisted lies . . . But still, like dust, I'll rise." The poem is defiant throughout, and it asks if this upsets you, the reader. It declares that shooting with words, cutting with eyes, and killing with hatefulness can happen, "But still, like air, I'll rise." Taunting, it continues and concludes its nine stanzas with: "I am the dream and the hope of the slave. / I rise / I rise / I rise."

CRITICAL COMMENTARY

The narrator of this poem is determined to rise above obstacles, RACISM, and defeat. No matter what anyone may do to hurt her or make her afraid, the narrator declares, confidently, "But still, [like dust or air], I'll rise." The literary critic Priscilla R. Ramsey, in her article "Transcendence: The Poetry of Maya Angelou," states that ". . . Stephen Henderson's *Understanding the New Black Poetry* . . . argue[s] that the 'I' of Black poetry is not a singular or individualistic referent but a symbol for the idea of a Black collective" (1999, 83). Using a collective voice and repetitive rhetorical questions, Angelou touches her audience and quickens their hope and confidence even at a time when the ordeal of verbal and physical abuse continues and equal rights seem far away and almost hopeless.

FURTHER READING

Angelou, Maya. *The Complete Collected Poems of Maya Angelou.* New York: Random House, 1994

Ramsey, Priscilla R. "Transcendence: The Poetry of Maya Angelou." In *Maya Angelou.* Modern Critical

Views, edited by Harold Bloom, 75–90. Philadelphia: Chelsea House, 1999.

"Take Time Out"

"Take Time Out" is in Part Five of *Oh Pray My Wings Are Gonna Fit Me Well,* published in 1975.

SYNOPSIS

With a choruslike repetition of "Take Time Out," the narrator in this poem is firmly reminding her readers to stop and try to understand each other and, further, to help people see they are in some kind of need. It is not an easy thing to do, and perhaps not even always a safe thing to do, but there are many people who simply need a kindness. In many of the examples Angelou gives in the poem, the ones in trouble are youths confused about their purpose in life and who they really are. In five stanzas, each describing a type that may need serious attention, the narrator tries to prick the consciousness of readers by reminding them of an assortment of people commonly seen on the streets of most cities.

The poem begins by saying, "When you see them / on a freeway hitching rides / wearing beads / with packs by their sides," perhaps you ought to think about what all this violence and jarring talk is about. Why is that person there? Does he have a home? Are her hopes dashed? That is followed by the line "Take Time Out." Perhaps it is time is to be reflective about how they got there. What can you do to help a down-and-out hitchhiker? In the second stanza, the narrator wonders about a fellow with a band around his head and an army surplus bunk for a bed. Again, the lines are asking what this is all about. In the next stanza, a barefoot girl in the rain is described, and soon the reader is also reminded about the confused ones on the street, "folks / who think tomorrow / is a place they / can call up / on the phone." Sons and daughters sharing dope stories are followed with a suggestion that their problem may have been brought about by whining, lying parents. So take time out to think about how these people got to this state of being and what an appropriate response might be.

CRITICAL COMMENTARY

In 1999, the scholar Elijah Anderson published *Code of the Street: Decency, Violence, and the Moral Life of the Inner City* (reprinted in 2000), a clear and revealing explanation of street behavior in some black neighborhoods. There is devastating crime in most large cities in the United States (and around the world), and Anderson's informed text reveals how these circumstances came about. He also shares stories about people who have climbed out of nearly hopeless backgrounds to become guides and leaders for the next generation.

Old Heads is a term used both derogatorily and positively in referring to older members of African-American culture. In Anderson's book, he has many entries under that title, and he explains that when African-American ghettos were less "rehabilitated" with INTEGRATION, there were "old heads" who would correct and chastise children and teens (and even older people) when they saw that their behavior was out of line (144–146). This is not as common as it once was because of the changing dynamic of urban living. Revitalization of old neighborhoods, different ethnic demographics, the rise in drug use, and other factors have changed the way the elders of the culture respond to trouble on the street. It is dangerous and sometimes futile to interfere with young people in this violent and often unreasonable climate. Respect for elders, once a commonplace in African-American culture, is no longer a certainty. Economic and political forces as well as RACISM have created urban decay.

Angelou's poem is a plea for people to "take time out" and pay attention to what is going on in neighborhoods like those Anderson describes. With understanding and patience, negative behavior can be recognized and changed.

FURTHER READING

Anderson, Elijah. *Code of the Street: Decency, Violence, and the Moral Life of the Inner City.* 1999. Reprint, New York: W. W. Norton, 2000.

Angelou, Maya. *The Complete Collected Poems of Maya Angelou.* New York: Random House, 1994.

"Tears"

"Tears" is included in Part One of Angelou's first collection of published poems, *Just Give Me a Cool Drink of Water 'fore I Diiie* (1971). This volume of poetry has two types of poems: those that depict romantic anguish and those that reflect oppression and black liberation ideology.

SYNOPSIS

This poem has only eight short lines. The title foreshadows the topic, and the words used to explain the cause of the tears are few, but even in their brevity, they create a somber mood. It begins, "Tears / The crystal rags," then the first stanza closes with "a worn-through soul." *Crystal rags* is a metaphor for profuse and transparent tears.

The second stanza begins with the word *Moans* representing the depth of sadness the narrator feels at the ending of her romance. It mentions a "swan song," a "Blue farewell," and a "dying dream," to create the poem's low-spirited mood.

CRITICAL COMMENTARY

Angelou reads widely, and though much of her poetry is written in black folk vernacular, much is written in standard English with literary allusions. In the second stanza of this poem, a "swan song" is mentioned. That phrase comes from an ancient mythological belief that the *Cygnus olor*, or mute swan, is unable to make sound until just before death, and then it is able to sing one beautiful melody. In spite of the demonstrable facts that the mute swan honks, grunts, hisses, and does not sing as it dies, this traditional belief persists. There are varied stories and poems recounting the lore.

The term has become a common theatrical expression to describe a final act or performance. In this poem, Angelou uses "swan song" to bid farewell to a dying dream. She had many romantic entanglements, but none ever developed into a lifetime companionship. Many of her poems reflect the pain and loneliness she has felt because of failed romance. Perhaps because of that, she has been able to focus on sharing so much of her talent with her readers. She has made a difference in the lives of many who wait for each new publication.

FURTHER READING

Angelou, Maya. *The Complete Collected Poems of Maya Angelou.* New York: Random House, 1994.

"Telephone, The"

"The Telephone" appears in Part One of Angelou's 1975 collection *Oh Pray My Wings Are Gonna Fit Me Well.* This poem is a reflection on an ordinary subject, the telephone.

SYNOPSIS

"The Telephone" is written in three stanzas and has an unrhymed, almost conversational style. It is a story about waiting for the telephone to ring. The first stanza describes the various colors phones may have and then goes on to express the instrument's power over her, "Sitting like a strict / and spinstered aunt," which implies a critical judgment.

The second stanza describes how the telephone, the vehicle for many conversations, "tats the day, crocheting / other people's lives / in neat arrangements, / ignoring me." The narrator wants it to ring, but it does not. She keeps busy and waits. The third stanza draws the poem to a close and, along with it, her longing. Another week, from Monday to "Sunday's dying," it has been silent.

CRITICAL COMMENTARY

Angelou's poetry is often reflective of her personal experience. Her everyday encounters, as with the telephone, are chosen with care, and she expresses a deep, familiar loneliness many people have. She is well aware that life is for living. In a 1977 interview, Judith Rich described Angelou as

> a handsome, statuesque woman in a shirt and long skirt, with a scarf on her head. She carries herself with grace, and is barefooted. Her voice is rich, melodious, deep. She chooses her words elegantly. Her feelings flicker always somewhere

close to the surface; her eyes brim with tears as she recalls someone dear, or she laughs her full, throaty joy. It's her capacity to transmit this warmth and humor, together with the inherent pain, through her work, that has made her a leading figure in writing and the performing arts. (77–78).

It is that "capacity to transmit this warmth and humor" that has captured the interest and loyalty of readers around the world. Her light verses are often universal and unbiased, simply reflecting the realities of ordinary life. Her empathy for the loneliness and despair of others is part of her talent. She chooses her words and the sounds they make very carefully. Using harsh consonants, she creates an environment that suits her topic. Crisp staccato sounds at the beginning of a word, repeated, have almost an onomatopoeic effect. This poem is particularly effective when read aloud.

FURTHER READING

Angelou, Maya. *The Complete Collected Poems of Maya Angelou.* New York: Random House, 1994.

Rich, Judith. "Westways Women: Life Is for Living." In *Conversations with Maya Angelou,* edited by Jeffrey M. Elliot, 77–85. Jackson and London: University Press of Mississippi, 1989.

"They Went Home"

This poem is found in Part One of Angelou's first poetry collection, *Just Give Me a Cool Drink of Water 'fore I Diiie* (1971). The critic John Alfred Avant has suggested that this is not one of the best in the collection, "but some readers are going to love it," and he suggests that it does "fit into the torchy unrequited love bag" (3,329), which was Angelou's intention.

SYNOPSIS

The most important line in this poem is "They went home." In 12 short, crisp lines, with simple rhyming, the narrator relates that many men came to her clean home and enjoyed her mysterious air, and they praised her smile, wit, and hips. But they would only spend a night or two and then, as expected, they would go home to their wives and lie, "that never once in all their lives, / had they known a girl like me."

CRITICAL COMMENTARY

This is really a short narrative, told from the perspective of a woman who feels she cannot win in a male-female relationship. A vulnerable, accommodating woman is described in just a few lines, and the reader immediately recognizes the loneliness she experiences over and over again. The men visit her, stay a while, and then go home to their wives. Perhaps it could be read both as the narrator's loneliness and as a warning.

FURTHER READING

Angelou, Maya. *The Complete Collected Poems of Maya Angelou.* New York: Random House, 1994.

Avant, John Alfred. Review of *Just Give Me a Cool Drink of Water 'fore I Diiie* by Maya Angelou. *Library Journal* 96 (1971): 3,329.

"Thirteens (Black), The"

This poem, and its contrasting poem, "The Thirteens (White)" appears in Part Two of Angelou's first published collection, *Just Give Me a Cool Drink of Water 'fore I Diiie* (1971).

SYNOPSIS

"The Thirteens (Black)" can be called a type of rap poem, and it is based on the insulting language of a traditional verbal exchange known as the "dozens." With rude, often clever street insults, the dozens is both a game and a can-you-top-this form of entertainment. An example might be: "Yo' Momma so ugly not even the Devil would take her on." Lyman B. Hagen writes that Angelou's "black 'Thirteens' lists the bitter realities of black street life in a manner that is matter-of-fact and accepting" (47).

The folklorist Roger Abrahams has studied the dozens by doing fieldwork in a Philadelphia ghetto. He writes:

> "Playing the Dozens" is one of the most interesting folkloristic phenomena found among contemporary Negroes, because in its operation it reflects so many of the cultural imperatives of the group from whom it is most often encountered, the lower-class Negro adolescent. . . . As sexual awareness grows, the vilification of the mother is changed to sexual matters, the contests become more heated and the insults more noteworthy. Many of them take the form of rhymes or puns, signaling the beginning of the bloom of verbal dexterity . . . (298, 300)

SYNOPSIS

The chantlike rhythm of this poem's three stanzas conveys the common behavior of luckless African Americans. Each stanza ends with the matter-of-fact statement, "The thirteens. Right on," as though shouting mothers, fathers gone to war, sisters prostituting themselves, and brothers drinking is just what many people do. Drugs, jail, and the gutter are a part of the chant. The last stanza expresses sorrow for the plight of many blacks and clearly regrets that there are not many alternatives. This behavior and the absurd stereotypes have to be accepted as part of the reality.

CRITICAL COMMENTARY

Playing the dozens is a substitute for physical violence. Roger Abrahams also speculates that "the adolescent boy would like to 'put down' his own mother . . . but he accomplishes this by putting down the mother of his opponent who he knows will in turn 'attack' the first speaker's mother" (1990, 295). However, this does not explain why females also play the dozens. It is speculation, but the term may have originated with the practice of selling old, damaged, or retarded black slaves by the dozen at slave auctions in past centuries in the United States.

The idioms used in black poetry serve as a counterpart to black power, which was in the forefront of American culture when this volume of poetry was published. Black poets like Angelou used their art to help heal blacks and create both understanding and pride. The goal was to help them overcome the political, economic, and social struggles they have been forced to face in the United States. "The Thirteens (Black)" stereotypes the black condition, but it also reveals the tragic outcomes that are all too frequent in oppressed cultures.

FURTHER READING

Abrahams, Roger. "Playing the Dozens." In *Mother Wit From the Laughing Barrel,* edited by Alan Dundes, 295–309. Jackson and London: University Press of Mississippi, 1990.

Angelou, Maya. *The Complete Collected Poems of Maya Angelou.* New York: Random House, 1994.

Hagen, Lyman B. *Heart of a Woman, Mind of a Writer, and Soul of a Poet.* Lanham, Md.: University Press of America, 1996.

"Thirteens (White), The"

This poem, and its contrasting poem, "The Thirteens (Black)" appears in Part Two of Angelou's first published collection, *Just Give Me a Cool Drink of Water 'fore I Diiie* (1971). "The Thirteens (White)" equally stereotypes whites and reveals the prejudice and generalities that many blacks feel toward them.

SYNOPSIS

The three stanzas, matching in rhythm and tempo "The Thirteens (Black)," suggest that whites, in their dominant and privileged position, are no better in morals and character than blacks. In the United States at the time *Just Give Me* was published, there were more choices for whites, but from common black perspectives, they had chosen to degrade themselves. The poem suggests that sexual immorality, exploiting servants, and other obscene behavior happen because "Your money thinks you're something." Each stanza ends with the line "The thirteens. Right On," in the same way as "The Thirteens (Black)," and those lines imply that the behavior is locked in and cannot (or will not) be changed.

CRITICAL COMMENTARY

These two poems, though stereotypical, reveal the prejudices and distrust both races seem to have for each other. The elements of behavior that both poems portray are common and generalized, and both racial differences and stereotypical thinking are clearly present. Angelou wanted people—all people—to come together. It has been written that she "has the unique ability to shatter the opaque prisms of race and class between reader and subject throughout her books of poetry and her autobiographies" (Wright State University). Based on the popularity of her work and the recognition and awards she has been given, that seems to be true. In revealing poems like "The Thirteens (Black)" and "The Thirteens (White)," the reader, no matter what his or her color, is taught about the assumptions that hurt both races.

FURTHER READING

Angelou, Maya. *The Complete Collected Poems of Maya Angelou.* New York: Random House, 1994.

Wright State University. "An Evening with Maya Angelou." Available online. URL: www.wright.edu/lecture/angelou.html. Accessed February 22, 2010.

"This Winter Day"

"This Winter Day" is the last poem in Part Five of *Oh Pray My Wings Are Gonna Fit Me Well,* published in 1975.

SYNOPSIS

"This Winter Day" transports the reader into a warm kitchen where soup is cooking with "white green and orange things" blending in it. The fragrance triggers saliva, "slipping in the liquid of its drip." The rainy day is blocked out by the eagerly awaited soup.

CRITICAL COMMENTARY

Behind closed doors, in the peace and safety of her warm kitchen, Angelou loves to cook, and she enjoys good food. This is a colorful, comfortable poem whose little vignette contrasts with "Chicken-Licken," in which a woman pulls the chain across the door and lets herself die. In "This Winter Day," one social woman reaches out to others to share the aromas of her kitchen. In Angelou's kitchen on a winter day, all that is lacking is a friend with whom to share her meal. She has many, but then she is also able to enjoy a pleasant solitude.

FURTHER READING

Angelou, Maya. *The Complete Collected Poems of Maya Angelou.* New York: Random House, 1994.

"Through the Inner City to the Suburbs"

"Through the Inner City to the Suburbs" was published in Angelou's *And Still I Rise* (1975), where it appears in Part Two.

SYNOPSIS

The narrative of this poem takes the reader through the decay and slums of a city ghetto and observes details of life there from the sooted window of a train. Grinning, smiling, sassy black people live and play near the tracks, and the narrator mentions "watermelon seeds on / A summer street." At night, the people seen from the train window dance and enjoy the hot summer evening, sweating, undulating, and enjoying the closeness and safety of the familiar.

From the window of the train, the white observers reflect on what they think they know of black life. They talk about what interests them, and they reduce the black people's needs down to a few elements. They are entertained ("delectation") and feel that somehow they understand the people they are observing. They might even say, "I had a colored Mammy . . . ," and they may think that gives them an insight or connection. And on the train goes, "bound for green lawns, / Double garages and sullen women," leaving the black figures still dancing and still "grinning / Still / Grinning."

CRITICAL COMMENTARY

Angelou uses many black stereotypes in describing the white commuters' view from train windows. She mentions the grinning faces, watermelon, "Dusky undulations," and dancing. These elements have been used over and over again to simplify a whole culture and reduce it to empty-headed foolishness. This marginalization alleviates any guilt felt for exclusion and abuse. The reality is that blacks and whites are, overall, both very smart; the great difference has to do with goals. Seen simplistically, the whites want overall economic superiority, while the blacks (though they would not refuse money) want to survive with the hope that at some point justice might be served and their reward will be equality.

Taking a brief look at the stereotypes mentioned above may provide further understanding. The first, which is mentioned several times in the poem, is grinning. Of course, black people, like any people, are happy sometimes, but there is more to that image than a simple happy face. For fear of reprisals, early American blacks learned to pretend they were happy and content. Slave masters feared uprisings but understood that there was never a time that slavery was really accepted by the black people. Intelligent, the blacks knew full well that they were being unjustly dominated, and they had to learn behavior that would allow them to survive.

Angelou also mentions "Watermelon seeds on / A summer street." Keith M. Woods, from the Poynter Institute (St. Petersburg, Florida) writes:

> Since the earliest days of plantation slavery, the caricature of the dark-skinned black child, his too-red lips stretched to grotesque extremes as they opened to chomp down on watermelon, was a staple of racism's diet. Over time, the watermelon became a symbol of the broader denigration of black people. It became part of the image perpetuated by a white culture bent upon bolstering the myth of superiority by depicting the inferior race as lazy, simple-minded pickaninnies interested only in such mindless pleasures as a slice of sweet watermelon. Like all racial and ethnic stereotypes, this one's destructive properties have, through the decades, stretched far beyond mere insult. It has helped poison self-esteem, pushing some people to avoid doing anything that seemed too "black," lest they be lumped into the company of Uncle Remus, Aunt Jemima, or some other relative of racism.

As far as the "dusky undulations" and dancing, these are also stereotypes aimed at denigrating black respectability and dignity. In the minstrel shows of the 1800s, white performers in blackface represented African Americans as happy and dancing. Al Jolson, who was a strong advocate for black performers on Broadway, is credited with introducing African-American song and dance to a white American audience in the 1927 film *The Jazz Singer*. The "dusky undulations" stemmed from the rhythmic dancing of the West Indies, though there are many other cultures that employ undulations in dancing as well. The traditional Hawaiian hula and other island performances, for instance, undulate and send strong, sensual messages.

Other stereotypes have plagued African Americans, reinforced by character actors such as Lincoln Perry, a black whose stage name was STEPIN FETCHIT. The roles he played epitomized the slow-moving, shiftless darky. The reality of his acting was that blacks and whites read him differently. For blacks, his slowness was a way to dupe the whites who were exploiting him. For whites, it reinforced a stereotype. Angelou knows the traditions and feelings of her people, her narratives are layered in way that blacks will understand, though many white readers perhaps will not. This poem helps to build racial pride through admiration and respect for those smiles that are often hiding deep pain.

FURTHER READING

Angelou, Maya. *The Complete Collected Poems of Maya Angelou.* New York: Random House, 1994.

Woods, Keith M. "Talking Race over a Slice of Watermelon" *PoynterOnline,* 29 July 2003. Available online. URL: http://poynter.org/column.asp?id=588&aid=42722. Accessed March 19, 2010.

"Times-Square-Shoeshine-Composition"

"Times-Square-Shoeshine-Composition" is included in Part Two of Angelou's first poetry collection, *Just Give Me a Cool Drink of Water 'fore I Diiie* (1971). This poem is in the liberation ideology tradition, a

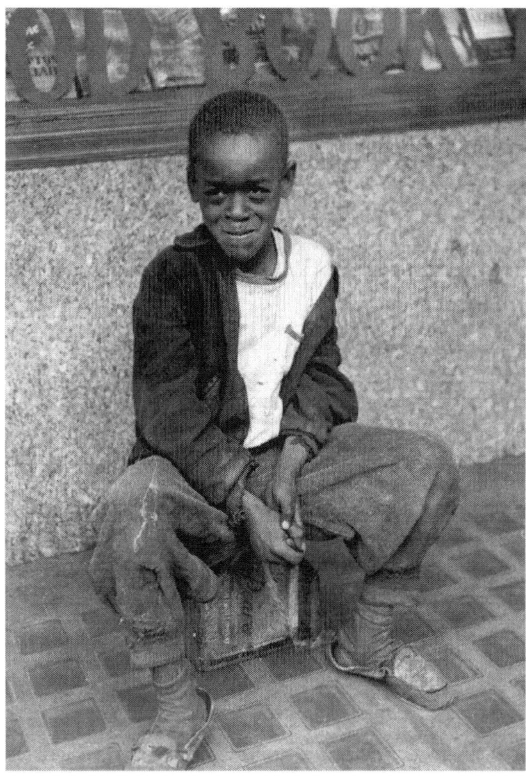

A tattered but smiling child, probably a shoeshine boy, sitting on a small wooden box *(Courtesy Library of Congress Prints and Photographs Division)*

topic she addresses in about half of the poems in this collection, which was nominated for the Pulitzer Prize.

SYNOPSIS

In this poem, the narrator is a shoeshine boy who tells his story with a rhythm and repetition that reflect the pace of his work and keep his tedious polishing of leather shoes stimulating and alive. The words *pow, pow,* mimicks sound of the cloth as it works across his customer's shoes and establishes the lyrics' steady rhythm. He confidently claims to be the best, and he claims that they call him "master mine." A customer tries to bargain him out of a dime, and the confident shoeshine boy refuses, saying, "Then you give that to your daughter."

The first line of the fourth stanza mentions the dozens, an insulting street game where participants spew out insults to one another about relatives, living circumstances, or even looks, but without anger or fighting. The first person who exhibits anger loses; composure is the key to the game. The boy is calm and confident with his customer, but he insists on the payment he has set. As the poem ends, he says he is greedy—"I'm a cap'talist, / can you dig it?"

CRITICAL COMMENTARY

Angelou used many African-American cultural elements to compose this poem. It is in part about black survival, and her plucky narrator is planning to make it big in life; he is already a capitalist. There is a BLUES quality to the poem, and several critics have remarked that Angelou sometimes writes in the same blues/protest style as LANGSTON HUGHES. The game known as "the dozens" is mentioned casually. It is a popular street game in African-American culture (briefly explained above and in the entry for "The Thirteens [Black]").

Lynn Z. Bloom writes: "In 'Times-Square-Shoeshine-Composition,' the feisty black shoeshine boy defends, in dialect, his thirty-five-cent price against the customer who tries to cheat him out of a dime, his slangy remarks [are] punctuated by the aggressive 'pow pow' of the shoeshine rag" (10–11). Carol E. Neubauer, a critic of Angelou's work, also comments:

> Two poems that embody the poet's confident determination that conditions must improve for the black race are "Times-Square-Shoeshine-Composition" and "Harlem Hopscotch." Both ring with a lively, invincible beat that carries defeated figures into at least momentary triumph. . . . Denying the charge that he is a "greedy bigot," the shoeshine man simply admits that he is a striving "cap'talist," trying to be successful in a city owned by the super-rich. (211)

Kathy M. Essick suggests: "Through the clever, rhetorical language of the trickster figure, the shoeshine boy 'Signifies' upon his tale in front of potential customers in a verbal play of figurative elements" (66–69). This poem again represents the liberation ideology that pervades Angelou's 1971 volume of powerful, pride-building poetry.

FURTHER READING

Angelou, Maya. *The Complete Collected Poems of Maya Angelou.* New York: Random House, 1994.

Bloom, Lynn Z. "Maya Angelou." In *Dictionary of Literary Biography,* vol. 38. Detroit: Gale, 1985, 10–11.

Essick, Kathy M. "The Poetry of Maya Angelou: A Study of the Blues Matrix as Force and Code." Ph.D. diss., Indiana University of Pennsylvania, 1994, 66–69.

Neubauer, Carol E. "Maya Angelou: Self and a Song of Freedom in the Southern Tradition." In *Maya Angelou.* Modern Critical Views, edited by Harold Bloom, 42. Philadelphia: Chelsea House, 1999.

"To a Freedom Fighter"

"To a Freedom Fighter" is in Part Two of Angelou's first published collection of poetry, *Just Give Me a Cool Drink of Water 'fore I Diiie* (1971).

SYNOPSIS

This poem describes the angst and deep anxiety an African freedom fighter feels for his cause and his black brothers who have suffered in the struggle to free their people from the oppression in South Africa. He is to "drink a bitter drought," the drought of responsibility, knowing full well the sacrifice and hardships he will have to face. In his "anger black and cold," he moans in vicarious misery from the knowledge that his brothers suffer blows of flogging by cane strap. The narrator hears his pain in his breath.

CRITICAL COMMENTARY

Maya Angelou lived with the African freedom fighter VUSUMZI MAKE for three years. When he was courting her, he told her of his capture by white oppressors and how he survived being deserted in the wasteland of the desert. At the time she met him in New York, he was working with the United Nations to try to free South Africa from apartheid (white oppression). In this poem, there are unfamiliar words, such as *lees* (dregs of sediment in a drink) and *herbane* (an ancient anesthetic potion of mandrake and deadly nightshade; a hallucinate), because the poem takes place in exotic Africa, a place of ancient and sometimes very dangerous herbal potions. Make used herbal mixtures to escape the difficult reality of his work. This is a poem of liberation that depicts the deep, emotional agony of his struggle.

FURTHER READING

Angelou, Maya. *The Complete Collected Poems of Maya Angelou.* New York: Random House, 1994.

"To a Husband"

"To a Husband" is included in Part One of Angelou's 1971 collection *Just Give Me a Cool Drink of Water 'fore I Diiie,* which was nominated for a Pulitzer Prize.

SYNOPSIS

The narrator in this short poetic narrative is a wife married to a strong African man. He is troubled and struggling, and his voice sometimes "Jabs ceaselessly at phantoms / In the room." He is powerful; she admires his graceful hands, like a "Skimming boat / Goes down the Nile," and he tells her about the antiquities of Egypt like Pharaoh's tomb. She admires him, and in the second, final stanza, she tells him, "You're Africa to me." She knows he is a freedom fighter, and with others, he is building the continent. She closes with "I sit at home and see it all / through you."

CRITICAL COMMENTARY

Maya Angelou's experience in Africa was a result of her relationship with VUSUMZI MAKE. He introduced Africa to her, and they lived together in Cairo for two years. She loved him, and she found in him an exotic beauty that lifted her and helped her to discover her own identity. The union, a form of marriage, did not last, but in this poem she describes both his unrest and the grace he possessed, which intrigued her. She was never comfortable with sitting at home, and when the realization came to her that he was a philanderer as well as a person in debt who did not pay his bills, she realized that she no longer loved him. Forced to take work as a journalist, her halcyon days as a wife and homemaker came to a sad end. At the time this poem represents, Angelou was still innocent of what would unfold in their future.

FURTHER READING

Angelou, Maya. *The Complete Collected Poems of Maya Angelou.* New York: Random House, 1994.

"To a Man"

This is the fourth poem in Maya Angelou's first published collection, *Just Give Me a Cool Drink of Water 'fore I Diiie* (1971).

SYNOPSIS

Described in this poem is a handsome, "Black Golden Amber" man, southern and sophisticated but aloof and secretive like a cat. Who is he? He is equated with "French tobacco" and "Brandy Fine" and described as always changing and reflecting upon himself like amber. It is an in-the-moment nugget of mystery—new, brief, and gentle. There are no breaks in this poem; it moves down the printed page almost as gracefully as "A big cat stalks." The word *Changing* stands alone in the third line and again almost at the end of the poem. The line "New. Now New" leaves the reader cautious. Who is he? Does she know?

CRITICAL COMMENTARY

Using the metaphor of golden amber, a stone with deep shadows that reflects elements of light within itself, like a mono-colored kaleidoscope, the beautiful black amber man is elusive. The poem's short lines, with carefully chosen words and phrases, take the reader deliberately "Into ever neverlessness," and impart a sense of wonder: "Still itself. / Still." The technique of repeating, almost chanting single words between the visual imagery, is mesmerizing—almost hypnotizing—and we wonder who this black man is.

FURTHER READING

Angelou, Maya. *The Complete Collected Poems of Maya Angelou.* New York: Random House, 1994.

"To Beat the Child Was Bad Enough"

"To Beat the Child Was Bad Enough" is included in Part Two of Angelou's collection *And Still I Rise* (1978).

SYNOPSIS

This is a poem of rage at the horror of child abuse. At the end of four stanzas, each reduced to fewer lines until the poem ends in just two—the last one with only one word, *Silently*—the child who is the subject of the poem is burned to death. The first lines begin with the image of a young child, light and full of promise. But, somehow, the child is placed in a world of misery with "Hunger" and "new hands, strange voices." The abuse comes as a form of neglect. The caretaker neglects to protect the child from danger, and the child dies.

In the next stanza, water boils gaily in a cheap, probably very light, pot. Out of curiosity, the child investigates and is burned, "The skin / Withdrew, the flesh submitted." The child screams and the sounds are like "shards / Of broken air." In last stanza, the child's body "floats / silently."

CRITICAL COMMENTARY

"To Beat the Child Was Bad Enough" is a message to the African-American community about child neglect and abuse. Yasmin Y. DeGout writes:

> By creating a community of . . . those who share in the pain or trauma of the speaker, such pieces undertake the healing process by creating a community of healers—those whose acknowledgment of the pain of the speaker allows healing to occur. The pieces [like this one] also offer such healing to readers who share similar stories. One may call this part of the blues mode in the Angelou canon. Such pieces not only create affinity among actual readers of the work, they

> also imply a community of listeners (whether actual readers or not)—what Benedict Anderson would call an "imagined community"—simply through the assumption that the pieces will find sympathetic listeners. (128)

In a society of people who most work away from home to survive financially, children, the most valuable resource of any country, are often neglected, abused, or abandoned. Angelou is horrified by all too frequent occurrences of child abuse, and this poem of rage and warning expresses that inexcusable travesty of human rights.

FURTHER READING

Anderson, Benedict. *Imagined Communities: Reflections on the Origins and Spread of Nationalism.* 1983. Reprint, New York: Verso, 1991.

Angelou, Maya. *The Complete Collected Poems of Maya Angelou.* New York: Random House, 1994.

DeGout, Yasmin Y. "The Poetry of Maya Angelou: Liberation Ideology and Technique." In *Maya Angelou.* Bloom's Modern Critical Views, edited by Harold Bloom, 121–132. New York: Bloom's Literary Criticism, 2009.

"Traveler, The"

"The Traveler" is included in Part Two of Angelou's collection *And Still I Rise* (1975).

SYNOPSIS

This eight-line, two-stanza poem narrates the anguish of a woman left alone. The first stanza mentions byways, implying travel in various places. The mention of "lone nights long" reveals the loneliness the narrator feels. The second stanza begins "Manless and friendless," and the narrator confesses that there is no cave that serves as her home; her torture is the long nights, alone.

CRITICAL COMMENTARY

Speaking about the frequent theme of loneliness, Angelou exposes her own frustration over being without a companion for much of her life. Traveling, particularly if it is frequent and without friends or family, is often unfamiliar and lonely. Angelou has a social personality, and like most people, though she needs private time to create her works, she also needs trusted companionship. That balance can be hard to find.

Poems about loneliness have been written since antiquity. Angelou has read widely and has probably encountered poetry expressing loneliness in the works of (among others) Gwendolyn Brooks ("To Be In Love"), Nikki Giovanni ("In Simpler Times"), Emily Dickinson ("The Loneliness One Dare Not Sound"), and Elizabeth Barrett Browning (*Sonnets from the Portuguese*). All humans experience loneliness at one time or another for various lengths of time, but gifted poets are well able to put the feelings that loneliness evokes into words of universal understanding. Angelou has spent much of her life alone, and she has expressed those moments in ways that may offer empathy and comfort to others experiencing the same kinds of lonely moments.

FURTHER READING

Angelou, Maya. *The Complete Collected Poems of Maya Angelou.* New York: Random House, 1994.

Brooks, Gwendolyn. *Selected Poems.* New York: Harper Perennial Modern Classics, 2006.

Browning, Elizabeth Barrett. *Sonnets from the Portuguese.* Charleston, S.C.: BiblioLife, 2009.

Dickinson, Emily. *The Complete Poems of Emily Dickinson.* Edited by Thomas H. Johnson. Boston: Back Bay Books, 1976.

Giovanni, Nikki. *The Collected Poetry of Nikki Giovanni: 1968–1998.* New York: Harper Perennial Modern Classics, 2007.

"Unmeasured Tempo"

"Unmeasured Tempo" is included in Angelou's 1983 collection *Shaker, Why Don't You Sing?* It is a melancholy poem about failure to find love in the time of youth.

SYNOPSIS

This free-verse poem has two stanzas with lines of varying length. It begins by using aging bodies as a metaphor for long awaiting happiness and companionship to arrive. The first stanza closes with the narrator saying: "Dreams are petted, like / cherished lapdogs / misunderstood and loved / too well." It is common for people to adopt pets for companionship, and often those pets are loved deeply and perceived to have human characteristics.

In the second stanza, the waiting continues. The narrator has learned much but has still gained little wisdom. Finally, the companion appears, smiling, but it is too late—much too late.

CRITICAL COMMENTARY

Angelou waited for many decades to establish a long-lasting companionship with a man she could love and one that could and would love her in return. She understood that this does not happen for everyone, and this poem is a tribute to those who seem to wait in vain for someone with whom to exchange love and companionship.

FURTHER READING

Angelou, Maya. *The Complete Collected Poems of Maya Angelou.* New York: Random House, 1994.

"Weekend Glory"

"Weekend Glory" was published in Angelou's 1983 collection *Shaker, Why Don't You Sing?* It is a reflection on sensible fun and recreation on Saturday, which helps make the tedious five-day workweek more endurable. It is also a brief narrative about living within one's means.

SYNOPSIS

This is a popular poem of Angelou's, and it is a good example of her ability to entertain and teach at the same time. The black male narrator begins by saying, "Some dichty [a word for uppity blacks] folks / don't know the facts." They strut, pose, and put on airs, and they live over their means, but he can teach them a thing or two if they will just come and "study me on Saturday night."

Rather than deal with a lot of picks and rakes, he gets his hair done, takes his "church money out," gets his girl, and joins his friends to "go to a joint / where the music is blues / and to the point." They laugh and dance for several hours, and they simply enjoy each other's company. He works all week at the factory, and this is his night out. His rich friends suggest he will never get ahead "livin' / from day to day," but he points out that they are doing the same thing. He is content with his economic station in life and is delighted to be "Black / on Saturday night."

CRITICAL COMMENTARY

Yasmin Y. DeGout writes that some of Angelou's most interesting poems are "the pieces that reference unnamed or representative cultural heroes in order to elicit racial pride and thereby liberate her readership from racist discourse within dominant ideology" (130). This poem is one of those, and with a steady tempo and rhythm, the anonymous narrator tells his story with optimism and an upbeat style.

To go out on the town on Saturday night, enjoying friends, music, and a few drinks, is a common activity worldwide and not limited to the African-American culture. The tradition among blacks has been noted in history and fiction, and there are many lively accounts of activities at juke (or jook) joints and other gathering places. Both ZORA NEALE HURSTON and Alice Walker wrote about these gathering places in their various works. Hurston, an anthropologist, defined a *juke joint* as "a fun house. Where they sing, dance, gamble, love and compose 'blues' songs incidentally" (63). Obviously, the juke joints were important social centers. Common among African Americans in the southeastern United States, these establishments were where music, dancing, gambling, and drinking took place. It was a place of fun after a weary week of toil, and sometimes there were cheap beds and a simple breakfast served the next morning.

"Weekend Glory" affirms the wisdom of a common man. He works, plays, pays his bills, and stays out of debt. He views the phony blacks for what they are, and he suggests that they could learn a lot from his choices. He is not rich, but he has a clear conscience and is a proud black male, living well and having fun on Saturday night.

FURTHER READING

Angelou, Maya. *The Complete Collected Poems of Maya Angelou.* New York: Random House, 1994.

DeGout, Yasmin Y. "The Poetry of Maya Angelou: Liberation Ideology and Technique." In *Maya Angelou.* Bloom's Modern Critical Views, edited by Harold Bloom, 121–132. New York: Bloom's Literary Criticism, 2009.

Hurston, Zora Neale. *Mules and Men.* Philadelphia: J. B. Lippincott, 1935.

"We Had Him"

This poem was written on the occasion of MICHAEL JACKSON's death in LOS ANGELES at the age of 50 on June 25, 2009. A singer, songwriter, and dancer, Jackson was sometimes called the "King of Pop," and he had millions of fans throughout the world. Maya Angelou wrote a poem for his memorial service held at the Los Angeles Staples Center on July 7, 2009. The singer and film star QUEEN LATIFAH read the poem.

SYNOPSIS

The words of this poem are a gentle tribute to Jackson, lamenting that "our bright and shining star can slip away like a puff of / summer wind." His death came as a deep shock to his family and to the vast number of fans who idolized him. In response to the shock, the poem states: "No oceans can rush our tides / with the abrupt absence of our treasure." Jackson had written many songs and choreographed many complicated dances. One of the most popular was the moonwalk, which Angelou refers to: ". . . and walk our dances across the face of the moon." The poem speaks of his passion, compassion, humor, and style. "We had him / Beautiful, delighting our eyes," with his "pose on his toes." The poem says that the world will miss Jackson: "But we do know we had him / And we are the world."

CRITICAL COMMENTARY

This poem reflects the heartfelt grief and shock that countless people felt when the unexpected death of Michael Jackson was announced. By selecting positive, nurturing words, Angelou conveys the respect and sorrow of millions of people. Jackson had been scheduled to perform a series of concerts in London beginning on July 13, 2009, and these concerts would have helped to repay debts that he had accrued over time. Tickets for the concerts had already set record sales, and his fans' excitement and anticipation of the performances added to the shock of his death. His enthusiasm, sense of humor, constant kindness to his fans, and gentle courtesy added to his popularity even more. Angelou reflects his personality in this poem by using words such as *beloveds, dear love, mother love,* and *family love,* and by emphasizing that "He gave us all he had been given." These words create a message of love and honor both from him and to him. Jackson was an icon to millions of fans, in spite of confusion and misunderstanding over some of his reported personal behavior. Angelou's poem warmly reflects the "doting embrace" of his people.

FURTHER READING

"Times Topics: Michael Jackson." *New York Times,* 26 June 2009. Available online. URL: http://topics.nytimes.com/top/reference/timestopics/people/j/michael_jackson/index.html. Accessed July 27, 2009.

Vena, Jocelyn. "Maya Angelou's Poem about Michael Jackson: 'We Had Him.'" *MTV News,* 7 July 2009. Available online. URL: www.mtv.com/news/articles/1615416/20090707/jackson_michael.jhtml. Accessed July 27, 2009.

"When Great Trees Fall"

This poem was published in 1990 in the collection *I Shall Not Be Moved.* Also published under the title of "Ailey, Baldwin, Floyd, Killens, and Mayfield," it is a tribute to the legacy of men who influenced not only Maya Angelou but the world at large.

SYNOPSIS

"When Great Trees Fall"—or "Ailey, Baldwin, Floyd, Killens, and Mayfield"—is a free-verse poem of five stanzas. The first line is "When great trees fall," and it refers to the giant contributions those named in the title—Alvin Ailey, JAMES BALDWIN, Pink Floyd, JOHN KILLENS, and JULIAN MAYFIELD have made. The line also refer to other greats who have passed on. How they existed and what they gave to the world will be remembered through the whisper of their memories.

The first stanza begins metaphorically, describing the consequences when great trees fall: "rocks . . . shudder, / lions hunker down," and "even elephants / lumber after safety." Silence befalls the observers when great world contributors die, and the information has to be processed while the listener absorbs the shock. In the third stanza, the narrator states that our sharpened memories remind us of "kind words / unsaid," and "promised walks / never taken." In the next stanza, the narrator reminds us that though we were "informed by their / radiance," we are reduced to "unutterable ignorance." But in the last stanza, the assurance comes that we will remember them "with a kind of / soothing electric vibration. . . . They existed," and we can be better because they did exist and left us their legacy.

CRITICAL COMMENTARY

Maya Angelou has generously and wisely offered tributes to people who have influenced her life and shaped her voice. In this poem of sadness and recovery, a work that exposes the process of loss and then the beauty of memory, she has paid tribute to Alvin Ailey, James Baldwin, possibly the music group Pink Floyd, John Killens, and Julian Mayfield.

Alvin Ailey (1931–89) founded the Alvin Ailey American Dance Theater (1959), and by the late 1970s, his dance troupe was one of the most popular in the United States. Maya Angelou danced with him on television variety shows in the 1950s.

James Baldwin (1924–87) was a writer whom Angelou met in Paris when she was on tour with PORGY AND BESS and then later in New York, when she became active in the HARLEM WRITERS GUILD. He befriended her, made her an honorary member of his family, and was instrumental in getting her to write her serial autobiographies.

John Killens (1916–87) was a black American fiction writer who received two Pulitzer Prize nominations for his fiction. He befriended Maya Angelou on a trip he made to California to work on the filming of his book *Youngblood* (1954) and invited her to move to New York and become a member of the Harlem Writers Guild. He and his wife and family were lifelong friends of Angelou and her son, Guy.

Julian Mayfield (1928–84) lived in Ghana, where he was an editor for the *African Review*. He was also a well-known New York actor and fiction writer. He and his wife befriended Maya and Guy when they all lived in Africa.

FURTHER READING

Angelou, Maya. *The Complete Collected Poems of Maya Angelou*. New York: Random House, 1994.

"When I Think About Myself"

"When I Think About Myself" appears in Part Two of Angelou's first volume of poetry, *Just Give Me a Cool Drink of Water 'fore I Diiie* (1971), which was nominated for the Pulitzer Prize.

SYNOPSIS

The poem begins with "When I think about myself, / I almost laugh myself to death," which is not to be taken literally. If the word *laugh* were to be changed to *cry* throughout the poem, the meaning would be clearer. The narrator, because of the necessity to survive, has made herself appear cooperative and cheerful to her employers in spite of insults, disappointments, and being demeaned. She has tried to laugh at the insults she has been subjected to and not let them break her pride.

In the second stanza, she reveals that people have been calling her "girl" for 60 years, and she has responded "Yes ma'am," even to young employers, such as "the child" she works for in this narrative. In the last stanza, she reflects on her family. They have grown the food and fruit they eat to survive, but they only consume the "rind," meaning the poorer parts of their labor. She says, "I laugh until I start to crying, / when I think about my folks." In this she is saying that generation after generation of her people have been maltreated, but they have survived with dignity, laughing on the outside but crying on the inside and waiting to be given equality and fair treatment. Even though she breaks down and cries "When she thinks about her folks," she maintains her self-pride and will at the end of the poem. She is determined to be respectful and faithful to those many generations who hoped that their sacrifice would help the next survive and reach the honest and democratic goals of equality.

CRITICAL COMMENTARY

Angelou often used the collective *I* as a pronoun representing "we." She begins this poem in that manner, and she speaks for many African Americans in service who have suffered insulting white behavior and yet have accepted it with quiet dignity instead of angrily demanding equal respect. Protective of the next generation, and fearful of losing their economic means of survival, they said nothing.

In his critical survey of Angelou's writing, Lyman B. Hagen writes:

> In "When I Think About Myself," Angelou explains why a black woman responds with a simple "yes, ma'am" for the sake of a job, even to a young white who insults her with the offensive word "girl." The servant does not pity herself and knows she is keeping her race alive. By being servile for an entire lifetime, she has provided sustenance for another generation who may find better conditions. Whenever appropriate, Angelou voices approval of those who endured indignities to feed, shelter, clothe, and educate the family. (129)

FURTHER READING

Angelou, Maya. *The Complete Collected Poems of Maya Angelou*. New York: Random House, 1994.

Hagen, Lyman B. *Heart of a Woman, Mind of a Writer, and Soul of a Poet: A Critical Analysis of the Writings of Maya Angelou*. Lanham, Md.: University Press of America, 1997.

"When You Come to Me"

"When You Come to Me" was published in Part One of Angelou's first collection of poems, *Just Give Me a Cool Drink of Water 'fore I Diiie* (1971).

SYNOPSIS

The metaphorical setting that Angelou chooses to use in this short, free-verse poem (two stanzas, 10 lines) is an attic visited by a child. The first line states that someone has come to the narrator, unbidden and from the past, tempting her to join him in revisiting "long ago rooms" where former memories are hidden. Just as a child is drawn to discover and explore pretty baubles and trinkets found tucked away in a dusty attic, the narrator suggests that this lover from the past is enticing her to do the same thing with him by exploring their past relationship. "Baubles of stolen kisses, / Trinkets of borrowed loves," but how long has it been? And to how many have his baubles and trinkets been given since they were together? The last line, in capital letters, simply says, "I CRY." Perhaps she cared very much for him, and he left her. She loved him in the past and was probably used for his pleasure. Now he wants to use her again.

CRITICAL COMMENTARY

Appropriately placing this poem in the section of this volume entitled "Where Love Is a Scream of Anguish," Angelou sensitively discloses the many ways in which she has been disappointed in romantic relationships. This poem about lost love, with its intriguing imagery, creates a scene of curiosity and exploration, and yet the poem also sounds a warning. Angelou is subtly but deliberately teaching that romance and the early, tender feelings of love and trust are not easily recaptured once someone has been abandoned and left hurting.

FURTHER READING

Angelou, Maya. *The Complete Collected Poems of Maya Angelou*. New York: Random House, 1994.

"Willie"

"Willie," a tribute to Maya Angelou's uncle, WILLIE JOHNSON, is included in Part Two of the collection *And Still I Rise* (1975). The narrator of the poem is Willie himself.

SYNOPSIS

"Willie" is a poem of triumph and self-respect. It begins with a statement of Willie's determination to live a normal life in spite of a crippled body. He just keeps moving and working throughout his life, "Movin' just the same." The second stanza discloses that his only partner in bed is emptiness, and that he is alone much of the time. Though he is in constant pain, he just keeps obeying and following those who lead him. He does his best to be cheerful, and in the third stanza, he says "That I'm present in all the songs that children sing."

Willie is subjected to the taunting that people with handicaps often have to learn to endure. People call him "Uncle," "Boy," and "Hey," but he does not defend himself or complain, he just assures them that he lives through the children and their play. In the fifth stanza, Willie confesses bad dreams, but he keeps his manners and both laughs and cries, just like "a summer breeze." In the last two stanzas, he assures everyone that he is present in the "surge of open sea" and the "rustle in the autumn leaves." He is present in the children's singing, and he says, "I am the Rhyme."

CRITICAL COMMENTARY

Angelou's Uncle Willie helped his mother, Annie Henderson, raise both Maya and her brother, Bailey. He was a stern taskmaster about their schoolwork and chores, and he worked hard to keep the family general store clean and well stocked. His body was injured when he was accidentally dropped by a babysitter in his early childhood, but he was not a complainer. He functioned normally with the aid of a cane, attending church and helping his mother in any way he could.

Occasionally in interviews, Angelou will sing the words to this poem in a loving, gentle voice. She trusted and respected Uncle Willie, much more than she was able to trust and respect her own father. She described a time once when he waited on some schoolteachers passing through STAMPS, ARKANSAS. He leaned against the counter, straightened his body, and did not let them see his cane. He talked to them, and Maya watched his pride as he presented himself as whole and unbent. He was a strong male example for both Maya and her brother, and he took care of his mother until her death. He was a good man who loved all of the children.

FURTHER READING

Angelou, Maya. *The Complete Collected Poems of Maya Angelou*. New York: Random House, 1994.

"Woman Me"

"Woman Me" is included in Part Five of Angelou's Collection *Oh Pray My Wings Are Gonna Fit Me Well* (1975).

SYNOPSIS

This is an ambiguous poem that raises questions about meaning and imagery. It has mixed metaphors, and the reader may be unsure about whether it describes a women or the vast, restive continent of Africa. At the beginning of the first of three stanzas, the delicateness of the smile leads the reader into thinking that the poem may be about a beautiful woman, yet it could also be Africa, mysterious and enticing. The first stanza refers to "Deafening revolutions," and then it mentions "Beggar-Kings" and "red-ringed Priests," which seems to identify obscure tribal chiefs of Africa.

The second stanza describes pharaohs who "ride deep in the bosom of the Nile." Lashed doors and "winds of death" describe violence. In the last stanza, laughter rings out loudly, and children try to map their lives between "your teeth." The final line—"A stomp of feet. A bevy of swift hands"—leaves the reader wondering about what part of liberation ideology this represents, and if it is about a woman, perhaps an anonymous woman Angelou knew or admired in Africa.

CRITICAL COMMENTARY

Many of Angelou's poems are about oppression and hoped-for liberation. Her fight for social justice for her people has been expressed largely through poetry, written in a manner that can be easily understood. Many of her poems are a strident protest against the injustices perpetrated upon her people, and she embraces all readers with the same defensiveness and determination to lift them to a higher level of pride and self-respect. In this lyrical and mysterious poem, she taunts the reader to decipher her metaphors. It is a narrative of empowerment and sublime gentleness, "A grasp of Lions. A lap of Lambs."

FURTHER READING

Angelou, Maya. *The Complete Collected Poems of Maya Angelou.* New York: Random House, 1994.

"Woman Work"

This poem is from Part Two of Angelou's collection *And Still I Rise,* published in 1975.

SYNOPSIS

"Woman Work" is a list of the daily round of chores that many housewives and mothers face. Its setting is in the South ("cane to be cut" and "cotton to pick"), and it may take place in a time long past or in the present. There are "children to tend, / The clothes to mend," and a long inventory of the daily work. But even though there is much to do, there is no hint of resentment or complaint. To the contrary, the woman finds daily solace, beauty, and strength-restoring restfulness by sensing and observing the natural loveliness of nature. "Fall gently snowflakes," and "Star shine, moon glow"—she basks in the generous sensory gifts of natural scenery. There is a wistful melancholy at the poem's end, when she says, "You're all that I can call my own." She sees and feels, and she gracefully accepts that her life is one of survival through constant service, but her daily reward comes from the beauty of the earth.

CRITICAL COMMENTARY

In this poem, Angelou discusses the mundane setting of many women's lives as repetitive, as represented by the daily list of things to do. The chores seem endless, and escape might seem futile; yet, with resourcefulness and a purposeful attitude, a reward can be found in the simple presence of nature. Both emotional and aesthetic pleasure can be found in the sublime beauty of the earth, and that is where Angelou turns in writing this poem to provide a sense of solace and restfulness for the hardworking mother described. The rhymed couplets of the list—*tend/mend, mop/shop, fry/dry, feed/weed, press/dress, cut/hut,* and *sick/pick*—convey a staccato rhythm. That staccato creates an image of steady tasks done efficiently, one by one, and when at last they are finished, there are still moments left to enjoy the natural magnificence of the earth, and to rest.

FURTHER READING

Angelou, Maya. *The Complete Collected Poems of Maya Angelou.* New York: Random House, 1994.

"Worker's Song"

This poem is the first included in Angelou's collection *I Shall Not Be Moved,* published in 1990.

SYNOPSIS

In the simple cadence of "Worker's Song," the rhythms of a work song convey powerful physical action. The repetitive chorus—"Whoppa, Whoppa / Whoppa, Whoppa"—pounds out the reality of the hard work and strength of the black laborers. Big ships and railroads run because of the workers' sweat. They struggle and hope for something better while they "work late and keep the whole world running." But there is "something . . . something coming."

CRITICAL COMMENTARY

The literary critic Hazel Rochman suggests that none of the other poems in *I Shall Not Be Moved* reach the level of excellence that this one does. Comparing this poem to others that have artistically noted the hard work and sacrifice of blacks, she writes: "Like Paul Robeson's singing, like Langston Hughes' 'Florida Road Workers,' rhythm and sense are one" (1,773). These workers, along with others from other nations, built America, and when Angelou speaks of their hard work and struggle to build the railroads, cars, planes, and factories, in a country where they had been oppressed for so long, she speaks from her own experience and knowledge. She presents the black people as hard workers, and as Lyman B. Hagen writes: "This poem sings the praises of those whose work contributes to the orderly function of vital activities" (133).

FURTHER READING

Angelou, Maya. *The Complete Collected Poems of Maya Angelou.* New York: Random House, 1994.

Hagen, Lyman B. *Heart of a Woman, Mind of a Writer, and Soul of a Poet: A Critical Analysis of the Writings of Maya Angelou.* Lanham, Md.: University Press of America, 1997.

Rochman, Hazel. Review of *I Shall Not Be Moved* by Maya Angelou. *Booklist* 8, no. 18 (May 1990): 1,773.

"Zorro Man, A"

SYNOPSIS

"A Zorro Man" is the third poem in Angelou's first published collection, *Just Give Me a Cool Drink of Water 'fore I Diiie* (1971).

SYNOPSIS

This poem creates a deeply sensual moment in a room metaphorically described as a womb. Reflective purple drapes create a mood of dark, private, enclosed space, removed from all other places, and it is a room of loss. Here she was loved, "in a gone time," and in those past moments, he trembled for her, and she enjoyed his lovemaking. Now the room and the man seem to be only a reflection of a time that was. The three unrhymed stanzas maintain the same rhythm in this short work, and the mirror serves as a trigger to throw her thoughts back into the past when he was, perhaps, a "booted and brave" soldier who loved her.

CRITICAL COMMENTARY

Angelou sometimes writes pages of words and thoughts before extracting what she wants to use in her typically brief poems. This poem subtly describes a woman's pleasure in sexual passion. It is a reverie in which a woman's intimate experience is savored and exposed. In this 20-line work, the imagery is strong and almost visual in its expression of his "trembling for me" and the orgasmic "when I was love." The literary critic Yasmin Y. DeGout states that "the poem both produces a rendering that transcends racialized perception of the human condition and creates an individual consciousness, a woman's interiority" (124). It is a reflection of a past relationship, but the intimacy and pleasure is remembered.

FURTHER READING

Angelou, Maya. *The Complete Collected Poems of Maya Angelou.* New York: Random House, 1994.

DeGout, Yasmin Y. "The Poetry of Maya Angelou: Liberation Ideology and Technique." In *Maya Angelou.* Bloom's Modern Critical Views, edited by Harold Bloom, 121–132. New York: Bloom's Literary Criticism, 2009.

Children's Books

Mrs. Flowers: A Moment of Friendship, A Perfect Present (1980)

This 32-page illustrated book tells the story of MRS. BERTHA FLOWERS. Angelou describes her as "the lady who threw me my first life line" (2004, 74). *Mrs. Flowers* includes most of chapter 15 of *I Know Why the Caged Bird Sings,* and it shares the experiences Angelou had with this gentle black lady who was also a scholar and teacher. Maya became mute after she was physically abused when she was seven or eight, and Mrs. Flowers, treating the child with respect and care, guided her back into speaking by teaching her to recite literature and poetry. She taught the child an important concept about language:

> "Now no one is going to make you talk—possibly no one can. But bear in mind, language is man's way of communicating with his fellow man and it is language alone which separates him from the lower animals." That was a totally new idea to me, and I would need time to think about it. (1986, 22)

FURTHER READING

Angelou, Maya. *The Collected Autobiographies of Maya Angelou.* New York: Modern Library Edition by Random House, 2004.

———. *Mrs. Flowers: A Moment of Friendship, A Perfect Friendship.* Illustrated by Etienne Delessert. Minneapolis, Minn.: Redpath Press, 1986.

Life Doesn't Frighten Me (1993)

This book is based on a poem included in Part Three of Angelou's collection *And Still I Rise,* published in 1975. The children's book bears the same title as the poem and is richly illustrated with paintings by the late Jean-Michel Basquiat, a New York painter whose first works appeared as urban street art, and who died in 1988, when he was only 27 years old. The stunning illustrations support the text. For example, the lines "Mean old Mother Goose / Lions on the loose / They don't frighten me at all" are illustrated with a colorful abstraction of a lion on the loose in a schoolyard.

On the book's cover leaf, a blurb states: "Angelou's strong words are matched by the daring vision of artist Jean-Michel Basquiat, whose childlike style reveals the powerful emotions and fanciful imaginings of childhood. Together, Angelou's words and Basquiat's paintings create a place where every child, indeed every person, may experience his or her own fearlessness." The book won the *Publishers Weekly* Best Book of 1993 award.

FURTHER READING

Angelou, Maya. *Life Doesn't Frighten Me.* Illustrated by Jean-Michel Basquiat. New York: Stewart, Tabori & Chang, 1993.

My Painted House, My Friendly Chicken and Me (1994)

This colorful book, illustrated with photographs by Margaret Courtney-Clark, is the story of an eight-year-old Ndebele girl named Thandi, who lives in a village of decoratively painted buildings in South Africa. The child lives with her family, including a mischievous younger brother, but her best friend is a chicken. The chicken listens to her secrets and never tells. The short story, printed in a large font, expresses the challenge of growing up in a world where two cultures clash, represented by the traditional African crafts passed from mother to daughter, and the modern art forms and clothing that the girl sees in her village. The houses are painted in careful designs that use many colors. Thandi tells us: "You have to have strong eyes to paint good, and your hand must not shake like the leaves on a tree, for you must fill a chicken's feather with paint and draw a line as straight as a spear."

FURTHER READING

Angelou, Maya. *My Painted House, My Friendly Chicken and Me.* Illustrated by Margaret Courtney-Clark. New York: Crown Books, 1994.

Kofi and His Magic (1996)

Kofi and His Magic is illustrated with vibrant photographs by Margaret Courtney-Clark. The story line is about Kofi, a young Ashanti boy who lives in a West African village where kente cloth is made. Kente—or *nwentoma,* as it is called locally—is made of silk fabric, is interwoven in strips, and is produced in many villages. The boy daydreams and transports himself and other children to many places in the region where he lives. The primary importance of the book lies in its photographs of West Africa, including a bustling marketplace, strong-looking men and women wearing fine gold decorations on their bodies, and people of all ages wearing kente cloth.

FURTHER READING

Angelou, Maya. *Kofi and His Magic.* New York: Crown Books, 1996.

Maya's World Series (2004)

The Maya's World books were published in 2004 by Random House Books for Young Readers. The four books in the series were written by Angelou and illustrated by Lizzy Rockwell.

Maya's World: Izak of Lapland
A story about Izak, who is from a family of reindeer herders. He has a pet reindeer named Totti, and it is Izak's responsibility to teach his little brother about his duties in the family.

Maya's World: Angelina of Italy
Angelina's story is about a little girl who lives in Italy and loves pizza. She somehow confuses pizza with the Leaning Tower of Pisa, and then she imagines that the tower is made of pepperoni and mozzarella. Her parents take her to see the tower, and her confusion is resolved.

Maya's World: Renée Marie of France
This story is about Renée Marie, who is very tall and afraid of heights. Her school class makes a field trip to the Eiffel Tower, and there she finds that she is afraid to go to the top.

Maya's World: Mikale of Hawaii
This is a story about Mikale, a little boy in Hawaii who is afraid of the ocean. He lives on the beautiful island of Oahu, and his uncle and little pet fish teach the boy about having more confidence.

Major Essays

"Why I Moved Back to the South" (1982)

Angelou begins this essay with a discussion of how misunderstood the South continues to be by many people. She suggests that white people from the rest of the United States, and even white people from the South, do not understand the underlying culture of the southern states. She writes: "Black people, on the other hand, comprehend the South. We understand its weight. It has rested on our backs. We recognize its violence. We have been its victim. We acknowledge its history. It was first written with our blood" (130).

After growing up in the segregated and dangerous town of STAMPS, ARKANSAS, Angelou never wanted to return to the South. As she relates in this essay, though she traveled throughout the world, she rejected invitations to speak in the South, and she would cringe when she overheard a southern accent in a northern restaurant. Finally, she was invited to speak at Wake Forest University in North Carolina, and she decided to make an exception and accept the invitation. Her friend, DOLLY MCPHERSON, accompanied her, and Angelou learned quickly that things had changed. Her talk was received positively by an integrated black and white audience, and she enjoyed talking to the students afterward.

Invited for drinks by the chair of the English department, Elizabeth Phillip, Angelou says, "We sat talking about the South, the changes which had taken place and the changes yet to come" (134). She received an invitation to join the faculty at Wake Forest and soon made the decision to accept it. She concludes: "Courageous black people in this state had called upon their fellow citizens to dare healthier ways of living. I knew that morning, that one day I would return to the south in general and North Carolina in particular" (134).

FURTHER READING

Angelou, Maya. "Way I Moved Back to the South." *Ebony,* February 1982, 130–134.

"My Grandson, Home at Last" (1986)

This essay is about the search for Colin Johnson, the son of Angelou's only child, Guy (born CLYDE BAILEY JOHNSON). The child was kidnapped by his mother, Guy's estranged wife, and neither Angelou nor Guy were able to locate him for four years. The literary critic Mary Jane Lupton writes: "The delicate personal essay in *Woman's Day* seems to be the antecedent of two books of prose reflections, what Angelou's publisher labels on the dust jacket of *Even the Stars Look Lonesome* a 'wise book'" (19).

FURTHER READING

Angelou, Maya. *Even the Stars Look Lonesome.* New York: Random House, 1997.

———. "My Grandson, Home at Last." *Women's Day,* August 1986, 46–55.

Maya, Guy, and Guy's son, Colin, at a family gathering in North Carolina, around 1985 *(Courtesy Angelou-Johnson Family Archives)*

Lupton, Mary Jane. *Maya Angelou: A Critical Companion.* Westport, Conn.: Greenwood Press, 1998.

"The Assurance of Caramel Cake" (2004)

Each section of Angelou's first cookbook *Hallelujah! The Welcome Table: A Lifetime of Memories with Recipes* begins with an essay that contextualizes the section and shares stories that often reveal the reason various recipes were included. This story tells of Grandmother Annie Henderson (Momma), Maya, Bailey, and the heavenly Caramel Cake (capitalized because it was so good). Maya writes, "I only saw Momma's anger become physical once" (14), and this was it.

Maya and Bailey had started school one fall, and they were in the same classroom. Bailey was in sixth grade, and Maya was in the fourth. The new teacher, a bit high-strung and perfectionistic, insisted that, one by one, the children stand and say their names and the grades they had received at the end of the last semester. The children, including Bailey, did what they were told. This was during the time Maya was mute, when the teacher got to her, she insisted that Maya speak. But Maya could not, and the teacher slapped her across the face. Maya ran from the classroom with Bailey running after her.

When they got home, Momma met them and asked what happened. Bailey stuttered and tried to explain. Maya was mute, but she wrote in her notebook, "Miss Williams slapped me because I wouldn't talk" (15). Bailey was able to say that the teacher had slapped Maya in the face. Momma told Bailey to go back to school, and she told Maya to wash her face. Then she put on a sparkling white apron, walked to the school with Maya, and had Maya show her where the classroom was. She entered the classroom and went up to the teacher, Miss Williams. Momma asked her if she was "somebody's grandbaby" (16). When Miss Williams said that she was, Momma slapped her and said, "Now, Sister, nobody has the right to hit nobody in the face. So I am wrong this time, but I am teaching a lesson" (16). Momma left, and after a stunned silence, everyone, including Maya and Bailey, got back to their schoolwork. Nothing more was said about it.

When the children got home, Momma and their Uncle Willie were both sitting on the porch. Uncle Willie asked Maya to get what was on the kitchen table and bring it to the porch. It was "the most wondrous Caramel Cake looking like paradise, oozing sweetness" (17). Bailey gasped when it was brought out onto the porch, and Uncle Willie said, "This cake can't pay you for being slapped in the face. Momma made it just to tell you how much we love you and how precious you are" (17).

Each section of the cookbook, from typical American pies to international cuisine, begins with a story. The recipes are clear and easy to follow, and they represent the broad range of Angelou's COOKING expertise.

FURTHER READING

Angelou, Maya. *Hallelujah! The Welcome Table: A Lifetime of Memories with Recipes.* New York: Random House, 2004.

Part III

Related People, Places, and Topics

abacus An abacus is a counting board that is still popular and used in some countries. An abacus is a frame with beads strung on wire or sometimes in slots and used for figuring math. In chapter 2 of *I Know Why the Caged Bird Sings,* Angelou reflects that when she and her brother, Bailey, were five and six, respectively, they could say their times tables quickly because of working in their grandmother's store. In SAN FRANCISCO, CALIFORNIA, later, she saw Chinese children using their abacuses.

Abernathy, Ralph (1926–1990) Maya Angelou and GODFREY CAMBRIDGE were inspired by addresses given by Ralph Abernathy and MARTIN LUTHER KING, JR., while the leaders were in HARLEM, New York, trying to raise interest in and money for the SOUTHERN CHRISTIAN LEADERSHIP CONFERENCE (SCLC). As a result, Angelou and Cambridge organized a successful musical revue, *Cabaret for Freedom,* which ran several weeks in Greenwich Village. They donated the money to the SCLC.

Abernathy was a close associate of King's in the SCLC. After King was assassinated, Abernathy was the leader of the SCLC Poor People's Campaign and led a march on Washington, D.C., that King had planned to conduct. Ralph Abernathy was born and raised on a farm in Lindon, Alabama. He received a master's degree in sociology from Atlanta University in 1951. He was also a professor of mathematics and a dean at Alabama State University. Abernathy was with King in Memphis, Tennessee, when the latter was assassinated on April 4, 1968. Abernathy died on April 17, 1990.

FURTHER READING

Abernathy, Donzaleigh. *Partners to History: Martin Luther King, Jr., Ralph David Abernathy, and the Civil Rights Movements.* Bethel, Conn.: Crown, 2003.

Abernathy, Ralph. *And the Walls Came Tumbling Down.* New York: Harper & Row, 1989.

abolition *Abolition* means to do away with something, and in the context of Angelou's work, it refers to the abolition of slavery. From the colonial days in early America, there were citizens who condemned slavery. In 1688, the Quakers of Germantown, Pennsylvania, spoke out against it, and in 1700, Samuel Sewall of Boston, a well-known judge, published a pamphlet called *The Selling of Joseph.* After the Revolutionary War, abolition sentiment grew, and organizations were formed to try to eliminate the slave trade and slavery in the United States. During the presidency of Andrew Jackson (1829–37), antislavery reached a furious pitch, leading in time to the Civil War: "After all, a free, supposedly civilized Christian people holding slaves and profiting from the institution of slavery seemed to many a contradiction of everything the nation espoused about freedom and democracy" (Remini 2008, 119).

Though the Civil War (1860–65) resulted in the Emancipation Proclamation and the freeing of slaves, it was not until the CIVIL RIGHTS MOVEMENT, more than halfway through the 20th century, that African Americans really began to gain all the freedoms and rights that were promised. Maya Angelou was involved in many aspects of the Civil Rights movement in the 1960s and 1970s. Abolition of slavery was technically a reality after the Civil War, but equal rights were long in coming.

FURTHER READING

Remini, Robert V. *A Short History of the United States.* New York: HarperCollins, 2008.

Schweikart, Larry, and Michael Allen. *A Patriot's History of the United States: From Columbus's Great Discovery to the War on Terror.* New York: Sentinel/Penguin Group, 2004.

Wright, Ronald. *What Is America?: A Short History of the New World Order.* Philadelphia: Da Capo Press/Perseus Books Group, 2008.

adage An adage is an old, traditional saying that has been generally accepted as truth. There are many adages in Angelou's writing and many sources for those adages. One example was from the time when VUSUMZI MAKE was engaged in an argument with a Yugoslavian at a diplomatic reception in Cairo. Another man, Joe Williamson (the Liberian chargé d'affaires), interrupted a heated conversation and said: "Ole man say in my country, 'Hurry, hurry, get dere tomorrow. Take time, get there today.' Or better yet, 'We come to party to show our teeth. We go to war to show our arms'" (Angelou 1980, 846).

FURTHER READING

Angelou, Maya. *The Heart of a Woman.* New York: Random House, 1980.

Ajax Maya Angelou wrote an adaptation of Sophocles' *Ajax* that was performed in 1974 in LOS ANGELES, CALIFORNIA, at the Mark Taper Forum. *Ajax* is one of the earliest of Sophocles' still surviving plays; the first performance may have been around 444 B.C., but the exact date is unknown. Homer, the blind Greek poet, also wrote about Ajax, one of many Greek heroes. Ajax was the son of Telamon, king of Salamis, and was named "Great Ajax" in part to distinguish him from another hero named Ajax; his name also indicated his huge size and strength. He was always ready for war, enjoyed leading attacks, and had the character of a noble warrior, one who was always ready to defend his country. However, Ajax also represents excessive pride, or hubris. He fought with Odysseus over the armor of Achilles, and Odysseus, considered more worthy, was awarded the armor.

Ajax was not stupid, but he was prideful and unimaginative. Because he rejected help from the goddess Athena, she cast a spell on him. He was full of anger because he did not receive the shield of Achilles, and under the influence of the spell, he mistook cows and sheep for Greek warriors and slaughtered all of them. He later fell on his own sword deliberately and killed himself.

Alger, Horatio (1832–1899) Angelou read Horatio Alger books when she was a child, and she was impressed with the concept of survival and success Alger continually stressed. Born on January 13, 1832, he was an American writer of rags-to-riches stories about boys who progressed from poverty to wealth and fame. He was a prolific author, even leaving a number of unpublished novels at his death on July 18, 1899.

Alley Oop *Alley Oop* is a syndicated comic strip originally created by an American cartoonist named V. T. Hamlin. Following Hamlin, other cartoonists have continued drawing the strip, which often satirizes American life. The main character is Alley Oop, an imaginary citizen of the ancient kingdom of Moo. He has a pet dinosaur, carries a stone hammer, and only wears fur shorts. The comic was begun on December 5, 1932, and is still a syndicated publication running in more than 600 newspapers.

Maya Angelou read the *Alley Oop* comic strip when she was a child, and she remembered the concept of caves "where all reality was unreal and even that changed every day" (68). She and her brother had been moved from STAMPS, ARKANSAS, to her mother's home in St. Louis, and the city seemed like a foreign country to her—perhaps a little like the imaginary kingdom of Moo. She mentioned the unfamiliar sounds of "flushing toilets, or the packaged foods, or doorbells or the noise of cars and trains and buses that crashed through the walls or slipped under the doors" (68).

FURTHER READING

Alley Oop. Comics.com. Available online. URL: http:www.comics.com/comics/alleyoop/html/about_comic.html. Accessed July 28, 2009.

Angelou, Maya. *I Know Why the Caged Bird Sings.* New York: Ballantine, 2009.

Amazon Because Maya Angelou is tall and strong, she has occasionally been referred to as an Amazon. An Amazon is a strong, tall, usually muscular woman, and in ancient times, she was called a warrior maiden. Folk stories from early Greece describe the Amazon name as being derived from a word that meant breastless, but the origin is really unknown. Amazon woman were said to have removed one breast in order to facilitate archery. They were trained for war and usually fought on horseback. They allegedly lived near the Black Sea in Scythia and would take occasionally take husbands to propagate, and the men were often imprisoned afterward. Male children were made slaves or were killed.

FURTHER READING

Stapleton, Michael. *The Illustrated Dictionary of Greek and Roman Mythology.* New York: Peter Bedrick Books, 1986.

Angelos, Enistasious "Tosh" (b. ca. 1930) Maya Johnson and Tosh Angelos met at the Melrose Music Store in the FILLMORE DISTRICT of SAN FRANCISCO. They married in 1952, when Angelou's son Guy (born CLYDE BAILEY JOHNSON) was five, and divorced in 1952. Angelos was a handsome American-Greek sailor. After his honorable discharge from the military after World War II, he worked as an appliance dealer. Though he did not formally adopt Maya's son, he was interested in the boy and was Clyde's first sustained father figure. Maya later adapted her stage name of Angelou from Tosh's last name.

aphorism An aphorism is a short, wise observation or statement pointing out a generally understood truth. It is similar to an ADAGE.

VIVIAN BAXTER often used aphorisms with Maya to drive home various principles. Because Vivian always had a quick, usually positive answer for people, she was well-liked. When people on the street saw her, they might say, "Hey baby. What's the news?"—and she might reply, "I can't win, 'cause of the shape I'm in" (201). To Maya, she might say, "Then nothing beats a trial but a failure. Give it everything you've got. I've told you many times, 'Can't do is like Don't Care.' Neither of them have a home" (258).

FURTHER READING

Angelou, Maya. *I Know Why the Caged Bird Sings.* New York: Ballantine, 2009.

arabesque In ballet, an arabesque is a position in which the arms are extended and one leg is lifted and pointed straight backward. Angelou was a trained dancer, and this was one of the many positions she mastered and mentions that she used.

autoethnography Maya Angelou wrote her autobiographies in a style now called autoethnography. It is a type of self-narrative wherein the writer tries to objectively and subjectively examine how his or her cultural/ethnic, social, religious, and political background has influenced the formation of his or her values, beliefs, and behavior. Angelou's work includes cultural and historical contextualization, and she describes her personal experiences and responses in relation to those contexts.

FURTHER READING

Ellis, Caroline. *Revisions: Autoethnographic Reflections on Life and Work.* Walnut Creek, Calif.: Left Coast Press, 2008.

Reed-Danahay, Deborah. *Auto/ethnography: Rewriting the Self and Social (Explorations in Anthropology).* Oxford, U.K.: Berg, 1997.

B

Bailey, Pearl (1918–1990) A popular black singer and entertainer, Pearl Bailey appeared in various show business venues throughout the United States from the time she was 15. Maya Angelou auditioned for a New York Broadway part in which she would have played opposite Bailey. Though she was offered the part in *Heart of Flowers,* she declined it because she preferred to take a part in the European traveling company of *PORGY AND BESS.* To appear in the Broadway play would have been a career boost for Angelou due to Bailey's fame. Pearl Mae Bailey was born on March 29, 1918, and made her debut as a singer onstage when she was 15. She went on to a remarkable career, singing and dancing in nightclubs and theaters. She performed with some of the big-band names of her era, including COUNT BASIE, and she also recorded many albums. Bailey appeared in Broadway musicals, films, and nightclubs, and her most memorable role was in an all-black production of the musical *Hello Dolly!* She often appeared on television and also had her own program, *The Pearl Bailey Show* (1971). When she was 67 years old, she enrolled in Georgetown University and graduated with a bachelor's degree in theology. She died on August 17, 1990, at the age of 72.

FURTHER READING

"Pearl Mae Bailey." Biography.com. Available online. URL: http://www.biography.com/articles/Pearl-Bailey-9195451. Accessed July 28, 2009.

Baldwin, James (1924–1987) Maya Angelou met James Baldwin for the first time when she was in Paris, France, performing in the opera Porgy and Bess. Over time, they became good friends and stayed in touch with each other regardless of where they were. Baldwin introduced Angelou to his mother and extended family in New York, and she was welcomed into the Baldwin clan as an additional daughter. As a fellow member of the HARLEM WRITERS GUILD, he was also directly involved in persuading her to write. He talked to the Random House editor ROBERT LOOMIS, who was trying to get Angelou to begin writing her autobiography, and suggested that Loomis challenge her in some way. Loomis told Angelou that autobiography was the most difficult genre in which to write, and that she may not be able to do it. That hooked her, just as Baldwin thought it would.

Born on August 2, 1924, raised in poverty, subjected to police brutality, Baldwin was the son of a fire-and-brimstone, authoritarian minister whose beliefs he first embraced and then rejected. When Baldwin was young, he actually preached in storefront churches, but ultimately, he renounced both the church and Christianity. Still, he incorporated black biblical rhetoric he had learned into his writing and was sometimes called a latter-day Jeremiah. He wrote both novels and penetrating essays, and according to *The Norton Anthology of African American Literature,* "Baldwin's knife-edged criticism of the failed promises of American democracy,

Maya Angelou and James Baldwin first met in Paris when she was on tour with *Porgy and Bess.* He reminded her of her brother, Bailey, and Baldwin believed in Maya's writing talent. Here they are shown with Rosa Guy, a lifelong friend of Maya's, and another friend, Jerome Bennett. *(Courtesy Angelou-Johnson Family Archives)*

and the consequent social injustices, is unrelenting and demonstrates a piercing understanding of the function of blacks in the white racial imagination, especially the function of black males" (Gates and McKay 1997, 1,652).

Emerging out of the African-American struggle to be recognized as full members of American democracy, and writing literary fiction was a whole cadre of black novelists: Richard Wright, Ralph Ellison, Chester Himes, Ann Petry, and James Baldwin, among others. These were protest writers, and their descriptions of ghettos, storefront churches, and abject poverty expressed the deprivation and hardships of the majority of American blacks. These writers believed in confronting the problems and putting aside racial prejudice to deal with the matters at hand. "It is the Negro," said James Baldwin, "who can make America what America must become" (quoted in Quarles 1987, 290).

Baldwin published many well-known novels: *Giovanni's Room* (1956), *Another Country* (1962), *Tell Me How Long This Train's Been Gone* (1968), *If Beale Street Could Talk* (1974), and *Just above My Head* (1979). His most famous essay collections were *Notes of a Native Son* (1955), *Nobody Knows My Name* (1961), and *The Fire Next Time* (1963). He was investigated by the FBI because of complaints about graphic representations of sexuality in *Another Country*. "However, Charles Newman, comparing Baldwin to Henry Adams, places *Another Country* within the larger spectrum of the American literary tradition" (Wallace 2007, 17). Newman writes:

> [In *Another Country*], the legend of America as refuge for the oppressed, opportunity for the pure in heart, is invoked only to be exposed. From the very first, [Baldwin] is saying

> our vision has been parochial. We have not accounted for the variety of man's motives, the underside of our settlers, the costs of a new life. . . . If *Another country* if formless, it is so because it rejects the theories of history available to it. (97)

James Baldwin died in France on November 30, 1987.

FURTHER READING

Gates, Henry Louis, Jr., and Nellie Y. McKay, eds. *The Norton Anthology of African American Literature.* New York and London: W. W. Norton, 1997.

Newman, Charles. "The Lesson of the Master: Henry James and James Baldwin." In *James Baldwin: A Collection of Critical Essays,* edited by Keneth Kinnamon, 52–65. Englewood Cliffs, N.J.: Prentice Hall, 1974.

Quarles, Benjamin. *The Negro in the Making of America.* 1964. Reprint, New York: Touchstone, 1987.

Wallace, David Shane. "*Another Country*—James Baldwin (1962)." In *Encyclopedia of African-American Literature,* edited by Wilfred D. Samuels, 16–17. New York: Facts On File, 2007.

Bardot, Brigitte (1934–) Brigitte Bardot is mentioned in Angelou's *Singin' and Swingin' and Gettin' Merry Like Christmas.* When Angelou was sailing to Alexandria, Egypt, from Greece, it was a very rough sea voyage. A champagne party had been planned, but Maya had been warned to eat lightly and not to drink anything—not even water. Bardot was on the ship with a movie company, and that group became ill after the party and stayed in their cabins for much of the trip.

Born in Paris on September 28, 1934, Bardot is an actress, model, singer, and animal rights activist. She starred in films and various musical shows, and she recorded many songs in the 1960s and 1970s. She was married several times and is reputed to have had many affairs. She has donated thousands of dollars for animal protection and has been in the news more recently because of her outspoken views on racial issues. She has one son, Nicolas-Jacques Charrier, born in 1960.

FURTHER READING

Singer, Barnett. *Brigitte Bardot: A Biography.* Jefferson, N.C.: McFarland & Company, 2006.

barrelhouse blues A barrelhouse was a juke joint, a place where the BLUES was often played and liquor was served. The term *barrelhouse* emerged when a plank of wood suspended between two barrels served as a bar. The term *barrelhouse blues* refers to deep soul music, a combination of blues and soul. In *I Know Why the Caged Bird Sings,* Angelou remarks that the music of the Christian revival meeting and the music of the juke joint were very similar.

Basie, Count (William James Basie) (1904–1984) Maya Angelou and her son, Guy Johnson (born CLYDE BAILEY JOHNSON), enjoyed the music of Count Basie and his various orchestras. His unique style was popular for many decades, and Maya enjoyed listening and dancing to his music.

William James Basie was born on August 21, 1904, in Red Bank, New Jersey. His father was a coachman and caretaker for a wealthy judge; his mother took in laundry, baked pies for sale, and was a piano player. She introduced her son to the piano and paid for his lessons from her earnings. Basie was not a particularly good student and dropped out of school in junior high school. He hung out at a local vaudeville theater where he would do odd jobs and learned to work the lights. One day, the pianist did not arrive by showtime, and Basie filled in playing by ear. For the next few years, he supplied the music for silent movies at the theater and played for pickup bands at local resorts, dances, and amateur shows. In 1924, he moved to HARLEM, a hotbed of JAZZ at the time, where he joined bands that toured on the vaudeville circuit. Around 1928, he became known as "Count Basie," while playing with Walter Page and his Famous Blue Devils.

By this time, Basie was playing with many of the most famous jazz musicians and singers of the time, including Louis Armstrong, Fats Waller, BILLIE HOLIDAY, Benny Morton, Jimmy Rushing, Willie "the Lion" Smith, and James P. Johnson. He formed a nine-member band known first as the Barons of Rhythm and later known as the Count Basie Orchestra. His troupe enjoyed an international reputation as one of the leading big bands of the swing era. They disbanded for a period of time and then regrouped in 1952 and toured the United States and Europe, where, especially in France, jazz was enjoying a resurgence. The group incorporated bebop into their repertoire as long as the audience understood the beat. The orchestra produced many recordings with noted vocalists, including Ella Fitzgerald, Tony Bennett, Bing Crosby, Frank Sinatra, Sarah Vaughan, and Sammy Davis, Jr. Over the length of Basie's career, his groups were awarded nine Grammy Awards (the first in 1958) and several Grammy Hall of Fame honors. On April 26, 1984, Basie died of pancreatic cancer in Hollywood, Florida; he was 79.

FURTHER READING

Dance, Stanley. *The World of Count Basie.* New York: Da Capo, 1980.

Southern, Eileen. *The Music of Black Americans: A History.* W. W. Norton, 1971.

Baxter, Vivian (Vivian Baxter Johnson) (fl. 1930s) Little is known of Vivian Baxter's life, except what has been shared about her by Maya Angelou in her autobiographies. Vivian was born in St. Louis, Missouri, one of six children (one sister and four brothers). She was a trained pediatric nurse but preferred to earn her living as a hostess and gambler. To her daughter, Maya, she was a very beautiful, quick-witted, fast-talking, and fast-living woman. When Vivian and Maya's father, BAILEY JOHNSON, SR., divorced, they shipped their two children—Maya, three, and BAILEY JOHNSON, JR., four—by rail to their paternal grandmother, who lived in STAMPS, ARKANSAS. Baxter may have realized that she was not a good mother for small children, but her maternal compassion was clearly evident when the children became teenagers and then adults. Maya felt her mother's care and affection and felt Vivian was an excellent role model for black female independence.

Vivian Baxter had diplomas from many training programs. She was particularly proud of her certificate of graduation from the U.S. Merchant Marine. She was a mature black female at the time she entered that training, and she underwent it primarily to prove that it could be done. Bright and witty, she knew many APHORISMs and MAXIMs, which gave shape to her worldview and helped her teach Maya the standards of conventional behavior for black women. She was generous with her children, and she did her best to support their choices and teach them how to succeed.

Belafonte, Harry (Harold George Belafonte, Jr.) (1927–) Maya Angelou became acquainted with Harry Belafonte and his singing partner, MIRIAM MAKEBA, a female vocalist from Africa, in New York. Guy, Maya's son, particularly enjoyed their music. Angelou performed calypso songs and dances at the Purple Onion in SAN FRANCISCO and was greatly influenced by Belafonte's rhythms and style.

Born Harold George Belafonte, Jr., in New York City on March 1, 1927, Belafonte is a renowned Jamaican-American singer, actor, and social activist. He lived in New York City during his youth, except for the period of 1935–40, when he lived with his grandmother in Jamaica. His goal was to become an actor, and he took classes at the Dramatic Workshop of the New School, in New York City. Fellow students at that same school included Marlon Brando, Tony Curtis, Walter Matthau, Bea Arthur, and SIDNEY POITIER. Belafonte paid for the acting classes by working as a club singer. At first he was a pop singer, but he developed an interest in folk music and began performing in that genre. In 1952, he received a recording contract with RCA Victor. "Matilda" was his first single release and became his signature song. In 1956, his album *Calypso* was the first LP to sell over a million copies, and he was soon dubbed the "King of Calypso." Millions of Americans danced to his lilting songs, and Angelou was one of them.

Belafonte left RCA in the 1970s and made fewer recordings. He received his first Grammy Award for the album *Swing Dat Hammer* (1960), and he was the first African American to receive an Emmy Award (for his solo TV special *Tonight with Belafonte* [1959]). He accomplished his dream of acting and starred and had supporting roles in many films, most notably *Bright Road* (1953), *Carmen Jones* (1954), *Island in the Sun* (1957), *Buck and the Preacher* (1972), and *Uptown Saturday Night* (1974). Belafonte was an outspoken critic of the embargo of Cuba in the early 1960s. He supported peace initiatives with the Soviet Union during the cold war, opposed the United States invasion of Grenada, and praised the policies of Fidel Castro. Belafonte harshly criticized President George W. Bush's administration, calling its world policies "morally corrupt." He married Marguerite Byrd in 1948, and they had two daughters. They were divorced in 1957, and that same year, he married his second wife, Julie Robinson, with whom he had a son and a daughter.

FURTHER READING

Fogelson, Genia. *Harry Belafonte (Black American)*. Los Angeles: Hollaway House, 2008.

Black Aesthetic movement (Black Arts Movement) Angelou's work, particularly her poetry, often reflects the liberation ideology of the Black Aesthetic movement. Her overriding message, however, is that all people should be free to pursue equal rights and self-respect.

The Black Aesthetic movement was an effort among the black artistic community to persuade all black artists to reflect principles in their work that would be in keeping with goals of the revolutionary African-American movement. Larry Neal, a leader in the movement for a defined Black Aesthetic, wrote a famous afterword entitled "And Shine Swam On" for *Black Fire: An Anthology of Afro-American Writing* (1971), which he and LeRoi Jones edited. In the afterword, Neal stated:

> Finally, the black artist must link his work to the struggle for his liberation and the liberation of his brothers and sisters. . . . The artist and the political activist are one. They are both shapers of the future reality. Both understand and manipulate the collective myths of race. Both are warrior priests, lovers, and destroyers. For the first violence will be internal—the destruction of a weak spiritual self for a more perfect self. (655–656)

Though the Black Aesthetic is sometimes defined as a movement born in the wake of the 1960s quest for civil rights, it could appropriately be defined as beginning with the cries for freedom by antebellum slaves and continuing into the 21st century with cries for equality.

FURTHER READING

Jones, LeRoi (Amiri Baraka), and Larry Neal, eds. *Black Fire: An Anthology of Afro-American Writing*. New York: William Morrow, 1971.

blackface Angelou has mentioned blackface in some of her poetry. The blackface style of entertaining is considered to be another racial slur against African Americans. Burnt cork, black grease paint, and sometimes black shoe polish have been used often to darken the skin of white theatrical entertainers who perform blackface. Blackface minstrel shows became popular in the 1830s when white male actors donned the makeup to portray stereotypically negative characteristics of African Americans while dancing, singing, and telling jokes in black dialect. Al Jolson (1886–1950), an American singer born in Lithuania, was a comedian and actor best remembered today for his role in the 1927 movie *The* JAZZ SINGER, in which he sang same songs in blackface. It was the first full-length talking movie, and it is the film credited with introducing contemporary white Americans to the sounds of JAZZ and the BLUES. African-American music of the time was emerging from the turn of the century through an awakening of African-American arts called the HARLEM RENAISSANCE.

See also MINSTREL TRADITION.

FURTHER READING

Lott, Eric. *Love and Theft: Black Minstrelsy and the American Middle Class*. New York: Oxford University Press, 1995.

Strausbaugh, James. *Black Like You: Blackface, Whiteface, Insult and Imitation in American Popular Culture*. New York: Tarcher Books, 2007.

Black Panther Party The Black Panther Party, originally formed as the Black Panther Party for Self-Defense, was founded in Oakland, California, on

October 15, 1966, by Huey P. Newton and Bobby Seale. An African-American organization, its principal goals initially were to provide self-defense for blacks and promote black power. The party created what was called a Ten-Point Program, listing many of the social and political grievances that had often been articulated by black radicals and liberals since the 1930s. At its height, the Black Panther Party created and supported many social programs for the black populations of several large cities in the United States. "The Black Panthers protested a May 1967 gun control law understanding that if only the police had guns, blacks would be helpless—and they organized community patrols to protect people from muggers as well as from mistreatment by police" (Schweikart and Allen 2004, 687).

The author and activist JAMES BALDWIN and Maya Angelou disagreed on Baldwin's traveling from New York City, his home, to California to join ELDRIDGE CLEAVER as a spokesman for the Black Panthers. Maya had misgivings about the kind of person Eldridge Cleaver was and suspected that his ideas were too violent.

The Black Panther leadership strongly supported the doctrines of socialism and communism, and as a result, the party came under the scrutiny of the FBI. J. Edgar Hoover stated that the party was a great threat to the internal security of the country. The FBI used tactics to disrupt the party and were very successful. Many believe these efforts, which included harassment, surveillance, infiltration, false testimony, eavesdropping, and perhaps even assassination, led to the demise of the party in the early 1970s.

FURTHER READING

Quarles, Benjamin. *The Negro in the Making of America.* New York: Touchstone/Simon & Schuster, 1987.

Schweikart, Larry, and Michael Allen. *A Patriot's History of the United States: From Columbus's Great Discovery to the War on Terror.* New York: Sentinel/Penguin Group, 2004.

Blacks, The In the Off-Broadway production of this satirical play by Jean Genet depicting white RACISM, Angelou played the role of the masked White Queen. Later, she played the same role in Berlin and Venice when the play was revived. "The thrust of *The Blacks* is that if power roles were reversed from whites to blacks, blacks would behave in the same fashion as whites" (Hagen 1997, 139). The play ran for 1,408 performances in New York City in the 1960s. It was the longest-running nonmusical Off-Broadway production during the decade. The original cast, which performed both in New York and Europe, included Angelou as well as JAMES EARL JONES; Louis Gossett, Jr.; GODFREY CAMBRIDGE; and CICELY TYSON.

FURTHER READING

Hagen, Lyman B. *Heart of a Woman, Mind of a Writer, and Soul of a Poet: A Critical Analysis of the Writings of Maya Angelou.* Lanham, Md.: University Press of America, 1997.

Lupton, Mary Jane. *Maya Angelou: A Critical Companion.* Westport, Conn.: Greenwood Press, 1998.

blues, the As a singer, dancer, and songwriter, Angelou was familiar with blues rhythms and both wrote and performed blues music. Her preference was for dancing, but during the years that she worked as an entertainer in nightclubs, she sometimes sang blues songs. Her autobiographies, poetry, plays, and essays often reflect the influence of her blues heritage. The rhythm of her poetry is often lyrical, and both the words and the tempo frequently have an underlying sadness and the lamenting wail of the blues.

Though there is wide speculation about how blues music originated, most scholars suggest that it emerged in the latter decades of the 19th century, primarily from African-American communities of the deep South. W. E. B. DUBOIS explained that the "striving in the souls of black folk" (371) was expressed through the blues:

> And so by fateful chance the Negro folk-song—the rhythmic cry of the slave—stands today now simply as the sole American music, but as the most beautiful expression of human experience born this side of the seas. It still remains as the singular spiritual heritage of the nation and the greatest gift of the Negro People. (536–537)

The blues in its various forms is both a musical form and a musical genre. SPIRITUALS, field hollers, work songs, shouts and chants, and simple narrative ballads are often named as being roots for the blues. Some musicologists have speculated that the blues are a blending of African rhythms and European structure. The blues are recognized as having great influence on other music genres such as JAZZ, rhythm and blues, rock and roll, and rap.

The first man to popularize the blues was W. C. Handy "[who] was struck with the possibilities of utilizing it in musical composition in 1903 when he heard a man singing a song in a Mississippi train station" (Davis 2003, 332). The man was dressed in rags and singing while strumming his guitar. Handy recognized that he was singing "an earthy kind of music that he [Handy] had known as a boy in Alabama" (332).

Ma Rainey (Gertrude Malissa Nix Pridgett Raine) has been credited as being the first professional blues singer. She sang sad, touching songs that were well received by her audiences. "She claimed that it was she who gave to the songs the name 'blues' after being asked time and time again about the kind of song she was singing and having finally answered in an inspired moment, 'It's the blues'" (332). Others claim that the blues had no specific beginning.

FURTHER READING

Davis, Francis. *The History of the Blues: The Roots, The Music, The People.* Cambridge, Mass.: Da Capo Press, 2003.

Du Bois, W. E. B. *The Souls of Black Folk. W. E. B. Du Bois Writings.* New York: Library of American College Edition, 1986.

Oakley, Giles. *The Devil's Music: A History of the Blues.* Cambridge, Mass.: Da Capo Press, 1997.

Southern, Eileen. *The Music of Black Americans: A History.* New York: W. W. Norton, 1971.

Boers In 1961, Maya Angelou and her son, Guy, moved to Cairo, Egypt, with VUSUMZI MAKE, a South African freedom fighter she had met in New York City. Make was passionate in the cause of ending apartheid in South Africa and had traveled to the United States to represent the cause to the United Nations.

The Cape of Good Hope area of South Africa was originally settled in the mid-17th century by the Dutch East India Company; the settlers were primarily Dutch Calvinists, but there were smaller populations of French Huguenots, Germans, Frisians, and Flemish. Over time, Afrikaans, which stems from Dutch, became the common language. (Today, people of European descent who speak Afrikaans are generally known as Afrikaners.) The British took control of the area in the early 19th century.

Starting in the mid-1830s, many people began migrating out of the area seeking independence and to escape British rule, thus splitting the original settlers into two groups: those who remained in the Cape area and those who migrated. The latter group—who became known as the *boers,* the Dutch word for farmers—established independent provinces and practiced segregation from the indigenous population (a practice that later became legitimized and known as apartheid). British expansionism provoked two wars around the end of the 19th century; the Boers won the first one, and the British won the second. The result was the incorporation of the independent provinces into the formation of the Union of South Africa. Currently, there are remnants of the Boer group, but INTEGRATION has blurred their ethnicity to a large extent.

FURTHER READING

Farwell, Byron. *The Great Anglo-Boer War.* New York: W. W. Norton, 1990.

Meredith, Martin. *Diamonds, Gold, and War: The British, The Boers, and the Making of South Africa.* Jackson, Tenn.: Public Affairs, 2007.

Thomas, C. H. *Origin of the Anglo-Boer Revealed: The Conspiracy of the 19th Century Unmasked.* Charleston, S.C.: Biblio Bazaar, 2008.

Brer Rabbit In *The Heart of a Woman,* Angelou uses the metaphor of Brer Rabbit's wily escape to describe her move from the main part of a news office in Cairo, where her first desk was among Egyptian male reporters, to a private library on the same floor that was lined with books written in English. She writes that she stood before the books and "felt just like Brer Rabbit in the briar patch" (842).

JOEL CHANDLER HARRIS wrote the first and perhaps the most authentic collection of Negro animal tales and published them as *Uncle Remus: His Songs and His Sayings* in 1880. Harris was raised near a Georgia plantation, and his collections were derived from stories he heard there during his early years. The origins of Brer Rabbit, a trickster figure, may be a cross between Africa and Native American Cherokee tales, but certainly his character is one of the best known in the published stories. The rabbit's ability to outwit the fox and the bear, his primary adversaries, are legendary. One theory concerning Brer Rabbit is that he may represent an enslaved African using his wits in seeking revenge on his white owner. Elizabeth McNeil writes: "In slavery, blacks did not intend whites to understand all of the survival humor or the double entendres that bespoke black intellectual autonomy and critiqued whites; such was the case with the Brer Rabbit category of tales that whites heard and enjoyed" (504).

Probably the most famous of all the Uncle Remus tales is the TAR BABY story, in which the fox tries to trick the rabbit by getting him stuck to a doll made of tar and therefore immobilized. Rather than falling for the ruse, the gummed-up Brer Rabbit insists to the fox that the worst thing he could do to him, much worse than boiling and eating him, would be to throw him into the briar patch. So that is what Brer Fox does, and Brer Rabbit is saved because, as he says, "'Bred en bawn in a brier-patch, Brer Fox—bred en bawn in a brier-patch!' en wid dat he skip out des ez lively ez a cricket in de embers" (Brewer 1968, 6).

FURTHER READING

Brewer, J. Mason. *American Negro Folklore.* New York: Quadrangle/New York Times Book Co., 1968.

McNeil, Elizabeth. "Trickster." In *Encyclopedia of African-American Literature,* edited by Wilfred Samuels, 504–506. New York: Facts On File, 2007.

Brewer, John Mason (1896–1975) Some of the lore and folk sayings used by Maya Angelou in her autobiographies and poetry, including "The Wonderful Tar-Baby Story," which is by JOEL CHANDLER HARRIS and can be found in John Mason Brewer's *American Negro Folklore* (1968). Brewer's work has been considered important by academics specializing in African-American FOLKLORE and culture and by myriad general readers.

An African-American folklorist, Brewer was born on March 24, 1896, in Goliad, Texas. He was also a poet, essayist, historian, anthologist, and educator whose primary area of interest was black culture. He taught as a distinguished visiting professor at East Texas State University and lectured at Yale University; Duke University; and the universities of Toronto, California, Colorado, Arizona, and Texas. He is most notable for his three collections of black Texas folklore published in the mid-1950s: *The Word on the Brazos: Negro Preacher Tales from the Brazos Bottoms of Texas* (1953), *Aunt Dicey Tales: Snuff-Dipping Tales of the Texas Negro* (1956), and *Dog Ghosts and Other Texas Negro Folk Tales* (1958). These collections were his effort to preserve the stories of former slaves and their immediate families.

Brewer published several books about black contributions to Texas history. He also wrote an award-winning collection of African slave-immigrant lore called *American Negro Folklore* (1968). During his career, he taught at several colleges and universities, and he was the first African American ever to be elected an officer of the American Folklore Society. He died on January 24, 1975.

FURTHER READING

Byrd, James W. *J. Mason Brewer: Negro Folklorist.* Austin, Tex.: Steck-Vaughn Company, 1967.

Glasrud, Bruce A. "From Griggs to Brewer: A Review of Black Texas Culture, 1899–1940." *Journal of Big Bend Studies* 15 (2003): 195–212.

Brown, John (1800–1859) Maya Angelou was a self-educated, voracious reader from early childhood. She knew well the history of John Brown and his failed rebellion and alluded to him in her work. John Brown was born on May 9, 1800, in Torrington, Connecticut. His father, who vehemently opposed slavery, moved the family to an area of northern Ohio populated by many strong abolitionists when

John was five. Brown married when he was 20, and he and his wife had seven children before she died in 1831. He married again that same year and fathered 13 children with his second wife.

Financial success eluded Brown, though he started and built several businesses. By the time he was 50, he had become a militant abolitionist, regarding himself as commissioned by God to free slaves. In 1855, taking five sons with him, he went to Kansas to help antislavery settlers. In 1856, he and six others hacked to death several unarmed proslavery men; this was believed to be in retaliation for the burning and pillaging of the free-state community of Lawrence earlier that same year. He also raided homes in Missouri without much success.

In 1859, Brown moved to western Virginia with a force of 21 men, and on October 16, he and his men raided the federal armory at Harpers Ferry with the intention of arming thousands who supported abolition. His plan was thwarted by a company of U.S. Marines, led by Robert E. Lee, who stormed the arsenal, killing 10 and capturing seven, including Brown. After being tried and found guilty of treason, he was hanged on December 2, 1859. Many northerners, including Henry David Thoreau, did not support his methods but spoke favorably of the militant abolitionist.

FURTHER READING

Davis, Kenneth C. *Don't Know Much about History: Everything You Need to Know about American History but Never Learned.* New York: Perennial/HarperCollins, 2003.

Quarles, Benjamin. *The Negro in the Making of America.* 3rd ed. New York: Touchstone, 1987.

Remini, Robert V. *A Short History of the United States.* New York: HarperCollins, 2008.

Brown v. Board of Education of Topeka, Kansas This 1954 Supreme Court ruling was a significant step in the early efforts of the 20th-century CIVIL RIGHTS MOVEMENT. Maya Angelou was deeply involved in the fight for African-American rights, and her own son was in American public school at the time this ruling was passed. Some of the earliest attempts at INTEGRATION took place in Little Rock, Arkansas, and Angelou followed the events closely because she was raised mainly in STAMPS, ARKANSAS.

In 1951, the Reverend Oliver Brown brought suit against the Board of Education of Topeka, Kansas, because his daughter had to pass a white school on the way to catching her bus to a black school. The case went to the U.S. Supreme Court under Chief Justice Earl Warren, who had been appointed by President Eisenhower. The outcome of the case in 1954 was that "the Supreme Court's ruling in *Brown v. Board of Education* overturned *Plessy v. Ferguson* [1896] and prohibited state-supported racial discrimination" (Schweikart and Allen 2007, 662).

FURTHER READING

Kluger, Richard. *Simple Justice: The History of Brown v. Board of Education and Black America's Struggle for Equality.* New York: Norton, 1990.

Schweikart, Larry, and Michael Allen. *A Patriot's History of the United States: From Columbus's Great Discovery to the War on Terror.* New York: Sentinel/Penguin Group, 2004.

Bunche, Ralph (Ralph Johnson Bunche) (1903–1971) In her works, Maya Angelou has mentioned Ralph Bunche's name in relation to the civil rights fight against RACISM in the United States. She read and kept herself informed about people and events during the CIVIL RIGHTS MOVEMENT, and she recognized the importance and influence of African-American leaders such as Bunche, a renowned American political scientist and diplomat.

Bunche was born on August 7, 1903 (possibly 1904), in Detroit, Michigan; his father was a barber, and his mother was an amateur musician. The family moved to Albuquerque, New Mexico, when he was young in the hope that the climate would be beneficial to his parents' health, but they both died shortly after the relocation. He was raised by a grandmother in LOS ANGELES, CALIFORNIA, and became an outstanding student both in high school and college, graduating summa cum laude from the University of California, Los Angeles, in 1927. He earned his master's and doctoral degrees in political science from Harvard University while also teaching at Howard University in the Department of Political Science. He chaired the department at Howard from 1928 to 1950.

Bunche was very involved in the preliminary planning of the United Nations and collaborated with Eleanor Roosevelt in the creation and adoption of the UN Declaration of Human Rights. His participation in the Arab-Israeli conflict as the principal secretary of the UN Palestine commission, and as the United Nations chief mediator of the talks, led to the 1949 Armistice Agreement. That leadership was the basis for his being awarded the Nobel Peace Prize in 1950.

Bunche actively and vocally participated in the Civil Rights movement. He was involved in the 1963 March on Washington with MARTIN LUTHER KING, JR., and the March from Selma to Montgomery, Alabama. He died on December 9, 1971, and is buried in the Bronx, New York.

FURTHER READING

Lindway, Beverly, ed. *Ralph Johnson Bunche: Public Intellectual and Nobel Peace Laureate.* Champaign: University of Illinois Press, 2008.

Urquhart, Brian. *Ralph Bunche: An American Odyssey.* New York: W. W. Norton, 1998.

Butler, Samuel (1835–1902) Samuel Butler is one of the authors Angelou mentions reading as a young schoolgirl in STAMPS, ARKANSAS. His writing was important to her, and whenever she is asked who some of her favorite early authors were, Samuel Butler is mentioned.

The Victorian-era English novelist and essayist was born on December 4 or 5, 1835, near Bingham, Nottinghamshire, England. His parents assumed that he would follow in the footsteps of his father and grandfather and go into the clergy. He followed this course until he noted no difference in the behavior of the baptized and unbaptized young men, which raised doubts in his faith. After a long correspondence with his father on the subject and finding no satisfactory answer, he elected to try a new vocation—painting. However, his father, on whom he was financially dependent, would not support this new direction, though he compromised by lending him some money to start a sheep business in New Zealand. The business was successful, so Butler sold it and returned to England thinking that he had enough money to live on for the rest of his life if he lived modestly.

While in New Zealand, Butler read Darwin's *On the Origin of Species* and, finding the theory in keeping with his views, wrote several newspaper articles, including "Darwin among the Machines." That was the antecedent of a later satire, *Erewhon* (an anagram of "No Where"). Subsequently, he found a scientist, Jean-Baptiste Lamarck, had published basically the same theory 50 years earlier, whereupon Butler thought Darwin was a fraud.

Upon returning to England, Butler took courses to further his interest in painting. He was not a successful painter and was judged by some to be naive. However, a few of his works were hung in the Royal Academy during those years. He continued writing and painting and started the satirical, utopian novel *Erewhon,* published in 1872. Erewhon is a land where moral failings and mental illness are cured by a "straightener," while physical illness and misfortune are considered crimes and are dealt with harshly. *Erewhon* brought Butler recognition and financial rewards. A follow-up novel, *Erewhon, Revisited* (1901), was also well received. In 1872, he started *The Way of All Flesh,* a semiautobiographical novel that was completed in 1885, but at his request, it was not published until after his death (June 18, 1902). It is the novel for which he is most famous.

FURTHER READING

Raby, Peter. *Samuel Butler: A Biography.* Iowa City: University of Iowa Press, 1991.

Calloway, Cab (1907–1994) Maya Angelou was familiar with the sounds of Cab Calloway and listened to them with great pleasure and admiration. He was one of the many artists whose music entertained Maya when she worked at the Melrose Record Store in the FILLMORE DISTRICT of SAN FRANCISCO, CALIFORNIA.

Cabell (Cab) Calloway was born on Christmas Day 1907 into a middle-class family in Rochester, New York. His father was an attorney; his mother, a teacher and church organist. Calloway enjoyed singing in the church choir, where his musical talent was recognized. The family moved to Baltimore, Maryland, in 1918, and it was there that he began private voice lessons and to frequent and perform in many of Baltimore's JAZZ clubs.

The summer after graduating from high school, Calloway went to Chicago, where his sister Blanche, an established jazz singer, lived. He credited his sister, who became a popular bandleader, with inspiring him to enter show business, and they became part of a touring production of a popular black musical revue. While in Chicago, Calloway held jobs as a singer, drummer, and emcee at some of the city's jazz clubs. It was at the Sunset Club that he met and performed with Louis Armstrong, who introduced him to the "scat" style of singing (in which meaningless syllables are improvised often in imitation of a musical instrument), and this became a trademark of his own singing.

By 1939, Calloway had taken over a floundering band called The Missourians and had built its reputation to the degree that they were then coupled with the DUKE ELLINGTON Band and played at the Cotton Club, the premier nightclub in HARLEM. The Missourians became the "house" band when the Ellington band was on the road. In the 1930s, the band's national popularity flourished, primarily because twice weekly they were featured on a nationally broadcast NBC show from the Cotton Club.

In 1931, Calloway recorded his most famous song, "Minnie the Moocher," and became known as the Hi-de-ho Man from a phrase in the chorus of that song. His band made many recordings in the 1930s and 1940s, and they were sometimes featured with Duke Ellington's band in several films made during this time. In the later years of his career, he personally performed in films and on the stage where his acting and singing talents were recognized. Cab Calloway died, age 86, on November 18, 1994, six months after suffering a stroke.

FURTHER READING

Shipton, Alyn. *Hi-de-ho-Man: The Life of Cab Calloway.* Oxford: Oxford University Press, 2007.

Travis, Dempsey, Jr. *Cab Calloway.* Holt, Minn.: Partners, 1997.

Cambridge, Godfrey (Godfrey MacArthur Cambridge) (1933–1976) In 1960, Godfrey Cambridge and Maya Angelou put together the successful fund-raiser *Cabaret for Freedom* in Greenwich Village in order to raise money for the MARTIN LUTHER KING, JR.'S SOUTHERN CHRISTIAN LEADERSHIP CONFERENCE. Cambridge and Angelou remained friends for many years until his premature death at age 43. Angelou admired his professionalism and respected his dedication to the CIVIL RIGHTS MOVEMENT through the arts.

An African-American actor and comedian, Godfrey MacArthur Cambridge was born on February 26, 1933, in New York City; his parents were immigrants from British Guiana. He was awarded a scholarship to study medicine, but after three years at Hofstra College, he decided to pursue a career in show business. He had many roles both on and off Broadway and in films. One of his most memorable film roles was in *Watermelon Man,* the story of a white bigot who one day awakens with black skin.

In the late 1960s and early 1970s Cambridge was a frequent guest as a standup comedian on *The Tonight Show* and other television shows. On November 29, 1976, at the age of 43, he had a heart attack and died. His death occurred on the set of a television movie, *Victory at Entebbe,* in which he was to play the part of Idi Amin.

FURTHER READING

"Godfrey Cambridge and New Family." *Jet,* 27 November 1975.

"Camptown Races" In poem "Forgive," an ironic poem about the oppression of African Americans in Richmond, Virginia, in the time of slavery, Maya Angelou refers to "camptown races." Stephen Collins Foster (1826–64) wrote the popular song "Camptown Races," which was published in 1850. Its original title was "Gwine to Run All Night," and it is also known as "Camptown Ladies" and "De Camptown Races." The origin of the song is unknown, but camptowns, or tent cities, were common temporary housing throughout the United States, especially during the period of the expansion of the American railroad system. At that time, horse racing was a popular form of entertainment. The song was not initially very popular; Foster's royalties for the first seven years after publication were only a little more than $100.

FURTHER READING

Emerson, Ken. *Doo-dah!: Stephen Foster and the Rise of American Popular Culture.* New York: Da Capo Press, 1998.

Capote, Truman (1924–1984) In 1954, Maya Angelou auditioned for a part in the play *House of Flowers,* written by Truman Capote. She was offered the part and would have played opposite the singer and actress PEARL BAILEY, but she declined the role to tour in Europe as a lead dancer for a production of *PORGY AND BESS.* Capote subsequently wrote a book called *The Muses Are Heard* (1956), which chronicled part of the *Porgy and Bess* tour when it played in Russia, but Angelou had left the company by then.

Born in New Orleans on September 30, 1924, to Lillie Mae and Archulus Persons, and originally named Truman Streckfus Persons, Capote was a noted novelist, playwright, and short story writer. His parents divorced when he was about four years old, and he was sent to live with relatives in Alabama for the next four to five years. While he was there, he met and became good friends with Harper Lee, who wrote *To Kill a Mockingbird.* Some critics suggest that he was the prototype for the character Dill in that book. Their friendship was a lifelong one.

His mother's second marriage was to Joseph Capote, a well-to-do businessman, and Truman moved to live with them in New York. There his stepfather renamed him Truman Garcia Capote. He began writing seriously at age 11, and it was an activity he thoroughly enjoyed; he would write for about three hours every day after school. He completed his formal education at age 17, feeling that further education would be of no benefit to his writing.

Capote wrote many novels and plays, some of which became screenplays. His best known book, which he called a "nonfiction novel," was *In Cold Blood,* an account of the murder of a Kansas farm family. He spent four years researching the facts, including many interviews with the murderers. The book brought him instant fame, and he also wrote the script for the film of the same name.

Capote was an outspoken, controversial person, short in stature, with a high-pitched voice—a man who dressed flamboyantly and enjoyed being the center of attention and associating with the jet set. He died on August 25, 1984, in LOS ANGELES, CALIFORNIA, age 59, at the home of his longtime friend Joanne Carson, the ex-wife of the late-night TV host Johnny Carson. The cause of death was a liver disease complicated by phlebitis and multiple drug ingestions.

FURTHER READING

Capote, Truman. *The Muses Are Heard.* New York: Random House, 1956.

Clarke, Gerald. *Capote, A Biography.* Cambridge, Mass.: Da Capo Press, 2005.

Plimpton, George. *Truman Capote: In Which Various Friends, Enemies, Acquaintances and Detractors Recall His Turbulent Career.* New York: Knopf, 1998.

Carmichael, Stokely (Kwame Ture) (1941–1998) Maya Angelou was friendly with several of the leaders in the American CIVIL RIGHTS MOVEMENT, and she knew of Stokely Carmichael through MARTIN LUTHER KING, JR.'s SOUTHERN CHRISTIAN LEADERSHIP CONFERENCE activities before Carmichael separated from King's nonviolent politics.

Stokely Standiford Churchill Carmichael was born on June 29, 1941, in Port of Spain, Trinidad. When he was two years old, his family moved to New York, seeking better socioeconomic conditions. Stokely, however, remained in Trinidad for several years, being cared for by his grandmother. Later, he joined his parents in New York. He attended the prestigious Bronx High School of Science in New York and graduated from Howard University in Washington, D.C., with a bachelor's degree in philosophy in 1964.

While at Howard, Carmichael joined the Student Nonviolent Coordinating Committee (SNCC), a civil rights activists' organization, and he participated in sit-ins and protest marches. With others, he helped raise the black voter registration in Lowndes County, Alabama, from 70 to over 2,700, which then exceeded the white voter registration by 300. In 1966, he was elected chairman of the SNCC. Shortly thereafter, he joined Martin Luther King, Jr., and others in continuing the "March Against Fear" initiated by James Meredith. Carmichael was arrested during the march, and upon his release, he gave his first "Black Power" speech, in which he encouraged African Americans to have black pride and social independence. He left the SNCC the following year, feeling that it should not allow white activists in the organization and that nonviolence was not the only way to achieve civil rights.

In 1967, Carmichael published *Black Power,* cowritten with Charles V. Hamilton, in which he expressed his political views, including his opposition to the Vietnam War. He started spending more of his time making speeches and lecturing throughout the world, and he visited North Vietnam, China, Cuba, and Guinea. In 1969, having married the South African performer MIRIAM MAKEBA the previous year (they separated in 1973), he moved to Conakry, Guinea, and became an aide to Prime Minister Ahmed Sekou Tourethan; he also become a student of the exiled Ghanian president KWAME NKRUMAH. He later changed his name to Kwame Ture to honor these men. While he was there, he organized the All-African Revolutionary party. Carmichael lived in Guinea the rest of his life and died of prostate cancer on November 15, 1998.

FURTHER READING

Carmichael, Stokely (Kwame Ture), and Charles V. Hamilton. *Black Power: The Politics of Liberation in America.* 1967. Reprint, New York: Random House, 1992.

Carson, Clayborne, David J. Garrow, Gerald Gill, Vincent Harding, and Darlene Clark Hine, eds. *The Eyes on the Prize Civil Rights Reader: Documents, Speeches, and Firsthand Accounts from the Black Freedom Struggle.* New York: Penguin, 1991.

Davis, Kenneth C. *Don't Know Much about History: Everything You Need to Know about American History but Never Learned.* New York: Perennial/HarperCollins, 2003.

Tindall, George Brown, and David E. Shi. *America: A Narrative History.* 4th ed. Vol. 2. New York: W. W. Norton, 1996.

Cheshire cat's smile Angelou has mentioned the Cheshire cat's smile in her poetry and writing.

A fictional animal, the Cheshire cat was popularized by Lewis Carroll in his book *Alice in Wonderland* and Walt Disney's film of the same name. The cat is depicted with a mischievous grin exposing teeth and gums; it also has the ability to appear and disappear in whole or in part at will. These are characteristics that have caused it to appear frequently in popular culture.

chifforobe Angelou has mentioned using a chifforobe in both her mother's and grandmother's homes. A chifforobe is a closetlike piece of furniture. A side-by-side combination of a chest of drawers, or chiffonier, and a wardrobe, it was designed to increase clothing storage space, which was lacking in many homes at the beginning of the 20th century. Sears, Roebuck and Co. first advertised the chifforobe in 1908. It is primarily used in the United States, mostly in the South.

Cisco Kid Maya and her brother, Bailey, enjoyed listening to episodes of *The Cisco Kid* on the radio when they were children. The Cisco Kid was a fictional heroic Mexican caballero or horseman popularized in several movies, on radio, in television series, and in comics. He was depicted as a Lone Ranger sort of character with a sidekick named Pancho, and the stories were their adventures in the West. His character was based on the main character in an O. Henry short story called "The Caballeros Way." In that story, he was a cruel outlaw and killer and not Mexican. He was responsible for at least 18 deaths, including a girlfriend whom he killed when he discovered that she meant to betray him.

More than 20 Cisco Kid movies were made mostly in the 1940s. During the same period, a radio series of over 600 episodes was aired. A series of 156 programs was telecast in the early 1950s.

Civil Rights movement Though Maya Angelou was not generally a placard-carrying or marching activist, she was deeply involved in and supportive of the American Civil Rights movement. Having been raised in the deep South, she knew personally the oppression, fear, and deprivation many African Americans were forced to live with on a daily basis. In 1960, she and GODFREY CAMBRIDGE put on a successful fund-raising show for MARTIN LUTHER KING, JR.'s SOUTHERN CHRISTIAN LEADERSHIP CONFERENCE (SCLC). *Cabaret for Freedom* played several weeks at a theater in Greenwich Village. Angelou and Cambridge enlisted many stars to present their specialties in the cabaret, and the effort raised a significant amount of money. Subsequently, because Angelou's administrative abilities were showcased by directing the cabaret, Martin Luther King, Jr., invited her to be the coordinator for the SCLC's northeast office, located in New York. She served successfully in that capacity for about a year and then moved to Africa.

The Civil Rights movement, whose direction was primarily to eliminate discrimination and disenfranchisement of African Americans, peaked during the 1954–68 period. Efforts had begun many years before this, and though they were ineffectual for the most part, they provided a foundation for the successes of the 1950s and 1960s. The movement was aimed at establishing the lawful rights of people of color and also addressed issues such as freedom, respect, dignity, and social and economic equality.

The tone of the movement was nonviolent protest and civil disobedience, taking the form of sit-ins, boycotts, marches, and other peaceful activities. Many civil rights organizations such as the NATIONAL ASSOCIATION FOR THE ADVANCEMENT OF COLORED PEOPLE (NAACP), the Student Nonviolent Coordinating Committee (SNCC), the CONGRESS OF RACIAL EQUALITY (CORE), and the SCLC provided leadership for these efforts. One of the most noted marches was the 1963 March on Washington, during which more than 250,000 persons heard Martin Luther King, Jr.'s famous "I Have a Dream" speech given in front of the Lincoln Memorial.

The results of the movement were numerous. In 1954, the U.S. Supreme Court decided that the education of black children in separate schools from white children was unconstitutional (see *BROWN V. BOARD OF EDUCATION OF TOPEKA, KANSAS*). In 1956, the local ordinance segregating blacks and whites on public transportation in Montgomery, Alabama, was lifted. Drives throughout the South significantly increased black voter registration and stimulated the passage of the Civil Rights Act of 1964 and the Voter Rights Act of 1965. The Civil Rights Act of 1964 outlaws racial segregation in schools, at the workplace, and at public facilities. The Civil Rights Acts of 1968 forbids discrimination in the sale, rental, and financing of housing based on race, religion, and national origin.

FURTHER READING

Bullard, Sara. *Free at Last: A History of the Civil Rights Movement and Those Who Died in the Struggle.* New York: Oxford University Press, 1994.

Dierenfield, Bruce J. *The Civil Rights Movement.* Rev. ed. Harlow, U.K.: Pearson Education, 2008.

Hampton, Henry, Steve Fayer, and Sarah Flynn, comps. *Voices of Freedom: An Oral History of the Civil Rights Movement from the 1950s through the 1980s.* New York: Bantam Books, 1990.

Cleaver, Eldridge (1935–1998) Though Maya Angelou, an advocate of nonviolent political persuasion, was wary of the potential violence in the civil rights philosophy of Eldridge Cleaver, she accepted the decision of her close friend, JAMES BALDWIN, to join Cleaver and the BLACK PANTHER PARTY in California.

Cleaver was born August 31, 1935, in Wabbaseka, Arkansas. His family later moved to Arizona and then to LOS ANGELES, CALIFORNIA. He spent time in juvenile detention centers in his teens as a result of petty crimes. In 1957, he was convicted of assault with intent to murder and was imprisoned. While in prison, he wrote several philosophical and political essays with unconventional views. The essays were later published in his book *Soul on Ice* (1968), which was very influential in the Black Power movement. After his release from prison, he became a spokesman for the Black Panther Party. His attraction to the party was because of its commitment to the use of arms in the struggle for equal rights for African Americans. In 1968, while a member of the party, he led an ambush on two police officers, was arrested and charged with attempted murder, jumped bail, and fled to Cuba and later to Algeria. He returned to the United States in 1975 and renounced his allegiance to the Black Panther Party. The murder charges were subsequently reduced to assault, and he was placed on probation.

Cleaver's political views changed substantially after returning to the United States. He became a conservative Republican and ran unsuccessfully for public office. He died on May 1, 1998, reportedly from prostate cancer and diabetes.

FURTHER READING

Cleaver, Eldridge. *Soul on Ice.* New York: Delta/Dell, 1999.

Cleaver, Eldridge, and Kathleen Cleaver, ed. *Target Zero: Life in Writing.* New York: Palgrave Macmillan, 2007.

Clinton, Bill (William Jefferson Clinton) (1945–) In 1993, Maya Angelou was invited to read a poem at the inauguration of President Bill Clinton—the first African-American woman to be given that honor. She was only the second poet to read at a presidential inauguration. The other was Robert Frost, who read at the inauguration of President John F. Kennedy in 1961. Frost had written a poem called "Dedication" for Kennedy, but because of the sun's glare, he could not see the

Maya Angelou reads her poem "On the Pulse of Morning" at the inauguration of Bill Clinton as president of the United States on January 20, 1993 *(Courtesy National Archives and Records Administration, William J. Clinton Presidential Library)*

words clearly and instead recited his poem "The Gift Outright," which he knew by heart. Angelou was able to read her poem "On the Pulse of Morning" in its entirety, speaking of the wonder of life and hope for the future of all humankind.

Colored Methodist Episcopal Church (C.M.E. Church) Maya Angelou and her brother, BAILEY JOHNSON, JR., attended this church with their grandmother during the years they lived with her in STAMPS, ARKANSAS. She refers to the church by this name on the opening page of *I Know Why the Caged Bird Sings.* The Colored Methodist Episcopal Church, renamed the Christian Methodist Episcopal Church in the 1950s, is a historically African-American church organized in 1870 by several black ministers. Its purpose was to create an organization that would allow African Americans to ordain their own ministers and bishops without the approval or endorsement of the white-dominated Methodist Episcopal Church, South. The C.M.E. Church came into being with the full support of the mother church. Today there are about 800,000 members in 3,000 churches in the United States.

FURTHER READING

Mead, Frank S. *Handbook of Denominations in the United States.* 9th ed. Revised by Samuel S. Hill. Nashville, Tenn.: Abingdon Press, 1990.

"Colored only" Angelou wrote that when the train carrying her and her brother, Bailey, from Long Beach, California, to their grandmother's home in STAMPS, ARKANSAS, reached the segregated South, she vaguely recalled that black people came forward and fed them fried chicken and potato salad. She was only three, but she has retained an obscure memory of some sort of change among the black people on that trip. Denoting separate but supposedly equal facilities, "Colored only" signs were prevalent throughout the South prior to the 1950s, when many of the JIM CROW laws were challenged for their illegality. The CIVIL RIGHTS MOVEMENT had many aims, and one was to rid the United States of that kind of discrimination. The signs designated racial restrictions in public facilities such as restaurants, public transportation, restrooms, and drinking fountains.

Congress of Racial Equality (CORE) The Congress of Racial Equality (CORE), a civil rights activist organization, was formed in Chicago by a group of pacifist students in 1942. CORE's goal was to help African Americans achieve equal rights through nonviolent civil disobedience.

In 1947, to test the Supreme Court ruling that racial discrimination in interstate travel was unconstitutional, CORE launched a two-week campaign, known as the Journey of Reconciliation, through North Carolina, Virginia, Kentucky, and Tennessee. Some members were arrested and jailed for breaking state JIM CROW laws, but the group attracted considerable publicity. Student sit-ins in 1961 in restaurants and at lunch counters helped eliminate SEGREGATION in these public facilities. CORE was also responsible for organizing Freedom Rides in the Deep South and was one of the civil rights organizations that planned the March on Washington in 1963. That same year, CORE, the NATIONAL ASSOCIATION FOR THE ADVANCEMENT OF COLORED PEOPLE, and the Student Nonviolent Coordinating Committee launched the Freedom Summer campaign, with the goal of increasing African-American voter registration in Mississippi. The drive was very successful: In some counties, black voter registration came to exceed white registration.

In the mid-1960s, CORE had more than 53 active chapters with about 100,000 members. In the late 1960s, the organization, under the leadership of Roy Innis, changed direction and became more concerned with black nationalism. James Farmer, one of CORE's founding members and its original leader, left the organization and began teaching at Lincoln University. He later entered government service, feeling that CORE had lost its main social agenda in favor of black nationalism.

CORE was an important organization, and Maya Angelou knew of its philosophy and activity through her own involvement in the American CIVIL RIGHTS MOVEMENT. However, she preferred to be active in MARTIN LUTHER KING, JR.'s organization, the SOUTHERN CHRISTIAN LEADERSHIP CONFERENCE.

FURTHER READING

Klarman, Michael J. *Unfinished Business: Racial Equality in American History.* New York: Oxford University Press, 2007.

Schweikart, Larry, and Michael Allen. *A Patriot's History of the United States: From Columbus's Great Discovery to the War on Terror.* New York: Sentinel/Penguin Group, 2004.

Tindall, George Brown, and David E. Shi. *America: A Narrative History.* 4th ed. Vol. 2. New York: W. W. Norton, 1996.

cooking One of Maya Angelou's jobs, when she was a young mother just out of high school, was as a short-order cook in a Creole-style restaurant, an episode of her life she narrates in *Gather Together in My Name* (1974). She did not know how to cook Creole food, but her mother's cook told her, "Ain't nothing but onions, green peppers and garlic. Put that in everything and you got Creole food. You know how to cook rice, don't you?" (235) Angelou learned to cook Creole, and as she matured and traveled, she learned to cook many other types of cuisine as well. Today she owns more than a hundred cookbooks, studies them, and serves her family and guests beautiful, healthful meals.

Angelou has simplified many complex dishes to make the taste available whenever she has a desire for it. In an early interview with Arline Inge, she prepared *kontumre,* a West African vegetable dish, and two side dishes to accompany it. She gave Inge some of the background and method for what she was preparing:

> "There [in Africa], this meal takes a day to prepare," she explains, "with the children and servants peeling, seeding and chopping the tomatoes for Jollof Rice. It takes at least two hours just to pick enough wild mustard greens for the Kontumre, another hour to wash them and another to chop them fine. But here at home, I just pick up some canned tomatoes and frozen spinach for greens, and I season with cumin and chilies in place of the native spices. It takes almost no time to put the ingredients together." Maya turns her attention to a pan of simmering peanut sauce for her golden Groundnut Stew. Now it's her turn to taste. "It's not bad, is it!" (Inge 1989, 97)

In 2004, Angelou published a cookbook entitled *Hallelujah! The Welcome Table.* There is a double dedication; the first reads: "I dedicate this book to every wannabe cook who will dare criticism by getting into the kitchen and stirring up some groceries." The second states: "To O, who said she wanted a big, pretty cookbook. Well, honey, here you are." Each chapter of recipes from around the world has a contextualizing introduction, and the chapter that explains when Angelou met OPRAH WINFREY is called "Oprah's Smothered Chicken." Angelou prepared the chicken dish when Oprah was a guest in her home. The next morning, she offered her guest an open choice for breakfast, and Oprah wanted to have some of the previous night's dinner again. She asked Angelou the name of the dish and was told that it was called Smothered Chicken. "Oprah said, 'No, this is too good for such a simple name. This is suffocated chicken.' She then added, 'This chicken never knew what hit it'" (203).

Great Food, All Day Long, Angelou's second cookbook, was published in 2010.

FURTHER READING

Angelou, Maya. *Great Food, All Day Long: Cook Splendidily, Eat Smart.* New York: Random House, 2010.

———. *Hallelujah! The Welcome Table.* New York: Random House, 2008.

Inge, Arline. "Maya Angelou." In *Conversations with Maya Angelou,* edited by Jeffrey M. Elliot, 97–101. London and Jackson: University Press of Mississippi, 1989.

coq au vin Maya Angelou's father, BAILEY JOHNSON, SR., was a cook in a U.S. Navy kitchen in San Diego. There were often leftovers, and he could create coq au vin out of leftover chicken and wine for his family. The term *coq au vin* is French for "rooster in wine." Because the rooster is usually old when it is eaten, braising, or slow COOKING, is often used to tenderize the meat. The chicken is covered with red wine and refrigerated the day before the final cooking and serving. Vegetables, some form of pork fat, mushrooms, garlic, and herbs are often added to the wine marinade, and the result is a tender, savory chicken dish.

cotton bolls The fibrous, prickly pods that encase growing fluffs of cotton, cotton bolls are hard and taloned, and unless protection for the hands is provided, they tear the skin. When she was young, Maya would watch the cotton pickers go to the fields in the morning and return exhausted in the late afternoon, often with their fingers cut by the cotton bolls. Angelou became passionately angry in later years after witnessing a stereotyped photograph of happy, singing cotton pickers as she knew firsthand of their suffering during the long days in the fields.

cracker This is a contemptuous name in parts of the South for poor whites. The term appears a few times in *I Know Why the Caged Bird Sings.*

Cullen, Countee (LeRoy Porter) (1903–1946) Maya Angelou enjoyed reading the poetry of Countee Cullen, one of the authors she read as a child. She occasionally quoted his work, and she admired him as an educated African American and one of her cultural heroes. She admired his high European style of writing and dedicated her poem "Lord, in My Heart" to him.

Cullen was born LeRoy Porter on May 30, 1903. Biographers cannot agree on his place of birth, which has been given variously as Louisville, Kentucky; New Orleans, Louisiana; Baltimore Maryland; or possibly New York City. He was abandoned by his parents shortly after his birth and raised by his grandmother until her death in 1918. After her death, he lived with the Reverend Frederick Ashbury Cullen and his wife in HARLEM. Reverend Cullen was the minister at Salem Methodist Episcopal Church. At this time, Porter changed his surname to Cullen, and even though he was never formally adopted, he considered the Cullens his parents.

Countee Cullen was an excellent student and achieved recognition for his poetry at an early age by winning several poetry contests. He attended DeWitt Clinton High School, which was primarily white, and was elected vice president of his senior class. After graduation from high school, he attended New York University. During his undergraduate years, he continued writing poetry, and many of his works appeared in leading periodicals of the day. In 1925, he graduated Phi Beta Kappa from New York University; distinguished himself by winning first place in the Witter Bynner poetry contest; and had his first collection of poems, *Color,* published. The collection won the Harmon Foundation in Literary Award and received critical acclaim in both black and white literary circles.

A contemporary of LANGSTON HUGHES, ZORA NEALE HURSTON, and Sterling Brown, Cullen was considered one of the outstanding HARLEM RENAISSANCE poets. He continued his education at Harvard University, graduating with a master's degree in literature in 1926. In the following years, he wrote a column for the Urban League's publication *Opportunity;* he put together an anthology of the works of 38 black poets; published further collections of his poetry; and wrote a novel, a play, and a collection of children's poems. In 1934, he turned down an offer to teach at Dillard University in New Orleans, choosing instead to teach French at DeWitt Clinton Junior High School in Harlem, a position he held for the rest of his life.

Cullen died unexpectedly on January 9, 1946, of poisoning from uremia coupled with high blood pressure. For a time after his death, he was celebrated as the most outstanding black writer of his time.

FURTHER READING

Hutchison, George. *The Harlem Renaissance in Black and White.* Cambridge, Mass.: Belknap Press of Harvard University, 1996.

Perry, Margaret. *A Bio-Bibliography of Countee P. Cullen 1903–1946.* Contributions in Afro-American and African Studies. Santa Barbara, Calif.: Greenwood Press, 1970.

Cultural Association for Women of African Heritage (CAWAH) The Cultural Association for Women of African Heritage, headed by JAZZ vocalist, songwriter, and actress ABBEY LINCOLN and Maya Angelou, was important for its inclusion of black entertainers in the nationalist African American CIVIL RIGHTS MOVEMENT. The murder in 1961 of Patrice Lumumba, the first prime minister of the Democratic Republic of the Congo and a strong proponent of nationalism in Africa, sparked an African-American nationalism movement in the United States. Several organizations supported the movement: the Nation of Islam, Muslim Brotherhood, United African Nationalist Movement, The Universal African Nationalist Movement, and CAWAH were the major groups.

FURTHER READING

Clark, John Henrik. *The New Afro-American Nationalism* (Fall 1961). Available online. URL: http://www.africawithin.com/clarke/new_afro.htm. Accessed February 25, 2010.

D

Davis, Bette (1908–1989) When they were children in STAMPS, ARKANSAS, Maya Angelou and her brother, Bailey, particularly enjoyed the films of Bette Davis. As Maya raised her only son, Guy, they often went to see films, and some of their favorites were the older films with stars from the past, including Davis.

Bette Davis, born Ruth Elizabeth Davis on April 5, 1908, was a very successful American film, stage, and television actress whose career spanned over 60 years. She played in more than 100 films, was nominated for the Academy Award 10 times, and twice received the Oscar for best actress. She was the first woman to receive a Lifetime Achievement Award from the American Film Institute. Her range of roles was broad, and she was noted for her willingness to play unsympathetic characters. In 1949, she was the highest paid woman in the United States, earning over $10,000 per week under a Warner Brothers four-film contract.

Davis was characterized as one of American film's leading ladies until the late 1940s and had a reputation as being forceful, combative, and perfectionist. Her forthright manner, clipped vocal style, and ever-present cigarette have often been imitated and satirized. One of the achievements of which she was most proud was cosponsoring the opening of the servicemen's club, Hollywood Canteen, during World War II. In early 1942, she sold more than $2 million dollars' worth of war bonds in two days. A picture of herself in the film *Jezebel* was auctioned off for $250,000 to support the war effort.

In 1983, Davis was diagnosed with breast cancer; had a mastectomy; and, over the next two weeks, suffered four strokes that left her face partially paralyzed and her speech slurred. After a lengthy period of physical therapy, she continued her career in film and television. She died on October 6, 1989, at the age of 81 as a result of the reoccurrence of breast cancer.

FURTHER READING

Fuller, Elizabeth. *Me and Jezebel: When Bette Davis Came to Dinner—And Stayed . . . And Stayed . . . And Stayed . . . And . . .* New York: Berkley, 1992.

Moseley, Roy. *Betty Davis.* 2nd ed. Lexington: University Press of Kentucky, 2003.

Quirk, Lawrence. *Fasten Your Seatbelts: The Passionate Life of Bette Davis.* New York: Signet, 1990.

Davis, Ossie (Raiford Chatman Davis) (1917–2005) Ossie Davis was a civil rights activist, director, actor, poet, and playwright. Maya Angelou knew him through his work in the CIVIL RIGHTS MOVEMENT and also through their work in the theater.

Born Raiford Chatman Davis on December 18, 1917, Ossie Davis was an African-American actor, playwright, author, director and social activist. The nickname "Ossie" came from a county clerk who misunderstood his mother's pronunciation of the initials of his first and middle names. Davis's acting career spanned seven decades and began in HARLEM with the Rose McClendon Players in 1939. His first film role was in SIDNEY POITIER's production of *No Way Out*. In the early years of his career, he tried to avoid playing subservient roles often allotted to black actors at the time. Later, he enjoyed success starring in several of Spike Lee's films.

With his wife, RUBY DEE, Davis was very active in the Civil Rights movement, and they were instrumental in the organizing the March on Washington for Jobs and Freedom in 1963. Their friends included MARTIN LUTHER KING, JR., MALCOLM X, and Jesse Jackson. Davis and Dee wrote a book together called *With Ossie and Ruby: In This Life Together* (1998). In the book, Davis states:

> It wasn't a matter of whether I had the talent, but of whether I was free enough, strong enough, bold enough, and confident enough to use it—to summon up at will, from memory and imagination, the authority and the power to assert myself, to stop hiding behind the ready smile of a free and easy good nature . . . and dare to become the man I was meant to be. . . . Such is the redemptive power of trying to become an artist. I couldn't be an artist unless first I became a man! (397)

Davis died of natural causes in Miami, Florida, on February 4, 2005, while working on a film called *Retirement*. He was 87 years old.

FURTHER READING

Davis, Ossie, and Ruby Dee. *With Ossie and Ruby: In This Life Together.* New York: William Morrow, 1998.

Dee, Ruby (Ruby Ann Wallace) (1924–) Along with her husband, OSSIE DAVIS, Ruby Dee was a strong activist in the CIVIL RIGHTS MOVEMENT. Angelou knew the couple well because of their work in the nonviolent civil rights work of MARTIN LUTHER KING, JR., and both Dee and Davis were active in helping to organize King's 1963 March on Washington.

A leading African-American stage, film, and television actress, Dee was born Ruby Ann Wallace on October 27, 1924, in Cleveland, Ohio. Her mother left the family shortly after her birth. After her father remarried, the family moved to HARLEM in New York City. Her stepmother, a teacher, made their home a creative and academic environment. Ruby was introduced to world literature and tutored in classical piano and violin. While at Hunter High School, her talents in writing and oratory led to school drama productions. Subsequently, at Hunter College, she earned a bachelor's degree in Romance languages and became active in the American Negro Theater with budding actors HARRY BELAFONTE and SIDNEY POITIER.

Dee had roles in several Off-Broadway plays in the early 1940s. In 1946, she had a role in *Jeb*, through which she met a young actor and playwright, Ossie Davis, whom she married two years later. The couple were linked both personally and professionally through their acting careers and civil rights activism. Dee's career has spanned more than seven decades, during which she played hundreds of roles on the stage, in film, and on television. In 2006, at age 83, she earned the Screen Actors Guild Award and was nominated for an Academy Award for best supporting actress for her role in the film *American Gangster*, starring Denzel Washington. She has continued to work since her husband's death in 2005, and she has received numerous awards and honors.

FURTHER READING

Davis, Ossie, and Ruby Dee. *With Ossie and Ruby: In This Life Together.* New York: William Morrow, 1998.

depression, the (Great Depression) Maya Angelou and her brother, BAILEY JOHNSON, JR., lived with their grandmother, Annie Henderson, in STAMPS, ARKANSAS, during the American depression of the 1930s. Their grandmother was able to keep her general store open by allowing her customers to trade government-issued foods they had received for items in the store. Annie Henderson made most of the clothes for the children and herself, and she managed her home and store with careful frugality. Maya recalled this time in *I Know Why the Caged Bird Sings,* but the impact on her life during that period was minimal. She and her brother were fed well, and they continued in school during that decade.

The Great Depression was a worldwide economic disaster. In the United States and in most other countries, it started with the stock market crash on October 29, 1929, a date that became known as Black Friday. The result was tremendous unemployment, as high as 25 percent in the United States and 33 percent in Germany. Starting in 1930, conditions were exacerbated by a severe drought in the agricultural heartland of the United States. The length of the depression varied from country to country. In the United States, it is generally agreed that it ended in 1939.

Economists have put forth several theories as to the cause of the depression. Most agree that widespread lack of confidence, fueled by reduction in spending, overproduction of goods, and overinvestment, led to a panic that turned a normal business cycle recession into a devastating depression.

FURTHER READING

Bernanke, Ben S. *Essays on the Great Depression.* Princeton, N.J.: Princeton University Press, 2004.

Powell, Jim. *FDR's Folly: How Roosevelt and His New Deal Prolonged the Great Depression.* New York: Three Rivers Press, 1004.

Shales, Amity. *The Forgotten Man: A New History of the Great Depression.* New York: HarperPerennial, 2008.

Diamond Lil Mae West (1893–1980), an American who wrote the play *Diamond Lil,* was one of ENISTASIOUS "TOSH" ANGELOS's favorite actresses. Tosh was a Greek-American sailor and Maya Angelou's first husband. Angelou was married to him for three years, and during that time she, her son, Guy, and Tosh frequented movie houses where old films were played. The sultry playwright and actress Mae West often appeared in the movies they saw. After the divorce, Maya and her son continued to attend old movies (and new) for entertainment.

West wrote and starred in *Diamond Lil* in 1928, which was her first successful play, and her role was the basis for her part in the 1933 film *She Done Him Wrong.*

FURTHER READING

West, Mae. *Diamond Lil.* New York: Macauley Company, 1932.

diaspora Angelou's poetry often refers to the African-American people of the diaspora. The word *diaspora* means a scattering of people away from their ancestral homeland. For Angelou and other African American, it refers primarily to the sub-Saharan black Africans who were sent to the Americas by way of the Atlantic slave trade. Starting in the 16th century, Africans were enslaved and shipped to North and South America and the Caribbean to work on the plantations of Spanish, Portuguese, and English (later American) landowners. The Atlantic slave trade ended in the 19th century.

FURTHER READING

Harris, Joseph E., ed. *Global Dimensions of the African Diaspora.* Washington, D.C.: Howard University Press, 1993.

Diller, Phyllis (1917–) Maya Angelou got her start in show business at the Purple Onion nightclub in SAN FRANCISCO, CALIFORNIA. Phyllis Diller was performing there at same time, and she and Angelou became acquainted. Diller, who is considered one of the pioneers of female stand-up comedy, was born Phyllis Ada Driver in Lima, Ohio, on July 17, 1917, and she married Sherwood Anderson Diller, who became the brunt of many of her jokes, in 1939. During World War II, she was a housewife, mother, and advertising copywriter. In the 1950s, she was employed as a secretary at a television station in San Francisco. One of the station's show hosts, Willard Anderson, conducted interviews and did skits with both celebrities and young people. He thought Diller was funny and invited her to join him on his show at the Purple Onion, where she launched her stand-up comedy career. She appeared at the Purple Onion for 87 consecutive weeks as she cultivated and perfected her act.

Diller made several guest appearances on *The Jack Paar Show* in the 1950s, and in the 1960s, she appeared to be everywhere. She costarred with Bob Hope in 23 special shows and in three films, and she appeared as a special guest on numerous television programs. She starred in two short-lived TV series in the late 1960s, and for three months, starting in December 1969, she played the lead role in *Hello Dolly*. She was one of a string of replacements for the original star, Carol Channing.

Diller published her autobiography, *Like a Lampshade in a Whorehouse,* in 2005. She did stand-up comedy on *The Tonight Show* in January 2007, and host Jay Leno asked her to come back later that year to celebrate her 90th birthday; she was unable to do so after fracturing her back. In her act, she was famous for her long cigarette holders, though she is a lifelong nonsmoker.

FURTHER READING

Diller, Phyllis. *Like a Lampshade in a Whorehouse: My Life in Comedy.* New York: Tarcher, 2006.

Lavin, Suzanne. *Women and Comedy in Solo Performance: Phyllis Diller, Lily Tomlin, and Roseanne.* New York: Tarcher, 2006.

Dostoyevsky, Fyodor (Fyodor Mikhaylovich Dostoyevsky) (1821–1881) Fyodor Dostoyevsky was one of Maya Angelou's favorite authors, and during difficult times in her life she would turn to his works (and other Eastern European writers) because of their insights and understanding of oppression and burdensome conflicts.

A world-renowned novelist and short story writer, Dostoyevsky was born on November 11, 1821 in Moscow, Russia. His father, a retired military doctor and an alcoholic, practiced at the Mariinsky Hospital for the Poor. The hospital was located in one of the most depressed areas of Moscow near a cemetery for criminals, a lunatic asylum, and an orphanage of abandoned children. Against his parents' wishes, Fyodor enjoyed visiting with the patients in the hospital garden and listening to their stories. It was perhaps here that his imagination began to create the characters and events that later appeared in his writings.

Dostoyevsky's mother died in 1837, and shortly thereafter, he was sent to a military engineering school in St. Petersburg. He despised mathematics, but he was able to study Western literature, including the works of WILLIAM SHAKESPEARE, Blaise Pascal, Victor Hugo, and E. T. A. Hoffmann. In 1842, he was commissioned as an army officer, but he left the military two years later to devote his time to writing. His first short novel, *Poor Folk,* published in 1846, had mixed reviews, but it brought him some celebrity in literary circles. In 1849, he and 30 others who were considered "radical socialists" were imprisoned in Siberia. He was released after four years of hard labor and an additional five years of military service.

Dostoyevsky's personal experiences are found throughout his writings, forming the background for his stories. He wrote of the basest human desires and the highest spiritual yearnings. At the core, his characters pursued man's eternal quest to understand himself and God. Many feel that Dostoyevsky had a deep understanding of human psychology. He wrote 15 novels, of which the best known are *Crime and Punishment* (1866) and *The Brothers Karamazov* (1880). He also wrote many short stories and novellas. He suffered from epilepsy from age nine until his death on February 9, 1881. The cause of death was a long hemorrhage associated with emphysema and epileptic seizure.

FURTHER READING

Frank, Joseph. *Dostoevsky: A Writer in His Time.* Edited by Mary Petrusewicz. Princeton, N.J.: Princeton University Press, 2010.

———. *Dostoevsky: The Mantle of the Prophet, 1871–1881.* Princeton, N.J.: Princeton University Press, 2002.

Grossman, Leonid Petrovich. *Dostoevsky: A Biography.* Indianapolis, Ind.: Bobbs-Merrill, 1975.

Lantz, Kenneth. *The Dostoevsky Encyclopedia.* Westport, Conn.: Greenwood Press, 2004.

Douglass, Frederick (Augustus Washington Bailey) (ca. 1817–1895) From her early years, Maya Angelou was familiar with the life and works of Frederick Douglass. He rose from the lowest socioeconomic conditions to become a spokesperson for ABOLITION and the improvement of his people. Angelou admired him and emulated his life in many ways by becoming active in the 20th-century CIVIL RIGHTS MOVEMENT and by speaking on behalf of her people through her books, poetry, essays, teaching, and many public addresses.

Augustus Washington Bailey was born a slave in Talbot County, Maryland, in February 1817 or 1818 and changed his surname to Douglass to avoid capture soon after he escaped to the North in 1838. When he was a boy, his mother was "rented out" to another farm, and therefore he was initially raised by his maternal grandmother, a slave woman who was married to a free black man. She was a strong, independent woman who Douglass felt influenced his lifelong respect for women. When he was six years old, his grandmother was told to take him to the farm of a slave owner named Aaron Anthony. There he experienced the fate of many slaves: beatings, starvation, and cruelty. However, Anthony's daughter, Lucretia Anthony Auld, recognized his potential, protected him, and selected him to be a companion of the farm master's young son.

It was at this time that Douglass, then Bailey, was exposed to white society and perhaps first thought of freedom from slavery. Lucretia Auld arranged for him to be sent to live with her brother-in-law, Hugh Auld, and his wife, Sophia, who lived in the shipbuilding area of Baltimore. Sophia Auld included Bailey in the lessons when she was teaching her children to read. When her husband discovered that Bailey was learning to read, he told her to stop; it was illegal in the United States at that time to teach slaves to read and write. However, Bailey continued to hone his reading skills, using whatever he could find, including *The Columbia Orator,* a textbook that included many speeches on the rights of freedom and democracy. He came to understand the power of words.

For the next several years, Bailey moved from farm to farm, the property of different owners, and one time he tried to escape but was captured and jailed. After his release, he became skilled in caulking ship's hulls; he also met and fell in love with Anna Murray, a free black woman who later became his wife. With money borrowed from her for a train ticket and identification given to him by a black seaman, he dressed in a sailor's uniform and escaped to Philadelphia, Pennsylvania, and then to New York City.

Douglass continued to travel north, finally settling in New Bedford, Massachusetts, where he regularly attended antislavery meetings. One evening, he was asked to talk about his experiences as a slave, and consequently, he became known as an eloquent speaker. He was asked to participate in the six-month tour of the Midwest and Eastern states sponsored by the American Anti-Slavery Society, and his reputation as a gifted orator brought him many more requests for antislavery speeches in the United States and the United Kingdom. While in England, Douglass said that he felt he was treated as a man rather than a man of color. Supporters there bought his freedom from slavery in the United States.

After his return to the United States, Douglass continued to lecture and speak about his enslavement and the need to end slavery. He also published several abolitionist newspapers in which he expressed his belief that the education of African-American people was the key to improving their lives. He strongly supported desegregation of schools and giving women the right to vote. He wrote three autobiographies, the first, *Narrative of the Life of Frederick Douglass, an American Slave,* in 1845. The second, *My Bondage and My Freedom,* was published in 1855. The final book, *Life and Times of Frederick Douglass,* was originally published in 1881 and then revised in 1892. *Narrative* was reprinted nine times in the first three years of publication, and over 11,000 copies were sold in the United States.

In February 1895, Douglass attended the National Conference of Women in Washington, D.C., and the audience gave him a standing ovation. Shortly after returning home, he suffered a massive heart attack or stroke, and he died on February 20, 1895. He was buried in Mount Hope Cemetery in Rochester, New York.

FURTHER READING

Lee, Maurice S., ed. *The Cambridge Companion to Frederick Douglass.* Cambridge: Cambridge University Press, 2009.

Myers, Peter C. *Frederick Douglass: Race and the Rebirth of American Liberalism.* Lawrence: University Press of Kansas, 2008.

Stauffer, John. *Giants: The Parallel Lives of Frederick Douglass and Abraham Lincoln.* New York: Twelve, 2009.

DuBois, W. E. B. (William Edward Burghardt DuBois) (1868–1963) Maya Angelou lived in Ghana at the same time as W. E. B. DuBois and became acquainted with his wife, Shirley Graham DuBois. Earlier, when Angelou lived in Cairo with VUSUMZI MAKE, the South African freedom fighter, she met David DuBois, Shirley's son and W. E. B.'s adopted son. David DuBois assisted Angelou in finding work as a journalist in Cairo when Angelou realized that Make was not providing enough money for their home and other expenses.

William Edward Burghardt DuBois—university professor, journalist, prolific writer, and black culture social scientist—was born on February 23, 1868, in Great Barrington, Massachusetts, to parents of French, Dutch, and African descent. His father left the family when he was very young, and shortly thereafter, his mother suffered a stroke, which left her unable to work. DuBois and his mother sustained themselves with money from relatives and his after-school jobs. Precocious and intelligent, he was the valedictorian at his high school graduation.

After high school, DuBois attended Fisk University and earned a bachelor of arts degree in 1888. During the summers at Fisk, he taught at rural black schools and saw for the first time the horrific living conditions, prejudice, and cruelty to which his people were subjected. He was awarded a scholarship to Harvard University, from which he graduated with a second bachelor's degree in 1890. He continued his education at Harvard, earning a master's degree in history in 1892. From 1892 through 1894, he did graduate work at the University of Berlin in Germany and traveled extensively throughout Europe. He then returned to Harvard and in 1895 became the first African American to receive a Ph.D. there. DuBois's doctoral dissertation, "The Suppression of the African Slave Trade to the United States, 1638–1870," became the first book in the Harvard Historical Series.

For the next two years, DuBois taught at Wilberforce University, a predominately black school in Ohio. In 1897, as an instructor for the University of Pennsylvania in Philadelphia, he completed a sociological study of an urban community. The result was a much-heralded book, *The Philadelphia Negro: A Social Study.* That same year, he was offered and accepted an assistant professorship at Atlanta University, where for the next 13 years he taught economics and history.

DuBois was a cofounder of the NATIONAL ASSOCIATION FOR THE ADVANCEMENT OF COLORED PEOPLE (NAACP), and from 1910 to 1934, he was the editor of the organization's monthly magazine, *Crisis,* which in 1913 had a circulation of 13,000 subscribers. From this platform, through his articles, and through the writings of other black authors, he was able to speak to the issues that most concerned him: widespread mistreatment of black people, social injustice, discrimination, lynchings, lack of education, unconditional and equal civil rights for all blacks, and African-American nationalism. On the issue of nationalism, whereby blacks would control their own schools, institutions, and economic cooperatives, he found himself at odds with the NAACP board and elected to return to teaching at Atlanta University.

DuBois was a strong proponent of higher education, especially liberal arts for African Americans, and he felt that blacks should challenge whites on all issues. He found opposition to this opinion in Booker T. Washington, who believed that African Americans should assimilate into the general population and would be economically successful by completing elementary school and vocational training.

In DuBois's later years, his writings moved progressively toward the left end of the political spectrum, and he was accused of supporting socialism as early as the 1940s. He admired the Soviet dictator Joseph Stalin, calling him "a great man," and felt that accounts of Stalin's purges were just propaganda. The HOUSE COMMITTEE ON UN-AMERICAN ACTIVITIES questioned him on his communist sympathies, and in 1959, he was awarded the Lenin

Peace Prize. He joined the Communist Party USA two years later.

A prolific writer, DuBois wrote more than 4,000 articles, books, and essays. One of the most important books he wrote was *The Souls of Black Folk* (1903), which most scholars consider to be the black master text. He clarified the black experience in the United States clearly and succinctly:

> If, however, the vistas disclosed as yet no goal, no resting place, little but flattery and criticism, the journey at least gave leisure for reflection and self-examination; it changed the child of Emancipation to the youth with dawning self-consciousness, self-realization, and self-respect. In those sombre forests of his striving his own soul rose before him, and he saw himself, darkly as through a veil; and yet he saw in himself some faint revelation of his power, of his mission. He began to have a dim feeling that, to attain his place in the world, he must be himself and not another. (368)

In 1959, DuBois emigrated to Ghana at the invitation of its president and began work on *Encyclopedia Africana,* a lifelong interest. He died in Ghana on August 27, 1963, age of 95, and was buried there.

FURTHER READING

DuBois, W. E. B. *The Souls of Black Folk.* In *W. E. B. Du Bois: Writings.* New York: Literary Classics of the United States, 1986, 357–546.

Marable, Manning. *W. E. B. Du Bois: Black Radical Democrat.* Boulder, Colo.: Paradigm, 2005.

Wolters, Raymond. *Du Bois and His Rivals.* Columbia: University of Missouri Press, 2003.

Zamir, Shamoon. *The Cambridge Companion to W. E. B. Du Bois.* Cambridge: Cambridge University Press, 2008.

Du Feu, Paul Paul Du Feu, a British-born working man, comic cartoonist, and master carpenter, was Maya Angelou's second legal husband though she had had a quasi-marriage (no official ceremony) with VUSUMZI MAKE of Cairo, between her first marriage (to ENISTASIOUS "TOSH" ANGELOS) and her second to Du Feu. Angelou and Du Feu met at a literary party in London and were married in 1973; she was seven years his senior. During the seven years of their marriage, he remodeled homes on the West Coast while Angelou expanded her career. During their marriage, she wrote short stories, articles, another autobiography, and poetry; composed music; produced plays; and lectured on the university circuit. She speaks little of her marriages, but friends feel that the marriage to Du Feu was her best. They are still good friends.

Du Feu's earlier marriage was to the feminist writer Germaine Greer. His celebrity fame was primarily based on being married to two famous women. He also received attention of a different kind when he was the first nude centerfold in the British *Cosmopolitan* magazine. Though he was nude, the photograph was somewhat modest. In a 1974 interview that Stephanie Caruana conducted with Maya Angelou, there is an explanation that the photograph of Du Feu was published the same month that the American *Cosmopolitan* ran a nude photograph of Burt Reynolds. Du Feu was sprayed lightly with gold paint by the photographer, and his navel was "airbrushed . . . ; his genitals were coyly hidden behind an upraised knee" (30).

FURTHER READING

Caruana, Stephanie. "Maya Angelou: An Interview." In *Conversations with Maya Angelou,* edited by Jeffrey M. Elliot, 29–37. Jackson and London: University Press of Mississippi, 1989.

Dunbar, Paul Laurence (1872–1906) Maya Angelou read Paul Lawrence Dunbar's poetry as a child, and he was one of her heroes. She was passionate about his work, and when she searched for a title for her first autobiography, focusing on her life from around age three to 16, she found it in his poem "Sympathy" (published 1899). The metaphor of a caged bird expressed her own sense of being locked into a life that was too constricting for her talent and energy, and so she borrowed the first line in the poem's third stanza to use for the title of her book: *I Know Why the Caged Bird Sings.*

Dunbar, an African-American poet, was born near Dayton, Ohio, on June 27, 1872. His parents were both former slaves and instilled a love of learning in him. He wrote his first poem when he was six years old. Dunbar attended the all-white Dayton Central High School, where he was a member of the debate society, editor of the school newspaper, and president of the literary society. He is credited with starting the *Dayton Tattler*, a newsletter for the black community. The newsletter was printed on a press owned by his classmates, Orville and Wilbur Wright, who later became known for their pioneering work in aviation.

Oak and Ivy, Dunbar's first collection of poetry, was published in 1892 when he was 20 years old. It attracted the attention of the famous writer and poet James Whitcomb Riley, known for writing in what became known as a Hoosier dialect. Similarly, Dunbar wrote his poems in both standard English and African-American dialect. His second book, *Majors and Minors*, gained him national attention and was praised in *Harper's Weekly* by William Dean Howells, a novelist and respected literary critic. Dunbar's fame spread, and he was invited to recite his works on a literary tour in England. When he returned to the United States, he took a job at the Library of Congress in Washington, D.C. The work was dusty and may have contributed to the development of his tuberculosis, which was diagnosed in 1900. After a year, he returned to writing and reciting full-time.

In the last years of his life, Dunbar became dependent on alcohol, which was probably the result of his deteriorating health and the failure of his marriage. He died of tuberculosis on February 9, 1906, at the age of 33. His writings included 12 collections of poetry, four books of short stories, five novels, and a play.

FURTHER READING

Best, Felton O. *Crossing the Color Line: A Biography of Paul Laurence Dunbar, 1872–1906.* Dubuque, Iowa: Kendall Hunt, 1996.

Wiggins, Lida Keck, and William Dean Howells. *The Life and Works of Paul Laurence Dunbar: Containing His Complete Poetical Works, His Best Short Stories, Numerous Anecdotes and a Complete Biography of the Famous Poet.* Whitefish, Mont.: Kessinger, 2007.

E

Eddy, Mary Baker (1821–1910) Maya Angelou briefly looked into Christian Science while she was working at the Melrose Record Store in SAN FRANCISCO, CALIFORNIA. The store's co-owner, Louise Cox, and her mother were active in the Christian Scientist Church and invited Maya to attend a service with them. The austere quiet of the church and its congregants' lack of emotion were unfamiliar to Angelou, so she did not feel comfortable there. In her solitude at night, she read the materials Cox and her mother had given her and carefully weighed many of the concepts presented by the Christian Science faith, but ultimately she decided that she could not affirm some of the beliefs she had read. For one thing, it was difficult for her to accept that God was really present everywhere and that she was never alone, as the materials suggested.

Mary Baker Eddy was the founder of the religious denomination known as Christian Science. Born on July 16, 1821, near Concord, New Hampshire, Eddy was afflicted by ill health until she sought help from Dr. Phineas Parkhurst Quimby. Dr. Quimby taught and practiced that disease was a mental condition, an invention of man, and that people were capable of being cured mentally, without medicine or other extraordinary measures. His method was to explain the mental causes of the malady and to teach people to replace fear with faith and believe in the expectation that they will heal completely. Being healed herself, Eddy spread his method of healing without medicine by tutoring and lecturing all across New England. She wrote several books and formed the Church of Christ, Scientist, in Boston in 1879. Many of her ideas and inspiration came from Dr. Phineas Parkhurst Quimby, and they spread throughout the United States. She died in Newton, Massachusetts, on December 3, 1910.

FURTHER READING

Brisbane, Arthur. *Mary Baker G. Eddy.* Boston: Ball, 1908.

Gill, Gillian. *Mary Baker Eddy.* Reading, Mass.: Perseus, 1998.

Smith, Clifford Pabody. *Historical and Biographical Papers: Sketches from the Life of Mary Baker Eddy and the History of Christian Science.* Boston: Christian Science, 1934.

We Knew Mary Baker Eddy. Boston: Christian Science, 1943.

Ellington, Duke (Edward Kennedy Ellington) (1899–1974) Maya Angelou, who loved the sounds of JAZZ and the BLUES, especially admired the music of Duke Ellington. Born Edward Kennedy Ellington into a middle-class family in Washington, D.C., he began his study of the piano at age seven and started playing professionally at age 17. In 1923, Ellington moved to New York City to lead a nightclub ensemble. He made hundreds of recordings, appeared on the radio and in films, and toured the world with his ensemble. His style was influenced by ragtime and swing. Besides his many jazz compositions, Ellington also wrote for ballet and theater, and he is often named as America's greatest composer. He continued to compose and lead his band until shortly before his death on May 24, 1974.

FURTHER READING

Bradbury, David. *Duke Ellington.* London: Haus, 2005.

Ellington, Duke. *Music Is My Mistress.* Garden City, N.Y.: Doubleday, 1973.

Yanow, Scott. *Duke Ellington.* New York: Friedman/Fairfax, 1999.

Emerson, Ralph Waldo (1803–1882) Maya Angelou enjoyed reading the works of Ralph Waldo Emerson when she was a child. Though her primary cultural icons and models were African-American writers, she learned from Emerson's works as well as from other white writers.

Born on May 25, 1803, in Boston, Massachusetts, Emerson was a poet, essayist, and lecturer. He graduated from Harvard University and worked for several years as a schoolmaster before returning to the Harvard Divinity School, where he was hired as a minister in 1829; however, he resigned three years later due to disagreements about church doctrine and practices. He subsequently lectured on the proper role of the scholar and the waning of the Christian tradition, and his philosophies fueled the transcendentalism movement in New England. Some of his famous works include the essays "Nature," "Self-Reliance," and "Experience," and his work became internationally famous during his lifetime.

Emerson was friends with Henry David Thoreau, Walt Whitman, Nathaniel Hawthorne, and other great thinkers of the 19th century. He had married, but his wife died of tuberculosis less than two years after their wedding. In July 1838, he was invited to speak at the Harvard Divinity School graduation; this address became famous because Emerson discounted biblical miracles and proclaimed that Jesus was not God. He was thereafter denounced as an atheist and was not invited back to speak at Harvard for 30 years. This did not diminish Emerson's popularity as a lecturer, and with the money he earned making presentations, he purchased property near Walden Pond, which would become the source of inspiration for Thoreau.

Emerson was an abolitionist, and he became involved in the antislavery movement prior to the Civil War. During the final years of his life, he had difficulty with his memory and withdrew from the public scene. He died of pneumonia on April 27, 1882.

FURTHER READING

Bosco, Ronald A., and Joel Myerson, eds. *Emerson in His Own Time: A Biographical Chronicle of His Life, Drawn from Recollections, Interviews, and Memoirs by Family, Friends, and Associates.* Iowa City: University of Iowa Press, 2003.

Emerson, Ralph Waldo. *The Complete Works of Ralph Waldo Emerson.* New York: William H. Wise, 1926.

Myerson, Joel, ed. *A Historical Guide to Ralph Waldo Emerson.* New York: Oxford University Press, 2000.

Ensenada, Mexico Maya Angelou and her father, BAILEY JOHNSON, SR., once drove from LOS ANGELES, CALIFORNIA, to Ensenada, Mexico, to get COOKING supplies. He became drunk while there, and at 16, Maya drove from Ensenada to the border without having any previous driving experience. Ensenada is a Mexican city located in the northwestern part of Baja California. The economy there boomed in the 1920s as hotels and casinos catered to Americans seeking alcohol and entertainment south of the United States's border. It remains a popular destination for cruise ships and tourists.

Equiano, Olaudah (Gustavus Vassa) (ca. 1745–1797) Also known as Gustavus Vassa, Olaudah Equiano was born in an Igbo village in Essaka, formerly in southeast Nigeria. After years of slavery, he became one of the most prominent and influential African intellectuals active in the British debate seeking the ABOLITION of the slave trade.

As children, Equiano and his sister were kidnapped by relatives in Africa and sold into slavery to a nearby chieftain. In time, he was sold to white slave traders and taken to Virginia. His second name was given to him by an owner in Virginia (a common practice), who was a naval officer; thus, Equiano was able to receive naval training. Later, he was sold to a Quaker merchant from Philadelphia who told him that he could purchase his own freedom if he could pay the 40 pounds the merchant had paid for him. He did so through honest trade and, subsequently, worked as a seaman, merchant, and explorer; he also became a popular speaker in England and a writer. His autobiography, *The Interesting Narrative of the Life of Olaudah Equiano,* first published in England in 1789, was one of the earliest known published writing by an African and fueled the growing antislavery movement in England. The book describes the horrors of the slave captivity, the slave industry, the terror of the Middle Passage, and careful descriptions of the treatment of slaves inside slave owners' homes in Virginia. Equiano was eventually instrumental in British lawmakers' decision to pass the Slave Trade Act of 1807, which abolished the British slave trade. He died in York, Pennsylvania, on March 31, 1797.

Maya Angelou has discussed Equiano and his autobiography in presentations about her own writing. It was in his work that Angelou read firsthand accounts of African captivity, the Middle Passage, and the abuse of slaves on Virginia plantations.

FURTHER READING

Equiano, Olaudah (or Gustavus Vassa, The African). *The Interesting Narrative of the Life of Olaudah Equiano.* Edited by Shelly Eversley. New York: The Modern Library, 2004. (Originally published in 1789.)

Evers, Medgar (1925–1963) Maya Angelou was familiar with Medgar Evers as a well-known figure in the American CIVIL RIGHTS MOVEMENT. She and Evers's widow, Myrlie Evers-Williams, attended and spoke at the 1997 funeral of Betty X Shabazz, the widow of MALCOLM X.

Medgar Evers was born on July 2, 1925, in Decatur, Mississippi. After serving in the U.S. Army during World War II, he graduated from Alcon College and settled in Mississippi. While working as an insurance salesman, he began organizing local affiliates for the NATIONAL ASSOCIATION FOR THE ADVANCEMENT OF COLORED PEOPLE (NAACP). In 1954, he moved to Jackson to become the NAACP's first field secretary in Mississippi. Evers was active in the Civil Rights movement until he was assassinated at his home on June 12, 1963. His death made him a nationally known figure, and he was buried with full military honors in Arlington National Cemetery.

FURTHER READING

Adler, David A. *Heroes for Civil Rights.* Edited by Bill Farnsworth. New York: Holiday House, 2008.

Brown, Jennie. *Medgar Evers.* Los Angeles: Melrose Square, 1994.

Nossiter, Adam. *Of Long Memory: Mississippi and the Murder of Medgar Evers.* Reading, Mass.: Addison Wesley, 1994.

Feelings, Tom (1933–2003) Tom Feelings was the illustrator for Angelou's collection of poetry *Now Sheba Sings Her Song* (1987) as well as her children's book *Soul Looks Back in Wonder*. Through his works, Feelings artistically represented the African-American experience. His most famous work is the rendering of the "Middle Passage." He was also celebrated as an author, teacher, and cultural activist.

Feelings was born on May 19, 1933, and raised in Brooklyn, New York. He attended the School of the Visual Arts and later lived in Ghana and Guyana, where he worked as a teacher. He was the recipient of a grant from the National Endowment for the Arts and worked for many years as an illustrator. Feelings was artist in residence at the University of South Carolina from 1990 to 1995. The winner of numerous awards for his work, he died in Mexico on August 25, 2003.

FURTHER READING

Bishop, Rudine Sims. "Tom Feelings and the Middle Passage." *Horn Book Magazine* 72, no. 4 (1996): 436–452.

Ford, Bernette, and George Ford. "Tom Feelings, Visionary: A Master of the Craft of Image Opened Doors in Publishing." *Black Issues Book Review* (January 2004): 70.

Feiffer, Jules and Judy Jules Feiffer (1929–) is a Pulitzer Prize–winning cartoonist and author who received awards for his editorial cartooning in the *Village Voice* (1986). Born on January 26, 1929, Feiffer has written plays, screenplays, and children's books and was inducted into the Comic Book Hall of Fame in 2004. He was a close friend of the author JAMES BALDWIN, who introduced Maya Angelou to Feiffer and his wife, Judy, shortly after the assassination of MARTIN LUTHER KING, JR. Baldwin's thoughtful idea was to help Maya learn to laugh again after the deep grief of King's sudden death, and because of a humorous story exchange at the Feiffer home, the Feiffers recommended Maya as a possible autobiographical writer to ROBERT LOOMIS, an editor at Random House. Jules Feiffer is currently an adjunct professor at Southampton College.

FURTHER READING

Angelou, Maya. *A Song Flung Up to Heaven*. New York: Random House, 2002.

Wikipedia. "Jules Feiffer." Available online. URL: http://en.wikipedia.org/wiki/Jules_Feiffer. Accessed July 1, 2009.

Fillmore District Maya Angelou was working in a record store in the Fillmore District in SAN FRANCISCO, CALIFORNIA, when she met her first husband, ENISTASIOUS "TOSH" ANGELOS. From 1910 to 1930, the Fillmore District was largely populated by Japanese immigrants. During World War II, these immigrants were forced to relocate, and the vacant housing attracted African Americans who had come to San Francisco to work in the shipyards.

The area also attracted many musicians and artists. For a time, the Fillmore District grew, but the economy was unstable. There was a series of redevelopment projects in the 1950s, and again in the 1990s, but the revitalization efforts had little success.

FURTHER READING

Bryant, Forrest. "Breaking Ground." *Downbeat* 75, no. 2 (2008): 13–14.

Doherty, Michael, and Meryl Block. "The Revitalization of Fillmore." *Urban Action* (2001). Available online. URL: http://bss.sfsu.edu/urbs/Urban%20Action%20Folder/ua2001/fillmore.html. Accessed November 16, 2010.

Flowers, Mrs. Bertha Bertha Flowers was an important character in Angelou's 1970 autobiography *I Know Why the Caged Bird Sings.* She was a genteel woman who lived in STAMPS, ARKANSAS, and treated the young Maya with patience and intelligence. Mrs. Flowers read great literature to Maya and helped teach the mute child to believe in herself. Maya had fallen silent for nearly five years from confusion and shock after having been brutally raped by her mother's boyfriend when she was around eight years old. Mrs. Flowers was instrumental in assisting Angelou to find the use of her voice again.

FURTHER READING

Angelou, Maya. *Mrs. Flowers: A Moment of Friendship.* Minneapolis, Minn.: Redpath Press, 1986.

folklore Much of Angelou's work, regardless of the genre, reflects the folklore of her people. Folklore is the expressed culture of a people—that is, their traditional stories, sayings, beliefs, customs, and art forms. In 1984, the American Folklore Society declared: "We now speak of folklore/folklife as song and story, speech and movement, custom and belief, craft and ritual—expressive and instrumental activities of all kinds learned and communicated directly or face-to-face in groups ranging from nations, regions, and states through communities, neighborhoods, occupations, and families" (quoted in Brunvand 1996, 286). All groups that stay together for more than a short length of time seem to develop various types of folklore. It can emerge from groups of any social or economic status, ethnicity, or age, from a family or from larger groups, but folklore emerges from a community where members find common meaning in some way and then create ways to demonstrate or express those cultural meanings. The items that emerge are often anonymous, but they carry the spirit or essence of the group.

Generally, academics delineate four basic categories in folklore, but each category has countless subcategories. *Oral* folklore, which is transmitted by word-of-mouth, is one of the main categories. Oral lore is often later written down as myth, legends, or FOLKTALES; folk and camp songs; jokes; anecdotes; riddles; APHORISMS; MAXIMs; names; and many more items. *Material* folklore refers to things that can be made and used or placed on display. From quilts to recipes, from hats to wooden shoes, from fences to barbecue pits, to lariats, whips, and saddles, things made by hand are often treasured by families or varied groups and are considered material folklore. *Customary* folklore has many categories, including seasonal holidays, religious traditions, folk dancing, etiquette and social behavior, traditional music, and other items. The folklore of *belief* can include weather lore, folk religion, folk cures, superstitions (these are in the oral category also), directional lore, and more.

FURTHER READING

Brunvand, Jan Harold, ed. *American Folklore: An Encyclopedia.* New York and London: Garland, 1996.

folktale Maya Angelou's serial autobiographies, poetry, essays, plays, presentations, speeches, and other works are often rich with folktales, FOLKLORE and folk speech. Allusions she occasionally makes in her autobiographies, essays, and poetry, as well as occasional titles, frequently have their origin in African-American folktales and music.

Angelou's first professional dancing performances were in the calypso style, which has its roots in island folkways and traditions. APHORISMS, soul food, the call and response of the church, and occasional superstitions are mentioned throughout her work and have enriched her depictions of the African-American people. It is important to remember that folklore belongs to all people, and many of the great American folklorists have reminded us that we are all folks.

Folktales are stories that are completely fictional and can take place in any time or place with animal or human characters, or both. Generally, the purpose of folktales is either to entertain or instruct. Folktales appear in all cultures, and many contain elements or motifs from different cultures that have been blended together, though the tales are considered to belong to everyone. In the African-American tradition, many folktales are a blend of African folk expressions and beliefs and Portuguese motifs derived from tales carried from the Cape Verde Islands, off the coast of West Africa. Virginia Hamilton, in a discussion of black folktales states: "Remember that these folktales were once a creative way for an oppressed people to express their fears and hopes to one another. They lend themselves well to being read out loud, as they were told out loud so long ago. . . . We must look on the tales as a celebration of the human spirit" (xii). Tales of animals personified with human characteristics were common, and like all folktale traditions around the world, the tales can be about heroes, beautiful women, magic, the supernatural, triumph, and sometimes loss.

FURTHER READING

Brewer, J. Mason. *American Negro Folklore.* New York: Quadrangle/The New York Times Book Company, 1968.

Dundes, Alan. *Mother Wit from the Laughing Barrel: Readings in the Interpretation of Afro-American Folklore.* Jackson and Mississippi: University of Mississippi Press, 1990.

Hamilton, Virginia. *The People Could Fly: American Black Folktales.* New York: Alfred A. Knopf, 1985.

Francis, Kay (1905–1968) BAILEY JOHNSON, JR., Maya Angelou's brother, thought that the movie star Kay Francis looked like his much beloved mother, VIVIAN BAXTER. He would often linger at the movie theater in STAMPS, ARKANSAS, if Francis was in the film being shown. Bailey told Maya about the resemblance and invited her to watch Kay Francis in films with him. Maya said that she thought their mother was much prettier.

Born Katharine Edwina Gibbs in Oklahoma City on January 13, 1905, Francis was a stage and film actress. She began performing on Broadway in 1925, and the success of her career led her to the film industry. In 1930, she signed a contract with the Warner Bros. film studio, staying there until 1936, and for a period of time she was the highest paid American film actress. She married five times and had numerous well-publicized affairs. In 1966, Francis was diagnosed with breast cancer from which she died on August 26, 1968.

French seams A French seam is a clothing seam that leaves no raw edges; the edges are sandwiched within a closed seam. Grandmother Henderson, who made many of Maya's childhood dresses, was skilled at making this kind of finished seam.

G

Gabriel See PROSSER, GABRIEL.

Garvey, Marcus (Marcus Mosiah Garvey, Jr.) (1887–1940) Maya Angelou mentions Marcus Garvey in her autobiographies in relation to popular African-American movements centered in HARLEM, New York. He was a part of her historical contextualization because he organized and led the first American black nationalist movement there.

He was born Marcus Mosiah Garvey, Jr., in Jamaica on August 17, 1887. Starting in 1910, he traveled across Central America, and he later lived in London, England, until his return to Jamaica in 1914. With friends, he organized the UNIVERSAL NEGRO IMPROVEMENT ASSOCIATION (UNIA), but the group failed to gain a following in Jamaica. In 1916, Garvey moved to New York City to establish a branch of UNIA in Harlem and other ghettos in the Northeast. By 1919, he was being called the "Black Moses" and had an estimated following of 2 million people.

Garvey taught that black people would only gain respect when they became economically independent, and he established several businesses to further the cause, including restaurants, grocery stores, the Black Star Line, and the Negro Factories Corporation. Garvey advocated the ideas of racial purism and separatism, and for that reason, he was actually in favor of the KU KLUX KLAN. This association with the Klan put him out of favor with other black leaders of the day. Garvey was tried for mail fraud in 1923 and was sentenced to five years in prison. President Calvin Coolidge eventually commuted his sentence, and he was deposited to Jamaica in 1927. Thereafter, he continued to travel and write. He died in London on June 10, 1940; his remains were exhumed in 1964 and reinterred in Jamaica, where he was proclaimed a national hero.

FURTHER READING

Garvey, Marcus. *Philosophy and Opinions of Marcus Garvey.* Edited by Amy Jacques Garvey. New York: Universal, 1923.

Hill, Robert A., ed. *The Marcus Garvey and Universal Negro Improvement Association Papers.* Berkeley: University of California Press, 1983.

McLean, Roderick Michael. *The Theology of Marcus Garvey.* Washington, D.C.: University Press of America, 1982.

Nembhard, Len S. *Trials and Triumphs of Marcus Garvey.* Millwood, N.Y.: Kraus, 1978.

Genet, Jean (1910–1986) Maya Angelou had a lead role as the White Queen in both a New York Off-Broadway production and then a European production of Jean Genet's play *The* BLACKS. Born in Paris on December 19, 1910, Genet was a French criminal turned writer; his mother was a prostitute who put him up for adoption. He was placed with a carpenter in the provinces of France and then with an older couple. After several attempts to run away and incidents of petty theft, Genet was sent to a reform school. He joined the Foreign Legion but was dishonorably discharged for practicing homosexuality. For a time he lived as a vagabond petty thief and male prostitute and wandered Europe. It was in prison that he began writing poetry and then wrote his first novel, *Our Lady of Flowers.* Genet became acquainted with Jean Cocteau and several other prominent writers who arranged to have his work published; Cocteau also protected Genet from being imprisoned again. Genet's plays, such as *The Blacks,* are known for being large-scale, stylized dramas in the Expressionist manner that depicted realistic struggles between outcasts and their oppressors. He died in Paris on April 15, 1986.

FURTHER READING

Haver, William. "The Art of Dirty Old Men: Rembrandt, Giacometti, Genet." *Parallax* 11, no. 2 (2005): 25–35.

Lavery, Carl. "Between Negativity and Resistance: Jean Genet and Committed Theatre." *Contemporary Theatre Review* 16, no. 2 (2006): 220–234.

Martin, Graham Duinstan. "Racism in Genet's 'Les Négres.'" *Modern Language Review* 70, no. 3 (1975): 517–525.

Gershwin, George (1898–1937) During the 1950s, Maya Angelou toured Europe with a theater company and played a leading role in the opera *PORGY AND BESS.* DuBose Heyward wrote the original book, which inspired brothers, George and Ira Gershwin, to write the well-received opera.

George Gershwin's family of Russian Jews emigrated to the United States in the 1890s; the original family name was Gershowiz. George was born on September 26, 1898, and raised in Brooklyn, New York. He began studying piano seriously at the age of 12, and later, because of his musical talent and drive, he quit high school. By the age of 20, he had produced his first hit, *Sewanee,* which was recorded by Al Jolson. Over the next 20 years, Gershwin wrote numerous scores and hit musicals, among them *Lady Be Good* (lyrics by his brother Ira), *Rhapsody in Blue, Strike Up the Band,* and *Girl Crazy.* He and his brother signed a contract with RKO film studios and wrote *Shall We Dance?, A Damsel in Distress,* and *The Goldwyn Follies. Porgy and Bess,* his one "serious" musical drama, opened on Broadway in 1935. Gershwin was one of the most talented and successful composers of the 20th century. He died on July 11, 1937, at the age of 38, struck down by a cancerous brain tumor.

FURTHER READING

Burroughs, John, ed. *Classical Music.* New York: DK, 2005.

Rimler, Walter. *George Gershwin: An Intimate Portrait.* Urbana: University of Illinois Press, 2009.

Gibson, Althea (1927–2003) At the beginning of her fourth autobiography, *The Heart of a Woman* (1981), Maya Angelou created a contemporary context for the books. Among other cultural and contemporary events of the time events, she mentions Althea as "the rangy tennis player who was the first black female to win the U.S. Women's singles" (623). Born in Silver, South Carolina, on August 25, 1927, Gibson grew up in New York City and won her first tennis tournament at age 15. At age 20, she won the American Tennis Association (ATA) women's singles championship, a title she would maintain for 10 consecutive years. She was known for her dominating serves and powerful play. In 1957, Gibson was voted Female Athlete of the Year by the Associated Press, becoming the first African American to receive the award. She was elected to the National Lawn Tennis Hall of Fame in 1971. Gibson was the first black player to win the French, Wimbledon, and the U.S. Open singles championships. She died on September 28, 2003.

FURTHER READING

Deans, Karen. *Playing to Win: The Story of Althea Gibson.* Edited by Elbrite Brown III. New York: Holiday House, 2007.

Evans, Howie. "Althea Gibson Was a Role Model for the Ages." *New York Amsterdam News,* 8 October 2003, 1.

Lamb, Yanick Rice. "Renaissance Woman: Althea Gibson Was a Tennis Legend, a Professional Golfer, Actress, Political Candidate, Education Advocate, and She Wrote a Memoir." *Black Issues Book Review* 6, no. 6 (2004): 60–61.

Gillespie, Dizzy (John Birks Gillespie) (1917–1993) Dizzy Gillespie was one of the great JAZZ artists Maya Angelou admired and mentioned in her work. He was a part of the jazz scene of the mid-20th century, a scene Angelou embraced and followed. Born in Cheraw, South Carolina, on October 21, 1917, John Birks Gillespie was a jazz trumpeter who pioneered the bebop sound. From an early age, he played in bands and other groups, following the lead of his trumpeter idol, Roy Eldridge. His clowning around on stage led to the nickname "Dizzy." Gillespie led an extremely prestigious career, and many rank him over Louis Armstrong as being the greatest jazz trumpeter of all time. Some of Gillespie's trademarks included his puffed-out cheeks, beret, horn-rim glasses, and bent-bell trumpet. He died in Englewood, New Jersey, on January 6, 1993.

FURTHER READING

"Gillespie, Dizzy." *Current Biography* 54, no. 1 (1993): 17.

Gillespie, Dizzy, and Al Fraser. *To Be, or Not . . . to Bop.* Duluth: University of Minnesota Press, 2009.

Leymarie, Isabelle. "Dizzie Gillespie, A Jazz Giant." *UNESCO Courier* 5115 (1998), 45.

Gladstone bag This style of overnight case was named after William Ewart Gladstone (1809–98), a British statesman. The Gladstone bag, mentioned in *I Know Why the Caged Bird Sings,* is a hinged traveling case that can open flat into two compartments of equal size. The bag is easy to pack, and the contents of the bag are easily accessible. In *Caged Bird,* Angelou writes that the Reverend Howard Thomas, presiding elder of the COLORED METHODIST EPISCOPAL CHURCH in the district including STAMPS, ARKANSAS, traveled with a Gladstone bag.

Graham, Martha (1894–1991) Maya Angelou studied dance with both Martha Graham and PEARL PRIMUS. Because of their tutoring, she mastered many of the graceful moves of interpretive modern dance and calypso.

Martha Graham was born on May 11, 1894, in Pittsburgh, Pennsylvania, to a prominent physician. Her family practiced strict Presbyterianism, which may have accounted for Graham's personal discipline. The Grahams were an upper middle-class family, and Martha was discouraged from entering a career in the performing arts. Nevertheless, she pursued her dream and became the premier American dancer and choreographer who was respected as a leading pioneer of modern dance. Graham danced and choreographed for over 70 years. She was the first dancer ever to perform at the White House in Washington, D.C. She established the Martha Graham Center of Contemporary Dance in 1926, and it is now the oldest continuing dance company in the United States. Graham performed for the last time on May 25, 1968; she died on April 1, 1991.

FURTHER READING

de Mille, Agnes. *Martha: The Life and Work of Martha Graham.* New York: Random House, 1991.

griot Some literary critics and scholars have suggested that Maya Angelou is, in spirit, a griot. A griot is a West African poet, praise singer, wandering musician, and storyteller. This role is often a hereditary responsibility, and the stories told may include local gossip and political commentary.

FURTHER READING

Thursby, Jacqueline S. *Story: A Handbook.* Westport, Conn.: Greenwood Press, 2006.

Guy, Rosa (Rosa Cuthbert Guy) (1925–) Maya Angelou and the writer Rosa Guy have been friends since they met at the HARLEM WRITERS GUILD. Born on September 1, 1925, Guy emigrated with her family from Trinidad in 1932 and grew up in Harlem. She became active in the American Negro Theatre during World War II and studied at the New York University. Along with other African-American writers, she formed the Harlem Writers Guild. Much of Guy's work deals with family relationships, identities, and conflicts; titles include *Bird at My Window* (1966), *The Disappearance* (1979), and *A Measure of Time* (1983). She is divorced from Warner Guy.

FURTHER READING

Guy, Rosa. *My Love, My Love, or, The Peasant Girl.* New York: Holt, Rinehart, and Winston, 1985.

Norris, Jerrie. *Presenting Rosa Guy.* Boston: Twayne Publishers, 1988.

Thigpen, D. "Rosa Guy." *Essence* 22, no. 7 (1991): 36.

Haley, Alex (1921–1992) The African-American writer Alex Haley was born on August 11, 1921. He is best known for his intergenerational ROOTS: THE SAGA OF AN AMERICAN FAMILY (1976). *Roots* won the Pulitzer Prize, though questions were raised about the accuracy of his history. Haley is credited with motivating African Americans to examine their genealogical histories, and many have been successful in uncovering their own African roots. Haley was also a ghost writer for *The Autobiography of Malcolm X* (1965). He died on February 10, 1992. Maya Angelou and CICELY TYSON played parts in the 1977 television adaptation of *Roots*.

Hallmark Cards On November 17, 2000, Hallmark Cards, Inc., announced that Maya Angelou had signed a licensing agreement "to collaborate on the creation of 'The Maya Angelou Collection from Hallmark,' a new line of products featuring exclusively penned poetry and sentiments. This offering will feature greeting cards and specialty gifts that may comprise framed sentiments, treasure keepers, and journals" *(Write News)*. Angelou stated that "My partnership with Hallmark creates a new way for my message to reach millions of women and families, many of whom may not be familiar with my work, but most of them seek an expanded viewpoint on courage, spirituality, and personal expression. . . . It is my hope that through this collaboration with Hallmark, I can help provide the inspiration to others to love life and persevere through all of its challenges" *(Write News)*.

FURTHER READING

"Hallmark Announces Maya Angelou Greeting Cards." *Write News*, 17 November 2000. Available online. URL: http://www.writenews.com/2000/111700_angelou_hallmark.htm. Accessed March 26, 2010.

Hansberry, Lorraine (1930–1965) Maya Angelou admired the work of the American author and playwright Lorraine Hansberry, whose most famous work, *A Raisin in the Sun*, was the first play written by an African-American woman to be performed on Broadway. Born on May 19, 1930, Hansberry grew up on the southern side of Chicago, and her parents were actively involved in the conflict against SEGREGATION. Her neighborhood and school were predominately white, and her childhood experiences greatly influenced her work. She briefly attended the University of Michigan and several schools in Chicago before moving to New York to work small jobs and develop her skills as a writer. She wrote two plays and many articles and essays before dying of cancer at the age of 35 on January 12, 1965.

FURTHER READING

Hansberry, Lorraine. *To Be Young, Gifted, and Black: Lorraine Hansberry in Her Own Words*. Adapted by Robert Nemiroff. New York: Vintage/Books, 1995.

Leeson, Richard M. *Lorraine Hansberry: A Research and Production Sourcebook.* Westport, Conn.: Greenwood Press, 1977.

McKissack, Pat, and Fredrick McKissack. *Young, Black, and Determined: A Biography of Lorraine Hansberry.* New York: Holiday House, 1998.

Harlem Maya Angelou was a member of the HARLEM WRITERS GUILD as well as being deeply involved in antidiscrimination efforts there during the CIVIL RIGHTS MOVEMENT. Harlem is a district of New York City and occupies the northern part of the borough of Manhattan. First established by a Dutch governor, the neighborhood transformed from pastoral farmland to a fashionable residential area as apartment houses were built during the building boom of the 1880s. Following the panic of 1893, the large amount of vacancies led property owners to rent to blacks, and by World War I, Harlem was firmly established as a black residential area. Currently there are many ethnic groups in Harlem, including African Americans, Puerto Ricans, and Italians.

FURTHER READING

Gurock, Jeffrey S. *When Harlem Was Jewish, 1870–1930.* New York: Columbia University Press, 1979.

Riker, James. *Revised History of Harlem (City of New York): Its Origin and Early Annals: Prefaced by Home Scenes in the Fatherlands; Or Notices of Its Founders before Emigration. Also, Sketches of Numerous Families, and the Recovered History of the Land-Titles.* Baltimore: Genealogical, 1996.

Harlem Renaissance In order to educate herself in the context and history of her people, their artists, and their intellectuals, the young Maya Angelou studied the important figures active during the Harlem Renaissance. The period of this African-American intellectual flowering was loosely defined as taking place between 1919 and the early or mid-1930s. Well-known figures included writers such as LANGSTON HUGHES, COUNTEE CULLEN, JAMES WELDON JOHNSON, Jean Toomer, ZORA NEALE HURSTON, Wallace Thurman, and many others. W. E. B. DUBOIS, whose wife Angelou would later meet in Africa, was among the leading intellectuals of the period, who also included MARCUS GARVEY and Booker T. Washington.

An unprecedented outpouring of artistic and professional works emerged from within the black community during the Harlem Renaissance, and there was a flowering of African-American cultural and intellectual life. It is considered the most influential movement in African-American cultural history, laying the groundwork for all subsequent African-American literature and impacting worldwide black consciousness. Although not confined to the New York borough, HARLEM served as the symbolic hub of this cultural awakening.

Participants in the Harlem Renaissance worked to reconceptualize "the Negro" apart from white stereotypes. New pride was taken in their heritage, and they sought to break away from values and bourgeois practices that might reinforce white racist beliefs. This movement helped to lay the foundation for the post–World War II CIVIL RIGHTS MOVEMENT.

The Harlem Renaissance is characterized by overt racial pride and the promotion of social INTEGRATION and progressive politics. The movement was characterized mostly by the creation of literature, art, and music, but it was more than artistic in nature. The Harlem Renaissance was also a sociological development as African Americans explored and began to define their identity and heritage.

FURTHER READING

Diepeveen, Leonard. "Folktales in the Harlem Renaissance." *American Literature* 58, no. 1 (1986): 64.

Long, Richard A. *One More Time: Harlem Renaissance History and Historicism.* Elizabeth, N.J.: Fire!! Press, 2006.

Mehra, Shaila. "Portraits of the New Negro Woman: Visual and Literary Culture in the Harlem Renaissance." *MELUS* 33, no. 3 (2008): 203–205.

Robinson, Edward L. "Word, Image, and the New Negro: Representation and Identity in the Harlem Renaissance." *Journal of African American History* 93, no. 4 (2008): 582–584.

Wintz, Cary D., ed. *The Emergence of the Harlem Renaissance.* New York: Garland, 1996.

Harlem Writers Guild The Harlem Writers Guild was founded in 1950 by ROSA GUY, JOHN KILLENS, Dr. John Henrik Clarke, Willard Moore, and Walter Christmas. Maya Angelou and others have received serious critical responses and writing tutelage through this organization. Guild members are all African-American writers, and it may be the oldest organization of its kind in the world. Its purpose is to aid in publishing works related to the African DIASPORA. A community service organization, it has won numerous awards.

Harris, Joel Chandler (1845–1908) In *The Heart of a Women,* Maya Angelou cites a story of BRER RABBIT as being analogous to her situation in the offices of the *Arab Observer,* where she worked in Cairo, Egypt. The Brer Rabbit stories were written by Joel Chandler Harris in a southern black dialect. Though Angelou has used black traditional vernacular frequently in her autobiographies and poetry, she more often uses standard American English, only seldom employing colloquialisms or common black dialect in her spoken lectures and interviews. Black English, such as Gulla (originating in Angola), is common among blacks in the United States and is identified as a language separate from standard American English.

Joel Chandler Harris, a white journalist and author, was known for his stories featuring the narrator of Uncle Remus. He was born in Eatonton, Georgia, on December 9, 1845; his parents were unmarried, and his father abandoned the family shortly after he was born. Harris's mother worked hard to support them and instilled in him a love for reading. His schooling was funded by a prominent physician in the area, and although Harris excelled in reading and writing, he was mostly known for his practical jokes and humorous mischief. At the age of 14, he quit school and went to work in the printer's shop on Turnwold Plantation, where he voraciously read through a library of great literature and began to write himself. In his time off, he would spend hundreds of hours in the slave quarters, soaking in the dialect and stories that would later inspire his Uncle Remus stories.

Harris moved frequently and worked in several positions as a writer and editor. He was eventually hired as associate editor of the *Savannah Morning News* (the most widely circulated newspaper in Georgia) and became established as Georgia's leading humor columnist. Around 1876, Harris accepted a job in Atlanta, and not long thereafter, he began writing the Uncle Remus tales, which were first published in the *Atlanta Constitution*. The stories featured cunning central characters such as Brer Rabbit and Brer Fox. The tales was published in collected form in 1880 as *Uncle Remus: His Songs and His Sayings* and became an instant best seller. Around 1890, Harris retired from the newspaper, but he continued to create children's fiction and articles for a local journal. In 1905, he was elected to the American Academy of Arts and Letters. He died in Atlanta on July 3, 1908.

The 185 tales that compose the Uncle Remus stories have undergone extreme scrutiny in the 20th century. Some critics doubt the legitimacy of the tales, citing the reluctance of the black population to divulge stories to white folklorists. Others criticize the racist promoting of white patronage. Another criticism levied at Harris's work is his use of phonetic dialect and exaggeration of the language of the black slaves. This has been interpreted as demeaning to blacks, though Harris often expressed his own philosophical view that blacks and whites were equal, and he felt that, given the same amount of education, they would both accomplish life with the same level of informed understanding. On a positive note, many place the Uncle Remus stories alongside the FOLKTALES of Aesop.

FURTHER READING

Bickley, R. B. *Joel Chandler Harris: A Reference Guide.* Boston: G. K. Hall, 1978.

Brasch, Walter M. *Brer Rabbit, Uncle Remus, and the "Cornfield Journalist": The Tale of Joel Chandler Harris.* Macon, Ga.: Mercer University Press, 2000.

Cochran, Robert. "Black Father: The Subversive Achievement of Joel Chandler Harris." *African American Review* 38, no. 1 (2004): 21–34.

Keenan, Hugh T., ed. *Joel Chandler Harris: An Annotated Bibliography of Criticism, 1977–1996: With Supplement, 1892–1976.* Westport, Conn.: Greenwood Press, 1997.

High John the Conqueror Angelou knew the FOLKTALES of High John the Conqueror, an African-American folk figure and trickster, and was familiar with some of the songs about him. She mentions him in *All God's Children Need Traveling Shoes* as she discusses black-owned newspapers in the United States carrying announcements of magic practitioners (1,038).

John was said to be an African prince captured and sold to be a slave in the southern United States. He was bright and played tricks on his masters, such as performing incredible tasks in short periods of time with the help of his sweetheart, the Devil's daughter. One story tells how he listened to a list of tasks his master, the plantation owner, planned for him, sharing his plans with his wife the day before giving his orders to John. High John listened at their kitchen window and then had the job finished or nearly finished when the master found him the next morning to give him the assignment. The master began to believe that High John was clairvoyant.

These were tales told by slaves in secret, and for the most part they never reached the ears of their white owners. The author and folklorist ZORA NEALE HURSTON wrote an article about High John in which she said: "It is no accident that High John de Conquer has evaded the ears of white people. They were not supposed to know" (543). Blacks knew that whites would not understand and would laugh. High John the Conqueror (spelled various ways) represented the cleverness of the blacks, and the whites did not know how often they were being outsmarted. The tales were told mostly in the time of slavery, but after the Emancipation Proclamation, they fell out of favor and were largely forgotten.

There is also a John the Conqueror root (*Ipomoea jalapa* or *Ipomea purga*) said to bring good luck to its carrier. It is inedible and well-known to African-American hoodoo practitioners in the United States.

FURTHER READING

Hurston, Zora Neale. "High John de Conquer." In *Mother Wit from The Laughing Barrel: Readings in the Interpretation of Afro-American Folklore*, edited by Alan Dundes, 541–548. Jackson and London: University of Mississippi Press, 1990.

Sanfield, Steve. *Adventures of High John the Conqueror.* Little Rock, Ark.: August House, 1989.

Holiday, Billie (Eleanora Fagan) (1915–1959) Maya Angelou describes Billie Holiday's visits to her home in the autobiography *The Heart of a Woman.* The visits were made just months before Holiday died. She was ill and had low energy and enjoyed just hanging out at Angelou's home in California during the daytime for several days. She also enjoyed Angelou's COOKING. Maya and her son, Guy, were both offended by her crude talk during her last visit to their home.

Holiday was born Eleanora Fagan on April 7, 1915, and grew up in Baltimore, Maryland. She became one of the great JAZZ vocalists of the 20th century, but her life was difficult, and she died prematurely, on July 17, 1959, because of heroin and alcohol addictions. Her lifelong friend, saxophonist LESTER YOUNG nicknamed her "Lady Day," and she called him "The Prez." Her own nickname was related to her mother's pet name for herself, "The Duchess."

FURTHER READING

American Masters. "Billie Holiday: About the Singer." Available online. URL: http://www.pbs.org/net/americanmasters/episodes/billie-holiday/about-the-singer/68. Accessed January 19, 2009.

Greene, Meg. *Billie Holiday: A Biography.* Westport, Conn.: Greenwood Press, 2007.

House Committee on Un-American Activities (House Un-American Activities Committee [HUAC]) Though Maya Angelou was never involved with the House Committee on Un-American Activities (HUAC), she was aware of it and mentioned it in her writing. The HUAC was prominent during a time of irrational fear of "Big Brother" as the government invaded and disrupted private lives.

Established in 1938 as a committee of the House of Representatives, the HUAC investigated alleged communist activities through the 1940s and 1950s. Many artists and entertainers were among those investigated. The results of investigation were contempt-of-Congress convictions and blacklisting of people who refused to cooperate with the investigation. Criticized for its tactics, the HUAC was renamed the Internal Security Committee in 1969 and was finally dissolved in 1975.

FURTHER READING

Donner, Frank J. "HUAC: From Pillory to Farce." *Nation* 203, no. 6 (1966): 174–176.

Gladchuck, John Joseph. *Hollywood and Anticommunism: HUAC and the Evolution of the Red Menace, 1935–1950.* New York: Routledge, 2007.

Jarrico, Bill. "The Blacklist through New Eyes." *Cinema Journal* 44, no. 4 (2005): 104–111.

O'Reilly, Kenneth. *Hoover and the Un-Americans: The FBI, HUAC, and the Red Menace.* Philadelphia: Temple University Press, 1983.

How to Make an American Quilt This film made in 1995 was based on the novel of the same title written by Whitney Otto. The screenplay was written by Jane Anderson, and the movie was directed by Jocelyn Moorhouse. It had an all-star cast, including Maya Angelou (who played the role of Anna), Winona Ryder, Anne Bancroft, Ellen Burstyn, Jean Simmons, Rip Torn, and other well-known stars. The story revolved around a romance, and the message was primarily about recognizing beauty in the patterns and coincidences of life.

Hughes, Langston (James Mercer Langston Hughes) (1902–1967) Maya Angelou greatly admired the poetry of Langston Hughes, and his short and meaningful poems influenced her own style. Poet, novelist, short story writer, and playwright, James Mercer Langston Hughes was born in Joplin, Missouri, on February 1, 1902, and grew up mostly with his grandmother in Kansas. He attended high school in Cleveland, Ohio, when his mother remarried and moved there. While in high school, he worked on the yearbook and newspaper staffs and began writing his first short stories. Hughes's father provided the tuition for him to attend Columbia University. Though he was a good student there, he left in 1922 because of prejudice. He became more and more involved in the area of HARLEM and continued writing, especially poetry.

Hughes then worked various odd jobs, including serving as a crewman on a freight ship. He traveled to Africa and across Europe and then returned to live with his mother in Washington, D.C. It was while working as a busboy that Hughes met the poet Vachel Lindsay. The story is that Hughes slipped some of his poetry underneath Lindsay's plate. The next day, newspapers nationwide reported that Lindsay had discovered an African-American busboy poet. Hughes was offered a scholarship and attended Lincoln University in Pennsylvania. His first two books were published before his graduation in 1929. He moved back to New York, and except for an occasional trip overseas, he remained in Harlem for the rest of his life. He died on May 22, 1967, from complications following abdominal surgery.

FURTHER READING

DeSantis, Christopher C., ed. *Langston Hughes: A Documentary Volume.* Detroit: Thomson Gale, 2005.

Leach, Laurie F. *Langston Hughes: A Biography.* Westport, Conn.: Greenwood Press, 2004.

Tidwell, John, and Cheryl R. Ragar. *Montage of a Dream: The Art and Life of Langston Hughes.* Columbia: University of Missouri Press, 2007.

Tracy, Steven Carl, ed. *A Historical Guide to Langston Hughes.* New York: Oxford University Press, 2004.

Hurston, Zora Neale (1891–1960) Maya Angelou read and respected the work of Zora Neale Hurston who had become well-known during the HARLEM RENAISSANCE. One of the great black female authors of the 20th century, she was a writer and folklorist who focused on African-American traditions in the South.

Hurston was born on January 7, 1891, in Notasulga, Alabama. When she was three, her family moved from Notasulga to Eatonville, Florida, the first all-black community in the United States. Her father had many jobs, including work as a preacher, sharecropper, and carpenter. Her mother, Lucy Potts Hurston, was a schoolteacher. After the death of her mother in 1904, Hurston joined a traveling theatrical company. She attended Baltimore's Morgan Academy in 1918, and then attended college at Howard University from 1919 to 1924. She went to New York during the peak of the Harlem Renaissance and was soon at its center as she worked with other young writers to create a literary magazine called *Fire!!* In 1925, she won a scholarship to attend Barnard College, where she was the only African-American student. She received her bachelor of arts in anthropology in 1928 at the age of 36 (she always claimed to be 10 years younger than she was), and she did fieldwork with the pioneering anthropologist Franz Boas.

Hurston next pursued a graduate degree in anthropology at Columbia and conducted FOLKLORE field studies among African Americans in the South. Her trips were funded by the folklorist Charlotte Mason, who was also a patron to LANGSTON HUGHES. Hurston collaborated with Hughes to write a play in 1930, but it was never finished. She published her first novel, *Jonah's Gourd Vine,* in 1934, and it received positive reviews. Her most famous work, *Their Eyes Were Watching God,* was published in 1937. For several years, she was on the faculty of North Carolina College for Negroes (now North Carolina Central University). Despite her early rise to literary popularity, she faded out of the spotlight by the time of her death in Florida on January 25, 1960.

The late 20th century saw a renewed interest in Hurston's work, largely due to the efforts of the writer Alice Walker. Walker located Hurston's grave and erected a dignified gravestone in her honor. "Celebrated as griot, actress, preacher, signifying ethnographer, blues singer, trickster, and literary artist, she is seen by many as the literary foremother of the 20th-century African-American and women's literary traditions" (Cronin, 261).

FURTHER READING

Beito, David T., and Linda Royster Beito. "Isabel Paterson, Rose Wilder Lane, and Zora Neale Hurston on War, Race, the State, and Liberty." *Independent Review* 12, no. 4 (2008): 553–573.

Bloom, Harold, ed. *Zora Neale Hurston.* New York: Chelsea House, 1986.

Cronin, Gloria L. "Hurston, Zora Neale (1891–1960)." In *Encyclopedia of African-American Literature,* edited by Wilfred D. Samuels, 259–261. New York: Facts On File, 2007.

Frydman, Jason. "Zora Neale Hurston, Biographical Criticism, and African Diasporic Vernacular Culture." *MELUS* 34 (2009): 99–118.

Hurston, Lucy Anne. *Speak, So You Can Speak Again: The Life of Zora Neale Hurston.* New York: Doubleday, 2004.

Nathiri, N. Y. *Zora!: Zora Neale Hurston, a Woman and her Community.* Orlando, Fla.: Sentinel Communications, 1991.

Newson, Adele S. *Zora Neale Hurston: A Reference Guide.* Boston, Mass.: G. K. Hall, 1987.

Seguin, Robert. "Cosmic Upset: Cultural Revolution and the Contradictions of Zora Neale Hurston." *Modernism/Modernity* 16, no. 2 (2009): 229–253.

I

integration Maya Angelou was active in the CIVIL RIGHTS MOVEMENT in the United States and, with others, worked diligently to end discrimination and SEGREGATION. Many of her poems include the theme of black oppression.

Integration means to bring together parts, and in racial terms, it means to bring together various racial or ethnic groups to achieve equality between them. Desegregation was viewed in the United States as the legal solution to segregation, the practice of restricting people to certain areas of residence, separate schools, churches, playgrounds, restaurants, parks, and so on, on the basis of race. It is a means for the majority group to maintain social and economic advantages and superiority over the minority. In the South, legal segregation in public facilities continued into the 1950s.

Following the formal Reconstruction period in the late 1870s, southern state legislatures began passing laws that required the separation of whites from persons of color in public transportation and schools. The idea of segregation quickly spread to restaurants, theaters, parks, and even cemeteries. The so-called JIM CROW laws were instituted in an effort to limit contact between blacks and whites in public places. These "separate but equal" laws were upheld in court until the famous case of *BROWN V. BOARD OF EDUCATION OF TOPEKA, KANSAS* in 1954, when the Supreme Court declared segregation in public schools to be unconstitutional. This ruling was applied to other public facilities, and in the following years, other Jim Crow laws were struck down.

The process of racial integration in the United States is ongoing. Early efforts at integration during the 1970s included busing students to other schools—black students would be bused to attend a predominantly white school or white students would be bused to attend a predominantly black school. Attitudes and traditions have been slow to change, particularly in the southern states. Racial integration is still an issue in much of the country because of the number of immigrants from Latin American and Asia; there are still regions and groups in the United States that discriminate against various minority groups.

FURTHER READING

Berghorn, Forrest J., Norman R. Yetman, and William E. Hanna. "Racial Participation and Integration in Men's and Women's Intercollegiate Basketball: Continuity and Change, 1958–1985." *Sociology of Sport Journal* 5, no. 2 (1988): 107–124.

Blissfield, Gwen. "White Attitudes toward Racial Integration and the Urban Riots of the 1960's." *Public Opinion Quarterly* 36, no. 4 (1972): 579.

Ellen, Ingrid Gould. "Race-Based Neighborhood Projection: A Proposed Framework for Understanding New Data on Racial Integration." *Urban Studies (Routledge)* 37, no. 9 (2000): 1,513–1,533.

———. "Stable Racial Integration in the Contemporary United States: An Empirical Overview." *Journal of Urban Affairs* 20, no. 1 (1998): 27.

Jackman, Mary R. "Education and Policy Commitment to Racial Integration." *American Journal of Political Science* 25, no. 2 (1981): 256.

———. "Individualism, Self-Interest, and White Racism." *Social Science Quarterly* 77, no. 4 (1996): 760–767.

Jackson, John P. *Science for Segregation, Race, Law, and the Case against Brown v. Board of Education.* New York: New York University Press, 2005.

———. *Social Scientists for Social Justice: Making the Case against Segregation.* New York: New York University Press, 2001.

Kushner, James A. *Apartheid in America: An Historical and Legal Analysis of Contemporary Racial Segregation in the United States.* Arlington, Va.: Carrollton Press, 1980.

Wells, Amy Stuart, et al. "Tackling Racial Segregation One Policy at a Time: Why School Desegregation Only Went so Far." *Teachers College Record* 107, no. 9 (2005): 2,141–2,177.

J

Jackson, Clidell (fl. 1940) Maya Angelou's mother, VIVIAN BAXTER, married Jackson Clidell—called Daddy Clidell by the family—shortly after the children were moved to California from STAMPS, ARKANSAS, in the early 1940s. After the marriage, the family relocated to SAN FRANCISCO, CALIFORNIA, and bought a 14-room house on Post Street in the FILLMORE DISTRICT. Clidell was an astute businessman with varied interests, including land in Texas. The marriage finally ended in divorce, but he was a positive influence on both Maya and Bailey. He spent time with them and set a good example.

Jackson, Michael (Michael Joseph Jackson) (1958–2009) Maya Angelou knew Michael Jackson well and wrote a eulogy poem entitled "We Had Him," which was read at Jackson's memorial funeral service by the entertainer and actress QUEEN LATIFAH. The "King of Pop," as he became known, Jackson was born on August 29, 1958, in Gary, Indiana, where his father created the group of child stars known as the Jackson 5, made up of Michael and his brothers. In 1970, the group scored four consecutive number-one pop hits. The Jackson 5 was noted for youthful exuberance, sharp choreography, large Afros, and loud fashions. They recorded albums for Motown Records until June 1975 and then continued on a successful streak with Epic Records as the Jacksons. The group was inducted into the Rock and Roll Hall of Fame in 1997.

Jackson released his first solo work in 1979, *Off the Wall,* which became a huge hit and ranks among his best-selling albums. Jackson had an energetic music style and innovative dance moves, such as his signature "moonwalk." Three years after *Off the Wall,* with the production of his album *Thriller,* he received much acclaim, including eight Grammys (a record) and the long-held distinction of the best-selling album in history, with more than 40 million copies sold worldwide. His music appealed to fans of disco, pop, and rhythm and BLUES. He was inducted into the Rock and Roll Hall of Fame in 2001.

Jackson led an eccentric and secluded lifestyle; his reputation was seriously damaged by accusations of child molestation in 1993 and again in 2003. On June 25, 2009, he died suddenly of cardiac arrest prior to a series of concerts he had hoped would spark a comeback.

FURTHER READING

Brown, Geoff. *Michael Jackson, Body and Soul: An Illustrated Biography.* New York: Beufort Books, 1984.

Haskins, James. *About Michael Jackson.* Hillside, N.J.: Enslow, 1985.

Johnson, Pamela K. "The Mirror of Michael Jackson." *International Review of African American Art* 22, no. 4 (2009): 36–37.

Silberman, Seth Clark. "Presenting Michael Jackson." *Social Semiotics* 17, no. 4 (2007): 417–440.

Terry, Carol D. *Sequins & Shades: The Michael Jackson Reference Guide.* Ann Arbor, Mich.: Pierian Press, 1987.

jazz Maya Angelou, as a performer and entertainer, enjoyed both jazz and the BLUES. She listened to music almost constantly and has a vast collection that represents music from many countries, periods, and styles. She has written that she finds music comforting; this was particularly when she was young and felt very lonely.

Emerging in the last half of the 19th century, and increasing in the early 20th, jazz was first recognized as a new art form in New Orleans. For decades, it was recognized as a black cultural phenomena, but in the 1930s, thanks to performances by Benny Goodman, who played jazz with black musicians, the sounds became accepted and sought by white audiences. Jazz was derived partially from ragtime and blues by African Americans in the southern states, and it slowly made its way to the northern states. It is the one genre of music that is truly American.

Jazz music is known for its syncopated rhythms, polyphonic playing, deviations of pitch, improvisation, and use of original timbres. Its development was influenced by both European harmonic structure and African rhythms. Jazz has never been an entirely composed piece of music. Each jazz musician is a composer in his or her own right, whereas the classical music performer interprets and expresses someone else's composition. Many subgenres have been created from jazz, including swing, bebop, Afro-Cuban, free jazz, and jazz funk.

The illicit speakeasies in the days of Prohibition (1920–33) became venues for the development of jazz, and this time is referred to as the "Jazz Age." The year 1933 saw the development of big swing-jazz orchestras and the emergence of virtuoso soloists such as Louis Armstrong, DUKE ELLINGTON, COUNT BASIE, and Artie Shaw. Swing music was dance music and was widely broadcast over the radio. But jazz allowed individual musicians to improvise on the melody and create thematic and complex solos. Over the next several decades, jazz would evolve and encompass new sounds, tempos, and harmonics. One reason that jazz is so versatile is its ability to incorporate new styles, such as rock and funk, and still maintain its distinctive sound.

In the earlier years of her life, music was an important outlet for Angelou, who loved the sounds of jazz and the blues and both sang and danced to these sounds. A blues aesthetic threads through her chronicles of troubles and survival in both her autobiographies and poetry. Her disappointments, frustrations, and realities were often expressed with lyrical sounds that were sometimes set to the rhythms of the blues and jazz.

FURTHER READING

DeVeaux, Scott. "Constructing the Jazz Tradition: Jazz Historiography." *Black American Literature Forum* 25, no. 3 (1991): 525.

Gennari, John. "Jazz Criticism: Its Development and Ideologies." *Black American Literature Forum* 25, no. 3 (1991): 449.

Gioia, Ted. *The History of Jazz.* New York: Oxford University Press, 1997.

Heldrich, Philip. "The History of Jazz." *Journal of Popular Culture* 34, no. 1 (2000): 167–168.

Mitchell, Bruce. "Jazz: A Multicultural Phenomenon." *Clearing House* 65, no. 4 (1992): 236.

Shipton, Alyn. *A New History of Jazz.* New York: Continuum, 2007.

Jim Crow When young Maya and her brother, Bailey, were transported by train from California to STAMPS, ARKANSAS, to live with their grandmother, Mrs. Annie Henderson, they became aware of when the train crossed into the segregated South because they then rode in a car that only carried black people. This was evidence of Jim Crow laws, enforcing SEGREGATION of the races, still in effect. The people took care of the children and shared their food with them. Growing up in Stamps under the Jim Crow laws left Angelou with a prejudice against whites that took many years and positive experiences to overcome. Ultimately, she did overcome her fear and disdain for whites and finally replaced her negative feelings with more positive understanding that there are good and bad people in all races.

In the late 1880s and 1890s, the children and grandchildren of slaves began to assert their rights as free citizens of the United States. They were known as the new Negroes. In response to their attempts to have equal rights, many states, cities, and other governing entities, primarily in the American South, passed laws that supposedly gave separate but equal rights to blacks and whites in voting, education, access to businesses, seating in buses and trains, drinking fountains, and other public facilities. These new laws were commonly called Jim Crow laws. This term *Jim Crow* came from the name of a song sung as part of a stage act in the 1820s by a white minstrel performer in BLACKFACE who derogatorily mimicked black men. Jim Crow laws were deemed unlawful during the 1950s and 1960s and were struck down during the CIVIL RIGHTS MOVEMENT.

FURTHER READING

Quarles, Benjamin. *The Negro in the Making of America.* New York: Touchstone: 1987.

Remini, Robert V. *A Short History of the United States.* New York: HarperCollins, 2008.

John Henry Maya Angelou alludes to the mythical John Henry in *A Song Flung Up to Heaven* as an analogy to describe the physical strength of her Aunt Lea's husband, Uncle Brother; she lived with her aunt and uncle for a while when she worked as a performer in Hawaii. Whether the legend of John Henry, an African-American folk hero, is based on fact or not is a matter of debate. The generally agreed story is that in the late 1880s, a "steel driver," who was a former slave, entered into a contest against a steam-powered hammer during the construction of a railway tunnel. Creating a tunnel at that time was accomplished by creating holes in the rock by pounding a steel drill with a sledgehammer, placing explosives in the holes, and igniting the explosive. The new steam-powered drill was touted to be able to outperform the manual steel drill and hammer. The legend has it that the contest was won by John Henry, but that he died from exhaustion shortly thereafter. Whether the tunnel was in Alabama or West Virginia is a point of contention, as is the identity of the person himself. However, the legend has been widely spread with the very popular ballad "John Henry, the Steel Driving Man."

FURTHER READING

Brewer, J. Mason. "The Ballad of John Henry." In *American Negro Folklore.* New York: Quadrangle/New York Times Book Company, 1968, 201–202.

Dorson, Richard M. "The Career of 'John Henry.'" In *Mother Wit from the Laughing Barrel: Readings in the Interpretation of Afro-American Folklore,* edited by Alan Dundes, 568–577. Jackson and London: University Press of Mississippi, 1990.

Nelson, Scott Reynolds. *Steel Drivin' Man: John Henry, the Untold Story of an American Legend.* New York: Oxford University Press, 2006.

Polly, Jane, ed. *American Folklore and Legend.* Pleasantville, N.Y.: Reader's Digest Association, 1978.

Johnson, Bailey, Jr. (ca. 1927–) Bailey was Maya's older brother by one year. They were great friends and mutually supportive and dependent upon one another, especially during their early years after having been abandoned by their parents to the care of their grandmother, Mrs. Annie Henderson (Momma). Bailey had a strong influence on Maya's childhood. He was her strongest supporter and ally, and Maya measured others by her small-framed brother, who was her hero, and whom she perceived as her "Kingdom Come." Maya and Bailey had an intense bond and enjoyed their private world of jokes. She was strengthened by his love and support; he was the only one able to comfort her after her rape, and he became her voice when they were returned to STAMPS ARKANSAS, from their mother's home in St. Louis after the tragedy. When he witnessed a disfigured and dead black man as his body was retrieved from water by a group of white men, he was confused and unable to understand their hateful comments and disrespect.

In many ways, Maya and Bailey were opposites. Maya was awkward; Bailey was graceful. Maya was plain; Bailey was attractive. Maya was introverted; Bailey was outgoing. They had mutual interests in language and poetry, but their points of view parted in the area of RACISM: Maya actively fought it; Bailey tried to ignore it. While still very young, 14, Bailey left Stamps, and got a job working on the railroad. He felt that he had matured to the point of being independent of the family.

Johnson, Bailey, Sr. (unknown–1969) Also called Big Bailey Johnson, this man was Maya Angelou's father. He left the family when she was about three years old, but he would surface occasionally in her life. Image played a major role in Big Bailey's life; his appearance was very important to him, not only in his clothing and cars, but in his ability to speak correctly. He has been described as using the language of an upper-class, educated white man of his time. From early in her childhood, Maya recognized his inability to genuinely have interest in his children's lives, and later she recognized his superficiality and selfishness.

Johnson, Clyde Bailey (Guy Johnson) (1944–) Maya Angelou's only child, Clyde Bailey Johnson was born when Maya was 16. He renamed himself Guy when he was still a boy, and the name was accepted by the family. Guy graduated from high school in Cairo, Egypt, and then took his first degree from the University of Ghana. A writer and poet, he has published two novels: *Standing at the Scratch Line* (1998) and *Echoes of a Distant Summer* (2002).

The following is from an online chat that Guy Johnson participated in on December 10, 1998; it was archived by BarnesandNoble.com.

> It is my desire to be a great writer. I know that I still have a mountain to climb to achieve that. With this first novel [*Standing at the Scratch Line*], I am just above the foothills, but I see the path to the top, and it is my desire to write compelling stories about everything that I find of interest. I hope to be with you as a writer for a very long time, and I hope that you will enjoy reading my work, because readers are the highest form of life on this planet.
>
> Truthfully, while I have been writing since I was 18, I didn't know that I wanted to be a writer. I thought I was going to be a painter and sketcher. Then I thought I was going to be a photographer. I tried a hand at darkroom technician. I played in a band. It took me quite some time to discover that I wanted to write The great thing about being the son of Maya Angelou is that I had the good fortune to grow up around some of the greatest black artists, dancers, singers, musicians, and actors of our time. My mother was in *The Blacks* in 1960, and in that cast were Ossie Davis, Ruby Dee, James Earl Jones, Godfrey Cambridge, Roscoe Lee Brown, Lou Gossett, Jr., and there were so many more I can't even remember. In terms of musicians, Billie Holiday, Clifford Brown, Eric Dolphy, et cetera. And on the political side she headed Martin Luther King's Southern Christian Leadership Conference, so of course I met Martin Luther King. Muhammad Ali met Malcolm X for the [first] time at my mother's house. So I would say I had the great fortune of living with one of the most inspiring creative people, and she was my mother.

FURTHER READING

Johnson, Guy. "About the Author." Interview, December 10, 1998. Available online. URL: http://www.authors.aalbc.com/guyjohnson.htm. Accessed March 29, 2010.

Johnson, James Weldon (1871–1938) At Maya Angelou's graduation from eighth grade, a white politician spoiled the excitement of the event by implying that the black children's future was destined to be limited. At the close of the ceremonies, after the man had left, the students, teachers, and their parents sang "Lift Every Voice and Sing," the Negro national anthem, and their spirits, hopes, and dreams were restored (142). The song was originally a poem by James Weldon Johnson, and it was set to music by his brother, John Rosamond Johnson.

Born on June 17, 1871, James Weldon Johnson had a diverse background. Working for several years as the principal of a high school in Florida, he studied law on the side and passed the Florida bar. He also wrote an impressive amount of poetry, of which his best known work is probably "Lift Every Voice and Sing" (1900). After his brother set it to music in 1905, the NATIONAL ASSOCIATION FOR THE ADVANCEMENT OF COLORED PEOPLE (NAACP) adopted the song in 1919 as the Negro national anthem.

In 1901, Johnson and his brother later moved to New York, where they wrote more than 200 songs for the Broadway musical stage. James Johnson was appointed the U.S. consul to Venezuela in 1906 and to Nicaragua in 1909. He later taught at Fisk University and wrote a novel, *The Autobiography of an Ex-colored Man.* In 1916, he became the leader of the NAACP. He engaged the organization in mass tactics, such as a silent protest in which 10,000 African Americans paraded down New York's Fifth Avenue in 1917. Throughout the 1920s, he was an inspiration for and promoter of the HARLEM RENAISSANCE by helping young blacks to be published. He died on June 26, 1938.

FURTHER READING

Chakkalakal, Tess. "'Making a Collection': James Weldon Johnson and the Mission of African American Literature." *South Atlantic Quarterly* 104, no. 3 (2003): 521–541.

Fleming, Robert Edward. *James Weldon Johnson.* Boston: Twayne, 1987.

Johnson, James Weldon. *Along This Way: The Autobiography of James Weldon Johnson.* New York: Viking Press, 1933.

Page, Amanda M. "The Ever-Expanding South: James Weldon Johnson and the Rhetoric of the Global Color Line." *Southern Quarterly* 46, no. 3 (2009): 26–46.

Routolo, Christina L. "James Weldon Johnson and the Autobiography of an Ex-Colored Musician." *American Literature* 72, no. 2 (2000): 249.

Johnson, Willie (fl. 1930s) Maya and Bailey's uncle and Annie Henderson's son, Willie Johnson was crippled at the age of three when a babysitter dropped him, as a result of which he walked with a cane. Early in *I Know Why the Caged Bird Sings,* Momma Henderson hid him in a bin of potatoes and onions to avoid his being detected by the KU KLUX KLAN. Willie helped Momma run her store and showed Maya kindness to the point that she wished that he could be her father. He was just as strict as Momma, however, and beat Maya and Bailey after they disrupted a church service with laughter. Sometimes he threatened to burn Maya on a hot potbelly stove if she did not learn her multiplication tables, but it was only a threat.

Jones, James Earl (1931–) Actor James Earl Jones was born in 1931, in Arkabutla, Mississippi, the son of a semiprofessional boxer and farmer. Known for his distinctive speaking voice, Jones made his Broadway debut in 1957. He performed with the New York Shakespeare Festival in plays such as *Othello* and *King Lear,* among many others. After his role in the play *The Great White Hope* (1968), he moved on to be one of the first African Americans to be cast as a regular on a soap opera, earning a part on *The Guiding Light.* Beginning in 1977, Jones was the voice of Darth Vader in the Star Wars saga and in 1994, he was the voice of Mufasa in the Disney cartoon *The Lion King.* Jones has also used his successful career as a commercial actor to support charitable causes. James Earl Jones was part of the star-filled cast when Maya Angelou performed as lead actress (the White Queen) in the 1960 Off-Broadway play *The* BLACKS by JEAN GENET.

FURTHER READING

Jones, James Earl, and Penelope Niven. *James Earl Jones: Voices and Silences.* New York: Limelight Editions, 2004.

Jones, Quincy (1933–) Quincy Jones and Maya Angelou admire each other's work, and on Thursday, April 30, 2009, Jones was awarded the "Maya Way" award in recognition of his work with youth, both in the United States and in Africa. Born on March 14, 1933, Jones cofounded the Institute for Black American Music and the Black Arts Festival in his hometown of Chicago. He is one of the United States' most noted musical icons. During his more than five decades as a conductor, record producer, musical arranger, film composer, and trumpeter, he has earned 79 Grammy Award nominations, 27 Grammys, and a Grammy Legend Award. He has also been nominated for seven Oscars, and the American Academy of Motion Picture Arts and Sciences awarded him the Jean Hershold Humanitarian Award in 1995.

Jones produced MICHAEL JACKSON's album *Thriller,* which has sold over 110 million copies worldwide. In 1985, he produced and conducted the charity song "We Are the World." When asked how he was able to achieve the collaboration of so many famous American artists for the song, he stated that he taped a sign at the entrance that read: "Check Your Ego At The Door."

FURTHER READING

Southern, Eileen. *The Music of Black Americans: A History.* New York: W. W. Norton, 1971.

Juneteenth Each summer in STAMPS, ARKANSAS, there is a black community celebration picnic where people of all classes and religions, laborers and professionals, come together for a day of fun and social mingling. In *I Know Why the Caged Bird Sings* (1970), Angelou describes the picnic in excellent detail, but she does not mention the specific date. It may have been a Juneteenth celebration.

June 19 is celebrated in 35 states as Freedom Day, or Emancipation Day. It commemorates the day in 1865 when Union general Gordon Granger read to the citizens of Galveston, Texas, General Order Number 3, which proclaimed "from the Executive of the United States, all slaves are free." For reasons not entirely clear, it took President ABRAHAM LINCOLN's Emancipation Proclamation, with an effective date of January 1, 1863, two and a half years to reach East Texas, where slavery was prevalent. "Juneteenth," as it is known, celebrates African-American freedom, achievements, and education.

FURTHER READING

Collins, Izola Ethel Fedfore. *Island of Color: Where Juneteenth Started.* Bloomington, Ind.: Author House, 2004.

K

Kerouac, Jack (Jean-Lebris de Kerouac) (1922–1969) Maya Angelou lived in SAN FRANCISCO, CALIFORNIA, during the early days of the Beat generation. The novelist and poet Jack Kerouac was there then, and apparently Angelou knew him as well as many other luminaries living there. In 2007, when Kerouac's Alley was established in Chinatown, San Francisco, a quote from Maya Angelou was included on a plaque there. It says: "Without courage, we cannot practice any other virtue with consistency."

Jean-Lebris de Kerouac, better known as Jack Kerouac, was born on March 12, 1922, in Lowell, Massachusetts to working-class immigrants from Quebec, Canada. His father ran a print shop and published a magazine, and Kerouac's interest in the written word and the literary world may have originated with this exposure. *On the Road,* written in 1951 and published in 1957, was his most noted work, but he also wrote more than 20 novels and numerous poems and other writings. Kerouac's work reflects his rejection of the values of his time and his adoption of the Bohemian lifestyle as he wandered throughout the United States. He called his writing style "spontaneous prose," which is similar to the stream-of-consciousness style of writing. His friends and traveling companions included Allen Ginsberg, William Burroughs, and Gregory Corso. Because of his lifestyle, Kerouac became known as "King of the Beatniks" and "Father of the Hippies," titles that he did not create himself. His death on October 21, 1969, age 47, was from an internal hemorrhage caused by cirrhosis of the liver.

FURTHER READING

Charters, Ann, and Allen Ginsberg. *Kerouac: A Biography.* New York: St. Martin's Griffin, 1994.

Christy, Jim. *The Long Slow Death of Jack Kerouac.* Toronto, Ontario: ECW Press, 1998.

Clark, Tom, and Carolyn Cassady. *Jack Kerouac: A Biography.* New York: Da Capo Press, 2001.

Kerouac, Jack. *On the Road.* New York: Viking Press, 1957.

Nicosia, Gerald. *Memory Babe: A Critical Biography of Jack Kerouac.* Berkeley: University of California Press, 1994.

Killens, John (John Oliver Killens) (1916–1987) The novelist John Killens was instrumental in persuading Maya Angelou to relocate from California to New York City so she could join and be critiqued by the HARLEM WRITERS GUILD. He and his family liked Maya and her son, Guy, and the two families became close friends.

Regarded by some as the spiritual father of the BLACK AESTHETIC MOVEMENT, John Oliver Killens was born in Macon, Georgia, on January 14, 1916. He was introduced to poetry by his mother, who was the president of the Dunbar Literary Club, and his great-grandmother filled his childhood with stories of the hardships of slavery. Killens had hopes of becoming a lawyer, but he found his true passion was writing novels about the lives of African Americans living in white America. Violence and RACISM in the United States were often depicted in his novels, but the improvement of society was his goal.

In the late 1940s, Killens moved to New York City, where he attended writing classes at Columbia University and New York University, and where he found other writers with similar perspectives. He cofounded the Harlem Writers Guild in the early 1950s, and his novel *Youngblood* (1954) was the first novel published by a guild member. Two of his other novels—*And Then We Heard the Thunder* (1962) and *The Cotillion, or One Good Bull Is Half the Herd*—were nominated for the Pulitzer Prize. From the mid-1960s until his death from cancer on October 27, 1987, he held writer-in-residence positions at, successively, Fisk University, Columbia University, Howard University, Bronx Community College, and MEDGAR EVERS College in the City University of New York.

FURTHER READING

Bloom, Harold. *Modern Black American Fiction Writers.* New York: Chelsea House, 1994.

Bolden, Tonya. *Strong Men Keep Coming: The Book of African American Men.* New York: J. Wiley and Sons, 1999.

King, Martin Luther, Jr. (1929–1968) Maya Angelou was the director of the northeast division of the SOUTHERN CHRISTIAN LEADERSHIP CONFERENCE (SCLC) for a year. Later, she was asked to assist King in raising funds by having black churches donate some of their congregational offerings for his planned Poor People's March to be held in Washington, D.C., but he was assassinated before she was able to join that campaign.

A renowned civil rights activist, King was born Michael King, Jr., on January 15, 1929, in Atlanta, Georgia, though his father later changed both their names in honor of the German Protestant Leader Martin Luther. Following in the footsteps of his father and grandfather, he attended Morehead College, graduating in 1948 with a B.A. degree. He continued his formal education at the Crozier Theological Seminary in Pennsylvania and was awarded a B.D. degree in 1951. While at Crozier, he received a scholarship for graduate studies at Boston University. King completed his doctorate in 1955. While at Boston University, he met and married Coretta Scott, a young woman known for her intellect and artistic talents. Together, they had two sons and two daughters. In 1954, the family moved to Montgomery, Alabama, where King became pastor of the Dexter Baptist Church.

In 1955, King was appointed to the executive committee of the NATIONAL ASSOCIATION FOR THE ADVANCEMENT OF COLORED PEOPLE, and in December that year, he accepted leadership of the bus boycott in Montgomery, Alabama—the first nonviolent demonstration by African Americans in the 20th century. The boycott lasted 382 days, and consequently, on December 21, 1956, the U.S. Supreme Court declared that laws segregating blacks and whites on public buses were unconstitutional.

In 1957, King was elected president of the Southern Christian Leadership Conference, a new civil rights organization. During his 11 years as president, he traveled extensively (over 6 million miles) and spoke frequently (more than 2,500 times), advocating Christian ideals and the nonviolent protest techniques advocated by Mohandas Gandhi. In those years, he led a massive protest in Birmingham, Alabama, which inspired his "Letter from Birmingham Jail" (1963); planned voter registration drives in Alabama; directed the peaceful march on Washington, D.C., by 250,000 people, to whom he delivered his "I Have a Dream" address (1963); was an adviser to Presidents John F. Kennedy and Lyndon B. Johnson; was arrested scores of times; was awarded five honorary degrees; wrote five books and numerous papers; named Man of the Year by *Time* magazine (January 3, 1964); and became the symbolic leader of black America. In 1964, he was awarded the Nobel Peace Prize at age 35, the youngest person to receive the award at that time. King was assassinated by JAMES EARL RAY on April 4, 1968, in Memphis, Tennessee,

Martin Luther King, Jr., was assassinated on April 4, 1968, Maya Angelou's 40th birthday. From that time on, Angelou no longer celebrated her birthday but instead sent flowers to King's widow, Coretta Scott King, until the latter's death in 2006. Maya's grandson Colin, Maya, and various young children appear here with Coretta Scott King. *(Courtesy Angelou-Johnson Family Archives)*

where he was leading a protest march in support of striking sanitation workers.

FURTHER READING

Quarles, Benjamin. *The Negro in the Making of America.* New York: Touchstone, 1996.

Remini, Robert V. *A Short History of the United States.* New York: HarperCollins, 2008.

Turner, Patricia A. *I Heard It through the Grapevine: Rumor in African-American Culture.* Berkeley: University of California Press, 1993.

Zinn, Howard. *The Twentieth Century: A People's History.* New York: Harper & Row, 1984.

Kipling, Rudyard (1865–1936) Rudyard Kipling was one of Maya Angelou's favorite authors when she was a child. A British short story writer and poet, Kipling was born on December 30, 1865, in Bombay, India (then under British control). At age six, he and his three-year-old sister, Alice, were sent to England for their education; this was a common custom for the children of British nationals who lived in India at the time. In 1878, Kipling was admitted to United Services College, a school founded to prepare boys for military service. It was a difficult period of time for him, but he made some lifelong friends and used the experience in several of his later works. In 1882, because his parents were not able to financially support his going to Oxford University (he was not academically strong enough to be awarded a scholarship), he returned to India.

Kipling's father had obtained a job for him as the assistant editor of a small local newspaper, the *Civil & Military Gazette*. Here, for the first time, he had the opportunity to get his stories and poems in print. He was a prolific writer, and during the period between November 1886 and June 1887, 39 of his stories appeared in the *Gazette*. The following year, he published six collections of stories. In 1889, after a dispute with the newspaper, he returned to England, specifically London, the literary center of the British Empire. For the next three decades, he continued to write and achieved much recognition. His most notable works included *The Jungle Book* (1894), *Kim* (1901), *The Seven Seas* (1896), *Captains Courageous* (1897), *The Second Jungle Book* (1895), and *Just So Stories* (1902). In 1907, Kipling was awarded the Nobel Prize in literature, the first English-language recipient to be awarded that honor. He continued writing until the early 1930s, and on January 18, 1936, at age 70, he died of an internal hemorrhage. His ashes were buried in the Poet's Corner of Westminster Abbey.

FURTHER READING

Cross, Thomas N. *East and West: A Biography of Rudyard Kipling.* Ann Arbor, Mich.: Luckystone Press, 1992.

Gilmour, David. *The Long Recessional: The Imperial Life of Rudyard Kipling.* New York: Farrar, Straus and Giroux, 2003.

Kitt, Eartha (Eartha Mae Kitt) (1927–2008) Eartha Kitt was a talented singer admired by Maya Angelou, who was asked to replace her in *New Faces of 1953*. Kitt's contract had run out, and she was headed for a job in Las Vegas. Maya could not take the position because she was still under contract at the Purple Onion in SAN FRANCISCO. Kitt was born in South Carolina on January 19, 1927, and died in Weston, Connecticut, on Christmas Day, 2008. Her mother was a sharecropper of mixed caucasian, African-American, and Native American heritage. Fostering an aloof and racially ambiguous image, she spoke out against racism and, later, the Vietnam War. Kitt performed as a singer in cabarets and recorded many live performances. Her most famous recording was "Santa Baby" (1953). Kitt worked in films, television, and nightclubs and also performed on Broadway and television. She won multiple awards for her work, including an Emmy award in 1966 and two Tony awards (1978, 2000).

Ku Klux Klan The Ku Klux Klan was in operation in the southern states during the time Maya and her brother, Bailey, lived in STAMPS, ARKANSAS. While they were there, an incident occurred between a black man and a white woman, and their Uncle Willie was told to take cover because the Klan would be riding that night. Momma Henderson, Maya, and Bailey hid Uncle Willie in an onion and potato storage bin, where he spent a cold and uncomfortable night.

The Civil War ended in 1865, and the following year, the Ku Klux Klan was founded in Pulaski, Tennessee, by former slave trader and Confederate general Nathan Bedford Forrest, who became the Klan's first Grand Wizard. By 1867, some white southerners, members of the terroristic Klan, were attacking carpetbaggers (whites from the North looking for ways to make money), politically active black southerners, and their white sympathizers. The primary fear in the South was that blacks would participate in government and be granted the vote. The Klan was formed to intimidate or destroy such outcomes and "it has been estimated that approximately four hundred hangings of African-Americans occurred between 1868 and 1871" (Remini 2008, 165). Bands of hooded members clad in ghostly white costumes, supposedly representing the ghosts of white Confederate soldiers who had died in the Civil War, rode through the countryside at night, stopping at various cabins and houses to issue warnings. When warnings failed, cabins and churches were burned, and many freed slaves were beaten or killed. During the Reconstruction period, the activities of the Ku Klux Klan diminished, only to be renewed in the early decades of the 1900s.

Between 1910 and 1930, the black population of the northern states rose from a little over 1 million to nearly 2½ million because of job opportunities in industry. Tensions grew because some white workers resented the hiring of blacks, and whites did not like blacks moving into white neighborhoods. A revived Ku Klux Klan operated in both the North and the South and harassed Jews, Catholics, foreign-born citizens, and particularly blacks. The Klan also carried out terrorist activities during the CIVIL RIGHTS MOVEMENT of the 1950s and 1960s. Today, the Klan is composed of numerous small chapters across the United States, with a total membership of about 8,000.

FURTHER READING

Collins, Joseph R. *The American Past, Part 2: A Survey of American History since 1865.* 4th ed. Fort Worth, Tex.: Harcourt Press, 1993.

Remini, Robert V. *A Short History of the United States.* New York: HarperCollins, 2008.

Todd, Lewis Paul, and Merle Curti. *Rise of the American Nation: Liberty Edition.* Orlando, Fla.: Harcourt Brace Jovanovich, 1982.

L

Lake, Veronica (Constance Frances Marie Ockelmen) (1922–1972) Veronica Lake is mentioned in Maya Angelou's serial autobiographies because of her roles in movies that Maya and her brother, Bailey, watched in STAMPS, ARKANSAS. An American film actress, she is best known for her film noir roles with Alan Ladd during the 1940s. Lake was born Constance Frances Marie Ockelman in Brooklyn, New York, on November 14, 1922. Her father died when she was 10, and her mother soon remarried. In 1938, the family moved to Beverly Hills, and Lake's mother enrolled her in the Bliss-Hayden School for Acting. She began performing in films while still a teenager, and she changed her name prior to signing a long-term contract with Paramount Pictures in 1941. Her breakthrough film was *I Wanted Wings* in 1941. Lake became famous for beginning the peek-a-boo hairstyle, with a wandering strand curling down over the right eye, which was popular in the 1940s. She went through several marriages and divorces, and her career took a downward turn with her role as a Nazi sympathizer in *The Hour before the Dawn* (1944). Lake's mental and physical health declined in the 1960s. The IRS seized her assets for unpaid taxes, and she died impoverished on July 7, 1972.

FURTHER READING

Lenburg, Jeff. *Peekaboo: The Story of Veronica Lake.* New York: St. Martin's Press, 1983.

Latifah, Queen (Dana Elaine Owens) (1970–) Queen Latifah read Maya Angelou's poem "We Had Him," at the memorial service for MICHAEL JACKSON in 2009. An African-American model, actress, singer, songwriter, record producer, and rapper, Dana Elaine Owens was born in Newark, New Jersey, on March 18, 1970, and is known by her stage name, Queen Latifah; she is also known as the Queen of Rap. In addition to her work in entertainment, she has a line of cosmetics designed for women of color called the CoverGirl Queen Collection. She is probably best known for her role as a jail matron in the 2002 film *Chicago,* for which she was nominated for an Academy Award as best actress in a supporting role. She has earned a Golden Globe Award, two Screen Actors Guild Awards, two Image Awards, a Grammy, six additional Grammy nominations, and an Emmy Award nomination.

FURTHER READING

Latifah, Queen, with Karen Hunter. *Ladies First: Revelations of a Strong Woman.* New York: William Morrow, 1999.

Queen Latifah Web site. Available online. URL: http://www.queenlatifah.com/. Accessed June 1, 2010.

Ruth, Amy. *Queen Latifah.* Minneapolis: Lerner, 2000.

Tracy, Kathleen. *Queen Latifah.* Hockessin, Del.: Mitchell Lane, 2004.

Lincoln, Abbey (Anna Marie Wooldridge) (1930–2010) An American JAZZ vocalist, songwriter, and actress, Abbey Lincoln became close friends with Maya Angelou through their mutual involvement in black music performance circles of LOS ANGELES in the late 1950s. They also worked together during rehearsals and preparations for JEAN GENET's Off-Broadway play *The* BLACKS. Abbey Lincoln and her future husband, MAX ROACH, withdrew from the play before the opening night, but Lincoln and Angelou remained friends.

Known for her passion and honesty, Lincoln was born on August 6, 1930, in Chicago, Illinois, under the name of Anna Marie Wooldridge. At age 19, she moved to California to sing in nightclubs. She was nominated for a Golden Globe award for her performance in the film *For Love of Ivy* (1969). She sang on the 1960s jazz civil rights recording *We Insist!—Freedom Now Suite,* following which she became connected with the political fight against RACISM in America. She has toured worldwide as a soloist, and she has appeared on radio and television as well as in films. In 2003, she was awarded the National Endowment for the Arts Jazz Masters' Award. Lincoln was married to Max Roach from 1962 to 1970. She died in New York City on August 14, 2010.

FURTHER READING

"Abbey Lincoln," Bold and Introspective Jazz Singer, Dies at 80." *New York Times,* 14 August 2010. Available online. URL: http://www.nytimes.com/2010.08/15/arts/music/15Lincoln.html. Accessed August 26, 2010.

Wikipedia. "Abbey Lincoln." Available online. URL: http://en.wikipedia.org/wiki/Abbey_Lincoln. Accessed August 26, 2010.

Lincoln, Abraham (1809–1865) Abraham Lincoln was one of the great heroes of the United States, particularly to the oppressed blacks of the South. Maya Angelou greatly admired Lincoln and studied his life and accomplishments. She felt that to understand the issues of the day, it was important to know the racial history of the United States.

The 16th president of the United States, Abraham Lincoln (no middle name) was born in rural Kentucky on February 12, 1809. His parents, native Virginians, were uneducated farmers, though based on personal religious convictions, Lincoln's father felt that slavery was wrong. Rather than contest a challenge in court over the ownership of their land, his father elected to move the family to southwestern Indiana when Lincoln was seven years old. The region where they moved was still wilderness at that time, and consequently, Lincoln's formal education only amounted to about a year to 18 months of classes. He was said to have remarked that when he was a young adult, he could read, write, and cipher to the rule of three, but that was about all he knew. It was probably his stepmother (his mother died two years after the family moved to Indiana), Sarah Bush Johnston, who influenced his interest in increasing his knowledge through reading. They seemed to have a special fondness for one another; he later referred to her as his angel mother.

In 1830, the family moved to Illinois. Lincoln, age 21, was tall (six feet, four inches) and lean, but muscular. Being of age, he struck out on his own. A local merchant was impressed with him and placed him in charge of his mill and store in New Salem. It was here that Lincoln had the opportunity to meet members of the community, and they soon found him to be a very amicable person.

In 1832, at the age of 23, Lincoln announced his candidacy for the Illinois General Assembly. He lost the election but received 277 of the 300 votes cast in his New Salem precinct. Two years later, he was elected to the Illinois legislature, and soon afterward, he decided to become an attorney. Although self-taught, he passed the bar examination in 1837, then moved to Springfield, the capital of Illinois, and began to practice law there. While in the Illinois legislature (he was reelected three times), he stated that slavery was founded on injustice and bad policy but recognized that being labeled an abolitionist would put him in disfavor with his constituency. In 1846, he ran for political office again and was elected to the U.S. House of Representatives. At the end of his two-year term, he returned to Springfield and his law practice.

Lincoln rode the circuit of the central Illinois counties, handling a variety of cases throughout the rural, prairie region. He soon built a reputation as a fair and able attorney. He argued 175 cases before the Illinois Supreme Court and won 31 of the 51 cases where he was the sole lawyer.

Lincoln first met Mary Todd in 1839 in Springfield, and they became engaged in December that year. A wedding was planned for January 1841, but it was canceled. They later met at a party, reconciled, and were married on November 4, 1842. Abraham and Mary Lincoln had four sons, but only one, Robert Todd Lincoln, lived to maturity. Their second son, Edward Baker Lincoln, lived from 1846 to 1850, while William "Willie" Wallace Lincoln, their third son, lived only eleven months. Son number four, Thomas "Tad" Lincoln, was born in 1853 and outlived his father, but died in 1871 in Chicago. (Mary Todd Lincoln, despondent over the loss of her husband and sons, was committed to a mental health hospital in 1875. She died in 1882.)

In October 1854 in Peoria, Illinois, Lincoln spoke in opposition to Illinois senator Stephen Douglas's position on the Kansas-Nebraska Act, which supported allowing territories to determine whether or not they would be pro-slavery. In his speech, Lincoln stated his position on slavery, which was an absolute conviction that it was a monstrous injustice. Later that year, he became a candidate for the U.S. Senate representing the Whig Party. After several votes in the Illinois legislature, he was leading, but he asked his supporters to solidify the fractured party by supporting another candidate, Lyman Trumball. This gave Trumball enough votes to win in the 10th round.

By 1856, Lincoln had identified himself as a member of the new Republican Party. He received national recognition as a result of his efforts to persuade the anti–Kansas-Nebraska Act factions of several other parties in Illinois to join with the new Republicans. He was nominated for vice president at the national convention in Philadelphia that year, but lost. In 1858, he accepted the Republican nomination for the U.S. Senate. During his acceptance speech, he made a statement adapted from the Book of Mark in the New Testament, chapter 3, verse 25: "A house divided against itself cannot stand." He went on to say that the government could not endure permanently half-slave and half-free and that it would have to become all one or the other. The Democratic Party nominee for the Senate from Illinois was Stephen A. Douglas. He and Lincoln had several debates over whether the federal government or the state/territorial government had constitutional authority to determine whether or not slavery was lawful in the state or territory. The debates were widely followed throughout the states and gave Lincoln greater national attention, and in 1860, he was nominated by the Republican Party as their candidate for the presidency of the United States.

Lincoln was elected president of the United States in November 1860; a major split in the Democratic party and the formation of the Constitutional Union Party had given him the election. After the election, and before Lincoln was inaugurated, South Carolina announced its secession from the Union. Soon six other southern states followed, and together they formed the Confederate States of America. Eventually, 11 states would join the confederacy.

Fort Sumter, a U.S. military base in South Carolina, was under construction in 1860. The Confederacy claimed it and, on April 12, 1861, fired upon it and forced the surrender of the garrison of U.S. soldiers. President Lincoln called for 75,000 troops to defend the capital and reestablish the union of all the states. With these actions, the Civil War began, pitting the North against the South. The next four years saw numerous devastating battles and a succession of generals at the head of the Union armies until Lincoln appointed General Ulysses S. Grant in overall command. In so doing, he turned the tide of the war in the North's favor.

On September 22, 1862, President Lincoln announced the Emancipation Proclamation. It stated that as of January 1, 1863, all slaves in the slave states that came under the authority of the United States as a result of Northern victories in the war were to be freed. By the end of the war, more than 3 million slaves had gained freedom from their former owners.

One of the bloodiest battles of the war was at Gettysburg, Pennsylvania, on July 1–3, 1863, which the North won. Later that year, President Lincoln, at the dedication of the Soldiers' National Cemetery in Gettysburg, gave his most renowned address. It was only about two minutes long and redefined the objectives of the Civil War, which was not only to preserve the union but also bring true equality to all its people.

The war was effectively ended with the signing of the surrender agreement by General Robert E. Lee representing the South and General Ulysses S. Grant representing the North at Appomattox Court House in Virginia on April 9, 1865. Over 620,000 soldiers had died during the war, though only one-third lost their lives as a result of the conflict; the other two-thirds had succumbed to disease.

During the latter part of the war, President Lincoln's efforts to pass the Thirteenth Amendment to the Constitution of the United States, which abolished slavery, came to fruition; the U.S. Congress approved the amendment on January 31, 1865, and it was ratified by the states on December 6 that year. However, Lincoln did not see this final chapter. On April 14, 1865, just five days after the end of the war, he and his wife were attending a play at Ford's Theatre when John Wilkes Booth shot him in the back of the head. Lincoln died early the next morning. Booth, a well-known actor, was also a confederate spy from Maryland. Twelve days later, he was cornered and shot by federal agents in a Virginia barn and died shortly thereafter.

FURTHER READING

Donald, David Herbert. *Lincoln.* New York: Simon & Schuster, 1996.

McPherson, James M. *Abraham Lincoln.* New York: Oxford University Press, 2009.

Thomas, Benjamin P. *Abraham Lincoln: A Biography.* Carbondale: Southern Illinois University Press, 2008.

White, Ronald C., Jr. A. *Lincoln: A Biography.* New York: Random House, 2009.

London, Jack (John Griffith Chaney) (1876–1916) Jack London was one of the many authors Maya Angelou has read and admired. She and her brother, Bailey, both read many of London's books while they were children.

Jack London is a pseudonym for John Griffith Chaney, an American novelist and short story writer. Born on January 12, 1876, and raised in Oakland, California, London led a life of poverty and quit school at age 14 to seek adventure. He worked for the government fish patrol (preventing illegal fishing) and then went to Japan as a sailor. He traveled the United States as a hobo on freight trains, was jailed for vagrancy, and in 1894 became a militant socialist. During this time, London utilized public libraries to educate himself in the theories of Charles Darwin, Karl Marx, and Friedrich Nietzsche. In 1897, he decided to earn a living as a writer and began a rigorous work schedule, producing sonnets, ballads, jokes, anecdotes, adventure stories, horror stories, and more. He completed 50 books in 17 years. Much of his work deals with the struggle for survival in the wilderness. Examples of his best writing include *The Call of the Wild* (1903), *White Fang* (1906), and *Burning Daylight* (1910). He became the highest paid author in America, but his expenses always outweighed his income. Toward the end of his life, he suffered from great pain, and it is possible that his death on November 20, 1916, was from an overdose of morphine, either accidental or deliberate.

FURTHER READING

Glass, Loren. "Nobody's Renown: Plagiarism and Publicity in the Career of Jack London." *American Literature* 71, no. 3 (1999): 529.

Gurian, Jay. "The Romantic Necessity in Literary Naturalism: Jack London." *American Literature* 38, no. 1 (1966): 112.

Haley, James L. *Wolf: The Lives of Jack London.* New York: Basic Books, 2010.

Pizer, Donald. "Jack London: The Problem of Form." *Studies in the Literary Imagination* 16, no. 2 (1983): 107.

Warner, Richard H. "A Contemporary Sketch of Jack London." *American Literature* 38, no. 3 (1966): 376.

Loomis, Robert (1926–) Throughout Maya Angelou's writing career, she has had only one editor: Robert Loomis. Loomis is an executive book editor at Random House, where he has worked since 1957, when the publishing company was founded. He is known for his "almost" editing style, saying that a manuscript is "almost good . . . except for the part between the beginning and the end." He has worked with several renowned authors besides Angelou, including Calvin Trillin, Edmund Morris, Shelby Foote, Neil Sheehan, Jim Lehrer, and William Styron. Several of the books he has edited have won the Pulitzer Prize and the National Book Award. The long-lasting relationship Loomis has with his authors is described by some as being legendary.

Loomis began his career as the editor of a student magazine at Duke University. He is a certified pilot who flies his Cessna 172 every weekend. Random House honored him in 2007 with a 50-year tribute. Many authors of books he edited were present for the celebration, including Maya Angelou, who credits Loomis with "tricking" her into writing her first book. As she has recalled, he prodded her into writing her first memoir after she had declined his request by challenging her with the statement, "And I must say, you may be right not to attempt an autobiography, because it is nearly impossible to write autobiography as literature. Almost impossible" (1,164). Since 1969, Loomis has been Angelou's editor for six memoirs and more than 20 books of poetry.

FURTHER READING

Angelou, Maya. *The Collected Autobiographies of Maya Angelou.* New York: Modern Library Edition by Random House, 2004.

Smith, Dinitia. "A Career in Letters, 50 Years and Counting." *New York Times,* 23 January 2007. Available online. URL: http://www.nytimes.com/2007/01/23/books/23loom.html. Accessed February 13, 2010.

Los Angeles, California Maya Angelou first visited Los Angeles in her early teens when her grandmother, Mrs. Annie Henderson, took her to California to return her to her parents. She visited her father in Los Angeles, but then went to live with her mother in SAN FRANCISCO. At a later time, Angelou and her son, Guy, lived in Los Angeles, where she performed in various clubs as a singer and dancer during part of his childhood. Guy attended several different schools there. After returning from Africa and moving to Los Angeles in the 1960s, she personally witnessed the riots in WATTS, which in part led to her active fight against RACISM and the economic deprivation of her people.

The southern California coastal region was home to several Native American tribes for thousands of years before the first Europeans explored the area and claimed it for Spain. However, it was not until 1769 that missionaries recommended that the current site of the city be developed. The city was formally founded in 1781 and became a part of Mexico when it gained its independence from Spain in 1821. After the U.S.-Mexican War ended in 1848, California was purchased by the United States, as agreed in the Treaty of Guadalupe Hidalgo. Los Angeles was incorporated in 1850, five months before California became part of the United States.

Los Angeles is the second-largest metropolitan area in the United States, with a population of about 4 million persons living in approximately 500 square miles. Los Angeles County, of which the city of Los Angeles is the seat, has a population of about 10 million people and is among the most culturally diverse counties in the country. The area is home to people from more than 140 countries speaking 224 identified languages. In the early 21st century, the combined population of ethnic minorities outnumbered the white population. More than 90 languages other than English are spoken in Los Angeles County, where more than 50 newspapers are published in other languages. The religious sphere of Los Angeles is equally diverse. Although the region has historically had a large number of Roman Catholics, it is now infused with traditions, creeds, and religious practices of every sort imaginable.

Los Angeles is a major world center for business, entertainment, international trade, culture, science, technology, fashion, and education. It is the home of Hollywood, which continues to be considered the film capital of the world. The contiguous ports of Los Angeles and Long Beach make it the most significant port in the Western Hemisphere, and it is the fifth-busiest harbor in the world. Fruit orchards were planted by the first Spaniards in the 1700s, but since then the financial services, construction, and film industries have superseded the food industry. This, the world's third-largest economic center, is surpassed only by the greater Tokyo and New York areas. Los Angeles has suffered earthquakes, fire, smog, gang warfare, and riots but is known positively for its mild climate and outdoor leisure.

An arts renaissance in the 1960s helped build Los Angeles's cultural scene. Over 1,000 murals play a prominent part in the cityscape. With the opening of several large auditoriums in the 20th century, Los Angeles became the country's second most important theater city. The *Los Angeles Times* Festival of Books is the largest literary event of its kind, drawing thousands of participants every year.

FURTHER READING

Banham, Reyner. *Los Angeles: The Architecture of Four Ecologies.* New York: Penguin Books, 1990.

Dreier, Peter. "America's Urban Crisis a Decade after the Los Angeles Riots." *National Civic Review* 92, no. 1 (2003): 35.

Los Angeles and Vicinity. Los Angeles: Los Angeles Chamber of Commerce, 1904.

Schneider, Jack. "Escape from Los Angeles: White Flight from Los Angeles and Its Schools, 1960–1980." *Journal of Urban History* 34, no. 6 (2008): 995–1,012.

Starr, Kevin. *Inventing the Dream: California through the Progressive Era.* New York: Oxford University Press, 1985.

Zach, Cheryl. *Los Angeles.* Minneapolis, Minn.: Dillon Press, 1989.

Zhou, Min. "How Neighborhoods Matter for Immigrant Children: The Formation of Educational Resources in Chinatown, Koreatown, and Pico Union, Los Angeles." *Journal of Ethnic and Migration Studies* 35, no. 7 (2009): 1,173–1,159.

Louis, Joe (Joseph Louis Barrow) (1914–1981) During the 1930s, the black people of STAMPS, ARKANSAS, gathered in the William Johnson General Merchandise Store to listen to radio broadcasts of the Joe Louis fights. At a time when boxing was dominated by gambling interests, Joe Louis, nicknamed the "Brown Bomber," established a reputation as an honest, hardworking fighter. In *I Know Why the Caged Bird Sings,* Angelou recounts the June 25, 1935, fight between Joe Louis and Primo Carnera. Louis won that fight, and for the blacks of Stamps, Arkansas, and many others throughout the United States, he had a powerful cultural impact as the first African American to achieve the national and international status of a genuine hero. Born on May 13, 1914, Louis was the world heavyweight boxing champion from 1937 to 1949, winning 65 out of 68 fights. He was the target of anti-Nazi sentiment prior to World War II. He also broke an important color barrier in the United States in golf by appearing under a sponsor's exemption in a PGA event in 1952. He died of a heart attack on April 12, 1981, at age 66.

FURTHER READING

Bak, Richard. *Joe Louis: The Great Black Hope.* New York: Perseus, 1998.

Erenberg, Lewis A. *The Greatest Fight of Our Generation: Louis v. Schmeling.* New York: Oxford University Press, 2005.

Libby, Bill. *Joe Louis, The Brown Bomber.* New York: Lothrop Lee & Shephard Books, 1980.

Louis, Joe, Edna Rust, and Art Rust, Jr. *My Life.* New York: Harcourt Brace Jovanovich, 1978.

Margolick, David. *Beyond Glory: Joe Louis vs. Max Schmeling and a World on the Brink.* New York: Vintage Books, 2005.

Lucullan feast Maya Angelou enjoyed COOKING for guests and sometimes referred to plentiful guest tables, her own and others, as Lucullan. A Roman general and patron of the arts named Lucius Licinius Lucullus was known for giving lavish banquets. His last name became the source of the adjective *Lucullan,* meaning "sumptuous" or "lavish."

M

Make, Vusumzi (Vusumzi [Vus] Linda Make) (1931–2006) Vusumzi Make was Maya Angelou's partner for approximately three years. Though they were engaged to be married, they never did so. Make was a South African civil rights activist and lawyer who met Angelou in 1960. The two had a whirlwind romance, and when Make moved to Cairo, Egypt, in 1961, Angelou and her son, Guy, went with him. They lived together for less than two years before separating late in 1962. He was a professor at the University of Liberia in Monrovia, Liberia, from 1968 to 1974. He died in Pretoria on April 15, 2006.

Makeba, Miriam (Zenzile Miriam Makeba) (1932–2008) Maya Angelou knew HARRY BELAFONTE and Miriam Makeba through their efforts in both the performance arts and in the CIVIL RIGHTS MOVEMENT. One of the world's leading African performers in the 20th century, Makeba was born on Marth 4, 1932, in Johannesburg, South Africa, during the time of apartheid. She sang in choirs at an early age, and her career as a professional singer began in 1954. Her appearance in the 1959 film *Come Back, Africa* attracted the interest of Harry Belafonte and other American performers who helped her gain entrance to the United States. She was denied reentry into South Africa in 1960 and lived in exile for the following three decades. She became increasingly popular, winning the Grammy Award in 1965 for the best folk recording for *An Evening with Belafonte/Makeba*. Her career declined, however, after her 1968 marriage to the civil rights activist STOKELY CARMICHAEL. Thereafter, she left the United States to perform and work in various European and African countries. In 1990, NELSON MANDELA invited her to come back to South Africa, which she did, and she continued to perform there and in other nations until her death on November 10, 2008.

FURTHER READING

Commey, Pusch. "Mama Afrika Goes Home in Song." *New African* 479 (2008): 32–34.

Makeba, Miriam. *Makeba: My Story.* Edited by James Hall. London: Bloomsbury Press, 1987.

Mohohlo, Thabiso P. "Miriam Makeba, a Life in Song and Activism." *New York Amsterdam News,* 13–19 November 2008, 21–38. Available online. URL: http://findarticles.com/p/articles/mi_8153/is_20081113/ai_n50781655. Accessed June 1, 2010.

Malcolm X (Malcolm Little) (1925–1965) Maya Angelou met Malcolm X in New York City around the time Patrice Lumumba was assassinated (1961). She met him again while she was living in Accra, Ghana, and Malcolm X was in Africa to meet leaders and dignitaries whose support he wished to enlist as he appealed to the United Nations for aid to oppressed African Americans.

He was born Malcolm Little on May 19, 1925, in Omaha Nebraska. His father, a supporter of MARCUS GARVEY, was killed in 1931 an event that led to his mother's nervous breakdown. Though Malcolm graduated at the top of his junior high class, he became a rebellious teenager, moving through detention homes and ending up living for a time with his half sister in Boston. Eventually, he moved to HARLEM, New York, where he became a street hustler, drug dealer, and the leader of a gang of thieves.

It was while serving in prison for robbery (from 1946 to 1952) that Malcolm converted to Islam. He read the teachings of Elijah Muhammad, leader of the African-American Nation of Islam, and was deeply influenced by them. He quit smoking and gambling, and he educated himself with the books he could access in the prison library. Following the Nation of Islam belief that surnames originated with white slaveholders, Malcolm replaced his birth surname of Little with X. After his release from prison, he became active in the Nation of Islam during the period of its greatest growth. He founded the Nation's newspaper, *Muhammad Speaks,* which he printed from his basement. Elijah Muhammad appointed Malcolm his second in command, and the two worked closely to promote the Nation of Islam and its ideals for many years.

Malcolm was a witty, charismatic, articulate speaker and organizer. He advocated civil rights in his speeches, whether from street corners in Harlem or auditoriums at Harvard and Oxford. He was critical, however, of mainstream civil rights activists, such as MARTIN LUTHER KING, JR., for their nonviolent approach. He argued that the issues of black identity, integrity, and independence were at stake. Malcolm X became responsible for the founding ideas of the Black Power and black consciousness movements across the United States in the 1960s and 1970s. He helped to change the terms referring to African Americans from *Negro* and *colored* to *black* and *Afro-American.*

A permanent rift developed between Malcolm X and Elijah Muhammad, and in 1964, Malcolm left the Nation to found Muslim Mosque, Inc. He traveled to Mecca, where he embraced Sunni Islam and the concept that all people, no matter their color, were brothers under one God. He gave up his rhetoric of separatist groups and of whites being blue-eyed devils, and he claimed that the solution to racial problems in America lay in orthodox Islam. In 1965, he founded the Organization of Afro-American Unity as a means to bring international attention to the plight of black Americans.

Growing hostility between Malcolm and the Nation of Islam led to open violence and death threats. On February 21, 1965, he was assassinated while delivering a lecture in Harlem. Malcolm's martyrdom, ideas, and speeches contributed to the development of the black nationalist ideology and helped to popularize the values of autonomy and independence among African Americans in the 1960s and 1970s.

FURTHER READING

Condit, Celeste Michelle, and John Louis Lucaites. "Malcolm X and the Limits of the Rhetoric of Revolutionary Dissent." *Journal of Black Studies* 23, no. 3 (1993): 291.

Cone, James H. "Demystifying Martin and Malcolm." *Theology Today* 51, no. 1 (1994): 291.

———. "Martin and Malcolm on Nonviolence and Violence." *Phylon* 49, no. 3 (2001): 173.

Davis, Lenwood G. *Malcolm X: A Selected Bibliography.* Edited by Marsha L. Moore. Westport, Conn.: Greenwood Press, 1984.

Goodheart, Lawrence B. "The Odyssey of Malcolm X: An Eriksonian Interpretation." *Historian* 53, no. 1 (1990): 47.

Kahn, Robert M. "The Political Ideology of Malcolm X." *Journal of Religious Thought* 38, no. 2 (1981): 16.

Malcolm X, with Alex Haley. *The Autobiography of Malcolm X.* 1965. Reprint, New York: Ballantine Books, 1992.

Morris, Jerome E. "Malcolm X's Critique of the Education of Black People." *Western Journal of Black Studies* 25, no. 2 (2001): 126.

Muhammad, Najee E. "The Educational Development of Malcolm X." *Western Journal of Black Studies* 26, no. 4 (2002): 240.

Sagon, Miriam. *Malcolm X.* San Diego: Lucent Books, 1997.

Smallwood, Andrew P. "The Intellectual Creativity and Public Discourse of Malcolm X: A Precursor to the Modern Black Studies Movement." *Journal of Black Studies* 36, no. 2 (2005): 248–263.

Strickland, Bill. "How Malcolm and Stokely and the Movement Redefined America." *Black Scholar* 27, no. 3 (1997): 41.

Tyner, James A. "Territoriality, Social Justice and Gendered Revolutions in the Speeches of Malcolm X." *Transactions of the Institute of British Geographers* 29, no. 3 (2004): 330–343.

Tyner, James A., and Robert J. Kruse. "The Geopolitics of Malcolm X." *Antipode* 36, no. 1 (2004): 24–42.

Mandela, Nelson (1918–) Maya Angelou was a supporter of black people's rights in South Africa and met many of the African leaders and freedom fighters through her relationship with VUSUMZI MAKE. Though she did not meet Nelson Mandela, she had great respect for the man who would become the first black president of South Africa after his negotiations with South African president F. W. de Klerk in the 1990s helped end apartheid. For this achievement, Mandela and de Klerk were jointly awarded the Nobel Peace Prize in 1993.

Born on July 18, 1918, Nelson Rolihlahla Mandela was the son of a chief in the Mandiba clan (Mandiba would become his nickname); however, he renounced his claim to the chieftainship and became a lawyer. In 1944, he joined the African National Congress (ANC), a black liberation group that opposed white apartheid, and he held several prominent positions in the organization. He established South Africa's first black law office with fellow ANC member OLIVER TAMBO. In 1955, Mandela was involved in drafting the Freedom Charter, a document calling for nonracial social democracy in South Africa. His activism in the antiapartheid movement made him a target for the authorities, and he was arrested and tried for treason, but he and his codefendants were acquitted in 1961.

Mandela's nonviolent resistance changed after the massacre of unarmed Africans by police forces in 1960 at Sharpeville and the subsequent banning of the ANC. He went underground and began advocating acts of sabotage against the South African regime, and in 1962, he traveled to Algeria for training in guerrilla warfare and sabotage. Arrested after his return, he was sentenced to prison for five years. In 1963, the imprisoned Mandela and several other men were tried for sabotage, treason, and violent conspiracy in the infamous Rivonia Trial. Mandela was sentenced to life imprisonment, and this cause rallied international support from those who opposed apartheid. After years of negotiations, Mandela was released from prison in 1990, and he soon became president of the ANC, which in turn led to his negotiations with de Klerk to end apartheid and transition to a nonracial democracy in South Africa.

In 1994, Mandela was elected as the first president of South Africa under universal suffrage. During his presidency, he began many initiatives to improve education, housing, living standards, and employment for South Africa's black population. After leaving office, he retired from politics, but he has maintained a strong international presence as an advocate for peace and equality.

FURTHER READING

Boehmer, Elleke. "Postcolonial Terrorist: The Example of Nelson Mandela." *Parallax* 37 (2005): 46–55.

Finlayson, Reggie. *Nelson Mandela.* Minneapolis: Lerner, 1999.

Laurence, Patrick. "Mandela's First 180 Days." *Africa Report* 39, no. 6 (1994): 63.

Lieberfeld, Daniel. "Peace Profile: Nelson Mandela." *Peace Review* 16, no. 3 (2004): 387–392.

Mandela, Nelson. *Long Walk to Freedom: The Autobiography of Nelson Mandela.* Boston: Little, Brown, 1994.

———. *A Prisoner in the Garden: Opening Nelson Mandela's Prison Archive.* Johannesburg: Penguin, 2005.

Sheckels, Theodore F. "The Rhetoric of Nelson Mandela: A Qualified Success." *Howard Journal of Communications* 12, no. 1 (2001): 85–99.

Yadiv, Arvind Kumar. "Nelson Mandela and the Process of Reconciliation in South Africa." *Journal of Communications* 12, no. 2 ((2007): 49–84.

Marshall, Herbert (Herbert Brough Falcon Marshall) (1890–1966) Herbert Marshall appeared in films Maya Angelou and her brother, Bailey, enjoyed when they were children living in STAMPS, ARKANSAS. A British actor and movie star, Marshall was born on May 23, 1890, into a theatrical family and originally had no intention to perform on the stage. After graduating from St. Mary's College in Harrow, a borough of London, he became an accounting clerk. When that profession ceased to interest him, he turned to acting. His first stage performance was in 1911, and within two years, he had attained stardom. He enlisted in the British Expeditionary Forces during World War I; his leg had to be amputated after it was severely wounded. Marshall obtained a prosthetic leg and continued his acting career, going on to play the romantic lover in many films such as *Trouble in Paradise* (1932), *The Little Foxes* (1941), and *The Razor's Edge* (1946). He was married five times and led a rambunctious social life. He died in Beverly Hills, California, on January 22, 1966.

FURTHER READING

Internet Movie Database. "Herbert Marshall (1890–1966)." Available online. URL: http://www.imdb.com/name/nm0003339. Accessed February 4, 2010.

Marshall, Paule (Valenza Pauline Burke) (1929–) Maya Angelou and Paule Marshall met at the HARLEM WRITERS GUILD and became close friends. Paule Marshall is a novelist whose works emphasize the need for black Americans to reclaim their African heritage. She was born Valenza Pauline Burke in Brooklyn, New York. After graduating from Brooklyn College, she worked as a librarian and then for a magazine named *Our World*. Her first novel, *Brown Girl, Brownstones* (1959), was an autobiographical account of her return as an adult to her parents' native country, Barbados. All of Marshall's work is influenced by her parents' Barbadian roots. She has taught at universities across the nation of the United States, including UC-Berkeley, Yale, and New York University. She is a MacArthur Fellow and is a past winner of the Dos Passos Prize in literature. Other novels she has published include *Soul Clap Hands and Sing* (1961), *Praisesong for the Widow* (1983), and *Triangular Road* (2009).

FURTHER READING

Evans, Mari. *Black Women Writers (1950–1980): A Critical Evaluation*. Garden City, N.Y.: Anchor Press/Doubleday, 1984.

Hedgepeth, Chester. *Twentieth-Century African-American Writers and Artists*. Chicago: American Library Association, 1991.

Kort, Carol. *A to Z of American Women Writers*. New York: Facts On File, 2000.

Pettis, Joyce. *Toward Wholeness in Paule Marshall's Fiction*. Charlottesville and London: University Press of Virginia, 1995.

Pryse, Marjorie, and Hortense J. Spillers. *Conjuring: Black Women, Fiction, and Literary Tradition*. Bloomington: Indiana University Press, 1985.

Willis, Susan. *Specifying: Black Women Writing the American Experience*. Madison: University of Wisconsin Press, 1987.

maxim A maxim is a statement of general truth, and it is often a proverbial saying. Maya Angelou's grandmother, Annie Henderson, and her mother, VIVIAN BAXTER, used many maxims that carried practical advice. Angelou carried these sayings in her mind, and she often used them in her serial autobiographies and in her poetry.

Mayfield, Julian (1928–1984) Julian Mayfield and his wife, Ana Livia, befriended Maya Angelou and her son, Guy, when they moved to Ghana. A few days after arriving there, Guy was in a serious automobile accident, and Mayfield and Ana Livia, a physician, took care of both Guy and his mother. They remained friends of Maya and Guy thereafter.

Mayfield had many professions, including novelist, journalist, playwright, scriptwriter, producer, Broadway and Hollywood actor, critical essayist, university lecturer, freedom fighter, and adviser to world leaders. Born in Greer, South Carolina, on June 6, 1928, he grew up in Washington, D.C., and served in the military immediately after high school. He then went to Lincoln University in Pennsylvania, where he majored in political science. He participated in several Off-Broadway productions until 1954, when he married Ana Livia Cordero and subsequently moved to Mexico. There he published his first novel, *The Hit* (1957), based on his one-act play *417*. From 1961 to 1966, Mayfield resided in Ghana, Africa, where he served as an adviser to the country's president, KWAME NKRUMAH. He returned to the United States in

1968 and lectured in universities and wrote articles for newspapers and magazines. He also had a leading role in *Uptight* (1968), a film about black militants.

Mayfield's contribution to African-American literature lies in his numerous critical essays as well as the important role his first two novels—*The Hit* and *The Long Night* (1958)—played in keeping the flame of protest alive at a time when few African Americans were being published. In 1959, he delivered a paper called "Into the Mainstream" at the First Conference of Negro Writers. In it, he urged black writers to use their unique voice and stay away from mainstream writing.

> The likelihood is that the Negro people will continue for several years to occupy, to a diminishing degree, the position of the unwanted child who, having been brought for a visit, must remain for the rest of his life. . . . [This means] the facade of the American way of life is always transparent. (1968, 560–561)

Julian Mayfield died in Washington, D.C., on October 20, 1984.

FURTHER READING

Davis, Arthur P. *From the Dark Tower: Afro-American Writers, 1960–1990.* Washington, D.C.: Howard University Press, 1974, 198–203.

Mayfield, Julian. *The Hit* and *The Long Night.* Boston: Northeastern University Press, 1989.

———. "Into the Mainstream." In *Dark Symphony: Negro Literature in America,* edited by James A. Emanuel and Theodore Gross. New York: Free Press, 1968.

Taylor, Estelle W. "Julian Mayfield." In *Dictionary of Literary Biography,* vol. 33, *Afro-American Fiction Writers after 1955,* edited by Thadious M. Davis and Trudier Harris, 174–178, Farmington Hills, Mich.: Gale, 1986.

West, Holly I. "The Goal of Julian Mayfield; Fusing Art and Politics." *Washington Post,* 7 July 1975, B1, B3.

McPherson, Dolly Dolly McPherson and Maya Angelou have been friends since they were young women; they were also colleagues at Wake Forest University in Winston-Salem, North Carolina. In 1991, McPherson published a book *Order Out of Chaos: The Autobiographical Works of Maya Angelou.* She is a native of New Orleans, Louisiana, and a graduate of Southern University. She received her Ph.D. from the University of Iowa and her M.A. from Boston University. She has studied and taught abroad on Fulbright and Ford Foundation grants. In 2002, she retired from Wake Forest University, where she was a professor of English and the literary executor of the Maya Angelou Papers, housed in the Smith Reynolds Library.

FURTHER READING

McPherson, Dolly A. *Order Out of Chaos: The Autobiographical Works of Maya Angelou.* London: Virago Press, 1991.

Medea Maya Angelou played the role of the nurse in Jean Anouilh's version of *Medea* in LOS ANGELES in the late 1950s. In that performance, the well-known African-American actress BEAH RICHARDS played the role of Medea. Maya felt somewhat marginalized by the director and Richards, so she decided to enhance the role of the nurse. Her costuming was excellent, and her portrayal of the old nurse, whose costume she designed herself, was convincing enough to earn some recognition in the reviews.

The play *Medea* was written by the Greek dramatist Euripides and first produced in 431 B.C.E. Medea, a sorceress, was the cast-off wife of Jason. They had two sons together, but he took a foreign wife who was the daughter of a powerful king. Medea had a nurse who knew her well and attended her. The play began with the nurse reflecting on Medea's situation because the king (Creon) plans to banish her from Corinth. Medea has a reputation for evil acts, and the nurse is worried. A visiting king, Agues, offers her sanctuary in Athens. Knowing she has a place to go, Medea prepares a golden dress and coronet laced with poison as a gift to Jason's new wife, Glace. The princess puts on the dress, and the poison burns and kills her. Her father tries to help her, and he is killed also. As further retribution to Jason for betraying her, Medea kills their sons, and with their bodies in her chariot, she leaves for Athens, where the boys' bodies will be buried in the region of Hera's temple. (In Greek mythology, Hera was a goddess and the wife of Zeus.)

Mendès-France, Pierre (1907–1982) Maya Angelou gave a song-and-dance performance at a celebration dinner party given for Pierre Mendès-France when she was in Paris with the traveling troupe of *Porgy and Bess.* Afterward, she expressed her view that she did not care for the politics and prejudices she had observed among the French.

A French socialist lawyer, statesman, and premier, Pierre Mendès-France was born in Paris on January 11, 1907, and became the youngest French deputy in 1932, at the age of 25. He was a member of the Radical Socialist Party and served under Leon Blum as an undersecretary of state for finance. Much of Mendès-France's political career was spent dealing with economics, and he was widely known for his competence in national economic affairs.

At the outbreak of World War II, Mendès-France joined the French air force, but he was taken prisoner by the Vichy government. He escaped in 1941 and joined the Free French air force. From 1943 to 1945, he served under General Charles de Gaulle as the commissioner of finance and then as the minister of national economy. However, he is known primarily for his involvement in the First Indochina War. Mendès-France became premier in 1954 with the promise that he would end France's involvement in the war within 30 days. His pledge was realized as an armistice line was drawn at the 17th parallel between North and South Vietnam, and at that point, France withdrew from the war.

Mendès-France's austere policies and proposal for an economic reform—that is, state regulations of prices and taxes to control inflation—made him unpopular among his colleagues, and he fell from power in 1955. He was still popular among the people, and he was looked to as the symbol of the Fifth Republic. Mendès-France published several books on political and economic topics. He died on October 18, 1982.

FURTHER READING

Daniel, Jean. "Why He Disagrees with De Gaulle." *New Republic* 150, no. 9 (1964): 9–11.

Lacouture, Jean. *Pierre Mendès France.* Translated by George Holoch. New York: Holmes & Meier, 1984.

Mendès France, Pierre. "French Policies." *Vital Speeches of the Day* 20, no. 19 (1954): 585.

———. *A Modern French Republic.* New York: Hill and Wang, 1963.

———. *The Pursuit of Freedom.* London and New York: Longmans, Green, 1956.

Werth, Alexandra. *Lost Statesman: The Strange Story of Pierre Mendès France.* New York: Abelard-Schuman, 1958.

Mickey Mouse Maya and Bailey enjoyed the Mickey Mouse cartoons when they were children. Mickey Mouse was a cartoon creature invented by Walt Disney and Ubbe Ert Iwerks, an animator and cartoonist who worked with Disney. Mickey's shape, large ears, and clever antics endeared him to audiences around the world from the time he was created. The first silent cartoon featuring Mickey Mouse was *Plane Crazy* (early 1928), and Disney's own children, two daughters, seeing the cartoon "years later, would be astonished by how primitive it looked. Mickey was crudely drawn with lines and arms sticking out of his circular torso" (Gabler, 115). Disney and Iwerks produced the "first animated cartoon with sound, *Steamboat Willie,* starring Mickey Mouse" (Zipes 1995, 34). One of the legends about Mickey's creation was that Disney played with and observed mice in his studio and was inspired to invent the Mickey Mouse character by watching the mice scamper across the top of his drawing board.

FURTHER READING

Gabler, Neal. *Walt Disney: The Triumph of American Imagination.* New York: Alfred A. Knopf, 2006.

Zipes, Jack. "Breaking the Disney Spell." In *From Mouse to Mermaid: The Politics of Film, Gender, and Culture,* edited by Elizabeth Bell, Lynda Haas, and Laura Sells, 21–42. Bloomington: Indiana University Press, 1995.

Million Man March On October 16, 1995, Louis Farrakhan, the Nation of Islam leader, led a mass gathering of black men in Washington, D.C., called the Million Man March. The purpose was to demonstrate to the United States a different perception of the black American male. On the same day, another event called the Day of Absence was organized by black female leaders. The purpose of this event was to encourage people not able to attend the gathering in Washington to attend teach-ins and religious services focusing on a positive black community rather than attend work, school, or social engagements. The actual number of participants in the Washington gathering has never been determined, but estimates range from 400,000 to nearly 2 million. Maya Angelou was one of the speakers at the event, and for the occasion she wrote and read the "Million Man March Poem."

FURTHER READING

Angelou, Maya. "Million Man March Poem." Available online. URL: www.poemhunter.com/poem/million-man-march-poem/. Accessed July 10, 2010.

Madhubuti, Haki R., and Maulana Karenga. *Million Man March/Day of Absence: A Commemorative Anthology: Speeches, Commentary, Photography, Poetry, Illustrations, Documents.* Chicago: Third World Press, 1996.

minstrel tradition In Maya Angelou's poem "A Brave and Startling Truth"—read in SAN FRANCISCO at the 50th celebration of the founding of the United Nations on June 26, 1995—and in other discussions, she mentions the minstrel tradition with its BLACKFACE figures and condescending presentation of blacks. It was a racist representation that continued for many decades in the 19th century, beginning before the Civil War and phasing out around the end of the century, though some small troupes continued in the early 1900s.

The minstrel show is an American form of entertainment. Originating in the 1830s, the shows were performed typically by white men in blackface. With great exaggeration, they portrayed stereotypical African Americans as lazy, guileful, noise, flashily dressed, but joyful. The shows consisted of dancing, singing, and joke telling in black dialect. The shows' popularity peaked about the time of the Civil War. After the war, other forms of entertainment such as vaudeville, musical comedies, and variety shows started drawing larger audiences, and peoples' interest in minstrel shows declined. They became almost nonexistent by 1910.

FURTHER READING

Sweet, Frank W. *A History of the Minstrel Show.* Palm Coast, Fla.: Backintyme, 2000.

Toll, Robert C. *Blacking Up: The Minstrel Show in Nineteenth-Century America.* New York: Oxford University Press, 1977.

Mitford, Jessica (1917–1996) Maya Angelou and Jessica Mitford were neighbors in Monterey, California, and became very good friends. Mitford read Angelou's early draft of *I Know Why the Caged Bird Sings* and was very supportive of her work. She encouraged Angelou to continue writing and publishing her autobiographies and poetry.

Born in Gloucestershire, England, on September 11, 1917, Jessica Lucy Mitford was an author, journalist, and political campaigner. Early in life, she became an adherent of communism. At age 19, she eloped with her second cousin, Esmond Romilly, and the two emigrated to the United States in 1939. They worked a series of odd jobs, and after Romilly went missing in action during World War II, Mitford married Robert Truehaft. The couple settled in California and became very active in civil rights campaigns. They resigned from the Communist Party in 1958, several years after having been summoned for questioning during the McCarthyism period.

Mitford published her first book, *Daughters and Rebels: The Autobiography of Jessica Mitford,* in 1960. It is an account of her childhood and early adult years. She became very involved in investigative journalism, researching and writing works such as *The American Way of Death* (1973), criticizing American funeral homes, and *Kind and Usual Punishment: The Prison Business* (1973), a harsh critique of the American prison system. Mitford taught a course at the San Jose State University on the "American Way" and tried her hand at music, recording two albums. One of those albums was with Maya Angelou, and the two sang duets on it. Jessica Mitford died of lung cancer at the age of 78 on July 22, 1996.

FURTHER READING

Degnan, James P. "Jessica Thumbs Her Toes." *Change* 26, no. 3 (1994): 97.

Long, Thomas G. "Why Jessica Mitford Was Wrong." *Theology Today* 55, no. 4 (1999): 496.

Mitford, Jessica. *Daughters and Rebels: The Autobiography of Jessica Mitford.* Boston: Houghton Mifflin, 1960.

———. *A Fine Old Conflict.* New York: Knopf, 1977.

Weir, Laila, and Cristina Martin. "Jessica Mitford: An Interview." *Nation* 250, no. 18 (1990): 642.

Montgomery Ward & Company The Montgomery Ward mail-order catalog was a welcome publication in STAMPS, ARKANSAS, during Maya Angelou's early years. Articles from house plans to socks could be found in its pages, and the items ordered were delivered to the door. At its height, Montgomery Ward was one of the largest retail stores in the United States. Founded in Chicago in 1872 by Aaron Montgomery Ward, the company distributed the first mail-order catalogs to facilitate the reselling of wholesale merchandise to farmers in rural communities. It enjoyed increasing sales through 1893, until the establishment of their competitor, Sears, Roebuck & Company. The first Montgomery Ward retail stores opened in 1926, and there were soon 556 of them across the country. Their mail-order catalog business ended in 1985. The company was bought and sold by larger corporations and, in 2000, announced that it was going out of business permanently, closing all its stores in the United States.

FURTHER READING

Latham, Frank Brown. *A Century of Serving Consumers: The Story of Montgomery Ward.* Chicago: Montgomery Ward, 1972.

mother wit Maya Angelou's mother and grandmother both used many APHORISMS and MAXIMS in their everyday speech, and due to their influence, Angelou used many of their sayings in her autobiographies. Mary Ardito quotes Angelou who repeated her mother's words in an interview: "You may not get what you paid for, but you will pay for what you get" (1982, 33).

Mother wit is a colloquial name for common sense or native intelligence. It was commonly used in England in the 19th century and was also a term used by African-American slaves. In Elizabeth Cleghorn Gaskell's book *North and South* (1854), the word was used in a sentence: "Raw, crude materials came together; men of the same level, as regarded education and station, took suddenly the different positions of masters and men, owing to the motherwit, as regarded opportunities and probabilities, which distinguished some, and made them far-seeing as to what great future lay concealed in that rude model of Sir Richard Arkwright's" (100).

The term is still used and is often conveyed through maxims, aphorisms, or clever observations. Common examples are: "He hasn't got the sense to come in out of the rain" or "Don't you know two and two *always* add up to four?"

FURTHER READING

Ardito, Mary. "It's the Thought that Counts." *Bell Telephone Magazine* 1 (1982): 32.

Gaskell, Elizabeth Cleghorn. *North and South.* Winnetka, Calif.: Norijana Books, 1854/2007.

N

National Association for the Advancement of Colored People (NAACP) Through her own civil rights efforts, Maya Angelou has supported the work of the National Association for the Advancement of Colored People (NAACP). Created in 1909, this interracial organization has worked to abolish SEGREGATION and discrimination in housing, education, transportation, and employment. Particularly, the NAACP works to oppose RACISM and ensure African Americans their constitutional rights. The group helped to denounce lynching in 1918 and was instrumental in the desegregation of schools in 1954. Since the start of the 21st century, the NAACP has sponsored campaigns against youth violence, encouraged economic enterprise among African Americans, and led voter drives to increase participation in the political process.

FURTHER READING

Boyd, Herb. "The Founders and Icons of NAACP." *New York Amsterdam News,* 9–15 July 2009, S3–S15.

———. "NAACP Milestones of Achievement." *New York Amsterdam News,* 9–15 July 2009, S2.

Collins, Stephen, and Katherine Scott Sturdevant. "The History and Rhetoric of the NAACP: The Origins." *Black History Bulletin* 71, no. 2 (2008): 12–14.

Jealous, Benjamin Todd. "We Are NAACP." *Vital Speeches of the Day* 75, no. 9 (2009): 426–431.

Miller, Jake C. "The NAACP and Global Human Rights." *Western Journal of Black Studies* 26, no. 1 (2002): 22.

Minchin, Timothy J. "Making Best Use of the New Laws: The NAACP and the Fight for Civil Rights in the South, 1965–1975." *Journal of Southern History* 74, no. 3 (2008): 669–702.

National Committee for Sane Nuclear Policy (SANE) Maya Angelou's son, Guy (see JOHNSON, CLYDE BAILEY), was involved with the National Committee for Sane Nuclear Policy (SANE) organization when he was a teenager. She had taught him to be concerned about important issues and become involved. SANE was founded in 1957 in response to the nuclear arms race and the Eisenhower administration's policies on producing and testing nuclear weapons. The name came from the concepts found in Eric Fromm's book *The Sane Society* (1955). The group's goal was to alert Americans of the threat of nuclear weapons. MARTIN LUTHER KING, JR., was closely aligned with the SANE efforts and often supported the organization's statements. SANE emerged from a 1957 meeting of pacifists and antinuclear activists and became a leader in the efforts for disarmament. By 1958, the organization's membership was 25,000. A SANE rally held in 1960 at Madison Square Garden attracted 20,000 people. As the conflagration in Vietnam escalated, SANE became increasingly active in the antiwar movement. In 1987, SANE joined with the Nuclear Weapons Freeze Campaign, and in 1993, the combination changed its name to Peace Action. Still active, it has a large grassroots network and is engaged in active political advocacy.

FURTHER READING

SANE. "We Are Facing a Danger Unlike Any Danger That Has Ever Existed." *New York Times,* 15 November 1957, advertisement.

Nisei The Nisei were second-generation people of Japanese descent born and educated in the United States. In *I Know Why the Caged Bird Sings,* Angelou mentions Nisei businesses that were taken over by black businessmen in the FILLMORE DISTRICT of SAN FRANCISCO, CALIFORNIA. Angelou notes that "the Japanese area became San Francisco's Harlem in a matter of months" (162). This was during the early months of World War II, and the Japanese residents were quietly relocated to internment camps for the duration of the war.

Nkrumah, Kwame (Osagyeto Kwame Nkrumah) (1909–1972) Kwame Nkrumah was the president of Ghana when Maya Angelou lived there, and also while her son, Guy, was a student at the University of Ghana. Nkrumah was a powerful Ghanaian nationalist leader who led the Gold Coast's drive for independence from Britain and presided over its emergence as the new nation of Ghana. He headed the country from independence in 1957 until he was overthrown by a coup in 1966.

Born on September 21, 1909, Nkrumah was raised in Ghana but came to the United States in 1935 to attend Lincoln University in Pennsylvania. He earned his master's degree in both education and philosophy from the University of Pennsylvania and began lecturing at colleges and Presbyterian churches. He moved to London in 1945 and helped organize the Fifth Pan-African Congress. He then founded the West African National Secretariat for the decolonization of Africa. He returned to Africa in 1947 and worked for years to rally the people for the independence of Ghana. He served as Ghana's first prime minister from March 1957 to July 1960 and then as its first president from July 1, 1960, until being overthrown on February 24, 1966. Thereafter, he lived in exile in Guinea. He died in Bucharest, Romania, on April 27, 1972.

FURTHER READING

Duffield, Ian. "Marcus Garvey and Kwame Nkrumah." *History Today* 31, no. 3 (1981): 24.

Gyasi, Stephen, Jr. "Nkrumah Never Dies." *New African* 486 (2009): 38.

Holden, Philip. "Modernity's Body: Kwame Nkrumah's Ghana." *Postcolonial Studies* 7, no. 3 (2004): 313–332.

Nkrumah, Kwame. *Ghana: The Autobiography of Kwame Nkrumah.* New York: Nelson, 1957.

Timothy, Bankole. *Kwame Nkrumah, from Cradle to Grave.* Dorchester, Dorset, U.K.: Gavin Press, 1981.

———. *Kwame Nkrumah: His Rise to Power.* Evanston, Ill.: Northwestern University Press, 1963.

Yoda, Lalbila. "The Influence of the USA on the Political Ideas of Kwame Nkrumah." *Round Table* 326, no. 1 (1993): 187.

numbers runners When Maya and Bailey were moved from STAMPS, ARKANSAS, to St. Louis to live with their mother, they observed their Grandmother Bailey, a precinct captain (the link between voters and a political party or machine), receive appeals from various criminals. There were "numbers runners, gamblers, lottery takers and whiskey salesmen not only in the loud streets but in our orderly living room as well" (*Caged Bird,* 51). The numbers is a type of illegal lottery game run by organized crime wherein a person picks three or four digits in the hope that those numbers will be drawn the following day. The numbers runner is the employee sent to collect the money from the bars, barbershops, corner groceries, and other shops where the customers picked their numbers. The runner then takes the money back to headquarters.

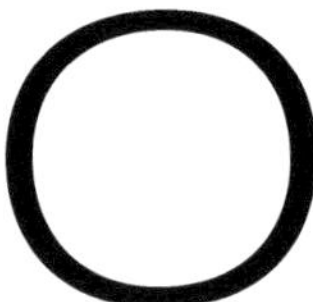

Oakland, California When Maya was a young teenager, her Grandmother Henderson took her to California to live with her mother, who at the time was living Oakland, California, with Maya's Grandmother Baxter and her sons. It was not long before her mother bought a large house in SAN FRANCISCO, and they moved there. Situated on San Francisco Bay opposite the city, Oakland was selected as the western terminus of the first transcontinental railroad (1869). After the 1906 San Francisco earthquake and fire, Oakland received an influx of refugees, which increased its population dramatically. Growth has also been stimulated over the years by military and naval installations, and also by the arrival of African Americans seeking work in the city's factories during World War II. Racial tension increased during the 1950s, and the BLACK PANTHER PARTY (founded in 1966), which became the leading force in the Black Power movement, was based in Oakland. After much remodeling and beautification, the city has continued to grow through the 1980s and 1990s.

FURTHER READING

Lamont, Deane Anderson. *America's "Healthiest" City: A History of Early Oakland, California*. Saarbrücken, Germany: VDM Verlag Dr. Müller, 2010.

———. "Oakland the Bay Area's Playing Field." *Journal of the West* 48, no. 1 (2009): 58–72.

Murch, Donna Jean. *Living for the City: Migration, Education, and the Rise of the Black Panther Party in Oakland, California*. Chapel Hill: University of North Carolina Press, 2010.

"Oakland, California." In *World Almanac & Book of Facts*. New York: World Almanac, 2008, 551.

Obama, Michelle (Michelle LaVaughan Robinson Obama) (1964–) Maya Angelou introduced Michelle Obama at the Women for Obama Rally held in Greensboro, North Carolina, on September 20, 2008. In that introduction, Angelou said that she had formerly supported Senator Hillary Rodham Clinton in the primaries, but she was now working for Barack Obama. Repeating the words of OPRAH WINFREY, Angelou said that Michelle Obama was the real deal.

Michelle Obama is the wife of the 44th president of the United States, Barack Obama, as well as the first African-American First Lady. Born Michelle LaVaughan Robinson on January 17, 1964, she grew up on Chicago's South Side and received her degree in sociology and African-American studies from Princeton University before attending Harvard Law School and receiving her J.D. degree in 1988. She returned to work in Chicago, specializing in intellectual property law, but she later became an assistant to the mayor. She married Barack Obama in 1992; the couple have two daughters. Michelle Obama subsequently became the associate dean of student services at the University of Chicago, where she helped organize the school's outreach programs. She became the executive director of community and external affairs for the university in 2002.

An excellent speaker, Obama took a prominent role in her husband's campaign for the 2008 Democratic presidential nomination. Campaign aides referred to her as "the closer" for her persuasiveness on the stump among uncommitted voters who attended rallies. She is also known for her fashion sense and has been listed in several magazines as one of the best-dressed American women. During her early months as First Lady, Obama visited soup kitchens and schools and advocated public service. She is now engaged in encouraging support for military families.

FURTHER READING

Cole, Harrett. "The Real Michelle Obama: Who Is This Woman . . ." *Ebony* 63, no. 11 (2008): 72–84.

Gibbs, Nancy, and Michael Scherer. "Michelle Up Close." *Time,* 21 May 2009, 26–33.

Samuels, Allison. "How Will Michelle Obama Make Her Mark?" *Newsweek* 24 October 2009, 69–76.

Savage, Luiza Ch. "Michelle Obama's Real Agenda." *Maclean's,* 12 April 2009, 24–28.

Senior, Jennifer. "Regarding Michelle Obama: The Many Meanings of a New American Icon." *New York,* 15 March 2009, 26–29.

Vaccariello, Liz. "Michelle Obama's Rules for Staying Healthy and Happy." *Prevention* 61, no. 11 (2009): 136–141.

Orient Express During Maya Angelou's tour of Europe with the opera *PORGY AND BESS,* she was able to travel on the famous Orient Express train from Yugoslavia to Athens, before boarding a ship headed for Africa. Europe's first transcontinental railroad was developed by Georges Nagelmakers, a Belgium businessman, and had its first run in 1883. It was noted for plush and luxurious comfort, with mahogany paneling, oriental rugs, velvet drapery, and fine cuisine. The glamour of the train inspired several writers, among them Agatha Christie and Graham Greene, who helped to make the train famous. The rail ran from Calais, France, to Constantinople. Interrupted by World Wars I and II, the Orient Express continued running until 1977. It was then revived in 1982 by an American, James Sherwood, with several routes between London and Venice.

FURTHER READING

Greene, Graham. *Orient Express.* Garden City, N.Y.: Doubleday, Doran, 1933.

Harmon, Melissa Burdick. "The Orient Express." *Biography* 5, no. 4 (2001): 102.

Phillips-Matz, Mary. "Hooked on the Orient Express." *Opera News* 60, no. 17 (1996): 20.

Rothenberg, Sheila, and Robert S. Rothenberg. "Splendors of the Orient-Express." *USA Today Magazine,* 1 July 1993, 35.

Sherwood, Shirley. *Venice Simplon Orient-Express: The Return of the World's Most Celebrated Train.* London: Weidenfeld & Nicolson, 1983.

Owens, Jesse (James Cleveland Owens) (1913–1980) When Maya Angelou was in Berlin, Germany, as part of the original cast of the play *The BLACKS* by JEAN GENET, a member of the troupe reminded the actors that it was Germany where Jesse Owens was denied the 1936 Olympic recognition he had earned because of the Nazis' political philosophies. The black cast members were warned to be sensitive to prejudices that may continue in Germany.

James Cleveland "Jesse" Owens was born in Oakville, Alabama, on September 12, 1913. His athletic abilities were evident at an early age, and he excelled in track-and-field events even during high school: As a student in Cleveland, Ohio, he won three events at the 1933 National Interscholastic Championships in Chicago. He went on to attend Ohio State University, and at one meet (in one day), he equaled the world record for the 100-yard dash, the 220-yard dash, the 220-yard low hurdles, and the long jump. On May 25, 1935, he set a world record in the long jump that stood for 25 years.

Owens won four gold medals at the 1936 Olympic Games in Berlin. His victories in the 100-meter run, the 200-meter run, the long jump, and the 4 × 100-meter relay were a blow to Adolf Hitler's intention to use the games to demonstrate Aryan superiority. A popular tale that came from these games was the idea that Hitler refused to shake hands with Owens because he was African American. In reality, Hitler had decided the previous day that he would no longer publicly congratulate any of the athletes. Unaware of the situation, American papers reported the "snub," and the myth perpetuated over the years.

For a time, Owens held or shared the world records for all sprint distances recognized by the International Amateur Athletic Federation. When he retired from competitive track, he worked in boys' guidance activities, made goodwill visits to India and East Asia for the United States Department of State, and served as secretary of the Illinois State Athletic commission. He was awarded the Presidential Medal of Freedom in 1976, and 10 years after his death on March 31, 1980, at age 66, he was awarded the Congressional Gold Medal.

FURTHER READING

Baker, William Joseph. *Jesse Owens: An American Life.* Urbana: University of Illinois Press, 2006.

Edmondson, Jacqueline. *Jesse Owens: A Biography.* Westport, Conn.: Greenwood, 2007.

Owens, Jesse. "1936: Golden Moment of Triumph." *Saturday Evening Post,* January/February 1976, 48–90.

Sanford, William Reynolds. *Jesse Owens.* Edited by Carl R. Green. New York: Maxwell Macmillan International, 1992.

Schaap, Jeremy. *Triumph: The Untold Story of Jesse Owens and Hitler's Olympics.* New York: Houghton Mifflin, 2007.

Snyder, Larry. "My Boy Jesse." *Saturday Evening Post,* 7 November 1936, 14–101.

Streissguth, Thomas. *Jesse Owens.* Minneapolis: Lerner, 1999.

Weatherford, Carole Boston. *Jesse Owens: Fastest Man Alive.* Edited by Eric Velasquez. New York: Walker, 2007.

P

pig latin Maya Angelou and her brother, Bailey, used pig latin in their conversation as children. It was a way to trick listeners, but often the listeners knew exactly what they were saying. Used mostly by children to converse in supposed privacy from adults or other children, pig latin is a language game of alteration in English. To change a word from standard English into pig latin, the beginning consonant sound is placed at the end of the word with the addition of *ay*. Therefore, "door" becomes "or-day" and "textbook" becomes "extbook-tay."

play pretties This term used to refer to black slave children who were brought into the households of slave owners to be playmates with their children. The languages the children used influenced one another's dialects. The idea is important to Angelou's poem "The Calling of Names."

Poe, Edgar Allan (1809–1849) During her childhood, Maya Angelou enjoyed reading the writing of Edgar Allan Poe, short-story writer, poet, critic, and editor known for creating gothic and mysterious moods in his writing. Poe was born in Boston, Massachusetts, on January 19, 1809. His mother died when he was young, and he was placed under the care of John and Frances Allan in Richmond, Virginia; he subsequently took their name for his middle name. After receiving a classical education abroad, Poe enrolled at the University of Virginia. His gambling losses were so great that the Allans would not allow him to continue at the university. He joined the army to pay off his debts, and John Allan later helped him to get an appointment to West Point military academy. By this time, Poe had already written and published several pamphlets of poetry, including *Aaraaff, Tamerlane, and Minor Poems* (1829). He was expelled from the academy and traveled to New York City and then to Baltimore, continuing to write stories. In August 1935, he became assistant editor of the *Southern Literary Messenger,* and his critical reviews made him popular. On September 22, 1835, married his young cousin, Virginia Clemm, and he seems to have been an affectionate husband and son-in-law.

Poe's drinking problem cost him his job, and that weakness was a bane throughout his life. He obtained work as an editor at various publications and moved up and down the East Coast. In 1841, Poe published the first detective story, "The Murders in the Rue Morgue," in *Graham's Magazine.* His most famous poem, "The Raven" (1845), gave him immediate national fame, and he was often asked to recite it during lectures. Poe was greatly affected by the death of his wife in 1847, and he experienced only brief relationships with women after that. It is uncertain whether his death on October 7, 1849, was caused by drinking or heart failure.

FURTHER READING

Fisher, Benjamin Franklin, IV, ed. *Poe and Our Times: Influences and Affinities.* Baltimore: Edgar Allan Poe Society, 1986.

Miller, John J. "Poe at 200—Eerie after All These Years." *Wall Street Journal,* 15 January 2009, D7.

Poe, Edgar Allan. *The Poetical Works of Edgar Allan Poe, with an Original Memoir.* New York: J. S. Redfield, 1858.

Stedman, Edmund Clarence. *Edgar Allan Poe.* Edited by Edmund Clarence Stedman. Boston: Houghton, Mifflin, 1881.

Tonkin, Maggie. "The 'Poe-Etics' of Decomposition: Angela Carter's 'The Cabinet of Edgar Allan Poe' and the Reading-Effect." *Women's Studies* 33, no. 1 (2004): 1–21.

Poitier, Sidney (1927–) Sidney Poitier and his wife attended *Cabaret for Freedom,* the revue that Maya Angelou and GODFREY CAMBRIDGE put together in Greenwich Village, New York City, to raise money for the SOUTHERN CHRISTIAN LEADERSHIP CONFERENCE. Poitier is the actor and motion-picture director credited with breaking the color barrier in the U.S. motion picture industry and expanding the horizons for the careers of other black actors.

Born in Miami, Florida, on February 20, 1927, Sidney Poitier grew up in the Bahamas but returned to the United States as a teenager. He enlisted in the U.S. Army during World War II, and upon his return, he applied for the American Negro Theater but was denied because of his accent. After six months of practicing his enunciation, he again applied and was admitted. His debut in a feature-length film was as Dr. Brooks in *No Way Out* (1950), which established a pattern for Poitier and black actors to follow in refusing roles that played to racial stereotypes.

Poitier won critical acclaim on Broadway in 1959 with his starring role in Lorraine Hansberry's *Raisin in the Sun* and its subsequent film adaptation. Other notable roles included the film version of PORGY AND BESS (1959) and his Oscar-winning role as Homer Smith in *Lilies of the Field* (1963); he was the first African American to win the award as best actor. Poitier made his directing debut in 1972 with *Buck and the Preacher.* In 1974, he was made a Knight Commander of the Order of the British Empire. He continued to direct films and made appearances in several himself, receiving many awards for his acting. Being a dual citizen of both the United States and the Bahamas, he was appointed ambassador to Japan for the Bahamas in 1997. Poitier was awarded the United States Presidential Medal of Freedom in 2009.

FURTHER READING

Brown, Jeremy K. "Poitier, Sidney." *Current Biography* 61, no. 9 (2000). 57.

Campbell, Christian. "'Island Boy': An Interview with Sir Sidney Poitier." *Callaloo* 30, no. 2 (2007): 482–486.

Frauenheim Ed. "Poitier's Dramatic, Trailblazing Career." *Workforce Management* (2008): 4.

Henderson, Shirley. "Sidney Poitier: Trailblazing Actor." *Ebony* 63, no. 10 (2008): 72.

Nipson, H. "Sidney Poitier Is Back." *Ebony* 43, no. 7 (1988): 31.

Spotnitz, F. "Sidney Poitier." *American Film* 16, no. 9 (1991): 18.

Porgy and Bess Maya Angelou toured with a government-sponsored troupe of black performers who performed *Porgy and Bess* in many European cities and in parts of northern Africa. She played the role of Ruby and was one of the lead dancers in the opera.

Considered by many to be GEORGE GERSHWIN's greatest masterpiece, *Porgy and Bess* was not readily accepted upon its premiere in 1935. The story line is based on *Porgy* (1925), a novel by DuBose Heyward. Gershwin conceived the piece as an "American folk opera" and made the daring decision to work with an entire cast of classically trained African Americans. The music is a synthesis of European orchestral techniques with American JAZZ and BLUES idioms. The story follows Porgy, a crippled black man in the slums of Charleston, South Carolina, as he tries to rescue Bess from her abusive lover and from Sportin' Life, a drug dealer.

The opera has continued to be controversial for its depiction of African Americans. Cast members have expressed concern that their characters might be playing into the stereotype that African Americans live in poverty, use illegal drugs, and settle their troubles with their fists. Over time, however, the opera has gained greater significance, and the musical score with its jazz roots and uniquely Gershwin touch, has become standard repertoire among opera houses.

FURTHER READING

Allen, Ray. "An American Folk Opera? Triangulating Folkness, Blackness, and Americaness in Gershwin and Heyward's Porgy and Bess." *Journal of American Folklore* 117, no. 465 (2004): 243–261.

Crawford, Richard. "Where Did Porgy and Bess Come From?" *Journal of Interdisciplinary History* 36, no. 4 (2006): 697–734.

Hutchisson, James M. *DuBose Heyward: A Charleston Gentleman and the World of Porgy and Bess*. Jackson: University Press of Mississippi, 2000.

Standifer, James. "The Tumultuous Life of Porgy and Bess." *Humanities* 18, no. 6 (1997): 8.

Thomason, Paul. "The Problem with Porgy and Bess." *Opera News* 63, no. 2 (1998): 18.

preachers By the time Maya Angelou was born, many black congregations met in peace both in the South and in the North. The preacher was the individual responsible to take care of the building and finances, to administer the rites of the church, and to exhort his congregation to righteous behavior. Within the black community, MARTIN LUTHER KING, JR., an ordained Baptist minister, and many others carried on the tradition of using strong measures to awaken the consciences of their people. Though Maya Angelou read voraciously and had many literary favorites including JAMES WELDON JOHNSON, PAUL LAURENCE DUNBAR, and WILLIAM SHAKESPEARE, "Angelou's style, her expression, and her tone, she admits, were, to a large extent, shaped by the lyricism of the black American preacher" (Elliot 1989, vii).

Oratory is a strong tradition in many denominations, and in the African-American tradition, it is the exhortation of the preacher that converts many people to the Gospel. In the early centuries of the United States, black people were separated from their belief systems in Africa, and "It is [E. Franklin] Frazier's position that the process of enslavement and the passing of earlier generations born in Africa destroyed the culture of the slaves. The vacuum was then filled by Christianity, which became the new bond of social cohesion. The new worldview which gave meaning to life was Christianity, articulated in the images and stories of the Bible, as accepted by the slaves and celebrated in their rituals" (Raboteau 1980, 52–53). Black people were allowed to attend some white church services, but as Albert J. Raboteau states:

> The revivalist impulse of the Great Awakening broke out anew on the frontier in 1800. The Great Western Revival, inaugurated by the Gasper River and Cane Ridge camp meetings in Kentucky, embraced blacks who eagerly participated in the tumultuous exercises which became characteristic of frontier revivalism. The camp meeting proved to be a powerful instrument for accelerating the pace of slave conversions. (132)

Soon, a tradition of powerful black preachers began to emerge. There were many black Baptist and Methodist lay preachers. "As such, they could not celebrate the sacraments, but were allowed to preach and to discipline black members within a restricted locale. . . . Methodists skirted legal restrictions against black preachers simply by licensing them as exhorters. . . . The majority of slaves, however, remained only minimally touched by Christianity by the second decade of the 19th century" (Raboteau 1980, 136, 149). Over time, plantation missions were established, and the slaves were regularly preached to on the Sabbath, another lecture was held on one weeknight of each week, and Sabbath schools were established for all ages.

FURTHER READING

Elliot, Jeffrey M. Introduction to *Conversations with Maya Angelou*, edited by Jeffrey M. Elliot, vii–xii. Jackson and London: University Press of Mississippi, 1989.

Frazier, E. Franklin. *The Negro Church in America*. New York: Shocken Books, 1964.

Raboteau, Albert J. *Slave Religion: The "Invisible Institution" in the Antebellum South*. Oxford and New York: Oxford University Press, 1980.

Primus, Pearl (1919–1994) Maya Angelou studied with both Pearl Primus and MARTHA GRAHAM to master the graceful movements of calypso dancing; she won a scholarship to study with Primus in 1952.

A recognized pioneer in African and Caribbean dance, Primus was a talented choreographer and teacher. Born in Trinidad on November 29, 1919, she graduated from Hunter College with a bachelor's degree in biology; she had also been an outstanding athlete in track and field as an undergraduate. After graduation, however, she was unable to find a job suited to her training because of her race, so she joined the National Youth Administration, where she was assigned to a dance group as an understudy. Later, she studied at the New Dance Group. Primus also studied anthropology and incorporated cultural traditions into her performances. Her abilities and dramatic presence onstage were recognized by such modern dance pioneers as Martha Graham, Doris Humphrey, Charles Weidman, Hanya Holm, and Louis Horst, all of whom invited her to study with them.

In the course of her career, Primus and her husband, Percival Borde, established collaborative performing arts projects in the United States and Africa. She eventually founded the Pearl Primus Dance Language Institute, where modern dance and ballet are taught and include African-American, Caribbean, and African influences. She died on October 29, 1994.

FURTHER READING

Creque Harris, Lea. *The Representation of African Dance on the Stage: From the Early Black Musical to Pearl Primus.* Atlanta, Ga.: Emory University, 1991.

DeFrantz, Thomas, ed. *Dancing Many Drums: Excavations in African American Dance.* Madison: University of Wisconsin Press, 2001.

Glover, Jean Ruth. *Pearl Primus: Cross-Cultural Pioneer of American Dance.* Ann Arbor, Mich.: UMI, 1989.

Sorrell, Walter. *The Dance Has Many Faces.* Chicago: Chicago Review Press, 1992.

Prosser, Gabriel (1775–1800) In her explorations of African-American history, Angelou learned of Gabriel Prosser's early efforts to assert the will to freedom of black slaves. (The name *Gabriel* is often thought to be more correct than *Gabriel Prosser*). Born into slavery in Virginia, Gabriel and his brothers lived on the tobacco plantation owned by Thomas Prosser. Gabriel was trained as a blacksmith and also taught to read and write. He became a deeply religious man, and he was strongly influenced by biblical examples. In 1800, he planned the first major slave rebellion in American history, an attack on Richmond that would see he and his fellow rebels seize the arsenal, take the powder house, and kill all whites except Frenchmen, Methodists, and Quakers. A violent rainstorm the night of the planned attack postponed the rebellion, and before the slaves could reassemble, Governor James Monroe was made aware of the plot and ordered out the state militia. Subsequently, Gabriel, his two brothers, and approximately 32 others were caught and hanged. Gabriel's rebellion greatly increased white fears of the slave population throughout the South.

FURTHER READING

Ayers, Edward L. "Virginia History as Southern History." *Virginia Magazine of History & Biography* 104, no. 1 (1996): 129.

Egerton, Douglas R. *Gabriel's Rebellion: The Virginia Slave Conspiracies of 1800 and 1802.* Chapel Hill: University of North Carolina Press, 1993.

Sidbury, James. *Ploughshares into Swords: Race, Rebellion, and Identity in Gabriel's Virginia, 1730–1810.* Cambridge: Cambridge University Press, 1997.

quotations There are myriad quotations attributed to Maya Angelou, and they are printed in many places, including in HALLMARK CARDS, on memorabilia, and on many Internet sites. The following are some of the nuggets of wisdom that she gave her readers and audiences in a January 20, 1997, interview on the occasion of her induction as a member of the Academy of Achievement, Museum of Living History in Washington D.C.

> I don't think modesty is a very good virtue, if it is a virtue at all. A modest person will drop the modesty in a minute. You see, it's a learned affectation. But humility comes from inside out. Humility says there was someone before me, someone found the path, someone made the road before me, and I have the responsibility of making the road for someone who is yet to come.
>
> . . . . .
>
> It has devolved upon me to—not preach, as it were—but to write about morals, about hope, about desolation, about pain and ecstasy and joy and triumph in the human spirit. So it seems to me, that is my calling. And I write about it for all of us, because I know that human beings are more alike than we are unalike. . . . Martin Luther King, Jr. always said human beings are more alike than we are unalike.
>
> . . . . .
>
> I believe that each of us comes from the Creator trailing wisps of glory.
>
> . . . . .
>
> Talk, use the language, men. Use the language, women. That is the only thing which really separates us from the rats and rhinoceros. It is the ability to say how we feel. "I believe this." "I need this." Start to talk, please.
>
> . . . . .
>
> Well, each one of us stepped on another's shoulders, you see? So you stand on my shoulders. I stand on Martin's and Malcolm's shoulders. And they stood on Dr. DuBois and Marcus Garvey, you see? So we make a wonderful pyramid. That's why it's always important to know you are in your place, because someone went before you, and paid for you.
>
> . . . . .
>
> Read ceaselessly. Read. Go into a library and just make yourself a list. Say, "I will read from A to BR." Read . . . all knowledge is spendable currency, depending on the market. Read. Put it in the old bean. You'll be amazed how it will serve you.

FURTHER READING

Academy of Achievement. "Interview: Maya Angelou, Poet and Historian." Available online. URL: www.achievement.org/autodoc/printmember/ang0int-1. Accessed March 29, 2010.

racism Maya Angelou had an early experience with discrimination because of race:

> I was very young, in that little village in Arkansas, and there was a movie house downtown. "Downtown" consisted of one paved street. There was a movie house, and the girl who worked selling tickets lived on land my grandmother owned. And I knew for a fact that she and her family hadn't paid any rent for three years. They lived behind the town, on our land. I went up to get a ticket. I may have been about eight or nine. My grandmother was very religious and didn't believe in the movies, but once she allowed me and my brother—every now and again. We went up to get a ticket. And the girl took my dime, and she wouldn't put her hand on it. I put it down. She had a cigar box, and she took the card and raked my dime into the cigar box. Now, the white kids got tickets. She took their money, and she gave them little stubs. She didn't give us anything. She just motioned, which meant that we had to go up the side steps, outside steps, and crawl through a really crummy little door, and sit perched on these three or four benches to watch the movie. And all because I was black. And I thought, "Well, I don't think I'll be going to the movies a lot. So I decided to boycott the movies." (Academy of Achievement).

Though they had experienced such blatant discrimination, Maya and her brother, Bailey, continued to attend the movie house as often as they could.

Racism is a belief that there is a superiority in intelligence and character in one race over another, and the predictable consequences of racism are political or economic domination by the more powerful group. Racists practice hatred and bigotry toward people who differ from themselves and believe that people can be grouped on the basis of biological traits—that is, that some groups have superior mental and behavioral traits. However, it is not merely a set of beliefs when it exercises unfair treatment of the group being dominated.

There are various types of racism; the scholar Geneva Gay has defined them as *individual, cultural,* and *institutionalized.* Gay stresses the behavioral aspects of racism: "It is an extension of an attitude into an action. Although the focus of attention is on *behavior,* attitudes are of crucial importance for they are the motivating forces which determine the nature of the actions one takes" (30).

FURTHER READING

Academy of Achievement. "Interview: Maya Angelou, Poet and Historian." January 22, 1997. Available online. URL: http://www.achievement.org/autodoc/printmember/ang0int-1. Accessed March 29, 2010.

Gay, Geneva. "Racism in America: Imperatives for Teaching Ethnic Studies." In *Teaching Ethnic Studies: Concepts and Strategies,* edited by James A. Banks, 27–49. Washington, D.C.: National Council for Social Studies, 1973.

Rains, Claude (William Claude Rains) (1889–1967) Claude Rains was one of the actors Maya and Bailey enjoyed watching when they went to the movie theater in STAMPS, ARKANSAS, as children. Rains was a British film and stage actor known for his smooth voice and polished, ironic style. Born in London on November 10, 1889, he began acting and working in theaters at the age of 11. After serving in World War I, he had a successful stage career upon his return to London and also taught at the Royal Academy of Dramatic Art. Rains's expressive face and commanding voice led to his making a screen test, and though the test was a failure, he was cast in the title role of *The Invisible Man* (1933), directed by James Whale. This role won him instant fame, and he went on to play a variety of leading and supporting roles, including learned professionals, politicians, spies, and criminals. He was nominated for an Academy Award for his part opposite BETTE DAVIS in *Mr. Skeffinton* (1944). Rains returned to the stage in the 1950s and continued to appear in films until 1965. He died in Laconia, New Hampshire, on May 30, 1967, at age 77.

FURTHER READING

Kemp, Philip. "Smooth as Old Cognac." *Sight & Sound* 15, no. 1 (2005): 32–35.

Skal, David J. *Claude Rains: An Actor's Voice.* Edited by Jessica Rains. Lexington: University of Kentucky Press, 2008.

Soister, John T., with JoAnna Wioskowski. *Claude Rains: A Comprehensive Illustrated Reference to His Work in Films, Stage, Radio, Television and Recordings.* Jefferson, N.C.: McFarland, 1999.

Ray, James Earl (1928–1998) The assassination of civil rights leader MARTIN LUTHER KING, JR., in 1968 left Maya Angelou in a deep, grief-stricken depression. King's killer was James Earl Ray, a petty criminal who had served time in prison on three counts. He escaped from the Missouri State Penitentiary in 1967, and it was the next year, on April 4, 1968, that he shot King on a hotel balcony, from the window of a neighboring rooming house. Ray fled the country and was eventually apprehended by the London police. Brought back to Memphis, he pled guilty and was sentenced to 99 years in prison. He escaped in 1977 and was at large for 54 hours before being recaptured in a massive manhunt. He died in prison on April 23, 1998.

FURTHER READING

Egerton, John. "The Enduring Mystery of James Earl Ray." *Progressive* 50, no. 11 (1996): 19–25.

Murdock, Deroy. "James Earl Ray Trial Could Free the Ghosts of Memphis." *Headway* 9, no. 4 (1997): 20.

White, Jack E. "James Earl Ray, Cause Celebre?" *Time,* 4 May 1998, 36.

Reese, Della (Delloreese Patricia Early) (1931–) When Maya Angelou was performing at a club in Hawaii, someone suggested that she visit a neighboring club and listen to the singer there. It was Della Reese, and after hearing her great voice and style, Angelou decided that she was not as dedicated to singing as Reese and never would be. From that time on, she decided, she would perform only as a dancer.

Reese is an African-American actress, singer, game-show panelist, and ordained minister. Born Delloreese Patricia Early on July 6, 1931, she began singing in church when she was six, and at the age of 13, she was hired to sing with Mahalia Jackson's gospel group. Reese attended Wayne State University but had to quit to take care of her ailing parents. She signed her first recording contract in 1953 and later that year joined the Erskine Hawkins Orchestra. She was voted the most promising singer in 1957 when her single "And That Reminds Me" became a top 20 pop hit and a million-record seller. In the following decades, Reese continued to record albums, and she received two Grammy nominations in the gospel category.

Reese transitioned into acting work in 1969, and in 1970, she was the first black woman to guest host *The Tonight Show Starring Johnny Carson*. She has appeared in several movies and television shows and is most popularly known for portraying the character of Tess in *Touched by an Angel* (1994–2003). She was ordained a minister in 2010.

FURTHER READING

Castro, Peter, and Cathy Free. "Counting Her Blessings." *People* 47, no. 7 (1997): 113.

Lipton, Michael A., et al. "Heaven Help Us!" *People* 51, no. 7 (1999): 113.

Reese, Della. *Angels along the Way: My Life with Help from Above*. Edited by Mime Richler. New York: G. P. Putnam's Sons, 1997.

"When God Spoke to Rev. Della." *Television Week* 22, no. 18 (2003): 2.

Richards, Beah (Beulah Richardson) (1920–2000) After Angelou returned to the United States from Africa and moved to California, Beah Richards, a talented actress on stage, screen, and television, played the lead role in a production of MEDEA; Angelou played a supporting though minor part in the play as an elderly nurse.

Born Beulah Richardson on July 12, 1920, in Vicksburg, Mississippi, Richards graduated in 1948 from Dillard University in New Orleans. Two years later, she moved to New York City. Her acting career began in 1955 with her portrayal of an 84-year-old grandmother in the Off-Broadway show *Take a Giant Step*. Thereafter, she often played the role of a mother or grandmother. Richards also appeared in the original Broadway production of LORRAINE HANSBERRY's *A Raisin in the Sun* (1959). She was nominated for a Tony award for her performance in *The Amen Corner* (1965) and received an Academy Award nomination for best supporting actress for her performance as SIDNEY POITIER's mother in *Guess Who's Coming to Dinner* (1967). Richards made numerous appearances on television, including *The Bill Cosby Show, Designing Women, The Practice,* and *ER*. The winner of two Emmy Awards, she was the subject of the 2003 documentary *Beah: A Black Woman Speaks*, which won the Grand Jury Prize at the AFI Film Festival.

Richards also wrote occasionally, and Angelou, in a 1973 interview with Bill Moyers, quoted part of a well-known poem by Richards called "A Black Woman Speaks of White Womanhood, of White Supremacy, of Peace." Angelou said to Moyers: "She [Richards] says, 'If they did appraise my teeth they checked out your thigh, and sold you to the highest bidder, the same as I.' And yet—she goes on in her poem to say, 'Yet you have settled down, and when you saw my children sold you gave no reproach, but for an added broach settled down in your pink slavery and thought that enduring my slavery or allowing it to happen would make yours less.' She says, 'You never noticed that the bracelet you took was really a chain, and the necklace you accepted throttled your speech.' Now, there's a great difference in the white American woman and the black American woman" (quoted in Moyers 1989, 21). Other parts of the poem boldly discuss crimes committed by whites against blacks, including the rape of and sexual violence committed against black women and the lynching of black men. Various dates are given for the date the poem was written, but it was in the early 1950s that Richards read it to a women's group in Chicago.

The talented Beah Richards died from emphysema in her hometown of Vicksburg, Mississippi, on September 14, 2000.

FURTHER READING

Chambers, Veronica, and Allison Samuels. "The Women of *Beloved*." *Newsweek* 132, no. 16 (1998): 74.

Gussow, Mel. "Beah Richards, 80, Actress in Stalwart Roles." *New York Times*, 16 September 2000, 13.

Moyers, Bill. "A Conversation with Maya Angelou." In *Conversations with Maya Angelou*, edited by Jeffrey M. Elliot, 18–28. Jackson and London: University Press of Mississippi, 1989.

Tait, George Edward. "July Profile: Beah Richards." *New York Amsterdam News*, 27 July 1996, 32.

Wilson, Brian. "Beah: A Black Woman Speaks." *Booklist* 100, no. 19 (2004): 1,761.

Roach, Max (Maxwell Lemuel Roach) (1924–2007) In the early 1960s, Maya Angelou struck up a close friendship with ABBEY LINCOLN and Max Roach, entertainers who were married from 1962 to 1970. They worked together on the Off-Broadway play *The Blacks* by Jean Genet, until Abbey and Max withdrew from participation.

An American jazz drummer and composer, Roach was one of the most influential and recognized percussionists in history. Born in North Carolina on January 10, 1924, he grew up in New York City playing drums for gospel bands. In the 1940s, he began playing in nightclubs, and his jam sessions with artists such as Charlie Parker and Dizzy Gillespie gave rise to the sound of bebop. Roach's percussive texture and manipulation of themes elevated the percussionist to the equal of the melodic soloist. He recorded with Parker and Miles Davis before starting his own quintet in 1954. A tragic accident killed two members of the original group, and Roach subsequently formed other ensembles. In 1972, he began teaching at the University of Massachusetts. He was frequently involved with unusual projects, including accompanying a rapper and playing for reading series. His compositions were for stage, film, and dance pieces. Roach continued to tour into the early part of the 21st century. He died at age 83 on August 16, 2007.

FURTHER READING

Corbett, John. "Max Roach." *Downbeat* 73, no. 6 (2006): 18.

Dais, Risasi Zachariah. "Max Roach Displays His Dynamic, Versatile Talents at 92nd Street Y." *New York Amsterdam News* 88, no. 52 (1997): 19.

McElfresh, Suzanne. "Max Attack." *Downbeat* 60, no. 11 (1993): 16.

Robeson, Paul (Paul LeRoy Bustill Robeson) (1898–1976) When Maya Angelou was on tour in Europe with the opera *Porgy and Bess*, she went to a music shop not far from her hotel in Yugoslavia. She purchased a beautiful mandolin inlaid with mother-of-pearl that the shopkeeper had retrieved from the back of his store. As she was in the process of paying for it, the shopkeeper's wife and several children emerged from the back room. The wife was introduced to Angelou and mentioned Paul Robeson, and then she began to sing "Deep River," a song Robeson had made famous. Soon the children and then the husband joined in the singing, and Maya also joined in to sing the moving lyrics: "Oh don't you want to go / To that gospel feast? . . . / That promised land / Where all is peace?" (Angelou 2004, 550). For Maya, it was a moment to reflect on the history of black people in the United States, and it was a poignant moment of recognition that people in Eastern Europe at that time had little more freedom than the blacks had suffered in the southern states.

An American actor, singer, and black activist, Robeson was born in Princeton, New Jersey, on April 9, 1898. He attended Rutger's University in New Brunswick, New Jersey, where he was an All-American football player and graduated at the head of his class. Refused a career as a professional athlete, he instead obtained a law degree from Columbia University in 1923. The legal profession lacked opportunity for blacks, and Robeson drifted to the stage. His part in the title role in Eugene O'Neill's *The Emperor Jones* (1923) caused a sensation in both New York and London. Robeson had a superb baritone voice and became world famous in *Show Boat* with his rendition of "Ol' Man River" (1925). He also became more politically active and was associated with strong left-wing ideas. In 1956, a slight scandal arose because Robeson refused to sign an affidavit saying that he was not a member of the Communist Party, though he had so testified before the House Committee on Un-American Activities 10 years earlier. Nonetheless, he was a defender of socialism and often spoke out against racism. Robeson died in Philadelphia, Pennsylvania, on January 23, 1976.

FURTHER READING

Angelou, Maya. *Singin' and Swingin' and Gettin' Merry Like Christmas.* In *The Collected Autobiographies of Maya Angelou.* New York: Random House, 2004.

Blockson, Charles L. "Paul Robeson." *American Visions* 13, no. 1 (1998): 14.

Boyle, Sheila Tully. *Paul Robeson: The Years of Promise and Achievement.* Amherst: University of Massachusetts Press, 2001.

Friedwald, Will. "Paul Robeson in His Depression-Era Prime." *Wall Street Journal,* 5 February 2009, D7.

Harrison, C. K., and Brian Lampman. "The Image of Paul Robeson: Role Model for the Student and Athlete." *Rethinking History* 5, no. 1 (2001): 117–130.

Jones, Ida E. "A Model for Tomorrow: Using Paul Robeson to Teach Human and Gender Rights." *Negro History Bulletin* 59, nos. 1–3 (1996): 26.

Keller, Robert H. "Paul Robeson at Blaine." *Columbia: The Magazine of Northwest History* 19, no. 4 (2005): 17–22.

Robeson Paul, Jr. "Paul Robeson." *Black Collegian* 28, no. 2 (1998): 160.

Weisberger, Bernard A. "The Ballad of Paul Robeson." *American Legacy: Celebrating African-American History and Culture* 4, no. 2 (1998): 32.

rococo When Maya Angelou was touring in Europe with the *PORGY AND BESS* opera, she took time out to enjoy the various cultures she was experiencing. She wrote about the different architectural and decorative styles she observed and mentioned the rococo style in particular.

Rococo is a modification of the more elaborate baroque style in architecture and indoor decor. Both were decorating styles popular among the wealthy in Europe. Baroque architecture uses large, elaborate arches, spires, and bulky moldings and carving in buildings, indoor room decorations, and in furniture. Both baroque and rococo are profuse and elaborate decorating styles common in the early 1800; rococo is characterized by elaborate but more delicate ornamentation on a smaller scale than baroque. The shell, among many other shapes, is a prominent motif for furniture, paneling, stage curtains, ceramics, and fabrics.

FURTHER READING

Marian, Mary Warner, and William Fleming. *Fleming's Arts and Ideas.* 10th ed. Beverly, Mass.: Wadsworth, 2005.

Romeo and Juliet When Maya Angelou was in Italy on tour with the opera *PORGY AND BESS*, she was told the group was in the city of Verona, the setting of the play *Romeo and Juliet.* When she reached Venice, she observed the Italian-style balconies and remembered WILLIAM SHAKESPEARE's famous play of love and loss, written around 1594–96.

Roots: The Saga of an American Family When Maya Angelou was living in Africa, she thought about ALEX HALEY's book *Roots,* as did many other black American expatriates. She lived first in Cairo, Egypt, and then in Accra, Ghana, where she searched, explored, and found a sense of heritage and perhaps some of her own roots. Even so, she returned to the United States realizing that the work she needed to do was in America rather than in Africa.

Roots is a novel written by Alex Haley and published in 1976. The story follows an African who is enslaved and brought to America, and then the African passes his story on to his descendants. Haley purportedly traced his own lineage back to Kunta Kinte—the "African"—captured by slave traders in 1767. For generations, the story of Kunta Kinte had been passed down the family line. For his novel, Haley researched the slave trade, researched African village customs, and even visited Gambia to learn from the oral historian there. Using this knowledge, he recreated the story of his ancestors.

While most of the story is fictional, *Roots* captured the imagination of the American people. Earning the Pulitzer Prize in 1977, the book was made into a television miniseries that earned nine Emmys, a Peabody, and many other rewards. The story of *Roots* spawned a surge of interest in genealogy. Most scholars agree that Haley probably did not locate the actual village of his ancestors, and that much of his story does not line up with fact, but it still has been one of the most influential works in American literature.

FURTHER READING

Bundles, A. L. "Looking Back at the *Roots* Phenomenon." *Black Issues Book Review* 3, no. 4 (2001): 12–15.

Duggan, Beth. "*Roots* Still Has Lessons to Teach." *Television Week* 26, no. 4 (2007): 24.

Haley, Alex. *Roots: The Saga of an American Family.* 30th anniv. ed. New York: Vanguard Books, 2007.

Hutchinson, Earl Ofari. "Saga Had an Impact on a Wide Audience." *Television Week* 26, no. 4 (2007): 24–.

Shute, Nancy. "New Routes to Old Roots." *Smithsonian* 32, no. 12 (2002): 76.

Taylor, Helen. "'The Griot from Tennessee': The Saga of Alex Haley's Roots." *Critical Quarterly* 37, no. 2 (1995): 46.

Rorschach test When Maya Angelou was contemplating entering the U.S. Army and officer's school, she had to take Rorschach tests. The Rorschach test is a personality and intelligence examination consisting of interpretations of black, gray, or sometimes colored ink blots. The interpretations of the one taking the test are thought to reveal certain intellectual and emotional factors. These types of tests are generically called Rorschachs.

Rustin, Bayard (1912–1987) Maya Angelou knew Bayard Rustin and was his replacement as Northeast coordinator of the SOUTHERN CHRISTIAN LEADERSHIP CONFERENCE (SCLC) when he left that position. Rustin was a black American civil rights activist. Born on March 17, 1912, he graduated from high school in West Chester, Pennsylvania, and then he worked a series of odd jobs while traveling widely. He enrolled in the City College of New York, but left after five years of study with no degree. Rustin actively opposed racial SEGREGATION and was a lifelong believer in pacifist agitation. He traveled to various countries to learn methods of peaceful protest and how to organize people. He organized the New York branch of the CONGRESS OF RACIAL EQUALITY (a reformist group) in 1941, and he worked for the Fellowship of Reconciliation from 1941 to 1953. In the 1950s, he worked as a close adviser to MARTIN LUTHER KING, JR., and with King, he was the chief organizer of the SCLC. He was also the chief organizer behind the March on Washington (1963), and in 1964, he directed a one-day student boycott of segregation in schools. In later life, he became an advocate for gay and lesbian rights. Bayard Rustin died on August 24, 1987.

FURTHER READING

"Bayard Rustin." *New Republic* 197, no. 13 (1987): 10–11.

"Bayard Rustin, R.I.P." *National Review* 39, no. 18 (1987): 20.

Carbado, Devon W., and Donald Weise. "The Civil Rights Identity of Bayard Rustin." *Texas Law Review* 82, no. 5 (2004): 1,133–1,195.

D'Emilio, John. "Invisible Man." *Crisis* 110, no. 4 (2003): 32.

———. "Remembering Bayard Rustin." *OAH Magazine of History* 20, no. 2 (2006): 12–14.

McKeen, Gayle. "The Doctrine of Non-Violence Revisited: Bayard Rustin, Rev. Joseph H. Jackson, and Malcolm X on the Strategies of the Civil Rights Movement." *Conference Papers—Midwestern Political Science Association* (2008): 1–13.

Podair, Jerold E. *Bayard Rustin: American Dreamer.* Lanham, Md.: Rowman & Littlefield, 2009.

S

San Francisco, California Maya Angelou moved to San Francisco in her early teens and lived with her mother and stepfather in the FILLMORE DISTRICT. At 16, she became a streetcar conductor in San Francisco, the first black woman to be given that responsibility.

The fourth most populous city in California, San Francisco was settled in 1776 by the Spanish, and the population in the region surged during the Gold Rush in 1848. In 1906, 75 percent of San Francisco was destroyed by an earthquake and fire, but the city quickly rebuilt and served as a port of embarkment for servicemen during World War II. After the war, massive immigration, liberalizing attitudes, and other factors led to the "Summer of Love" and the gay rights movement, cementing San Francisco as the center for liberal activism in the United States. It is known for its steep rolling hills, eclectic architecture, and famous landmarks, including the Golden Gate Bridge, Chinatown, and cable cars.

FURTHER READING

Beebe, Morton. *San Francisco.* Rev. ed. New York: Harry N. Abrams, 1993.

Haddock, Patricia. *San Francisco.* Minneapolis, Minn.: Dillon Press, 1989.

Visalli, Santi. *San Francisco.* New York: Rizzoli, 1990.

Schulberg, Budd (1914–2009) Budd Schulberg appears in Angelou's sixth autobiography, *A Song Flung Up to Heaven* (2002), because he went to WATTS in LOS ANGELES after the 1965 riots and founded the Watts Writers Workshop. His presence and support to the writers there helped to tell the story of life in Watts prior to the riots. Those narratives contributed to reform and helped eliminate exploitation of people living in depressed neighborhoods and neglected communities.

An American novelist, screenwriter, and journalist, Schulberg was born in New York City on March 27, 1914, and grew up in Hollywood, the son of a motion picture producer. He graduated from Dartmouth College in 1936 and began to work as a screenwriter, in addition to writing and publishing short stories. Schulberg was a member of the Communist Party until they demanded that his first novel be written to reflect Marxist dogma. During World War II, he was an officer in the U.S. Navy and Office of Strategic Forces. Throughout his life, he continued to publish novels and write screenplays, including *On the Waterfront,* which won an Academy Award in 1954. After the 1965 riots, Schulberg established the Douglass House Watts Writers Workshop in Los Angeles, and in 1971, he founded the Frederick Douglass Creative Arts Center in New York. Married four times, he died on August 5, 2009.

FURTHER READING

Gross, K. "Budd Schulberg." *People* 32, no. 25 (1989): 93.

Jacobson, Mark. "What Makes Budd Run?" *New York* 35, no. 28 (2002): 28.

Newfield, Jack, and Mark Jacobson. "An Interview with Budd Schulberg." *Tikkun* 15, no. 3 (2000): 9.

Steyn, Mark. "What Made Budd Schulberg Run?" *Maclean's* 122, no. 32 (2009): 56–57.

Vonnegut, Kurt. "Budd Schulberg." *Paris Review* 43, no. 160 (2001): 96–111.

Seeger, Pete (1919–) Pete Seeger appears in Angelou's sixth autobiography, *A Song Flung Up to Heaven*. He was one of many prominent white and African-American luminaries who participated in the celebration of what would have been W. E. B. DuBois's 100th birthday (February 23, 1968).

Born on May 3, 1919, into a musical family, Seeger left Harvard after two years of study to hitchhike around the country and ride freight trains, gathering country ballads, work songs, and hymns. He became a virtuoso on the banjo and is credited with popularizing American folk music. In 1948, Seeger formed a folk group, the Weavers, and the group became quite popular at concerts, on college campuses, and on records. Just as they achieved national recognition, Seeger became the target for controversy over his left-wing activities and labor practices. The Weavers had difficulty booking concerts or selling records, and therefore they disbanded in 1952. After this, Seeger preferred to work alone, though the Weavers reunited in 1955 and enjoyed popular success until they disbanded again in 1964; Seeger had left them in 1958. During that time, he was faced with blacklist issues, especially after he refused to answer questions from the House Committee on Un-American Activities during the McCarthy era. For several years, major television networks refused to let him appear on their channels, but over time the controversy and uproar settled down, and he was able to perform more frequently. He and the original Weavers reunited for one last wildly successful concert at Carnegie Hall in 1980. Seeger has received several Grammy Awards and numerous other awards and honors. He was inducted into the Rock and Roll Hall of Fame in 1996. He is a longtime campaigner for civil rights and environmental causes.

FURTHER READING

Dunaway, David King. *How Can I Keep from Singing? The Ballad of Pete Seeger*. New York: Villard, 2008.

Ferris, William R., and Michael K. Honey. "Pete Seeger, San Francisco, 1989." *Southern Cultures* 13, no. 3 (2007): 3–38.

Harris, Scott "Pete Seeger: Folk Music's Granddad Plays It Green." *E—The Environmental Magazine* 5, no. 6 (1994): 10.

Ratliff, Ben. "Love or Die: Will We Ever Learn?: Pete Seeger—at 89." *New York Times*, 29 September 2008, 1.

Sacks, Leo. "Pete Seeger." *Billboard* 118, no. 26 (2006): 22.

Thurmaier, David. "Seeger, Springsteen, and American Folk Music." *Phi Kappa Phi Forum* 86, no. 4 (2006): 11–14.

segregation, racial Maya Angelou has worked diligently all of her adult life to help end segregation in the United States, which is the practice of restricting people to separate schools, housing, churches, businesses, playgrounds and other institutions based on race. Segregation is a means of maintaining the social, economic, and political dominance of the ruling group. Recently, white populations have used segregation to maintain legal clout, but historically, other groups (African Bantu, Asian Mongols, American Aztecs) have also imposed segregation. Segregation has been an issue all over the world wherever multiracial groups have coexisted. In the United States, segregation of public facilities was in place from the late 19th century through the 1950s through legislation often referred to as Jim Crow laws. Southern blacks in the 1950s and 1960s began the Civil Rights movement to try and end the patterns of segregation. This movement led to the Civil Rights Act of 1964, which contained strong provisions against segregation in the use of public facilities, education, and voting.

See also INTEGRATION.

FURTHER READING

Brown, Leslie, and Anne Valk. "Behind the Veil: Behind Brown." *OAH Magazine of History* 18, no. 2 (2004): 38–42.

Chin, Gabriel J., and Randy Wagner. "The Tyranny of the Minority: Jim Crow and the Counter Majoritarian Difficulty." *Harvard Civil Rights-Civil Liberties Law Review* 43, no. 1 (2008): 65–125.

Kusher, James A. *Apartheid in America: An Historical and Legal Analysis of Contemporary Racial Segregation in the United States.* Arlington, Va.: Carrollton Press, 1980.

Loevy, Robert D. *The Civil Rights Act of 1964: The Passage of the Law That Ended Racial Segregation.* Albany, N.Y.: State University of New York Press, 1997.

López, Ian F. Haney. "'A Nation of Minorities': Race, Ethnicity, and Reactionary Colorblindness." *Stanford Law Review* 59, no. 4 (2007): 985–1,063.

Service, Robert (Robert William Service) (1874–1958) Robert Service was among the many poets Maya Angelou enjoyed reading. A popular Canadian author, Service was noted for his writings about the Canadian North, including his poems "The Shooting of Dan McGrew" and the "Law of the Yukon." Born in Preston, England, on January 16, 1874, he moved to Canada at the age of 21 and took a position in a bank, whose officials posted him to the Yukon wilderness. Inspired by his surroundings, Service wrote poetry about the things he saw. His first book, *The Songs of a Sourdough,* was published in 1907 (in the United States, under the title of *The Spell of the Yukon and Other Verses*), and Service was dubbed the "Canadian Kipling." He subsequently moved to France and was known to dress as a working man (despite his reputation as the wealthiest author in the French Riviera) and observed everything around him. During World War I, Service worked as an ambulance driver, and thereafter he wrote much poetry on the duty to country during times of war. He died in France on September 11, 1958.

FURTHER READING

Klinck, Carl Frederick. *Robert Service: A Biography.* New York: Dodd, Mead, 1976.

Mackay, James Alexander. *Robert Service, Vagabond of Verse: A Biography.* Edinburgh: Mainstream, 1995.

Mayes, Hubert G. "A 'Sourdough' in France." *Beaver* 70, no. 1 (1990): 39.

Service, Robert William. *Yukon Poems of Robert W. Service.* Palmer Lake, Colo.: Filter Press, 1967.

Shabazz, Betty (Betty X, Betty Dean Sanders) (1934–1997) Maya Angelou met MALCOLM X in New York City and planned his itinerary when he visited Africa to encourage African dignitaries to engage in African/African-American dialogue and support. Malcolm X spoke often of his wife and family with fondness, and Angelou noted this in her book *All God's Children Need Traveling Shoes* (1986).

Malcolm was very close to his wife, Betty Shabazz, also known as Betty X; the *X* represented her unknown African family name. Her maiden name was Betty Dean Sanders, and she was born on May 28, 1934, in either Pinehurst, Georgia, or Detroit, Michigan (records in either possible birthplace do not include her birth certificate). She began her university education at the Tuskegee Institute (now Tuskegee University) in Alabama but relocated to New York City, where she completed nurses' training at the Brooklyn State Hospital School of Nursing. Betty met Malcolm X at a Nation of Islam lecture in HARLEM. She converted to the Nation of Islam and married Malcolm on January 14, 1958, in Lansing, Michigan; he changed their last name to Shabazz. Betty Shabazz was present at the assassination of her husband in New York City in 1965. Thereafter, she dedicated herself to raising their six daughters, though she also returned to school and earned an M.A. in public health education at Jersey City State College and a Ph.D. in education administration at the University of Massachusetts, Amherst. She worked as a professor and director of the communications department and public relations at Medgar Evers College in Brooklyn. She also gave lectures on civil rights and racial tolerance.

On June 1, 1997, Shabazz suffered burns over 80 percent of her body when her grandson, Malcolm Shabazz, set fire to her apartment. She died of her injuries on June 23, 1997. The grandson was sentenced to 18 months in juvenile detention for manslaughter.

FURTHER READING

Angelou, Maya. *All God's Children Need Traveling Shoes.* New York: Random House, 1986.

Armstrong, Linda. "Dr. Maya Angelou Cooks to Raise Money for Dr. Betty Shabazz Foundation." *New York Amsterdam News* 88, no. 40 (1997): 21.

Barker, Cyril "Josh," and Tanangachi Mfuni. "Center Pays Tribute to the Legacy of Malcolm X and Betty Shabazz." *New York Amsterdam News* 96, no. 22 (2005): 4.

"Betty Shabazz." *Biography Today* 7, no. 2 (1998): 85.

Jeffries, Bayyinah. "First Ladies of the Nation of Islam: The Life and Work of Sister Clara Muhammad, Betty Shabazz, and Khadijah Farrakhan." *Conference Papers—Association for the Study of African American Life & History* (2006): 1.

Rickford, Russell J. *Betty Shabazz: A Remarkable Story of Survival and Faith before and after Malcolm X.* Naperville, Ill.: Sourcebooks, 2003.

Shadow, The When Maya and Bailey were children in STAMPS, ARKANSAS, they would regularly listen to the stories of the Shadow on the radio. A popular half-hour radio program, broadcast every Sunday night, that began in 1937 and continued until 1954, *The Shadow* was based on Walter Gibson's serialized novels in *Street and Smith Magazine.* It followed the psychic title character through crime-fighting escapades, and the Shadow became one of the most famous heroes in radio and fiction magazines. He could influence the minds of his opponents to make himself appear several feet to the side of where he was. The show began with the ominous words, "Who knows what evil lurks in the hearts of men? The Shadow knows!" That statement was followed by a foreboding laugh and a musical theme from Camile Saint-Saëns's *Le Rouet d'Omphale.* The Shadow was originally played by Jack LaCurto, then by Orson Wells, beginning in 1937. *The Shadow* inspired cartoon strips, films, and a television series.

Shakespeare, William (1564–1616) Maya Angelou said many times that William Shakespeare was one of her first great loves. To help her emerge from her long period of silence after being brutally raped at about eight years old, a teacher, MRS. BERTHA FLOWERS, helped her by introducing the child, who was then 11 or so, to good books and poetry. Shakespeare became a favorite, and Mrs. Flowers said that Maya would not really love and understand poetry until it literally rolled across her tongue, through her teeth, and out of her lips. As a result of this training, Maya memorized many poems and learned to use her voice once again.

Shakespeare was an English poet, actor, and dramatist, and he is considered by many to be the greatest dramatist of all time. His works are notable for their powerful poetry, ingenuity, creativity, and structure. His subject was humanity, with all of its emotions, complexities, and characters. Shakespeare's clever words and images are memorable, and his works continue to be read worldwide.

Shakespeare's date of birth is unknown, but he was baptized on April 26, 1564. He grew up in Stratford-upon-Avon, England, and attended the local grammar school, where he studied Latin and the classics. He did not go on to the university but instead married Anne Hathaway when he was 18. There are many stories of how Shakespeare made a living during the first years of his marriage, but all that is known for sure is that by the 1590s, he was heavily involved in the theater. One of his patrons was Henry Wriothesley, the third earl of Southampton, to whom Shakespeare dedicated his first published poems, *Venus and Adonis* and *The Rape of Lucrece.* Shakespeare was a member of Lord Chamberlain's theatrical company (called the King's Men after James I's ascent to the throne in 1603). The group had some of the best actors in London, and with Shakespeare as the professional dramatist, the company prospered. For 20 years, he also wrote dramatic poetry of the highest quality. He died in Stratford-upon-Avon on April 23, 1616, at age 52.

FURTHER READING

Bach, William B. "Shakespeare and Received Opinion." *Sewanee Review* 101, no. 4 (1993): 549.

Jolliffe, Lee. "Shakespeare's Words: Quotes, Misquotes, and Lost Contexts." *ETC.: A Review of General Semantics* 66, no. 3 (2009): 345–348.

Levine, Lawrence W. "William Shakespeare and the American People: A Study in Cultural Transformation." *American Historical Review* 89, no. 1 (1984): 34.
McMillin, Scott. "Shakespeare and the Chamberlain's Men in 1598." *Medieval & Renaissance Drama in England* 17 (2005): 205–215.
Smith, Cheryl Hogue. "No Reason without Rhyme: Rhetorical Negotiation in Shakespeare." *English Journal* 99, no. 1 (2009): 91–98.
Thompson, Ayanna. "Rewriting the 'Real': Popular Shakespeare in the 1990s." *Journal of Popular Culture* 40, no. 6 (2007): 1,052–1,072.
Weis, René. "Was There a Real Shakespeare?" *Textual Practice* 23, no. 2 (2009): 215–228.

Shannon, Kentucky (Kentucky Wofford) (1850–?) Kentucky Shannon was Maya Angelou's great-grandmother. Genealogist Rafi Guber and actor-comedian Billy Crystal discovered that Kentucky's father's name was Washington Wofford, and they informed Angelou of this news a few years ago. Angelou in turn posted an article on February 6, 2008, entitled "Why My Great Grandmother's Name Matters," which expresses how overwhelmed she was to learn a little more about this woman she had only known by her name and a passed-down "steely" reputation. Angelou writes: "I knew that my great grandmother, who was born in 1850 had been a slave. But Kentucky Shannon was not her slave name. It was the name she gave herself, seemingly as a renunciation of the institution of slavery. Family members had asked her where the name came from, whether she had been born in Kentucky or had some other connection to the place. She would never discuss it." She further explains that it was the PBS African American Lives project that used DNA testing and historical research to find this information. Angelou also learned that she is a descendant of the Mende people, whose homelands are Sierra Leone and Liberia in Western Africa.

FURTHER READING

Angelou, Maya. "Why My Great Grandmother's Name Matters." *The Root*, February 6, 2008. Available online. URL: http://www.theroot.com/views/why-my-great-grandmothers-name-matters. Accessed August 20, 2009.

sharecroppers The girls who taunted Grandmother Henderson in Angelou's *I Know Why the Caged Bird Sings* were from a family of sharecroppers who lived on land behind the Johnson store. A sharecropper is a tenant farmer, particularly in the southern United States, who becomes indebted to their employer for seed, tools, living quarters, and food. The sharecropper works the land and receives a percentage of the profit from the crops minus the indebtedness.

siddity This is an African-American colloquial word used occasionally throughout Angelou's work; it means "pretentious" or "putting on airs."

signifying Maya Angelou uses the traditional African-American style known as *signifying* in her poetry. In such a style, there are meanings embedded in some of the words, phrases, and rhythms used that are not readily apparent. Signifying is saying one thing and meaning something else. It separates the informed from the uninformed and creates an insider/outsider group. Angelou has used this device in much of her writing. Lyman B. Hagen calls it "indirection" and gives examples from Angelou's writing—for instance, Hagen cites a passage from *Gather Together in My Name* and notes the "white myth that all blacks looked alike and that they all stuck together" (39). Angelou has reversed that in her book, saying that whites still look alike to her, and that everyone knows they stick together better than blacks (paraphrased here). Hagen continues, "This quote is immediately recognized by African Americans as an indirection" (39).

In the introduction to his book *The Signifying Monkey: A Theory of African-American Literary Criticism* (1988), Henry Louis Gates, Jr., states: "I have tried to define a theory of African-American criticism not to mystify black literature, or to obscure its several delightful modes of creating meaning, but to begin to suggest how richly textured and layered that black literary artistry indeed is" (xx). Using "two signal trickster figures, Esu-Elegbara and the Signifying Monkey, in whose myths are registered certain principles of both formal language use and its interpretation" (xx), Gates takes his readers on an interesting journey into the use and traditions of signifying in the African-American culture.

Gates also writes: "Signifyin(g) is the black rhetorical difference that negotiates the language user through several orders of meaning. In formal literature, what we commonly call figuration [or figurative language] corresponds to Signification" (79). It is a complex use of language, but as Hagen said, "this use of indirection to avoid denial or lying, has become embedded in black folk culture to exclude whites or to talk around them" (39). He adds that "a knowledge of black linguistic regionalisms and folklore enhances the appreciation of Angelou's poems. Thus a Whorfian 'linguistic relativity' in which language shapes the way we view the world may be at work here. . . . But most of Angelou's poems can be understood and appreciated on their own merits, sans [without] special insight" (132).

FURTHER READING

Gates, Henry Louis, Jr. *The Signifying Monkey: A Theory of African American Literary Criticism.* New York and Oxford: Oxford University Press, 1988.

Hagen, Lyman B. *Heart of a Woman, Mind of a Writer, and Soul of a Poet: A Critical Analysis of the Writings of Maya Angelou.* Lanham, Md.: University Press of America, 1997.

slave narratives As a child and into adulthood, Maya Angelou read voraciously, and stories of the African-American past, including slave narratives, were a part of her own history. Though she knew little about her, Angelou's great-grandmother, KENTUCKY SHANNON, "declared her personal independence when slavery was abolished by taking the name Kentucky Shannon" (Gillespie, Butler, Long, 15). That in itself is a brief slave narrative. Many African Americans still carry the surname of their ancestor's owner, and one of the practices of the Black Muslims (Nation of Islam) was to drop the slave owner's surname and adopt the letter X as their last name. MALCOLM X adapted this form.

Henry Louis Gates, Jr., writes: "The birth of the Afro-American literary tradition occurred in 1773, when Phillis Wheatley published a book of poetry" (vii). In time, other African Americans, as they learned to read and write, put the pen to paper and began to tell their stories. In the 18th and 19th centuries, many slave narratives were published, emerging from the experience of enslaved Africans in Great Britain, Canada, the United States, and the Caribbean. Among the most well-known were FREDERICK DOUGLASS's autobiography *Narrative of the Life of Frederick Douglass, an American Slave* (1845) and Harriet Jacobs's *Incidents in the Life of a Slave Girl* (1861). The Library of Congress in Washington, D.C., houses many slave narratives. *Born in Slavery: Slave Narratives from the Federal Writer's Project, 1936–1938,* contains more than 2,300 first-person accounts of slavery and 500 black-and-white photographs of former slaves. These records of the past were collected as part of the Federal Writers' Project of the Works Progress Administration (WPA), and they were assembled and microfilmed for the 17-volume *Slave Narratives: A Folk History of Slavery in the United States from Interviews with Former Slaves* (1941). These materials are available to the public, and many are available online.

Virginia Hamilton, an award-winning children's author, tells the story of her own grandfather, Levi Perry, who was a black man born into slavery and who escaped across the Ohio River with his mother around 1854. They were rescued by a white man, John Rankin, who helped many slaves escape from the South. Twice a year, Levi Perry would tell his ten children the story. He would begin, "Now listen, children. I want to tell you about slavery and how my mother and I ran away from it" (quoted in Hamilton 1985, 146). Hamilton's mother, Etta Belle Perry, who was Levi Perry's oldest daughter, told her the tale.

Other interesting slave narratives are accounts of marriages during slave times in the United States. There was a time when slaves were forbidden to marry, though secret marriage ceremonies took place even before it was officially legal to do so. As the Christian religion (mostly Baptist, Methodist, or Presbyterian) started to be taught to the slaves in earnest throughout the southern states and western frontier (not west of the Mississippi), the slaves were allowed to be baptized and marry, and many "legalized" weddings took place. These marriages posed new difficulties for both the slaves and the slave owners because of the real possibility of one or the other being sold and thus separating a married couple. Though that was not entirely resolved until after the Civil War, many couples were married either in private home ceremonies or in their various denominations after the turn of the 1800s. "Jumping the broom" was an African custom practiced by many slaves before and after the marriage was legalized for them. For many, this constituted a binding and permanent marriage. Albert Raboteau includes the following account in his book *Slave Religion* (1980):

> The most frequent method of marrying two slaves was the custom of jumping the broomstick. One of several variations of the ritual was described by William Davis: "Dey lays de brooms on de floor and de woman put her broom front de man and he put the broom front de woman. Dey face one 'nother and step' cross de brooms at de same time to each other and takes hold of hands and dat marry dem." Another variation was to hold the broomstick a foot off the ground and then require the bride and groom one after the other to jump over it backwards. William Wells Brown asserted that "this custom had a binding force with Negros as if they had been joined by a clergyman; the difference being the one was not so high-toned as the other. Yet, it must be admitted that the blacks always preferred being married by a clergyman. (228–229)

"Jumping the broom," thought to be imported from Nigeria, is practiced today by many during formal or informal wedding ceremonies. It became popularly revived in the United States after *Roots: The Saga of an American Family* was televised to millions of viewers in the 1970s. There is a "dramatic scene in which Kunta Kinte and Bell took their step into married life. Since the 1970s countless African-American couples have incorporated this tradition into their weddings with the intention of creating a bridge between them and their cultural heritage" (Cole 2003, 11).

FURTHER READING

Cole, Harriette. *Jumping the Broom: The African-American Wedding Planner.* 2nd ed. New York: Henry Holt, 2003.

Gates, Henry Louis, Jr., ed. *The Classic Slave Narratives.* New York: New American Library, 1987.

Gillespie, Marcia Ann, Rosa Johnson Butler, and Richard A. Long. *Maya Angelou: A Glorious Celebration.* New York: Doubleday/Random House, 2008.

Hamilton, Virginia. *The Black People Could Fly: American Black Folktales.* New York: Alfred A. Knopf, 1985.

Lane, Lunsford. *Narrative of Lunsford Lane.* 3rd ed. Boston: Hewes and Watson's Print, 1845.

Library of Congress. *Born in Slavery: Slave Narratives from the Federal Writers' Project, 1936–1938.* Available online. URL: http://memory.loc.gov/ammem/snhtml. Accessed July 1, 2010.

Raboteau, Albert J. *Slave Religion: The "Invisible Institution" in the Antebellum South.* Oxford and New York: Oxford University Press, 1980.

Sloan's Liniment Maya's grandmother, Annie Henderson, sold Sloan's Liniment in her general store to cotton-field workers who used it to relieve their aching bodies. Liniment is a topical medication usually used to treat sore muscles; the treatment consists of rubbing the medication into the skin. Sloan's Liniment—a concoction developed by Andrew Sloan, a self-taught Ohio veterinarian—was originally used to ease the sore shoulder and leg muscles of horses during spring plowing. It was a popular liniment, and in 1871, Sloan's sons, Earl and Foreman, took several bottles to St. Louis and sold the preparation at horse shows and auctions in the area. At some point, someone used it on his own body and found that it eased sore muscles and pain. It was then advertised as being good for man or beast. The active ingredient in the liniment is capsaicin (in topical form), which is found in chili peppers. Other ingredients are methyl salicylate, oil of camphor, turpentine, and oil of pine.

This particular liniment was invented early in the commercial production of liniment creams. The glass bottles had the words *Sloan's Liniment* in raised letters on them, and their frequent presence in today's antique and flea market sites attest to the popularity of the product, which is still sold today.

FURTHER READING

Calbert, Robert Noah. *The History of Massage: An Illustrated Survey.* Rochester, Vt.: Healing Arts Press, 2002.

Southern Christian Leadership Conference (SCLC) In 1960, Maya Angelou replaced BAYARD RUSTIN as Northwest coordinator in the New York office of the Southern Christian Leadership Conference in New York City. The arrest of Rosa Parks, an African-American woman, for refusing to give up her seat on a bus to a white man on December 5, 1955, in Montgomery, Alabama, is considered by many as the spark that ignited the modern CIVIL RIGHTS MOVEMENT. The ensuing Montgomery bus boycott, a nonviolent protest by the community, lasted 381 days and culminated in the desegregation of the Montgomery bus system. The boycott was directed by the Montgomery Improvement Association (MIA) with MARTIN LUTHER KING, JR., as its president and RALPH ABERNATHY as its program director. As other bus boycotts developed throughout the South, MIA and other protest groups met to organize and coordinate their efforts to end SEGREGATION through nonviolent protests. The new organization, known as the Southern Leadership Conference on Transportation and Nonviolent Integration, was founded in Atlanta, Georgia, on January 10–11, 1957. At its first conference in August of that year, the name Southern Christian Leadership Conference was adopted. Nonviolent mass action is the basic tenet of the organization.

FURTHER READING

Garro, David. *Bearing the Cross: Martin Luther King, Jr., and the Southern Christian Leadership Conference.* Perennial Classics. New York: Harper Perennial Modern Classics, 2004.

spirituals Maya Angelou was raised in the COLORED METHODIST EPISCOPAL CHURCH, later named the Christian Methodist Episcopal Church. It was her Grandmother Henderson's faith, and when Maya and her brother, Bailey, lived in STAMPS, ARKANSAS, with their grandmother, they spent several hours each Sunday at the church. The music there was heartfelt, rhythmic, and carried the message of the gospel into the very fiber of the singers and the listeners. Angelou loved the music and the way it made her feel. When she visited other denominations as a young adult, it was the spirited music she seemed to miss the most.

Spirituals are religious songs created and originally sung by enslaved African Americans in the United States. They often include a call-and-response pattern common in community meetings and worship services in West Africa, the original home of many slaves. Spirituals are communal songs whose authors are not known. The songs, often plaintive, were a means by which the slaves could share their sorrows, hopes, and joys with one another. Some spirituals appear to have double meanings. On the surface, they may express hopes of spiritual salvation, but on a deeper level, there may be a covert wish for physical freedom.

Black gospel songs had been popular since the mid-1920s and have their roots in the older black spirituals, but a distinguishing feature is that for the most part, the authors of the more recent songs are known.

FURTHER READING

Chenu, Bruno. *The Trouble I've Seen: The Big Book of Negro Spirituals.* Valley Forge, Pa.: Judson Press, 2003.

Smith, Jeffrey. *The Concept of Religion Reflected in the Early Negro Spirituals.* Bloomington, Ind.: iUniverse, 2008.

Southern, Eileen. *The Music of Black Americans: A Story.* New York: W. W. Norton, 1971.

Stamps, Arkansas Stamps, Arkansas, is located in Lafayette County in the southwestern corner of the state. It had a population of about 2,100 people in 2000. Its claim to fame is that it is where the writer Maya Angelou spent her childhood, and it is described in her first autobiography, *I Know Why the Caged Bird Sings* (1970).

Stepin Fetchit (Lincoln Theodore Monroe Andrew Perry) (1902–1985) As children, Maya Angelou and her brother, Bailey, both enjoyed the movie antics of Stepin Fetchit, a popular comedian and film actor. He was born Lincoln Theodore Monroe Andrew Perry on May 30, 1902, in Key West, Florida. In his mid-teens, he left home and performed in carnivals, medicine shows, and vaudeville, where he danced, sang, and did comedy. The origin of Perry's stage name, Stepin Fetchit, may have been from the name of a horse on which he made a lot of money or the name of a vaudeville team of which he was a part. He is said to have given both explanations.

Perry's film career in Hollywood began in the late 1920s. He developed a comedic persona as a stereotypical lazy, shuffling, mindless Negro, but with timing that made people laugh. Members of the African-American community criticized his acting, finding it demeaning to their race. Some fans, however, saw him as a sly trickster pretending not to understand simple directions so that his white boss ended up doing the work. Perry became very successful; he was the first black man to earn a million dollars in the film industry. His career waned in the late 1930s as civil rights leaders continued to express their disapproval of the stereotype he was portraying. He lived a high lifestyle and by 1947 had to declare bankruptcy. During his career, Perry played in about 50 films, three of them with fellow comic Will Rogers. Stepin Fetchit died in Woodland Hills, California, on November 19, 1985, at age 83.

FURTHER READING

Clark, Champ. *Shuffling to Ignominy: The Tragedy of Stepin Fetchit.* Bloomington, Ind.: iUniverse, 2005.

Watkins, Mel. *Stepin Fetchit: The Life & Times of Lincoln Perry.* New York: Vintage Books, 2006.

T

Tambo, Oliver (Oliver Reginald Tambo) (1917–1993) Maya Angelou met Oliver Tambo and VUSUMZI MAKE at JOHN KILLENS's home in New York City in 1960. Tambo and Make were African freedom fighters and had come to speak to both the United Nations and the people of the United States to gain support in their fight against apartheid in South Africa.

Oliver Reginald Tambo was born to subsistence farmers in a small village in Pondoland, South Africa, on October 27, 1917. His parents recognized the value of education and sent him to St. Peter's School in Johannesburg. After graduating from St. Peter's, he was awarded a scholarship to the University College of Fort Hare, which was then the only college blacks could attend. There, he became involved in politics and was expelled for taking part in a student boycott. After leaving Fort Hare, he returned to St. Peter's in Johannesburg in 1942 and taught mathematics and science. While at St. Peter's he earned a law degree by correspondence course and, with NELSON MANDELA and others, cofounded the African National Congress—Youth League (ANC–YL), an antiapartheid organization. The ANC–YL believed that proactive tactics were required to achieve their goals, and its members organized nonviolent boycotts, strikes, and civil disobedience demonstrations, in addition to supporting noncollaboration. Their activities seemed to enliven the more sedate mother organization, the African National Congress (ANC), especially after Tambo became its secretary general in 1955.

In 1959, the South African government banned Tambo from political activities in the country; he and his family, at the request of the ANC, moved to London. The following year, the ANC was banned and went underground, and Mandela and others were arrested for sabotage and attempting to overthrow the government. The group was found guilty of the charges and sentenced to life in prison. During the 30 years Tambo was out of the country, he established ANC missions in 27 countries. In 1961, suppression by the South African government had reached such a point that the ANC adopted a more militant role in striving for the removal of apartheid laws. Tambo developed ties with other African nations, which allowed the ANC to establish training facilities in their countries. As strikes, boycotts, and demonstrations became larger, more numerous, and militant, foreign investors started leaving the country. By the late 1980s, economic production had declined, the currency had collapsed, and there was chronic inflation. The government began secret negotiations with Mandela, which resulted in his release from prison, removal of the ban on the ANC, and ultimately a referendum in 1992 in which the white population strongly supported reform of the apartheid laws. Oliver Tambo died on April 24, 1993, as a result of a stroke.

FURTHER READING

Callinicos, Luli. *Oliver Tambo: His Life and Legacy.* Johannesburg, South Africa: STE Publishers, 2006.

Johns, Sheridan, and Hunt R. Davis, Jr., eds. *Mandela, Tambo, and the African National Congress: The Struggle against Apartheid, 1948–1990. A Documentary Survey.* New York and Oxford: Oxford University Press, 1991.

Tar Baby In *The Heart of a Woman* (1981), Maya Angelou compares her delight over being moved to the library in a newspaper office in Cairo with BRER RABBIT's escape to the briar patch. She was at first assigned to a desk in a room full of Egyptian male journalists who were suspicious of her presence among them. When they suggested that they move her desk into the partially glass-walled library, which happened to be lined with books written in English, Angelou was relieved and happy, just like Brer Rabbit when he was stuck to the Tar Baby and about to be thrown into a stew pot.

The Tar Baby episode appears in one of the Brer Rabbit stories by JOEL CHANDLER HARRIS. A doll made out of tar and turpentine sits beside the road, and Brer Rabbit, thinking it is a living thing, strikes it again and again and becomes stuck to it because it will not respond to his greeting. Brer Fox and Brer Bear set the Tar Baby as a trap for Brer Rabbit, but the rabbit escapes again. He tells the fox that whatever else he does, he must not throw Brer Rabbit into the briar patch—throwing him there would be the most horrible end he could imagine. Of course, that is what Brer Fox does. When he is free, he turns to Brer Fox and says that he is delighted to be in the briar patch, because that is where he was born and bred.

Virginia Hamilton, a scholar and children's writer, writes:

> There are some three hundred versions of the Tar Baby tale. Variants of the tale appear in many countries. In the Bahamas the elephant creates the tar baby; in Brazil an old woman or man traps a monkey in a sticky wax baby. There is a version from India, and there are African versions among the Ewes and Yurubas, all showing great antiquity and universality in this tale.
>
> Long ago, in certain localities of Georgia the tar baby was considered an actual, living, monstrous creature. The monster was composed of tar and haunted isolated places on the plantation. It would insult people to the point at which they would strike out at it and thus become trapped in its sticky substance. (19)

FURTHER READING

Hamilton, Virginia. *The People Could Fly: American Black Folktales.* New York: Alfred A. Knopf, 1985.

Texarkana, Arkansas Located on the border of Texas and Arkansas, Texarkana is the city where, in *I Know Why the Caged Bird Sings,* Momma (Grandmother Henderson) had to take Maya to a black dentist. The white dentist in STAMPS, ARKANSAS, refused to treat her.

Thackeray, William Makepeace (1811–1863) Maya Angelou enjoyed reading the works of the English novelist William Makepeace Thackeray when she was a child. Thackeray was born on July 18, 1811, in Calcutta, India, where his father worked for the British East India Company. When William was four years old, his father died. His mother elected to remain in India but sent her young son to England for his education. Thackeray entered Trinity College, Cambridge University, in 1829, but not being much of a scholar, he left the following year. However, some of his earliest writings were published there. He spent some time on the Continent and, after returning to England, studied law for a short period. At age 21, he came into a sizable inheritance but lost a large portion to an Indian bank failure. He also spent a fair amount gambling and publishing two unsuccessful newspapers.

In 1836, Thackeray married Isabella Gethin Shawe, with whom he had three daughters. To support his family he began, as he put it, "to write for life." He wrote art criticism and fictional pieces for *Fraser's Magazine,* a conservative publication, often signing them with pseudonyms. Thackeray gained notoriety satirizing English snobbery with "The Snobs of England," which appeared in *Punch.* His most famous novel, *Vanity Fair,* in which he created a most immoral female character, Becky

Sharp, was published in serialized form in 1847–48. His popularity grew, and when not writing, he spent considerable time lecturing and touring in England, Europe, and the United States. During his lifetime, he wrote more than 30 novels, short stories, and essays, many of them were serialized in various publications. Thackeray died in London on December 24, 1863, at age 52.

FURTHER READING

Ferris, Ina. *William Makepeace Thackeray.* New York: Macmillan, 1983.

Thurmond, Strom (James Strom Thurmond) (1902–2003) Maya Angelou and many of her friends and colleagues did not hold a high opinion of Strom Thurmond, who was among many feared politicians discussed in conversations between Angelou and artists/performers in the Black Arts Movement (BLACK AESTHETIC MOVEMENT) and Black Power movement. An American politician and noted segregationist, James Strom Thurmond was born in Edgefield, South Carolina, on December 5, 1902. He was raised and educated in Edgefield before attending and graduating from Clemson College (now Clemson University) with a degree in horticulture. After studying law with his father, he was admitted to the South Carolina bar in 1930. Thurmond was elected to the South Carolina Senate in 1933 and served until he was elected a judge of the 11th Circuit Court. He gave up his judgeship early in World War II, enlisted in the U.S. Army, and served in both the European and Pacific campaigns.

In 1947, Thurmond was elected governor of South Carolina, serving until 1951. Though a Democrat at that time, he opposed President Harry S. Truman's DESEGREGATION policies and ran against Truman as the presidential candidate for the States' Rights Democratic Party. He won only four states and 39 electoral votes. Upon the resignation of U.S. Senator Charles E. Daniel, Thurmond was appointed to fill the seat in 1954. He was elected to the position in 1956 and held it until his retirement at age 100, 46 years later. In an unsuccessful attempt to stop the Civil Rights Act of 1957, he filibustered for over 24 hours. Increasingly, he found himself at odds with the Democratic Party's support of civil rights legislation, and in 1964, he switched to the Republican Party where he strongly supported the candidacies of Barry Goldwater (1964) and Richard Nixon (1968) for president.

Thurmond was president pro tempore of the U.S. Senate from 1981 to 1987 and again in 1995. For six years, he chaired the Judiciary Committee, and he was chair of the Armed Services Committee from 1995 to 1999. He did not seek reelection in 2002 and ended his career in 2003. He died on June 26, 2003, and was buried in his boyhood town of Edgefield, South Carolina.

FURTHER READING

Bass, Jack, and Marilyn W. Thompson. *Strom: The Complicated Personal and Political Life of Strom Thurmond.* Jackson, Tenn.: Public Affairs, 2006.

Cohodas, Nadine. *Strom Thurmond & the Politics of Southern Change.* Macon, Ga.: Mercer University Press, 1994.

Till, Emmett (1941–1955) Angelou has mentioned the murder of Emmett Till in conveying horrid truths about southern RACISM in her work. On August 28, 1955, Till, a 14-year-old African-American boy from Chicago, was murdered in Tallahatchie County, Mississippi. He had gone there to visit his cousin, and his mother had warned him that interactions between blacks and whites were not at all the same in Mississippi as in Chicago. Leaving his cousin and other friends outside, Emmett entered the white Bryant's Grocery and Meat Market, and the clerk was an attractive young white woman, Carolyn Bryant, who was married to the store's owner. His friends had dared him to ask her for a date since he carried a photograph of a white girl in his wallet. He entered the store alone, and no one knows for certain what words were said between Till and Bryant. Whatever happened, it exploded into violence, and several days later, his body was found in the Tallahatchie River badly decomposed and bearing clear evidence of vicious torture and a violent beating. He had been shot just above the right ear, and his neck was wrapped with barbed wire. Photographs of his body lying in a casket revealed the severe damage to his face and head. His mother wanted the casket open to show the nation the face of brutal racism, and the picture appeared in the widely circulated September 15, 1955, issue of *Jet* magazine and the *Chicago Defender*. His murderers were Carolyn's husband, Roy Bryant, and Bryant's half brother, J. W. Milam. On September 23, 1955, both were acquitted by a white jury.

There have been many texts published since Till's murder expressing outrage. Among the books and theatrical works that were produced, JAMES BALDWIN wrote *Blues for Mister Charlie* (1964). "Mr. Charlie" is a black colloquialism for a white man, and Baldwin's "play dramatizes the murder to emphasize the insidious arrogance of a culture that refused to see itself as accountable for such crimes. In the state of Mississippi, blacks had no rights that whites were bound to respect" (Hudson-Weems 2007, 499).

Chris Crowe's young-adult book about the tragedy, *Getting Away with Murder* (2003), states that Till's murder was one of the triggers for the American CIVIL RIGHTS MOVEMENT.

> Emmett's murder in August 1955 and the sham trial that followed it infuriated African Americans everywhere. For many, the brazen murder of a boy by two white men was the last straw in centuries of racial oppression and abuse. Even before Emmett's death, African activists had been working to formalize a civil rights movement, but the outrage that followed his death and the acquittal of his murderers finally launched the movement to combat racism in the United States. (12–13)

FURTHER READING

Baldwin, James. *Blues for Mister Charlie, a Play.* New York: Dial Press, 1964.

Crowe, Chris. *Getting Away with Murder: The True Story of the Emmett Till Case.* New York: Phyllis Fagdman, 2003.

Hudson-Weems, Clenora. "Till, Emmett (1941–1955)." In *Encyclopedia of African-American Literature*, edited by Wilfred Samuels, 498–499. New York: Facts On File, 2007.

toby Maya Angelou said she felt her "toby" quiver just moments before she learned of her son Guy's terrible automobile accident a few days after arriving in Ghana in 1963. A toby is a charm or token that has been prepared by a conjurer of hoodoo or voodoo to bring good luck to the one who carries it. It is sometimes believed to be magic, and the tradition stems from practices common in ancient Africa. Many people carry good-luck charms of one kind or another from Ohio buckeyes to rabbits' feet.

Truth, Sojourner (Isabella Baumfree) (ca. 1797–1883) When Maya Angelou was in London with VUSUMZI MAKE, accompanying him while he attended an international conference, she told a story about Sojourner Truth, abolitionist and women's rights activist. The narrative was shared with wives of African diplomats and freedom fighters who were attending the conference. Many of the women told stories from their homeland and their personal experiences in the fight for equal rights in Africa. Some had been beaten and had scars to prove it. The setting for Maya's story was prior to the Civil War in the 19th century.

Born into slavery in Swartekill, New York, Sojourner Truth—née Isabella Baumfree—was a charismatic black spiritual leader and prominent spokeswoman for the rights of women. At an antislavery rally in Indiana, a man yelled at Sojourner, "I don't believe you are a woman" (quoted in hooks 1981, 159). Truth then "bared her breasts to prove that she was indeed a woman" (159). There are varied reports and stories about Truth's later "Ain't I a Woman" speech that she delivered in 1851 at the Ohio Women's Rights Convention in Akron, Ohio. Versions of the speech were published both by Marius Robinson and Frances Dana Barker Gage, both of whom had been in the audience and heard it. One of the versions of her speech is included in Virginia Hamilton's book *Many Thousand Gone* (1993), and though it is not in the original vernacular, it reveals the passion whith which she spoke:

> That man over there says that women need to be helped into carriages, and lifted over ditches, and to have the best place everywhere.

Nobody ever helps me into carriages, or over mud puddles, or give me any best place. And ain't I a woman? Look at me! Look at my arm. I have ploughed and planted, and gathered into barns, and no man could head me! And ain't I a woman? I could work as a man and eat as much as a man—when I could get it—and bear the lash as well! And ain't I a woman? I have borne thirteen children, and seen them most all sold off to slavery, and when I cried out with my mother grief, none but Jesus heard me! And ain't I a woman? (74)

Over the years, Truth continued to give speeches against slavery, and during the Civil War, she helped to recruit black soldiers for the Union army. She was also an advocate for women's nights and prison reform, and she spoke out against capital punishment. She died at her home in Battle Creek, Michigan, on November 26, 1883.

FURTHER READING

Hamilton, Virginia. *Many Thousand Gone: African Americans from Slavery to Freedom.* New York: Alfred A. Knopf, 2003.

hooks, bell. *Ain't I a Woman: Black Women and Feminism.* Boston: South End Press, 1981.

Tubman, Harriet (Araminta Ross) (ca. 1820–1913) Maya Angelou shared stories about Harriet Tubman and the UNDERGROUND RAILROAD with African women in London who had accompanied their husbands (African diplomats and freedom fighters) to a conference there. Tubman was born a slave in Maryland around 1820–22; her birth name was Araminta Ross. In 1849, she escaped to Philadelphia, and then she returned to Maryland to help her family escape to safety. She subsequently assisted innumerable slaves to freedom in the north by helping to establish safe houses along the route known as the Underground Railroad. Robert Remini states: "It was estimated that by the 1850s, the Underground Railroad helped 1,000 or more runaways a year escape their servitude" (134). During the Civil War, Tubman worked for the Union army as a cook, nurse, scout, and spy, and she helped even more slaves to freedom.

In 1869, Sarah Bradford published the first biography of Harriet Tubman's life and work, and her expanded second edition was published in 1886. This early biography attests to the recognition Tubman was accorded by numerous grateful people during her lifetime and how well-known and respected she was. The following information is from the second edition of the biography, reprinted in 1994: "After her almost superhuman efforts in making her own escape from slavery, and then returning to the South *nineteen times,* and bringing with her over three hundred fugitives, she was sent by Governor Andrew of Massachusetts to the South at the beginning of the War, to act as spy and scout for our armies and to be employed as hospital nurse when needed" (6). Tubman later became a suffragette and civil rights activist. She died in Auburn, New York, on March 10, 1913, at age 93.

FURTHER READING

Bradford, Sarah. *Harriet Tubman: The Moses of Her People.* 1886. Reprint, New York: Carol, 1994.

Remini, Robert V. *A Short History of the United States.* New York: HarperCollins, 2008.

Turner, Nat (1800–1831) Maya Angelou has mentioned Nat Turner in her discussions of the history of African Americans. Though she did not support the violence that he espoused, she sympathized with the desperation of his times and the dangers for blacks, which lingered well into the 20th century.

Turner was born into slavery in Southampton County, Virginia, on October 2, 1800, and learned to read and write at an early age. Intelligent and religious, he frequently had visions and became convinced that God intended him for a higher purpose, and by February 1831, he was preparing a rebellion of slaves. On August 21 that year, he and a few fellow slaves began going to houses to free other slaves and kill the white people they encountered; as they spread through the countryside, more joined the rebellion. Armed with little more than farm tools, Turner and his gang moved across Southampton County, eventually killing 55 white men, women, and children. However, his poor planning and organization led to a counterattack, and within two days Turner had gone into hiding. For two months, he was able to evade capture, and he became widely feared; people were terrified that he might strike at any time and kill again. He was finally captured on October 30, and on November 11, he was hanged. Of the other 44 slaves and five free blacks who took part in the rebellion, 15 were acquitted, 18 were hanged, and the rest were sold out of state. For many years afterward, slave owners feared Turner's influence. New slave laws were passed, and military patrols made their presence known throughout the South.

FURTHER READING

Conlin, Joseph R. *The American Past, Part I: A Survey of American History to 1877.* 4th ed. Fort Worth, Tex.: Harcourt Press, 1993.

Davis, Kenneth C. *Don't Know Much about History: Everything You Need to Know about American History but Never Learned.* New York: Perennial/HarperCollins Publishers, 2004.

Greenberg, Kenneth S. *Nat Turner: A Slave Rebellion in History and Memory.* Oxford and New York: Oxford University Press, 2003.

Quarles, Benjamin. *The Negro in the Making of America.* New York: Touchstone, 1987.

Tyson, Cicely (1933–) Cicely Tyson was one of the original cast members in the controversial Off-Broadway play *The* BLACKS, by JEAN GENET. Her fellow actors in the play included Maya Angelou, JAMES EARL JONES, GODFREY CAMBRIDGE, and Louis Gossett, Jr.

An accomplished actress of television, stage, and film, Cicely Tyson was born in HARLEM on December 19, 1933. After graduating from high school, she worked as a secretary for the American Red Cross, but as she shouted to her fellow office workers, "I know that God did not put me on the face of this earth to bang on a typewriter for the rest of my life." She tried fashion modeling and had a mostly successful career, but she said she felt like a machine. She turned to acting after being asked to play a role in a film (which was never released), and she subsequently attended several acting schools in the New York area. She had parts in a few Off-Broadway shows and played uncredited roles in films in the late 1950s and early 1960s, in addition to acting in TV series such as *East Side/West Side* (1963–64). Tyson preferred to play parts where she could portray a strong, positive black woman image; consequently, she limited her opportunities.

In the early 1960s, Tyson's career was mostly in Off-Broadway stage productions and guest appearances on television, but her cinema opportunities increased, and she had a few feature film roles before she starred in *The Heart Is a Lonely Hunter,* in 1968. In 1972, she was nominated for an Academy Award for best actress for her performance in *Sounder.* Tyson was awarded two Emmys in 1974 for her outstanding portrayal of a 110-year-old woman in *The Autobiography of Miss Jane Pittman.* The most productive years of her career were in the 1960s and 1970s, and she was nominated for and received many awards for her performances. To this day, she continues to be seen on television and in films.

FURTHER READING

Bogle, Donald. *Primetime Blues: African Americans on Network Television.* New York: Farrar, Straus and Giroux, 2002.

U

Underground Railroad The Underground Railroad and its most famous "conductor," HARRIET TUBMAN, are well-known in African-American history, and Maya Angelou knew their stories and shared them with African women. Many anonymous people helped black slaves escape from the South via an informal system known as the Underground Railroad. It ran from the south northward through Ohio, Pennsylvania, and New York. The people found freedom in either Canada or the northeast United States. "While many of these [helpers] were white abolitionists, often Quakers, the ranks of conductors were also joined by escaped slaves who risked far more by returning to help other slaves out. Of these, the most famous was Harriet Tubman" (Davis 2003, 198).

FURTHER READING

Bradford, Sarah. *Harriet Tubman: The Moses of Her People.* New York: Carol, 1994.

Davis, Kenneth C. *Don't Know Much about History: Everything You Need to Know about American History but Never Learned.* New York: HarperCollins, 2003.

Universal Negro Improvement Association (UNIA) Founded in 1914 by Marcus Garvey, the organization was intended to unite all of Africa and its scattered people into one united group. It still exists today, but it is now called Universal Negro Improvement Association and African Communities League (UNIA/ACL). The current president-general is Redmond Battle.

Garvey was a pan-Africanist and believed that African Americans should force European colonial powers to leave Africa. As a black separatist, Garvey wanted to establish close economic and political ties to the African nations. MALCOLM X's father was a follower of Garvey, and Malcolm always believed that his father had been murdered by white racists.

Benjamin Quarles writes of Garvey:

> A self-dramatizer as well as a man of amazing energy and persuasiveness, Garvey established himself in Harlem and literally catapulted himself into the limelight. Branches of his brainchild, the Universal Negro Improvement Association, mushroomed in Negro urban centers, and his well edited weekly, the *Negro World*, effectively spread the Garvey Gospel. With a sure sense of mass psychology, Garvey utilized plumed hats and cockades, street parades with brass bands playing martial airs, "African Redemption" medals, and the conferring of such titles of nobility as "knight" and "duke." At the height of his influence in the mid-twenties, Garvey had upwards of a million followers. (229)

Garvey had many business ventures and was eventually brought to trial for fraud. He was jailed but pardoned by President Coolidge and fled to

London, where he died in obscurity some years later.

Though Maya Angelou was not a part of the UNIA, she recognized the influence that Garvey had particularly on the people of HARLEM.

FURTHER READING

Davis, Kenneth C. *Don't Know Much about History: Everything You Need to Know about American History but Never Learned.* New York: HarperCollins, 2003.

Quarles, Benjamin. *The Negro in the Making of America.* 3rd ed. New York: Simon & Schuster, 1996.

V

VE-day Maya Angelou was living in SAN FRANCISCO, CALIFORNIA, with her infant son at the end of World War II, and she has described it as a time of high spirits, hope, and celebration. Victory in Europe day was May 8, 1945. This was the date when the Allies accepted the surrender of Nazi Germany and the end of Adolf Hitler's Third Reich. By this time, Hitler had committed suicide, and so his replacement, the German president Karl Dönitz, authorized the surrender. Massive celebrations took place, but they were somewhat subdued by the reality of the many tragedies that had taken place. Millions of people had been killed or mutilated. Estimates were that at least 6 million Jews alone had been exterminated. It was a time of relief, but also a time of mourning for many. Though the war had ended, rationing of food and clothing continued. The United States was still mourning the death of Franklin D. Roosevelt on April 12, just a month before. The largest VE-day celebration took place in New York City's Times Square.

FURTHER READING

Tindell, George Brown, and David E. Shi. *America: A Narrative History*. 4th ed. New York: W. W. Norton, 1996.

Watts In summer 1965, Watts—a mostly black and depressed neighborhood in LOS ANGELES, CALIFORNIA, located near the highway approaching Los Angeles International Airport—experienced a frenzy of riots and looting. Watts was pocket of poverty and overcrowding. There was high unemployment, drugs, and crime, and often young people were roaming the streets unsupervised and looking for fights. On August 11, a young black man was pulled over by a policeman for suspected drunken driving. When he was put under arrest, a crowd gathered and began jeering and taunting, and then they began pushing and shoving. Before long, stones, bottles, and chunks of concrete were being thrown, and the policeman called for backup. In a few hours, the crowd had swelled to a mob, and the riots began. Watts was sealed off, and for a little while things were quiet. "By nightfall the small, roving bands had grown to a mob of thousands, hostile, angry, and beyond control" (Davis 2003, 480).

The black comedian Dick Gregory tried to calm the crowds and instead was shot in the leg. The riots continued for days, and thousands of National Guardsmen came into the area. Watts had become a war zone, which was ironic because "the Urban League had rated Los Angeles as the most prosperous and desirable city for black urban residents in the United States" (Tindall and Shi 1996, 1,422). The riots, which lasted six days before finally dying down on August 15, left 34 dead, nearly 4,000 rioters in jail, and in excess of $35 million in damages.

Maya Angelou had been working in the Watts neighborhood doing door-to-door canvassing shortly before the riots began. She entered Watts twice during the conflagration out of curiosity, but she emerged unnoticed and unhurt.

FURTHER READING

Davis, Kenneth C. *Don't Know Much about History: Everything You Need to Know about American History but Never Learned.* New York: HarperCollins, 2003.

Tindell, George Brown, and David E. Shi. *America: A Narrative History.* 4th ed. New York: W. W. Norton, 1996.

Winfrey, Oprah (1954–) Maya Angelou first met Oprah Winfrey in Maryland after a series of seminars Angelou had presented there. Winfrey approached her courteously to request an interview, the fifth request that day, and Angelou intended at first to turn her down. Winfrey persisted and said, "Doctor, I only need five minutes of your time. You have my word that you will be free to go in five minutes" (quoted in Angelou 2004, 201). Angelou was impressed. Giving one's word is a powerful thing, she thought, and she decided to test Winfrey to see if her word was good. It was, and the impression she made on Angelou has been permanent and long-lasting. Their relationship has grown so strong that they are much like a mother and daughter.

Oprah Winfrey was born on January 29, 1954, in Kosciusko, Mississippi, and she was reading aloud and reciting at the age of three. Her broadcasting career began at age 17 when she was hired by WVOL radio in Nashville, Tennessee. She was there for two years and then became a reporter/anchor for WTVF-TV in Nashville. She graduated from Tennessee State University, where she majored in speech communications and performing arts. She worked in Baltimore as a coanchor and discovered her talent as a talk-show host. Building on that, she moved to Chicago to host WLS-TV's *AM Chicago,* which she built into one of the most popular shows in Chicago. In 1985, it was renamed *The Oprah Winfrey Show,* and the rest is history.

Several years ago, Oprah Winfrey requested an interview with Maya and promised it would last only five minutes. She kept her word and won Angelou's respect and admiration. Over time, the two women have become close, sharing a bond very much like that of mother and daughter, characterized by mutual trust and affection. *(Photo by Evan Agostini/AP)*

A public-minded leader, Winfrey was named one of the 100 Most Influential People of the 20th Century by *Time* magazine. As noted by *Forbes* magazine in 2003, she was the first African-American woman to become a billionaire. Informed, generous, and energetic, Winfrey has contributed time and money to the public good. She has organized charitable schools for underprivileged children in Africa, and she is one of the partners in a cable channel and interactive network called Oxygen Media, Inc., that is designed particularly for women. On January 1, 2001, OWN, the Oprah Winfrey Network, debuted on cable television.

FURTHER READING

Academy of Achievement. "Biography: Oprah Winfrey, Entertainment Executive." Available online. URL: http://www.achievement.org/autodoc/printmember/win0bio-1. Accessed February 13, 2009.

Angelou, Maya. *Hallelujah! The Welcome Table: A Lifetime of Memories with Recipes.* New York: Random House, 2004.

Garson, Helen S. *Oprah Winfrey: A Biography.* Westport, Conn.: Greenwood Press, 2004.

womanist Angelou has often identified herself as a womanist. During the feminist movement in the United States, African-American female intellectuals wrote that they viewed the white feminist struggle as different from their own. White women were working toward female/male equality in education and the professions, liberation from homemaking if they so choose, voice in the public arena, equal pay for equal labor, protection against sexual harassment, and other important concessions to provide equitable privilege and legal protection in all areas. Black women, on the other hand, felt that they had never had the privilege of staying home and being cloistered, and that neither they or their males had been given a strong voice in the public arena. There were other contrasting issues as well. From the time they were first brought to American shores (1619), black women had worked, had been used and abused, and had been disenfranchised and negated. Their men had been humiliated, damaged, and often lynched during centuries of neglect, lack of access to education, and consequent menial unemployment.

The term *womanism* was coined by Alice Walker, an African-American writer and intellectual. In her 1983 book *In Search of Our Mother's Gardens,* she defined a *womanist* as someone "committed to survival and wholeness of entire people, male *and* female. Not a separatist, except periodically, for health. Traditionally universalist, as in: 'Mama, why are we brown, pink, and yellow, and our cousins are white, beige, and black?' Ans.: 'Well, you know the colored race is just like a flower garden, with every color flower represented'" (xi). She added: "Womanist is to feminist as purple is to lavender" (xii).

This is not a new perspective among African-American intellectuals. Patricia Hill Collins, in *Black Feminist Thought: Knowledge, Consciousness, and the Politics of Empowerment* (1990), quotes a speech made in 1893 by Anna Julia Cooper:

> We take our stand on the solidarity of humanity, the oneness of life, and the unnaturalness and injustice of all special favoritisms, whether of sex, race, country, or condition. . . . The colored woman feels that women's cause is one and universal; and that . . . not till race, color, sex, and condition are seen as accidents, and not the substance of life; not till the universal title of humanity to life, liberty, and the pursuit of happiness is conceded to be inalienable to all; not till then is woman's lesson taught and woman's cause won—not the white woman's nor the black woman's, not the red woman's but the cause of every man and of every woman who has writhed silently under a might wrong. (37)

Collins also states: "Whether we advocate working through separate Black women's organizations, becoming part of women's organizations, working within existing political structures, or supporting Black community institutions, African-American women intellectuals repeatedly identify political actions such as these as a *means* for human empowerment rather than ends in and of themselves" (37).

FURTHER READING

Collins, Patricia Hill. *Black Feminist Thought: Knowledge, Consciousness and the Politics of Empowerment.* New York: Routledge, Chapman and Hall, 1990.

Cooper, Anna Julia. "Speech to Women." In *Black Women in Nineteenth-Century American Life,* edited by Bert J. Lowenberg and Ruth Bogin, 330–331. University Park: Pennsylvania State University Press, 1976.

Walker, Alice. *In Search of Our Mother's Gardens.* Orlando, Fla.: Harcourt Brace Jovanovich, 1983.

Young, Lester (1909–1959) Maya Angelou greatly enjoyed the music of Lester Young. She often listened to it when she worked at the Melrose Record Shop on Fillmore Street in SAN FRANCISCO, CALIFORNIA. A great and widely recognized tenor saxophone player, Young—born in Woodville, Mississippi, on August 27, 1909—was sometimes called a musician's musician. He was nicknamed "Prez" by JAZZ vocalist BILLIE HOLIDAY, which she explained stood for "President of the Saxophone." He was particularly famous for playing the lead sax with the COUNT BASIE Band during the 1930s, and he was well-known for his recordings with Holiday. It was Young who gave Holiday her nickname, "Lady Day," and also gave her mother the nickname of "Duchess." Young often held the saxophone at unusual angles, and his porkpie hat was copied by many other jazz musicians. He died in New York City on March 15, 1959, at age 49.

FURTHER READING

Gelly, Dave. *Being Prez: The Life and Music of Lester Young.* New York: Oxford University Press, 2007.

Porter, Lewis. *Lester Young.* Ann Arbor: University of Michigan Press, 2005.

Z

zoot suit Maya's brother, Bailey, wore a zoot suit during the time he and Maya lived in SAN FRANCISCO, CALIFORNIA, with their mother after moving there from STAMPS, ARKANSAS, in 1941. Particularly popular in the 1940s, but first emerging in the late 1930s, the zoot suit (occasionally spelled *zuit suit*) was a two-piece man's suit with trousers that had a high waist, wide legs, and a tightly cuffed pegged leg. The jacket was long, nipped in at the waist, and had both wide lapels and wide, padded shoulders. This was a style mostly adapted and made popular by African Americans, Mexican Americans, Puerto Ricans, Italian Americans, and Filipino Americans. Sometimes zoot suiters wore a felt hat decorated with a long feather, a dangling watch chain, and pointy shoes. The clothing was controversial because of the excessive material and careful tailoring it took to produce a suit. Because of the war effort, it was considered a waste of time and materials.

FURTHER READING

Quarles, Benjamin. *The Negro in the Making of America.* 3rd ed. New York: Touchstone, 1996.

PART IV

Appendixes

Chronology of Maya Angelou's Life

1928

Maya Angelou (Marguerite Ann Johnson) was born on April 4, 1928, in St. Louis, Missouri, the second child of Bailey Johnson, Sr., a doorman and Navy dietician, and Vivian Baxter Johnson, a licensed real estate agent, trained nurse, and merchant marine. Her older brother, Bailey Johnson, Jr., was credited with giving her the name of Maya. When they were very young, he called her "My Sister." It has been suggested, though not verified, that he encountered the Mayan culture in his reading and renamed his sister Maya.

1931

Because of their parents' divorce, Maya and Bailey were sent to Stamps, Arkansas, to live with their paternal grandmother, Annie (Momma) Johnson Henderson, and her son, their Uncle Willie. Unescorted, they rode the train from Long Beach, California, to Stamps, Arkansas. Reportedly, Maya was three and Bailey was four. The children wore identifying name tags, and their grandmother met them in Stamps. Later, in *Wouldn't Take Nothing for My Journey Now*, Maya wrote:

> One of my earliest memories of Mamma [Momma], of my grandmother, is a glimpse of a tall cinnamon-colored woman with a deep, soft voice, standing thousands of feet up in the air on nothing visible. That incredible vision was the result of what my imagination would do each time Mamma drew herself up to her full six feet, clasped her hands behind her back, looked up into the distant sky and said "I will step out on the word of God." (1993, 73–74)

Maya and Bailey were loved and carefully looked after by their Grandmother Henderson.

1935

In summer 1935, Bailey Johnson, Sr., arrived unexpectedly at Momma's general store in Stamps, Arkansas. He was very handsome, visited for a while, and then took Maya and Bailey, Jr., to St. Louis for an extended visit with their mother. It was a difficult adjustment for Maya, who was content to stay with her grandmother, but Bailey was excited to be with his mother, whom he adored. The children had known only a frugal, rural life. Their mother took them to ethnic restaurants in St. Louis and to the bars where she worked, and she introduced them to convenience foods (thinly sliced ham and treats like jelly beans and peanuts mixed) and various board games. In the bars where their mother worked as a gambler, the children learned to perform the Time Step, a basic dance step, and Maya discovered that she loved to dance. The children thoroughly enjoyed the excitement and variety of urban living.

1936

Maya and Bailey attended school a full year in St. Louis. In late spring 1936 (though the date is somewhat uncertain), when she was eight, Maya was brutally raped by her mother's boyfriend, Mr. Freeman, who was a foreman at the Southern Pacific railroad yards in St. Louis.

Maya had been left alone with him one morning, and unknown to anyone but her, he had touched her intimately prior to that morning. Freeman told Maya he would kill her beloved brother if she revealed what he had done to her. She felt so ill after the violation that she went to bed, and her mother, a nurse, thought she was sick with the measles. Soon, soiled bedding and underclothing revealed the injury, and Maya finally told Bailey what had happened. Subsequently, there was a court trial, and though Mr. Freeman was found guilty and sentenced to a year and a day in prison, he was jailed for less than a day.

Shortly after his release, he was found dead, apparently been kicked to death in an alley; no one was ever arrested for his murder. When Maya and Bailey heard that Mr. Freeman was dead, Maya slipped into shock and imagined that her words had condemned the man to a brutal death. She reacted to the trauma with self-imposed muteness. (Years later, she explained later that she thought that if she spoke, it might condemn someone else to death.)

Though her mother wanted to keep her children close to her, it was decided that Maya and Bailey should be returned to Stamps, Arkansas, to live with Momma Johnson and Uncle Willie. Bailey, who was devoted to his mother and called her "Mother Dear," was upset by the move, but he knew he needed to take care of Maya. He was the only person she talked to for many years. Bailey, an intelligent and caring child, continued to be protective of Maya. During the time of silence, Maya read and memorized many passages of prose and poetry. "And in her silence she became—and remains—an intense listener and observer, attuned to words spoken and things unsaid" (Gillespie, Butler, and Long 2008, 23).

1937–1939

Mrs. Bertha Flowers, a teacher and a gentle woman, lived in Stamps and was both a customer and friend of Grandmother Henderson. Mrs. Flowers learned of the silent child and carefully established a trust with the still-traumatized Maya. She invited Maya into her immaculate home, where she treated the child like an honored guest with freshly baked cookies and cold lemonade. She began what they called "lessons in living" (Angelou 2004, 79) and initiated their literary journey with a reading from *A Tale of Two Cities* to Maya. Over time and with careful tutoring, Mrs. Flowers pulled Maya into a world of literature and mother wit, encouraging her to listen to the finest writers of the world as well as the wisdom of country people's homely sayings. Maya absorbed Mrs. Flowers's lessons, and as she was coaxed to memorize and recite the work of the great poets and writers, she slowly regained her voice.

1940–1941

Maya graduated from eighth grade with honors from Lafayette County Training School in Stamps. It was decided that she and Bailey should be returned to their mother, who had moved to California. They were bright children, and the family thought they would receive a better education and have more opportunity for success there than in Stamps. Further, Bailey was so outspoken that there was fear among the family that someone might hurt him in the South's segregated and violent atmosphere. Grandmother Henderson escorted Maya to California, and Bailey followed about a month later. After several weeks of adjusting to California with their grandmother in a temporary apartment in Los Angeles, the children were picked up by their mother and driven to Oakland, near San Francisco, where Vivian lived with her mother and brothers.

1941

Their mother remarried, and she and her husband, Clidell Jackson, known to the children as Daddy Clidell, purchased a large boardinghouse in the Fillmore District of San Francisco. Maya and Bailey moved there with them and were enrolled in school. Jackson was good to the children and was a stable father figure. Vivian's boardinghouse was a lively place. There was music, dancing in the living room, and people coming and going. It was a welcoming atmosphere for Maya and Bailey. Maya was sent to a private day school for girls near their home. The United States entered World War II in December 1941, and though Maya was young and safe, she felt deep anxiety about the violence of war.

1942

Maya did well at the girls' school, but she was not comfortable with the students there. She was soon transferred to George Washington High School, located about 60 blocks from the neighborhood where she lived. It was in a white residential district, and soon she was given a scholarship to the California Labor School to attend night classes in dance, drama, and pantomime. She was treated with respect at both schools and came to realize that she had a good mind.

1943

In the summer, Maya visited her father in San Diego. He took her on a trip to Ensenada, Mexico, with a plan of buying food supplies for his home. He partied with friends there and passed out in the backseat of the car. Maya was 15 and had never driven, but she drove them back to the border. Staying with him in San Diego did not work out because of a jealous girlfriend, so she ran away. For a month or so before returning to her mother in San Francisco, she lived in a junkyard car and survived by associating with a multicultural and fairly well-organized group of homeless teens.

1944

For about one semester, Maya became the first black conductor on the San Francisco trolley car system. She graduated from Mission High School in San Francisco at 16, and just after graduation, her son and only child, Clyde Bailey Johnson (later called Guy), was born.

1944–1947

Sixteen years old with a two-month-old child, Maya both wanted and needed to live independent of her mother and stepfather. She wanted to find a room of her own and take care of Clyde as well. Welfare support was never a consideration in her mind. Her first real job was as a cook at a Creole restaurant. She did not know how to prepare the food, but her mother's cook instructed her, and she became financially independent. She had a short-lived relationship with a handsome customer she met at the restaurant. He told her at the beginning of their relationship that he was committed to another woman, and soon he left her. Maya was brokenhearted afterward, lost weight, and stopped taking good care of herself.

After Maya turned 18, Bailey counseled her to make a change and move to another city. She and baby Clyde relocated to San Diego, where she found a babysitter named Mother Cleo and took a job as a waitress at the Hi Hat Club. In time, she met a lesbian couple there, and after they revealed their source of income as prostitution, she became their pimp. When that became dangerous, she quickly took the baby and left San Diego for Stamps, Arkansas, to visit Grandmother Henderson. Maya was then 19, and baby Clyde was about two.

Momma loved and enjoyed baby Clyde, but the visit did not last long. The South was still deeply segregated, and Maya had become accustomed to a different, much more open and integrated environment in San Diego. After some weeks in Stamps, Momma felt that Maya's behavior with whites had put not only Maya but possibly the whole family in danger, and she demanded that her granddaughter leave town. Her grandmother and uncle put Maya, the baby, and all of their luggage in a horse-drawn wagon driven by a friend named Brother Wilson, who took her to Lewisville (spelled as Louisville in the book), about five miles west of Stamps. Maya soon returned to San Francisco, where she and Clyde moved in with her mother.

Maya took a job as a short-order cook and found an excellent record shop across from the restaurant where she worked. Hating the job, she decided that she would join the U.S. Army and become an officer. She thought that the military would provide a trade, and the GI Bill would enable her to buy a home and get an education afterward. As it turned out, her application was turned down because of suspected communist links to the California Labor School, which she had attended during her high school years.

1947–1948

Maya lived at home with her mother and worked as a swing-shift waitress at a restaurant called the Chicken Shack. For a brief period of time, she was the dance partner of R. L. Poole; their performance name was Poole and Rita.

1948–1949

During these years, Maya met a customer at the Chicken Shack who was actually a pimp. He courted and deluded her, and she ended up working for him for a short time as a prostitute in Stockton, California. Again, Bailey rescued her, and she and her child returned to San Francisco. While employed at the Melrose Record Shop on Fillmore, Maya met Enistasious "Tosh" Angelos, a white Greek-American and sailor who was seriously interested in black music. He had hopes of becoming a professional musician. He loved both Maya and her son and told her that he wanted to marry her. Marriage between the races in the United States at this point of the 20th century was generally not acceptable. It was illegal in some states and rarely accepted by white or black communities. But Maya was looking for security for her son and herself, so she decided to accept Tosh's proposal. She considered him to be a Greek rather than a typical white American. Maya and Tosh were married at the San Francisco City Hall in 1949, and they set up housekeeping in San Francisco.

1949–1952

During this time, Maya won a scholarship to study dancing with Pearl Primus, a great New York dancer and teacher who was combining African dance with African-American styles. Tosh approved of her study there, so Clyde and Maya went to New York for about a year. They stayed with musicians Tosh knew, and soon he joined them. When her course of study was finished, they moved back to San Francisco. Tosh worked as an appliance salesman, and Maya became a full-time homemaker. He was a good parent to Clyde and a devoted husband to her for some time, but because of religious, racial, and power struggles, the marriage ended in divorce in 1952 after two years. By this time, Maya was 25 and Clyde was 9. Though Bailey had supported the marriage, her mother had not because of the racial issue. After the divorce in 1952, Maya began to pursue her career in performance in earnest.

1952

Maya had a variety of jobs in the San Francisco area, and for a few months she worked at the Garden of Allah as a dancer and B-girl (she visited with customers and got a percentage of their liquor bill). In a 1974 interview with Stephanie Caruna, Angelou said:

> My costume consisted of two sequins and a feather. . . . I danced fifteen minutes of every hour, six times a night. The other ladies would go out and strip, and the band would play, "Tea for Two," or something like that, because the women weren't into what they were doing, and the band was bored with all that grind, grind, grind. But I was a dancer and I loved it. Each time they *played* for me—all sorts of wonderful things like "Caravan." And we had a fabulous time. (quoted in Caruna 1989, 52–53)

1955

Maya's reputation as an excellent dancer at the Garden of Allah began to spread, and one evening a group of singers, dancers, and musicians from the Purple Onion went to the Garden to watch her perform. (The Purple Onion in San Francisco was a club noted for giving starts to many famous stars of show business, including Phyllis Diller.) At a house party with this same group soon after that first evening, Maya sang and danced to the calypso song "Run Joe." They were not sure about calypso music and dance until that moment, and they were very impressed with her performance. The group of new friends helped her become one of the acts at the Purple Onion. She soon adopted the stage name of Maya Angelou and began to seriously pursue a professional dancing and singing career. She became a popular and sought-after performer.

Through connections, professional recognition, and critical praise, Maya went to New York City to audition for an Off-Broadway play (*House of Flowers* by Truman Capote), starring Pearl Bailey, and she also auditioned for a European tour of George Gershwin's *Porgy and Bess.* Offered contracts after both auditions, Maya chose to tour with *Porgy and Bess,* sponsored by the U.S. State Department. While she was abroad, Maya met James Baldwin for the first time in Paris, and over time they became good friends. During the tour, she also taught modern dance at the Habima Theatre in Tel Aviv, Israel, and at the Rome Opera House in Italy. Her mother, who still lived in San Francisco, took care of Clyde who, by the time she returned to the States, was around 11 years old.

1955–1957

Maya went back to the United States before the tour was completed because her mother's circumstances had changed and Clyde was having serious skin problems. Clyde recovered his health quickly after her return, and she promised she would take him along on her performance commitments thereafter. Soon, she and Clyde traveled to Hawaii, and after a gig there, she continued to perform at clubs on the West Coast. When she traveled out of town, Clyde always accompanied her. During this time, she also wrote song and lyrics and recorded six songs for Liberty Records.

For about a year, Maya and Clyde lived in a commune in Sausalito, but they found it uncomfortable and needed more privacy. It was during this time that Clyde announced he would be like to be called Guy, permanently. His mother had changed her name, so he felt that he could do the same. Maya accepted his request, as did other family members. Also during this period, John Killens, a black writer from New York, had traveled to Los Angeles to write a screenplay for his book *Youngblood.* Killens read some of Maya's work, and he strongly encouraged her to develop her writing talent. Killens suggested that Maya relocate to New York City, where she could improve her writing by joining the Harlem Writers Guild.

In 1957, Maya made her first film when she performed in the Hollywood musical *Calypso Heatwave.* She appeared as herself, a star performer who sang "Run Joe." She had continued to work at mastering calypso dancing, and her talent was broadly recognized and acclaimed.

1958

With the help of the John Killens family, Maya and Clyde relocated to the Brooklyn area of New York City. Maya went ahead of her son, found an apartment, and then he joined her. They both adjusted well to the change and felt comfortable there.

1959–1960

Maya became a participant in the Harlem Writers Guild, where new writing efforts by the black members were read and critiqued. Her talent was immediately recognized, but the criticism was hard for her to accept at first. Soon she realized the benefit of more experienced voices, and she continued in the guild. She made many lasting friendships there, including Rosa Guy, Paule Marshall, and Julian Mayfield.

In 1960, an early period in the civil rights efforts, Martin Luther King, Jr., conducted a challenging rally at a church in Harlem to inform people about the continuing inequality in the South. He needed people to get involved and work for change. Maya attended the speeches with her friend Godfrey Cambridge, and after the talks they heard there, Cambridge and Maya developed a fund-raising scheme. In 1960, they wrote, produced, and performed in *Cabaret for Freedom,* a musical revue presented at a theater in Greenwich Village. It was put on to raise funds for the Civil Rights movement and Martin Luther King, Jr.'s Southern Christian Leadership Conference (SCLC). There was a full house for every performance.

Because of the success of *Cabaret for Freedom,* Maya's organizational skills were recognized, and King invited her to serve as northern coordinator for the SCLC. She doubted her skills for management, but she was given support and succeeded at the work. She did so well that King showed up at the office unannounced one day and had a get-acquainted visit with her. During the time she worked in the SCLC office, she became engaged to a bail bondsman named Thomas Allen. He was fairly successful at his work and a kind, stable individual, but he was not interested in politics or any kind of activism. Maya knew that if she married him, she would be isolated and no longer involved in the work she loved. Things changed unexpectedly in Maya's life, and she broke the engagement before the wedding ceremony.

1960

Maya met a South African freedom fighter, Vusumzi Make (called Vus), at a house party in New York City. After a whirlwind romance, she traveled to London with him for a conference he needed to attend. Afterward, he had other countries to visit, so he gave Maya money and instructed her to return to New York City to find and furnish an upscale apartment. When he returned after his travels, the three of them (Maya, Vus, and Guy) lived in a spacious Manhattan apartment. Make did not like Maya's furniture choices, so he went to expensive furniture stores himself and bought what he wanted. Maya soon found that she was trapped as a housewife inside the luxuriously appointed apartment. Vus did not want her to work, and his standards for the upkeep of their home were unrealistically demanding.

1961

Max Roach and his future wife, Abbey Lincoln Roach, were professional performers and close friends of Maya's. Maya had met Abbey in Los Angeles when they both lived there. They asked her to look over *The Blacks,* a play by Jean Genet. Though Maya disliked the script, Vus encouraged her to accept a role in it, and she played the White Queen. The cast included many well-known stars, including Godfrey Cambridge, James Earl Jones, Roscoe Lee Brown, Cicely Tyson, Louis Gossett, Jr., and others. The play was performed Off-Broadway at the St. Mark's Playhouse, and it was a success.

Vus and Maya had been living together less than a year, and he decided to move back to Africa and take Maya and Guy with him. He had a position in Cairo, where he would be a representative of the South African United Front. Maya suspected he was not being faithful to her, and he was also failing to pay their bills. They were evicted from the luxury apartment and stayed in a budget flat for a few weeks before moving to Africa. Guy was 16 and quickly made a circle of friends in Cairo. He and his mother competed to see who would learn the language first, and they both made quick and successful adjustments to their new home in Egypt.

1962

Maya, Guy, and Vus made their home in another beautiful apartment with deluxe furnishings in a choice area of Cairo. Maya soon learned that, once again, Vus was not making the payments on the furniture or paying the rent. She needed a secure place to live for Guy and herself, and she also needed to pay tuition for her son's education. She turned to a journalist friend, David DuBois, and he helped her find work. She became an associate editor at the newly founded magazine the *Arab Observer* (an English-language newsweekly). This was an all-new experience for Maya, as she stated:

> I got the Africa Desk-Politics. It was really interesting, because I was, at once, a female, non-Muslim, non-Arab, American, Black, and six feet tall. All I needed was that I should be Jewish! It was a shock to the community. It was really terrifying that each time I spoke, each time the magazine came out, there was the question of: Was that my point of view, or was I speaking for my husband? . . . All the other journalists were male and the idea of having a woman even work there, let alone a woman as boss, was ridiculous. But we worked it out. (quoted in Rich, 78)

While Maya worked as an associate editor of the *Arab Observer,* her relationship with Vus was deteriorating because of his infidelity and undependable money management. Maya made friends with some women in Cairo, but by the end of the year, she could see no reason to stay in Cairo. Guy graduated from high school and wanted to attend college at the University of Ghana at Accra. Maya was offered a job that appealed to her in Liberia at the Department of Information. The new plan was to take Guy to Ghana, settle him at the university in Accra, and then move on to Liberia.

1963–1964

Relocated to Accra, Ghana, Maya (34) and Guy (18) were just there a few days before Guy was seriously injured in a car accident. She was told that his convalescence would take at least two months. Though she had planned to take a job in Liberia, Guy's convalescence required that she find work in Accra. Both of them were made to feel welcome in part by friendly black American expatriates such as Julian and Ana Livia Mayfield. New friends helped her find work as an assistant administrator at the School of Music and Drama, University of Ghana, and before long Maya was also employed by the Ghanian Broadcast Corporation and the *Ghanian Times* newspaper. While she lived in Accra, she appeared in Bertolt Brecht's play *Mother Courage* at the National Theatre in Ghana.

In 1964, Malcolm X visited Ghana to try to persuade dignitaries there to support his appeal to the United Nations in behalf of African Americans. Maya helped him by planning his itinerary while he was in Ghana, and they maintained regular correspondence after he returned to the United States.

1965

Upon returning to the United States, Angelou had planned to work with Malcolm X in the Civil Rights movement. He was working on enlarging the Organization for African American Unity (OAAU) and hoped that she would become the organization's coordinator. After leaving Ghana and arriving in New York, Maya decided that she needed to see her mother and brother in California before beginning her work with the OAAU. She flew west, planning to return to New York, but Malcolm X's sudden and shocking assassination left her temporarily without direction. She stayed in California and worked for a period of time as a survey taker in the Watts neighborhood of Los Angeles, just before the tragic riots in that area in August.

1966–1967

Angelou became a lecturer at the University of California, Los Angeles, and she also played a minor role in Jean Anouilh's play *Medea,* starring her neighbor, Beah Richards. She also wrote a two-act drama, *The Least of These,* which was first produced in Los Angeles. She wrote two other plays during this time this time in California: a two-act drama called *The Clawing Within* and another play called *Adjoa Amissah.* Neither of these plays have been presented to the public. During most of this time, Guy was a student at the University of Ghana in Accra. Just before Maya left for New York, Guy returned to California from Ghana and was in another serious automobile accident. She waited until he was out of the hospital and in no danger, and then her mother, a nurse, undertook the remainder of Guy's convalescence, and Maya was able to return to the East Coast.

1968

While living in New York, Maya was invited to write, produce, and narrate a 10-part National Educational Television series in San Francisco on African traditions in American life; it was called *Blacks, Blues, Blacks.* While preparing dinner for guests in celebration of her 40th birthday on April 4, 1968, she learned that Martin Luther King, Jr.., had been assassinated in Memphis, Tennessee. This was a great shock to her, and she isolated herself to mourn. She slipped into a depression, and James Baldwin who had become a close friend, came to her rescue. He talked her out of her depression and invited her to a dinner party at Jules and Judy Feiffer's home.

After enjoying her stories, Baldwin and the Feiffers encouraged Maya to write an autobiography. They contacted Robert Loomis at Random House in her behalf. Maya resisted the idea at first, but when she finished *Blacks, Blues, Blacks.* (which she also narrated), she began to write her life story. During this time she also performed a song for the film *For Love of Ivy.*

1969

The Poetry of Maya Angelou, with Angelou performing the poems, was recorded on GWP records. This same year she began writing *I Know Why the Caged Bird Sings,* which was copyrighted in 1969 and published in 1970. The book was an immediate best seller.

1970

I Know Why the Caged Bird Sings, which narrates the story of Maya's first 16 years, was published in January. It was nominated for the National Book Award, and Maya was also appointed writer in residence at the University of Kansas and awarded a Yale University Fellowship. The book is still in print and continues to be assigned reading in many colleges and universities. It is a book of survival and affirmation.

1971–1972

Angelou published a collection of poems called *Just Give Me a Cool Drink of Water 'fore I Diiie.* Many of the poems included in this volume were recorded by GWP records in 1969, and the collection was nominated for a Pulitzer Prize. Angelou also wrote the screenplay *Georgia, Georgia* for Independent-Cinerama during this time, and she was the first African-American woman to have an original script produced and filmed. It was made in Sweden, but Maya was not allowed to direct it. In 1972, she also appeared on television as a narrator, interviewer, and hosted several African-American special presentations.

1973

Maya married the British builder and architect Paul Du Feu, and they made their home in California. The marriage ended in divorce eight years later. She made her Broadway debut with a performance in the play *Look Away,* for which she was nominated to receive the Tony Award.

1974

Maya Angelou directed the film *All Day Long* and published the second of her autobiographies, *Gather Together in My Name.* She also wrote an adaptation of Sophocles' *Ajax,* which was performed in Los Angeles at the Mark Taper forum. She became a Distinguished Visiting Professor at Wake Forest University, Wichita State University, and California State University, Sacramento.

1975

Angelou published her second collection of poems, *Oh Pray My Wings Are Gonna Fit Me Well.* She was awarded the Rockefeller Foundation Fellowship in Italy, and she received honorary degrees from Smith and Mills Colleges. Angelou recorded *An Evening with Maya Angelou* for the Pacific Tape Library. This same year, she was appointed to the board of trustees of the American Film Institute. In addition, President Gerald R. Ford appointed her to the American Revolution Bicentennial Council.

1976

Angelou published the third book of her serial autobiographies, *Singin' and Swingin' and Gettin' Merry Like Christmas.* She also wrote two African-American television specials, *The Inheritors* and *The Legacy.* She was awarded an honorary degree from Lawrence University and received the *Ladies' Home Journal* Woman of the Year Award. In addition, she wrote the play *And Still I Rise,* which was performed at the Ensemble Theatre in Oakland, California.

1977

Angelou earned an Emmy nomination for her role as Kunta Kinte's grandmother, Nyo Boto, in the television miniseries *Roots,* based on the book by Alex Haley. She also appeared in a Richard Pryor television special as an actor. President Jimmy Carter appointed Angelou to the National Commission on the Observance of International Women's Year, and she received the coveted Golden Eagle award from the Public Broadcasting System for her documentary series *Afro-Americans in the Arts.*

1978

Maya Angelou published her third book of poetry, *And Still I Rise,* which she dedicated to close friends: "This book is dedicated to a few of the Good Guys. You to laugh with / You to cry to / I can just about make it over: Jessica Mitford, Gerald W. Purcell, and Jay Allen." She also published a small book entitled *Phenomenal Woman: Four Poems Celebrating Women,* which is dedicated to the memory of her mother, Vivian Baxter, "the most phenomenal."

1979

Angelou wrote screenplays for the television movies *I Know Why the Caged Bird Sings* and *Sister, Sister.*

1981–1982

The marriage of Angelou and Paul Du Feu ended in divorce. Angelou published the fourth book in her serial autobiographies, *The Heart of a*

Woman. Angelou received a lifetime appointment as Reynolds Professor of American Studies, Wake Forest University, North Carolina, and settled there as her permanent home. She teaches in the humanities, and thoroughly enjoys her students, mostly focusing on what it means to be a member of the human family. She was also invited to appear on television as an actor on *The Richard Pryor Special* in 1982.

1983

Angelou published a collection of poetry called *Shaker, Why Don't You Sing?,* and she was honored with the Matrix Award given by Women in Communications, Inc.

1984–1985

In addition to her frequent talks, presentations, and prolific writing, as well as receiving numerous honorary degrees, Angelou continued to teach at Wake Forest University.

1986

Angelou published her fifth autobiography, *All God's Children Need Traveling Shoes,* a rich account of her years in Ghana. She also published *Mrs. Flowers: A Moment of Friendship* and *Poems,* a collection of her previous volumes of poetry: *Just Give Me a Cool Drink of Water 'fore I Diiie, O Pray My Wings Are Gonna Fit Me Well, And Still I Rise,* and *Shaker, Why Don't You Sing?* She was also awarded the Fulbright 40th Anniversary Distinguished Lecturer, Liberia Award.

1987

Angelou published *Now Sheba Sings the Song,* a poem illustrated with sketches by Tom Feelings. She also received the North Carolina Award for Literature. Late in the year, reporter, Carol Sarler interviewed Angelou for an article in the *Sunday Times Magazine,* in which the author is quoted as saying:

> In the afternoon I read—if I'm teaching I read works coming out of the theme of my class and I put on the music to complement the reading. For instance, if I'm doing a course on African culture's impact on the world I will read Basil Davidson's *Last Kingdoms of Africa* and I'll put on tapes of African music, Odetta singing 19th-century slave songs, Mahalia Jackson singing anything—and I turn it up very loud, it's all over my house, that insistence of the music which helps to entrench me into the era. (quoted in Sarler 1987, 50)

1988

Angelou appeared on Bill Moyer's PBS program *The Face of Evil.* She also directed a film of Errol John's *Moon on a Rainbow Shawl* in London. An extremely active 60-year-old woman, she continued meeting with the public at frequent book-signing occasions.

1989

Angelou was listed in *USA Today*'s list of 50 black role models. She appeared in a TV special, *The Price of a Ticket,* with James Baldwin.

1990

Angelou published *I Shall Not Be Moved,* a collection of poems dedicated to Vivian Baxter and Mildred Garris Tuttle. She also received the Candace Award and delivered the Nancy Hanks Lecture for the American Council of the Arts in Washington, D.C. She appeared in the television special *R.A.C.E.* and the televised 22nd Annual NAACP Image Awards.

1991

Angelou received the Langston Hughes Medal and also appeared as an actor in a television special about Jacqueline Kennedy Onassis, the former First Lady.

1992

Angelou performed as an actor in television specials called *Who Cares about the Kids?* and *Kindred Spirits: Contemporary African American Artists.* She also took part in the Essence Awards, a television special. The Essence Awards pay tribute to the achievements of exceptional African Americans.

1993

Angelou was an actor in the television specials *Changing of the Guard—a Pre-Inaugural Special* and *The Alistair Cooke Salute*. She read her poem "On the Pulse of Morning" at Bill Clinton's presidential inaguration in Washington, D.C.; the poem was written at his request. Angelou published *Wouldn't Take Nothing for My Journey Now,* a collection of memoir essays; and *Life Doesn't Frighten Me,* a children's book. She also won the Grammy Award for best spoken-word album, and she performed as the character June, with Janet Jackson and Tupac Shakur, in John Singleton's urban drama *Poetic Justice.* Angelou also played a role in the film *And Still I Rise;* was an actor in *One Child, One Dream: The Horatio Alger Awards,* a television special; and was an actor in *Malcolm X: The Real Story.*

1994

The Complete Collected Poems of Maya Angelou was published by Random House. Angelou also wrote and published a children's book, *My Painted House, My Friendly Chicken, and Me.* She appeared in several television specials: *There Are No Children Here* (in the role of Leila Mae); *Malcolm X: Make it Plain;* a show on the Horatio Alger Awards; as a presenter at the Essence Awards; as an actor in the *Dvorák Concert from Prague—A Celebration;* as herself in *Century of Women;* and in the presentation *The 12 Most Fascinating People of 1993.* She also received the first Medal of Distinction from the University of Hawaii Board of Regents.

1995

In recognition of the popularity of *I Know Why the Caged Bird Sings,* on February 26, a representative of Bantam Books commended Angelou for being the first African American to have the longest-running title (2 years) on the *New York Times* Paperback Nonfiction Best-Seller List. She was interviewed on the David Frost show, and later that same year, on June 26, Angelou read her poem "A Brave and Startling Truth" at the 50th anniversary of the founding of the United Nations in San Francisco; following this, the poem was published. She also read her poem "A Black Woman Speaks to Black Manhood" (also called the "Million Man March Poem") at the Million Man March in Washington, D.C., on October 16. She published *Phenomenal Woman: Four Poems for Women,* and she appeared in the film *How to Make an American Quilt* in the role of Anna. This same year, she narrated the film *The Journey of August King,* appeared as a presenter at the televised Horatio Alger Awards, and appeared as an actor in the television specials: *Generation X: Black Voices of Reason, Rage, and Responsibility;* the *Fourth Annual Environmental Media Awards;* and the *Concert of the Americas.*

1996

Angelou published the children's book, *Kofi and His Magic;* received the Martin Luther King, Jr., Legacy Association National Award; and served as an ambassador for UNICEF International. She appeared in the following television shows and special presentations: *Touched By an Angel,* as Clarice Mitchell; *Maya Angelou Talking with David Frost; Gospel According to Jesus; Ark of the Spirit with Avery Brooks; American Dreamers;* and *American Dream.*

1997

Angelou's book *The Heart of a Woman* (1981) was recognized as *USA Today's* "Best-Selling Book." She published *Even the Stars Look Lonesome,* a collection of essays, and she also performed as narrator in the film *Perfect Moment.* Her television appearances included: *Images of Life: Photographs That Changed the World; How Do You Spell God;* and *Elmo Saves Christmas.* This year she also appeared at a pajama party on *The Oprah Winfrey Show.*

1998

Angelou directed the drama *Down in the Delta,* produced by Miramax. She appeared on television in *Quincy Jones—The First 50 Years, Porgy and Bess: An American Voice,* and *Century of Women.*

1999

Angelou was recognized by *Writer's Digest* as one of the 100 best writers of the 20th century. She was also presented with the Lifetime Achievement Award for Literature. She appeared on television as a narrator for *Madagascar: A World Apart;* as an interviewee in *Intimate Portrait: Maya Angelou;* as a narrator of *Dare to Compete:*

The Struggle of Women in Sports; as a presenter at the 30th NAACP Image Awards; and as an actor in the 1999 Special Olympics—World Summer Games.

2000

Angelou signed a contract with Hallmark Cards to help create "The Maya Angelou Collection from Hallmark." The products are an assortment of greeting cards and specialty gifts, including frames with sentiments, vases, mugs, journals, and other items. Though some critics have decried the collection as inspirational kitsch, Angelou expressed a hope that her message of loving and positive perseverance would reach many more people through this medium.

Angelou also published a new edition of *Phenomenal Woman: Four Poems Celebrating Women;* it was edited by Linda Sunshine and illustrated using paintings by the 19-century French impressionist Paul Gauguin. She was presented with the National Medal of Arts and appeared on television in *Rip Van Winkle: An Animated Special from the "Happily Ever After: Fairy Tales For Every Child" Series* as a voice; as an interviewee on *Phyllis Diller: First Lady of Laughter;* as an interviewee on *Oprah Winfrey: Heart of the Matter;* as herself in *Moesha;* and as an actor on *Great American History Quiz: Pursuit of Happiness* and *Great American History Quiz: Heroes and Villains.*

2001

Angelou appeared in the television specials *Jessye Norman Sings for the Healing of AIDS* and in the role of a conjure women in the television movie *Runaway.*

2002

Angelou published the sixth and last of her serial autobiographies: *A Song Flung Up to Heaven.* She won a Grammy Award for her recording of this book. She was interviewed four times on television: *We Are Not Vanishing; Roots—Celebrating 25 Years: The Saga of an American Classic; Quincy Jones: In the Pocket;* and *Billy Holiday: Sensational Lady.* She also acted in the television special *American Responds: A National Celebration.*

2004

I Know Why the Caged Bird Sings: The Collected Autobiographies of Maya Angelou was published by Random House. Angelou also played herself in the television special *America beyond the Color Line.*

2005

Angelou published *Amazing Peace: A Celebration.* She read the poem "Amazing Peace" at the lighting of the National Christmas Tree, Washington, D.C., on December 1, 2005.

2006

Angelou became a weekly radio talk show host for XM Satellite Radio on the Oprah & Friends station. She also published *Mother: A Cradle to Hold Me* and published *Celebrations: Rituals of Peace and Prayer. Celebrations* is dedicated to Brandon Bailey Johnson, Caylin Nichole Johnson, Elliott Jones, and Lydia Stuckey. It contains poems written for particular celebrations and includes: "On the Pulse of Morning," "A Brave and Startling Truth," "Continue," "Sons and Daughters," "When Great Trees Fall," "A Black Woman Speaks to Black Manhood," "Amazing Peace," "Mother: A Cradle to Hold Me," "In and Out of Time," "Ben Lear's Bar Mitzvah," "Vigil," and "Prayer." Angelou also received the Mother Teresa Award and appeared in Tyler Perry's film *Madea's Family Reunion,* playing the role of May. Her 2005 poem "Amazing Peace" (published in book form as *Amazing Peace: A Celebration*) won the Quill Award for poetry. Angelou also appeared on television twice as an honoree at *Oprah Winfrey's Legends' Ball* and as an interviewee on *Iconoclasts.*

2007

Angelou narrated the film *As Seen through These Eyes* and was given the Martha Parker Legacy Award.

2008

Angelou became the first recipient of The Hope for Peace and Justice Voice of Peace Award. She was inducted into the International Civil Rights Walk of Fame at the Martin Luther King, Jr.,

National Historic Site, and she received both the Gracie Allen Award and the Cornell Medallion. She published *Letter to My Daughter,* a collection of essays dedicated to women who played different roles in her life, writing: "My thanks to some women who mothered me through dark and bright days, Annie Henderson, Vivian Baxter, Frances Williams, Berdis Baldwin, Amisher Glenn; My thanks to one woman who allows me to be a daughter to her, even today, Dr. Dorothy Height; My thanks to women not born to me but who allow me to mother them, Oprah Winfrey, Rosa Johnson Butler, Lydia Stuckey, Gayle B. King, Valerie Simpson, Stephenie Floyd Johnson, Dinky Weber, Brenda Crisp, Bettie Clay, Araba Bernasko, Frances Berry." Angelou also wrote the poetry for and narrated the M. K. Asante, Jr., film entitled *The Black Candle.* She wrote the televised *Live from Lincoln Center Jazz at Lincoln Center Red at Holiday Stomp,* played the role of herself in *African American Lives 2,* and was an interviewee on *Joe Louis: America's Hero . . . Betrayed.*

2009

Angelou appeared in Chris Rock's film *Good Hair* as herself. She also appeared on *Dateline NBC* as an interviewee. Angelou wrote a poem called "We Had Him," read by Queen Latifah, for entertainer Michael Jackson's memorial service on July 7, 2009.

2010–2011

Maya Angelou is still teaching occasionally at Wake Forest University, giving benefit talks, and cooking for friends and family. In a 1974 interview with Stephanie Caruna, as they were talking about life, she expressed how she felt about the end of her life on earth. She said:

> I'm here for you to use. Life! When it's through with me, I hope to be through with it. I'll tip my hat, and split. . . . But in that way, I disagree with Dylan Thomas and what he said in his poem, "Do not go gentle into that good night. . . ." When life is through with me, I want to say to it as you would say to a lover, or a friend, or a child: "Goodbye! It's been a ball . . . truly. And thank you." (Caruna 1974, 37)

Angelou was 83 on April 4, 2011, and she is still joyfully letting life use her. All who read her work have been enriched by her understanding and profound teaching of what it means to be human. She recently published her second cookbook, *Great Food, All Day Long: Cook Splendidly, Eat Smart,* a collection of recipes and autobiographical sketches.

FURTHER READING

Angelou, Maya. *The Collected Autobiographies of Maya Angelou.* New York: Modern Library Edition by Random House, 2004.

———. *Wouldn't Take Nothing for My Journey Now.* Toronto, Ontario: Random House of Canada, 1993.

Caruna, Stephanie. "Maya Angelou: An Interview." Reprinted in *Conversations with Maya Angelou,* edited by Jeffrey M. Elliot, 29–37. Jackson and London: University Press of Mississippi, 1989.

Gillespie, Marcia Ann, Rosa Johnson Butler, and Richard A. Long. *Maya Angelou: A Glorious Celebration.* New York: Doubleday, 2008.

Rich, Judith. "Westways Women: Life Is for Living." In *Conversations with Maya Angelou,* edited by Jeffrey M. Elliot, 77–85. Jackson and London: University Press of Mississippi, 1989.

Sarler, Carol. "A Life in the Day of Maya Angelou." *Sunday Times Magazine,* 27 December 1987, 50.

Chronologies of Individual Autobiographies

The individual autobiographies in the series of six cover the period of Maya Angelou's life from 1931 to 1968. The following descriptions provide a selected overview of each year during this time period, and it includes some quotations from the books. Citations in this chronology are taken from *The Collected Autobiographies of Maya Angelou* (New York: Modern Library Edition by Random House, 1994).

I Know Why the Caged Bird Sings (1931–1944)

1931

Three-year-old Maya and four-year-old Bailey, her brother, were shipped from Long Beach, California, to Stamps, Arkansas, by their divorced parents. The children had a safe journey, and when they reached the segregated South, black people on the train, strangers, fed them chicken and potato salad and looked after them as they traveled.

1932

The children quickly adjusted to living with their grandmother, Annie Henderson, and Uncle Willie. They were welcomed "Warmly, but not too familiarly" (10). They lived comfortably with their grandmother and uncle in the rear of their grandmother's general store.

1933–1934

Each year, Maya looked at the fields across from her grandmother's store as the seasons and colors changed. She watched the cotton pickers climb onto big wagons to be taken to the fields to work. Grandmother Henderson—or Momma, as she was called—got up early and opened the store so the people could buy snacks for the day before going to their labor for the day.

Uncle Willie helped train the children in their times tables. Though he would never have hurt them, he now and then made threats to shove them into the red-hot potbellied stove that heated the store if they made too many mistakes in math. As a very young child, Maya began to read the works of William Shakespeare. She said, "He was my first white love" (16). She also read Rudyard Kipling, Edgar Allan Poe, Paul Lawrence Dunbar, and other fine writers.

1935–1936

The children's father arrived in Stamps without any warning. Maya took an immediate dislike for him because he teased and made fun of her and also had a peculiar way of talking. He used "ers" and "errrers" rather erratically. He announced that he was taking the children to St. Louis to live with their mother. Maya was upset and thought, "For all I knew, we were being driven to Hell and our father was the delivering devil" (49).

Their father took them to St. Louis, where they were welcomed into their Grandmother Baxter's home (their mother's mother), but their mother was not at home. She arrived soon, and the children were amazed by her beauty and, most particularly, her red lipstick. Their father left a few days later for California, and

Maya thought, "He was a stranger, and if he chose to leave us with a stranger, it was all of one piece" (50). The children attended school there a full year. Their mother was a professional nurse, but she preferred to work in a bar named Louie's. The children learned to dance the Time Step there and enjoyed soft drinks and boiled shrimp.

Sometime during the late spring or early summer, Maya was brutally raped by her mother's live-in boyfriend, Mr. Freeman. There was a court trial, and the child was deeply traumatized. Freeman was found dead in an alley soon after serving only one day in jail for his crime. Maya, in her child's mind, felt that her words had killed him. Fearful that she might kill someone else in the same way, she ceased talking. She did communicate occasionally with her beloved brother, Bailey. Both children were soon returned to Grandmother Henderson and Uncle Willie in Stamps, Arkansas. She wrote later that as she lived her life, "Mr. Freeman . . . was a nagging passenger in my mind" (193).

1937

After returning to Stamps, Maya remained silent. "I discovered that to achieve perfect personal silence all I had to do was attach myself leechlike to sound. I began to listen to everything" (70). On the other hand, Bailey regaled the local people with stories about "watermelons [in St. Louis] twice the size of a cow's head and sweeter than syrup. . . . And if you can count the watermelon's seeds, before it's cut open, you can win five zillion dollars and a new car" (72).

1937–1939

Mrs. Bertha Flowers, a friend of Maya's grandmother, occasionally purchased things at the general store and befriended Maya. She taught the silent child to recite and patiently coaxed her into talking again. Maya wrote: "She said that I must always be intolerant of ignorance but understanding of illiteracy. . . . She encouraged me to listen carefully to what country people call Mother Wit. That in those homely sayings was couched the collective wisdom of generations" (79). Mrs. Flowers encouraged Maya, gave her excellent classics to read, and brought her back to life with what she and Maya called "my lessons in living" (79).

1939

Maya worked for Mrs. Cullinan, a white woman who treated her poorly. Mrs. Cullinan even had the audacity to suggest that Maya (using the name Margaret) be renamed Mary for Mrs. Cullinan's convenience. Maya hated her and her friends, and she did what she could to get fired. Finally, following Bailey's advice, she broke some of Mrs. Cullinan's favorite china, and that was the end of her job. Mrs. Cullinan yelled at her, called her names, and threw a piece of broken plate at her, but it missed and hit the kitchen maid.

1940

Maya graduated from eighth grade with honors from Lafayette Country Training School in Stamps. At the graduation, the joy of the occasion was nearly spoiled by the speaker, a white politician. He spoke of the professional potential of white students in a nearby school, and he offered little future hope for the black graduates. After he left, the community of adults and children were demoralized; as Maya later wrote, "The man's dead words fell like bricks around the auditorium and too many settled in my belly" (139). However, before the ceremonies were over, a better feeling was restored by the class valedictorian. He had a prepared talk and gave it, but then he turned from the audience to the graduating students sitting behind him and began to sing James Weldon Johnson's poem, set to J. Rosamond Johnson's music, which was "Lift Ev'ry Voice and Sing." "It was the Negro national anthem. Out of habit we were singing it" (142). The group's spirits were lifted, and their calm restored thanks to the young speaker's presence of mind and the support of the parents and students.

1941

After a negative racial encounter with a white dentist while seeking needed help for Maya, and after Bailey saw a bloated black corpse being dragged out of a pond by white men, arrangements were made for the children to rejoin their divorced parents in California. Bailey saw one of the white men look down at the misshapen body and grin disrespectfully, and there were also rude comments. Bailey was puzzled by the horror and was beginning to try to understand "the humorless puzzle of inequality and hate" (154). Grandmother Henderson and Uncle Willie decided it was time to remove the children from this dangerous environment, and soon Maya was traveling on the train to California with her grandmother. Bailey would follow a month later when there was money for his ticket.

1941–1942

Grandmother Henderson and Maya, now 14, first went to Los Angeles where their father lived. In a month, Bailey joined them, and their mother picked them up and drove them to her home in San Francisco. Maya attended a girl's school near their home in the Fillmore neighborhood, but she was soon transferred to the George Washington High School, which was situated in a white neighborhood located some 60 blocks from home. She also received a scholarship to attend night classes in dance, drama, and pantomime at the California Labor School. Maya was treated with respect at both schools, and one teacher she remembered through her life was Miss Kirwin, who "never seemed to notice that I was Black and therefore different" (166).

1943

In the summer, Maya visited her father in San Diego. He lived in a trailer and had a girlfriend named Dolores who was jealous of Maya. Bailey Johnson, Sr., wanted to make a trip to Ensenada, Mexico, for some cooking supplies and told Maya that she would be going with him. He got drunk there and fell asleep in the backseat of the car. Maya, who had never driven a car, drove the stick-shift vehicle to the border, where she had a slight accident. Her father awakened and drove the rest of the way. The relationship between Maya and Dolores was so bad that it ended up with Dolores actually stabbing Maya with a pair of sharp scissors. Her father was visiting a neighbor when it happened, and Maya, injured, ran from the trailer to her father's car, rolled up the windows, and waited for her father to return. He got medical help for her, and the next day, Maya ran away. She lived with homeless teens in a lot for old used cars before returning home, weeks later, to her mother in San Francisco.

Maya decided to get a job, and after intense wrangling, she was hired to be the first black conductor on the San Francisco streetcar line. She was given peculiar shifts, perhaps deliberately because of her color, but she worked rather than attend school for a time. She did return to school in the spring but did not attend regularly. Maya became pregnant after an encounter with a handsome white boy, a neighbor she barely knew. She was experimenting, and three weeks after the one-time encounter, she found herself pregnant.

1944

Maya graduated from the San Francisco Summer School class at Mission High School. About three weeks later, she gave birth to her son, Clyde Bailey Johnson. Her mother and stepfather, Daddy Clidell Jackson, took good care of her, and she stayed with them for a few months after the baby was born.

Gather Together in My Name (1944–1949)

1944–1945

After living at home for the first few months of Clyde's life, Maya decided that she wanted to be independent rather than live in her mother's home. Her first job was as a cafeteria bus girl, and that one lasted only a week. The second job, as a Creole cook at a café, worked for her, though at the time she was hired, she did not know how to prepare Creole food. She asked questions of people who did know the style, and she quickly became an excellent cook of Creole cuisine. She rented a room in a San Francisco Victorian house and bought her first furniture. She found a dependable babysitter and enjoyed her independent life, her privacy, and most of all her baby. Before long she met a male customer named Curly, and though he informed her that he was engaged, she had an affair with him. When it was over, she was brokenhearted, and her brother suggested that she move to a different city. She was going to move to Los Angeles, but after stopping there and visiting with a rather unsupportive extended family, she changed her plan and moved on to San Diego.

1946–1947

Maya found a good babysitter named Mother Cleo, and she quickly got a job as a cocktail waitress at the Hi Hat Club. Mother Cleo and her husband, Mr. Henry, offered her a room for $15 a week, and so Maya was again independent and able to take care of her son. She met two lesbians at the Hi Hat Club who were working as prostitutes and eventually became their pimp. Things began to fall apart with that arrangement, and Maya, thinking she may be caught and arrested, ran away from San Diego and returned to Stamps, Arkansas, for a visit with her grandmother.

1947

Grandmother Henderson enjoyed baby Clyde very much, but Maya had to run away from Stamps as well. She had become accustomed to the more integrated and less prejudiced openness of San Diego, and she offended white shopkeepers in Stamps. Grandmother Henderson, fearing for Maya's safety, put Maya, her baby, and all of her luggage in a horse-drawn wagon and told Maya, "Brother Wilson is coming to drive you to Louisville" (294). (Lewisville, Arkansas, is about five miles west of Stamps.) Maya returned to her mother's home in San Francisco and soon found work as "a short-order cook in a tiny greasy spoon" (295).

Maya quit the job at the greasy spoon and considered joining the U.S. Army. Because she had attended the California Labor School, which had some communist connections, Maya's application for the military was turned down. She was able to get another job as a cook at a restaurant called the Chicken Shack. For a while, she performed in a dance act called "Poole and Rita" (315), but that only lasted until Poole's girlfriend returned.

Maya's mother told her about an opening for a fry cook in Stockton, California. She moved there, found a woman called Big Mary to take care of Clyde, and hoped to meet the man of her dreams. L. D. Tolbrook came into her life as a customer at the restaurant. He was an older man, but he was handsome, suave, and well-dressed. He was a smooth-talking pimp and gambler, and he ran several houses of prostitution not far from Stockton. Feigning fear of retribution from gambling debts, L. D. tricked Maya into becoming a prostitute to help him pay what he owed. Thinking that he was telling the truth, Maya accommodated him. She was using marijuana for her nerves, and he said he did not like that, but he enlisted her anyway.

Bailey's wife died unexpectedly of tuberculosis and pneumonia, and Maya went to San Francisco to see him. She also comforted her mother, who had had surgery and, because of postsurgical complications, was in the same hospital at the time Bailey's wife died. The truth about what Maya was doing in the Stockton region came out, and Bailey told her to get out of the prostitution business immediately. He gave Maya enough money for a round-trip ticket to Stockton to get the baby from Big Mary, pay her, and come back home.

Maya went to get baby Clyde from the babysitter, but the house was closed up and empty. Both Big Mary and Clyde were gone. Maya went to Tolbrook for help and learned immediately that he was married. His attractive wife answered the door, and at last Maya realized that she had been used. The next day, Maya located Clyde in Bakersfield, California. A neighbor who lived near the house where Big Mary babysat knew that Big Mary had a brother in Bakersfield, and she said that was probably where the babysitter had taken Clyde. When Maya found him, he began crying. He was three and she was 19, and she recognized that he was a real person with feelings rather than simply her pretty little doll-baby. He was tenderhearted and had missed her terribly. Maya suddenly realized that her son was not just her "beautiful appendage" (368), and they promptly returned to San Francisco.

1948–1949

Maya took a job as the manager of a restaurant in Oakland. The owner wanted to make the menu more sophisticated, and Maya redesigned it, but that did not work. The customers wanted the soul food they were accustomed to. Maya was then given a job as a driver of boxers who worked out at Lake Merrit, but she became nearly hysterical with fear for the boxers when she saw her first boxing match—so hysterical, in fact, that she lost her job. Maya had met a man named Troubadour at the restaurant. About a week after she was fired, he visited her home and asked Maya if he could use her apartment in Oakland as a place to store clothes he sold, and as a place for women to try them on. Maya knew they were stolen clothes, but she agreed to let him use her place. He was a drug addict, and when he learned that Maya was using marijuana, he took her to a dismal place full of drug-using losers, shot heroin into his own arm in front of her, and passed out. She learned the lesson he wanted her to learn, gathered the clothes he said she could keep, and returned to her mother's home. By this time, she was 21, and she never used illegal substances again.

Singin' and Swingin' and Getting Merry Like Christmas (1949–1957)

1949–1952

When Maya returned to San Francisco, she worked two jobs and frequented the Melrose Record Shop on Fillmore Street. In time, she started working there. She lived in her mother's big house, but she paid rent. Clyde was five, in school, and already reading well. Maya met a white man at the record store. He was a Greek American, had been discharged from the navy, and worked in an electrical appliance shop. He seemed to want to court both Maya and five-year-old Clyde. By spending time with Clyde and taking him places, he became a father figure to him. The three of them went to movies and enjoyed each other's company.

Tosh proposed to Maya, and she accepted, though she was not sure of her love for him. Bailey told her that he could tell that Tosh (Angelos) was in love with her, and he thought that she should marry him. They were married in 1952 at a courthouse in San Francisco, and Maya's mother was so upset at the thought of her only daughter marrying a white man that she took all of her furniture and moved to Los Angeles a few days before their wedding took place.

1953–1954

Tosh did not want Maya to work. They rented a large flat, and she became a full-time homemaker. Tosh would accept very few of Maya's friends into their home, and Clyde was never to have friends over. Over time, tensions began to develop that could not be ignored. Maya believed in God, and she was teaching her son the same beliefs. She longed for church services and began to go secretly. Tosh did not approve of this, and negative remarks and sarcasm slowly crept into the relationship. One morning, he said, "I think I'm just tired of being married." The marriage did not end just then; unexpectedly, Maya had to undergo surgery for appendicitis. It became complicated, and she had to stay in the hospital several weeks. Her grandmother had died the day of Maya's surgery, but Tosh felt it best not to tell her while she was so sick, so she did not learn about the death until later.

1954–1957

Maya and Tosh stayed together for one more year after the surgery. When it ended, Maya again had to find work to take care of herself and her child. She got a job as a nightclub dancer and a B-girl, which meant that she would make a percentage of money from drinks she could sell to the customers. She became popular and was making a lot of money, and she was anticipating making even more when she was unexpectedly fired. She was suspected of turning tricks, or promising to, because she was making so much more money than the other B-girls. The manager put her on two weeks' notice, but before she left the club, people from another club, the Purple Onion, visited one evening to watch her perform. Ultimately, after auditioning, she was hired as a performer at the Purple Onion, and this was the true beginning of her professional singing and dancing career. She changed her name to Maya Angelou from Maya Johnson, and the public began to embrace her.

When her contract at the Purple Onion was almost up, Maya was invited to audition for a show called *House of Flowers* in New York. She had also hoped to audition in New York for a role in the opera *Porgy and Bess.* The opera was going on a 22-nation tour sponsored by the U.S. Department of State. As it turned out, she was offered roles in both and had to make a decision. She chose *Porgy and Bess* and made arrangements for her mother and a close friend, Aunt Lottie, to take care of Clyde. She soon headed for Montreal, where the troupe of *Porgy and Bess was* located and prepared to leave for Europe. She toured with the company for about a year.

Circumstances for Maya's mother were changing in San Francisco, and she was planning to move to Las Vegas. Clyde was pining for his mother and had developed a serious skin disorder, so as soon as she could, Maya returned home. Shortly after she arrived in San Francisco, his skin improved, and he announced that from then on he would be called Guy. Maya promised him that should she ever take a performing job outside of the area where he was, she would always take him with her. Her brother, Bailey, was working as a cook in Hawaii and urged her to take a job there. When she accepted a contract to perform at a Hawaiian club for several weeks, she took Guy with her.

The Heart of a Woman (1957–1963)

1957–1959

After they returned to the mainland, Maya and Guy moved onto a houseboat with friends in Sausalito and lived the hippy life. Tiring of that, and concerned about the impact it was having on Guy, she rented a house in Laurel Canyon in the Los Angeles area. It was there that Billie Holiday visited them. Because the neighborhood and school were not comfortable for them, they relocated to the Westlake district. It was a mixed ethnic neighborhood and much better for them.

Maya wrote a lot during this time, and she met John Killens, a family man and writer, when he was in Los Angeles for the filming of his book *Youngblood.* He recognized her writing talent and persuaded her to move to New York to become a member of the Harlem Writers Guild. Maya was excited by this opportunity. By 1957, Guy was 13 and had become a "tall, aloof stranger" (641). She hoped the change might be good for him, so they made the move. That same year, she appeared in the Off-Broadway play *Calypso Heat Wave,* and she recorded *Miss Calypso* for Liberty Records. Guy made a good adjustment to the change, and he became good friends with the Killens's son, who was about the same age.

1960

Maya met Godfrey Cambridge at a Greenwich Village party, became friends, and attended a presentation by Martin Luther King, Jr., and other civil rights leaders who were in New York City to raise money for the Southern Christian Leadership Conference (SCLC). After the talks they heard, they decided to put on a fund-raiser for the SCLC. With the organization's support, they put together *Cabaret for Freedom* in Greenwich Village, and Maya, collaborating with Cambridge, wrote, produced, and performed in it. Soon, she was asked to be the northern coordinator of the SCLC.

Maya was briefly engaged to a man named Thomas Allen, but broke it off abruptly when she met and fell in love with Vusumzi Make, an African freedom fighter who swept her off her feet. Make was in the United States to raise money for the cause of freedom in South Africa. They began a romantic relationship, and with Make's encouragement, Maya performed a leading role in the Off-Broadway play *The Blacks,* by Jean Genet. Maya traveled with Make to a conference in London and then returned to the United States.

1961–1962

Maya, Make, and Guy had a luxurious apartment in New York, but they moved in 1961 to Cairo, where Guy completed high school. Maya worked in Cairo as an associate editor at the *Arab Observer,* and in 1962, she separated from Make.

1963

Maya and Guy relocated to Accra, Ghana. After recovering from a serious automobile accident that took place just a few days after arriving in Ghana, Guy enrolled in the University of Ghana at the age of 19. Maya worked as an assistant administrator of the School of Music and Drama and for both the Ghanaian Broadcast Corporation and the *Ghanaian Times* newspaper. She also appeared in the play *Mother Courage* at the University of Ghana.

All God's Children Need Traveling Shoes (1963–1965)

1963

A part of this year was spent supporting Guy as he convalesced from his automobile accident, in which he had suffered severe injuries, including a broken neck. His primary physician was Ana Livia Mayfield, wife of the writer and actor Julian Mayfield. When Guy recovered, he enrolled immediately at the university. Maya lived at the YWCA and made many new friends among the women there. Eventually, she rented a house with Vicki and Alice, her new American expatriate friends from the YWCA, and she continued working for the *Ghanaian Times.* Maya was embraced by many of the people she met in Ghana, and she enjoyed being invited to traditional ceremonies. She and her housemates accepted an African child named Kojo into their household; he served them, and they in turn tutored him with his schoolwork.

President Kwame Nkrumah was Ghana's leader, and both Ghanaians and Americans respected and admired him. Maya met many of the leading dignitaries of the country, and she met many foreign dignitaries as they visited Ghana. Dr. W. E. B. DuBois and his wife lived there, though he was in failing health. Maya became acquainted with his wife, Shirley Graham.

1964–1965

Malcolm X made two visits to Africa in 1964, and one of these was to Ghana. Maya met him at an evening gathering at Julian Mayfield's home. Malcolm X told the group that he had come to Ghana to try to make as many government contacts as possible "so when he took the case of the Black American before the General Assembly of the United Nations, he could be sure at least of some African and maybe other nationals' support" (990). The group present at that small dinner party had many government contacts, and some of them had even met Kwame Nkrumah. Malcolm was pleased, "Black Americans! You are really something. . . . You people just got here and already you know the President" (991).

Maya was part of the group that escorted Malcolm X to various events and appointments so that he could meet as many African dignitaries and official representatives from other countries as possible. After he left, an opportunity came to Maya go to Berlin and then Venice to join the troupe who had performed *The Blacks* in New York. They were presenting the play in those cities, and she would play the White Queen, the same role that she had played in the Off-Broadway production. The play was well-received in both cities, and then Maya returned to Ghana by way of Cairo and visited with friends she had met when she had lived there with Vusumzi Make.

Malcolm X had begun a civil rights group called the Organization of Afro-American Unity, and Maya wanted to help them succeed. She and Malcolm exchanged several letters, and it was her plan to work with him when she returned to New York. Before she left Ghana, friends took her to a small village to help her have another view of the people of Africa. She had a sense that her people may have originated there because she observed familiar features in the faces and also familiarity in the tones and sounds of the voices. A few days after that interesting visit, she was "not sad departing Ghana" (1,051). She had enjoyed her stay there, but she was ready to return to the United States and devote her energy to the important quest for change happening there.

A Song Flung Up to Heaven (1965–1968)

1965–1967

When Maya arrived in New York after being away for four years, she made a decision to visit her mother and friends in California before beginning her work for Malcolm X. Her mother and brother, Bailey, met her at the airport in San Francisco, and the three of them thoroughly enjoyed being reunited. Two days after Maya arrived in the United States, Malcolm X was assassinated in New York City. Maya was devastated, and after a few days, Bailey invited her to return to performing as a singer and dancer in Hawaii, where he was a cook at a fine hotel. He found a nightclub that offered her a job, and she could stay with her mother's married sister who lived there. She went, and while she was there, she heard Della Reese sing. After hearing Reese's fantastic voice, Maya decided never to sing again, having realized that she was not as talented in singing or as dedicated to performance as Reese was. She therefore resolved to direct her energies to writing and the Civil Rights movement.

Maya returned to the mainland and decided to live in Los Angeles. She quickly found a place to live among writers and performers and found a job as a survey taker in Watts. She had an opportunity to play the part of the old nurse in Jean Anouilh's *Medea,* and while she enjoyed the performance, she then decided to return to New York, where she could be a part of the Harlem Writers Guild again, and she could begin writing seriously. Friends in New York offered places for her to stay, but before she left, Guy, having returned from Africa to San Francisco three days earlier, was in another serious automobile accident. His neck was broken, so Maya remained in San Francisco until he could be safely moved from the hospital to her mother's care (Vivian Baxter was a professional nurse).

In New York, Maya received sponsorship from a wealthy club owner, Jerry Purcell. He told her, "I manage artists who make more in one night than you have ever made in a year. Yet I know no one more talented than you" (1,127). With his "no strings" patronage, she found an apartment, many friends made gifts of furnishings, and she began writing. Her close friendship with Dolly McPherson developed during this time, and Maya worked on improving her writing skills.

1968

At the 100th birthday anniversary of W. E. B. DuBois, there was a great celebration held at Carnegie Hall. Many star performers, writers, and political figures appeared and gave tribute to the great man, who had passed away five years earlier at the age of 95 in Ghana. Maya was invited to sit in the box with the friends and family of James Baldwin, and she watched as Ossie Davis, James Baldwin, Pete Seeger, Martin Luther King, Jr., and others paid tribute to DuBois.

After the ceremonies, Martin Luther King, Jr., took Maya aside and said he wanted to talk with her. She had worked for him as the northern coordinator of the Southern Christian Leadership Conference years before in New York. He was planning a poor people's march in Washington, D.C., and he needed to raise funds for tent cities to accommodate people who would participate in case they needed them. He hoped that Maya would travel around the country to "talk to black Preachers. I'd like each big church to donate one Sunday's collection to the poor people's march" (1,148). Maya accepted the challenge. He wanted one month of her time, and she agreed to do it, but she wanted to wait until after her 40th birthday on April 4.

When that day arrived, Maya spent it happily cooking and preparing her apartment for the celebration that night. The phone rang, and it was her friend Dolly, who told her not to turn the radio or television on, and that she would be right over. When she arrived, she told Maya that King had been assassinated. Maya, in deep mourning and depression, hibernated for a few weeks in her apartment. She told her friends what she needed to do, and both Dolly and Jerry Purcell saw that she had food. One day, James Baldwin stopped by, told her to get dressed, and then explained that he was taking her along to a dinner party with friends of his. He told her they were funny, and that she would enjoy it. The friends were Jules and Judy Feiffer, and along with their 10-year-old daughter, they enjoyed visiting in the living room. The adults had dinner and regaled each other with funny stories.

Not long after that evening, Maya was invited to write a public television series of 10-hour-long programs on African-American culture and history. She accepted the challenge and wrote *Black, Blues, Black* for National Educational Television's station KQED in San Francisco.

While she was working on that project, Robert Loomis, an editor at Random House, called her. She was recommended to him by Jules and Judy Feiffer, who felt Angelou had talent and stories to tell. Loomis invited Maya to write an autobiography for Random House, but she resisted. He pursued her and finally, on the advice of James Baldwin, he said, "I won't bother you again. And I must say, you may be right not to attempt an autobiography, because it is nearly impossible to write an autobiography as literature. Almost impossible" (1,165). She responded with, "I'll start tomorrow." She soon returned to New York and wrote her first book, *I Know Why the Caged Bird Sings*.

Selected Bibliography of Maya Angelou's Works

Note: Bibliographic citations are arranged chronologically.

Autobiographies

Angelou, Maya. *I Know Why the Caged Bird Sings.* New York: Random House, 1970.

———. *Gather Together in My Name.* New York: Random House, 1974.

———. *Singin' and Swingin' and Gettin' Merry Like Christmas.* New York: Random House, 1976.

———. *The Heart of a Woman.* New York: Random House, 1981.

———. *All God's Children Need Traveling Shoes.* New York: Random House, 1986.

———. *A Song Flung Up to Heaven.* New York: Random House, 2002.

———. *The Collected Autobiographies of Maya Angelou.* New York: Modern Library Edition by Random House, 2004.

Nonfiction Essay Collections

Angelou, Maya. *Wouldn't Take Nothing for My Journey Now.* New York: Random House, 1993.

———. *Lessons in Living.* New York: Random House, 1993.

———. *Even the Stars Look Lonesome.* New York: Random House, 1997.

———. *Hallelujah! The Welcome Table.* New York: Random House, 2004.

———. *Letter to My Daughter.* New York: Random House, 2008.

———. *Great Food, All Day Long: Cook Splendidly, Eat Smart.* New York: Random House, 2010.

Poetry Collections and Single Published Poems

Angelou, Maya. *Just Give Me a Cool Drink of Water 'fore I Diiie.* New York: Random House, 1971.

———. *Oh Pray My Wings Are Gonna Fit Me Well.* New York: Random House, 1975.

———. *And Still I Rise.* New York: Random House, 1978.

———. *Shaker, Why Don't You Sing?* New York: Random House, 1983.

———. *Now Sheba Sings the Song.* Illustrated by Tom Feelings. New York: Dutton, 1987.

———. *I Shall Not Be Moved.* New York: Random House, 1990.

———. *On the Pulse of Morning.* New York: Random House, 1993.

———. *The Complete Collected Poems of Maya Angelou.* New York: Random House, 1994.

———. *Phenomenal Woman: Four Poems Celebrating Women.* New York: Random House, 1994.

———. "Million Man March Poem." 1995. Available online. URL: www.poemhunter.com/poem/million-man-march-poem/. Accessed July 10, 2010.

———. *A Brave and Startling Truth.* New York: Random House, 1995.

———. *Poems: Maya Angelou.* New York: Bantam Books, 1997.

———. *Amazing Peace: A Christmas Poem.* New York: Random House, 2005.

———. *Celebrations: Rituals of Peace and Prayer.* New York: Random House, 2006.

———. *Mother: A Cradle to Hold Me.* New York: Random House, 2006.

———. *Poetry for Young People: Maya Angelou.* Edited by Edwin Graves Wilson. New York: Sterling Publishing Company, 2007.

Vena, Jocelyn. "Maya Angelou's Poem about Michael Jackson: 'We Had Him,'" *MTV News,* 7 July 2009. Available online. URL: www.mtv.com/news/articles/1615416/20090707/jackson_michael.jhtml. Accessed July 27, 2010.

Children's Books

Angelou, Maya. Mrs. *Flowers: A Moment of Friendship.* Minneapolis: Redpath Press, 1986.

———. *Life Doesn't Frighten Me.* Edited by Sara Jane Boyers. Illustrated by Jean-Michel Basquiat. New York: Stewart, Tabori & Chang. 1993.

———. *My Painted House, My Friendly Chicken, and Me.* Photographs by Margaret Courtney-Clarke. New York: C. Potter, 1994.

———. *Kofi and His Magic.* New York: C. Potter, 1996.

———. *Maya's World: Izak of Lapland.* New York: Random House, 2004.

———. *Maya's World: Angelina of Italy.* New York: Random House, 2004.

———. *Maya's World: René Marie of France.* New York: Random House, 2004.

———. *Maya's World: Mikale of Hawaii.* New York: Random House, 2004.

Angelou, Maya, et al. *Soul Looks Back in Wonder.* Illustrated by Tom Feelings. New York: Dial Books, 1993.

Speeches

Angelou, Maya. Nancy Hanks Lecture. American Council of the Arts, Washington, D.C., March 20, 1990.

Cinematic, Theatrical, Musical, Poetic, Television, and Dance Productions

Author

Cabaret for Freedom. Musical revue, coauthored with Godfrey Cambridge, 1960.

The Least of These. Two-act play, 1966.

The Best of These. Play, 1966.

The Clawing Within. Two-act play, 1966.

Getting Up Stayed on My Mind. Play, 1967.

Adjoa Amissah. Two-act musical, 1967.

Black, Blues, Black. TV Series, National Educational Television, 1968.

Georgia, Georgia. Screenplay, 1972.

AJAX. Two-act drama, adapted from Sophocles' play, 1974.

All Day Long. Screenplay, American Film Institute, 1974.

Assignment America. Series of six half-hour PBS programs, 1975.

And Still I Rise. One-act musical, 1976.

The Legacy and *The Inheritors.* Two-part program for the U.S. Information Agency, 1976.

I Know Why the Caged Bird Sings. TV movie, cowritten with Leonora Thuna, 1979.

Sister, Sister. TV drama, also producer, 1982.

On a Southern Journey. One-act play, 1983.

Theatrical Vignette. One-act play, 1983.

Trying to Make It Home. Byline. TV, 1988.

Maya Angelou's America: A Journey of the Heart. Documentary; also host, 1988.

Brewster Place. TV series, coauthor, 1990.

"The Reunion." Episode in *America's Dream,* TV miniseries, 1996.

How Do You Spell God? Screenplay, TV movie, 1996.

Angelou on Burns. Documentary, United Kingdom, 1996.

Kwanzaa. Cowritten with M. K. Asante, Jr., 2008.

Director

Visions. TV Series, one episode, 1976.

Moon on a Rainbow Shawl. Play by Errol John, London, 1988.

Down in the Delta. Film, 1998.

Producer

Afro-Americans in the Arts. Documentary, PBS, 1977.

Spoken Word Albums

The Poetry of Maya Angelou. GWP Records, 1969.

Women in Business. University of Wisconsin, 1981.

On the Pulse of Morning. Ingram audio production, 1993.

Phenomenal Women. Ingram audio production, 1995.

Been Found. Music & Spoken Word album with Nicholas Ashford and Valerie Simpson, Record Label Ichiban/Ryko, 1996.

A Song Flung Up to Heaven. Library Edition, 2002.

Hallelujah! The Welcome Table. Random House Audio Voices Unabridged Edition, 2004.

Angelou's Work has Appeared in These Periodicals

Black Scholar
California Living
Chicago Daily News
Cosmopolitan
Ebony
Essence
Ghanaian Times
Harper's Bazaar
Life
Mademoiselle
New York Times
Redbook

SELECTED BIBLIOGRAPHY OF SECONDARY SOURCES

Abrams, M. H. A. *A Glossary of Literary Terms.* 6th ed. New York: Harcourt, 1993.

Adams, Phoebe. Review of *Gather Together in My Name. Atlantic* (1 June 1974): 233.

Almeida, Ruth E. Review of *Gather Together in My Name. Library Journal* (1 June 1974): 1,538.

Als, Hilton. "Songbird: Maya Angelou Takes Another Look at Herself." *New Yorker,* 5 August 2002, 72–76.

Anderson, Jervis. *This Was Harlem: A Cultural Portrait.* New York: Farrar Straus Giroux, 1982.

Andrews, William L. *To Tell a Free Story: The First Century of Afro-American Autobiography: 1760–1865.* Urbana: University of Illinois Press, 1986.

Arensberg, Liliane K. "Death as a Metaphor of Self in *I Know Why the Caged Bird Sings.*" *College Language Association Journal* (December 1976): 293–291.

Avant, John Alfred. Review of *Just Give Me a Cool Drink of Water 'fore I Diiie* by Maya Angelou. *Library Journal* 96 (1971): 3,329.

Baker, Houston. Review of *All God's Children Need Traveling Shoes. New York Times Book Review,* 11 May 1986: 14.

Benson, Carol. "Out of the Cage and Still Singing." *Writer's Digest* (January 1975): 18–20.

Bertolino, James. "Maya Angelou Is Three Writers: *I Know Why the Caged Bird Sings.*" In *Censored Books,* edited by Nicholas J. Karolides, Lee Burress, and John M. Kean, 299–305. Metuchen, N.J.: Scarecrow Press, 1993.

Bethel, Lorraine. "Maya." *Equal Times* 20 (November 1978): 14–16.

Black Elk. 1932. *Black Elk Speaks.* Edited by John Neihardt. New York: Pocket Books, 1972.

Bloom, Lynn Z. "Maya Angelou." In *Dictionary of Literary Biography,* vol. 38, 3–12. Detroit, Mich.: Gale, 1985.

Bloom, Lynn Z., and Ning Yu. "American Autobiography: The Changing Critical Canon." *a/b: Auto/Biography Studies* 9, no. 2 (Fall 1994): 167–180.

Blundell, Joyce Boyarin. Review of *All God's Children Need Traveling Shoes. Library Journal* (March 15, 1986): 113.

———. Review of *And Still I Rise* by Maya Angelou. *Library Journal* 103 (1978): 1,640.

———. Review of *Shaker, Why Don't You Sing?* by Maya Angelou. *Library Journal* 103 (1978): 746, 748.

Braxton, Joanne M. *Black Women Writing Autobiography.* Philadelphia: Temple University Press, 1989.

———. "Maya Angelou." In *Modern American Women Writers,* edited by Elaine Showalter, 108. New York: Scribner's, 1991.

Brent, Linda (Harriet Jacobs). *Incidents in the Life of a Slave Girl.* Edited by L. Maria Child. New York: Harcourt Brace Jovanovich, 1973.

Brooks, Gwendolyn. *Report from Part One.* Detroit: Broadside, 1972.

Buss, Helen M. "Reading for the Doubled Discourse of American Women's Autobiography." *a/b: Auto/Biography Studies* 5, no. 1 (1991): 95–108.

Butterfield, Stephen. *Black Autobiography in America.* Amherst: University of Massachusetts Press, 1974.

Carby, Hazel V. *Reconstructing Womanhood: The Emergence of the Afro-American Woman Novelist.* New York: Oxford University Press, 1987.

Carson, Benjamin S. *Gifted Hands: The Ben Carson Story.* New York: HarperCollins, 1993.

Chevalier, Tracy, ed. *Contemporary Poets.* 5th ed. Chicago: St. James Press, 1991.

Chick, Nancy. "Maya Angelou: A Twentieth Century Scheherazade." Master's thesis, University of Georgia, 1992.

Chrisman, Robert. "*The Black Scholar* Interviews Maya Angelou." *Black Scholar* (January–February 1977): 44–52.

Cole-Leonard, Natasha. "Maya Angelou's *Hallelujah! The Welcome Table, A Lifetime of Memories with Recipes* as Evocative Text, or, 'Ain't' Jemima's Recipes." *Langston Hughes Reviews* 19 (Spring 2005): 66–69.

Collier, Eugenia. "Maya Angelou: From 'Caged Bird' to 'All God's Children.'" *New Directions* (October 1986): 22–27.

Cordell, Shirley J. "The Black Woman: A Focus on 'Strength of Character' in *I Know Why the Caged Bird Sings.*" *Virginia English Bulletin* 36 (1986): 36–39.

Cosgrave, Mary Silva. Review of *And Still I Rise* by Maya Angelou. *Horn Book Magazine* 55, no. 1 (1979): 97.

———. Review of *The Heart of a Woman. Horn Book Magazine* (February 1982): 84.

———. Review of *Oh Pray My Wings Are Gonna Fit Me Well* by Maya Angelou. *Horn Book Magazine* 52 (1976): 78.

———. Review of *Shaker, Why Don't You Sing?* by Maya Angelou. *Horn Book Magazine* 59, no. 3 (1983): 336.

Cotter, James Finn. Review of *Oh Pray My Wings Are Gonna Fit Me Well* by Maya Angelou, *The Women and The Men* by Nikki Giovanni, and *The Peacock Poems* by Shirley Williams. *America* 134, no. 2 (1976): 103–104.

Crockett, Sandra. "Poetic Angelou Can Sing, Cut a Ring." *Baltimore Sun,* 9 September 1997, E18.

Cudjoe, Selwyn R. "Maya Angelou and the Autobiographical Statement." In *Black Women Writers (1950–1980): A Critical Evaluation,* edited by Mari Evans, 6–24. Garden City, N.Y.: Doubleday, 1984.

———. "Maya Angelou: The Autobiographical Statement Updated." In *Reading Black, Reading Feminist,* edited by Henry Louis Gates, Jr., 272–306. New York: Penguin, 1990.

Dance, Daryl C. "Black Eve or Madonna?" In *Sturdy Black Bridges,* edited by Roseann P. Bell, Bettye J. Parker, and Beverly Guy-Sheftall, 123–132. Garden City, N.Y.: Doubleday, 1979.

Demetrakopoulos, Stephanie A. "The Metaphysics of Matrilinearism in *Women's Autobiography.*" In *Women's Autobiography,* edited by Estelle C. Jelinek. Bloomington: Indiana University Press, 1980.

Douglass, Frederick. *Narrative of the Life of Frederick Douglass.* In *The Classic Slave Narratives,* edited by Henry Louis Gates, Jr., 323–436. New York: New American Library, 1987.

Dundes, Alan, ed. *Mother Wit from the Laughing Barrel.* Englewood Cliffs, N.J.: Prentice-Hall, 1973.

Egan, Susanna. *Patterns of Experience in Autobiography.* Chapel Hill: University of North Carolina Press, 1984.

Elliot, Jeffrey M., ed. *Conversations with Maya Angelou.* Jackson: University Press of Mississippi, 1989.

Equiano, Olaudah. *Gustavus Vassa, the African, or the Interesting Narrative of the Life of Olaudah Equiano.* In *The Classic Slave Narratives,* edited by Henry Louis Gates, Jr., 15–248. New York: New American Library, 1987.

Essick, Kathy M. *The Poetry of Maya Angelou: A Study of the Blues Matrix as Force and Code.* Indiana: Indiana University of Pennsylvania, 1994.

Estes Hicks, Onita. "The Way We Were: Precious Memories of the Black Segregated South." *African American Review* 27, no. 1 (Spring 1993): 9–18.

Evans, Mari, ed. *Black Women Writers (1950–1980): A Critical Evaluation.* Garden City, N.Y.: Anchor Press, 1984.

Felton, Keith. "Womanflight on the Wings of Words." *Los Angeles Times,* 28 December 1975, 70–71.

Fleischner, Jennifer. *Mastering Slavery.* New York: New York University Press, 1996.

Fleming, Margaret, and Joe McGinnis, eds. *Portraits: Biography and Autobiography in the Secondary School.* Urbana, Ill.: National Council of Teachers of English, 1984.

Foster, Frances. "Parents and Children in Autobiography by Southern Afro-American Writers." In *Home Ground: Southern Autobiography,* edited by Bill Berry, 98–109. Columbia: University of Missouri Press, 1992.

Fox-Genovese, Elizabeth. "'Myth and History': Discourse in Origins in Zora Neale Hurston and Maya Angelou." *Black American Literature Forum* 24, no. 3 (Summer 1990): 221–235.

Freeman, Sharon. *Voice Youth Advocates* 9 (August–October 1986): 170.

Froula, Christine. "The Daughter's Seduction: Sexual Violence and Literary History." *Journal of Women in Culture and Society* 11, no. 4 (1986): 621–644.

Fulghum, Robert. "Home Truths and Homilies." *Washington Post Book World,* 19 September 1993, 4.

Gabbin, Joanne V. "Maya Angelou: The People's Poet Laureate: An Introduction." *Langston Hughes Review* 19 (Spring 2005): 3–7.

Gates, Henry Louis, Jr. "The Blackness of Blackness: A Critique of the Sign of the Signifying Monkey." In *Black Literature and Literary Theory,* edited by Henry Louis Gates, Jr., 285–321. New York: Methuen, 1984.

———. *Colored People.* New York: Vintage, 1995.

———. *Reading Black, Reading Feminist: A Critical Anthology.* New York: Meridian, 1990.

———. *The Signifying Monkey: A Theory of African-American Literary Criticism.* New York: Oxford University Press, 1988.

Gates, Henry Louis, Jr., and Nellie Y. McKay, eds. *The Norton Anthology of African American Literature.* New York: Norton, 1997.

Georgoudaki, Ekaterini. "Contemporary Women's Autobiography: Maya Angelou, Gwendolyn Brooks, Nikki Giovanni, Lillian Hellman, and Audre Lourde." *Diavazo* 237 (April 1990): 62–69.

———. *Race, Gender, and Class Perspectives in the Works of Maya Angelou, Gwendolyn Brooks, Rita Dove, Nikki Giovanni, and Audre Lourde.* Thessaloniki, Greece: Aristotle University of Thessaloniki, 1991.

Gilbert, Sandra M. "A Platoon of Poets." *Poetry* 128 (1976): 290–299.

Gilbert, Susan. "Maya Angelou's *I Know Why the Caged Bird Sings:* Paths to Escape." *Mount Olive Review* (1987): 39–50.

Giovanni, Nikki. *Gemini: An Extended Autobiographical Statement on My First Twenty-Five Years of Being a Black Poet.* Indianapolis: Bobbs-Merrill, 1971.

Goldberg, Doris. "Poetry of Angelou." *Blade,* 5 November 1978, G10.

Golden, Marita. *Migrations of the Heart.* 1983. Reprint, New York: Ballantine Books, 1987.

Goodman, G., Jr. "Maya Angelou's Lonely Black Chick Outlook." *New York Times,* 24 March 1972, 28.

Gottlieb, Annie. "Growing Up and the Serious Business of Survival." (Review of *Gather Together in My Name*) *New York Times Book Review,* 16 June 1974, 16, 20.

Gropman, Jackie. Review of *All God's Children Need Traveling Shoes. Southern Literacy Journal* (August 1986): 113.

Gross, Leslie. "Parent Calls Required Book Explicit, Racially Divisive." *Capital,* 27 October 1997, A1, A10.

Gross, R. A. "Growing Up Black." (Review of *I Know Why the Caged Bird Sings*) *Newsweek,* 2 March 1970, 90–91.

Grusser, John C. "Afro-American Travel Literature and Africanist Discourse." *Black American Literature Forum* 24, no. 1 (Spring 1990): 5–20.

Guiney, E. M. Review of *I Know Why the Caged Bird Sings. Library Journal* (16 March 1970): 1,018.

Hagen, Lyman B. *Heart of a Woman, Mind of a Writer, and Soul of a Poet: A Critical Analysis of the Writings of Maya Angelou.* Lanham, Md.: University Press of America, 1997.

Harmon, William. *A Handbook to Literature.* 10th ed. Upper Saddle River, N.J.: Prentice-Hall, 2006.

Harris, Kathryn Gibbs. Review of *Oh Pray My Wings Are Gonna Fit Me Well* by Maya Angelou. *Library Journal* 100, no. 17 (1975): 1,829.

Hemenway, Robert E. *Zora Neale Hurston.* Urbana: University of Illinois Press, 1977.

Hiers, John T. "Fatalism in Maya Angelou's *I Know Why the Caged Bird Sings.*" *Notes on Contemporary Literature* 6, no. 1 (1976): 5–7.

Hill-Lubin, Mildred A. "The Grandmother in African and African-American Literature: A Survivor of the Extended Family." In *Ngambika: Studies of Women in African Literature,* edited by Carol B. Davies and Anne A. Graves, 257–270. Trenton, N.J.: African World, 1986.

Hirsch, Marianne. "Maternal Narratives: 'Cruel Enough to Stop the Blood.'" In *Reading Black, Reading Feminist,* edited by Henry Louis Gates, Jr., 415–430. New York: Penguin, 1990.

hooks, bell. *Bone Black: Memories of Girlhood.* New York: Henry Holt, 1996.

Hord, Fred Lee. "Someplace to Be a Black Girl." In *Reconstructing Memory: Black Literary Criticism.* Chicago: Third World Press, 1991, 75–85.

Howe, Michele. "Angelou's Poetry Builds Bridges between Peoples." *Star-Ledger* (Newark, N.J.), 3 June 1990, C4.

Hughes, Langston, and Arna Bontemps, eds. *Book of Negro Folklore.* New York: Dodd, Mead, 1958.

Jelinek, Estelle C. "Introduction: Women's Autobiography and the Male Tradition." In *Women's Autobiography: Essays in Criticism,* edited by Estelle C. Jelinek, 1–20. Bloomington: Indiana University Press, 1980.

Jones, George E. "Maya Angelou's *I Know Why the Caged Bird Sings* and Black Autobiographical Tradition." *Kansas Quarterly* 7 (1975): 72–78.

Jordan, June. Review of *Singin' and Swinging' and Gettin' Merry Like Christmas. Ms.* (January 1977): 40–41.

Kelley, Ken. "Visions: Maya Angelou." *Mother Jones* (May/June 1995). Available online. URL: http://www.motherjones.com/media/1995/05/visions-maya-angelou. Accessed February 24, 2010.

Kent, George E. "Maya Angelou's *I Know Why the Caged Bird Sings* and Black Autobiographical Tradition." *Kansas Quarterly* 7 (1975): 75–78.

King, Sarah E. *Maya Angelou: Greeting the Morning.* Brookfield, Conn.: Millbrooke Press, 1994.

Kinnamon, Keneth. "Call and Response: Intertextuality in Two Autobiographical Works by Richard Wright and Maya Angelou." In *Studies in Black American Literature: Belief versus Theory in Black American Literary Criticism,* vol. 2, edited by Joe Weixlmann and Chester J. Fontenot, 121–134. Greenwood, Fla.: Penkeville, 1986.

Kuehl, Linda. Review of *Singin' and Swingin' and Gettin' Merry Like Christmas. Saturday Review,* 30 October 1976, 46.

Lehmann-Haupt, Christopher. "Books of the Times: Masculine and Feminine." Review of *I Know Why the Caged Bird Sings. New York Times,* 25 February 1970, 45.

Lewis, David Levering. "A Transitional Time: *The Heart of a Woman.*" In *Readings on Maya Angelou,* edited by Mary E. Williams, 152–155. San Diego, Calif.: Greenhaven, 1997.

Liddy, Martha. Review of *Just Give Me a Cool Drink of Water 'fore I Diiie* by Maya Angelou. *Library Journal* 96 (1972): 3,916.

Lippmann, Ellen. Review of *And Still I Rise* by Maya Angelou. *School Library Journal* 25, no. 3 (November 1978): 108.

Lupton, Mary Jane. "Maya Angelou." In *American Writers,* supp. IV, part 1, edited by Leonard Unger, 1–19. New York: Scribner's, 1996.

——— "Singing the Black Mother: Maya Angelou and Autobiographical Continuity." *Black American Literature Forum* 24 (1990): 257–276.

———. "Talking with an Icon: An Interview with Maya Angelou." 16 June 1997. Unpublished.

MacKethan, Lucinda H. "Mother Wit: Humor in Afro-American Women's Autobiography." *Studies in American Humor* 4 (1985): 51–61.

Magill, Frank N., ed. *Masterpieces of African-American Literature.* New York: HarperCollins, 1992.

Maierhofer, Roberta. "'Hold! Stop! Don't Pity Me': Age, Gender, and Ethnicity in American Studies." *Arbeiten aus Anglistik und Amerikanistik* 25, no. 1 (2000): 107–118.

Manora, Yolanda. "'What You Looking at Me For? I Didn't Come to Stay': Displacement, Disruption, and Black Female Subjectivity in Maya Angelou's *I Know Why the Caged Bird Sings.*" *Women's Studies: An Interdisciplinary Journal* 34, no. 5 (July–August 2005): 359–375.

Mayfield, Julian. "Black on Black: A Political Love Story." *Black World* (February 1972): 55–71.

McCall, Cheryl. "Maya Angelou." *People,* 8 March 1982, 92–97.

McDowell, Deborah E. "Traveling Hopefully." *Women's Review of Books* 4 (October 1986): 17.

McMurry, Myra K. "Role-Playing as Art in Maya Angelou's *Caged Bird.*" *South Atlantic Bulletin* 41, no. 2 (May 1976): 106–111.

McPherson, Dolly A. "Defining the Self through Place and Culture: Maya Angelou's *I Know Why the Caged Bird Sings.*" *MAWA Review* 5, no. 1 (June 1990): 12–14.

———. *Order Out of Chaos: The Autobiographical Works of Maya Angelou.* New York: Peter Lang, 1990.

Megna-Wallace, Joanne. "Simone de Beauvoir and Maya Angelou: Birds of a Feather." *Simone de Beauvoir Studies* 6 (1986): 49–55.

Metzger, Linda, et al., eds. *Black Writers: A Selection of Sketches from Contemporary Authors.* Detroit, Mich.: Gale Research, 1989.

Meyers, Linda Mae Zarpentine. "Maya Angelou and the Multiplicity of Self." Master's thesis, Morgan State University, 1995.

Minudri, Regina. Review of *Gather Together in My Name. Library Journal* (15 May 1974): 99.

———. Review of *I Know Why the Caged Bird Sings. Library Journal* (June 15, 1970): 2,320.

Mitchell, Lisa. "Maya Angelou: Sometimes She Feels Like a Motherless Child." Review of *Singin' and Swingin' and Gettin Merry Like Christmas. Los Angeles Times,* 21 November 1976, 5.

Moore, Opal. "Learning to Live: When the Bird Breaks from the Cage." In *Censored Books,* edited by Nicholas J. Karolides, Lee Burress, and John M. Kean, 306–316. Metuchen, N.J.: Scarecrow Press, 1993.

Moyers, Bill. "Portraits of Greatness." PBS Home Video, Pacific Arts, 1982.

Nero, Clarence. "A Discursive Trifecta: Community, Education, and Language in *I Know Why the Caged*

Bird Sings." *Langston Hughes Review* 19 (Spring 2005): 61–65.

Neubauer, Carol E. "Displacement and the Autobiographical Style in Maya Angelou's *The Heart of A Woman.*" *Black American Literature Forum* 17 (1983): 123–129.

———. "An Interview with Maya Angelou." *Massachusetts Review* 28 (1987): 286–292.

———. "Maya Angelou: Self and a Song of Freedom in the Southern Tradition." In *Southern Women Writers: The New Generation,* edited by Tonette Bond Inge. Tuscaloosa: University of Alabama Press, 1990.

O'Neale, Sondra. "Reconstruction of the Composite Self: New Images of Black Women in Maya Angelou's Continuing Autobiography." In *Black Women Writers (1950–1980): A Critical Evaluation,* edited by Mari Evans, 25–36. Garden City, N.Y.: 1984: Anchor/Doubleday.

Pascal, Roy. *Design and Truth in Autobiography.* Cambridge, Mass.: Harvard University Press, 1960.

Pascal, Sylvia. Review of *The Heart of a Woman. Southern Literary Journal* (December 1981): 88.

Plimpton, George. "The Art of Fiction CXIX: Maya Angelou." *Paris Review* 32, no. 116 (1990): 145–167.

Premo, Cassie. "When the Difference Becomes Too Great: Images of the Self and Survival in a Postmodern World." *Genre* 16 (1995): 183–191.

Ramsey, R. Priscilla. "Transcendence: The Poetry of Maya Angelou." *Current Bibliography of African Affairs* 17, no. 2 (1984–85): 139–153.

Rehm, Diane. "Maya Angelou: *Letter to My Daughter.*" Interview. *The Diane Rehm Show,* November 20, 2008.

Rich, Marney. "In Maya Angelou, A Caged Bird Sings." In *Conversations with Maya Angelou,* edited by Jeffrey M. Elliot, 125–130. Jackson: University Press of Mississippi, 1989.

Robinson, Kathryn. Review of *Singin' and Swingin' and Gettin' Merry Like Christmas. Southern Literary Journal* (Summer 1976): 144.

Sample, Maxine. "Gender, Identity, and the Liminal Self: The Emerging Woman in Buchi Emecheta's *The Bride Price* and Maya Angelou's *I Know Why the Caged Bird Sings.*" In *North-South Linkages and Connections in Continental and Diaspora African Literature,* edited by Edris Makward, Mark Lilleheht, and Ahmed Saber, 213–215. Trenton, N.J.: Africa World, 2005.

Sarler, Carol. "A Life in the Day of Maya Angelou." In *Conversations with Maya Angelou,* edited by Jeffrey M. Elliot, 214–217. Jackson: University Press of Mississippi, 1989.

Saunders, James Robert. "Breaking Out of the Cage: The Autobiographical Writings of Maya Angelou." *Hollins Critic* 28, no. 4 (October 1991): 1–11.

Schramm, Katharina. "Imagined Pasts–Present Confrontations: Literacy and Ethnographic Explorations into Explorations into Pan-African Identity Politics." In *Africa, Europe, and (Post) Colonialism: Racism, Migration and Diaspora in African Literatures,* edited by Susan Arndt and Marek Spitezok von Brisinki, 243–256. Bayreuth, Germany: Bayreuth University, 2006.

Schultz, Elizabeth. "To Be Black and Blue: The Blues Genre in Black American Autobiography." *Kansas Quarterly* 7 (1975): 81–96.

Shelton, Austin, ed. *The African Assertion: A Critical Anthology of African Literature.* New York: Odyssey, 1968.

Showalter, Elaine, ed. *Modern American Women Writers.* New York: Charles Scribners, 1991.

Shuker, Nancy. *Maya Angelou.* Englewood Cliffs, N.J.: Silver Burdett Press, 1990.

Smith, Sidonie Ann. "The Song of a Caged Bird: Maya Angelou's Quest after Self Acceptance." *Saturday Review,* 9 May 1970, 70.

Spigner, Nieda. Review of *The Heart of a Woman. Freedomways* 1 (1982): 55.

Stepto, Robert B. "The Phenomenal Woman and the Severed Daughter (Maya Angelou, Audre Lorde)." *Parnassus: Poetry in Review* 8, no. 1 (Fall–Winter 1979): 312–320.

Sukenick, Lynn. Review of *Gather Together in My Name. Village Voice,* 11 July 1974, 31.

Sylvester, William. "Maya Angelou." In *Contemporary Poets,* edited by Harold Bloom. New York: Chelsea House, 1986.

Tate, Claudia. *Black Women Writers at Work.* New York: Continuum, 1983.

Tawake, Sandra Kiser. "Multi-Ethnic Literature in the Classroom: Whose Standards?" *World Englishes: Journal of English as an International and Intranational Language* 10, no. 3 (Winter 1991): 335–340.

Tinnie, Wallis. "Maya Angelou." In *The History of Southern Women's Literature,* edited by Carolyn Perry, Mary Louise Weaks, and Doris Betts, 517–524. Baton Rouge: Louisiana State University Press, 2002.

Toppman, Lawrence. "Maya Angelou: The Serene Spirit of a Survivor." In *Conversations with Maya Angelou,* edited by Jeffrey M. Elliot, 140–145. Jackson: University Press of Mississippi, 1989.

Vermillion, Mary. "Reembodying the Self: Representations of Rape in *Incidents in the Life of a Slave Girl* and *I Know Why the Caged Bird Sings.*" *Biography* 15 (1992): 243–260.

Wall, Cheryl. "Maya Angelou." In *Woman Writers Talking,* edited by Janet Todd, 59–67. New York: Holmes & Meier, 1983.

Weller, Sheila. "Work in Progress/Maya Angelou." *Intellectual Digest* (June 1973).

Maya Angelou's Honors, Appointments, Awards, and Honorary Degrees

The list below is adapted from the list on the Maya Angelou page on Wikipedia (http://en.wikipedia.org/wiki/List_of_awards_and_nominations_received_by_Maya_Angelou) and from Wright State University's Presidential Lecture Series page on Maya Angelou (http://www.wright.edu/lecture/angelou2.html).

Honors, Appointments, and Awards

Chubb Fellowship Award, Yale University, 1970

National Book Award nomination, *I Know Why the Caged Bird Sings,* 1970

Pulitzer Prize nomination for *Just Give Me a Cool Drink of Water 'fore I Diiie,* 1972

Tony Award nomination for performance in *Look Away,* 1973

Distinguished Visiting Professor, Wichita State University, 1974

Member, American Revolution Bicentennial Council (appointed by Gerald Ford), 1975–76

Rockefeller Foundation Scholar in Italy, 1975

Board of Trustees, American Film Institute, 1975

Ladies' Home Journal Award ("Woman of the Year in Communication"), 1976

Golden Eagle Award for *Afro-Americans in the Arts* (documentary), 1977

Member, Presidential Commission for International Women's Year (appointed by Jimmy Carter), 1977

Emmy Award nomination for performance in *Roots,* 1977

Reynolds Professor of American Studies, Wake Forest University (lifetime appointment), 1981

Ladies' Home Journal, "Top 100 Most Influential Women," 1983

Matrix Award, Field of Books from Women in Communication, Inc., 1983

Member, North Carolina Arts Council, 1985

Fulbright Program 40th Anniversary Distinguished Lecturer, 1986

North Carolina Award in Literature, 1987

Inductee, American Academy of Achievement, 1990

Candace Award, National Coalition of 100 Black Women, 1990

Langston Hughes Medal, City College of New York, 1991

Horatio Alger Award, 1992

Distinguished Woman of North Carolina, 1992

Women in Film Crystal Award, 1992

Presidential Inauguration Poet, 1993

Arkansas Black Hall of Fame, 1993

Grammy Award for Best Spoken Word Album, *On the Pulse of Morning,* 1993

Rollins College Walk of Fame, 1994

Spingarn Medal (NAACP), 1994

Black History Makers Award, 1994

Citizen Diplomat Award, 1993

Frank G. Wells Award, 1995

Grammy Award for Best Spoken Word or Non-Musical Album, *Phenomenal Woman,* 1995

Lifetime Membership, NAACP, 1996

President's Award, Collegiate of Language Association for Outstanding Achievements, 1996

Southern Christian Leadership Conference of Los Angeles and Martin Luther King, Jr., Legacy Association National Award, 1996

The New York Black 100, 1996

American Ambassador, UNICEF, 1996

National Conference of Christians and Jews, Distinguished Merit Citation, 1997

NAACP Image Award, Outstanding Literary Work, Nonfiction *(Even the Stars Look Lonesome)*, 1997
W. K. Kellogg Foundation, Expert-in-Residence Program, 1997
North Carolina "Woman of the Year" Award, North Carolina Black Publishers Association, 1997
Presidential and Lecture Series Award, University of North Florida, 1997
Black Caucus of American Library Association, Cultural Keepers Award, 1997
Humanitarian Contribution Award, 1997
Homecoming Award, Oklahoma Center for Poets and Writers, 1997
Board of Governors, Winston-Salem State University, Maya Angelou Institute for the Improvement of Child and Family Education, 1998
Alston/Jones International Civil and Human Rights Award, 1998
Inductee, National Women's Hall of Fame, 1998
Christopher Award, 1998.
American Airlines Audience, Gold Plaque Choice Award for *Down in the Delta* from Chicago International Film Festival, 1998
City Proclamation, Winston-Salem, North Carolina, from Mayor Jack Cavanaugh, 1998
Sheila Award, Tubman African American Museum, 1999
Speaker, Special Olympics World Games, Raleigh, North Carolina, 1999
Lifetime Achievement Award for Literature, 1999
Named one of "the top 100 best writers of the 20th Century," *Writer's Digest*, 1999
Presidential Medal of Arts, 2000
Member, U.S. Holocaust Memorial Museum Committee, 2001
Ethnic Multicultural Media Awards (EMMAS), Lifetime Achievement, 2002
Grammy Award for Best Spoken Word Album, *A Song Flung Up to Heaven*, 2002
American Geriatrics Society's Foundation for Health in Aging Award, 2002
Charles Evans Hughes Award, National Conference for Community and Justice, 2004
Honoree, Howard University Heart's Day, 2005
John Hope Franklin Award, June 2006
Black Caucus of American Library Association, Joint Conference of Librarians of Color Author Award, 2006
New York Times Best Seller List, May 2006
John Hope Franklin Award, 2006
Mother Teresa Award, 2006
Martha Parker Legacy Award, 2007
Inductee, International Civil Rights Walk of Fame, Martin Luther King, Jr., National Historic Site, 2008
Voice of Peace Award (first recipient), Hope for Peace and Justice, 2008
Cornell Medallion, 2008
Gracie Allen Award (Gracie), 2008
Lincoln Medal, 2008
Marian Anderson Award, 2008
Andrus Award (NAACP)
Presidential Medal of Freedom, 2011

Honorary Degrees

Portland State University, 1973
Smith College, 1975
Mills College, 1975
Lawrence University, 1976
Wake Forest University, 1977
Columbia College, 1979
Occidental College, 1979
Atlanta University, 1980
University of Arkansas at Pinebluff, 1980
Wheaton College, 1981
Northeastern University, 1982
Kean College of New Jersey, 1982
Claremont Graduate School, 1982
Spelman College, 1983
Boston College, 1983
Winston-Salem State University, 1984
Rollins College, 1985
Howard University, 1985
Tufts University, 1985
University of Vermont, 1985
North Carolina School of the Arts, 1986
Mount Holyoke College, 1987
University of Southern California, 1990
Northeastern University, 1992
Skidmore College, 1993
University of North Carolina, 1993
Academy of Southern Arts and Letters, 1993
American Film Institute, 1994
Bowie State University, 1994
University of Durham, 1995
Shaw University, 1997
Lafayette College, 1999
Hope College, 2001
University of Illinois at Urbana-Champaign, 2003
Columbia University, 2003
Eastern Connecticut University, 2003
Chapman University, 2007
Shenandoah University, 2008

INDEX

Boldface page numbers indicate major treatment of a topic. *Italic* page numbers denote photos or illustrations.

A

C

I